NEW GMAT® PREMIER 2012-2013

KAPLAN
PUBLISHING
New York

GMAT® is a registered trademark of the Graduate Management Admission Council, which neither sponsors nor endorses this product.

This publication is designed to provide accurate and authoritative information in regard to the subject matter covered. It is sold with the understanding that the publisher is not engaged in rendering legal, accounting, or other professional service. If legal advice or other expert assistance is required, the services of a competent professional should be sought.

© 2012 Kaplan, Inc.

Published by Kaplan Publishing, a division of Kaplan, Inc.
395 Hudson Street
New York, NY 10014

All rights reserved. The text of this publication, or any part thereof, may not be reproduced in any manner whatsoever without written permission from the publisher.

Printed in the United States of America

10 9 8 7 6 5 4 3 2 1

ISBN: 978-1-60978-217-7

Kaplan Publishing books are available at special quantity discounts to use for sales promotions, employee premiums, or educational purposes. For more information or to purchase books, please call the Simon & Schuster special sales department at 866-506-1949.

CONTENTS

How to Use This Book vii

The GMAT is Changing in 2012 xi

PART ONE: THE GMAT

Chapter 1: Introduction to the GMAT 3

GMAT Format 3

GMAT Scoring 5

GMAT Attitude 6

GMAT Checklist 9

Chapter 2: CAT Test Mechanics 15

The CAT Explained 15

Navigating the GMAT: Computer Basics 17

Pros and Cons of the Computer-Adaptive Format 18

Kaplan's CAT Strategies 20

PART TWO: STRATEGIES AND PRACTICE

Chapter 3: Verbal Section Strategies and Practice 23

How to Manage the Verbal Section 23

How the Verbal Section Is Scored 25

Chapter 4: Critical Reasoning 27

Question Format and Structure 27

The Basic Principles of Critical Reasoning 28

Critical Reasoning Question Types..34

The Kaplan Method for Critical Reasoning 41

Practice Quiz..46

Answers and Explanations 70

Chapter 5: Sentence Correction 95

Question Format and Structure 95

The Basic Principles of Sentence Correction 97

Sentence Correction Rules 109

The Kaplan Method for Sentence Correction 110

Practice Quiz..114

Answers and Explanations 130

Chapter 6: Reading Comprehension.....................................145

Question Format and Structure 146

The Basic Principles of Reading Comprehension..........................146

Reading Comprehension Question Types 152

The Kaplan Method for Reading Comprehension 156

Practice Quiz..167

Answers and Explanations 188

Chapter 7: Quantitative Section Strategies and Practice..............221

What the Quantitative Section Tests 221

Quantitative Analysis..222

How to Manage the Quantitative Section 222

How the Quantitative Section Is Scored 224

Chapter 8: Problem Solving...227

Question Format and Structure 228

The Basic Principles of Problem Solving................................228

The Kaplan Method for Problem Solving..................................248

Practice Quiz..253

Answers and Explanations 264

Chapter 9: Data Sufficiency 291

    Question Format and Structure 292

    The Basic Principles of Data Sufficiency 293

    The Kaplan Method for Data Sufficiency 303

    Guessing in Data Sufficiency 318

    Practice Quiz 321

    Answers and Explanations 340

Chapter 10: Word Problems 371

    The Basic Principles of Word Problems 372

    Word Problems in Problem Solving 375

    Common Word Problem Categories 381

    Word Problems in Data Sufficiency 387

Chapter 11: Analytical Writing Assessment (AWA) Strategies and Practice 391

    Essay Format and Structure 392

    The Basic Principles of Analytical Writing 393

    How the AWA Is Scored 395

    The Kaplan Method for Analytical Writing 398

    Breakdown: Analysis of an Argument 399

    Breakdown: Analysis of an Issue 404

    GMAT Style Checklist 409

    Practice Essays 410

Chapter Preview: Integrated Reasoning

Chapter 12: Take Control of the Test 415

    Develop Good Mental Conditioning 415

    Manage Stress 417

    Prepare the Week before the Exam 419

    Cancellation and Multiple Scores Policy 420

PART THREE: GETTING INTO BUSINESS SCHOOL

Chapter 13: Where and When to Apply 425

    Considering Where to Apply 425

Considering Where You Can Get In. 431

Deciding When to Apply 432

Useful Business School Resources 434

Chapter 14: How to Apply 437

How Schools Evaluate Applicants 437

Who Reviews Your Application? 440

What Decisions Are Made 440

Preparing Your Application 441

Maximizing the Various Parts of Your Application 442

Before You Submit Your Application 446

A Special Note for International Students. 447

PART FOUR: PRACTICE TEST

How to Take This Test. 450

GMAT Practice Test Answer Sheet 450

Analysis of an Argument Essay. 451

Analysis of an Issue Essay. 454

Quantitative Section 457

Verbal Section. 470

PART FIVE: PRACTICE TEST ANSWERS AND EXPLANATIONS

Practice Test Answer Key 492

Quantitative Section Explanations. 493

Verbal Section Explanations 503

PART SIX: RESOURCES

Appendix: Math Skills Refresher 523

Arithmetic 524

Algebra. 579

Geometry 591

Answers and Explanations for Math Skills Refresher Practice Sets 626

HOW TO USE THIS BOOK

WELCOME TO KAPLAN GMAT PREMIER 2012–2013!

Kaplan's *GMAT Premier* gives you everything you need for test day. We'll walk you through everything you need to know to take advantage of the book and online companion. We'll help you prep smarter and score higher.

QUICK START GUIDE

YOUR BOOK

Kaplan's *GMAT Premier* is packed with resources to help you get ready for test day, including:

- Targeted review of essential verbal and math concepts
- Strategies for every question type
- One practice test and chapter-end practice questions with detailed answer explanations
- Advanced questions: the hardest questions to help you prep smarter
- Expert exclusive tips from Kaplan GMAT instructors who have scored in the 99th percentile

YOUR ONLINE COMPANION

Your online companion lets you access additional instruction and practice materials to reinforce key concepts and sharpen your GMAT skills. Resources include:

- A diagnostic quiz
- Five computer-adaptive practice tests

- Additional practice for the Verbal, Quantitative, and Analytical Writing sections of the GMAT, including quizzes and essay prompts
- "Fast Fact" videos featuring top Kaplan GMAT instructors reviewing key concepts and problems
- Access to a Classroom Anywhere event—an interactive, instructor-led GMAT prep lesson
- GMAT Study Sheet

GETTING STARTED

1. Register your online companion for extra practice.
2. Sign up for a Classroom Anywhere event.
3. Take the online diagnostic quiz to identify your strong and weak areas.
4. Create a study plan.
5. Practice, practice, practice!

REGISTER YOUR ONLINE COMPANION

Register your online companion using these simple steps:

1. Go to **Kaptest.com/booksonline**.
2. Follow the on-screen instructions. Please have a copy of your book available.

Access to the online companion is limited to the original owner of this book and is nontransferable. Kaplan is not responsible for providing access to the online companion for customers who purchase or borrow used copies of this book. Access to the online companion expires one year after you register.

SIGN UP FOR A CLASSROOM ANYWHERE GMAT TRAINING SESSION

Kaplan's GMAT Classroom Anywhere classroom events are interactive, instructor-led GMAT prep lessons that you can participate in from anywhere you can access the Internet.

Classroom Anywhere events are held in a state-of-the-art virtual classroom—actual lessons in real time, just like a physical classroom experience. Interact with your teacher and other classmates using audio, instant chat, whiteboard, polling, and screen-sharing functionality. And just like in-person courses, a GMAT Classroom Anywhere event is led by an experienced Kaplan instructor.

To register for a free GMAT Classroom Anywhere event, go to **kaplanGMAT.com** and search for a free event. (You may be asked for a U.S. or Canadian zip code; Classroom Anywhere events are available for all zip codes.)

Take the Online Diagnostic Quiz

Your online companion features a diagnostic quiz. The quiz provides you with samples of each question type, enabling you to familiarize yourself with the question formats. It also allows you to accurately gauge the content you know and identify areas for practice and review.

After you've taken the diagnostic quiz, check your answers carefully. Note how many questions you got right and wrong, how long it took you to answer each question, and how often you skipped questions. Look for patterns. Were you stronger in some areas than others?

Then review the detailed answer explanations to better understand your strengths and weaknesses. This will help you target your practice time to specific concepts.

Create a Study Plan

Use what you've learned from your diagnostic quiz to identify areas for closer study and practice.

Schedule time to study, practice, and review each GMAT skill and Kaplan strategy. Initially, your practice should focus on the skills of each section and not on timing. Add timing to your section and test practice as you improve fundamental proficiency.

Practice, Practice, Practice!

Your book and online companion come with practice, practice, and more practice.

Remember, Kaplan's *GMAT Premier* is designed to meet your individual needs. Use the book and online companion when and how they work best for you.

Take time to familiarize yourself with some of the key components of your book. It has all the tools you'll need to conquer the GMAT on test day!

GOOD LUCK!

THE GMAT IS CHANGING IN 2012

INTEGRATED REASONING

The Graduate Management Admission Council (GMAC), the organization that owns and administers the GMAT, has announced the addition of a new section to the test. The 30-minute section, called Integrated Reasoning, will debut June 2012. It will replace the Analysis of an Issue essay prompt. GMAC calls the new version of the test the Next Generation GMAT.

GMAC developed the new section with the input of 740 business school faculty and with the objective of creating a test that can better predict a student's success in a business school program. The new Integrated Reasoning section will require test takers to integrate information from multiple sources in a variety of formats to solve problems. GMAC's decision to eliminate the Analysis of an Issue essay was based on research that showed that most test takers get comparable scores on both essays, making it possible to use only a single essay to assess test takers' abilities.

The Integrated Reasoning section will differ from other areas of the test in terms of form, content, and navigation. There will be 12 questions in the Integrated Reasoning section, and some questions may include multiple parts. The four new question types in the Integrated Reasoning section are as follows:

- Graphics Interpretation
- Multi-Source Reasoning
- Table Analysis
- Two-Part Analysis

As with the other sections of the GMAT, you will not need prior business knowledge to answer the Integrated Reasoning questions. A full discussion of the four question types can be found in the Integrated Reasoning chapter of this book.

THE SCORING SCALE OF THE REVISED GMAT

The scoring scale for the Total score, based on the Quantitative and Verbal scores, will remain 200 to 800 points. The Integrated Reasoning section will be scored separately from the rest of the exam. The single Analytical Writing Assessment will continue to be scored separately on a 0- to 6-point scale in half-point increments. Admissions officers will receive your Integrated Reasoning score alongside your Total score and your Analytical Writing score.

At the time of this book's publication, GMAC had not yet released the scoring scale of the Integrated Reasoning section or disclosed whether partial credit would be given for questions with multiple parts. GMAC plans to announce the new scoring scale in April 2012. As the launch of the Next Generation GMAT approaches, we will post updated information about the test at **kaplanGMAT.com**.

WHICH TEST SHOULD I TAKE?

For most test takers, taking the GMAT before the test changes in June 2012 is the right choice. Taking the current test will reduce the overall time investment required to prepare for the GMAT. Even if you're not planning to apply to business school this year, you can take the GMAT now and use your scores later, since GMAT scores are good for up to five years.

Some students may think taking the new test will improve their chances of getting into business school. This is not necessarily the case. Admissions officers may differ in the way they interpret the new scores, bringing uncertainty to the admissions process. The changes will also affect how you study for the test. You will need to find time to prepare for Integrated Reasoning without sacrificing any of the effort you would spend on other areas of the test.

Those who feel more comfortable taking the current test may do so up until June 2012. Register for the exam well in advance, as the availability of GMAT appointments varies based on the test center. There will also be a rush to take the GMAT in its current form before the test changes. If you'd prefer to take the new test, you can register for the Next Generation GMAT beginning in December 2011. To register for either version of the test, go to **mba.com**.

PREPARING FOR THE CURRENT OR NEW TEST

If you are taking the GMAT before June 2012, you do not need to prepare for Integrated Reasoning. That section will not appear formally on the test prior to June 2012. GMAC may include Integrated Reasoning questions in a nonscored research section on the GMAT in January 2012, but you do not need to study for this section. You do, however, want to be fully prepared for the Quantitative, Verbal, and Analytical Writing sections of the test. Use this entire book *except* the chapter on Integrated Reasoning.

If you are taking the GMAT after June 2012, you do need to prepare for Integrated Reasoning. You will also want to be ready for all of the other sections of the test, except for the Analysis of an Issue essay, which will not appear on the test beginning June 2012. To prepare for the Next Generation GMAT, use this entire book *except* the section about the Analysis of an Issue essay within the chapter on Analytical Writing Assessment (AWA) Strategies and Practice. Be sure, however, to study the rest of the chapter, as the Analysis of an Argument essay will still be an important part of the Next Generation GMAT. Also, keep in mind that the Introduction to the GMAT chapter is an introduction to the *current* GMAT. If you are taking the test after June 2012, supplement that chapter with the information in the introduction you are reading now and in the Integrated Reasoning chapter.

Your online resources can also help you prepare for Integrated Reasoning. Your first practice test has a complete 30-minute Integrated Reasoning section. This section includes 12 questions with answers and explanations. This practice test will give you hands-on experience with the new navigation methods and answer formats so that you will feel confident using them on test day. You can also get additional practice with the new navigation methods and question types at **gmac.com**.

No matter which version of the GMAT you choose to take, this book, along with your online resources, can help you succeed. Let's get started.

kaptest.com/publishing

The material in this book is up-to-date at the time of publication. However, the Graduate Management Admission Council may have instituted changes in the tests or test registration process after this book was published. Be sure to read carefully the materials you receive when you register for the test.

If there are any important late-breaking developments—or changes or corrections to the Kaplan test preparation materials in this book—we will post that information online at **kaptest.com/publishing.** Check to see if any information is posted there regarding this book.

kaplansurveys.com/books

What did you think of this book? We'd love to hear your comments and suggestions. We invite you to fill out our online survey form at **kaplansurveys.com/books.**

Your feedback is extremely helpful as we continue to develop high-quality resources to meet your needs.

## Part One

THE GMAT

CHAPTER 1: INTRODUCTION TO THE GMAT

- GMAT Format
- GMAT Scoring
- GMAT Attitude
- GMAT Checklist

Let's start with the basics. The GMAT is, among other things, an endurance test. It is a computerized test, consisting of 150 minutes of multiple-choice testing plus two 30-minute analytical essays. Add in the administrative details, plus two 8-minute breaks, and you can count on being in the test center for about 4 hours.

It's a grueling experience, to say the least. And if you don't approach it with confidence and rigor, you'll quickly lose your composure. That's why it's so important that you take control of the test, just as you take control of the rest of your application process to business school.

Here are the basics.

GMAT FORMAT

The GMAT begins with the Analytical Writing Assessment (the AWA). You will be required to compose two different essays, typing them each into the computer using a simple word-processing program. You are given 30 minutes for each essay.

The first essay is the "Analysis of an Argument" topic, for which you'll have to analyze the reasoning behind a given argument, explain its weaknesses or flaws, and recommend how to correct them to improve the argument. Your own personal views on the topic are not relevant.

The second essay is the "Analysis of an Issue" topic. You'll have to analyze a given issue or opinion and then explain your point of view on the subject. You will be required to cite relevant reasons and/or examples drawn from your own experience, observation, or reading.

After the essay sections and an 8-minute break, there are two 75-minute multiple-choice sections—one Quantitative (Math) and one Verbal. The Quantitative section contains 37 questions in two formats, Problem Solving and Data Sufficiency, which are mixed together throughout the section. The Verbal section contains 41 questions in three formats, Reading Comprehension, Sentence Correction, and Critical Reasoning, which are also mixed throughout the section. Within each section, question types appear in random order, so you never know what's coming next.

This is how the sections break down:

- AWA: 60 minutes, 2 essay assignments
  - Analysis of an Argument topic (30 minutes)
  - Analysis of an Issue topic (30 minutes)
- Quantitative (Math) Section: 75 minutes, 37 questions
  - Data Sufficiency questions
  - Problem Solving questions
    - Verbal Section: 75 minutes, 41 questions
      - Reading Comprehension questions
      - Sentence Correction questions
      - Critical Reasoning questions

Some important things to note:

- After you have completed the second essay, you'll get an 8-minute break. Then, between the two multiple-choice sections, you will get another break.
- So-called "experimental" questions will be scattered throughout the test. They will look just like the other multiple-choice questions but won't contribute to your score.

We'll talk more about each of the question types in later chapters. For now, note the following. You'll be answering 78 multiple-choice questions in 2½ hours. That's less than 2 minutes per question, not counting the time it takes to read the Reading Comprehension passages. Clearly, you'll have to move fast. But you can't let yourself get careless. Taking control of the GMAT means increasing the speed of your work without sacrificing accuracy!

EXPERT EXCLUSIVE

Don't assume just because a question *seems* easy that it's experimental. The question might be harder than you think. You don't want to get a scored question wrong because you thought it wouldn't count. Do your best on every question!

GMAT SCORING

You'll receive four scores for the GMAT:

- Overall scaled score, from 200 to 800
- Quantitative scaled subscore, from 0 to 60
- Verbal scaled subscore, from 0 to 60
- AWA score, from 0 to 6. This score is separate from your overall score for Quantitative and Verbal.

> **EXPERT EXCLUSIVE**
>
> As of the printing of this book, the 99th percentile for Quant is a subscore of 51; for Verbal it's 46. You can get several questions wrong and still be in the top 1 percent!

Because the test is graded on a preset curve, the scaled score will correspond to a certain percentile, which will also be given on your score report. A 650 overall score, for instance, corresponds to the 80th percentile, meaning that 80 percent of test takers score at or below this level. The percentile figure is important because it allows admissions officers at business schools to get a sense quickly of where you fall in the pool of applicants.

Percentile	Approximate Score
99th percentile	760
95th percentile	720
90th percentile	700
80th percentile	650
75th percentile	640
50th percentile	550

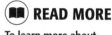 **READ MORE**

To learn more about how schools use your scores, go to **mba.com**.

Though many factors play a role in admissions decisions, the GMAT score is usually an important one. And, generally speaking, being average just won't cut it. While the median GMAT score is around 550, you need a score of at least 650 to be considered competitive by the top B-schools. According to the latest Kaplan/Newsweek careers guide, the average GMAT scores at the best business schools in the country—such as Stanford, Sloan (MIT), Kellogg (Northwestern), and Wharton (Penn)—are above 700. That translates to a percentile figure of 90 and up!

Fortunately, there are strategies that can give you an advantage on the computer-adaptive GMAT. You can learn to exploit the way that the computer-adaptive test (CAT) generates a score. We'll explain how in the next section.

SCORE REPORTS

About 20 days after your test date, your official score report will be available online. You'll receive an email when yours is ready. Reports will only be mailed to candidates who request that service. The official score report includes your scores for the Analytical Writing Assessment (AWA), Verbal, and Quantitative sections, as well as your total score and percentile ranking. **Test takers who skip the AWA do not receive score reports.**

Your report also includes the results of all the exams you've taken in the previous five years, including cancellations. Any additional reports are US$28 each. All score-report requests are final and cannot be canceled.

GMAT ATTITUDE

In the chapters that follow, we'll cover techniques for answering the GMAT questions. But you'll also need to go into the test with a certain attitude and approach. Here are some strategies.

THE ART OF USING NOTEBOARDS

Test takers are given noteboards, which are spiral-bound booklets of laminated paper, and a black wet-erase pen. Here are the specs so you know what to expect on test day.

Noteboard
- 5 sheets, 10 numbered pages
- Spiral-bound at top
- Legal-sized (8.5" × 14") in United States, Canada, and Mexico; A4 elsewhere
- First page has test instructions and is not suitable for scratchwork. Pages 2–10 consist of a gridded work surface.
- Pale yellow in United States, Canada, and Mexico; a different color possible elsewhere

Pen
- Black fine-print Staedtler wet-erase pen

You will not be given an eraser, and you are not supposed to reuse the noteboard. Each time you fill up your noteboard during the test, the administrator will replace your used noteboard with a clean one. You can also request a new pen, if necessary. The noteboard cannot be removed from the test room during or after the exam, and you must return it to the administrator when your exam is complete.

We know how important it is for test takers to be as prepared as possible for the actual testing experience. That's why we have always recommended that students use scratch material with our GMAT preparation program, including with the practice questions and tests in this book. Since the noteboards will be your only option on test day, we suggest that you use an eraser board (or anything with a similar surface) and a non-permanent marker while doing the practice tests. Although using them won't mimic the test day experience exactly, at least you'll get the feel of working in a comparable medium. And at the very least, using the noteboard and pen on test day won't be jarring or unfamiliar, as it might be otherwise. In fact, students who take a Kaplan classroom course receive a noteboard that mimics the writing surface that GMAT test takers use, as well as the same type of pen.

Most test takers have not had any difficulties using the noteboards and pens on test day. Plus, practicing with the eraser board and marker will help you feel even more comfortable and in control. However, nothing is perfect, so based on all the feedback we've received from test takers, here are two snags and how to tackle them:

(1) **Erasable ink you're not supposed to erase:** Say you make a mistake during a calculation or you smudge your work with your hand. The noteboard's surface probably won't lend itself to quick-and-easy erasing (not surprisingly, since you are not meant to reuse it). You can't write on top of the smudge or error because you'll just be left with a blob of ink that you can't read. So what should you do? Just start over. Seriously. Think of it this way—you won't waste precious time in a futile attempt to save what is essentially a sinking ship. Left-handed test takers (and some right-handed ones, too) might find that their writing styles make them particularly susceptible to smudging. If this sounds like you, practicing with the eraser board will help you work out any such problems before test day.

> **EXPERT EXCLUSIVE**
> You don't get to use a pencil on the GMAT, so don't give yourself the luxury of using one during your prep. Get comfortable using ink now, and test day will be much less stressful!

(2) **A problematic pen:** Difficulties with pens are not common at all. The test administrators are careful to provide good writing utensils so test takers don't have any extra anxieties. Also, keep in mind that you should recap your pen when you are not using it so that it doesn't dry out.

However, you could get a pen that's simply dry from the get-go or dries out quickly no matter how careful you are. Don't sweat it. The best thing to do is just to get a new pen. And should you be saddled with a pen that leaves wayward blobs of ink, don't waste time with it either. Ask the administrator for a new pen as soon as it starts to act up.

More Noteboard Strategies

Using one booklet for an entire section and requesting a replacement during breaks is the most efficient method for using the noteboards. Since you are given nine pages to write on, this technique can be used without difficulty, especially with planning and practice. However, should you need a new noteboard (or pen) during a section, hold the used one in the air to clarify immediately the nature of the request (rather than just raising your hand).

GO ONLINE

Work on the Diagnostic Quiz in your Online Companion.

DRAW A GRID

If you find crossing off answer choices on paper tests particularly helpful (as a process of elimination), consider doing the same thing here. It's an obvious challenge, since you're working on computer, but it can be done with your noteboard.

Your noteboard is already gridded, so reserve five lines at the top of one of the pages and label them A through E before you begin the exam. Use the grid to mark off answer choices that you have eliminated, as shown below. That way, you can tell at a glance which answer choices are still in the running. If you end up using it often, it'll be worth the 10 seconds it takes to draw it up.

A	✗	✗		✗		✗			✗		✗		
B		✗	✗	✗			✗	✗	✗	✗		✗	
C				✗				✗					✗
D	✗		✗		✗		✗		✗		✗		
E	✗	✗		✗		✗			✗				

BE SYSTEMATIC

EXPERT EXCLUSIVE

The penalty for an unreached question is severe—one question that you don't reach counts against you almost as much as two wrong answers would.

Because it's so important to get to the hard questions as early as possible, work systematically. Use your noteboard to organize your thinking. If you eliminate choices, cross them off on your noteboard using the grid just described and guess intelligently. Make sure to leave enough time to answer every question in the section. You'll be penalized for questions you don't reach.

PACE YOURSELF

Of course, the last thing you want to happen is to run out of time before you've done all the questions. Pace yourself so that this doesn't happen. We're not saying you have to spend exactly 90 seconds, for instance, on every Critical Reasoning question. But you should have a sense of how much time to spend on each question. (We'll talk about general timing guidelines later.)

Before you go in to take the exam, you must get a sense of how long is too long to spend on a question. This is something you can do only with practice, so while working on the practice questions in this book, time yourself. (If you're using your watch, take it off and set it on the table in front of you.)

STOP THE CLOCK

The timer in the corner of the GMAT screen can work to your advantage, but if you find yourself looking at it so often that it becomes a distraction, turn it off for 10 or 15 minutes and try to refocus. Even if you lose track a bit without the clock, there is no replacement for focus and accuracy.

No matter what your preference is for the clock, when there are five minutes left, the clock turns on permanently, counts down the seconds, turns red, and flashes.

> **EXPERT EXCLUSIVE**
>
> Some people work best with the clock off from the beginning. If that's you, be sure to check in with the clock every five questions. You don't want to fall too far behind pace.

DON'T WASTE TIME ON QUESTIONS YOU CAN'T DO

Skipping a tough question is easier said than done. It's natural to want to plow through a test and answer every question as it appears. But that doesn't pay off here. If you dig in your heels on a tough question, refusing to move on until you've cracked it, you're letting your test macho get in the way of your test score. Like life itself, a test section is too short to waste on lost causes.

REMAIN CALM

It's imperative that you remain calm and composed during the test. You can't let yourself get rattled by one hard question or a Reading Comp passage to the degree that it throws off your performance on the rest of the Verbal section.

When you face a tough question, remember that you're surely not the only one finding it difficult. The test is designed to challenge everyone who takes it. Having trouble with a difficult question isn't going to ruin your score, but getting upset and letting it throw you off track will. When you understand that part of the test maker's goal is to reward those who keep their composure, you'll recognize the importance of not panicking when you run into challenging material.

GMAT CHECKLIST

The GMAT is offered by appointment, at your convenience, almost every day of the year. You will be required to register online before making an appointment.

CHOOSE A TEST CENTER

Before you register to take the exam, search for a test center that's convenient for you and determine whether that site has available seats. Each test center operates on its own schedule and can accommodate varying numbers of test takers throughout the day. To locate a test center near you, go to **mba.com**.

REGISTER AND SCHEDULE YOUR APPOINTMENT

Available time slots change continuously as people register for the test. You will find out what times are available at your chosen test center when you register. You may be able to schedule an appointment within a few days of your desired test date, but popular dates (especially weekends) fill up quickly.

Admissions deadlines for business schools vary. Check with the schools and make your test appointment early enough to allow your scores to be reported before the schools' application deadlines.

You may register and schedule your appointment online, by phone, by mail, or by fax:

- Online: Go to **mba.com**.
- Phone: Use one of the following numbers, based on your location:
  - The Americas: Call toll-free (within the United States and Canada only) 800-717-GMAT (4628) or call the customer service line (952) 681-3680. The lines are operational from 7:00 A.M. to 7:00 P.M. Central Time.
  - Asia Pacific: +60 38318-9961, 9:00 A.M. to 6:00 P.M. AEST
  - India: +91 120 439-7830, 9:00 A.M. to 6:00 P.M. Indian Standard Time
  - Europe/Middle East/Africa: +44 (0) 161 855 7219, 9:00 A.M. to 6:00 P.M. GMT
- Mail or fax (slowest options):
  - Download the Test Center List, Country Code List, and GMAT Appointment Scheduling form, available at **mba.com**.
  - Fill out the GMAT Appointment Scheduling form.
  - If you wish to fax your form, use one of the following fax numbers, based on your location:
    - The Americas: (952) 681-3681
    - Asia Pacific and India: +60 38319 1092
    - Europe/Middle East/Africa: +44 (0) 161 855 7301
  - If you wish to mail your form, send your completed form to the following address. Keep in mind that mail from some countries can take as long as eight weeks to arrive in the United States:

Pearson VUE
Attention: GMAT Program
P.O. Box 581907
Minneapolis, MN 55458-1907
USA

The fee to take the GMAT is US$250 worldwide (at the time of printing). It is payable online by credit card or by mailing in a check. If you have questions about GMAT registration, visit **mba.com** or call 800-717-GMAT (4628).

Identify Yourself Correctly

When scheduling your test appointment, be sure that the spelling of your name and date of birth match the ID you will present at the test center. If those do not match, you will not be permitted to take the test, and your test fee will be forfeited.

RESCHEDULING OR CANCELING AN APPOINTMENT

If you need to reschedule the date, time, or location of your appointment, there is a US$50 fee (at the time of printing) as long as you reschedule at least seven days before your original appointment. If you need to reschedule fewer than seven days before your original date, you have to pay the full registration amount again. Rescheduling can be done online at **mba.com** or by calling one of the numbers listed previously, based on your location. If you reschedule over the phone, you may be subject to an additional fee. You cannot reschedule an appointment by mail or fax.

If you need to cancel your appointment, you will receive a US$80 refund (at the time of printing) as long as you cancel at least seven days before your original appointment. If you cancel fewer than seven days before your original date, you forfeit the entire registration fee. For registration fees paid by credit card, the refund amount will be credited to the card. If the fee was paid by check or money order, you will receive a check in the mail. Cancellations can be made online at **mba.com** or by calling one of numbers listed previously, based on your location. If you cancel over the phone, you may be subject to an additional fee. You cannot cancel an appointment by mail or fax.

THE DAY OF THE TEST

You should arrive at your testing center 30 minutes before the time of your scheduled appointment. A late arrival (15 minutes or more) may result in you being turned away from the test center and the forfeiture of your test fee. Plus, you must complete a number of security measures before you will be allowed to take the exam.

Presentation of Proper Identification

You will be asked to present ID—no exceptions. The following are the only acceptable forms:

- Passport
- Government-issued driver's license
- Government-issued national/state/province identity card (including European ID card)
- Military ID card

If you aren't a citizen of the country in which you take your test, you'll probably need your passport. In some countries—including (as of this printing) China, India, Japan, and South Korea—you'll need your passport no matter what. Visit **mba.com** for the current requirements.

The ID must be current (not expired) and legible, and it should contain all four of the elements listed below. If you do not have one ID with all four of these elements, you will need to bring a second ID (also from the list above) that shows the missing elements.

(1) Your name in the Roman alphabet. It must be exactly the same as what you provided when you made your appointment.
(2) Your date of birth. The date of birth must also exactly match the date provided when you made your appointment.
(3) A recent, recognizable photograph
(4) Your signature

If these elements do not match what the test administrator has on file for you, you will not be allowed to take the GMAT, and your test fee will be forfeited.

Before you schedule your test appointment, make sure you understand all the requirements that are particular to your situation and have acquired or renewed the ID you will use. Also, note that if your ID is found to be fraudulent or invalid after you take the exam, your scores will be canceled and your test fee forfeited.

Fingerprint, Palm Scans, Signature, and Photograph

Once your government-issue ID is approved, the administrator will take your fingerprint or palm scan, signature, and photograph using digital equipment. The testing rooms are also equipped with audio and video recorders, which are active during the exam. If you do not complete the entire check-in process or refuse to be recorded, you will not be allowed to take the GMAT, and your test fee will be forfeited.

Agreements

When you arrive at the center, you will be asked to agree to the GMAT Examination Testing Rules & Agreement. Once you are seated at a workstation, you will electronically confirm that you agree to the GMAT Nondisclosure Agreement and the General Terms of Use statement. If you do not agree, you will not be allowed to take the GMAT, and your test fee will be forfeited.

> **EXPERT EXCLUSIVE**
> The GMAT takes this agreement seriously. If you are caught violating it, your schools will be informed of this fact, and you may be liable for civil penalties!

Prohibited Items

The following items cannot be brought into the testing room:

- Electronics such as cell phones, beepers, pagers, personal data assistants (PDAs), cameras, stereos, radios, and photographic devices
- Any timepieces, including wristwatches, stopwatches, and watch alarms
- Notes, scratch paper, books, pamphlets, dictionaries, translators, or thesauruses
- Pens or pencils
- Measuring tools such as rulers
- Calculators or watch calculators

Essentially, you can't bring anything that may cause distractions, provide aid during testing, or be used to remove exam content from the testing room. It is possible that your test center has storage space available, such as lockers, where you can leave possessions that are prohibited from the testing room. However, this may not be the case at all centers. Call your test center to inquire about storage and plan accordingly.

Disruptive Behavior

You will not be allowed to smoke, eat, drink, or use a cell phone in the testing room. In fact, you can't use a phone or send a text message at all once the test has begun, even at breaks.

You also cannot leave the testing room without the administrator's permission. Some test centers offer the use of headphones to keep noise to a minimum; if this interests you, call your test center for details. Should you have any questions or problems during the exam, raise your hand and wait for the administrator to approach you.

Breaks

The length of your appointment is approximately four hours. Two breaks are scheduled into the exam—one after the second essay is complete and another between the two multiple-choice sections. Each time you leave and return to the testing room, you will be digitally fingerprinted or palm scanned. If you exceed the allotted time, the excess time will be deducted from the next section of your exam. For more information on administrative regulations and testing procedures, visit **mba.com**.

Bring the Names of Five Business Schools You Wish to Receive Your Scores

You may select up to five schools to receive your scores before you take the test. Your registration fee will cover that cost. Before test day, decide which schools you want to get your GMAT scores and bring that list with you. You will not be able to change the list once you have made your selection.

Bring Your Study Sheet to the Test Center

Arrive early and, as you wait for your test time, review the key items on your Study Sheet, which you can download from your Online Companion. It will give you a quick refresher—and will put you in the right mindset for the exam.

CHAPTER 2: CAT TEST MECHANICS

- The CAT Explained
- Navigating the GMAT: Computer Basics
- Pros and Cons of the Computer-Adaptive Format
- Kaplan's CAT Strategies

The GMAT is a computer-adaptive test—a CAT. A CAT is designed to assess your abilities using fewer test questions than traditional paper-based tests. Several things make a CAT unique:

- It is a computer-based test that you take at a special test center, by yourself, at a time you schedule. You will sit at a private workstation, though there will be other test takers around you.
- It adapts to your performance. Each person's test is unique, with the multiple-choice questions adjusting to your ability level. In other words, each test taker is given different questions. The questions are weighted according to their difficulty and other statistical properties—not their position in the test.
- It bases your score on two things:

  (1) The number of questions you answer—whether you answer them correctly or incorrectly

  (2) The level of difficulty (and other statistical characteristics) of each question

> **EXPERT EXCLUSIVE**
> The biggest myth about CATs is that early questions count more than later ones. They don't. The test maker has exhaustively demonstrated this to us, and we've verified it with our own research. If you spend too long on the first 10 questions because you think they are more valuable, you may not finish the section, thus incurring a severe penalty.

THE CAT EXPLAINED

The computer-adaptive format of the GMAT takes some getting used to—in fact, it's pretty unusual at first. Here's how it works.

There's a large pool of potential questions, ranging from moderately easy to very difficult. To start, you're given a question of moderate difficulty. If you get it right, the computer

EXPERT EXCLUSIVE

Most tests start off with the easiest questions and work their way up to the hard ones. But the GMAT starts right in the middle. So if you find the first few questions a little challenging, that's pretty normal.

will give you a harder question next. But if you get it wrong, the computer will give you an easier question next. In other words, the computer scores each question and then uses that information—along with your previous responses and the requirements of the test design—to determine which question to present next. The process continues throughout, and by the end the computer will have an accurate assessment of your ability level.

If you keep getting questions right, the test will get harder and harder; if you slip up and make some mistakes, it will adjust and start giving you easier problems. But if you begin to answer those easier problems correctly, the test will go back to the hard ones.

The GMAT is trying to find a level of difficulty at which you get the right answer half the time. Ideally, that's your "score level." The practical consequence for you, the test taker, is that you shouldn't be surprised to see a number of questions that you can narrow down to two answer choices but then struggle to figure out which is right. That'd give you a 50 percent chance of getting the question right—exactly what the test is trying to achieve. You're not failing; the test is just doing its job.

Ideally, you are given enough questions to ensure that scores are not based on luck. If you get 1 hard question right, you might just have been lucky, but if you get 10 hard questions right, then luck has little to do with it. So the test is self-adjusting and self-correcting.

You will see only one question at a time. The computer must score a question before providing you a new one, so you'll be required to answer every question. For this reason, too, once you have confirmed your response and moved on to the next question, you will not be able to return to a question. The computer has already scored your response and has selected a new question for you.

EXPERT EXCLUSIVE

Solidify your performance on the intermediate-range questions, and you'll set yourself a "floor" below which you won't fall.

Because a string of wrong answers can significantly lower your score, making several random guesses at the end of a section is very dangerous. So whenever you don't know how to answer a question, eliminate whatever answer choices you can and then select the answer you think is best. Otherwise, you'll run out of time at the end of the section and be forced into a lower score.

Another major consequence of the GMAT format is that hard questions are worth more than easy ones. It has to be this way, because the very purpose of this adaptive format is to find out at what level you reliably get about half the questions right; that's your scoring level.

GO ONLINE

Your Diagnostic Quiz will give you an idea of what it is like to take a computer-based test.

Imagine two students—one who does 10 basic questions, only half of which she gets right, and one who does 10 very hard questions, only half of which she gets right. The same number of questions have been answered correctly, but this does not reflect an equal ability.

In fact, the student who got 5 out of 10 hard questions wrong could still get a very high score on the GMAT. But to get to these tough questions, she first had to get medium-difficulty questions right.

So no matter how much you want to start practicing those tough questions now, first make sure that you can get most of the intermediate questions right. You can struggle with some tough questions and still earn a high score because if you dip back into the intermediate range, you'll get a bunch right and bounce right back up. But if you struggle at the intermediate questions, you'll never reach the high-scoring tough ones in the first place. GMAT success is built from the bottom up, not from the top down.

> **EXPERT EXCLUSIVE**
> Most tough GMAT questions are composed of several intermediate concepts tested at once. So mastering the intermediate questions allows you to handle most tough questions too!

NAVIGATING THE GMAT: COMPUTER BASICS

Let's preview the primary computer functions that you will use to move around on the GMAT. The screen below is typical for an adaptive test.

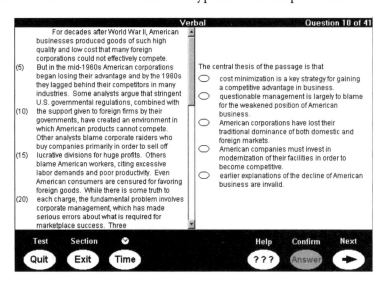

As you can see, there are empty bubbles for the answer choices—no letters (A), (B), (C), (D), (E). This is different from most multiple-choice tests.

To make the questions in this book appear as testlike as possible, the five answer choices in practice questions are not identified by letters. You will see blank ovals, just as you will on test day. However, for the purposes of discussion, we identify each answer choice using the corresponding letter in the answer explanation.

Here's what the various buttons do.

THE SCROLL BAR

Similar to the scroll bar on a Windows-style computer display, this scroll bar is a thin, vertical column with up and down arrows at the top and bottom. Clicking on the arrows moves you up or down the page you're reading.

THE NEXT BUTTON

Hit this when you want to move on to the next question. After you press Next, you must hit Confirm.

THE CONFIRM BUTTON

This button appears in a pop-up window after you click the Next button. The Confirm button tells the computer you are happy with your answer and are really ready to move to the next question. You cannot proceed until you have hit this button.

THE TIME BUTTON

Clicking on this button turns the time display at the top of the screen on and off. When you have five minutes left in a section, the clock flashes in red, and the display changes from hours/minutes to hours/minutes/seconds.

THE HELP BUTTON

This one leads to directions and other stuff from the tutorial. You should know all this already, and besides, the test clock won't pause just because you click on Help.

THE EXIT BUTTON

This allows you to exit the section before the time is up. If you budget your time wisely, you should never have to use this button—time will run out just as you are finishing the section.

THE QUIT BUTTON

Hitting this button ends the test.

PROS AND CONS OF THE COMPUTER-ADAPTIVE FORMAT

There are both good and annoying things about the GMAT's computer-adaptive format. The following are a few things you should be thankful for—or watch out for—as you prepare to try your luck on the test.

7 Good Things about the CAT

(1) There's a timer at the top of the computer screen to help you pace yourself. (You can hide it if it distracts you.)

(2) There will be only a few other test takers in the room with you—it won't be like taking an exam in one of those massive lecture halls with distractions everywhere.

(3) You get an eight-minute pause between each section. The pause is optional, but you should always use it to relax and stretch.

(4) You'll find the CAT much more convenient for your schedule than the pencil-and-paper exam. It's offered at hundreds of centers almost every day of the year.

(5) Registering to take the exam is very easy, and sometimes you can sign up just a few days before you'd like to go. However, depending upon the time of the year and the availability of testing centers in your area, you may have to register several weeks in advance for a desired test date.

(6) The CAT format gives you more time to spend on each question than you had on the paper-based test.

(7) Perhaps the CAT's best feature is that it gives you an immediate score and your chosen schools will receive it just 20 days later.

> **EXPERT EXCLUSIVE**
>
> Since you can't go back, reread the question before you submit your answer. Fixing a few careless errors is worth the extra few seconds.

7 Annoying Things about the CAT

(1) You cannot skip around. You must answer the questions one at a time in the order the computer gives them to you. There is only one question on the screen at a time.

(2) If you realize later that you answered a question incorrectly, you cannot go back and change your answer.

(3) If the person next to you is noisy or distracting, the proctor cannot move you or the person, since your test is on the computer.

(4) You cannot cross off an answer choice and banish it from your sight (it's on a computer screen, after all), so you have to be disciplined about not reconsidering choices you've already eliminated.

(5) You have to scroll through Reading Comp passages, which means you won't be able to see the whole thing on the screen at once.

(6) You can't write on your computer screen the way you can on the paper test, so you have to use the scratch paper they give you, which will be inconveniently located away from the computer screen.

(7) Lastly, many people find that computer screens tire them and cause eyestrain—especially after four hours.

> **EXPERT EXCLUSIVE**
>
> Eyestrain is especially likely on the Verbal section because you won't be looking away from the screen to scratchwork as often. So look away from the screen for a moment after every few Verbal questions. Your eyes will feel better, and you'll be able to focus better—mentally as well as visually.

KAPLAN'S CAT STRATEGIES

Using certain CAT-specific strategies will have a direct, positive impact on your score:

- At the start of the section, each question you get right or wrong will rapidly move the computer's estimate of your score up or down. Your goal is to get the computer's estimate of your score up to where you're handling the hard questions. That's because getting a hard question right will help your score a lot but getting a hard question wrong will hurt your score only slightly.

  - It's great to get as many of the first 10 questions right as you can, because this moves you very quickly into the high-value questions. But you can't afford to take much extra time to do so, because that will force you (1) not to answer several questions at the end, (2) to make many random guesses at the end, or (3) to rush your way into many careless errors at the end. Needless to say, each of those options would hurt your score. At Kaplan, we've run countless experiments on the GMAT scoring engine, and the best approach is always to move at a steady pace at the beginning, not taking much extra time.

  - As you progress through the middle part of the section, try your best not to get several questions in a row wrong, as this will sink your score on the CAT. If you know that the previous question you answered was a blind guess, spend a little extra time trying to get the next one right.

- The CAT will switch from one question type to another within a section (going from Reading Comprehension to Sentence Correction, for example) without automatically showing the directions for each new question type. Knowing the format and directions of each GMAT question type beforehand will save you a lot of time—and aggravation—during the exam.

- Because the level of difficulty of questions on the CAT is not predictable, always be on the lookout for answer-choice traps.

- Because each right or wrong answer directly affects the next question you get, the CAT does not allow you to go back to questions you've already answered. In other words, you cannot go back to double-check your work. So be sure about your answers before moving on.

- If you're given a question you cannot answer, you'll have to guess. Guess intelligently and strategically by eliminating any answer choices that you know are wrong and guessing among those remaining.

- Don't get rattled if you keep seeing really tough questions. It just means you're doing very well! Keep it up!

EXPERT EXCLUSIVE

You may be tempted to speed through the early questions so that you'll have more time on the harder ones. Be careful not to rush yourself into a careless error! A missed intermediate question will hurt you more than a missed difficult one.

STRATEGIES AND PRACTICE

CHAPTER 3: VERBAL SECTION STRATEGIES AND PRACTICE

- How to Manage the Verbal Section
- How the Verbal Section Is Scored

A little more than half of the multiple-choice questions that count toward your overall score appear in the Verbal section. You'll have 75 minutes to answer 41 Verbal questions in three formats: Reading Comprehension, Sentence Correction, and Critical Reasoning. These three types of questions are mingled throughout the Verbal section, so you never know what's coming next. Here's what you can expect to see.

Verbal Question Type	Approximate Number of Questions
Critical Reasoning	12
Reading Comprehension	14
Sentence Correction	15
Total:	41 questions

EXPERT EXCLUSIVE
You may see a few more of one question type and a few less of another. Don't panic. It's likely just a slight difference in the types of "experimental" questions that you get.

In the next three chapters, we'll show you strategies for each of these question types. But first, let's look at some techniques for managing the whole section.

HOW TO MANAGE THE VERBAL SECTION

The GMAT will give you four Reading Comp passages. Two will be longer and have four questions each, and two will be shorter and have three questions each. With less than two minutes per question, where will you find the time to read those passages?

Part of the answer, of course, is that chapter 6 of this book will give you great tips about how to read the passages efficiently. Another big part, though, is how you handle Sentence Correction. Follow the Kaplan Method for Sentence Correction, which you will see in chapter 5, and your average time for SC questions will be down to 60 seconds. That's a savings of 15 minutes for the average test taker—more than enough time to read the passages! You also want to pace yourself so that you have time to work on the questions at the end of the section.

One of the most persistent bits of bad advice out there is to take more time at the beginning of the test. Don't! Running short of time at the end of the test will cost you much more than you gain from those few extra right answers. You'll be penalized for not reaching a question, and long strings of wrong answers due to random guessing or rushing will hurt your score as well.

What this all means is that you are under some conflicting pressures. It might seem like a good idea to take extra time at the beginning to ensure that you get all the first questions right, since then the test would give you those difficult, high-value questions. But if you use up a lot of time early on, you won't have time to finish, and your score will suffer a severe penalty. Just a handful of unanswered final questions can lower a score from the mid-90th percentile to the mid-70th percentile! Plus, if you spend all that time early on, you won't have time to solve those hard questions, and you won't be able to take advantage of their extra value.

So if taking more time at the beginning isn't a good idea, should you rush through the beginning? No way! Most GMAT problems are as much analytical puzzles as math problems, so trying to rush almost guarantees missing some crucial aspect of the problem. And if you get a lot of midlevel questions wrong, the test will never give you those difficult, high-value questions that you want to reach.

EXPERT EXCLUSIVE

What makes for a "good guessing question"? One that you know plays to your weaknesses, one that requires lots of reading, or an EXCEPT question (these are notoriously time consuming).

If you are stuck on a question, make a guess. And if you start to fall behind pace, look for good guessing questions. That way you'll reach the end of the section.

STRATEGIC GUESSING

Whether because you're running short of time or you've hit a question that totally flummoxes you, you will have to guess occasionally. But don't just guess at random. Try to narrow down the answer choices before you guess. This will greatly improve your chances of guessing the right answer. When you guess, you should follow this plan.

(1) **Eliminate answer choices you know are wrong.** Even if you don't know the right answer, you can often tell that some of the answer choices are wrong. For instance, on Sentence Correction questions, you can eliminate answer choice (A) as soon as you find an error, thus reducing the number of choices to consider.

(2) **Avoid answer choices that make you suspicious.** These are the answer choices that just "look wrong" or conform to a common wrong-answer type.

For example, if an answer choice in a Reading Comprehension question mentions a term you don't remember reading, chances are it is wrong. (The next three chapters will have more information about common wrong-answer types on the Verbal section.)

(3) **Choose one of the remaining answer choices.** The fewer options you have to choose from, the higher your chances of selecting the right answer. It's like the 50-50 on *Who Wants to Be a Millionaire!*

TREAT EVERY QUESTION AS IF IT WERE SCORED

Some questions on the test are experimental—questions that the test makers are checking out for possible use on future tests. These questions do not contribute to your score, and there is no way of identifying them. Treat every question as if it were scored.

HOW THE VERBAL SECTION IS SCORED

The Verbal section of the GMAT is quite different from the Verbal sections of most paper-and-pencil tests. The major difference is that the GMAT "adapts" to your performance. Each test taker is given a different mix of questions, depending on how well he or she is doing on the test. In other words, the questions get harder or easier depending on whether you answer them correctly or not. Your GMAT score is not directly determined by how many questions you get right but by how hard the questions you get right are.

When you start a section, the computer

- assumes you have an average score (500); and
- gives you a medium-difficulty question. What happens next depends on whether you answer the question correctly.

If you answer the question correctly,

- your score goes up; and
- you are given a slightly harder question.

If you answer the question incorrectly,

- your score goes down; and
- you are given a slightly easier question.

This pattern continues for the rest of the section. As you get questions right, the computer raises your score and gives you harder questions. As you get questions wrong, the computer lowers your score and gives you easier questions. In this way, the computer tries to "home in" on your score.

 GO ONLINE
Complete your Diagnostic Quiz as soon as you can. That way, you can get started focusing on your weak areas. Concentrate on quality—not on the number of questions you got right.

CHAPTER 4: CRITICAL REASONING

- Question Format and Structure
- The Basic Principles of Critical Reasoning
- Critical Reasoning Question Types
- The Kaplan Method for Critical Reasoning

Critical Reasoning (CR) tests reasoning skills involved in making arguments, evaluating arguments, and formulating or evaluating a plan of action. These questions are based on materials from a variety of sources, though you will not need to be familiar with any subject matter beforehand.

Specifically, you are measured on your ability to reason in the following areas:

- **Argument construction.** Recognizing the basic structure of an argument, properly drawn conclusions, underlying assumptions, explanatory hypotheses, or parallels between structurally similar arguments
- **Argument evaluation.** Analyzing an argument, recognizing elements that would strengthen or weaken it, identifying reasoning errors committed in the argument or aspects of the argument's development
- **Formulating and evaluating a plan of action.** Recognizing the relative appropriateness, effectiveness, and efficiency of different plans of action, as well as factors that would strengthen or weaken a proposed plan of action

> **EXPERT EXCLUSIVE**
>
> A skill that pertains to each of these three areas is the ability to recognize the "scope" of an issue. This is perhaps the most important Critical Reasoning skill, and you'll be reading a lot about it in the pages to come!

QUESTION FORMAT AND STRUCTURE

The directions for Critical Reasoning questions are short and to the point. They look like this:

> **Directions:** Select the best of the answer choices given.

About 12 Critical Reasoning questions appear on the GMAT. Here's an example of one:

> A study of 20 overweight men revealed that each man experienced significant weight loss after adding SlimDown, an artificial food supplement, to his daily diet. For three months, each man consumed one SlimDown portion every morning after exercising and then followed his normal diet for the rest of the day. Clearly, anyone who consumes one portion of SlimDown every day for at least three months will lose weight and will look and feel his best.
>
> Which one of the following is an assumption on which the argument depends?
>
> ○ The men in the study will gain back the weight if they discontinue the SlimDown program.
>
> ○ No other dietary supplement will have the same effect on overweight men.
>
> ○ The daily exercise regimen was not responsible for the effects noted in the study.
>
> ○ Women won't experience similar weight reductions if they adhere to the SlimDown program for three months.
>
> ○ Overweight men will achieve only partial weight loss if they don't remain on the SlimDown program for a full three months.

EXPERT EXCLUSIVE

Notice that the question comes after the argument? You'll save a lot of time if you skip down to the question first and read the argument second.

On the GMAT, in business school, and in your career you'll need the ability to see and understand complex reasoning. It's not enough to sense whether an argument is strong or weak; you'll need to analyze precisely why it is so. This presumes a fundamental skill that's called on by nearly every Critical Reasoning question—the ability to isolate and identify the various components of any given argument. And that brings us to the basic principles of Critical Reasoning.

EXPERT EXCLUSIVE

Over 70% of Critical Reasoning questions use arguments, so understanding their structure will be of great help on test day.

THE BASIC PRINCIPLES OF CRITICAL REASONING

Here are the basic skills that you need to succeed on CR questions.

UNDERSTAND THE STRUCTURE OF AN ARGUMENT

First, you must know how arguments are structured so that you can break them down into their core components. When we use the word *argument,* we don't mean a conversation where two people are shouting at each other. An argument in Critical Reasoning means any piece of text where an author puts forth a set of ideas and/or a point of view and attempts to support it. Every GMAT argument is made up of two basic parts:

(1) The conclusion (the point that the author is trying to make)

(2) The evidence (the support that the author offers for the conclusion)

Success on this section hinges on your ability to identify these parts of the argument. There is no general rule about where the conclusion and evidence appear in the argument—it could be the conclusion first followed by the evidence, or it could be the other way around. Consider this stimulus (in other words, the passage):

> The Brookdale Public Library will require extensive physical rehabilitation to meet the new building codes passed by the town council. For one thing, the electrical system is inadequate, causing the lights to flicker sporadically. Furthermore, there are too few emergency exits, and even those are poorly marked and sometimes locked.

Suppose that the author of this argument was allowed only one sentence to convey her meaning. Do you think she would waste her time with the following statement? Would she walk away satisfied that her main point was communicated?

> The electrical system [at the Brookdale Public Library] is inadequate, causing the lights to flicker sporadically.

No. Given a single opportunity, she would have to state the first sentence to convey her real purpose:

> The Brookdale Public Library will require extensive physical rehabilitation . . . .

That is the conclusion. If you pressed the author to state her reasons for making that statement, she would then cite the electrical and structural problems with the building. That is the evidence for her conclusion.

But does that mean that an evidence statement like "The electrical system is inadequate," can't be a conclusion? No, we're just saying it's not the conclusion for this particular argument. Every idea, every new statement, must be evaluated in the context of the stimulus in which it appears.

For the statement above to serve as the conclusion, the stimulus could be the following:

> The electrical wiring at the Brookdale Public Library was
> installed over 40 years ago and appears to be corroded in
> some places [evidence]. An electrician, upon inspection of
> the system, found a few frayed wires as well as some blown
> fuses [evidence]. Clearly, the electrical system at the Brookdale
> Public Library is inadequate [conclusion].

> **EXPERT EXCLUSIVE**
>
> Words such as *because, since,*
> *for, as a result of,* and *due*
> *to* signal evidence. Words
> such as *consequently, hence,*
> *therefore, thus, clearly, so,* and
> *accordingly* signal a conclusion.

To succeed in Critical Reasoning, you'll have to be able to determine the precise function of every sentence in the stimulus. The easiest way to do this is to use structural signals, or "keywords" as we call them at Kaplan, to identify conclusion and evidence. Words such as *because, for,* and *since* are clear indications of evidence; words such as *therefore, hence, thus, so,* and *consequently* usually signal the conclusion. Notice how the word *clearly* in the argument above provides a strong signal that the last sentence is the conclusion.

Not every Critical Reasoning stimulus will have these keywords, but most do; look for them every time, because using them to identify the conclusion and evidence will greatly increase not only your ability to get the right answer but also your ability to do so quickly.

The explanations for the practice test in the back of this book discuss the structure of many of the Critical Reasoning arguments on the test, so read these carefully to shore up your understanding of this crucial aspect.

STUDY THE QUESTION

Before you read the stimulus, look over the question. This will give you some idea of what you need to look for as you read. Suppose the question with the first library argument above asked the following:

> The author supports her point about the need for rehabilitation
> at the Brookdale Library by citing which of the following?

If you had read the question before the stimulus, you'd know what to look for in advance—only the evidence, the "support," provided. You wouldn't have to pay much attention to the conclusion at all! But suppose the question were this:

> **EXPERT EXCLUSIVE**
>
> Some CR problems put very
> important information—
> sometimes even the conclusion
> itself—into the question. Read it
> carefully!

> The author's main point is best expressed by which of the
> following?

In this case you'd do the opposite—you'd focus only on the conclusion and wouldn't care much about the evidence.

Reading the question first allows you to save valuable time because you will know how to attack the stimulus. As you'll soon see, this technique will be especially handy when you have a great working knowledge of the strategies for the different types of Critical Reasoning questions.

PARAPHRASE THE ARGUMENT

After you read the stimulus, paraphrase the author's main argument to yourself. That is, restate the author's ideas in your own words. Frequently, the authors in Critical Reasoning say pretty simple things in complex ways. So if you mentally translate the verbiage into a simpler form, the whole thing will become be more manageable.

In the library argument, for instance, you probably don't want to deal with the full complexity of the author's stated conclusion:

> The Brookdale Public Library will require extensive physical rehabilitation to meet the new building codes passed by the town council.

Instead, you want to paraphrase a much simpler point:

> The library will need fixing up to meet new codes.

Similarly, the evidence is pretty bulky:

> For one thing, the electrical system is inadequate, causing the lights to flicker sporadically. Furthermore, there are too few emergency exits, and even those are poorly marked and sometimes locked.

You could paraphrase it like this:

> The library's electrical system is bad, and the emergency exits are too few, hard to find, and locked.

So the whole argument might be said simply:

> The library's electrical system is bad, and the emergency exits are too few, hard to find, and locked. Therefore, the library will need fixing up to meet new codes.

EXPERT EXCLUSIVE

Paraphrasing serves as a valuable test. If you can't paraphrase the stimulus, you probably don't understand it yet. If you don't understand the stimulus, the odds of getting the right answer are not high, so keep trying. If you can't paraphrase after several tries, you should probably make a guess and move on to the next problem.

Often, by the time you begin reading through the answer choices, you run the risk of losing sight of the gist of the stimulus. So restating the argument in your own words will not only help you get the author's point in the first place, it will also help you hold onto it until you've found the correct answer.

Explain questions and certain Inference questions consist of collections of facts rather than complete arguments. Nonetheless, paraphrasing that information will be helpful in making sure you get the gist of the stimulus.

HUNT FOR POTENTIAL PROBLEMS WITH THE ARGUMENT

You must read actively, not passively, on the GMAT. Active readers are always thinking critically, analyzing what they're reading, and forming reactions as they go along. Instead of accepting an argument at face value, they look for potential problems. This pays huge dividends on most Critical Reasoning questions.

Here are some common potential problems in Critical Reasoning questions:

- **Shifts of scope.** The argument suddenly introduces a new term or idea that wasn't mentioned before and isn't connected to the rest of the argument.
- **Confusing correlation for causation.** Just because two things happen at the same time doesn't mean that one caused the other!
- **Plans and predictions.** Could there be something inherently self-defeating about a proposed course of action? Any unintended consequences? Any important factors unaccounted for? The GMAT asks many questions about plans and predictions, because they are like miniature business plans!

Consider the argument about the library again. Seems pretty reasonable at first glance—good lighting and working emergency exits are pretty important for a public building. But the critical reader might ask, "Wait a sec—I've got a lot of information about the problems but no information about the codes. Do the codes apply to flickering lights, for example?"

Since part of what you're called on to do here is to evaluate arguments, don't let yourself fall into the bad habits of the passive reader—reading solely for the purpose of getting through the stimulus. Those who read this way invariably find themselves having to read stimuli two or even three times. Then they're caught short on time. Read the stimulus right the first time—with a critical eye and an active mind.

ANSWER THE QUESTION BEING ASKED

One of the most disheartening experiences in Critical Reasoning is to understand the author's argument fully but then supply an answer to a question that wasn't asked.

EXPERT EXCLUSIVE

For a Strengthen question, a common trap is a statement that nicely weakens the argument among the answer choices. Don't fall for it!

The classic example of this error occurs on "Strengthen/Weaken" questions. When you're asked to strengthen or weaken an argument, you can be sure that there will be one, two, even three answer choices that do the opposite of what's asked. Choosing such a wrong choice is less a matter of failing to understand the argument than of failing to remember the task at hand.

The question stem will always ask for something very specific. It's your job to follow the test makers' line of reasoning to the credited response.

Also, be on the lookout for "reversers," words such as *not* and *except*. These little words are easy to miss, but they change entirely the kind of statement you're looking for among the choices.

TRY TO PREDICT AN ANSWER

This principle, which is really an extension of the last one, is crucial. You must try to approach the answer choices with at least a faint idea of what the answer should look like. That is, predict the answer in your own mind before looking at the choices. This isn't to say you should ponder the question for minutes—it's still a multiple-choice test, so the right answer is on the screen. Just get in the habit of framing an answer in your head.

Once you have made a prediction, scan the choices. Sure, the correct choice on the exam will be worded differently and will likely be more fleshed out than your vague idea. But if it matches your thought, you'll know it in a second. And you'll find that there's no more satisfying feeling in Critical Reasoning than predicting correctly and then finding the correct answer quickly and confidently.

> **EXPERT EXCLUSIVE**
>
> Notice how the question asks not just for an assumption in general but for one specifically about the new codes? By studying the question, we're able to predict the answer much more effectively.

Continuing with the library situation, suppose you were asked this:

> The author's argument depends on which of the following assumptions about the new building codes?

Having hunted for potential problems and realized that the argument gives no information about whether the codes apply to the problems in the library, you could quickly realize that the answer must say something like "The new building codes apply in this situation." Then an answer like this one would jump off the screen as clearly correct:

- ○ The new codes apply to existing buildings, as well as to buildings under construction.

Alternately, the correct answer could be worded like this:

- ○ The new codes would force renovation to the ventilation systems and improved handicapped access, as well as improvements to the electrical system and emergency exits.

> **EXPERT EXCLUSIVE**
>
> The most effective predictions are vague enough to fit with unexpected ideas (like "existing buildings") but specific enough about the scope of the argument to allow you to eliminate most wrong answers.

EXPERT EXCLUSIVE

A remarkable number of wrong answer choices in CR contain scope problems. Be wary of choices that are too extreme or that don't match the stimulus in tone or subject matter.

KEEP THE SCOPE OF THE STIMULUS IN MIND

When you're at the point of selecting one of the answer choices, focus on the scope of the stimulus. Most of the wrong choices on this section are wrong because they are "outside the scope." In other words, the wrong answer choices contain elements that don't match the author's ideas or that go beyond the context of the stimulus.

Some answer choices are too narrow, too broad, or have nothing to do with the author's points. Others are too extreme to match the scope—they're usually signaled by such words as *all*, *always*, *never*, *none*, and so on. For arguments that are moderate in tone, correct answers are more qualified and contain such words as *usually*, *sometimes*, and *probably*.

To illustrate the scope principle, let's look again at the question mentioned above:

> The author's argument depends on which of the following assumptions about the new building codes?

Let's say one of the choices read as follows:

> The new building codes are far too stringent.

EXPERT EXCLUSIVE

A common error is to think that scope is purely about terminology. It's much more about the impact of the ideas in the answer choice on the ideas in the stimulus. If it has the right impact, the answer is in scope, regardless of its terminology.

Knowing the scope of the argument would help you to eliminate this choice very quickly. You know that this argument is just a claim about what the new codes will require: that the library be rehabilitated. It's not an argument about whether the requirements of the new codes are good, or justifiable, or ridiculously strict. That kind of value judgment is outside the scope of this argument.

Recognizing scope problems is a great way to eliminate dozens of wrong answers quickly.

CRITICAL REASONING QUESTION TYPES

Now that you're familiar with the basic principles of Critical Reasoning, let's look at the most common types of questions. Certain question types crop up again and again on the GMAT, and it pays to understand them beforehand.

ASSUMPTION QUESTIONS

An assumption is a piece of support that isn't explicitly stated but is necessary for the argument to remain valid. It bridges the gap between two pieces of the argument, usually between conclusion and evidence but sometimes between two unconnected pieces of evidence. Without it, the argument falls apart. When a question asks you for what's missing from the argument or what the argument depends on, then it's asking you to find an assumption.

Predicting the Answer for Assumption Questions

As we've just seen, you can often predict an answer to an Assumption question. By previewing the question stem, you'll know what to look for. Once you understand the argument's structure, you may well see a missing piece. Consider this simple stimulus:

> Allyson plays volleyball for Central High School. Therefore, Allyson must be over 6 feet tall.

The conclusion is pretty clearly the second sentence, and the evidence is the first. Where's the problem? Well, who's to say that all high school volleyball players have to be over 6 feet tall? So we can pretty confidently predict that an answer would say something like this:

> All volleyball players at Central High School are over 6 feet tall.

But what if the assumption doesn't just jump out at you? Can you track it down? Of course you can! One of the most common ways the GMAT uses assumptions is to cover over a scope shift in the argument. Notice how the argument above starts by talking about playing volleyball and then all of a sudden is talking about being over 6 feet tall. Look closely at the terms in each part of the argument. Could the scope be slightly different?

Consider this seemingly solid argument:

> Candidate A won the presidential election, carrying 40 out of 50 states. Clearly, Candidate A has a strong mandate to push for her legislative agenda.

Sounds pretty good. But take a close look at the terms of the argument. The evidence is a win representing a sizeable majority of states. The conclusion is about a strong mandate for an agenda. Even if you don't immediately see why those two things don't have to be the same, you could still make a prediction like this: "Candidate A's big victory means she has a mandate for her agenda." You'd be much more likely to recognize the right answer between these two possibilities:

○ No other candidate in the last 24 years has won as many states as did Candidate A.

○ Most of the people who voted for Candidate A support her legislative agenda.

The first answer choice doesn't deal with Candidate A's agenda at all. The second one shows a connection between her victory and her agenda, so it must be the right answer.

But what if you still aren't sure that your answer choice is correct? Or what if the assumption is so subtle that you can't predict the answer at all? In those cases, you can use the Denial Test.

The Denial Test

Because an assumption must be true for the conclusion to be valid, we can test each answer by seeing whether the conclusion could still be valid even if the answer were negated (e.g., rewritten to say the opposite). If the argument falls apart, then that answer choice is a necessary assumption. If the argument is unaffected, then the choice is wrong. Let's look at the volleyball prediction:

All volleyball players at Central High School are over 6 feet tall.

Now let's negate it:

Some volleyball players at Central High School are not over 6 feet tall.

Would Allyson still have to be over 6 feet tall? Of course not! That's why that prediction would be a necessary assumption.

And now look at the Candidate A answer choices:

○ No other candidate in the last 24 years has won as many states as did Candidate A.

○ Most of the people who voted for Candidate A support her legislative agenda.

And now we'll negate them:

○ Some candidates in the last 24 years have won as many states as did Candidate A.

Could Candidate A still enjoy a strong mandate? Definitely. Just because others in the past were as popular doesn't mean that she doesn't enjoy support for her agenda as well.

○ Most of the people who voted for Candidate A do not support her legislative agenda.

Now can Candidate A claim a mandate for her agenda? Of course not. That's why the second choice would be credited as correct.

> **EXPERT EXCLUSIVE**
>
> Don't be too extreme when you negate answer choices. The denial of *hot* isn't *cold* but rather *not hot*. Similarly, the denial of *all are* isn't *none are* but rather *some aren't*.

> **EXPERT EXCLUSIVE**
>
> There are many ways to write a Critical Reasoning question. Any wording that suggests that you need to find a missing but vital piece of information indicates an Assumption question.

Sample Question Stems

Assumption questions are worded in some of the following ways:

- Which one of the following is assumed by the author?
- Upon which one of the following assumptions does the author rely?
- The argument depends on the assumption that . . .
- Which one of the following, if added to the passage, would make the conclusion logical?

- The validity of the argument depends on which one of the following?
- The argument presupposes which one of the following?

STRENGTHEN AND WEAKEN QUESTIONS

Determining an argument's necessary assumption, as we've just seen, is required to answer an Assumption question. But it also is required to answer another common type of question: Strengthen or Weaken.

In the real world, we can weaken someone's argument by attacking their evidence. But the GMAT is testing not your ability simply to find evidence but rather your ability to analyze how that evidence is used. The right answer to a Weaken question on the GMAT will always weaken the connection between the evidence and the conclusion—in other words, the assumption.

The answer to many Weaken questions is the one that reveals an author's assumption to be unreasonable; conversely, the answer to many Strengthen questions provides additional support by affirming the truth of an assumption.

Let's use the same stimulus as before but in the context of these other question types:

> Allyson plays volleyball for Central High School. Therefore, Allyson must be over 6 feet tall.

Remember the assumption holding this argument together? It was that all volleyball players for Central High are over 6 feet tall. That's the assumption that makes or breaks the argument. So if you're asked to weaken the argument, you'd want to attack that assumption:

> Which one of the following, if true, would most weaken the argument?

Prediction: Not all volleyball players at Central High School are over 6 feet tall.

Answer:

- ○ Some volleyball players at Central High School are under 6 feet tall.

We've called into doubt the author's basic assumption, thus damaging the argument. But what about strengthening the argument? Again, the key is the necessary assumption:

> Which one of the following, if true, would most strengthen the argument?

Prediction: All volleyball players at Central High School are over 6 feet tall.

Answer:

- ○ No member of the Central High School volleyball team is under 6'2".

EXPERT EXCLUSIVE
Notice that we don't have to prove the conclusion wrong, just make it less likely. Allyson *could* still be over 6 feet tall, but now she doesn't have to be.

Here, by confirming the author's assumption, we've in effect bolstered the argument.

 KAPLAN STRATEGY

- For a Strengthen or Weaken question, keep the following in mind: Weakening an argument is not the same as disproving a conclusion—and strengthening is not the same as proving it. A weakener tips the scale toward doubting the conclusion, while a strengthener tips the scale toward believing in the validity of the conclusion.

- The wording often takes the form of "which of the following, if true, would most [weaken or strengthen] the argument?" The "if true" part means that you have to accept the validity of the answer choice right off the bat, no matter how unlikely it may sound.

- Many wrong answers have the opposite of the desired effect. If you're asked to weaken an argument, watch out for wrong answers that would strengthen it. Asked to strengthen? Be wary of weakeners. Pay close attention to what the question asks.

Sample Stems

The stems associated with these two question types are usually self-explanatory. Here's a list of some you can expect to see on test day:

Weaken:

- Which one of the following, if true, would most weaken the argument above?
- Which one of the following, if true, would most seriously damage the argument above?
- Which one of the following, if true, casts the most doubt on the argument above?
- Which of the following, if true, would most seriously call into question the plan outlined above?

Strengthen:

- Which one of the following, if true, would most strengthen the argument?
- Which one of the following, if true, would provide the most support for the conclusion in the argument above?
- The argument above would be more persuasive if which one of the following were found to be true?

It's also common for the question stem to refer explicitly to part of the argument. You might, for example, see the following:

> Which of the following, if true, casts the most doubt on the author's conclusion that the Brookdale Public Library does not meet the requirements of the new building codes?

Reading the question stem first, here we would be told outright what the author's conclusion is, making the reading of the stimulus much easier to manage.

INFERENCE QUESTIONS

The second most common question type in Critical Reasoning is the Inference question. The process of inferring is a matter of considering one or more statements as evidence and then drawing a conclusion from them. A valid inference is something that must be true if the statements in the stimulus are true. Not *might* be true, not *probably* is true, but *must* be true.

Think of an inference as a conclusion that requires no assumption whatsoever. But the answer to an Inference question is just as likely to be drawn from only one or two details as it is to take into account the stimulus as a whole. For this reason, it can be very difficult to predict an exact answer. Nevertheless, you can make a general prediction: The answer is the one that *must* be true based on the facts in the stimulus. You can use this prediction to help eliminate choices answer by answer, ruling out options that clearly don't match the facts as you paraphrased them. This is the beauty of a multiple-choice test—find four wrong answers, and you've also found the right one!

> **EXPERT EXCLUSIVE**
> Success on Inference questions often depends on not eliminating answer choices that you aren't sure about. Eliminate only when you're sure it's a wrong answer.

Let's examine a somewhat expanded version of the volleyball team argument:

> Allyson plays volleyball for Central High School, despite the team's rule against participation by nonstudents. Therefore, Allyson must be over 6 feet tall.

Wrong answer: Allyson is the best player on the Central High School volleyball team.

Certainly Allyson *might* be the best player on the team. It's tempting to think that this would *probably* be true—otherwise the team would not risk whatever penalties violating the rule might entail. But *must* it be true? No. Allyson could be the second best. Or the third best. Or perhaps the coach owed Allyson's dad a favor. We have no support for the idea that she's the best on the team.

Valid inference: Allyson is not a student at Central High School.

Clearly, if Allyson plays volleyball *despite* the team's rule against participation by nonstudents, she must not be a student. Otherwise, she wouldn't be playing despite the rule; she'd be playing in accordance with the rule. But note that this inference is not an essential assumption of the argument because the conclusion about Allyson's height doesn't depend on it.

So be careful: Unlike an assumption, an inference need not have anything to do with the author's conclusion. In fact, many Inference questions don't have conclusions at all—they consist solely of individual facts. Make sure you are prepared for Inference questions, as they require a different approach than do other Critical Reasoning questions. Remember, everything that you'll need will be contained in the stimulus, so focus on the information as it's presented and avoid answers that twist the facts (or make up new ones).

Sample Stems

Inference questions probably have the most varied wording of all the Critical Reasoning question stems. Some question stems denote inference fairly obviously. Others are more subtle, and still others may even look like other question types entirely. The bottom line is that if a question asks you to take the stimulus as fact and find something based on it, then you're looking at an Inference question. Here's a quick rundown of various Inference question stems that you may see on your test:

- Which one of the following can be inferred from the argument above?
- Which one of the following is implied by the argument above?
- The author suggests that . . .
- If all the statements above are true, which one of the following must also be true?
- The statements above, if true, support which of the following?
- Which of the following is best supported by the statements above?
- Which of the following is the conclusion toward which the author is probably moving?
- The statements above best support which of the following conclusions?

OTHER QUESTION TYPES

Assumption, Strengthen, Weaken, and Inference make up about 85 percent of all Critical Reasoning questions, but you might run into other question types as well.

Explain Questions

These ask you to find an explanation for a seeming discrepancy in the question stem. Your paraphrasing skills are the key to this problem type—in your own words, restate not only the details in the stimulus but also the nature of the apparent inconsistency. Then, look for an answer that explains how the apparently contradictory facts in the stimulus could both be true.

Here are some example question stems:

- Which of the following would best explain the discrepancy above?
- Which of the following would best resolve the paradox described above?

Flaw Questions

These are similar to Weaken questions, but instead of asking you for some new fact that, if true, would make the argument questionable, flaw questions ask what's already wrong. So your prediction should focus on reasoning errors made in the argument.

Here are some example question stems:

- Which of the following is a flaw in the reasoning above?
- The argument above is vulnerable to which of the following criticisms?

Boldface Questions

Boldface questions ask for the role that specific sentences play in relation to an author's argument. The relevant sentences are, as the name implies, written in bold font. The answers to these questions will be abstract, using language such as "The first provides a counterexample to an opinion, while the second reaffirms that opinion by dismissing the counterexample." This technical language may make these problems seem intimidating.

Fortunately, these questions are rare, appearing only occasionally on the tests of high-scoring test takers. Moreover, if you do see one of these questions on test day, they shouldn't be nearly as scary as they look. Remind yourself that boldface questions test the same core skill as the rest of the Critical Reasoning section: the ability to identify the evidence and the conclusion of an argument.

One caution: Unlike most GMAT stimuli, boldface questions often contain multiple arguments. Make sure that you note not only which parts of the argument are evidence and which are conclusions but also which evidence is connected to which conclusion. In addition, use keywords in the stimulus to identify which conclusion (if any) the author agrees with. Once you've done so, you should be able to make a prediction about the role of the bolded statements. Then you can turn these difficult questions into points.

Here is an example question stem:

- The portions of the argument in **boldface** play which of the following roles?

THE KAPLAN METHOD FOR CRITICAL REASONING

Now it's time to learn how to orchestrate all of this background information into a strategy for attacking Critical Reasoning questions. We've developed a method that you can use to attack each and every CR question.

STEP 1: IDENTIFY THE QUESTION TYPE

As we mentioned in the discussion of basic principles, reading the question stem first is a great way to focus your reading of the stimulus. Determine the question type, and you'll know exactly what you're looking for. There may be other important information in the question stem as well—possibly even the conclusion itself.

> **EXPERT EXCLUSIVE**
>
> If you aren't sure about the question type, don't rush on to Step 2. Take the time you need to understand what the question is asking.

STEP 2: UNTANGLE THE STIMULUS

With the question stem in mind, read the stimulus. Read actively, paraphrasing to make sure you understand the argument's construction and hunting for any potential problems.

ONLINE

Revisit the questions in your Diagnostic Quiz. This time through, predict an answer for each one and see if that makes a difference in helping you answer them correctly.

STEP 3: PREDICT THE ANSWER

Form an idea of what the right answer choice should say or do.

STEP 4: EVALUATE THE CHOICES

Attack each answer choice critically. Keep your prediction in mind and see whether the answer choices match it. If you don't find a "clear winner," start looking through the answers that you haven't eliminated. You know what you *like* about each; now focus on what might be *wrong*.

Here's how your Prediction and Evaluation steps will work for the major question types:

- **Assumption Question:** Predict what the central assumption should say and hunt for the answer that matches your prediction. If that fails, use the Denial Test.
- **Strengthen/Weaken the Argument:** Identify the central assumption and predict an answer explaining why that assumption is more (for a Strengthen question) or less (for a Weaken question) likely to come true.
- **Inference:** It's often difficult to form a prediction beyond "The right answer must be true." Work through the answers one by one, eliminating choices that are clearly wrong. Don't eliminate an answer that you're unsure of—it may be right.
- **Explain:** Predict the answer that explains how seemingly discrepant facts can both be true.
- **Flaw:** Predict the reasoning error committed by the argument.
- **Bolded Statement:** Predict an answer based on your understanding of the author's use of logic.

Now let's apply the Kaplan Method to the Critical Reasoning item we saw earlier:

> A study of 20 overweight men revealed that each man experienced significant weight loss after adding SlimDown, an artificial food supplement, to his daily diet. For three months, each man consumed one SlimDown portion every morning after exercising, then followed his normal diet for the rest of the day. Clearly, anyone who consumes one portion of SlimDown every day for at least three months will lose weight and will look and feel his best.

Which one of the following is an assumption on which the argument depends?

- ○ The men in the study will gain back the weight if they discontinue the SlimDown program.
- ○ No other dietary supplement will have the same effect on overweight men.

EXPERT EXCLUSIVE

Read the question first and take a moment to plan your strategy before you start reading the stimulus.

- ○ The daily exercise regimen was not responsible for the effects noted in the study.

- ○ Women won't experience similar weight reductions if they adhere to the SlimDown program for three months.

- ○ Overweight men will achieve only partial weight loss if they don't remain on the SlimDown program for a full three months.

STEP 1: IDENTIFY THE QUESTION TYPE

We see, quite clearly, that we're dealing with an Assumption question. So we can immediately adopt an "assumption mindset," which means we know before we even read the stimulus that there will be some missing link in the chain of reasoning—a missing piece of support without which the conclusion wouldn't be valid. Now we turn to the stimulus, ready to find that link.

STEP 2: UNTANGLE THE STIMULUS

Sentence 1 introduces a study of 20 men using a food supplement product, resulting in weight loss for all 20. Sentence 2 describes how they used it: once a day, for three months, after morning exercise. So far so good; it feels as if we're building up to something. The key word *clearly* usually indicates that some sort of conclusion follows, and in fact it does: Sentence 3 says that anyone who has one portion of the product daily for three months will lose weight, too.

We might paraphrase the argument like this:

> Each of 20 overweight men lost weight by consuming some SlimDown every morning after exercise, then eating normally. So anyone who consumes SlimDown will lose weight.

> **EXPERT EXCLUSIVE**
>
> Notice how the argument asserts that there could only have been one cause for a certain effect even though other causes might, in reality, be possible? That's a very common GMAT pattern, which you can use to help form your paraphrase.

Reading critically, do we see any scope shifts or other potential problems? Sure—what happened to the exercise? It's in the evidence as part of the study regimen but is totally dropped from the conclusion. That's a pretty significant change in scope, and we can use that as the basis of our prediction in Step 3.

We could, if we were so inclined, look at the argument even more abstractly:

> A bunch of guys did A and B and had X result. So if someone does A, they'll get X result too.

> **EXPERT EXCLUSIVE**
>
> There's rarely one "perfect way" to figure out the right answer; as long as you read critically, you'll be moving in the right direction.

Sounds pretty fishy—who says A (SlimDown) caused X (weight loss)? Why couldn't it have been B (exercise)? We can use this insight to make a prediction in Step 3, too. Notice that no matter how abstractly or concretely we analyze the question stem, we arrive at the same basic issue—that the author isn't accounting for the exercise.

STEP 3: PREDICT THE ANSWER

We've realized that the argument forgot to consider the exercise. So we might predict something like "The author assumes exercise doesn't matter." That's it. There's no need to paraphrase with something fancy and glamorous. A vague paraphrase, as long as it's focused on the right scope, is enough to find the right answer.

📖 READ MORE

For more practice with Critical Reasoning questions, turn to Kaplan's *GMAT Verbal Workbook*.

STEP 4: EVALUATE THE CHOICES

Judge the answer choices based on how well they fulfill the requirements of your prediction. And sure enough, only (C) even mentions the exercise regimen! Reading it closely, we see it fits our prediction perfectly, clearing up the question of whether the exercise caused the weight loss.

Since the difficulty of Critical Reasoning is often in the answer choices (rather than the stimulus), you can't let them make you indecisive. Pick (C) with confidence and move on.

We also could have used the Denial Test. Let's look at what the answer choices would look like when negated:

- Answer choice (A): The men in the study will not gain back the weight if they discontinue the SlimDown program. There's no reason to think that just because the weight loss is permanent, it wasn't caused by SlimDown. Wrong answer.
- Answer choice (B): Other dietary supplements would have the same effect. That's no reason to think that SlimDown wouldn't work. (The conclusion says that SlimDown will work, not that *only* SlimDown could work.) Wrong answer.
- Answer choice (C): The daily exercise regimen was responsible for the effects noted in the study. If it was the exercise, it wasn't the SlimDown. Now the conclusion isn't possible . . . so this is definitely the right answer!
- Answer choice (D): Women will experience similar weight reductions if they adhere to the SlimDown program for three months. That's no reason to think that it didn't work for the men. Wrong answer.
- Answer choice (E): Overweight men could achieve total weight loss if they don't remain on the program for a full three months. If anything, this makes it more likely that SlimDown caused the weight loss. Wrong answer.

EXPERT EXCLUSIVE

You can see how the Denial Test is more time consuming than a successful prediction, so form a prediction if you can.

OTHER POSSIBLE QUESTION STEMS

Grasping the structure of an argument and locating the author's central assumption allows you to answer many different kinds of questions.

- Flaw question: Which of the following best describes the flaw in the argument above?
  - Prediction: What about the exercise?
  - Right answer: It fails to consider whether the exercise regimen could have been responsible for the weight loss.
- Weaken question: Which of the following, if true, casts the most doubt on the argument above?
  - Prediction: The exercise, and not the SlimDown, caused the weight loss.
  - Right answer: Daily exercise contributed significantly to the weight loss experienced by the men in the study.

SUMMARY

The Basic Principles of Critical Reasoning are the following:

- Understand the structure of an argument.
- Study the question.
- Paraphrase the argument.
- Hunt for potential problems with the argument.
- Answer the question being asked.
- Try to predict an answer.
- Keep the scope of the stimulus in mind.

The most common question types are the following:

- Assumption questions
- Strengthen and Weaken questions
- Inference questions

The Kaplan Method for Critical Reasoning is as follows:

Step 1: Identify the question type.
Step 2: Untangle the stimulus.
Step 3: Predict the answer.
Step 4: Evaluate the choices.

Address the common Critical Reasoning question types as follows:

- Assumption question: Find the missing link.
- Strengthen question: Make the assumption more likely.
- Weaken question: Make the assumption less likely.
- Inference question: Find what *must* be true.

PRACTICE QUIZ

Directions: Select the best answer for each question.

1. In Los Angeles, a political candidate who buys saturation radio advertising will get maximum name recognition.

   The statement above logically conveys which of the following?

   ○ Radio advertising is the most important factor in political campaigns in Los Angeles.

   ○ Maximum name recognition in Los Angeles will help a candidate to win a higher percentage of votes cast in the city.

   ○ Saturation radio advertising reaches every demographically distinct sector of the voting population in Los Angeles.

   ○ For maximum name recognition, a candidate need not spend on media channels other than radio advertising.

   ○ A candidate's record of achievement in the Los Angeles area will do little to affect his or her name recognition there.

2. In recent years, attacks by Dobermans on small children have risen dramatically. Last year saw 35 such attacks in the continental United States alone, an increase of almost 21 percent over the previous year's total. Clearly, then, it is unsafe to keep dogs as pets if one has small children in the house.

   The argument above depends upon which of the following assumptions?

   ○ No reasonable justification for these attacks by Dobermans on small children has been discovered.

   ○ Other household pets, such as cats, don't display the same violent tendencies that dogs do.

   ○ The number of attacks by Dobermans on small children will continue to rise in the coming years.

   ○ A large percentage of the attacks by Dobermans on small children could have been prevented by proper training.

   ○ The behavior toward small children exhibited by Dobermans is representative the behavior of dogs in general.

Advanced

3. An investigation must be launched into the operations of the private group that is training recruits to fight against the Balaland Republic. The U.S. Neutrality Act plainly forbids U.S. citizens from engaging in military campaigns against any nation with which we are not at war. Since no war has been declared between the United States and the Balaland Republic, we should bring charges against these fanatics, who are in open defiance of the law.

   Which of the following, if true, would most weaken the argument above?

   ○ The Balaland Republic is currently engaged in a bloody and escalating civil war.

   ○ Diplomatic relations between the United States and the Balaland Republic were severed last year.

   ○ The recruits are being trained to fight only in the event the United States goes to war against the Balaland Republic.

   ○ The training of recruits is funded not by U.S. citizens but rather by a consortium of individuals from abroad.

   ○ Charges cannot be brought against the private group that is training the recruits unless an investigation is first launched.

Advanced

4. Critics of strict "promotional gates" at the grade school level point to a recent study comparing students forced to repeat a grade with those promoted despite failing scores on an unscheduled, experimental competency test. Since there was no significant difference between the two groups' scores on a second test administered after completion of the next higher grade level, these critics argue that the retention policy has failed in its expressed purpose of improving students' basic skills.

   Which of the following best expresses the argument made by critics of promotional gates?

   ○ Anxiety over performance on standardized tests often hinders a student's ability to master challenging new material.

   ○ A student's true intellectual development cannot be gauged by a score on a standardized competency test.

   ○ The psychological damage a child suffers by repeating a grade outweighs the potential intellectual benefits of a second chance at learning.

   ○ Strict requirements for promotion do not lead to greater mastery of fundamentals among students.

   ○ Socioeconomic factors as well as test scores influenced whether a given student in the study was promoted or forced to repeat a grade.

Advanced

5. Statistics show that more than half of the nation's murder victims knew their assailants; in fact, 24 percent last year were killed by relatives. Nor was death always completely unexpected. In one study, about half the murder victims in a particular city had called for police protection at least five times during the 24 months before they were murdered. Nonetheless, most people are more likely to fear being killed by a stranger in an unfamiliar situation than by a friend or relative at home.

Which of the following, if true, best explains the attitude of most people to the likelihood of being murdered?

○ Statistics are likely to be discounted no matter what the source, if their implication seems to run counter to common sense.

○ In the face of such upsetting problems as murder and assault, most people are more likely to react emotionally rather than rationally.

○ A study taken in only one city is not likely to have an effect on attitudes until similar studies have been undertaken at the national level and have yielded similar results.

○ Most people do not consider themselves to be in the high-risk groups in which murder occurs frequently between relations, but they do see themselves as at least minimally susceptible to random violence.

○ People who seek police protection from relatives and friends are often unwilling to press charges once the emotions of the moment have cooled.

6. Freedom of expression can easily be violated in even the most outwardly democratic of societies. When a government arts council withholds funding from a dance performance that its members deem "obscene," the voices of a few bureaucrats have in fact censored the work of the choreographer, thereby committing the real obscenity of repression.

Which of the following, if true, would most seriously weaken the argument above?

○ Members of government arts councils are screened to ensure that their beliefs reflect those of the majority.

○ The term *obscenity* has several different definitions that should not be used interchangeably for rhetorical effect.

○ Failing to provide financial support for a performance is not the same as actively preventing or inhibiting it.

○ The council's decision could be reversed if the performance were altered to conform to public standards of appropriateness.

○ The definition of *obscenity* is something on which most members of a society can agree.

7. The local high school students have been clamoring for the freedom to design their own curricula. Allowing this would be as disastrous as allowing three-year-olds to choose their own diets. These students have neither the maturity nor the experience to equal that of the professional educators now doing the job.

Which of the following statements, if true, would most strengthen the above argument?

○ High school students have less formal education than those who currently design the curricula.

○ Three-year-olds do not, if left to their own devices, choose healthful diets.

○ The local high school students are less intelligent than the average teenager.

○ Individualized curricula are more beneficial to high school students than are the standard curricula, which are rigid and unresponsive to their particular strengths and weaknesses.

○ The ability to design good curricula develops only after years of familiarity with educational life.

8. The rate of violent crime in this state is up 30 percent from last year. The fault lies entirely in our court system: recently our judges' sentences have been so lenient that criminals can now do almost anything without fear of a long prison term.

The argument above would be weakened if it were true that

○ 85 percent of the other states in the nation have lower crime rates than does this state.

○ white-collar crime in this state has also increased by over 25 percent in the last year.

○ 35 percent of the police in this state have been laid off in the last year due to budget cuts.

○ polls show that 65 percent of the population in this state opposes capital punishment.

○ the state has hired 25 new judges in the last year to compensate for deaths and retirements.

9. The education offered by junior colleges just after World War II had a tremendous practical effect on family-run businesses throughout the country. After learning new methods of marketing, finance, and accounting, the sons and daughters of merchants returned home, often to increase significantly the size of the family's enterprise or to maximize profits in other ways.

   Which of the following statements is best supported by the information above?

   ○ The junior colleges principally emphasized methods of increasing the size of small businesses.

   ○ The business methods taught in the junior colleges were already widespread before World War II.

   ○ The business curricula at junior colleges did not include theoretical principles of management.

   ○ Without the influence of junior colleges, many family-run businesses would have been abandoned as unprofitable.

   ○ Business methods in many postwar family-run businesses changed significantly as a result of the junior colleges.

10. Techniques to increase productivity in the performance of discrete tasks, by requiring less human labor in each step of the production process, are widely utilized. Consultants on productivity enhancement point out, however, that although these techniques achieve their specific goal, they are not without drawbacks. They often instill enough resentment in the workforce eventually to lead to a slowdown in the production process as a whole.

    Which of the following can be reasonably inferred from the statements above?

    ○ Productivity enhancement techniques do not attain their intended purpose and should not be employed in the workplace.

    ○ The fact that productivity enhancement techniques are so widely employed has led to a decline in the ability of American businesses to compete abroad.

    ○ If productivity enhancement consultants continue to utilize these techniques, complete work stoppages will eventually result.

    ○ Ironically, an increase in the productivity of discrete tasks may result in a decrease in the productivity of the whole production process.

    ○ Production managers are dissatisfied with the efforts that productivity enhancement consultants have made to increase productivity.

11. Time and time again, it has been shown that students who attend colleges with low faculty/student ratios get the most well-rounded education. As a result, when my children are ready for college, I'll be sure they attend a school with a very small student population.

    Which of the following, if true, identifies the greatest flaw in the reasoning above?

    ○ A low faculty/student ratio is the effect of a well-rounded education, not its source.

    ○ Intelligence should be considered the result of childhood environment, not advanced education.

    ○ A very small student population does not, by itself, ensure a low faculty/ student ratio.

    ○ Parental desires and preferences rarely determine a child's choice of a college or university.

    ○ Students must take advantage of the low faculty/student ratio by intentionally choosing small classes.

12. The increase in the number of newspaper articles exposed as fabrications serves to bolster the contention that publishers have become more interested in boosting circulation than in printing the truth. Even minor publications have staffs to check such obvious fraud.

    The argument above assumes that

    ○ newspaper stories exposed as fabrications are a recent phenomenon.

    ○ everything a newspaper prints must be factually verifiable.

    ○ fact-checking is more comprehensive for minor publications than for major ones.

    ○ only recently have newspapers admitted to publishing intentionally fraudulent stories.

    ○ the publishers of newspapers are the people who decide what to print in their newspapers.

13. Our architecture schools must be doing something wrong. Almost monthly, we hear of domes and walkways collapsing in public places, causing great harm to human life. In their pursuit of some dubious aesthetic, architects design buildings that sway, crumble, and even shed windows into our cities' streets. This kind of incompetence will disappear only when the curricula of our architecture schools devote less time to so-called artistic considerations and more time to the basics of good design.

Which of the following, if true, would most seriously weaken the argument above?

○ All architecture students are given training in basic physics and mechanics.

○ Most of the problems with modern buildings stem from poor construction rather than poor design.

○ Less than 50 percent of the curriculum at most architecture schools is devoted to aesthetics.

○ Most buildings manage to stay in place well past their projected life expectancies.

○ Architects study as long and as intensively as most other professionals.

14. World War II had a profound effect on the growth of nascent businesses. The Acme Packaging Company netted only $10,000 in the year before the war. By 1948, it was earning almost 10 times that figure.

The argument above depends upon which of the following assumptions?

○ Acme's growth rate is representative of that of other nascent businesses.

○ An annual profit of $10,000 is not especially high.

○ Wars inevitably stimulate a nation's economy.

○ Rapid growth for nascent businesses is especially desirable.

○ Acme is not characterized by responsible, far-sighted managers.

15. This editorial cannot be a good argument because it is barely literate. Run-on sentences, slang, and perfectly dreadful grammar appear regularly throughout. Anything that poorly written cannot be making very much sense.

Which of the following identifies an assumption in the argument above?

○ This editorial was written by someone other than the usual editor.

○ Generally speaking, very few editorials are poor in style or grammar.

○ The language of an argument is indicative of its validity.

○ Generally speaking, the majority of editorials are poor in style and grammar.

○ The author of the editorial purposely uses poor grammar to disguise what he knows is a bad argument.

16. Electrical engineers have developed an energy-efficient type of lightbulb that is likely to replace the traditional incandescent bulb for household use. The new bulb, known as the electronic lamp, operates by using a high-frequency radio signal rather than the filament featured in incandescent bulbs. Although the electronic lamp currently costs 20 times as much as its traditional counterpart, its use will prove more cost-effective in the long run. While a 100-watt incandescent bulb lasts 6 months if burned for 4 hours daily, a 25-watt electronic lamp used for the same amount of time each day lasts up to 14 years.

    The argument above assumes that

    ○ the typical household use of a lightbulb is approximately four hours a day.

    ○ aside from its greater efficiency, the electronic lamp resembles the incandescent lightbulb in most aspects.

    ○ the type of light cast by the electronic lamp is different from that cast by an incandescent bulb.

    ○ the price of electronic lamps will decrease as they are produced in greater quantities.

    ○ a 100-watt incandescent light bulb does not provide significantly more or otherwise better light than a 25-watt electronic lamp.

Advanced

17. In interviews with jurors inquiring how they arrived at their verdicts, researchers found that 40 percent of the references jurors made were to factors that had not been included in courtroom testimony. To improve the jury system, the researchers suggested that judges give instructions to the jury at the beginning of a trial rather than at the end. They argued that this would permit jurors to concentrate on the most relevant evidence rather than filling in gaps with their own assumptions, which have little to do with the legality of a case.

    The answer to which of the following questions is LEAST directly relevant to evaluating the researchers' suggestion above?

    ○ Is it possible for a judge to instruct a jury at the end of a trial in such a way that jurors will disregard any irrelevant factors they had been using to weigh the evidence?

    ○ Will a jury that hears a judge's instructions at the beginning of a trial be able to weigh the evidence accordingly once that evidence has actually been presented?

    ○ Will having judges give instructions at the beginning of a trial rather than at the end significantly alter the customary procedures employed by the judicial system?

    ○ When jurors are queried as to how they arrived at their verdicts, does their interpretation of their decision-making process include many references to factors that were not, in fact, influential?

    ○ If jurors hear the judge's instructions at the beginning of a trial, what percentage of the factors that influence their decisions will be matters that were not presented in the evidence?

18. Privatization of the large state enterprises that compose the industrial sector in Russia is proceeding slowly due to competing claims of ownership by various groups. Continued government subsidization of these enterprises creates large deficits, which drive up the inflation rate and cause the ruble's value to decline. Since further decline in the value of the ruble could be disastrous, it is unlikely that the government will make the ruble freely convertible to Western currencies until the question of ownership of state enterprises has been resolved.

If the author's prediction concerning the ruble is accurate, which of the following conclusions can most reliably be drawn?

○ The industrial sector accounts for at least 50 percent of Russia's economic activity.

○ Making the Russian ruble freely convertible to Western currencies will not cause the ruble's value to increase.

○ The Russian government can indefinitely withstand the expense of subsidiary state enterprises.

○ The Russian government is among the groups claiming ownership of certain state enterprises.

○ The Russian government is under pressure from the West to make the ruble freely convertible to Western currencies.

Advanced

19. Attempts to blame the mayor's policies for the growing inequality of wages are misguided. The sharp growth in the gap in earnings between college and high school graduates in this city during the past decade resulted from overall technological trends that favored the skills of more educated workers. Nor can the mayor's response to this problem be criticized, for it would hardly be reasonable to expect him to attempt to slow the forces of technology.

Which of the following, if true, casts the most serious doubt on the conclusion drawn in the last sentence above?

○ The mayor could have initiated policies that would have made it easier for less-educated workers to receive the education necessary for better-paying jobs.

○ Rather than cutting the education budget, the mayor could have increased the amount of staff and funding devoted to locating employment for graduating high school seniors.

○ The mayor could have attempted to generate more demand for products from industries that paid high blue-collar wages.

○ Instead of reducing the tax rate on the wealthiest earners, the mayor could have ensured that they shouldered a greater share of the total tax burden.

○ The mayor could have attempted to protect the earnings of city workers by implementing policies designed to reduce competition from foreign industries.

20. In a survey of freshmen at University X, two-thirds claimed never to have plagiarized while in high school. However, the survey may overstate the proportion of freshmen at University X who did not plagiarize in high school because_____.

    Which of the following best completes the passage above?

    ○ some people who do not attend University X probably plagiarized in high school.

    ○ some people who plagiarized in high school may not do so in college.

    ○ some people who claimed to have plagiarized once may have done so many times.

    ○ at University Z, one-half of the freshmen admitted to having plagiarized in high school.

    ○ some freshmen who did plagiarize in high school might have claimed on the survey that they did not do so.

21. Smith Products fabricates machine tools that are essentially identical to those produced by Jackson Manufacturing. For both companies, raw materials represent about two-thirds of the cost of manufacturing the machine tools. To gain an edge over Jackson Manufacturing, Smith Products should purchase its raw materials from a new supplier advertising much lower prices.

    Which of the following, if true, would most weaken the argument above?

    ○ Smith Products spends more on employee wages than Jackson Manufacturing does.

    ○ Smith's current supplier provides raw materials of exceedingly high quality.

    ○ The market for machine tools has been declining for several years.

    ○ The new supplier's materials are of low quality and would reduce the life span of Smith machine tools by half, causing sales to decline.

    ○ The plant manager for Smith Products is planning to increase the plant's efficiency.

22. According to a recent study, a diet that is free of meat and dairy products greatly reduces the risk of suffering a heart attack. The study cites the fact that only 10 percent of those who consume such a diet suffer a heart attack at some point in their lives.

    Which of the following would most seriously weaken the argument above?

    ○ Diets free of meat and dairy are low in calcium, which can lead to bone density decreases.

    ○ Those who consume only dairy but not meat are twice as likely to suffer a heart attack as those who consume neither meat nor dairy.

    ○ Some people who consume neither dairy nor meat suffer two or more heart attacks over the course of a lifetime.

    ○ Meat and dairy products are high in low-density cholesterol, which is known to harden arteries and cause other heart problems.

    ○ Of those who consume dairy and meat, 7 percent regularly suffer heart attacks over the course of their lifetime.

Questions 23–24

23. In 2001, a local high school implemented a new program designed to reduce the incidence of teenage pregnancy. The program, however, failed to produce the desired result. If the program had been successful, the dropout rate for female students would not have increased substantially in 2001.

    The argument in the passage depends on which of the following assumptions?

    ○ The number of teen pregnancies nation-wide increased in 2001.

    ○ The number of teen pregnancies in 2001 was greater than the number of teen pregnancies in 1991.

    ○ Teenage pregnancy is a leading reason that female students leave school.

    ○ The program was mandatory for all female students.

    ○ Most 2001 female dropouts were not pregnant at any time during the year.

24. The argument in the passage would be most seriously weakened if it were true that

    ○ the number of female students in the school has remained constant for the past decade.

    ○ nationwide, the teen pregnancy rate and the female high school dropout rate both increased significantly in 2001.

    ○ some female students who dropped out were pregnant at the time.

    ○ many female high school dropouts said that poor economic conditions forced them to leave school and find jobs.

    ○ the school also implemented a program designed to reduce the incidence of drug use among teenagers in 2001.

25. The workers' union of GrainCorp, a grain-processing plant, is attempting to obtain a pay raise from GrainCorp management. To pressure GrainCorp management into accepting the union's proposal, the president of the union has proposed organizing a consumer boycott against SquareMart food stores, which are owned by MegaFood, the parent company of GrainCorp.

    The answer to which of the following questions is LEAST directly relevant to the union president's consideration of whether a boycott of SquareMart will lead to acceptance of the union's pay rate proposal?

    ○ Would the loss of business at SquareMart stores materially affect MegaFood?

    ○ Are the staple food products purchased by consumers at SquareMart stores readily available at other stores not owned by MegaFood?

    ○ How many SquareMarts are within the region of the GrainCorp plant?

    ○ Have other unions successfully employed the same strategy?

    ○ Is MegaFood the only corporation that operates both grain-processing plants and food stores?

26. An ecology magazine regularly publishes articles on tree diseases. This year, the number of articles on *Ophiostoma ulmi*, the fungus that causes Dutch elm disease, is significantly smaller than the number of such articles that appeared last year. Clearly, fewer researchers studied *Ophiostoma ulmi* this year than did so last year.

    Which of the following, if true, weakens the above conclusion?

    ○ Many researchers publishing articles are currently studying *Stegophora ulmea*, a fungus that causes elm leaf spot.

    ○ Since its introduction, Dutch elm disease has killed half of the elm trees in North America.

    ○ Research on Dutch elm disease that focuses on prevention receives more funding than research that focuses on finding a cure.

    ○ A new strain of the fungus *Rhytisma acerinum* infested maple trees at an unprecedented rate this year.

    ○ All articles go through at least a one-year review process before publication.

27. Saguaro kangaroo rats generally leave watering holes, where food and water are abundant, during the day, while Sonoran kangaroo rats remain near these same watering holes and continue foraging throughout the day. Although Sonoran kangaroo rats have larger and more frequent litters, they are generally outnumbered by the Saguaro kangaroo rat.

    Which of the following, if true, would best resolve the apparent paradox described above?

    ○ Several species of successful rodents also leave the streams and watering holes during the day.

    ○ The Saguaro kangaroo rat matures much more slowly than the Sonoran kangaroo rat because of its relatively limited food supply.

    ○ Many of the predators of kangaroo rats, such as falcons and rattlesnakes, are only active around streams during the day.

    ○ Saguaro kangaroo rats are more sensitive to sunlight than are Sonoran kangaroo rats.

    ○ Sonoran kangaroo rats are reproductive to a greater age than are Saguaro kangaroo rats.

28. National regulations that limit the sale of meat to within five days of packing should be changed. Under optimal conditions, meat kept at 40°F will not spoil for 16 days. If the regulations were changed, prices for meat would drop due to increased shelf life and reduced waste, but the safety of the food supply would not be compromised.

    Which of the following, if true, would most seriously weaken the conclusion drawn above?

    ○ After cooking their meat, many consumers save leftovers for more than 11 days.

    ○ Seven of 10 shopkeepers favor extending the limitation on meat to 9 days.

    ○ Approximately 65 percent of the meat display cases nationally maintain temperatures between 47°F and 54°F.

    ○ Approximately half the meat stored for 25 days is still safe to consume.

    ○ Meatpacking operations are more efficient when they can make fewer, larger deliveries than when they must make more frequent, smaller deliveries.

29. The owner of a four-story commercial building discovered termites in the building's first and second floors and called an exterminator. The exterminator pumped gas into the walls on both the first and second floors. Due to the exterminator's work, the termites on those floors were killed quickly.

    Which of the following, if true, most seriously undermines the validity of the explanation for the speed with which the termites were killed?

    ○ The third floor had no termite infestation.

    ○ Even though the exterminator did not pump gas into the walls of the fourth story, the previously undiscovered termites there died as quickly as they did on the first and second stories.

    ○ The speed at which termites are killed increases as the concentration of an exterminator's gas increases.

    ○ The speed with which the exterminator's gas kills termites drops off sharply as the gas dissipates throughout the building's walls.

    ○ The exterminator's gas-pumping system works efficiently even when pumping gas into both the first and second stories of the building simultaneously.

30. Recent surveys show that many people who left medical school before graduating suffer from depression. Clearly, depression is likely to cause withdrawal from medical school.

    Which of the following, if true, would most strengthen the conclusion above?

    ○ Many medical schools provide psychological counseling for their students.

    ○ About half of those who leave medical school report feeling depressed after they make the decision to leave.

    ○ Depression is very common among management consultants who have a similarly difficult work schedule as that of many young doctors.

    ○ Medical students who have sought depression counseling during medical school leave medical school at a higher rate than the national average.

    ○ Career change has been shown to be a strong contributing factor in the onset of depression.

31. The performance of Southport's two high schools has been quite consistent over the past five years. In each of those years, Suburban High has enrolled 40 percent of Southport's students and produced 75 percent of the town's high school graduates, while Lakeside High has accounted for the remainder.

    Which of the following can properly be inferred regarding the past five years from the passage above?

    ○ The total number of students attending each high school has remained roughly constant.

    ○ Students attending Suburban High come from a larger geographical area than students attending Lakeside High.

    ○ Lakeside High has graduated a lower percentage of its attendees than has Suburban High.

    ○ The respective geographic areas from which the schools draw their student populations have remained unchanged.

    ○ Students attending magnet programs accounted for a higher percentage of the graduating students at Lakeside High than at Suburban High.

32. A chemical company recently introduced a new type of foam spray that it claims will reduce the rate of erosion from the walls of road cuts. A study by the company showed that the rate of erosion was low on a road cut where the foam was applied.

    Which of the following, if true, would most seriously weaken the company's conclusion?

    ○ Road cuts similar to the one studied typically show low rates of erosion without the foam.

    ○ Because the foam itself weathers, the foam would have to be reapplied every four years to maintain protection against erosion.

    ○ Studies by the company that produces the material are very reliable.

    ○ The foam manufacturer's computer models of the road cut in the study predicted even less erosion than actually occurred.

    ○ Other foams made from similar materials have failed to halt erosion from certain types of road cuts.

33. A researcher has discovered that steel containing Element X is stronger and more flexible than ordinary steel because Element X reduces the occurrence of microscopic fractures. The level of Element X in much of the steel produced in Canada is naturally high because the ore deposits from which the steel is produced also contain Element X.

    Which of the following can be correctly inferred from the statements above?

    ○ Steel from Canada is stronger and more flexible than steel from any other country.

    ○ Steel that is not from Canada is highly likely to develop microscopic fractures after years of use.

    ○ Producing steel from ore deposits containing Element X is the best way to make steel that is stronger and more flexible.

    ○ Some steel produced in Canada is less likely to develop microscopic fractures than other steel.

    ○ Steel produced from Canadian ore deposits contains the highest levels of Element X found in any steel.

34. The Laysan Rail, an insectivore bird once present on several of the Hawaiian Islands, can no longer be found and is thought to be extinct. Scientists originally thought that a decrease in the amount of ground vegetation available for nesting was responsible for the decline of the bird. However, they now believe that increased competition for food was ultimately responsible for the Laysan Rail's inability to survive.

Which of the following would best help to account for the change in the accepted explanation for the Laysan Rail's extinction?

○ The vegetation on the Laysan Rail's home island was decimated when rabbits were introduced to the island in the 1910s.

○ When attempts were made to relocate the Laysan Rail to other islands, the birds lost the geographical cues that they relied on for finding mating sites.

○ The Laysan Rail builds nests under dense ground cover to protect the eggs.

○ A recent study found that an increase in the use of pesticides resulted in a decrease in the numbers of flies and moths present in the Laysan Rail's territory.

○ Many species nested in the same types of vegetation as the Laysan Rail.

Advanced

35. Retail clothing stores should hold "one-day-only" sales to clear merchandise that has been returned because it is defective in some way. The stores should sell this merchandise for up to 70 percent less than the original retail price. Stores will find these sales to be an effective way of getting rid of defective merchandise as long as they inform customers that the discounted merchandise is nonreturnable.

The author assumes which of the following about the "one-day-only" sale merchandise in predicting the effectiveness of these sales?

○ The defects in the merchandise are not so significant that customers will be unwilling to pay even the sale price.

○ The rate of returns when merchandise is new makes these "one-day-only" sales key to a store's profitability.

○ Too few shoppers purchase merchandise at full retail price.

○ If these sales become popular, stores will have to have them more often.

○ The majority of the "one-day-only" sale merchandise will be purchased by shoppers who would otherwise not shop at those stores.

36. A brochure for City X highlights the reasons why residents should move there rather than to other cities in the state. One reason that the brochure mentions is the relative ease of finding a job in City X, where the unemployment rate is 4.7 percent.

    Which of the following statements, if true, casts the most doubt on the validity of the reason to move to City X mentioned above?

    ○ Most of the jobs in City X are hourly rather than salary jobs.

    ○ The state where City X is located has an average unemployment rate of 3.9 percent.

    ○ Other reasons to move to City X include the school system and easy access to recreational activities.

    ○ The national unemployment rate, calculated during the last census, is 4.3 percent.

    ○ City Y, located in the same state as City X, recently built a new factory that will employ 5,000 workers.

Advanced

37. If participation in the honors creative writing class were limited to graduate students and those undergraduates who had received at least a B+ in composition, most of the undergraduate students would be forced to take the regular creative writing class. Such a reduction in undergraduate enrollment would reduce the percentage of failing grades in the honors class.

    Which of the following, if true, would most strengthen the conclusion drawn in sentence 2 above?

    ○ Graduate students have all scored at least B+ in composition.

    ○ The honors creative writing course is experiencing overcrowding due to increases in graduate enrollment.

    ○ Many undergraduates would work harder to score B+ in composition rather than be excluded from honors creative writing.

    ○ The number of failing grades in honors creative writing has decreased in recent years.

    ○ Undergraduates who scored lower than B+ in composition are responsible for a disproportionate percentage of failing grades in honors creative writing.

Questions 38–39

Advanced

---

38. In a certain state, the rate at which inhabitants of City X contract a certain disease is significantly lower than the rate at which inhabitants of City Y contract the disease. So if a couple originally from City Y relocates to City X and raises a family there, their children will be significantly less likely to contract this disease than they would had they remained in City Y.

Which of the following, if true, would most seriously weaken the conclusion drawn in the passage?

○ Many health experts do not believe that moving to City X will lead to a significant increase in the average person's immunity to the disease.

○ The mayor of City Y has falsely claimed that statistics relating to the incidence of the disease in his city are not accurate.

○ The lower incidence of the disease in City X can be ascribed mostly to genetically determined factors.

○ Some inhabitants of City Y possess a greater immunity to the disease than do the healthiest inhabitants of City X.

○ Smog levels in City X are significantly lower than those of any other city in the state.

39. Which of the following statements, if true, would most significantly strengthen the conclusion drawn in the passage?

○ The rate at which inhabitants of City X contract the disease will increase as the overall population of City X increases.

○ In contrast to City Y, City X is characterized by an abundance of environmental factors that tend to inhibit the occurrence of the disease.

○ Of those inhabitants of City Y who move to City X, 23 percent live beyond the average life span of native inhabitants of City X.

○ Over the last two decades, the incidence of the disease has decreased in City Y but has remained unchanged in City X.

○ Studies indicate that the incidence of the disease among inhabitants of City X who move to City Y is roughly equal to that of inhabitants of City X who remain in City X.

40. A recently published article on human physiology claims that enzyme K contributes to improved performance in strenuous activities such as weight lifting and sprinting. The article cites evidence of above-average levels of enzyme K in Olympic weight lifters and sprinters.

    Which of the following, if true, would most strengthen the article's conclusion?

    ○ Enzyme K levels tend to peak when people feel most alert.

    ○ Enzyme K has no other function in the human body.

    ○ Enzyme K is required for the performance of strenuous activities.

    ○ Enzyme K helps weight lifters more than it helps sprinters.

    ○ Strenuous activities do not cause the human body to produce unusually high levels of enzyme K.

41. In the state of Michigan, from 1980 to 1989, total spending on books purchased from all sources increased by 34 percent. But during the same period, spending on fiction books, most of which were purchased from bookstores selling only new books, grew just 16 percent.

    Which of the following statements about the period from 1980 to 1989 is best supported by the statements above?

    ○ Spending on nonfiction books increased by more than 34 percent.

    ○ Shoppers were more likely to buy fiction books when they went to a bookstore than they were to buy nonfiction.

    ○ The prices of books purchased at bookstores are higher than those of books purchased elsewhere.

    ○ Individual spending on books increased, while institutional spending declined.

    ○ The number of people who bought books from secondhand bookstores increased during this period.

42. The state legislature has proposed a new law that would provide a tax credit to people who install alarm systems in their homes. Members of the legislature claim that the new law will reduce crime, citing studies showing that crime rates fall as the percentage of homes with alarm systems rises.

    Which of the following, if true, would cast the most doubt on the claim that the new law will reduce crime?

    ○ No law can prevent crime altogether.

    ○ The amount of the tax credit is so low relative to the cost of alarm systems that very few people will install alarm systems to obtain this credit.

    ○ Neighborhood crime prevention programs can reduce crime as effectively as alarm systems can.

    ○ The state would have to build more prisons to house all the people caught by the new alarm systems.

    ○ The state can afford to reduce taxes further.

43. Countries A and B are in competition to draw tourists to their countries. In Country A, about 2,500 violent crimes are reported per year. In Country B, about 1,000 violent crimes are reported per year. Trying to draw tourists away from Country A, officials in Country B use these violent crime statistics to claim it has a lower violent crime rate than Country A.

    Which of the following, if true, would expose the flaw in Country B's argument that it has the lower violent crime rate?

    ○ Most violent criminals in Country B are repeat offenders.

    ○ White-collar crime is higher in Country B than in Country A.

    ○ The population of Country A is 20 times greater than the population of Country B.

    ○ Country B has fewer tourists than Country A.

    ○ Country A has a better prison system than Country B.

44. If a poor harvest season in a major corn-producing state results in higher prices for a bushel of corn, corn prices in all other states will rise as well, whether or not those states are net importers of corn.

    Which of the following conclusions is best supported by the statement above?

    ○ Agricultural commodities companies in states that are not net importers of corn are excluded from the national corn market when there is a disruption in the national corn supply.

    ○ National corn supply disruptions have little, if any, effect on the price of local corn as long as the locality is in a state that is not a net importer of corn.

    ○ The corn market in any state is part of the national corn market, even if most of the corn consumed in the state is produced in the state.

    ○ Poor harvesting seasons come at predictably regular intervals.

    ○ Higher prices for corn tend to lead to increased prices for livestock, which rely on corn feed.

45. Town X and Town Y are roughly equal in size and local population. A survey was done measuring traffic patterns during the summer months for each of the past five years. The survey found that, on average in Town Y, there were 28 minor car accidents in June as well as 28 in July. During the same two months in Town X, the average was only 14 minor car accidents each month. Thus, if the Dentco Autobody Repair franchise were looking to open a new shop in one of the two towns, it would be more likely to succeed in Town Y.

    Which of the following, if true, would most seriously damage the conclusion drawn in the passage?

    ○ More people walk to work or use mass transit in Town Y.

    ○ The state is planning to add a thruway exit for Town Y.

    ○ The traffic volume in Town Y quadruples in the summer because it is a beach town.

    ○ In June and July six years ago, Town X had double the amount of accidents than Y.

    ○ There are rumors of a mega mall possibly being constructed in Town X.

46. Ronald is a runner on the track team and is a great hurdler. All runners on the track team are either sprinters or long-distance runners, but a few long-distance runners do not run the sprint because they are too slow. Hurdlers never run long-distance because they lack the endurance necessary. Therefore, Ronald must be fast.

    For the conclusion drawn above to be logically correct, which of the following must be true?

    ○ Sprinters are faster than hurdlers.

    ○ All runners on the track team who run hurdles also run long-distance.

    ○ Hurdling requires more endurance than running long-distance.

    ○ All sprinters are fast.

    ○ Every runner on the track team who is fast is a sprinter.

47. The latest census of the town in which Jacob's hardware store is located has revealed that the population of new residents has increased tenfold since 1980. Though Jacob has not encountered any new competition for business during this time period, his inventory records indicate that the average number of lawnmowers and snowblowers that he sells per year has risen only slightly over the average number of lawnmowers and snowblowers he sold yearly prior to 1980.

    Which of the following, if true, best explains the discrepancy outlined above?

    ○ Since 1980, many of the single home properties have been subdivided into smaller single home parcels.

    ○ Inflation has caused the prices of the machines to increase every year since 1980.

    ○ All of the housing built in Jacob's town since 1980 has been large apartment complexes.

    ○ The average snowfall since 1980 has decreased from 6 feet per year to 4 feet per year.

    ○ Jacob's store only carries two brands of lawnmowers and snowblowers.

ANSWERS AND EXPLANATIONS FOLLOW ON THE NEXT PAGE

ANSWERS AND EXPLANATIONS

1. D	11. C	21. D	31. C	41. A
2. E	12. E	22. E	32. A	42. B
3. C	13. B	23. C	33. D	43. C
4. D	14. A	24. D	34. D	44. C
5. D	15. C	25. E	35. A	45. C
6. C	16. E	26. E	36. B	46. D
7. E	17. C	27. C	37. E	47. C
8. C	18. B	28. C	38. C	
9. E	19. A	29. B	39. B	
10. D	20. E	30. D	40. E	

DIAGNOSTIC TOOL

Tally up your score and write down your results below.

Total Correct: _____ out of 47

Approximate Percentage Correct: # you got right × 100 ÷ 47: _____

DIAGNOSE YOUR RESULTS

Look back at the questions you got wrong and think back on your experience answering them.

STEP 1: FIND THE ROADBLOCKS

Did you struggle to answer some questions? To improve your score, you need to pinpoint exactly what element of these roadblocks tripped you up. To do that, ask yourself these three questions:

1. Did I not know what I was looking for when I read the stimulus?

If that's the case, you either didn't identify the question type or forgot what strategies to employ when solving it. Go back and review the Kaplan principles and strategies for the question types you struggled with. Make sure that you understand them and how to apply them. Get as much practice as you can with this question type. Try out the Kaplan's *GMAT Verbal Workbook*, which includes practice sets for each question type and a full-length Verbal practice section!

2. Did I understand the question stem but struggle with the stimulus?

Were you unable to digest the dense language? Did you struggle to identify the central assumption or to form a confident prephrase? Did you misread the scope of the argument? Try out Kaplan's *GMAT Verbal Workbook*, which contains valuable strategies for breaking down a Critical Reasoning argument, as well as exercises to build speed and accuracy. You should also read the answer explanations, as they will guide you through these skills as well.

3. Did I do fine with both the question stem and the stimulus but struggle with the answer choices?

Did more than one answer seem correct? Did no answer seem correct? Either you misread the scope of the stimulus, or you struggled to connect the ideas in the answer choices to the ideas in the stimulus. Closely read the answer explanations for more guidance on how to work with answer choices.

STEP 2: FIND THE BLIND SPOTS

Did you answer some questions quickly and confidently—but get them wrong anyway?

When you come across wrong answers like these, you need to figure out what you thought you were doing right, what it turns out you were doing wrong, and why that happened. The best way to do that is to read the answer explanations.

They give you a detailed breakdown of why the correct answer is correct and why all the other answer choices are wrong. This helps to reinforce the Kaplan principles and method for each question type and helps you figure out what blindsided you so it doesn't happen again. Also, just like with your roadblocks, try to get in as much practice as you can.

STEP 3: REINFORCE YOUR STRENGTHS

Now read through all the answer explanations for the ones you got right. Again, this helps to reinforce the Kaplan principles and method for each question type, which in turn helps you work more efficiently so you can get the score you want. Keep your skills sharp with more practice.

> **EXPERT EXCLUSIVE**
>
> Don't ignore the explanations for the ones you got right. Could you have solved more efficiently? Could you have eliminated answers more easily? The stronger your skills become, the higher your GMAT score will be.

As soon as you are comfortable with all the GMAT question types and Kaplan methods, complete a full-length practice test under timed conditions. In this way, practice tests serve as milestones; they help you to chart your progress! So don't save them all for the final weeks.

If you are aiming for that top score, try out Kaplan's *GMAT 800*, which includes only the toughest GMAT questions and most focused strategies.

For even more practice, you can also try out the GMAT Quiz Bank! You get more than 1,000 questions that you can access 24/7 from any Internet browser, each with comprehensive explanations. You can even customize your quizzes based on question type, content, and difficulty level. Take quizzes in Timed Mode to test your stamina or in Tutor Mode to see explanations as you work. Best of all, you also get detailed reports to track your progress.

Visit **kaptest.com/GMAT** for more details on the Quiz Bank and for more information on other online and classroom-based options.

EXPERT EXCLUSIVE

Words like *most important* in (A) and *every* in (C) are hallmarks of answers that are too extreme to be correct.

1. D

The question stem is a little unusual, but since it asks what conclusion the argument seems to make, we can treat this as an Inference question—we want to find something completely supported by the stimulus. So after reading the stimulus and making sure that we understand it, we'll go through the answers one by one.

The stimulus says that in L.A., buying saturation radio advertising will get maximum name recognition. In other words, saturation radio ads are enough, on their own, to guarantee maximum name recognition.

(A) claims that radio ads are the most important factor to campaigns. That's too broad to be supported, as the stimulus discusses only name recognition, not campaigns as a whole. (B) is *possibly* true but ultimately a wrong answer because there's nothing that tells us for certain what the results of maximum name recognition would be. Similarly, (C) is out of scope; the stimulus gives us no information on the role of distinct voting sectors in name recognition. (D) claims that the only thing a candidate needs to do to get maximum name recognition is advertise on the radio; the stimulus says that radio advertising, in large enough quantities, would guarantee maximum name recognition. They say the same thing! So (D) is the credited answer. Finally, just because radio advertising alone is sufficient, that doesn't necessarily mean that other factors have no effect, so we can rule out (E).

2. E

Pretty clearly, this is an Assumption question, so we are looking for the "missing link" in the argument. The evidence discusses attacks by Dobermans, but the conclusion is about dogs—all dogs. That's a big change of scope. The author must be thinking that all dogs behave as Dobermans do. So there's our prediction: "All dogs behave like Dobermans." That's exactly what (E) says, although of course the GMAT phrases it more densely. (Notice, though, how specific answer (E) is about the scope of the argument—dogs' behavior around small children!) The Denial Test would also work well here. If Dobermans' behavior toward children isn't typical of dogs in general, then the argument falls apart.

(A), whether the attacks were justified, is beside the point. Even if the kids were pulling the dogs' tails, the author's point that the dogs aren't safe still holds. Other pets are beyond the scope, so (B) is out. As for (C), the argument doesn't deal with the future, so the author needn't assume anything about it. And it certainly wouldn't weaken the argument if, contrary to (D), many of the attacks could not have been prevented, so (D) is not assumed.

3. C

This is a Weaken question, so we need to find the central assumption and then find the answer that makes it more questionable. The argument basically says that charges should be brought against a group that is training recruits to fight against Balaland. Why? Because we aren't at war with Balaland, and citizens are forbidden to engage in military campaigns against countries with which we aren't at war. Where's the problem with this argument? Note the scope shift—the law forbids "military campaigns," but the group is only "training." The author must be assuming that the group is actively engaged in military campaigns, as well. So to weaken this argument, we want to look for the answer that says, "The group is only training; they aren't actually fighting." (C) fits the bill; as the group would only start fighting if the United States declared war, they aren't in violation of the law.

(A) is no weakener; aside from the problem that it has nothing to do with our prediction, the bloodiness of a civil war doesn't justify a military campaign—only a declaration of war can. Neither does severing diplomatic ties, so (B) is out. (D) seems tempting, as the law only prohibits *U.S. citizens* from fighting. But the answer choice commits a subtle scope shift—it's only discussing who's *funding* the group, not who would be fighting. And as for (E), the author starts off calling for an investigation, but we can't say that charges should not be brought without one.

4. D

This is an unusual question stem, but it's just asking for a paraphrase of an argument. Since we *always* want to paraphrase what we read, this is hardly a new task. And we also notice from the question stem whose argument we want to focus on. Basically, the argument against "promotional gates" is that they don't achieve improvement in basic skills, as evinced by a competency test. That's what (D), in the GMAT's puffed-up style, says—that the program didn't work. Every other answer choice is outside the scope of the argument. (A) discusses "challenging material" and (B) discusses "true intellectual development," but the argument is only about "basic skills." The argument never discusses, as (C) does, "psychological damage"; nor does it discuss "socioeconomic factors" or reasons for repeating grades, so (E) is also outside the scope.

5. D

This is a rare Explain question. We want to predict an answer that explains how seemingly discrepant pieces of data could both be true. So as you read the stimulus, look for the contradictory information. The key word *nonetheless* shows us the contrast we're looking for: that despite the fact that most murder victims know their attackers, most people are more afraid of being killed by a stranger. So people's fears don't connect with the actual facts and data; we can predict that the correct answer will show that the general population has a skewed perspective. That's exactly what we find in choice (D).

(A) is out of scope, as we don't know what "common sense" might tell us. (B) makes an irrelevant comparison between reacting emotionally and reacting rationally, and it doesn't explain the attitude of most people toward murder. (C) looks good at first, but it contradicts the evidence, as the first sentence shows the study to be national. The right answers to Explain questions show how *all* the evidence can be true. (E) might explain why people who knew they might be killed ended up dead, but it hardly resolves the discrepancy.

6. C

To weaken an argument, knock out the central assumption. The author shifts from *withholding funds* to *censorship*, which is active repression. It's a subtle change of scope but enough of one to form the prediction for a weakener: "Withholding funds isn't the same as censorship." (C), which says exactly that, destroys the argument.

(A) is out of scope, as the author never claims that an act isn't censorship if it reflects majority beliefs. (B) dwells on how the author uses the word *obscenity*, but it is the use of *censorship* that is the issue. If anything, (D) strengthens the argument by reinforcing the link between censorship and the denial of funds. And (E), like (A), discusses the irrelevant idea of majority opinion.

7. E

> **EXPERT EXCLUSIVE**
>
> Watch out for weakening answers in Strengthen questions, and vice versa.

First, we have to understand the argument. The author claims that high school students should not design their own curricula, because they don't have the maturity or experience of professional educators. What if experience and maturity weren't necessary for the design of good curricula? The author's argument would completely fall apart. So to strengthen it, we need the answer to explain why curriculum design requires both experience and maturity. (E) does exactly that and is the credited answer.

(A) just restates the last piece of evidence, and right answers on the GMAT always deal with the assumption, not the evidence. (B) reinforces the author's rhetorical flourish about three-year-olds, but that is just window dressing, not the heart of the author's point; we didn't need to bring three-year-olds into our paraphrase at all. So (B) does not strengthen the main argument. The comparison made in (C) is irrelevant; teenagers who don't go to the local high school are outside the scope of the argument, which is about what one needs to design curricula. Besides which, "intelligence" is not exactly the same thing as "experience and maturity." (D) is also out of scope, as it discusses what kind of curriculum is best, not who designs it (and if anything, (D) weakens the argument, as it suggests that there needs to be a change in curriculum design).

8. C

The author notes that crime is up significantly and that judges' sentences have been getting more lenient lately. He concludes that the blame for the rise in crime belongs "entirely" to the court system. That's a very strong claim—the author must be assuming that there could be no other contributing factors whatsoever. A great Weaken prediction would be something like "any other reason that crime might have gone up." (This is a *classic* GMAT weakener, by the way: if you have to weaken a causality-based argument, look for another cause.) (C) gives us a great other reason—fewer cops. Please notice that it doesn't matter that police weren't explicitly mentioned in the argument. Scope is more about impact than terminology, and the number of police could definitely have an impact on the crime rate.

EXPERT EXCLUSIVE

The assumption that there couldn't be any other possible cause is very common on the GMAT.

(A) is a faulty comparison, as the argument is only about this state; it doesn't really matter what's happening elsewhere. (B) hardly weakens the idea that lenient sentencing is causing a rise in violent crime—why wouldn't white-collar criminals respond to lenient sentencing as well? (D) doesn't impact the argument either; even if the percentage of state residents who opposed the death penalty *did* have an impact on crime rate, we aren't told that this number changed since last year. (E) is out of scope, as it's the leniency of the judges that's at issue, not their tenure; we can't say for sure that a newer judge would be more lenient.

9. E

This question asks, "Which of the following statements is best supported by the information above?" In other words, what can be inferred from the stated material? The author in this question asserts that junior college education had a big impact on family-run businesses after WWII, as the new methods of accounting, marketing, and finance allowed business size to grow and profits to be maximized.

It's difficult to make a specific prediction on most Inference questions. It's often best to say, "The answer *must* be true based on the stimulus; it won't go beyond the scope or read a detail in an extreme way."

In (A), the disqualifying word is *principally*. The information presented does not specify what the junior colleges emphasized. This choice reads too much into the fact that often family businesses increased in size because of the newly acquired knowledge. (B) is wrong because we really can't infer how popular or widespread these methods were before the war. For all we know, these could have been revolutionary techniques or well-kept secrets. In (C), we know junior colleges taught new methods of marketing and finance and stuff like that; we do not know how much management theory was or was not presented. This choice relies on data we aren't given—a sure sign of an incorrect or unwarranted inference. (D) takes the facts in the stimulus too far. We're told that profits increased thanks to the influence of junior colleges, so we could infer that family-run businesses would have been less profitable without them. But there's a world of difference between *less profitable* and *unprofitable*. (E) is certainly true. Business methods did change because of the education—the stimulus calls them "new methods," after all. It's a common mistake to throw out an answer because it seems somehow "too obvious." Some Inference answers are tough to prove right, yes . . . but many are very straightforward.

10. D

The author presents the idea that productivity increases in discrete tasks can actually lower overall productivity, as worker resentment often builds to the point that it slows down the production process as a whole. A valid inference can't stray far from this.

Note that the stimulus uses words like *drawbacks*, *often*, and *slowdown*. These are very different from *catastrophes*, *always*, and *stoppage*. The hedged language of the stimulus creates the possibility for answers to be wrong because they take things too far. Sure enough, (A), (B), and (C) do just that. (A) alleges that these techniques *never* work, not even once. This is too extreme; all the stimulus says is that they "often" don't work. (B) takes the ideas much too far. Some slowdown in the production process doesn't mean that businesses are less competitive abroad. Besides, the stimulus never claims that these techniques are exclusive to American businesses. (C) also goes too far—a slowdown is very different from a stoppage. (D), by contrast, matches the tone of the stimulus, using nonextreme language: "may result." In fact, (D) is a great paraphrase of the stimulus as a whole, and it is the right answer. (E) is out of scope—production managers are never mentioned, so we have no idea how they feel.

11. C

We are asked to find a flaw, which means that our prediction will concern what's wrong with the argument already. We might paraphrase the argument like this: "The most well-rounded education comes from schools with low student-to-faculty ratios, so I will send my kids to colleges with low student populations." The author assumes that a low student population is the same thing as a low student/faculty ratio. That's an error—a school with a large student population could have a low student/faculty ratio by hiring lots of faculty. Similarly, a school with few students could have proportionally even fewer faculty, resulting in a high ratio. So our prediction would be something like this: "Having a low student population doesn't mean a school must have a low student/faculty ratio." That's exactly what (C) says, which is why it's the right answer.

> **EXPERT EXCLUSIVE**
> Mistaking a ratio or rate for an actual number or amount is a common mistake, both in stimuli and wrong answer choices.

(A) claims that the author confuses cause and effect, but that isn't a big flaw here; even if (A) is right, the stimulus points out that the two are highly correlated, so the author's strategy would still likely work. (B) is out of scope, as *intelligence* and *well-rounded education* don't mean the same thing. (D) touches on the issue of whether the plan is practical, which is outside the scope of the argument. Nothing in the argument indicates whether *this* parent has influence. (E) is also outside of the scope because it addresses not college choice but what happens after admission.

12. E

There are actually many assumptions in this argument, so it's entirely possible that you made a valid prediction even if you didn't find the answer right away. The argument basically says that because more newspaper articles are being exposed as fabrications, publishers must care more about raising circulation than printing the truth. There are two scope shifts here: (1) the author gives evidence about *newspaper articles* but draws a conclusion about *publishers*, and (2) the author shifts from *fabrications* to *boosted circulation*. So if your prediction was something like either (1) "Publishers have influence over newspaper articles," or (2) "Fabricated articles boost circulation," give yourself a pat on the back, because you were right. It so happens that the GMAT used (1) as the basis of the right answer—you can see that it matches with (E) quite nicely. So you may have needed the Denial Test to evaluate the answer choices. Let's examine them that way.

> **EXPERT EXCLUSIVE**
>
> If you can't find your predicted answer, don't go back and rework the stimulus. If you've already read critically, understood the argument's construction, and thought about its scope, then you'll be able to eliminate many wrong answers quickly.

(A) What if newspaper articles have been exposed as fake for a while? That wouldn't mean that such exposures couldn't have been on the rise lately. (B) What if a newspaper prints at least one article that doesn't need to be verified? That tells us nothing about the publisher's priorities overall. (C) What if major publications were as comprehensive while fact-checking as minor ones? That certainly wouldn't damage the author's argument—if anything, it would strengthen it! (D) is very similar to (A)—newspapers could have been admitting to this behavior for a while, and that wouldn't mean that the behavior isn't on the rise. But if we deny (E) and claim that publishers make no decisions about what's printed, then it's hardly possible to pin the blame for the fabrications on them, and the argument collapses.

13. B

The argument tells us that buildings are collapsing and concludes that the architecture schools aren't teaching enough of "the basics of good design." Like most GMAT questions that assert a cause-and-effect relationship (this one does so by assigning blame), the central assumption is that there are no other possible causes. So our predicted Weaken answer might be "another reason that the buildings are falling down." (B) hands us that other reason on a silver platter. (A) Basic physics and mechanics don't mean the same thing as "the basics of good design." And even if they did, the argument never claims that they aren't taught, just that they aren't taught *enough*. (C) commits a similar error—the argument doesn't claim that most of the curriculum is aesthetics, just that however much aesthetics is taught is too much. (D) is out of scope; the issue of *when* the buildings started to crumble is not the same as *why*. (E) is also irrelevant—it's not the *length of study* that the author criticizes but *what is studied*.

EXPERT EXCLUSIVE

Notice the word *inevitably* in answer (C). Extreme language is a good sign that an answer choice is wrong.

14. A

The author uses the single case of Acme to conclude that the war profoundly affected "nascent businesses." This assumes that Acme's growth rate is typical, or representative, of such businesses as in (A); otherwise, why hold it up as an example?

As for (B), the author needn't assume that $10,000 isn't much of a profit. Maybe he thinks it started out high and got even higher. (C), which brings up other wars, is beyond the scope—the argument concerns World War II, period. (D) is tricky, but it's not assumed. Notice that the author claims only that World War II had a profound, not salutary, effect on nascent businesses, so we don't know just how he feels about rapid growth rates. As for (E), the author needn't assume Acme's managers had nothing to do with the company's success, just that the war also had an effect—and a marked one.

15. C

The author argues, basically, that the editorial has to be wrong because it's written poorly. Here's yet another scope change—shifting from bad *writing* to bad *reasoning*. So we can predict an assumption like "Bad writing guarantees bad reasoning." (C) uses more formal word choices but says the same thing.

(A) is wrong because the argument isn't about who wrote the editorial, only how well it's written. (B) and (D) are both irrelevant because it doesn't really matter how other editorials are written—we need a connection between writing and reasoning. (E) comes close, but the argument doesn't depend on whether the author intentionally writes poorly; he could have done so by accident and still be making a bad point.

16. E

Here we need to identify an assumption. The author concludes that the "electronic lamp" can replace the incandescent bulb. The supporting evidence is essentially that one electronic lamp is more cost-effective in the long term (and lots of numbers to back that up). So what's missing from this argument? Whenever the GMAT asks you to consider proposals or predictions, think about whether there might be any unintended consequences, or unconsidered factors, or anything about the evidence that might prevent the prediction from coming true. One electronic lamp will clearly cost less long-term than one incandescent bulb. But what if something other than cost is more important to homeowners? (E) is a good match, since it rules out the possibility that the incandescent bulb is superior in some other way.

(A) isn't assumed because the *4 hours a day* figure was only a standard of comparison between the bulbs, not their expected workload. (B) is tempting but goes too far. The new lamp has to work as well as the old bulb but can be dissimilar in other ways. It could be a different shape, for example. In fact, the stimulus explicitly says that the bulbs are different in how they work. (C) is a weakener; if the type of light were different, the new lamp might not be an acceptable replacement. (D) just amplifies the evidence that the new lamp will be cheaper. But that doesn't affect the assumption that price was the only difference. (In the real world, we can strengthen and weaken evidence, but the GMAT tests *how evidence is used*.)

17. C

This is an unusual question stem, so make sure you understand it before you move on to the stimulus. We're asked to find a question that's *least* relevant to evaluating a suggestion. In a way, this is very similar to the previous question; it asks us to evaluate a plan. Look closely at what the plan intends to achieve and how it intends to achieve it. Think critically about what might prevent the plan from working. The plan is to give jurors instructions at the beginning of trials rather than at the end. It is hoped that this will improve the jury system by helping jurors consider fewer factors not mentioned in the courtroom testimony. Four of the five answer choices will reveal potential problems in this plan—factors that the plan didn't consider or ways in which the plan would actually work against its goal.

If the answer to (A) is yes, then the plan isn't even necessary—the present system just needs some tweaking. If the answer to (B) is yes, then the plan is sound, but if the answer is no, then the plan will definitely fail. The question posed by (C) is ultimately irrelevant to the issue of whether the jury system will work better—whether or not other procedures would have to be adjusted isn't the point. So (C) is the correct answer. (D) strikes at the whole reason for the plan. If the factors that didn't come from the courtroom testimony actually didn't influence the decision, then there's no reason to change the system. Lastly, (E) asks straightforwardly whether the plan would work at all; if the jurors would still spend 40 percent of their time considering factors that didn't come from the evidence, then the plan wouldn't work!

18. B

This question asks for the most reliable conclusion based on the author's prediction concerning the ruble. That makes this an Inference question, so we need to find the answer that must be true. The author describes a chain of cause and effect and ends with a prediction: Competing claims of ownership are slowing efforts to privatize state enterprises; these enterprises must still be subsidized by the government; government subsidies lead to large deficits; deficits drive up the inflation rate; high inflation causes the ruble's value to decline. In a nutshell, the disagreement over ownership is causing the ruble to decline in value. The author's conclusion, which we're told to accept as accurate, is that because further decline in the ruble's value could spell disaster, the government is unlikely to allow unrestricted conversion to Western currency until the ownership issue has been resolved.

Notice the big new idea that comes along right at the end, in the author's conclusion. All of a sudden she's talking about making the ruble "freely convertible to Western currencies." Let's look for an answer that must be true based on what we know. (A) doesn't have to be true. If the industrial sector is smaller, privatization could still gum up the works. (B) has to be true because preventing further decline in the ruble is given as the reason for delaying the conversion of the ruble.

> **EXPERT EXCLUSIVE**
>
> Inference questions differ from Assumption questions. An assumption must be true for an argument to be correct. An inference must be true based on any of the facts presented.

(C) contradicts the spirit of the passage, which says that government subsidies are creating a strain on the economy. Contrary to (D), the argument doesn't state that the government is among the parties seeking ownership of state enterprises but only that until the issue is resolved, the enterprises must remain in state hands. (E) would explain why the Russian government might want to make the ruble convertible in the first place, but (1) there's no hint of it in the passage and (2) it doesn't jibe with the conclusion that the government will probably wait to make the ruble convertible.

19. A

The question stem lets us know that we're dealing with a Weaken question, but it gives even more help than that. We're told exactly where the argument's conclusion is. We can start by reading the last sentence to understand what it is we'll need to weaken: the notion that the mayor's response to some problem can't be criticized. Immediately the critical reader says to herself, "Oh yes, it can!" And what's the problem? That's given to us in the first sentence: "the growing inequality of wages." Already we can make a prediction: Since the argument is essentially "The mayor couldn't have done anything about the inequality of wages," our prediction should be "The mayor *could* have done something about the growing inequality of wages." There's only one piece of the puzzle missing—the overall scope of the argument, which has to do with technological trends favoring the skills of more educated workers. Understanding the scope turns out to be a crucial aspect of this problem, as all four wrong answers seem like valid weakeners but get the scope wrong. (A) is the only answer that explains how the mayor could have helped people get the education necessary to get higher-paying jobs.

(B) doesn't really weaken the argument, because the argument explicitly says that high school grads earn less money. The issue isn't getting more of them jobs but getting them *higher-paying* jobs. (C) also doesn't address the issue of education, so it's out of scope. (D) doesn't explain how the mayor could have helped narrow the income gap. Perhaps it explains how the mayor could have ameliorated the *results* of that gap, but that's a different issue. Many people would still be stuck with low-paying jobs. That's the same problem that (E) has—(E) discusses protecting the jobs that people already have, not getting them better-paying ones.

20. E

These "fill-in-the-blank" questions are a kind of Inference question; we're looking for the phrase that *must* make logical sense when put into the stimulus. So any answer that doesn't deal directly with the ideas in the stimulus will be wrong. We know that the survey says that most freshmen at University X *claim* not to have plagiarized in high school and that we're looking for the reason that this survey may be inaccurate. The right answer will do so while staying within the scope of the stimulus.

(A) is out of scope; we're only concerned with students at University X who answered the survey. (B) is irrelevant to the argument; the survey is concerned only with how many students plagiarized in high school, not how many may plagiarize in college. (C) doesn't work because the survey asks only whether a student ever plagiarized, not how often. (D) tells us that the proportion of those who did not plagiarize is lower at another school, but that has no bearing on the proportion at University X as reported by the survey. (E) is correct: it tells us that some plagiarizers might have denied doing so on the survey. If that's true, then the survey results are inaccurate, and the actual proportion who did not plagiarize is lower than two-thirds.

21. D

By now you've seen several questions that ask you to weaken plans. This is a common GMAT question, and you should approach it in a standard way—look for the answer that explains why the plan will fail even though the evidence is true. In this case, our prediction would be "something that explains why the Smith product will lose its competitive edge, even though its new supplier offers much lower prices." (D) does so by stating that the low quality of the new materials will cause a drop in sales. If that occurs, using the new supplier will not create an advantage for Smith Products, so (D) is the answer. (A) and (E) indicate other ways that Smith might gain an advantage, but they don't have any bearing on whether changing suppliers would create an advantage. (B) is similarly irrelevant; even if true, it doesn't provide any information about the quality of the new supplier. (C) is out of scope of the argument, because it explains why both Smith and Jackson would lose sales but not why Smith would lose more.

22. E

The argument that we are asked to weaken concludes that a diet free of meat and dairy products reduces one's risk of having a heart attack. This is based on the fact that 10 percent of those who eat such a diet have heart attacks. But we are given no facts about the risks of eating meat and dairy. The argument assumes that more than 10 percent of people who do eat meat and dairy have heart attacks. Our prediction should be something like "Fewer than 10 percent of people who eat meat and dairy get heart attacks." This is exactly what (E) says.

(A) is a sneaky wrong answer. It provides a good reason for eating meat and dairy but not one that weakens *this* argument, which is that such diets would increase risk of heart attack. (B) comes closer to strengthening the argument than weakening it by providing evidence that people who eat dairy are more likely to have heart attacks. But it is still out of scope, since the passage doesn't mention people who eat dairy but not meat. (C) tells us that some of the people who eat neither meat nor dairy have more than one heart attack. Because we do not have a parallel statistic telling us how many dairy- and meat-eating heart attack sufferers experience more than one heart attack, this information does little to affect the argument in either direction. (D) strengthens the argument because it explains in more detail exactly how meat and dairy consumption is responsible for heart problems.

23. C

EXPERT EXCLUSIVE

Watch out for out-of-scope wrong answers like (A) that seem to attack the conclusion in a general way but don't address the argument itself.

This stimulus begins with the conclusion that a 2001 school program to reduce teenage pregnancy was a failure. The evidence is that the female dropout rate increased during 2001. The assumption must be that pregnancy is an important reason for females to drop out of school. (C) says this correctly.

(A) is out of scope; we're concerned only with the pregnancy numbers in one school, not the numbers nationwide. Though it might be true that an overall increase in nationwide teen pregnancy was somehow related to the failure of the program at this school, any such connection is outside the scope of this argument, which has to do with the connection between pregnancy and the dropout rate. (B) is irrelevant: Comparing the number of pregnancies in 2001 to the number in 1991 might be one way of measuring the program's success or failure, but it has nothing to do with the argument that the increased female dropout rate in 2001 proves the program failed. (D) is out of scope because the argument concerns the dropout rate, not the number of students in the program. Also notice the extreme words *all* and *mandatory*; they should make us suspicious that this answer is wrong. (E) provides a reason to doubt the conclusion as opposed to stating the argument's assumption.

24. D

EXPERT EXCLUSIVE

Be on the lookout for cause-and-effect reasoning. The GMAT uses it often!

The way the GMAT usually weakens these cause-and-effect arguments is to suggest that another factor was influencing the outcome. So to weaken the assumption that pregnancy caused all those dropouts, look for an answer that would give us another reason. (D) does just that, so it is correct.

(A) makes the classic error of confusing rate and number. Even if the number of female students has stayed the same, the rate of female students who dropped out could have varied drastically. (B) is out of scope because it only deals with a nationwide statistics, and if anything, it would strengthen the argument by suggesting a link between pregnancy and dropout rates. (C) doesn't affect the argument because we don't know what *some* means. It could mean only one, but it could mean a sizeable majority. (E) is also out of scope. If we learned that many dropouts quit school for drug-related reasons, that might weaken the argument, but the mere existence of an antidrug program hardly lets us conclude that.

> **EXPERT EXCLUSIVE**
> On the GMAT, *some* really only means "at least one." We can't read much into it.

25. E

We need to find the one question that does not help us decide whether the boycott of SquareMart would lead to the acceptance of the pay rate proposal. The question stem itself gave us a lot of info! There's one important piece of evidence in the stimulus—namely that SquareMart and the company that employs the union workers in question are owned by the same parent company. As with any question that asks us to evaluate a plan, we need to consider other factors that might influence the situation and whether the proposed solution would be effective.

With (A), if a loss of business would hurt the parent company's bottom line, the boycott would put a great deal of pressure on management and would be more likely to work. Similarly, if SquareMart were an insignificant piece of the MegaFood empire, the boycott wouldn't work. So this is an important question. (B) raises the possibility that SquareMart might be the only place some people can buy staple items. That would make the boycott less likely to succeed, as people couldn't refuse to patronize the store. If, per (C), there are many SquareMarts in the area, then a boycott could be easily organized and highly effective. But if no SquareMart stores are nearby, the union members may not be able to execute a successful boycott. For one thing, they wouldn't be customers themselves and couldn't take their business away from a store that they already didn't use! As for (D), if boycotts have been successful before, they may well be so again. And if they've failed in the past, they'd be more likely to fail now. (E) is the correct answer, as whether other companies have a similar corporate structure has no bearing on the likelihood of the boycott's success.

26. E

As with all Weaken questions, we want to understand the argument and look for its assumption. The argument basically says that because the number of articles on a particular topic dropped this year, we can safely conclude that fewer researchers are working on that topic this year. The argument shifted scope from number of articles in a given year to the number of researchers, so it must assume that there's a correlation between those two numbers in

> **EXPERT EXCLUSIVE**
> Pay close attention to the time frame of the stimulus. Many right (and wrong) answers are based on it.

any one year. To weaken this, we need to find the answer that explains how fewer articles doesn't mean fewer researchers. (E) does this—if it takes more than a year to clear an article for publication, then the number of articles in one year can't be representative of anything else in that same year.

(A) might explain why there are fewer articles on *Ophiostoma ulmi*, but it hardly weakens the connection between number of articles and number of researchers. (B) is wrong because the extent of Dutch elm disease is outside the scope of the question, which is only concerned with how many people are studying the fungus that causes the disease. (C)'s information is irrelevant to the actual number of research studies completed. (D) concerns a different type of fungus, so it is incorrect. And, if anything, it would strengthen the argument by giving a possible reason for a decline in research related to *Ophiostoma ulmi*.

EXPERT EXCLUSIVE

Watch out for answers that explain the evidence but that do not strengthen or weaken the central assumption.

27. C

The "apparent paradox" refers to the fact that although Saguaro kangaroo rats have smaller, less frequent litters and spend less time foraging where resources are abundant, they nevertheless outnumber the Sonoran kangaroo rats. Our prediction must be something like "an answer that explains why Saguaro rats are more populous, even though they don't have as many kids and spend less time foraging."

(B) and (E) make the paradox even harder to explain. They both discuss further inherent weaknesses of the Saguaro species, which, if anything, would lead us to believe that there should be more Sonoran rats rather than the other way around. (A) isn't relevant to the comparison between the Sonoran and Saguaro species. (D) only does half the job; it may explain why the Saguaro rats leave watering holes during daylight hours, but that doesn't explain why they have greater population numbers. Only (C) provides a plausible explanation. The fact that Sonoran rats spend more time in areas where predators are active could explain why they are outnumbered by the Saguaro rats. More Sonoran rats are getting eaten!

28. C

The argument proposes that safety of the food supply will not be compromised if regulations are changed because meat can be safely stored at 40°F for well over five days. Perhaps you saw the big assumption here—namely, that the vast majority of meat is stored at or below 40°F. If so, your predicted Weaken answer would have been "A lot of meat is stored at temperatures above 40°." If you didn't see this assumption, you could have used what should be your standard paraphrase when asked to weaken a plan, proposal, or prediction: explain why the proposal won't work even though the evidence is true. In this case, that means "an answer that explains why the food supply will become unsafe, even though it's perfectly safe to store meat at 40°F for much longer than five days." (C) fits either paraphrase. If most meat is kept well above 40°F, we can't assume it will last as long as 16 days.

(A) is out of scope because we know nothing of the shelf life of meat after it has been cooked; the stimulus only tells us about the life of raw meat. (B) is irrelevant, as a shopkeeper's opinion doesn't affect the safety of a piece of food. Besides, this seems to agree with the argument's conclusion, not weaken it. (The author doesn't advocate that the shelf life be extended to 16 days, just that it be extended.) (D) doesn't address the temperature issue. Furthermore, knowing that half the meat stored at 25 days is still safe doesn't tell us much about what happens on day 5 or day 6. (E) also ignores the temperature issue and could, in fact, be viewed to strengthen the argument by providing a reason that longer shelf life will result in lower prices.

29. B

The question stem tells us very clearly what we are to weaken—the explanation for the speed with which the termites were killed. Reading the stimulus tells us the reason: gas was pumped directly into the walls in the first and second floors. This is another classic example of the GMAT's cause-and-effect arguments. Our prediction should be along the lines of "Something other than the direct pumping of gas was responsible for the speedy deaths." (B) does this. It doesn't outright tell us what the other factor was. But if termites died with equal speed on floors into which no gas was being pumped, then it's pretty likely that the direct pumping wasn't the cause of the rapid deaths.

Taken by itself, (A) is irrelevant. (C) and (D) appear to support, rather than weaken, the argument, because they suggest that a higher density of gas kills termites more rapidly. (E) doesn't weaken the argument because it offers no information to help us compare the speed of termite deaths in gassed and nongassed areas of the building.

30. D

Questions that ask you to strengthen are rarer than ones that ask you to weaken. Work carefully; it's easy to fall into the habit of picking weakeners after doing so many. The conclusion is that depression is likely to cause withdrawal from medical school. The evidence is that many people who have left medical school suffer from depression. This is classic correlation/causation confusion. The evidence only shows a strong correlation between the two groups. We don't really know which caused which—perhaps they first left school and only later became depressed. The author takes for granted that the depression caused the withdrawal and not the other way around. We need to find the answer that confirms that assumption. Since (D) discusses medical students who seek counseling *when they are students*, it's very clear that the onset of depression happened prior to withdrawal from school. This makes it clear that the withdrawal didn't cause the depression, strengthening the assumption that it is the other way around.

(A) is irrelevant; the counseling provided may or may not be for depression. (B) and (E) both support the idea that the withdrawal came first. Either one weakens this argument, but we want to strengthen it. (C) is out of scope since we're discussing medical students, not consultants or young doctors.

31. C

The most proper inference will be the choice that *must* be true if the statements in the stimulus are true. Any choices that might be true but do not have to be true can be eliminated. Suburban High enrolled 40 percent of the town's students and produced 75 percent of its graduates, so Lakeside High must have enrolled 60 percent of the town's students, producing 25 percent of its graduates. It's pretty tough to make a prediction for most Inference questions, but you might have been able to do so here because there's a firm mathematical deduction to be made: Lakeside has more students but fewer graduates, meaning that it graduated a lower percentage of its students than Suburban did. With that as your prediction, you'd find (C) pretty quickly. Of course, you could have solved this problem by eliminating the wrong answers instead.

(A) could be true but doesn't necessarily follow from the stimulus. We know that the percentage of enrollees and graduates at each school has been constant, but that doesn't say anything about the total number of students, which may have increased, decreased, or stayed the same. (B) and (D) discuss the geographic areas in which the students live, which are never mentioned. Nor does the argument relate graduation rates to attendance in a magnet program—it never mentions magnet programs at all, actually—so (E) is out of scope.

32. A

This Weaken question could have been approached many different ways. One way would be to look at this with the traditional conclusion-evidence-assumption approach. The conclusion is that the foam spray will reduce erosion on road cuts. The evidence is that it has done so on one particular road cut. The assumption here is that this one road cut is representative of all road cuts. So our prediction would be "That one road cut was not like most other road cuts." (A) is a good match, as it shows that the tested road cut probably had a lower erosion rate to begin with. We also could have treated this as a cause-and-effect argument, because it says essentially, "The spray caused the low erosion." To weaken this, we'd find the answer that showed another reason the erosion on the tested road cut was low. (A) again—there's something about the cut itself that gives it a low rate of erosion.

> **EXPERT EXCLUSIVE**
>
> If you see more than one way of approaching a question, go with what your gut tells you will be the most efficient—easy to think about and likely to pay off. If that doesn't lead you quickly to an answer, then you can try another approach.

Lastly, we could have approached this as we've been approaching other questions that ask us to evaluate a proposal, with the standard "Explain why the plan won't work even though the evidence is true." In this case, that's "Explain why the foam won't lower erosion rates, even though the tested road cut had a low erosion rate." As we've seen, (A) does exactly that.

(B) is concerned with the long-term use of the foam and its maintenance; that the foam has to be reapplied doesn't mean that it won't work to lower erosion while it's on. (C) actually strengthens the argument because it makes the study more credible. (D) is out of scope—that the computer model predicted better results doesn't mean that the foam completely failed. It may still have lowered erosion, even if not by as much as was hoped. (E) is tempting, but *similar materials* doesn't mean *the same materials*. Those other foams are therefore not relevant to this study.

33. D

We need to find the choice that must logically follow if the stimulus is true. If making steel with Element X reduces the level of microscopic fractures, and if some Canadian steel contains Element X, it follows that some Canadian steel will be less likely to develop such fractures. So (D) can be inferred.

(A) is too extreme to be inferred. It *might* be true, but nothing says that at least one other country can't produce steel as strong and flexible as Canada's. (B) wrongly introduces the idea of "years of use"; we know nothing about when these fractures would start to appear. Furthermore, the stimulus only tells us about some Canadian steel. We know nothing about steel from other countries. Perhaps many countries make steel with Element X; perhaps none do. We just don't know. (C) and (E) are both too extreme. The stimulus never says that there isn't a better steel out there somewhere, nor does it say that Canadian ore has more Element X than any other kind, only that it has a lot.

34. D

The question is very specific about what we're looking for: evidence that would explain why scientists changed their theory about why the Laysan Rail is now extinct. We'll look closely in the stimulus to find the new theory. Scientists first attributed the extinction to a loss of ground vegetation, which the birds used for nesting. But now they believe that it was a loss of food. Since the birds are insectivores, this means a loss of insects. What evidence would support this new conclusion? A reasonable prediction would be "data showing a decrease in the availability of insects." Sure enough, that's what (D) says.

Perhaps you missed the word *insectivore* in the stimulus, so your prediction was "less food available." In that case, both (A) and (D) might have seemed tempting to you. When this happens, check the stimulus again to get a clearer sense of the scope. Asking yourself, "So, do these birds eat plants, per (A), or do they eat flies and moths, per (D)?" would lead you to the word *insectivore*.

(A) actually explains the original theory but not the new one. (B) is out of scope; neither theory deals with why relocation attempts failed. (C), like (A), supports the original theory by explaining why the vegetation was important. (E) does this as well—as vegetation got scarcer, competition for available nesting space probably got

EXPERT EXCLUSIVE
Don't worry too much about advanced vocabulary. Perhaps you didn't know right away what *insectivore* meant. But after working the answers down to (A) or (D) and searching critically for a clue about whether the birds eat plants or bugs . . . the "insect" in insectivore would make it clear.

fiercer. Note how important reading the question stem is—three choices are right answers, just to the wrong question!

> **EXPERT EXCLUSIVE**
>
> Because the test is adaptive, you'll often get down to two answers. When that happens, either make a guess or investigate the stimulus more closely, depending on how much time you have left.

35. A

Once again, the question stem gives us a lot. We know not only that it's an Assumption question but also that the conclusion is a prediction about the effectiveness of a "one-day-only" sale. Treat predictions just like plans and proposals—the central assumption is that there's nothing inherently self-defeating about the prediction. As we read, we'll hunt for anything that catches our eye as a possible problem.

The prediction is that "one-day-only" sales will be a good way of getting rid of merchandise that has previously been returned as defective. The stores will offer steep discounts and be clear that the merchandise is nonreturnable. If you don't see the potential problem that the assumption has to clear up (namely, that people might not want to buy defective merchandise in the first place), the Denial Test can lead you to the right answer.

If (A) were negated, then no one would be willing to pay even the sale price for the defective merchandise. If that were the case, then the sale wouldn't be effective. So this is the right answer. If (B) were negated, then the stores would be profitable without the sales. That doesn't damage the argument, as the author is only speculating about the store's ability to get rid of defective merchandise. (C) isn't necessary for similar reasons; the store could be selling plenty of merchandise and still need to clear out the returns. If (D) is negated, then the store could get away with having very few sales. That hardly implies that the sales are failing to meet their goal of clearing out defective merchandise. In fact, it would seem to indicate the sales' success! (E) is out of scope, as the issue of who'd buy the merchandise doesn't matter—it only matters whether it would be bought.

36. B

The argument we have to weaken is that people should move to City X rather than to other cities in the same state because City X has an unemployment rate of 4.7 percent. There's a big piece of data missing—the unemployment rate in the rest of the state. For this argument to make sense, that rate would have to be above 4.7 percent. So your prediction should be "The unemployment rate in the rest of the state is below 4.7 percent." Since 3.9 percent is lower than 4.7 percent, (B) is the right answer.

The exact types of jobs (salary or hourly) available in City X are not part of the argument, so (A) is out of scope. Similarly, other possible reasons to move to City X, such as schools and recreation, are also not at issue, so (C) is incorrect. (D) cites the national unemployment rate, something outside the scope of this argument, which seeks only to compare City X to its home state, not to the nation as a whole. (E) may seem tempting initially but commits the flaw of confusing a value for a rate. We have no idea whether 5,000 new jobs would represent a significant reduction of City Y's unemployment rate (if City Y had 5 million residents, 5,000 jobs would represent only 0.1 percent). Furthermore, we don't know City Y's current unemployment rate, so we don't know how it compares to that of City X.

37. E

The argument here is that eliminating undergraduates who did not receive a B+ or better in composition will reduce the failure rate in the honors class. The assumption must be that undergraduates who did not receive a B+ or better in composition have previously been the ones responsible for the failure rate and are expected to continue to be responsible if they're allowed in the class. To strengthen the argument, we'd look for confirmation of that assumption. Our prediction might be "Undergrads with less than a B+ in composition compose a sizeable proportion of those who fail honors creative writing." (E) hits the nail right on the head.

EXPERT EXCLUSIVE

Did this question seem familiar to you? Many GMAT arguments are similar to one another. The more you practice, the more you'll find those similarities, and the more accurate and confident you'll be on test day.

(A) may seem tempting but is irrelevant. The passage speaks only of eliminating undergraduates. Graduate students would still be allowed to take the course regardless of their composition grade. Whether or not the honors class is overcrowded in (B) is out of scope; reducing the failure rate, not overcrowding, is the focus of the stimulus. (C) tells us nothing about the failure rate, because it doesn't explain how the hard work in composition would pay off in a higher grade in creative writing. (D) is an answer that confuses absolute numbers with rates. We want to lower the failure *rate*, not the absolute number of failures.

38. C

To weaken the argument, we need to find the choice that contradicts its key assumption. The conclusion is that moving from City Y to City X will lower the likelihood of contracting the disease, since the disease occurs at a much lower rate in City X. The assumption is that living in City X reduces the risk of contracting the disease; in other words, environmental factors (such as lifestyle, air quality, or health care costs) in City X are responsible for the low incidence of the disease. Whenever we have to weaken a cause-and-effect assumption, we want to look for an answer that suggests another cause. In this case, then, our prediction would be "a reason other than the environment in City X that explains the lower incidence of the disease." That's what (C) does; if genetic factors are the reason for the lower incidence of the disease, moving won't help. Moving might change your environment but will not change your genetics.

(A) is out of scope; the rates of incidence in the two cities, not the opinion of professionals, are at issue here. Also, this type of "appeal to authority" is rarely correct on the GMAT. (B) would strengthen the argument; the statistics state that

EXPERT EXCLUSIVE

Answers like (B) that seem to attack the evidence (instead of the assumption) are usually wrong.

the incidence is higher in City Y, and if the mayor were proven to have falsely suggested otherwise, it would still make sense to move to City X, where the incidence is lower. (D) is irrelevant. Even if true, it would not imply that the risk for the average person is lower in City Y. (E) is out of scope; we have no information on whether smog has anything to do with the disease in question. Furthermore, this would, if anything, strengthen the conclusion by providing at least one sense in which City X is a more healthful place to live.

39. B

The key assumption is that environmental factors in City X are responsible for the low incidence of the disease in that city. To strengthen the argument, we need to find the choice that confirms this assumption. And that is what (B) does.

(A) suggests that an increase in population will increase the rate of the disease. This would suggest that newcomers would be more, not less, likely to contract the disease. (C) is too general, speaking of life span and not the specific disease in question. (D) is irrelevant; the fact remains that the incidence in City Y is still significantly higher than in City X. (E) would weaken the argument. If City X inhabitants show the same resistance to the disease even in City Y, the reason for their immunity must be inherent—probably genetic, not environmental.

40. E

Because the article claims that enzyme K caused better performance, this is an example of a causality argument—an "X causes Y" situation. The evidence is that Olympic weight lifters and sprinters have above-average levels of enzyme K. This is evidence only of correlation. It could be that the strenuous activities of weight lifting and sprinting produce enzyme K (as part of the body's recovery process, perhaps). In other words, it could be that "Y causes X." The author assumes that high levels of the enzyme cause better athletic performance (X does cause Y), not that athletic performance produces the enzyme (Y does not cause X). Our prediction, then, should be something like "The enzyme does, in fact, aid athletic performance," or "Athletic performance does not, in fact, produce the enzyme." (E) matches the second prediction. It removes "Y causes X" as a possibility, making it much more likely that "X caused Y."

(A) simply adds another correlation, this time between enzyme K and alertness. It does nothing to strengthen the causal relationship in the argument. (B) is also too extreme—enzyme K could serve another purpose and still improve athletic performance. (C) distorts what the article claims; the article says only that enzyme K improves performance, not that it is required. (D) is an irrelevant comparison; both weight lifters and sprinters are presented as equal evidence.

41. A

When the question asks you for what's "best supported" by the stimulus, it is an Inference question. The right answer *must* be true. If spending on all books from all sources grew by 34 percent but spending on fiction books grew only 16 percent, then spending on other types of books must also have increased. In fact, since all books are either fiction or nonfiction, it must be the case that spending on nonfiction books grew more than 34 percent. So (A) must be true based on the information in the stimulus.

(C), (D), and (E) introduce the ideas of purchase price, source of spending, and location of purchase. We know only that some books were purchased at bookstores; we can infer nothing about where the rest of the books were purchased, who bought them, or how much the books cost. These all *might* be true, but none of them *must* be true. (B) draws the false conclusion that because fiction books were largely bought in bookstores, nonfiction books must not have been. In fact, there's no discussion about where nonfiction books were bought.

42. B

This argument has elements of both causality ("X causes Y") and plans/proposals/predictions. So there are many good ways to approach this question. As with all Weaken questions, we begin by understanding the argument. We are to believe that a new law that will give people a tax credit if they install an alarm system will reduce crime. The evidence is a correlation between lower crime and more alarm systems. There are several assumptions. Perhaps you noticed that the link between alarm systems and low crime is only a correlation. The argument assumes that the alarm systems are causing the reduction in crime. There's also the assumption that the tax credit will cause more alarm systems to be installed. Or we could look at this argument through the plan/proposal/prediction lens and say that it assumes that there's nothing self-defeating about the plan.

> **EXPERT EXCLUSIVE**
>
> Some GMAT arguments have more than one assumption. If your prediction doesn't lead to the answer, it doesn't mean that you don't understand what's going on. Use your knowledge of the argument's scope to eliminate wrong answers.

To weaken the first assumption, we'd look for an answer to say, "The drop in crime noted by the studies was caused by something other than installation of alarm systems." To weaken the second, we'd say, "The tax credit won't lead to more alarm installations." To weaken the third, we'd say, "Explain why the tax credit won't lead to lower crime, even though alarm sales correlate with low crime." Answer (B) fits nicely with the second two, as it explains how the tax credit would fail to result in more alarm system installations. It turned out that the right answer wasn't built on the first assumption. But kudos to you for noticing it, as differentiating between correlation and causation will serve you well on many GMAT questions.

(A) uses extreme language and is also out of scope; the issue is whether this particular law can reduce crime, not whether crime can ever be eradicated. (C) presents an irrelevant comparison. Even if it is true, it does not provide any reason why the new tax law would not reduce crime. (D) is a 180; if the new law reduces crime, the state should need fewer prisons, not more. (E) actually makes the proposal more likely to work and thus strengthens the assumption.

43. C

The flaw in Country B's argument is that it does not properly distinguish between totals and rates or percentages. Country B has fewer violent crimes, but that doesn't mean that it has a lower crime rate, or fewer violent crimes *per person*. If you're very comfortable with number/rate issues, your prediction might have been very specific: "Country A has more people than Country B." If not, you'd have used "something that explains why Country A has a lower *crime rate*, even though it has more *actual crimes*." Either way, (C) fits the bill—Country A has 2.5 times more crimes but a population 20 times larger. That's actually a crime rate *one-eighth* of Country B's!

(A), (B), and (E) aren't relevant to the relative rates of violent crime in the two countries. (D) is irrelevant because the crime rates in the two countries are not determined by how many tourists they have but by their total populations.

44. C

As with all Inference questions, we need to find the answer that *must* be true, assuming that the info in the stimulus is true. The stimulus says that if corn prices rise because of a poor harvest in one state, then all states will see corn prices rise, even those states that grow most of their own corn. Perhaps you were able to predict an answer here, as this only makes sense if, as (C) suggests, the corn market is not local but national. If not, you could move through the answers, eliminating the wrong ones.

(A) is a 180, the exact opposite of what the stimulus says. If states that could grow their own corn were excluded from the national corn market, they wouldn't see prices rise. But the stimulus says that they do. (B) is wrong for the exact same reason—it directly contradicts the stimulus. (D) is out of scope, as the argument merely discusses what happens in the event of a bad harvest, not whether such harvests are predictable. (E) is also out of scope, since the argument only discusses corn prices. It certainly *could* be true—in fact it *probably* is true—but it does not *have to be* true based on the stimulus, so it is not the right answer.

45. C

The argument that we need to weaken is that an autobody repair franchise would do better in Town Y than in Town X. The supporting evidence is that there are more accidents in Town Y in June and in July. That's a pretty narrow sample—the argument must be assuming that the number of accidents in June and July is representative of the annual number of accidents. A reasonable prediction is "There's something about June and July that would cause an abnormally large number of accidents in Town Y—or fewer in Town X." Answer (C) does this—if the traffic volume quadruples in those months, then we might reasonably estimate the normal number of monthly accidents to be seven. If so, the repair shop should actually open in Town X!

(A) is out of scope because the high number of accidents in Town Y could still occur even if many people walk or use mass transit. Be wary of answers that seem to question the evidence; they are usually out of scope. (B) would strengthen the argument, as the traffic volume would likely increase year-round. (D) doesn't weaken the argument, because the figures predate the survey. Since then, something has happened to reverse the trend, as the figures have been consistent five years in a row. (E) The construction of a mega mall would certainly draw more vehicular traffic to Town X, but a rumor does not qualify as actual evidence.

> **EXPERT EXCLUSIVE**
>
> Kudos if you realized that there might be a numbers/rates problem here, but the stimulus corrected for this by noting that the towns were of equal size and population.

46. D

The question asks for something that must be true for the conclusion to be true. In other words, we are looking for the assumption. The argument says that hurdlers never run long-distance. All runners on the team are either long-distance or sprinters. If no hurdler runs long-distance, we can deduce that all the hurdlers must be sprinters. Since Ronald is a hurdler, we can also deduce that Ronald must be a sprinter. Therefore, the conclusion claims, Ronald must be fast. Here's a great example of the sort of assumption that will pass us by if we aren't reading critically. We normally think of sprinters as being fast. But *sprinter* and *fast* are, technically, different terms. Since the author doesn't explicitly say that all sprinters are fast, he must be assuming it. (D) captures this exactly.

> **EXPERT EXCLUSIVE**
>
> A small number of Critical Reasoning questions use chains of "formal logic." Carefully work through the relationships and notice what deductions you can make.

(A) directly contradicts the stimulus, since the argument implies that *all* hurdlers are sprinters. No one can be faster than himself! (B) also directly contradicts the stimulus. (C) also contradicts the stimulus, which says that hurdlers lack the endurance required for long-distance. (E) sounds tempting at first but commits a logical error. "All sprinters are fast," doesn't mean, "All fast runners are sprinters." The abstract version of this is " 'All A are B,' doesn't mean that 'all B are A.' " Here's a clear example: "All dogs are four-legged animals," is true, but "All four-legged animals are dogs," is not.

47. C

As with any Explain question, you should make sure that you understand what the discrepant pieces of information are. The stimulus tells us that despite no increase in competition and a large increase in local population, a hardware store has seen little increase in snowblower or lawnmower sales. Our prediction should be "the answer that explains why snowblower and lawnmower sales have not gone up, even though there are more people and the same number of competitors."

EXPERT EXCLUSIVE

Did this seem similar to other questions you have seen so far? Many stimuli assume one time period to be representative of another. Keep noticing these similarities; by test day, many GMAT arguments will feel like old friends.

(A) doesn't explain the slow sales, because although the area to be mown or blown may not be increasing, the number of people responsible for doing the job is going up; there's no reason to think that they're all sharing equipment. (B) doesn't explain things because wages may have risen right along with inflation. Inflation tells us nothing about relative buying power or the demand for equipment. (C) is the right answer, because apartment owners don't require snowblowers or lawnmowers. The maintenance crews of the buildings do, but sales have increased a little—so those sales are accounted for in the stimulus. (D) may explain the slow sales of snowblowers (they may be used less and therefore need replacement less often) but not of lawnmowers. (E) is ruled out by the stimulus, which explicitly says that Jacob's store has no competition; there's no better selection anywhere else in town.

CHAPTER 5: SENTENCE CORRECTION

- Question Format and Structure
- The Basic Principles of Sentence Correction
- Sentence Correction Rules
- The Kaplan Method for Sentence Correction

The GMAT includes about 16 Sentence Correction questions, which are mixed in with Critical Reasoning and Reading Comprehension. Sentence Correction tests your command of standard written English—the rather formal language that is used in textbooks and scholarly periodicals. It's the language that's used to convey complex information precisely, as opposed to the casual language that we use for everyday communication.

> **EXPERT EXCLUSIVE**
>
> Unsurprisingly, Sentence Correction uses common informal usage in some of its wrong answers. It pays to learn the formal rules for the most frequently tested areas of grammar.

QUESTION FORMAT AND STRUCTURE

The directions for these questions look like this:

> **Directions:** The following question presents a sentence, part or all of which is underlined. Below each sentence you will find five ways to phrase the underlined portion. Choice (A) repeats the original version, while the other four choices are different. If the original seems best, choose choice (A). If not, choose one of the revisions.
>
> This question tests correctness and effectiveness of expression. Choose an answer that follows the norms of standard written English: grammar, word choice, and sentence construction.
>
> Choose the answer that produces the most effective sentence, aiming to eliminate awkwardness, ambiguity, redundancy, and grammatical error.

EXPERT EXCLUSIVE

Spelling and capitalization are not tested on the GMAT. Certain answer choices differ in their punctuation, but it's never punctuation itself that's being tested.

EXPERT EXCLUSIVE

Grammar trumps style on the GMAT. Some right answers have awkward style but are still correct, because the other four choices commit grammatical errors.

Sentence Corrections cover a range of grammar and style errors, some of which are so obscure that even good writers commit them. The good news is that you don't have to be a grammar expert to do well on this section. All you need is a mode of attack and some knowledge about what does—and does not—constitute good GMAT English.

You do not need to know every grammar rule for these questions. Errors reflecting certain rules show up repeatedly on the GMAT. Focus on mastering these rules—that's how to get the biggest bang for your study-time buck.

Another key element in GMAT English is style, or what the directions call "effectiveness of expression." That means English that is clear and exact and without awkwardness, ambiguity, or redundancy. (Note that it doesn't have to be interesting. In fact, the test is set up to see whether you get worn down by difficult, often boring prose or whether you rise above that to stay involved—and awake.)

The typical Sentence Correction question contains two or more errors. Time is of the essence with these; the sentences vary in length and complexity, so you'll have to move considerably faster on the short ones to leave time for the long ones. Here's an example:

Several consumer protection agencies have filed suit, seeking to bar distributors from advertising treatments for baldness <u>that brings no discernible improvement and may even result in potential harm.</u>

- ○ that brings no discernible improvement and may even result in potential harm.
- ○ that bring no discernible improvement and may even prove harmful.
- ○ bringing no discernible improvement and even being harmful.
- ○ that brings no discernible improvement and may even potentially result in harm being done.
- ○ that bring no discernible improvement, maybe even resulting in harm.

We'll look at the Kaplan method for this question, discuss the grammar rules being tested, and go over the basic principles and strategies to keep in mind on every Sentence Correction question.

THE BASIC PRINCIPLES OF SENTENCE CORRECTION

Here are the basic things that you need to do to succeed on Sentence Correction questions.

EXPERT EXCLUSIVE

Answer (A) is right as often as any other choice, so one in five SC sentences are correct as written. Don't be afraid of (A) if you spot errors in the other four choices.

UNDERSTAND THE DIRECTIONS COMPLETELY

There's no greater waste of your precious testing time than rereading the directions. Essentially, you're given a sentence in which some or all the words are underlined. Answer choices (B) through (E) present four other ways of expressing the underlined portion, and (A) repeats the original sentence's wording. You have to choose the best version of the sentence. So if you think that the original sentence is fine and none of the rewrites are better, pick (A). If, however, you feel that the original sentence is awkward or contains a grammatical error, pick the answer that presents the best rewrite.

On a related note, always read the entire original sentence carefully. Don't try to save time by reading only the underlined portion and simply comparing it to the answer choices. You'll need to see how the underlined portion relates to the nonunderlined portion.

KEEP AGREEMENT BETWEEN SUBJECT AND VERB

Verbs must agree with their subjects. Singular subjects have singular verbs, and plural subjects have plural verbs. If you're a native speaker, this is probably so automatic that you may wonder why the GMAT tests it at all. But the test makers craftily separate subject and verb with lots of text to make it harder to recognize whether the subject and verb agree. Also, it is often hard to tell whether the subject is singular or plural.

EXPERT EXCLUSIVE

If you aren't a native speaker, don't panic. Odds are that you learned the formal English that the GMAT tests and that you don't have to unlearn nearly as much improper usage as native speakers do.

As a result, Sentence Correction questions often feature separated subjects and verbs or subjects that aren't obviously singular or plural. You should look out for the following:

- Long modifying phrases or clauses following the subject
- Phrases and clauses in commas between the subject and the verb
- Subjects joined by *either/or* and *neither/nor*
- Sentences in which the verb precedes the subject
- Collective nouns, such as *majority, system, audience,* and *committee*
- Singular subjects (frequently collective nouns) followed by a prepositional phrase that contains a plural noun (e.g., *a group of students*). It is the first noun, not the second, that is the subject.

Drill: Subject-Verb Agreement

Correct each of the following subject-verb errors.

1. The depletion of natural resources, in addition to the rapid increase in utilization of these resources, have encouraged many nations to conserve energy.

   _____

2. There is, without a doubt, many good reasons to exercise.

   _____

3. Among the many problems plaguing suburbanites is the ubiquity of shopping malls, the increasing cost of gasoline, and the unavailability of mortgages.

   _____

4. The neighbors told police investigators that neither Annette nor her brother are capable of telling the truth.

   _____

5. The majority of the voters want to unseat the incumbent.

   _____

EXPERT EXCLUSIVE

Only the word *and* creates a compound subject, which is always plural. *In addition, also,* and other such words do not.

Answers and Explanations

(1) *Depletion* is the subject. Correct by changing *have* to *has* or by changing *in addition to* to *and*.

(2) There *are* many good reasons. A good strategy is temporarily to ignore parts of the sentence that are set off by commas.

(3) If the sentence ended at *malls, is* would be correct. But because more than one problem is listed, *are* is the correct verb here.

(4) "Neither Annette nor her brother *is* capable." In *or/nor* constructions, the verb agrees with the subject to which it is closest. So if it were "Neither Annette nor her friends," *are* would be called for.

(5) As a general rule, the number of the verb depends on the sense of the sentence. Because unseating a politician is an action taken by the voters as a group, *majority* acts as a singular collective noun: "The majority wants to unseat."

KEEP A MODIFIER AS CLOSE AS POSSIBLE TO THE WORD OR CLAUSE THAT IT MODIFIES

A modifier is a word, phrase, or clause that describes another part of the sentence. It should be placed as close as possible to whatever it is modifying. Adjectives modify nouns; adverbs modify verbs or adjectives. Modifiers describe the word that they are right next to. (The only exception is the case of two modifiers; one has to be first.) The GMAT often creates modification errors by making a modifier appear to describe a word that it actually doesn't.

The most common GMAT modification error is a long modifier at the beginning of the sentence. It should modify the subject of the sentence but will likely not do so properly. A long modifier that comes in the middle or end of the sentence will seem to describe the word immediately before it. Also look out for the following:

- Sentences beginning or ending with descriptive phrases
- *That/which* clauses, especially ones that come at the end of sentences

Drill: Modification

In each of the following sentences, first identify what each clause or phrase is modifying. Then, fix each error you find.

1. Upon landing at the airport, the hotel sent a limousine to pick us up.

   _____

2. Based on the most current data available, the company made plans to diversify its holdings.

   _____

3. Small and taciturn, Joan Didion's presence often goes unnoticed by those she will later write about.

   _____

4. I took several lessons to learn how to play tennis without getting the ball over the net even once.

   _____

5. The house overlooked the lake, which was set back from the shore.

   _____

> **EXPERT EXCLUSIVE**
>
> Does sentence #4 sound okay as written? Our ear accommodates subtle modification errors, so we have to be very strict about the rule when considering modifiers. Look closely at what "without getting the ball over the net" is describing.

Answers and Explanations

(1) The sentence seems to be saying that the *hotel* landed at the airport. Your common sense will tell you that *upon landing at the airport* really intends to modify the unnamed *we*, instead. So you could say, "Upon landing at the airport, we were met by a limousine sent by the hotel."

EXPERT EXCLUSIVE

Modification errors can be fixed three ways: moving the modifier to where it belongs, rewriting the modifier to describe the subject properly, or changing the subject to fit the modifier properly.

(2) As written, it sounds as though the company was based on current data. *Based on the most current data available* modifies the subject *company*. Obviously, though, what was based on the data were the *plans*, not the company. "Based on the most current data available, plans were made to diversify the company's holdings."

(3) It's Joan Didion—not her presence—who is small and taciturn. "Small and taciturn, Joan Didion often goes unnoticed ..."

(4) As written, *without hitting the ball over the net* is describing *how to play tennis*. The intended meaning is much more likely to be "I took many tennis lessons before I could hit the ball over the net even once."

(5) Misplacement produces an absurd image: a lake that's set back from its own shore. Of course, the *which* clause should follow *the house*: "The house, which was set back from the shore, overlooked the lake."

MAKE SURE A PRONOUN AGREES WITH ITS ANTECEDENT AND REFERS TO ONLY ONE ANTECEDENT

Luckily, the GMAT doesn't test every kind of pronoun error. Errors fall into two categories: reference and agreement. Pronoun reference errors mean that a given pronoun does not refer to—or stand for—a specific noun or pronoun in the sentence (its antecedent).

For pronoun agreement errors, it's a question of numbers: perhaps a pronoun that refers to a singular noun is not in singular form, or a pronoun that refers to a plural noun is not in plural form.

As usual, the GMAT presents camouflaged examples of these two mistakes. Look out for the following:

EXPERT EXCLUSIVE

On the GMAT, *they* cannot refer to singular nouns of unspecified gender. *They* must refer to a plural noun.

- Pronouns, such as *it* and *they*, that are often misused on the GMAT (and in everyday life)
- Pronouns that don't clearly refer to a specific noun
- Pronouns that don't agree in number with their antecedents

Drill: Pronoun Agreement

Correct the following common pronoun reference errors.

1. Beatrix Potter's stories depict animals in an unsentimental and humorous manner, and she illustrated them with delicate watercolor paintings.

   _____

2. There is no known cure for certain forms of hepatitis; they hope, though, that a cure will be found soon.

   _____

3. If the partners cannot resolve their differences, the courts may have to do it.

   _____

4. In order to boost their name recognition, the Green Party sent canvassers to a busy shopping mall.

   _____

5. It is now recognized that the dangers of nuclear war are much graver than that of conventional warfare.

   _____

Answers and Explanations

(1) *She* is clearly intended to refer to Beatrix Potter, but notice that the proper noun *Beatrix Potter* doesn't appear anywhere in this sentence; a pronoun cannot refer to a modifier, even a possessive modifier such as *Beatrix Potter's*. There's a second problem as well: it's not clear whether the *them* that are illustrated are the stories, or just the animals. Here's a rewrite that solves all the problems: "Beatrix Potter not only wrote stories that depicted animals in an unsentimental and humorous manner but also illustrated each story with delicate watercolor paintings."

(2) It's unclear what *they* refers to. The only plural noun is *forms*, but it can't be the *forms of hepatitis* that are hoping for a cure. It must be *scientists* or some other group of people: "scientists hope to find a cure soon."

(3) *It* is the unclear pronoun here. There's no singular noun in the sentence for *it* to refer to. The main clause should read: ". . . the courts may have to do so."

> **EXPERT EXCLUSIVE**
>
> Pronouns cannot refer to verbs. But you can use an adverb (such as *so*) or an auxiliary (such as *does*).

(4) A pronoun or possessive should match the form of the noun it refers to. Use *its* and not *their* in place of the Green Party, because party, like *audience*, is a singular noun that stands for a collective group: "In order to boost its name recognition, the Green Party . . . ."

(5) *Dangers* is plural, so ". . . than those of conventional warfare."

MAKE SURE THAT A VERB TENSE REFLECTS THE SEQUENCE OF EVENTS

A verb tense indicates the order in which separate actions or events occur. Deciding which verb tense is appropriate in a given situation isn't just a matter of grammar; it's also a question of logic. Many GMAT sentences are long and complicated, involving or implying several different actions. The correct tenses make the sequence of events clear.

To determine whether the verbs in a sentence are in the proper tenses, pick one event as a standard and measure every other event against it. Ask yourself whether the other events are supposed to have happened before the standard event took place, after it took place, or while it took place. Those aren't mutually exclusive options, by the way: it is possible in English to have one action start before a second action and continue during that second action.

A frequent GMAT verb error is the inappropriate use of *-ing* forms: "I am going, I was going, I had been going," and so on. As far as the GMAT is concerned, the only reason to use an *-ing* form is to emphasize that an action is continuing or that two actions are occurring simultaneously. To remember this rule, think of the word *during* and its *-ing* ending. When this rule is being tested, pick a simpler tense—one that doesn't use the *-ing* form. In other words, avoid *-ing* forms as much as possible.

Most Commonly Tested Verb Tenses

- **Simple Present**—*I am*—Used for an action happening now, with no contextual information about when it started.
- **Simple Past**—*I was*—Used for an action that happened at a specified time in the past.
- **Simple Future**—*I will*—Used for an action that will happen in the future.
- **Past Perfect**—*I had been*—Used for an action that happened *before* another past action (e.g., "I had been on the subway for 30 minutes before I realized that I was going the wrong direction.")
- **Present Perfect**—*I have been*—Used for an action that started in the past but is still continuing now (e.g., "I have been on the subway for two hours now, and I still don't know where I'm going!") or for past events that happened at an unspecified time (e.g. "He has read *Don Quixote* seven times.")

 GO ONLINE

Once you have mastered each basic principle, go back to the Diagnostic Quiz and reconsider each question.

EXPERT EXCLUSIVE

On the GMAT, *-ing* forms are usually incorrect when the question is testing verb rules. But *-ing* forms are often used correctly to avoid modification errors.

EXPERT EXCLUSIVE

The GMAT tests usage only, not terminology. You don't need to know these names, just when it's appropriate to use the *had* or *has/have* auxiliaries with a verb. Many people think of "past perfect" as "past past" to remember the usage rule.

There are other verb tenses in the English language, but these are the ones that are tested most often.

Drill: Verb Tense Reflection

Correct the verb tenses.

1. The criminal escaped from custody and is believed to flee the country.

   _____

2. Some archaeologists believe that the Minoans of 3,700 years ago had practiced a religion that involved human sacrifice.

   _____

3. If the experiment works, it will be representing a quantum leap forward for pharmaceutical chemistry.

   _____

4. He had seen that movie recently, so he doesn't want to see it tonight.

   _____

5. By the time she retires, she will save enough money to allow her to live comfortably.

   _____

6. She already closed the door behind her when it occurred to her that she wasn't able to get back in later.

   _____

Answers and Explanations

(1) The *criminal escaped* correctly uses simple past tense to refer to an event that happened at a specific time. The believing happens now, so simple present *is believed* is correct. However, the fleeing happened at an unknown and unspecified time in the past, so the present perfect should be used: "...is believed to *have fled* the country."

(2) Here, there's no indication the Minoans practiced human sacrifice for a while and then did something else. So use the simple past *practiced* instead of *had practiced*.

(3) The experiment won't *be representing* a quantum leap; it will *represent* a quantum leap.

(4) *Had* plus a past tense verb is used to indicate which of two things that went on in the past occurred earlier. That's not necessary in this sentence. "He *saw* that movie recently, so he doesn't want to see it tonight." ("He had seen the movie recently, so he didn't want to see it tonight," also works, although it changes the meaning of the sentence to indicate that the desire happened earlier tonight instead of happening now.)

(5) Here, we're indicating an action that began in the past but will end in the future. Think of it this way: At some future time, what will have happened? ". . . she *will have saved* enough money."

(6) *Closed, occurred,* and *wasn't able to get back in* are all in the simple past tense. But you need to indicate that she first closed the door and then something occurred to her—namely, that she wouldn't be able to do something in the future. "She *had* already *closed* the door behind her when it occurred to her that she wouldn't be able to get back in."

KEEP SIMILAR ELEMENTS IN A SENTENCE PARALLEL TO EACH OTHER

Similar elements in a sentence—such as items in a list or verbs in a series—must be in similar form, as must two-part constructions (such as *from* X *to* Y, *either* X *or* Y, X *and* Y, and *as much* X *as* Y).

Though this principle has several components, the basic concept behind parallelism is pretty simple: ideas with the same importance and function—nouns, verbs, phrases, or whatever—should be expressed in the same grammatical form. Look out for the following:

- Lists of items or a series of events
- Such expressions as *both* X *and* Y, *either* X *or* Y, *prefer* X *to* Y

Prepositions, articles, and auxiliaries can begin a list without needing to be repeated throughout. But if they are repeated, they must be in every element of the list.

- Right: "Will you travel by plane, by car, or by boat?"
- Also right: "Will you travel by plane, car, or boat?"
- Wrong: "Will you travel by plane, car, or by boat?"

Drill: Parallelism among Similar Elements

For each of the following sentences, put parallel items into the same form.

1. The city's decay stems from governmental mismanagement, increasing unemployment, and many businesses are relocating.

2. Tourists' images of France range from cosmopolitan to the pastoral.

   _____

3. Excited about visiting New York, Jasmine minded neither riding the subways nor to cope with the crowded sidewalks.

   _____

4. To visualize success is not the same as achieving it.

   _____

5. I remember my aunt making her own dandelion wine and that she played the fiddle.

   _____

6. In my favorite Armenian restaurant, the menu is fascinating and the entrées exquisite.

   _____

Answers and Explanations

(1) *Many businesses are relocating* should be written as *business relocation* to parallel *governmental mismanagement* and *increasing unemployment*.

(2) If you say *the* pastoral, you have to say *the* cosmopolitan. Or you could say "... from cosmopolitan to pastoral."

(3) To parallel *riding*, you need *coping*—not *to cope*.

(4) *To visualize* should be *visualizing* to parallel *achieving*. Alternately, *achieving* could be written as *to achieve* to parallel *to visualize*.

(5) "I remember *that* my aunt *made* . . . and that she played . . . ."

(6) You say *is fascinating*, so you must say *are exquisite*.

COMPARE LIKE THINGS ONLY

Faulty comparisons account for a significant number of errors in GMAT Sentence Correction questions. Most relate to the very simple idea that you can't compare apples to oranges. Of course, you want to compare things that are grammatically similar, but you also want to compare things that are logically similar. You can't logically compare, say, a person to a quality or an item to a group. You have to compare one individual to another, one quality to another, one group to another. Look out for the following:

- Key comparison words, such as *like, as, compared to, less than, more than, other, that of,* and *those of*
- Long modifying phrases between compared elements. Don't be distracted! Ignore the modifying phrase at first so you can see the compared elements clearly.

Drill: Comparing Like Things

Fix the comparisons in the sentences below.

1. Like a black bear that I once saw in the Buenos Aires Zoo, the Central Park Zoo polar bear's personality strikes me as being sadly neurotic.

   _____

2. The article questioned the popularity of jazz compared to classical music.

   _____

3. The challenger weighed 20 pounds less than that of the defender.

   _____

4. The Boston office contributes less to total national sales than any other U.S. branch.

   _____

5. The host paid more attention to his celebrity guest than the others.

   _____

EXPERT EXCLUSIVE

The GMAT often uses a more formal inverted structure for the second element of comparisons. For #3, "... less than did the defender"; for #4, "... than does any other U.S. branch."

Answers and Explanations

(1) *Like* creates a comparison, and you can compare only similar things. Here, you have to compare bears to bears or personalities to personalities. "Like a black bear I once saw in the Buenos Aires Zoo, the Central Park Zoo polar bear strikes me as being sadly neurotic."

(2) "The article questioned the popularity of jazz compared to *that of* classical music."

(3) "The challenger weighed 20 pounds less than the defender did," or "The challenger's weight was 20 pounds less than that of the defender."

(4) There are two ways to read this sentence as it's written. We could be comparing the Boston office's contribution to national sales and other branches' contributions, but we also could be comparing the Boston office's contribution to national sales and the Boston office's contribution to those other branches!

The former comparison is more logical, so we clarify: ". . . than any other U.S. Branch *does*."

(5) A similar problem—you need to repeat the verb after *than* ("than *he paid to* the others") or refer to the verb by placing *to* after *than* ("than *to* the others").

USE YOUR "EAR" TO DETECT CORRECT IDIOMS

This frequently tested principle concerns forms of expression that have established themselves in standard English as the "right" way to say things. There's no grammar rule that applies here; it's just that these particular expressions are generally agreed upon as correct by all English speakers.

If you're a native English speaker, you probably know most idioms already. You'll hear them and be able to instinctively tell what's "right" and what's not. For example, if someone were to say to you, "I am aware about these problems, because I saw the newscast yesterday," you'd pick up on the error right away. The correct idiom is "aware *of*," not "aware *about*." But some idioms are commonly, through incorrectly, used in informal English. For example, your brother says to you, "Here's a tip—Mom prefers platinum over gold." Did you spot the error? The correct idiom is "prefers X *to* Y." So it's a good idea to review idioms and to keep a list of those you encounter but don't know.

> **EXPERT EXCLUSIVE**
> Some people find flashcards to be a more effective learning tool than lists and notebooks. On the front, write the verb (*prefer*), and on the back, write the verb and the correct preposition (*prefer* X *to* Y).

If you're a nonnative English speaker, you'll likely know fewer idioms. Jot down all the idioms that you come across and make sure you know all the correct forms.

Also, look out for the following:

- Prepositions (*to, from, at, over,* etc.) in the underlined portion of the sentence. Their usage is often dictated by idiomatic rules.

- Verbs whose idiomatic usage you've seen frequently tested. Common examples are *prefer, require,* and *regard*.

Kaplan's *GMAT Verbal Foundations* offers intensive review of common English idioms.

Drill: Correct Idioms

Circle the word(s) that completes the idiom correctly in the sentence. In some cases, the correct idiom requires no additional words, and neither answer should be circled.

1. Mathew Brady is regarded (as/to be) one of the greatest 19th-century American photographers.

_____

2. The destruction of tropical rain forests is generally considered (as/to be) a major threat to the environment.

_____

 READ MORE

To develop your ear for idioms, read newspapers, magazines, and websites that use complex and formal language. Periodicals and websites aimed at a general audience frequently use informal grammar and idioms, which are *incorrect* on the GMAT!

3. It took me four times as long to write the report collaboratively (than/as) it would have taken me to write it by myself.

    _____

4. The Geneva Convention covers such questions (like/as) the proper treatment of prisoners of war.

    _____

5. Hiram plays guitar (likc/as) his father does.

    _____

6. The gas was being produced (in/at) a rate of 12 million cubic feet a day.

    _____

7. I prefer Korean food (to/over) Japanese.

    _____

8. My mother tried to discourage me (from attending/to attend) law school.

    _____

9. Many consumers buy inferior products when forced to choose (among/between) price and value.

    _____

10. Off-off-Broadway theaters seat significantly (fewer/less) patrons than do Broadway theaters.

    _____

Answers and Explanations

(1) The idiom is *regarded as.*

(2) The idiom is *considered a major threat.* While *considered to be* is also correct according to some grammarians, it's not correct on the GMAT. *Considered as* is always wrong.

(3) The idiom is *as long . . . as.* The collaboration lasted four times as long as the solo work would have. *As far . . . as* works in the same way.

(4) You have to say, "The Geneva Convention covers such questions *as* the proper treatment."

(5) "He plays *as* his father does." *As* is used to compare actions, such as playing the guitar. *Like* is used to compare people or things: "He plays a guitar like his father's," means that the guitars are similar.

(6) The idiom is *at a* rate of, not *in a* rate of.

(7) The idiom is *prefer . . . to.*

(8) You don't discourage someone *to attend*; you discourage that person *from attending*.

(9) Use *between* to distinguish two things, such as *price* and *value* here. Use *among* for more than two things. They divided the pie *among the four of them.*

(10) *Fewer* is correct. *Fewer* is used when you can count the items in question (fewer people or lawnmowers). *Less* is used when the items in question are more abstract in number and cannot be counted (less sand or flour).

> **EXPERT EXCLUSIVE**
> The word *like* never means *for example* on the GMAT. *Like* should be used only in comparisons.

> **EXPERT EXCLUSIVE**
> Other common countable/ uncountable pairs are *number/ amount* and *many/much.*

> **EXPERT EXCLUSIVE**
> On the GMAT, when the word *which* does not follow a comma, it is almost always wrong. In contrast, it is almost always correct when it follows a preposition. There have been exceptions, but if you have to guess, using this guideline will put the odds strongly in your favor.

KAPLAN STRATEGY

Know this about *which*, *where*, and *when*:

- *Which* must come directly after a comma, and it must refer to the noun just before the comma (except when it follows a preposition, as in the phrase "in which").

- *Where* must refer to an actual location.

- *When* must refer to an actual time.

SENTENCE CORRECTION RULES

There are some rules that you should know about certain types of Sentence Correction errors.

PARALLEL STRUCTURE ERRORS

The key to handling parallel structure questions is *consistency, consistency, consistency.*

Rule 1: Items in a list must have parallel form.

Rule 2: Many two-part constructions set up parallel elements; for example, "from A to B" and "just as A, so B."

Rule 3: Two-part constructions are often tested idiomatically. For example, "not only" *must* be followed by "but also," not just by "but."

EXPERT EXCLUSIVE

When the sentence begins with a modifier, there is almost certainly a modification error.

MODIFICATION ERRORS

Many modification errors involve misplaced modifiers that appear at the beginning of the sentence.

Rule 1: A modifying phrase must clearly refer to what it modifies, so it must be placed as close as possible to what it modifies.

Rule 2: Adjectives modify nouns, while adverbs modify verbs, adjectives, or other adverbs.

PRONOUN ERRORS

The pronouns that cause the most trouble on the GMAT are *it, its, they, their, them, which,* and *that.*

Rule 1: A pronoun must refer unambiguously to a specific noun.

Rule 2: A pronoun must agree in number with the noun it replaces.

VERB ERRORS

The rules sound simple, but the test maker has a way of making these errors less than obvious.

Rule 1: A verb must agree with the subject of the sentence. That means plural subjects go with plural verbs and singular subjects go with singular verbs.

Rule 2: The verb tense must make sense with the rest of the sentence.

THE KAPLAN METHOD FOR SENTENCE CORRECTION

Now we come to the Kaplan method for tackling a Sentence Correction question.

STEP 1: READ THE ORIGINAL SENTENCE CAREFULLY, LOOKING FOR ERRORS

Read the sentence. Look for things that sound wrong but also keep your eyes peeled for signs of the classic errors that the GMAT loves to repeat. If you spot an error, eliminate (A) immediately. If you don't spot an error the first time through, don't bother rereading. You're no more likely to spot a problem the second time around—especially because there may not be an error at all! Instead, move straight to Step 2.

EXPERT EXCLUSIVE

Once you become proficient at the Kaplan method, your pace on SC will increase. By test day, you'll finish most SC questions in less than a minute. Think of the time that will save for Reading Comp!

STEP 2: SCAN AND GROUP THE ANSWER CHOICES

Instead of wasting time reading each answer choice individually, quickly scan and compare the answers with one other. If you spotted an error in Step 1, sort the answer choices into two groups: those that do not fix the error (which you can eliminate) and those that do fix it.

If you *didn't* spot an error, try to zero in on a grammatical or stylistic difference that splits the answer choices into distinct groups. This will let you identify one of the issues that the question is testing. Once you know what is being tested, you can apply your knowledge of English grammar to determine which group is correct—thereby eliminating multiple answers at once.

STEP 3: ELIMINATE CHOICES UNTIL ONLY ONE REMAINS

If more than one choice remains, go back to Step 2 and scan again to find another difference. Then eliminate accordingly. Repeat this process until only one answer remains.

Important Pacing Tip: If more than one choice remains after you have eliminated all of the answers that you are sure are wrong, just go with your best guess. If you don't know the rule by test day, you probably won't successfully teach it to yourself while taking the exam. You'll get a much higher score by investing that time in other questions.

If you are working on a quiz or a practice test, of course, reading the answer explanation closely will help you to learn the important rules so you can use them successfully on test day.

Now let's apply the Kaplan method to the Sentence Correction question we saw earlier:

> Several consumer protection agencies have filed suit, seeking to bar distributors from advertising treatments for baldness <u>that brings no discernible improvement and may even result in potential harm.</u>

- ○ that brings no discernible improvement and may even result in potential harm.

- ○ that bring no discernible improvement and may even prove harmful.

- ○ bringing no discernible improvement and even being harmful.

- ○ that brings no discernible improvement and may even potentially result in harm being done.

- ○ that bring no discernible improvement, maybe even resulting in harm.

STEP 1: READ THE ORIGINAL SENTENCE CAREFULLY, LOOKING FOR ERRORS

The underlined phrase is a clause that is describing something in the first part of the sentence. (The use of the word *that* is a good clue.) What in the first part of the sentence "brings no discernible improvement" and may cause harm? *Treatments.* But you can't say *treatments brings*.

EXPERT EXCLUSIVE

If you don't spot an error quickly, immediately go to Step 2. By scanning for differences, you'll discover what rule is being tested.

We've found a problem with this sentence (subject-verb agreement), so (A), the original structure, can't be correct.

STEP 2: SCAN AND GROUP THE ANSWER CHOICES

Now you'd quickly scan among the choices, looking for ones that repeat the error. That's (D).

If you didn't spot the error at first, you'd look for the main differences among the choices: two say *brings*, two say *bring*, and one says *bringing*. Which is correct?

> **EXPERT EXCLUSIVE**
>
> We at Kaplan refer to such a pattern as a "2-2-1 split." Unfortunately, there are no trends to help you guess which element of a split is right, but it does help you to think of the choices as grouped together, making for quick elimination of wrong answers.

> **EXPERT EXCLUSIVE**
>
> Notice that we never had to consider that *may* and *potential(ly)* were redundant in (A) and (D). If you follow the Kaplan method, you can find the right answer even without considering all the errors!

STEP 3: ELIMINATE CHOICES UNTIL ONLY ONE REMAINS

If you spotted the error, you eliminated (A) and (D) as wrong, which leaves *bring* and *bringing*.

If you didn't spot the error, you'd now say to yourself, "Hmm . . . two answer choices say *brings*, two say *bring*—one is plural, the other singular. This is very likely about the subject-verb agreement. So what *brings* no improvement? Is it *baldness*? There's an *of* before *baldness*, so *baldness* can't be the subject. Plus "Baldness brings no discernable improvement," just doesn't make sense. It has to be *treatments*. Now that makes sense! Sneaky, GMAT, but I figured it out!" Now you'd eliminate (A) and (D) and turn your attention to *bring/bringing*.

You'd eliminate *bringing*, either because you recognize that the continuous tense is awkward and unnecessary here or because you know that on the GMAT, *–ing* forms are almost always wrong in verb questions. Plus, only one answer choice uses *bringing*, so eliminate it and move on.

Scanning between (B) and (E), you spot a difference at the end: *and may even prove harmful* versus *maybe even resulting in harm*. *Prove* is parallel with *bring*, and *resulting* is not. Eliminate (E). That leaves only one answer, (B).

SUMMARY

The Basic Principles of Sentence Correction are the following:

- Understand the directions completely.
- Keep agreement between subject and verb.
- Keep a modifier as close as possible to the word or clause that it modifies.
- Make sure a pronoun agrees with its antecedent and refers to only one antecedent.
- Make sure that a verb tense reflects the sequence of events.
- Keep similar elements in a sentence parallel to each other.
- Compare like things only.
- Use your "ear" to detect correct idioms.

Common rules for Sentence Correction are the following:

For Parallel Structure Errors:

Rule 1: Items in a list must have parallel form.

Rule 2: Many two-part constructions set up parallel elements; for instance, "not only . . . but also," or "from A to B."

For Modification Errors:

Rule 1: A modifying phrase must clearly refer to what it modifies, so it must be placed as close as possible to what it modifies.

Rule 2: Adjectives modify nouns, while adverbs modify verbs, adjectives, or other adverbs.

For Pronoun Errors:

Rule 1: A pronoun must refer unambiguously to a specific noun.

Rule 2: A pronoun must agree in number with the noun it replaces.

For Verb Errors:

Rule 1: A verb must agree with the subject of the sentence. That means plural subjects go with plural verbs and singular subjects go with singular verbs.

Rule 2: The verb tense must make sense with the rest of the sentence.

The Kaplan Method for Sentence Corrections is as follows:

Step 1: Read the original sentence carefully, looking for errors.

Step 2: Scan and group the answer choices.

Step 3: Eliminate choices until only one remains.

PRACTICE QUIZ

Directions: The following question presents a sentence, part or all of which is underlined. Below each sentence you will find five ways to phrase the underlined portion. Choice (A) repeats the original version, while the other four choices are different. If the original seems best, choose (A). If not, choose one of the revisions.

This question tests correctness and effectiveness of expression. Choose an answer that follows the norms of standard written English: grammar, word choice, and sentence construction. Choose the answer that produces the most effective sentence, aiming to eliminate awkwardness, ambiguity, redundancy, and grammatical error.

1. The concert this weekend promises to attract <u>an even greater amount of people</u> than attended the last one.

   ○ an even greater amount of people

   ○ an even larger amount of people

   ○ an amount of people even greater

   ○ a number of people even larger

   ○ an even greater number of people

2. <u>Compared with the time period of John Steinbeck's *The Grapes of Wrath*,</u> the poor of today would be considered wealthy.

   ○ Compared with the time period of John Steinbeck's *The Grapes of Wrath*

   ○ Compared with the time period during which John Steinbeck's *The Grapes of Wrath* took place

   ○ Compared with the characters in John Steinbeck's *The Grapes of Wrath*

   ○ In comparison to the time of John Steinbeck's *The Grapes of Wrath*

   ○ In comparison to John Steinbeck's *The Grapes of Wrath*

3. Although the square root of a negative number has no real value, it is not necessarily true that <u>equations involving imaginary numbers like these are practically inapplicable.</u>

   ○ equations involving imaginary numbers like these are practically inapplicable

   ○ equations involving such imaginary numbers have no practical applications

   ○ equations involving these inapplicable imaginary numbers are practical

   ○ equations involving imaginary numbers such as these are inapplicable practically

   ○ there is no practical applications for equations involving such imaginary numbers as these

4. Anarchists believe that the ideal society is one in which the motivation to maintain law and order <u>lies in the innate reasonableness of human nature rather than in the threat of force</u>.

    ○ lies in the innate reasonableness of human nature rather than in the threat of force

    ○ lie in the innate reasonableness of human nature rather than in the threat of force

    ○ lays in the innate reasonableness of human nature rather than the threat of force

    ○ lay in the innate reasonableness of human nature instead of the threat of force

    ○ lies in the innate reasonableness of human nature instead of the threat of force

5. The public's widespread belief in the existence of <u>UFOs and their general curiosity about extraterrestrial life has</u> generated considerable interest in science fiction.

    ○ UFOs and their general curiosity about extraterrestrial life has

    ○ UFOs and they are generally curious about extraterrestrial life which has

    ○ UFOs, as well as their general curiosity about extraterrestrial life, have

    ○ UFOs, as well as its general curiosity about extraterrestrial life, has

    ○ UFOs, as well as general curiosity about extraterrestrial life, have

6. In some countries, the political system works by a simple logic: the more an organization contributes to politicians' campaign funds, <u>its interests are better served by the policies and actions of the government</u>.

    ○ its interests are better served by the policies and actions of the government

    ○ its interests are the better served through the policies and actions of the government

    ○ the better its interests are served by the policies and actions of the government

    ○ by the policies and actions of the government, its interests being better served

    ○ by the policies and actions of the government, service is the better for its interests

7. Many of the thousands of students currently enrolled in night courses hope <u>for the exchanging of their drab jobs for new careers that are challenging</u>.

    ○ for the exchanging of their drab jobs for new careers that are challenging

    ○ for exchanging drab jobs for new careers that will challenge them

    ○ to exchange their drab jobs with new careers that will be new and challenging

    ○ to exchange their drab jobs for new and challenging careers

    ○ to exchanging their drab jobs and find careers that will be new and challenging

8. Records of the first 736 British convicts deported to Australia reveal <u>convictions for crimes against property in all cases and they ranged</u> from highway robbery to forgery.

   ○ convictions for crimes against property in all cases and they ranged

   ○ convictions in all cases were crimes against property and ranging

   ○ the ranging of convictions for crimes against property in all cases

   ○ that all were convicted of crimes against property ranging

   ○ that all of them had convictions for crimes that were against property; the range was

9. The symptoms of the participants in a recent decongestant effectiveness study, such as a "stuffy nose," <u>parallel that of the multitudes of Americans afflicted with</u> the common cold each winter.

   ○ parallel that of the multitudes of Americans afflicted with

   ○ parallel the multitudes of Americans afflicted with

   ○ parallel those of the multitudes of Americans afflicted with

   ○ parallels those of the multitudes of Americans afflicted from

   ○ parallels that of the multitudes of Americans afflicted from

10. A group of students who have begun to clean up Frederick Law Olmsted's Morningside Park in New York City <u>believes that the park needs not to be redesigned but to be</u> returned to its former condition.

    ○ believes that the park needs not to be redesigned but to be

    ○ believe that the park needs to not be redesigned but to be

    ○ believes that the park needs not to be redesigned but could be

    ○ believe that the park needs to be not redesigned but to be

    ○ believe that the park needs not to be redesigned but that it be

11. <u>Having recently published a series of science fiction books influenced by Sufism, Doris Lessing will likely</u> be remembered best for her early novels about Africa.

    ○ Having recently published a series of science fiction books influenced by Sufism, Doris Lessing will likely

    ○ Although she has recently published a series of science fiction books influenced by Sufism, Doris Lessing is likely to

    ○ She has recently published a series of science fiction books influenced by Sufism, and Doris Lessing will likely

    ○ In spite of recently publishing a series of science fiction books influenced by Sufism, Doris Lessing should likely

    ○ Recently publishing a series of science fiction books influenced by Sufism, Doris Lessing may likely

Advanced

12. In February 1983, brush fires had swept the drought-parched southeastern coast of Australia, at least 69 people being killed, and thousands of homes and acres of farmland were left smoldering.

    ○ had swept the drought-parched southeastern coast of Australia, at least 69 people being killed, and thousands of homes and acres of farmland were left smoldering

    ○ swept the drought-parched southeastern coast of Australia, having killed at least 69 people, and thousands of home and acres of farmland were left smoldering

    ○ swept the drought-parched southeastern coast of Australia, killing at least 69 people, and had left thousands of homes and acres of farmland smoldering

    ○ swept the drought-parched southeastern coast of Australia, killing at least 69 people, and leaving thousands of homes and acres of farmland smoldering

    ○ swept the drought-parched southeastern coast of Australia, killing at least 69 people, and left smoldering thousands of homes and acres of farmland

13. Scoliosis, a condition when the spine curves abnormally and throws the body out of line, can cause heart and lung problems as well as physical deformity.

    ○ a condition when the spine curves abnormally and throws the body out of line

    ○ a condition in which an abnormal curvature of the spine throws the body out of line

    ○ a condition of the spine curving abnormally and in which the body is thrown out of line

    ○ where the body is thrown out of line by an abnormal curvature of the spine

    ○ a condition of an abnormal curvature of the spine throwing the body out of line

14. Although some ornithologists contend that the precursors of birds are arboreal creatures that glide from tree to tree, others believe that they were runners whose front limbs evolved into wings.

    ○ Although some ornithologists contend that the precursors of birds are arboreal creatures that glide from tree to tree

    ○ However it may be that some ornithologists contend that the precursors of birds were arboreal creatures that glide from tree to tree

    ○ Despite that the precursors of birds were, according to some ornithologists, arboreal creatures that glide from tree to tree

    ○ Although some ornithologists contend that the precursors of birds were arboreal creatures that glided from tree to tree

    ○ According to some ornithologists gliding from tree to tree, the precursors of birds are arboreal creatures, that

Advanced

15. The newly elected baseball commissioner has asked that a federal arbitrator would mediate negotiations between representatives of the umpire's union, which has threatened to go on strike, and the lawyers representing major league franchise owners.

    ○ that a federal arbitrator would mediate negotiations between representatives of the umpire's union, which has threatened

    ○ that a federal arbitrator mediate negotiations between representatives of the umpire's union, which have threatened

    ○ of a federal arbitrator that he mediate negotiations between representatives of the umpire's union, which have threatened

    ○ a federal arbitrator that he mediate negotiations between representatives of the umpire's union, which has threatened

    ○ a federal arbitrator to mediate negotiations between representatives of the umpire's union, which has threatened

16. In the conflict between the Israelis and the Palestinians, the refusal of each side to acknowledge the other as a legitimate national movement is closer to the heart of the problem than is any other issue.

    ○ the refusal of each side to acknowledge the other as a legitimate national movement is closer to the heart of the problem than

    ○ that the refusal of each side to acknowledge the other as a legitimate national movement is closer to the heart of the problem as

    ○ the refusal of each side to acknowledge another as a legitimate national movement is closer to the heart of the problem than

    ○ that the refusal of each side to acknowledge another as a legitimate national movement is closer to the heart of the problem than

    ○ the refusal of each side to acknowledge the other as a legitimate national movement is closer to the heart of the problem as

17. In this year's negotiations, unionized workers will fight to improve job security in many industries but will seek large wage increases in some others, <u>such as the prospering telecommunications industry.</u>

    ○ such as the prospering telecommunications industry

    ○ such industries like telecommunications, which is prospering

    ○ as in that of the prospering telecommunications industry

    ○ as is the prospering telecommunications industry

    ○ as in an industry like telecommunications, which is prospering

18. To tackle the issue of congressional campaign spending is <u>becoming embroiled in a war which is raging between those who support public financing with</u> those who would lift the limits on the amount political parties and individuals may donate.

    ○ becoming embroiled in a war which is raging between those who support public financing with

    ○ becoming embroiled in a war raging among those who support public financing with

    ○ to become embroiled in a war raging between those who support public financing and

    ○ to become embroiled in a war which is raging among those who support public financing and

    ○ becoming embroiled in a war raging between those who support public financing and

Advanced

19. <u>A scientist has determined that a recently discovered ancient Chinese weapon, buried since approximately 1300 BCE, is enclosed in silk, a fabric previously thought to have been invented 1,000 years later.</u>

    ○ A scientist has determined that a recently discovered ancient Chinese weapon, buried since approximately 1300 BCE, is enclosed in silk, a fabric previously thought to have been invented 1,000 years later.

    ○ Buried since approximately 1300 BCE, an ancient Chinese weapon had been recently determined by a scientist to be enclosed in silk, a fabric previously thought to be invented 1,000 years later.

    ○ A scientist had determined that a recently discovered ancient Chinese weapon is enclosed in silk, a fabric previously thought to be invented 1,000 years later, after having been buried since approximately 1300 BCE.

    ○ After being buried since approximately 1300 BCE, a scientist has determined that a recently discovered ancient Chinese weapon is enclosed in silk, a fabric previously thought to have been invented 1,000 years later.

    ○ A recently discovered ancient Chinese weapon, buried since approximately 1300 BCE, has been determined to be covered with silk by a scientist, a fabric previously thought to have been invented 1,000 years later.

20. When he had run for mayor of Cleveland in 1968, Carl Stokes won the election, proving that an African American candidate can be elected in a city in which African Americans constitute a minority of the population.

    ○ When he had run for mayor of Cleveland in 1968,

    ○ He ran for mayor of Cleveland in 1968, and

    ○ Running, in 1968, for Mayor of Cleveland,

    ○ When he ran for mayor of Cleveland in 1968,

    ○ In 1968 he had run for mayor of Cleveland, and

Advanced

21. Brief psychotherapy requires far fewer hours and costs far less money than traditional psychoanalysis and so will hopefully prove to be an effective treatment for many of the large amount of people currently seeking therapy.

    ○ will hopefully prove to be an effective treatment for many of the large amount

    ○ will prove hopefully to be an effective treatment for many of the large amount

    ○ hopefully will prove to be an effective treatment for many of the large number

    ○ will, it is hoped, prove to be an effective treatment for many of the large number

    ○ will, it is hoped, prove to be an effective treatment for many of the large amount

22. Having often been thought of as still a city of working-class neighborhoods, Chicago is increasingly populated by poor people.

    ○ Having often been thought of as still a city of working-class neighborhoods, Chicago is increasingly populated by poor people.

    ○ It is still often thought of as a city of working-class neighborhoods, and Chicago is increasingly populated by poor people.

    ○ In spite of still often being thought of as a city of working-class neighborhoods, the people who populate Chicago are increasingly poor.

    ○ It is still often thought of as a city of working-class neighborhoods, but the people who populate Chicago are increasingly poor.

    ○ Although still often thought of as a city of working-class neighborhoods, Chicago is increasingly populated by poor people.

23. To control public unease over the regime's impending economic collapse, the government ordered local officials should censor records of what were their communities' unemployment figures.

    ○ should censor records of what were their communities' unemployment figures

    ○ would do the censorship of records of their communities' unemployment figures

    ○ censoring records of unemployment figures in their communities

    ○ the censoring of a record of unemployment figures in their communities

    ○ to censor records of unemployment figures in their communities

24. As a result of having nostrils, called nares, connected to olfactory bulbs that go back to the brain, sharks are capable of smelling even a few molecules of blood in the water.

    ○ As a result of having

    ○ As a result of it having

    ○ Because they have

    ○ Because of having

    ○ Because of their having

25. In the past few months, there has been extensive dispute over if fare hikes should be a first or last recourse in improving the transit system.

    ○ over if fare hikes should be a first or last recourse

    ○ about if fare hikes is a first or last recourse

    ○ about hiking fares being first or last recourses

    ○ over whether fare hikes should be a first or last recourse

    ○ concerning hikes in fares and their being first or last recourses

Advanced

26. Psycholinguists know that a child produces speech sounds by imitating adults, but they do not know how he learns to distinguish significantly different phonemes or how the child comes to ignore meaningless variations among speech sounds.

    ○ by imitating adults, but they do not know how he learns to distinguish significantly different phonemes or

    ○ by imitating adults, but they do not know either how he learns to distinguish significantly different phonemes nor

    ○ through the imitation of adults, but they neither know how he learns to distinguish significantly different phonemes or

    ○ through the imitation of adults, but they do not know either how he learns to distinguish significantly different phonemes nor

    ○ by imitating adults, but they do not know how he learns to distinguish significantly different phonemes nor

27. In response to higher oil prices, window manufacturers have improved the insulating capability of their products; their windows have been built to conserve energy, and they are.

   ○ have been built to conserve energy, and they are

   ○ are built to conserve energy, and they have

   ○ are built to conserve energy, and they do

   ○ are being built to conserve energy, and have

   ○ had been built to conserve energy, and they are

28. Though initially opposed to the measure, the governor approved the new needle exchange program at the urging of his own doctor, his chief advisers, and a coalition of some 20 social action groups.

   ○ at the urging of his own doctor, his chief advisers, and a coalition of some

   ○ as a consequence of having been urged by his own doctor, his chief advisers, and a coalition of some

   ○ on account of being urged by his own doctor, chief advisers, and a coalition of

   ○ as he was urged to do by his own doctor, his chief advisers, and a coalition of some

   ○ as his own doctor was urging him to do, along with his chief advisers, and a coalition of

29. Since the new manufacturing process for plastic containers was introduced 10 years ago, the average size of plastic manufacturing plants have dropped from 200,000 square feet to 50,000 square feet, an area that is about a football field's size.

   ○ have dropped from 200,000 square feet to 50,000 square feet, an area that is about a football field's size

   ○ have dropped from 200,000 square feet to 50,000 square feet, about the size of a football field

   ○ has dropped from 200,000 square feet to 50,000 square feet, about the size of a football field

   ○ has dropped from 200,000 square feet down to 50,000 square feet, about the size of football field's

   ○ has dropped from 200,000 square feet down to 50,000 square feet, about a football field's size

Advanced

30. In order to document their contribution to the field of structural engineering, the curators at the university's art museum organized a comprehensive exhibition of the work of leading Swiss designers, including photographs, diagrams, and models of their most famous bridges and buildings.

   ○ In order to document their contribution to the field of structural engineering, the curators at the university's art museum organized a comprehensive exhibition of the work of leading Swiss designers, including photographs, diagrams, and models of most famous bridges and buildings.

   ○ In order to document the contribution of the Swiss to the field of structural engineering, the curators at the university's art museum organized a comprehensive exhibition of the work of leading Swiss designers, including photographs, diagrams, and models of their most famous bridges and buildings.

   ○ In order to document the contribution of the Swiss to the field of structural engineering, the curators at the university's art museum organized a comprehensive exhibition of the work of leading Swiss designers, including photographs, diagrams, and models of its most famous bridges and buildings.

   ○ In order to document their contribution to the structural engineering field, a comprehensive exhibition was organized by the curators at the university's art museum of their photographs, diagrams, and models of the most famous bridges and buildings of leading Swiss designers.

   ○ The curators at the university's art museum, in order to document their contribution to the field, organized a comprehensive exhibition of the work of leading Swiss designers, including photographs, diagrams, and models of their most famous bridges and buildings.

31. It can be difficult for small investors to sell their shares of stock in companies whose policies they disagree with, because small investors' assets are less robust <u>than</u> large investors.

   ○ than

   ○ than those of

   ○ than is true of

   ○ compared with

   ○ relatively to those of

32. Unable to keep up with the new competitors that had recently entered its industry, the company was forced to begin closing plants, laying off workers, and <u>reduced</u> its research and marketing budgets.

   ○ reduced

   ○ it reduced

   ○ reducing

   ○ would reduce

   ○ it had reduced

Advanced

33. Those who study ancient European history soon realize that <u>before Greece was Greece, it was a collection of small city-states</u> that were intensely jealous of one another and were only occasionally able to work together for common goals.

    ○ before Greece was Greece, it was a collection of small city-states

    ○ before there was Greece, it was a collection of small city-states

    ○ before Greece, it was a collection of small city-states

    ○ it was a collection of small city-states that was Greece

    ○ Greece had become a collection of small city-states

34. <u>Compiled from documents provided by several government agencies</u>, the investigative commission produced a report clearly indicating that federal officials had frequently authorized expenditures far above statutory limits.

    ○ Compiled from documents provided by several government agencies

    ○ Compiling it from several government agencies' documents

    ○ A compilation of documents from several government agencies

    ○ Documents provided by several government agencies

    ○ Working from documents provided by several government agencies

35. In addition to being more expensive than manual research, <u>the compounds identified by machine-based research are often of lower quality than those identified by</u> manual research, which are more likely to become marketable pharmaceutical products.

    ○ the compounds identified by machine-based research are often of lower quality than those identified by

    ○ machine-based research often identifies compounds that are of lower quality than those identified by

    ○ machine-based research is lower in quality than those compounds identified by

    ○ the compounds identified by machine-based research are often lower in quality than

    ○ compounds identified by machine-based research often had lower quality than those identified by

36. Since 1993, when it passed a referendum <u>approving casino gambling, the town of Riverside, Missouri, was using</u> casino tax revenue to improve its streets, sewers, buildings, and other public works.

    ○ approving casino gambling, the town of Riverside, Missouri, was using

    ○ for the approving of casino gambling, the town of Riverside, Missouri, has used

    ○ approved casino gambling, the town of Riverside, Missouri, has used

    ○ approving casino gambling, the town of Riverside, Missouri, has used

    ○ approving casino gambling, the town of Riverside, Missouri, was to be using

37. Disappointed by his students' refusal to complete the assigned reading, <u>a pop quiz from the teacher was chosen to surprise them</u> the next day.

    ○ a pop quiz from the teacher was chosen to surprise them

    ○ they were surprised by the choice of a pop quiz from the teacher

    ○ the teacher chose to surprise his class with a pop quiz

    ○ the teacher was surprised by a pop quiz from them

    ○ a pop quiz as the choice of the teacher surprised them

38. Many freshmen find the first year of college quite challenging and are unable to balance responsibilities such as attending class, <u>reading assignments, and to write</u> papers with the wide and sometimes bewildering array of new social opportunities.

    ○ reading assignments, and to write

    ○ reading assignments, and writing

    ○ to read assignments, and write

    ○ to read assignments, and to write

    ○ to read assignments, writing

39. Without hiding the fact that the destruction of Athens <u>was one of their most important objectives</u>, the multitudinous Persian army, led by Xerxes and nine of his generals, marched westward toward Greece in the spring and summer of 480 BCE.

    ○ was one of their most important objectives

    ○ was one of its most important objectives

    ○ was one of the objectives they considered to be most important

    ○ having been one of its most important objectives

    ○ is one of its most important objectives

40. As evidence of sushi's drastically increasing popularity, the most recent studies show that the number of sushi restaurants in the state <u>increased by more than three times</u> in the past five years.

    ○ increased by more than three times

    ○ increased by more than triple

    ○ was increased more than three times

    ○ has more than tripled

    ○ was more than tripled

41. Researchers have found that the human body can use protein derived from whey more efficiently than it can use protein from other sources such as soy, eggs, or drinking milk.

    ○ protein from other sources such as soy, eggs, or drinking milk

    ○ protein from other sources like soy, eggs, or drinking milk

    ○ protein from other sources such as soy, eggs, or milk

    ○ protein which it has derived from other sources such as soy, eggs, or drinking milk

    ○ its protein from other sources such as soy, eggs, or milk

42. At 60 inmates per 100,000 citizens, Norway has one of the lowest incarceration rates of all Western countries, reflecting their long humanitarian tradition.

    ○ reflecting their long

    ○ being a reflection of its long

    ○ reflection of their long

    ○ reflecting its long

    ○ reflecting its greater

43. Despite offering significant discounts, Detroit automakers were losing U.S. market share to lower-cost rivals from Japan and South Korea, which are gaining ground even while offering smaller discounts.

    ○ Despite offering significant discounts, Detroit automakers were losing

    ○ Despite offering significant discounts, Detroit automakers are losing

    ○ Despite significant discounts, the Detroit automakers lost

    ○ Despite significant discounts, the Detroit automakers continuing to lose

    ○ The Detroit automakers, despite significant discounts, were losing

Advanced

44. Sky Airlines recently announced aggressive cost-cutting measures ranging from new airport check-in procedures that encourage passengers to use self-service kiosks and reductions in the size of its fleet.

    ○ ranging from new airport check-in procedures that encourage passengers to use self-service kiosks and reductions

    ○ ranging from new airport check-in procedures that encourage passengers to use self-service kiosks and to reductions

    ○ such as improvement of airport check-in procedures, encouragement of passengers to use self-service kiosks and reducing

    ○ ranging from new airport check-in procedures that encourage passengers to use self-service kiosks to reducing

    ○ ranging from new airport check-in procedures that encourage passengers to use self-service kiosks to reductions

45. The Dancing Doll line sold slightly more than $3.5 million worth of toys last year, 40 percent more than <u>the Teeny Tiny Trucks line did and nearly three times as much as the Basic Blocks line's sales</u>.

    ○ the Teeny Tiny Trucks line did and nearly three times as much as the Basic Blocks line's sales

    ○ the Teeny Tiny Trucks did and nearly three times what the Basic Blocks' sales were

    ○ the Teeny Tiny Trucks line sold and nearly three times as much as Basic Blocks' sales

    ○ the Teeny Tiny Trucks line and nearly three times more than Basic Blocks' sales

    ○ the Teeny Tiny Trucks line and nearly three times more than the Basic Blocks line

Advanced

46. <u>It was decided by the National Weather Service to purchase a forecasting system that combines 44 computers linked together with each other to form the world's sixth-largest supercomputer.</u>

    ○ It was decided by the National Weather Service to purchase a forecasting system that combines 44 computers linked together with each other to form the world's sixth-largest supercomputer.

    ○ A forecasting system that combines 44 computers linked together with each other to form the world's sixth-largest supercomputer was selected to be purchased by the National Weather Service.

    ○ It was decided by the National Weather Service to purchase a forecasting system that links 44 computers together to form the world's sixth-largest supercomputer.

    ○ The National Weather Service decided to purchase a forecasting system that links 44 computers together to form the world's sixth-largest supercomputer.

    ○ The National Weather Service decided to purchase a forecasting system that combines 44 computers linked together with each other to form the world's sixth-largest supercomputer.

47. The Democratic Republic of Congo <u>not only has one of the world's largest populations, with over 56 million people, but also has</u> one of the world's fastest-growing populations, with an annual growth rate of 3.5 percent.

   ○ not only has one of the world's largest populations, with over 56 million people, but also has

   ○ not only has one of the world's largest populations, with over 56 million people, it also has

   ○ not only has one of the world's largest populations, with over 56 million people, but moreover it is

   ○ with 56 million people, making it one of the world's most populous countries, but also has

   ○ has one of the world's largest populations, with over 56 million people, but also has

Advanced

48. <u>Corporation X spends a larger percentage of its revenue on insurance than Corporation Y does on employee salaries.</u>

   ○ Corporation X spends a larger percentage of its revenue on insurance than Corporation Y does on employee salaries.

   ○ In Corporation X, a larger percentage of the revenues is spent on insurance than is spent on employee salaries in Corporation Y.

   ○ In Corporation X, they spend a larger percentage of revenues on insurance than Corporation Y does on employee salaries.

   ○ A larger percentage of Corporation X's revenue is spent on insurance than Corporation Y spends on employee salaries.

   ○ Of the Corporations X and Y, a higher percentage of revenues is spent on insurance by the former than the latter spends on employee salaries.

49. Because the city's files covered only the years 1934 through <u>2002, so the potential buyers were unable to determine the year of originally</u> construction.

    ○ 2002, so the potential buyers were unable to determine the year of originally

    ○ 2002, and the potential buyers were unable to determine the year of originally

    ○ 2002, the potential buyers were unable to determine the year of original

    ○ 2002, therefore the potential buyers were unable to determine the year of originally

    ○ 2002; therefore, the potential buyers were unable to determine the year of original

50. Museumgoers who glanced up into the building's five-story atrium often <u>notice birds nesting in the rafters, whose behavior was being studied by the museum's staff.</u>

    ○ notice birds nesting in the rafters, whose behavior was being studied by the museum's staff

    ○ notice birds nesting in the rafters, which were being studied by the museum's staff

    ○ notice that birds, whose behavior was being studied by the museum's staff, are nesting in the rafters,

    ○ noticed that birds, whose behavior was being studied by the museum's staff, were nesting in the rafters

    ○ noticed that birds, with the behavior that was being studied by the museum's staff, were nesting in the rafters

ANSWERS AND EXPLANATIONS

1.	E	11.	B	21.	D	31.	B	41.	C
2.	C	12.	D	22.	E	32.	C	42.	D
3.	B	13.	B	23.	E	33.	A	43.	B
4.	A	14.	D	24.	C	34.	E	44.	E
5.	D	15.	E	25.	D	35.	B	45.	E
6.	C	16.	A	26.	A	36.	D	46.	D
7.	D	17.	A	27.	C	37.	C	47.	A
8.	D	18.	C	28.	A	38.	B	48.	A
9.	C	19.	A	29.	C	39.	B	49.	C
10.	A	20.	D	30.	B	40.	D	50.	D

DIAGNOSTIC TOOL

Tally up your score and write down your results below.

Total Correct: _____ out of 50

Percentage Correct: # you got right × 100 ÷ 50: _____

DIAGNOSE YOUR RESULTS

Look back at the questions you got wrong and think back on your experience answering them.

STEP 1: FIND THE ROADBLOCKS

Did you struggle to answer some questions? To improve your score, you need to pinpoint exactly what element of these roadblocks tripped you up. To do that, ask yourself these two questions.

1. Did I have trouble finding the differences among the answer choices?

If so, you need to practice scanning answer choices to compare them rather than reading each one individually. Sometimes answer choices differ only by one or two letters! In these cases, we're highly unlikely to spot the difference if we're reading each one instead of comparing. Sometimes answer choices have radically different structures. (This is often the case when the whole sentence is underlined.) These are more challenging to compare, as you need to hunt through each answer choice to find the comparable pieces. Try out Kaplan's *GMAT Verbal Workbook*, which has Sentence Correction practice sets and a full-length Verbal section.

2. Did I find the differences but have difficulty knowing which choices to eliminate?

Were you unable to identify errors? Did lots of answer choices seem "equally right"? If so, you need to solidify your understanding of the grammar, style, and idiom rules that puzzled you. Review the rules in this chapter and read the answer explanations thoroughly for even more specific guidance. You should also try out Kaplan's *GMAT Verbal Workbook*, which contains review of the fundamental rules for English grammar and usage, as well as exercises to build speed and accuracy.

STEP 2: FIND THE BLIND SPOTS

Did you answer some questions quickly and confidently—but get them wrong anyway?

When you come across problems like these, you probably misunderstood the grammar, style, or idiom rule in question. Odds are that you've learned "informal" usage instead of the more formal rules that the GMAT is using. You need to unlearn what you think is right and learn the formal rule instead. Pick up a copy of the *GMAT Verbal Foundations* book for a back-to-basics review of these key concepts.

Also, read the answer explanations for a detailed breakdown as to why the correct answer is correct and why all the wrong choices are wrong. Study these rules very closely so you don't make the same mistakes on test day. And as with your roadblocks, try to get in as much practice as you can.

STEP 3: REINFORCE YOUR STRENGTHS

Now read through all the answer explanations for the ones you got right. This helps to reinforce the Kaplan method and your facility with the rules being tested. The more quickly and confidently you handle the questions that you are strong on, the more time you'll have for the tougher questions, and the more confidence you'll build as you move through the test. Keep your skills sharp with more practice.

As soon as you are comfortable with all the GMAT question types and Kaplan methods, complete a full-length practice test under timed conditions. In this way, practice tests serve as milestones; they help you to chart your progress! So don't save them all for the final weeks.

If you are aiming for that top score, try out Kaplan's *GMAT 800*, which includes only the toughest GMAT questions and most focused strategies.

You can also try out the GMAT Quiz Bank! You get more than 1,000 questions that you can access 24/7 from any Internet browser, each with comprehensive explanations. You can even customize your quizzes based on question type, content, and difficulty level. Take quizzes in Timed Mode to test your stamina or in Tutor Mode to see explanations as you work. Best of all, you also get detailed reports to track your progress.

Visit **kaptest.com/GMAT** for more details on the Quiz Bank and for more information on other online and classroom-based options.

IMPORTANT NOTE REGARDING THESE ANSWER EXPLANATIONS

These explanations show you all the groups in the answer choices. Different people work with different splits first, so we have to write them this way. But don't construe this to mean that you should be revisiting answers that you've eliminated. *Once you know an answer choice is wrong and have eliminated it, do not reconsider it!*

> **EXPERT EXCLUSIVE**
>
> By choosing to work on the easiest differences, you won't have to figure out every error. There is virtually no difference between *larger number* and *greater number* and no need to worry about the difference to solve this question.

1. E

Scanning the answer choices, note that three choices contain the word *amount* and two contain *number*. Because people can be counted, they come in numbers—not amounts. So (A), (B), and (C) are out. (C) and (D) misplace the modifier; *even larger* and *even greater* next to *people* suggests that the people themselves are bigger. (E) is best: ". . . to attract an even greater number of people" clearly refers to more people.

2. C

Notice that the very first word you read is *compared*. Right away you should start hunting for comparison errors as you read. In standard English, only similar things can be compared. So "the poor" can be compared only with other people, including fictional characters. People cannot be compared with a "time period," as in (A) and (B); or with a "time," as in (D); or with a book, as in (E). Only (C) presents a valid comparison. Also note the 3-2 split between *compared with* and *in comparison to*. The GMAT prefers shorter constructions whenever possible; if you can say the same thing with two words instead of three, choose the two-word version. (D) and (E) could be eliminated for this reason as well.

3. B

Choices (A), (C), (D), and (E) use the plural pronoun *these* to refer to the singular noun *square root*. That's not a problem in (B); the phrase *such imaginary numbers* means "numbers like the one mentioned." You may have noticed other differences. For example, (E) starts differently than the others. Aside from being wordier ("there is no practical applications for equations . . ." as opposed to "equations . . . have no practical applications"), (E) has an agreement error between *is* and *applications*. (A) and (D) say *practically* instead of *practical*, and the meanings are different. *Practically* has a connotation of "almost completely," but *practical* means "in practice" or "actual." Lastly, (C) creates a modifying error by moving *inapplicable* next to *numbers*, thereby violating the original meaning of the sentence, which uses *inapplicable* to describe the equations.

4. A

You may have focused first on the verb *lies*, which is often confused with *lay*. The two words have too many different meanings to list here (*lay*, for example, has almost 70 definitions!). But the basic difference is that *lay* means *to lay something down* (an action you do to something else—grammarians call this is a "transitive verb"), while *lie* means *to lie down* (you're doing that to yourself—this is an "intransitive verb"). For example, you'd say, "Before you *lie* down for a nap, you *lay* down new sheets." To complicate matters, *lay* is also the past tense of *lie*.

Lie means something slightly differently here (*to reside in*), but it is used in the intransitive sense, which is correct. Eliminate (C) and (D), which use *lay*. There's also a 3-2 split between singular verbs and plural verbs. What's the subject? In true GMAT style, it's far away from the verb—*motivation*, which is singular. Eliminate (B).

As you can see, there are *two* different reasons to discard (D)! But remember, you need only eliminate an answer once—after finding just one reason, you'd eliminate and *move on*. There's no need to look at it again.

In (E), the phrase *instead of* should signal replacement or a substitution, whereas the intended meaning is a comparison. (A) is correct.

5. D

It is unclear what *their* refers to—public or UFOs. Logically, it would seem the reference is to the public, but *public* is singular, so we'd have to use *its*, not *their*. Using the pronoun error, you'd eliminate (A), (B), and (C). Perhaps you noticed a subject-verb agreement error—the word *and* creates a compound subject, which is always plural. But the sentence uses the singular *has*. (A) and (B), if not eliminated before, could be thrown away for this reason. (C), (D), and (E) change *and* to *as well as*, which does not create a plural noun but a modifying phrase; the subject is now *belief*, so the plural *have* in (C) and (E) should be eliminated. (D) is correct. Additionally, there is no main verb for the subject *belief* in (B).

> **EXPERT EXCLUSIVE**
> Only the word *and* creates a compound subject.

6. C

If you noticed the parallelism error in the original sentence, you'd quickly select (C). What is that error? Notice the 2-1-2 split at the beginning of the answers: *its interests are, the better its interests are,* and *by the policies*. These words need to be parallel to *the more an organization contributes.* Only (C) meets this test with *the more...the better.* Here are other differences you could have used to eliminate. *Served through* is idiomatically wrong in (B); *served by* is correct. Placing *by the policies* . . . at the beginning of the

> **EXPERT EXCLUSIVE**
> The parallelism rule here is the same one used in "*the bigger they are, the harder they fall.*"

sentence removes it from its verb, thus violating the modification rule. Eliminate (D) and (E). You could also eliminate the last two for being awkwardly worded.

7. D

One idiom being tested here is *hope for* versus *hope to*. One can hope for something to happen or for a thing—hope for a peaceful resolution to the problem. One can also hope to do something—hope to travel the world one day. In this sentence, the students want to do something: change careers. The proper idiom is *hope to.* Eliminate (A) and (B). Another idiom tested here is *exchange for*, so (C)'s *exchange with* is wrong. (E) doesn't specify what the "drab jobs" are being exchanged for. Furthermore, (E)'s *careers that will be new and challenging* is wordy compared to *new and challenging careers.* (A), (B), and (C) also all have overly wordy constructions. The basic wordiness rule is the fewer words the better, as long as no meaning is lost.

EXPERT EXCLUSIVE

Note that the shortest choice is correct. The most concise answer is usually (not always, but usually) the right answer on the GMAT.

8. D

The original sentence likely hit your ear as wrong, since it is very awkward. The underlined pronoun *they* is also ambiguous, as it is unclear whether it refers to *crimes* or to *convictions*. Eliminate (A). Scanning reveals lots of structural differences. *The ranging* in (C) is unidiomatic and puts a lot of distance between *ranging* and *from*. Another difference is the *and* in (B), which requires parallelism; also, *were* doesn't match *ranging*, so (B) should be eliminated. (E) is too wordy—*all of them had convictions* and *crimes that were against property*—compared to (D). Perhaps you looked at the 3-2 split of *(not that)/ that.* The word *that* is often required after verbs in complex sentences—it subordinates a clause. "All were convicted" and "all of them had convictions" are full clauses in themselves (they have subjects and verbs) and must be subordinated to the main clause, "records reveal." Thus, the word *that* is necessary.

9. C

There is a 3-2 split at the beginning between plural and singular verbs. What's the subject? What parallels? It's *symptoms*, so we can eliminate (D) and (E), both of which can also be eliminated on idiomatic grounds. There's a 3-2 split at the end between *afflicted with* and *afflicted from*, and the latter is unidiomatic. There's also a 2-2-1 split after the verb—*that/those/the multitudes. Symptoms* don't parallel *multitudes of Americans*, so eliminate (B). *That* is singular, but it refers to the plural *symptoms.* Eliminate (A) and, if needed, (E).

10. A

Many students are thrown by the plural verb "have" at the beginning of this sentence. However, the whole phrase containing the word *have* is a modifier: The *group* is composed of *students who have begun to clear up . . .* The subject is *group*, which is singular, so the main verb has to be *believes*, as in (A). Eliminate (B), (D), and (E). There's also a split at the end—*but to be/but could be/but that it be.* What's the first element? The basic structure is "the park needs not A but B." So we need to match *to be redesigned*; we need *to*, so eliminate (C) and, if you haven't done so already, (E).

11. B

(B), using *Although*, makes clear the contrast between Lessing's recent work and her better-known early work. *In spite of* in (D) provides the needed contrast, but because it has three words compared to just one (*although*) and it uses the *-ing* form, it should be eliminated for wordiness. (A), (C), and (E) don't make that contrast clear. (D) can also be eliminated because the word *should* at the end changes the meaning of the sentence. Also, *is likely to be* is more idiomatic than *will likely be* in (A) and (C), *should likely be* in (D), or *may likely be* in (E). (B) is correct.

12. D

(A) uses the past perfect *had swept* for no reason, given that there's no sequence of events; they all took place at essentially the same time. *Having* in (B) illogically implies that the fires killed people before sweeping through the area. Perhaps you puzzled over parallelism; it seems at first that the fires did a list of three things linked by *and*—swept, killed, and left. But no answer choice is in that form! Why not? It's because this question is correctly using the continuous tense; the sense of the sentence is that people were killed and homes were left smoldering *as the fires swept*. So *killing* and *leaving* are correct (and parallel to each other). That eliminates everything but (D).

> **EXPERT EXCLUSIVE**
> Not many GMAT questions use the continuous tense (you may have learned it as "the progressive tense") correctly. Study this question closely to understand its proper use.

13. B

When should be used only for references to a time, and *where* should be used only for references to a place, so (A) and (D) are incorrect. (C) and (E) are both awkward, and they use the unidiomatic phrase *a condition of*.

14. D

Since the sentence is about *precursors,* or forerunners, and since the nonunderlined part of the sentence uses the past tense verb *were*, the answer has to use *were*, not *are* as in (A) and (E). Also, *however it may be that* in (B) and *despite that* in (C) are unidiomatic. (E) drops the contrast altogether. Note that (E) also makes it seem that the ornithologists are the ones gliding from tree to tree. (D) is correct.

15. E

There are clear differences at the beginning of the choices: *that a federal arbitrator/of a federal arbitrator/a federal arbitrator*. In (C), *asked of* is unidiomatic. For verbs like *ask*, there are two correct forms: *ask + object + to* or *ask + that + (subject of clause) + (infinitive without* to*)*. The former construction is attempted by (D) and (E), but (D) uses *that* inappropriately. (A) and (B) try the latter, but (A) uses *would* inappropriately. Scanning

> **EXPERT EXCLUSIVE**
> All verbs that are synonyms of *request* or *order*, such as *ask*, *mandate*, or *require*, can be used in either of the two ways described in this explanation: "The GMAT requires test takers to be on time," or "The GMAT requires that test takers be on time."

between (B) and (E), and ignoring the differences at the beginning because both forms are acceptable, we see a difference at the end: *have* or *has*. The verb in question is part of a modifying phrase that describes *union*, so the singular *has* is correct. Eliminate (B) (and (C), if it hasn't already been eliminated). (E) is correct.

16. A

There is a 3-2 split between *the refusal* and *that the refusal* at the beginning of the choices. *That the refusal* would create a sentence composed entirely of modifying phrases with no subject at all. So eliminate (B) and (D). There's another 3-2 split at the end between *than* and *as*. Look upstream to find the beginning of the two-part construction, which is *closer*. *Closer . . . than* is correct, so eliminate (E). The final split is between *the other* and *another*. *Another* is properly used for an unspecified other. Since we know the two parties involved, we can eliminate (C). (A) is correct.

17. A

Such . . . like in (B) is unidiomatic. The proper form meaning "for example" is *such as*. *That of* in (C) is illogical: *that* can stand only for *industry*, and it doesn't make sense to talk about the industry of an industry. *Is* in (D) doesn't have an object. In (E), the use of both *as* and *like* is redundant. Also, (B) and (E) both use the phrase *which is prospering*, when the single word *prospering* will do. (A) is correct.

18. C

Kudos if you noticed that the word *is* mandated parallelism: A *is* B. If you did, you could quickly eliminate all but (C) and (D), which are the only answers parallel to *to tackle*. There is also a 3-2 split between *between* and *among*. Since there are only two sides in the war, *between* is correct. Eliminate (B) and (D). If you hadn't already eliminated (A) because of the parallelism error, you could do so because it uses an incorrect idiom, *between. . . . with*, or because *a war which is raging* is wordy compared to *a war raging*.

> **EXPERT EXCLUSIVE**
>
> When words or phrases change positions between choices, it's likely that the modification rule is being tested. Look closely at what the word or phrase is next to.

19. A

This is a long and complex sentence, just the sort that makes us say, "Yech, I wouldn't write that way." But our job isn't to find the best way in the universe to express an idea, just to find the one correct way of the five given to us. Let's do a scan of the answers and see what's being tested. There's a 2-2-1 split among the beginnings: *a scientist/(after being) buried/a recently discovered*. It seems that the placement of phrases is the issue, so let's pick one of these phrases and compare the answers to see where they belong. *Scientist* and *weapon* are both subjects; *buried* is a modifier. We have a nice, clear rule about the placement of modifiers, so looking at the *buried* phrase will probably be easiest. (A), (B), and (E) all put the phrase next to *weapon*, which is where it belongs. (D) claims that the scientist has been buried since 1300 BCE, which is probably not the case. (C) is a little tougher, as the *buried* phrase follows another modifying phrase. They both modify *silk*, which isn't what the *buried* phrase is meant to describe. Since we've discovered another modifier (the *fabric* phrase), let's see where it's placed. All but (E) place it properly; (E) claims that the scientist is a fabric. We've gotten things down to (A) and (B). One big difference is the subject; (A) is "a scientist has determined that a weapon . . . ," and (B) is "weapon had been recently determined by a scientist . . . ." The latter is what grammarians call "passive voice," and it is considered stylistically weak; since we have an "active" option, we can eliminate (B). The original structure, (A), is best. Incidentally, there are also verb tense errors: (B) and (C) use the past perfect *had been* for no reason, and since the invention of silk happened in the past, *previously thought to be* is wrong.

> **EXPERT EXCLUSIVE**
>
> "Active voice" has the subject *doing the action*. Since the weapon isn't determining, (B) isn't active.

20. D

(D) makes the sequence of events perfectly clear: Stokes ran for mayor at essentially the same time he won the election. (A) and (E) use the past perfect *had run*, which makes it sound as if Stokes ran for mayor long before actually winning; the use of *when* makes it clear that the actions are meant to be understood as happening together. Two past tense verbs in the same sentence create the sense that the actions happened at the same time. The continuous tense in (C) makes it seem that the winning triggered the running, which makes no sense. The *and* at the end of (B) and (E) creates an awkward construction, making it seem that the *he* is referring to someone other than Carl Stokes.

21. D

People can be individually counted, so they come in numbers, as in (C) and (D). That means (A), (B), and (E), which all use *amount*, are incorrect. And strictly speaking, the adverb *hopefully* cannot be used to mean "it is hoped." (Though most of us use it this way in everyday speech, standard written English has more rigorous requirements.) As an adverb, *hopefully* modifies only the action *prove,* so the meaning becomes "prove in a hopeful manner." Since *psychotherapy* is not a person, it can't do anything in a hopeful manner! That would eliminate (C), as well as (A) and (B) were they not already eliminated. (D) is correct, with "it is hoped" and "the large number [of people]."

22. E

You don't always have to start eliminating based on differences at the front of the choices; you can use the end or middle, too. There is a 3-2 split in the middle between *Chicago* and *the people*. Which is right? Since the modifying phrase describes a city, it must be *Chicago*. Eliminate (C) and (D). There's a clear split at the beginning, too: *having often been/it is still often/in spite of still often/although still often*. If we hadn't eliminated (C) because of the modification error, we certainly could do so because of wordiness—*in spite of* takes three words to say what *although* does in one. We also need some sense of contrast, given the meaning of the sentence, so (A) and (B) get eliminated as well. (The word *but* in (D) captures the contrast—it's the modification that's wrong.) The last difference to note is *having often been* in (A), which is unnecessarily complicated as there's no sequence of events.

23. E

EXPERT EXCLUSIVE

Order and all its synonyms follow the same rules as *ask*. This is a commonly tested rule and one you want to learn!

This is a great example of the payoff you get from knowing some commonly tested rules. If you picked up the verb *order* as a commonly tested verb form, you'd have started looking for an answer to begin with *to*—you order someone *to* do something. That would immediately lead you to (E), and you'd have the right answer in a matter of seconds! Your ear may well have led you to (E), as (A), (B), and (D) are awkwardly constructed on their own—the awkwardness of (D) becomes apparent when read in the context of the nonunderlined text.

24. C

You'll find that *-ing* verbs often make sentences or phrases unnecessarily wordy. That's the case here. Four answers use *of having*; one uses the much less awkward *have* and is therefore correct. Also note another example of a one-word phrase (*because*) preferred to a four-word phrase (*as a result of*). Lastly, note how *they* in (C) (and *their* in (E)) provide clear references to the subject *sharks*, something the other three choices do not.

25. D

EXPERT EXCLUSIVE

The GMAT almost always prefers *whether* to *if*. And the GMAT almost always dislikes *being*.

There is a 2-2-1 split among the word used to indicate the two disputed options: *if*, *being*, and *whether*. *Whether* is the appropriate word for a choice between two. The GMAT tests this rule often. Only (D) gets it right! Note also the 2-2-1 split among *over*, *about*, and *concerning*. The idiomatically proper match with *dispute* is *over*. And, in case you're curious, there is a subject-verb disagreement in (B)—*hikes is*.

26. A

This choice illustrates the importance of knowing your idioms and of working strategically. Scan the answer choices quickly to zero in on the significant differences, the clearest of which is at the end: *or/nor*. This is a nice, clear rule: *or* by itself is correct, as are *either . . . or* and *neither . . . nor*. (*Nor* is not correct on its own as in (E).) (A) is the only answer to get this right! Also note the awkward construction in (C) and (D) of *through the imitation of adults*.

27. C

EXPERT EXCLUSIVE

Remember, verb tenses don't always need to be in parallel; rather, they need to make logical sense given the sequence of events.

The windows in question "have been built to conserve energy, and they are." Are what? Conserving energy, of course. The verb that follows *are* is left out, but its meaning is implied. Problem is, the verb is *to conserve* energy, not *conserving*. *Are* makes no sense. You can't say "they are [conserve energy]," as in (A) and (E). Nor can you say "have [conserve energy]," as in (B) and (D). You may also have noticed the verb tense difference. *Had been* in (E) is incorrect, as the building of the windows did not happen before a past event. The continuous *are being* in (D) is not necessary here, as it usually is not in verb tense questions. *Have been* in (A) may be tempting, but the improvement and the building didn't happen at the same time (the improvement must have been achieved before the windows could be built).

28. A

There's a split at the beginning: *at/as a consequence/on account of/as*. They all have the sense of "because," but (B) and (C) take too many words to create this sense and should be eliminated. (E) adds *along with* improperly. Lists only need one conjunction: "X, Y, and Z"; not "X, along with Y, and Z". Lastly, notice that (B), (C), and (D) are all in the passive voice. (A) solves that problem—instead of a verb form, it uses *the urging*, which we know to be a noun because of the *the*. (*-ing*'s used as nouns are called "gerunds," by the way.) Also note that (C) and (E) drop the word *some*, thereby changing the meaning. (When used with a number, *some* means "approximately.")

> **EXPERT EXCLUSIVE**
> The word *by* should raise a red flag—it often signals the passive voice.

29. C

Notice the descriptive phrase *of plastic manufacturing plants* between the subject *size* and the verb *have dropped*. That's our clue to check for subject-verb agreement. In fact, *size* is singular, but *have dropped* is plural. (A) and (B) contain *have* and should be eliminated. There's also another split: the *down* in (D) and (E) is redundant with *dropped*. If something has dropped, it's gone down! This quickly leaves you with only (C). To improve your ear's ability to spot awkward phrasing, check out the end of (A), (D), and (E). (D)'s ending is not only awkward but also redundant, as the implied word at the end is *size*: "about the size of a football field's [size]."

30. B

Yeesh, what a long sentence. When faced with choices that are this long, it may be easier to scan two answers at a time rather than all five at once. Scanning (A) and (B), we notice *their contribution* versus *the contribution of the Swiss*. So pronoun ambiguity may be the issue. Is *their* ambiguous? It sure is, as it may refer either to *leading Swiss designers* or to *the curators*. Eliminate answers that repeat that error; a quick scan shows those to be (A), (D), and (E). Comparing the two that remain shows you only one difference: *their most famous bridges* versus *its most famous bridges*. *Its* could only possibly refer to the museum, which makes no logical sense—these are the designers' buildings. So (B) is correct. Also note the passive construction of (D): "organized by the curators." (D) also has a modification error. The beginning of the sentence is describing the curators, but "exhibition" follows the comma.

> **EXPERT EXCLUSIVE**
> Don't panic when you see a long underlined portion. If you are scanning for differences instead of reading each choice individually, you can answer even scary-looking problems with relative ease.

EXPERT EXCLUSIVE

See how quickly you can answer some SC problems when you spot an error in Step 1? That's the payoff of active reading!

31. B

The fact that the word *than* is underlined is a clue that there may be a comparison problem here. As written, the sentence actually compares the assets of small investors to the large investors themselves, which doesn't make sense. We need to compare either investors to investors or assets to assets. Only (B) and (E) make the comparison clear: *small investors' assets* are being compared to *those of large investors*. Those two differ at the beginning: *than/relatively to*. The correct construction is only *less . . . than*. (E), as well as (D), can be eliminated on those grounds.

32. C

When you see items in a list, consider whether there is a problem with parallelism. Here we have a list of three things the company was forced to do: close plants, lay off workers, and reduce budgets. In the original sentence, the first two items have the gerund *-ing* form (*closing, laying*), so the third item must be *reducing*. (C) is correct.

33. A

The underlined portion includes the pronoun *it*. At first glance, it seems like *it* could refer either to *Greece* or to the phrase *ancient European history*. However, the logical structure of the sentence clearly identifies the pronoun: "before A was X, it was Y," makes the meaning of *it* unambiguously *Greece*. Things look good, but we might still be hesitant; we should check the rest of the answers.

(E) removes the *it*, playing it safe. However, (E) incorrectly uses the past perfect tense; the *had become* would imply that becoming city-states happened before some other event, but there isn't a second past event anywhere else in the sentence. (B), (C), and (D), meanwhile, keep the *it* but eliminate the sentence structure in (A) that identifies the pronoun; in all three, *it* seems to refer to *European history*, which logically cannot be a *collection of small city-states*.

34. E

The sentence begins with a long descriptive phrase, so we should check to see if this modifying phrase is used correctly. The phrase should modify the noun that immediately follows it, which in this case is *the investigative commission*. But the commission itself was not compiled from government documents; its report was. The phrase should modify *report*, not *commission*. But the subject is not part of the underlined portion, so we'll have to look for an opening phrase that correctly modifies *commission*.

In (B), the change to *compiling*—an active participle—means that the phrase now modifies *commission* and is possibly correct. But the pronoun is awkward and fairly ambiguous due to the long distance between *it* and *report*. Eliminate (B). (C) and (D) do not solve the problem; those phrases do not describe *commission*. (E) changes the phrase so that it modifies *commission*; the commission must have worked with the documents to produce the report. (E) is correct.

35. B

If you noticed the comparison error as you read, that's great. Otherwise, seeing the 3-2 split between [*the*] *compounds* and *machine-based research* would have led you to test the agreement with the preceding modifying phrase, which makes a comparison with *manual research*. We can't compare *compounds* to *research*, so we eliminate all but (B) and (C).

(C) incorrectly makes *machine-based research* of a lower quality rather than the *compounds* identified by machine-based research. (This error is repeated in (D), incidentally, which compares *compounds* to manual research.) (B) is correct.

36. D

The word *since* in a sentence is a big clue that verb tenses are being tested. Sure enough, there's a 1-3-1 split at the end of the choices involving verbs: *was using/has used/was to be using*. When was the casino tax revenue used? *Since 1993* lets us know that the use of the revenue began in the past but is still continuing, so eliminate (A) and (E). The other split is at the beginning: *approving/for the approving of/approved*. (B) is awkward, and it should be tossed for that. (C) incorrectly changes the active participle *approving* to the passive *approved*. (D) is the right answer.

> **EXPERT EXCLUSIVE**
>
> Look out for words like *since*, *during*, *before*, and *after*. They indicate sequence of events, so noticing them will make verb tense questions much easier.

37. C

There are two warning signs of problems in this question: the underlined pronoun *them* and the initial modifying phrase set off by a comma. Both are incorrect in (A). The modifier, beginning with *disappointed*, clearly is meant to refer to the teacher. Only (C) and (D) correct that modification error by putting *the teacher* immediately after the comma. However, we can answer this question without even addressing the modification issue. *Them* in this sentence is meant to refer to the teacher's students, but the noun *students* doesn't appear anywhere, only the possessive modifier *students'*. For that reason, the only answer that removes the pronoun—(C)—is correct.

> **EXPERT EXCLUSIVE**
>
> You've seen by now how often sentences that begin with modifying phrases have modification errors. Look for that on test day, and you'll get many right answers quickly.

38. B

The underlined portion of this sentence follows a comma, includes another comma and the conjunction *and*, and is preceded by the keywords *such as*. These clues indicate a series in which all the elements must have parallel form. The first element is *attending class*. Because it is not underlined, the rest of the series must be adapted to match it. The correct answer choice must therefore contain *reading*, which only (A) and (B) do. It must also contain *writing*, which only (B) and (E) do. (B) is the right answer. Note that (E) omits the *and*, thus failing to end the list properly.

39. B

If you saw the pronoun error as you read, you quickly eliminated (A) and (C), as the pronoun refers to the singular *army*, not to the plural *Xerxes and nine of his generals*.

You could also have seen that pronoun agreement was being tested by scanning the answer choices, as *their/its* is the only difference between (A) and (B). The other major split among the answer choices is a 3-1-1—*was/having been/is*. The sentence is clearly set in the past (it's describing 480 BCE). So the present *is* and the present perfect *having been* are wrong; (D) and (E) can be eliminated. Only (B) remains, and it is correct. To continue training your ear to spot awkward sentences, compare (C) to (B).

40. D

There is a 2-2-1 split among verb tenses: *increased/was/has*. Immediately after the underlined portion is the critical clue letting us know what tense to use: *in the past five years*. Clearly the increase started in the past and has continued to the present. That's what the present perfect *has* form is for, so (D) has to be correct. Also note that *increased by more than three times* is unidiomatic. The proper way to say that idea is simply *more than tripled*. And (C), was *increased more than three times*, changes the meaning to imply that there were more than three increases.

41. C

The underlined portion contains a list of three sources of protein. These three sources must have parallel forms, but *soy, eggs,* and *drinking milk* do not. A parallel construction would be *soy, eggs, or milk*. So (A), (B), and (D) are out. (E) adds *its*, which seems to refer to *the human body*. The sentence is not about protein in the human body but rather protein that the human body can use, so (E) can be eliminated. Note the *like* in (B) is incorrectly used—on the GMAT, *like* cannot mean "for example."

42. D

The plural pronoun *their* incorrectly refers to the singular Norway. *Their* should be *its*. So (A) and (C) are out. (B) corrects this error but changes *reflecting* to the awkward *being a reflection of* (*reflection of*, in (C), is also incorrect). (E), too, uses the proper pronoun, but the word *greater* changes the meaning of the sentence. That leaves (D), which is the correct choice.

43. B

These choices have a difference among the verbs: *were losing/are losing/lost/continuing to lose*. The sentence's only indication of what tense to use is the other action: *are gaining ground*. Because the two actions are happening at the same time, they both require the same tense. Since *are gaining* is not underlined and must be correct, we need *are losing* in the right answer. That means (B).

> **EXPERT EXCLUSIVE**
> Whenever you see a list, check for parallel structure.

> **EXPERT EXCLUSIVE**
> This is an example of how the GMAT uses an *-ing* verb to avoid modification errors.

> **EXPERT EXCLUSIVE**
> Whenever a sentence has two actions (in this case "losing market share" and "gaining ground"), verb tense errors are likely.

44. E

The sentence contains two parallel elements—procedures and reductions—that are incorrectly joined by the construction *from . . . and*. The construction should be *from . . . to*. Eliminate (A) and (B). (C) changes the parallel structure format with *such as*, but *reducing* is not parallel with *improvement* and *encouragement*. Moreover, *reducing* can't be followed by the preposition *in* from the original sentence. Eliminate (C). (D) correctly uses *from . . . to* but includes the nonparallel *procedures* and *reducing*. That leaves (E), which is correct.

45. E

The word *than* preceding the underlined portion of the sentence tells us that the underlined portion is a comparison. Items compared must be parallel. Here, the money the Dancing Doll (DD) line received from sales is compared to that received by the Teeny Tiny Trucks (TT) and Basic Blocks (BB) lines, so all of these quantities should be stated the same way. Only the name of the toy line and the amount should change from item to item, and the verb *sold* does not need to be repeated for each item. Since (A) includes *did* with the TT sales but no verb with the BB sales, these forms are not parallel; eliminate (A).

(B) is not parallel because it uses *did* with TT sales and *were* with BB sales. (C) includes *sold* with TT sales but no additional verb with BB, so it's out. (D) and (E) both eliminate the verbs and make the comparison more parallel by using *more than* for both items, but (D) uses *Basic Blocks' sales*—something not parallel to *Dancing Dolls line* and *Teeny Tiny Trucks line*. (E) uses exactly the same form for all three items, so it is correct.

46. D

While this sentence is long and wordy, we needn't be intimidated as long as we scan for differences. There's a pretty clear 2-1-2 split right at the start: *It was decided by the National Weather Service/A forecasting system/The National Weather service decided*. The first of these, *It was decided by . . .*, is passive construction and not preferred by the GMAT. That eliminates (A) and (C). What about (B)? It's structured slightly differently, but does it share the passive voice error? It sure does! The whole thing reads "A forecasting system . . . *was selected* to be purchased by the National Weather Service." Eliminate (B) as well. Comparing (D) to (E), we see this difference: *links 44 computers together* versus *combines 44 computers linked together with each other*. (E) is amazingly redundant. Just saying *linked together* is enough—if things are "linked together," they are already "combined" and "with each other." (This redundancy error is shared by (A), (B), and (E).) (D) remains, and it is correct.

> **EXPERT EXCLUSIVE**
>
> See how spotting the word *by* as a signal for passive voice can save you lots of time and earn you lots of right answers?

EXPERT EXCLUSIVE

One of the GMAT's favorite idiomatic constructions is *not only . . . but also*.

47. A

A *not only* construction must be completed with *but also*. The original sentence does so and has no other errors, so (A) is correct. (B) is missing the *but*. (C) uses *moreover it is*. (D) too drops the *not only* but also creates a sentence fragment by changing the verb into a participle (*making*). It also drops the word *over*, changing the meaning. (E) drops the *not only* while keeping the *but also*.

48. A

The sentence compares the percentage of revenue that Corporation X spends on insurance with the percentage that Corporation Y spends on salaries. Since these two things have the same form, the comparison is clear and grammatically correct. (A) is the right answer. In (B), the phrase *In Corporation X* modifies the rest of the sentence, illogically making it seem as if X spends a percentage of its revenue on employee salaries in Corporation Y. It also needlessly uses the passive voice. In (C), *they* has no clear antecedent; because *corporation* is singular, *they* seems to refer to some other, unspecified subject. (D) compares Corporation X's percentage with Corporation Y's actual amount. (E) is awkwardly worded and seems to compare a percentage to an amount.

49. C

There are two splits among these choices, one at the beginning and one at the end. The former is *so/and/the/therefore.* Since the sentence already contains a connecting word that links the two clauses (that word is *because*), no other such word is needed. Only (C) can be correct! Had you started with the difference at the end, you'd be comparing *originally* to *original*. Since the word modified is a noun (*construction*), we need an adjective; (A), (B), and (D) must go.

50. D

There are two problems with this sentence. First, the unchangeable verb *glanced* is in the past tense, but the underlined *notice* is in the present tense. Since museumgoers would have *noticed* the birds at the same time that they *glanced up,* both verbs must be in the past tense. So *notice* must become the past tense *noticed*. On this basis, we can eliminate (A), (B), and (C).

The other problem involves modification, as evidenced by the changing position and wording of the modifying phrase among the answer choices. The clause that begins *whose behavior* is intended to describe *birds*, as *rafters* do not have behavior. This also gets rid of (A). (B) solves the problem but by changing the meaning, so it should be eliminated. (C) and (D) get the modification right. (E) attempts to do so but rewrites the modifier awkwardly. (D) is correct.

CHAPTER 6: READING COMPREHENSION

- Question Format and Structure
- The Basic Principles of Reading Comprehension
- Reading Comprehension Question Types
- The Kaplan Method for Reading Comprehension

Reading Comprehension tests critical reading skills. Among other things, it tests whether you can do the following:

- Summarize the main idea of a passage.
- Understand logical relationships between facts and concepts.
- Make inferences based on information in a text.
- Analyze the logical structure of a passage.
- Deduce the author's tone and attitude about a topic from the text.

In Reading Comp, you are presented with a reading passage (in an area of business, social science, biological science, or physical science) and then asked three or four questions about that text. You are not expected to be familiar with any topic beforehand—all the information is contained in the text in front of you. In fact, if you happen to have some previous knowledge about a given topic, it is important that you not let that knowledge affect your answers. Naturally, some passages will be easier than others, though all will present a challenge. The passages will have the tone and content that one might expect from a scholarly journal.

> **EXPERT EXCLUSIVE**
>
> Many Reading Comp questions have wrong answers based on information that is actually true but not mentioned in the passage. So if you know the subject, be careful. And if you don't know the subject, be happy—some wrong answers won't be tempting!

You will see four Reading Comp passages—two shorter passages with 3 questions each and two longer passages with 4 questions each, for a total of 14 questions. However, you will see only one question at a time on the monitor and you will have to answer each question before you can see the next question.

CAUTION

A common misconception is that the shorter passages are easier. They aren't! The longer passages may have more text, but the structure is often more clear.

The passage will be visible on one side of the monitor as long as you have a question on that passage. If the text is longer than the available space, you'll be given a scroll bar to move through it.

QUESTION FORMAT AND STRUCTURE

The directions for these questions look like this:

Directions: The questions in this group are based on the content of a passage. After reading the passage, choose the best answer to each question. Base your answers only according to what is stated or implied in the text.

Here's an example of a typical question:

Which of the following does the author suggest about the importance of the emigration of Southerners to Brazil?

- ○ Without the Southern presence, Brazil would never have been settled.

- ○ The Southerners' sole purpose in immigrating was to introduce new inventions to the Brazilians.

- ○ If the Southerners had not emigrated, they would have gone to prison for war crimes.

- ○ Dom Pedro II feared the condition Brazil would be in without the presence of the Americans.

- ○ The Southerners' arrival had a great impact on the development of education and agriculture in Brazil.

THE BASIC PRINCIPLES OF READING COMPREHENSION

Usually we read to learn something or to pass the time pleasantly. Neither of these goals has much to do with the GMAT. On test day, we have a very specific goal—to get as many right answers as we can. So our reading needs to be tailored to that goal. There are really only two things a Reading Comp question can ask you about: the "big picture" of the passage or its "little details."

Since the passage is right there on the screen, we don't need to worry much about the "little details" as we read. (In fact, doing so may hinder our ability to answer questions, as you'll soon see.) So our main goal as we read is to prepare ourselves to get the "big-picture" questions right, while leaving ourselves as much time as possible to find the answers to the "little-detail" questions.

Here are the four basic things you need to do to accomplish this.

LOOK FOR THE TOPIC AND SCOPE OF THE PASSAGE

Think of the Topic as the first big idea that comes along. Almost always, it will be right there in the first sentence. It will be something broad, far too big to discuss in the 150–350 words that most GMAT passages provide. Here's an example of how a passage might begin:

> The great migration of European intellectuals to the United States in the second quarter of the 20th century prompted a transmutation in the character of Western social thought.

What's the topic? The migration of European intellectuals to the United States in the second quarter of the 20th century. It would also be okay to say that the Topic is the effects of that migration on Western social thought. Topic is a very broad concept, so you really don't need to worry about how exactly you word it. You just need to get a good idea of what the passage is talking about so you feel more comfortable reading.

Now, as to Scope. Think of Scope as a narrowing of the Topic. You're looking for an idea that the author might reasonably focus on for the length of a GMAT passage. If the Topic is "the migration of European intellectuals to the United States in the second quarter of the 20th century," then perhaps the Scope will be "some of the effects of that migration upon Western social thought." More likely it will be more specific: "one aspect of Western social thought affected by the migration." But perhaps something unexpected will come along. Might the passage compare two different migrations? Or contrast two different effects? We need to think critically about what's coming and look for clues in the text that let us know on what specific subject(s) the author intends to focus.

> **EXPERT EXCLUSIVE**
>
> It's important to jot down brief summaries of each paragraph's main point(s). You'll need this later to help you answer questions.

Finding the Scope is critically important to doing well on Reading Comp. As in Critical Reasoning, many Reading Comp wrong answers are wrong because they are outside the Scope of the passage. It's highly unlikely that there will be a "topic sentence" in the traditional sense—but the first paragraph probably will have some indication of what the author intends to focus on.

Note: Some passages are only one paragraph long. In these cases, the Topic can still be in the first sentence. The passage will probably (but not necessarily) narrow down to Scope somewhere in the first third of the paragraph, as the author doesn't have much text to work with and needs to get down to business quickly.

GET THE GIST OF EACH PARAGRAPH AND ITS STRUCTURAL ROLE IN THE PASSAGE

The paragraph is the main structural unit of any passage. At first, you don't know Topic or Scope, so you have to read the first paragraph pretty closely. But once you get a sense of where the passage is going, all you need to do is understand what role each new paragraph plays. Ask yourself the following:

- Why did the author include this paragraph?
- What's discussed here that's different from the content of the paragraph before?
- What bearing does this paragraph have on the author's main idea?
- What role do the details play?

Notice that last question—don't ask yourself, "What does this mean?" but rather, "Why is it here?" Many GMAT passages try to swamp you with boring, dense, and sometimes confusing details. Consider this paragraph, which might show up on a difficult science-based passage:

> The Burgess Shale yielded a surprisingly varied array of fossils. Early chordates were very rare, but there were prodigious numbers of complex forms not seen since. *Hallucigenia*, so named for a structure so bizarre that scientists did not know which was the dorsal and which the ventral side, had fourteen legs. *Opabinia* had five eyes and a long proboscis. This amazing diversity led Gould to believe that it was highly unlikely that the eventual success of chordates was a predictable outcome.

Wow. Pretty dense stuff. But if we don't worry about understanding all of the science jargon and focus on the gist of the paragraph and *why* the details are there, things get easier. The first sentence isn't that bad:

> The Burgess Shale yielded a surprisingly varied array of fossils.

Okay, the "Burgess Shale," whatever that is, had a lot of different kinds of fossils.

> Early chordates were very rare, but there were prodigious numbers of complex forms not seen since. *Hallucigenia*, so named for a structure so bizarre that scientists did not know which was the dorsal and which the ventral side, had fourteen legs. *Opabinia* had five eyes and a long proboscis.

EXPERT EXCLUSIVE

Notice that we don't have to know what any of these scientific terms mean in order to know why the author brings them up!

Oh, this is just a list of the different kinds of fossils and some facts about them. Not a lot of "chordates," whatever they are, but lots of other stuff.

This amazing diversity led Gould to believe that it was highly unlikely that the eventual success of chordates was a predictable outcome.

Notice how the beginning of this sentence tells us *why* those annoyingly dense details are there; they are the facts that led Gould to a belief—namely that the rise of "chordates" couldn't have been predicted. So, on our noteboard, we'd jot down something like this:

Evidence for Gould's belief—chordate success not predictable.

Doing this for every paragraph allows you to create a map of the passage's overall structure. We'll call this a "Passage Map" from here on. This map will help you keep a clear understanding of the "Big Picture." And making it will give you a sense of mastery over the passage, even when it deals with a subject you don't know much about.

> **EXPERT EXCLUSIVE**
> Notice how the word *amazing* puts a little extra emphasis on the author's point. Look out for "charged" words; they show us the author's voice saying "Hey! Pay attention to this!"

LOOK FOR OPINIONS, THEORIES, AND POINTS OF VIEW—ESPECIALLY THE AUTHOR'S

An important part of critical reading is distinguishing between factual assertions and opinions/interpretations. It's the opinions/interpretations that the Reading Comp passages are built on, and you should pay the most attention to them. Let's say you come upon a paragraph that reads:

The coral polyps secrete calceous exoskeletons, which cement themselves into an underlayer of rock, while the algae deposit still more calcium carbonate, which reacts with sea salt to create an even tougher limestone layer. All of this accounts for the amazing renewability of the coral reefs despite the endless erosion caused by wave activity.

In a sense, this is just like the Burgess Shale paragraph; it begins with a lot of scientific jargon and later tells us why that jargon is there. In this case, it shows us how coral reefs renew themselves. But notice a big difference—the author doesn't tell us how someone else interprets these facts. She could have written "scientists believe that these polyps account for . . . ," but she didn't. This is the author's own interpretation.

> **EXPERT EXCLUSIVE**
> If you happen not to personally agree with the author's viewpoints, keep it to yourself. In this situation, that's irrelevant. The questions are going to test your command of the author's views, so you can only get in trouble by imposing your own.

It's important to differentiate between the author's own voice and other people's opinions. GMAT authors can disagree with other people but won't contradict themselves. So the author of the Burgess Shale passage might well disagree with Gould in the next paragraph. But the author of the Coral Reef passage has laid her cards on the table—she definitely thinks that coral polyps and algae are responsible for the renewability of coral reefs.

Spotting the opinions and theories also helps you to accomplish the goal of reading for structure. Once you spot an idea, you can step back from the barrage of words and attack the passage critically, saying, "Okay, but where's the support for this idea? Does the author agree? Or disagree?"

Consider how the critical reader would react to this:

> Abraham Lincoln is traditionally viewed as an advocate of freedom because he issued the Emancipation Proclamation and championed the Thirteenth Amendment, which ended legal slavery in the United States. And indeed this achievement cannot be denied. But he also set uncomfortable precedents for the curtailing of civil liberties.

EXPERT EXCLUSIVE

Notice how vocabulary is treated on the GMAT. You won't have to know what a "calceous exoskeleton" or a "coral polyp" is, but you would have to know that "civil liberties" and "personal freedoms" are basically interchangeable.

"Ah," the critical reader says, "that phrase *traditionally viewed* lets me know how people usually think about Lincoln. But the author might not completely agree. Sure enough, I see that she brings up the fact that he restricted civil liberties. And the word *uncomfortable* is a pretty big sign that the author is not at all pleased with Lincoln because of it! I should note, though, that the phrase *this achievement cannot be denied* means that she won't go so far as to say that Lincoln was an enemy of freedom."

"In fact," the reader continues, "I bet I know what the author is going to do structurally. She'll have to have at least one paragraph describing these precedents and how they restricted civil liberties. It might even be possible, since she uses the word *precedents*, that she goes on to describe how later presidents used Lincoln's actions as justification for their own restrictions. Holy smokes! Three sentences in, and I bet I've got the passage already!"

 ONLINE

Test your Reading Comprehension knowledge each month with your new quiz.

Put together, the passage's structure and its opinions/theories (especially the author's) will lead you to understand the author's primary Purpose in writing the passage. This is critical, as most GMAT passages have a question that directly asks for that Purpose. For the Lincoln passage, you might get a question like this:

> Which of the following best represents the main idea of the passage?
>
> ○ The Emancipation Proclamation had both positive and negative effects.
>
> ○ Lincoln's presidency laid the groundwork for future restrictions of personal freedoms.
>
> ○ The traditional image of Lincoln as a national hero must be overturned.

○ Lincoln used military pressure to influence state legislatures.

○ Abraham Lincoln was an advocate of freedom.

Just from a critical reading of the first few sentences, you could eliminate (A) as being a distortion of the first and third sentences, (C) as being too extreme because of the *cannot be denied* phrase, (D) as out of scope—either too narrow or just not there at all, and (E) as missing the author's big point—that Lincoln helped restrict civil liberties. And just like that, you've gotten a right answer and increased your score!

> **EXPERT EXCLUSIVE**
>
> Answer (D) from the Lincoln question is an example of an extra-tempting wrong answer—if there were a long paragraph describing how Lincoln used the army to influence Maryland's secession to vote and if we'd read that paragraph too closely, then we'd be drawn to that answer.

DON'T OBSESS OVER DETAILS

On the GMAT, you'll need to read only for short-term—as opposed to long-term—retention. When you finish the questions on a certain passage, that passage is over, gone, done with. You're promptly free to forget everything about it.

What's more, there's certainly no need to memorize—or even fully comprehend—details. You need to know why they are there so you can answer Big-Picture questions, but you can always go back and reread them in greater depth if you're asked a little-detail question. And you'll find that if you have a good sense of the passage's scope and structure, the ideas and opinions in the passage, and the author's Purpose, then you'll have little problem navigating through the text as the need arises.

Furthermore, you can hurt your score by reading the details too closely. Here's how:

- **Wasted time.** Remember, there will only be three or four questions per passage. They can't possibly ask you about all the little details. So don't waste your valuable time by focusing on what you don't need to know! If you do, you won't have nearly enough time to deal with the questions.

- **Extra-tempting wrong answers.** There just isn't time to read and understand fully every last little detail, so trying to do so inevitably causes us to jumble all the details together in a confusing blob. Since most of the wrong answers in GMAT Reading Comp come from irrelevant or distorted bits of the passage, uncritical readers find almost every answer choice tempting! The critical reader who doesn't read the details too closely doesn't recognize those answers as familiar and thus isn't tempted by them. Instead, she takes advantage of the open-book nature of the test to find the answer when asked.

- **Losing the Big Picture.** It's very easy to miss the forest for the trees. If you get too drawn into the details, you can pass right by the emphasis and opinion signals that you'll need to understand the author's main Purpose.

Here's a great trick for cutting through confusing, detail-laden sentences: focus on the subjects and verbs first, throwing away modifying phrases, and don't worry about confusing terminology. Let's revisit some unpleasant text from before:

> The coral polyps secrete calceous exoskeletons, which cement themselves into an underlayer of rock, while the algae deposit still more calcium carbonate, which reacts with sea salt to create an even tougher limestone layer. All of this accounts for the amazing renewability of the coral reefs despite the endless erosion caused by wave activity.

Yuck. But look at what happens if we distill this to main subjects and verbs, ignore modifiers, and don't worry about words we don't understand:

> Coral polyps (whatever they are) secrete something . . . and algae deposit something. This accounts for the amazing renewability of the coral reefs.

Not too bad! And now the bulkiness of that first sentence isn't slowing us down, so we can understand its role in the big picture.

 KAPLAN STRATEGY ———————————————————

The Basic Principles of Reading Comprehension are the following:

- Look for the Topic and Scope of the passage.
- Get the gist of each paragraph and its structural role in the passage.
- Look for opinions, theories, and points of view—especially the author's.
- Don't obsess over details.

READING COMPREHENSION QUESTION TYPES

Though you might want to break down the Reading Comp section according to the kinds of passages that appear—business, social science, biological science, or physical science—it's more effective to do so by question type. While passages differ in their content, we read them in essentially the same way, employing the same critical reading techniques for each.

Earlier, we looked at questions in two ways: "Big Picture" and "little detail." That basic difference holds true, but that terminology has more to do with what the questions focus on. (Some focus on both.) It's ultimately more effective to categorize questions more specifically. The four main question types on GMAT Reading Comp are **Global, Detail, Inference**, and **Logic.**

GLOBAL QUESTIONS

Any question that explicitly asks you to consider the passage as a whole is a Global question. Here are some examples:

- Which one of the following best expresses the main idea of the passage?
- The author's primary purpose is to . . .
- Which of the following best describes the organization of the passage?
- Which of the following would be an appropriate title for this passage?

The correct answer will be consistent with the passage's Topic, Scope, Purpose, and Structure. If you've jotted them down on your noteboard— and you should!—then it will only take a few seconds to select the right answer. Most wrong answers will either get the Scope wrong (too narrow or too broad) or misrepresent the author's point of view.

The GMAT will probably word the answer choices rather formally, so by "few seconds," we mean closer to 45 than to 10. But that's still significantly under your average time per question, meaning that you can spend more time dealing with the more time-consuming Inference questions.

DETAIL QUESTIONS

Detail questions ask you to identify what the passage explicitly says. Here are some sample Detail question stems:

- According to the passage, which of the following is true of X?
- The author states that . . .
- The author mentions which of the following in support of X?

"Wait a minute, Kaplan," you might be saying. "Didn't you just tell me not to read the details too closely? What's the deal?"

Good question! Reading carefully through all the details at once would be a big waste of time because you're likely to get only one, possibly two, Detail questions per passage. Plus, most Detail questions point you straight to the detail, anyway. That is, they reference a specific word or phrase that's easily located or give you line numbers to specify the detail's location. Occasionally, the screen even highlights the referenced phrase both in the question stem and in the passage.

So between highlighting, line references, and your Passage Map, finding the detail that the GMAT is asking about is usually not much of a challenge. What, then, could they possibly be testing? They are testing whether you understand that detail *in the context of the passage*. The best strategic approach, then, is to read not only the sentence that the question stem sends you to but also the sentence before and after it. Usually

EXPERT EXCLUSIVE

Be wary of Global answer choices based on details from the first or last paragraph. These are usually traps laid for those who wrongly assume that GMAT passages are traditional essays with "topic sentences" and "concluding sentences."

 ONLINE

Using the questions on your online Practice Test, practice taking notes on a separate sheet of paper. On test day, you will not be able to mark the passage directly.

EXPERT EXCLUSIVE

The phrase *according to* always signals a Detail question.

EXPERT EXCLUSIVE

Initially, you won't read details closely. But when solving a Detail question, take the time to understand the sentences that you know will help you get the right answer. If you need to read the sentences in the question two or three times, that's just fine.

EXPERT EXCLUSIVE

Make sure that you read whole sentences when solving Detail questions. A common GMAT trick is to have the right answer depend on a faraway part of the sentence. Notice here that the question stem sends you to the end of the last sentence, but it's the "no evidence" and "however" at the *beginning* of the sentences that form the support for the right answer.

the context you need comes before the detail from the question stem. Consider this question:

According to the passage, which of the following is true of the guinea pigs discussed in line 17?

Let's say that line 17 goes like this:

. . . a greater percentage of the guinea pigs that lived in the crowded, indoor, heated area survived than did the guinea pigs in the outdoor cages.

If we don't read for context, we might think that the right answer would be this:

Guinea pigs survive better indoors.

But what if we read the full context, starting one sentence before?

Until recently, scientists had no evidence to support the hypothesis that low temperature alone, and not other factors such as people crowding indoors, is responsible for the greater incidence and severity of influenza in the late fall and early winter. Last year, however, researchers uncovered a journal from a Yellowstone Park camp that suffered an influenza outbreak in October of 1945; this journal documented that a greater percentage of the guinea pigs that lived in the indoor, heated area survived than did the guinea pigs in the outdoor cages.

Now we know that the right answer will be

Researchers discovered that some guinea pigs survived better indoors than outdoors during a flu outbreak.

By reading not just line 17 but the information before it, we realize that not all guinea pigs survive better indoors; only a specific subset did. If we had picked an answer that matched our first prediction, we would be distorting the facts—we need to understand the information in context.

INFERENCE QUESTIONS

Reading Comp Inference questions, like Critical Reasoning Inference questions, ask you to find something that must be true based on the passage but is not mentioned *explicitly* in the passage. In other words, you need to read "between the lines."

Inference questions come in two types. The first type is Inference questions with a specific reference. Like Detail questions, these prompts will use key phrases and line numbers to point you directly to a part of the passage—and like Detail questions, they are best solved by reviewing the context of that detail and then making a prediction about what the answer will be.

Consider the following Inference question, once again asking about the guinea pigs we discussed earlier:

> Which of the following is implied about the guinea pigs
> mentioned in line 17?

Just like last time, we want to review the context around the line reference. Doing so, we'll find that "until recently," there was "no evidence" that temperature affected the flu; "however," last year these guinea pig records appeared. The logical inference is not explicitly stated, but we can easily put two and two together. The answer will be something like this:

> Their deaths provided new evidence that influenza may be
> more dangerous in lower temperatures.

Other Inference questions make no specific references, instead asking what can be inferred from the passage as a whole or what opinion the author might hold. Valid inferences can be drawn from anything in the passage, from Big-Picture issues like author opinion to any of the little details. But you will probably be able to eliminate a few answers quickly because they violate the Big Picture.

> **EXPERT EXCLUSIVE**
> Don't throw away an answer because you aren't sure about it or "don't like it." If you can't *prove* an answer choice wrong, don't eliminate it.

Then you'll investigate the remaining answers choice by choice, looking to put each answer in one of three categories—(1) proved right, (2) proved wrong, or (3) not proved right but not proved wrong either. It's distinguishing between the second and third categories that will give you success on Inference questions.

Here are some sample Inference question stems:

- Which of the following can be most reasonably inferred from the passage?
- The author would most likely agree that . . .
- Which of the following is suggested about X?

> **EXPERT EXCLUSIVE**
> The words *agree* and *suggest* indicate an Inference question.

LOGIC QUESTIONS

Logic questions ask why the author does something—why he cites a source, why he includes a certain detail, why he puts one paragraph before another, and so forth. Another way of thinking of this is that a Logic question asks not for the purpose of the passage as a whole but for the purpose of a part of the passage. As a result, any answer choice that focuses on the actual content of a detail will be wrong.

Here are some sample Logic question stems:

- The author mentions X most probably to . . .
- Which of the following best describes the relationship of the second paragraph to the rest of the passage?
- What is the primary purpose of the third paragraph?

Most Logic questions can be answered right from your Passage Map—the written summary of each paragraph and the passage's overall Topic, Scope, and Purpose. If the question references a detail, as does the first sample question stem above, then you should read the context of that detail as well—just as you should for any Detail or Inference question that references a specific detail.

> **EXPERT EXCLUSIVE**
>
> Make sure that you read the entire question stem. Many Logic questions start off sounding like Detail or Global questions and only reveal themselves to be Logic questions at the end.

THE KAPLAN METHOD FOR READING COMPREHENSION

Most test takers read the entire passage very closely from beginning to end, taking detailed notes and making sure that they understand everything, and then try to answer the questions from memory. But this is *not* what the best test takers do.

The best test takers attack the passages and questions critically in the sort of aggressive, energetic, and goal-oriented way we've described earlier. Working this way pays off because it's the kind of pragmatic and efficient approach that the GMAT rewards—the same type of approach that business schools like their students to take when faced with an intellectual challenge.

STEP 1: READ THE PASSAGE STRATEGICALLY

To read strategically, be on the lookout for structural keywords and phrases. They will help you to distinguish important things (like opinions) from unimportant (like supporting examples) and to understand why the author wrote each sentence.

> **EXPERT EXCLUSIVE**
>
> Reading the passage strategically doesn't mean going on a scavenger hunt for keywords ("Aha! I found a *however*! My work here is done!"). Rather, it means using those keywords to identify the important parts of the passage—its opinions and structure—so you can focus on them and not on little details.

- **Contrast** keywords such as *but, however, nevertheless,* and *on the other hand* tell you that a change or disagreement is coming.
- **Continuation** keywords such as *moreover, also,* and *furthermore* tell you that the author is continuing on the same track or general idea.
- **Evidence** keywords let you know that something is being offered in support of a particular idea. The specifics of the support are usually unimportant for the first Big-Picture read, but you do want to know what the idea is! Examples of evidence keywords are *since, because,* and *as.*

- **Conclusion** keywords such as *therefore* and *hence* are usually *not* associated with the author's main point in Reading Comp. Rather, they indicate that the next phrase is a logical consequence of the sentence(s) that came before.

- **Illustration** keywords let you know that what follows is an example of a broader point. One example, of course, is *example*. *For instance* is another favorite.

- **Sequence** is a broader category of keywords. These are any words that create lists or groupings. *First, second,* and *third* are obvious examples. But you could also get a chronological sequence (*17th century, 18th century,* and *today*). Science passages may also group complicated phenomena together using simpler sequence keywords (*at a high temperature* and *at a low temperature,* for example).

- **Emphasis** keywords are used when the author wants to call attention to a specific point. These come in two varieties: generic emphasis, such as *very* and *critical,* and charged emphasis, such as *beneficial* or *dead end.*

- **Opinion/Idea** keywords are perhaps the most important of all. The GMAT cares much more about the ideas in a passage and how details support or attack those ideas than about the details themselves. Be sure to distinguish between the author's opinion and that of others. Others' opinions are easier to spot and will be triggered by words like *believe, theory,* or *hypothesis.* The author's opinion is more likely to reveal itself in words that imply a value judgment, such as *valid* or *unsupported.* (If the passage gives you something in the first person, like *I disagree,* that's also a pretty clear sign.)

> **EXPERT EXCLUSIVE**
> Conclusion keywords are very powerful and important in Critical Reasoning stimuli but not nearly as important in Reading Comprehension passages.

With this strategic analysis as a guide, you should construct a Passage Map—a brief summary of each paragraph and its function in the passage's structure—and note the author's Topic, Scope, and Purpose. Start by identifying the Topic and then hunt for Scope, trying to get a sense of where the passage is going, what the author's going to focus on, and what role the first paragraph is playing. Then jot down the gist of each paragraph, noting the structure and the role it plays in the passage. Finish by double-checking to make sure that you got the Topic and Scope right (sometimes passages can take unexpected turns) and note the author's overall Purpose.

Topic will be the first big, broad idea that comes along. Almost always, it will be right there in the first sentence. There's no need to obsess over the exact wording of the Topic; you just want to get a general idea of what the author is writing about so it gets easier to understand.

Scope is the narrow part of the Topic that the author focuses on. If the author expresses her own opinion, then the thing she has an opinion about is the Scope. Identifying Scope is crucial because many wrong answers are wrong because they are outside the Scope of the passage. Remember that even though the first paragraph usually narrows the Topic down to the Scope, there won't be a "topic sentence" in the traditional sense.

EXPERT EXCLUSIVE

The GMAT does not use *analyze* or its synonyms (*assess, review, critique,* etc.) unless the author has an opinion or conclusion of his own. Think of the noun versions—*analysis, assessment,* and *criticism.* They all imply conclusion or value judgment.

Purpose is what the author is doing. You'll serve yourself well by picking an active verb for the Purpose. This helps not only by setting yourself up to find right answers—many Global and Logic answer choices use active verbs—but also by forcing you to consider the author's opinion. Here are some "neutral" verbs: *describe, explain, compare.* Here are some "opinionated" verbs: *advocate, argue, rebut, analyze.*

Like most sophisticated writing, the prose you will see on the GMAT doesn't explicitly reveal its secrets. Baldly laying out the why and how of a passage up front isn't a hallmark of GMAT Reading Comprehension passages. And even more important (as far as the test makers are concerned), if ideas were blatantly laid out, the test makers couldn't ask probing questions about them. So to set up the questions—to test how we think about the prose we read—the GMAT uses passages in which authors hide or disguise their statement of purpose and challenge you to extract it.

After you finish reading, your Passage Map would look something like this example:

EXPERT EXCLUSIVE

There's no need to write full sentences in your Passage Maps. Since ideas will repeat, arrows connecting words or phrases would be just fine.

¶1 Critics: current election system unfair, suggest alternatives

¶2 Alternative—approval voting. Pros & cons.

¶3 Alternative—rank voting. Pros & cons.

¶4 Change unlikely

Topic: U.S. Presidential Election System ◄─┐

Scope: Alternatives to ─┘↑

Purpose: Describe two alternatives to ──────┘

You don't want to take any more than four minutes to write the Passage Map. In fact, as long as you get the Topic, Scope, and Purpose right, you want to spend as little time as possible reading. After all, you get points for answering questions, not for nicely detailed Passage Maps. So the more time you can spend working on the questions, the better your score will be!

Your Passage Map can be as complete or as cryptic as you need it to be. Don't waste time trying to write out entire sentences if fragments and abbreviations will do. And notice in the above example how effective arrows can be. For example, there's no sense writing out the Purpose as "Describe the advantages and disadvantages of two possible, if unlikely, alternatives to the current American presidential election system."

STEP 2: ANALYZE THE QUESTION STEM

The next step is to identify the question type: Global, Detail, Inference, or Logic. Ask yourself, "What should I do on this question? What is being asked?" Here are some guidelines:

If you see "purpose of the passage" or "main idea" = Global Question

If you see direct language like "according to" or "states" = Detail Question

If you see indirect language like "agree" or "suggest" = Inference Question

If you are asked for the purpose of a detail or paragraph = Logic Question

Also, be sure to focus on exactly what the question is asking about. Let's say you see this question:

> The passage states which of the following about the uses of fixed nitrogen?

Don't look for what the passage says about "nitrogen" in general. Don't even look for "fixed nitrogen" alone. Look for the *uses* of fixed nitrogen. (And be aware that the GMAT may ask you to recognize that *application* is a synonym of *use*.)

Finally, the GMAT occasionally asks questions that do not fall into one of the four major categories. Don't obsess over these outliers. They make up less than 10 percent of GMAT Reading Comp questions, so chances are you won't even see one. But if you do, don't worry. These unusual questions usually involve paraphrasing or analyzing specific points of reasoning in the passage. Because you can use your Passage Map to understand the author's reasoning and Kaplan's principles of Critical Reasoning to deconstruct that reasoning, you will be prepared to crack even these rare problems.

STEP 3: RESEARCH THE RELEVANT TEXT IN THE PASSAGE

Since there just isn't enough time to memorize the whole passage, you shouldn't rely on your memory to answer questions.

STEP 4: MAKE A PREDICTION

As you've already seen, it really helps to know what you're looking for before you consider the answer choices. Doing so will help the right answer jump off the screen at you. Here is how you should form your predictions for each question type:

- **Global.** Use your notes on the Passage Map and the Topic, Scope, and Purpose as the basis of your prediction.

EXPERT EXCLUSIVE

"I don't understand why it's right," doesn't mean "I know it's wrong." If you've proved four answers wrong, confidently select the one that's left, even if you aren't wild about it. This is the beauty of multiple-choice—knowing the four wrong answers means knowing the right one!

- **Detail.** Predict an answer based on what the context tells you about the detail.
- **Inference.** The right answer *must* be true based on the passage. (Since many valid inferences could be drawn from even one detail, it's often best not to make your prediction more specific than that.)
- **Logic.** Predict an answer that focuses on *why* the paragraph or detail was used, not on *what* it says.

Some answers are very tempting because they have the correct details and the right scope, but have a *not, doesn't,* or other twist that flips their meanings, to the opposite of what the text provides. Watch out for these "180s."

STEP 5: EVALUATE THE ANSWER CHOICES

Hunt for the answer choice that matches your prediction. If only one answer does, it's the right answer!

If you can't find a match for your prediction, if more than one seems to fit your prediction, or if you weren't able to form a prediction at all (this happens for some Inference questions), then you'll need to evaluate each answer choice looking for errors. Eliminating four wrong answers is the same as finding the one right answer!

Here are some common wrong answer traps to look out for:

- **Global.** Answers that misrepresent the Scope or Purpose of the passage and answers that focus too heavily on details from the beginning or end of the passage
- **Detail.** Answers that distort the context or focus on the wrong details entirely
- **Inference.** Extreme language or exaggerations of the author's statements, distortions of the passage's meaning, and the exact opposite of what might be inferred
- **Logic.** Answers that get the specifics right but the purpose wrong

Always be on the lookout for Scope shifts and for "half-right/half-wrong" answers, which are mostly okay except for one or two words.

Now let's try the Kaplan method on an actual GMAT-length passage and some of its questions. On test day, you won't be able to take notes on the passage or skip forward or back between questions. So challenge yourself to take notes on separate paper and to answer the questions in order.

Since 1980, the notion that mass extinctions at the end of the Cretaceous period 65 million years ago resulted from a sudden event has slowly gathered support, although even today there is no scientific consensus. In the Alvarez scenario, an asteroid struck the earth, creating a gigantic crater. Beyond the immediate effects

(5) of fire, flood, and storm, dust darkened the atmosphere, cutting off plant life. Many animal species disappeared as the food chain was snapped at its base.

Alvarez's main evidence is an abundance of iridium in the KT boundary, a thin stratum dividing Cretaceous rocks from rocks of the Tertiary period. Iridium normally accompanies the slow fall of interplanetary debris, but in KT boundary

(10) strata, iridium is 10–100 times more abundant, suggesting a rapid, massive deposition. Coincident with the boundary, whole species of small organisms vanish from the fossil record. Boundary samples also yield osmium isotopes, basaltic sphericles, and deformed quartz grains, all of which could have resulted from high-velocity impact.

(15) Paleontologists initially dismissed the theory, arguing that existing dinosaur records showed a decline lasting millions of years. But recent studies in North America, aimed at a comprehensive collection of fossil remnants rather than rare or well-preserved specimens, indicate large dinosaur populations existing immediately prior to the KT boundary. Since these discoveries, doubts about

(20) theories of mass extinction have lessened significantly.

Given the lack of a known impact crater of the necessary age and size to fit the Alvarez scenario, some scientists have proposed alternatives. Courtillot, citing huge volcanic flows in India coincident with the KT boundary, speculates that eruptions lasting many thousands of years produced enough atmospheric debris to cause

(25) global devastation. His analyses also conclude that iridium in the KT boundary was deposited over a period of 10,000–100,000 years. Alvarez and Asaro reply that the shock of an asteroidal impact could conceivably have triggered extensive volcanic activity. Meanwhile, exploration at a large geologic formation in Yucatan, found in 1978 but unstudied until 1990, has shown a composition consistent with

(30) extraterrestrial impact. But evidence that the formation is indeed the hypothesized impact site remains inconclusive.

1. It can be inferred from the passage that supporters of the Alvarez and Courtillot theories would hold which of the following views in common?

   ○ The KT boundary was formed over many thousands of years.

   ○ Large animals such as the dinosaurs died out gradually over millions of years.

   ○ Mass extinction occurred as an indirect result of debris saturating the atmosphere.

   ○ It is unlikely that the specific cause of the Cretaceous extinctions will ever be determined.

   ○ Volcanic activity may have been triggered by shock waves from the impact of an asteroid.

2. The author mentions "recent studies in North America" (lines 16–17) primarily in order to

○ point out the benefits of using field research to validate scientific theories.

○ suggest that the asteroid impact theory is not consistent with fossil evidence.

○ describe alternative methods of collecting and interpreting fossils.

○ summarize the evidence that led to wider acceptance of catastrophic scenarios of mass extinction.

○ show that dinosaurs survived until the end of the Cretaceous period.

STEP 1: READ THE PASSAGE STRATEGICALLY

Take a couple of minutes to read the passage. Aim at the Topic, Scope, and author's Purpose or point of view. Where is the text going?

Here's an example of how the passage should be analyzed. We've reprinted the passage through the lens of critical reading. On the left is the passage as you might read it, with keywords in bold. On the right is what you might be thinking as you read.

PASSAGE	ANALYSIS
. . . **the notion** that mass extinctions at the end of the Cretaceous period 65 million years ago resulted from a sudden event **has slowly gathered support, although** even today there is **no** scientific **consensus**. In the **Alvarez scenario**, [bunch of details about an asteroid]	Wow, what a rich first sentence. Not only do we get Topic (*mass extinctions at the end of the Cretaceous period*—whatever that is), but we also get an idea (*the notion that [the mass extinction] resulted from a sudden event*), the fact that some people agree with it (*slowly gathered support*), and the fact that not everyone does (*no scientific consensus*). Wow! I'll bet the passage goes on to talk not only about the support but also about why not everyone agrees. We also get one specific theory (*the Alvarez scenario*) and an elaborate description of what that is— seems to involve an asteroid.
Alvarez's main evidence is [lots of detail]	The keywords are pretty clear—here's some evidence in support of one "sudden event" theory.
	Don't care what the evidence is until there's a question about it.

Paleontologists initially dismissed the theory, arguing that [something] last[ed] **millions of years. But** recent studies . . . **doubts** about theories of mass extinction **have lessened significantly**.

With *dismissed the theory*, it's clear that this paragraph opposes the "sudden event" idea (just what we predicted!). Note how *millions of years*, not normally a keyword, creates contrast with "sudden event." But what's this? *But* announces a change. Are we going to get more support for "sudden event"? Yep! *Doubts have lessened significantly.*

Given the **lack** of [evidence] to **fit the Alvarez scenario, some scientists have proposed alternatives. Courtillot, citing** [evidence], **speculates** that eruptions . . . cause[d] global devastation. **His analyses also conclude** [something about iridium]. **Alvarez and Asaro reply . . . But evidence . . . remains inconclusive.**

Alvarez lacks some evidence still, so there are some other theories. This Coutillot guy says something about volcanoes and iridium. Looks like Alvarez has something to say about Courtillot, too. And there isn't enough evidence either way, so the author doesn't pick a "winner."

Your Passage Map would look something like this:

¶1 Mass ext & sudden event—Alvarez/asteroid

¶2 Alvarez evidence

¶3 Initial disagreement, now less doubt

¶4 Courtillot/volcanoes; Alvarez reply; not enough evidence to choose

Topic: Mass extinctions at end of Cret. period

Scope: Theories about ⤴

Purpose: Describe two "sudden event" theories.

> **EXPERT EXCLUSIVE**
> This isn't the only way to word the Passage Map, of course. Anything along these lines would work—so long as you note that there are two theories and that the author doesn't prefer one to the other.

STEP 2: ANALYZE THE QUESTION STEM

Now identify the question type. Question 1 is a clearly an Inference question: it uses the phrase *can be inferred*. Luckily, this Inference question contains referents that will point us to a specific part of the passage. This will save us a lot of time. Question 2 is a Logic question. The phrase *in order to* shows us that we're asked to identify *why* the detail was used.

STEP 3: RESEARCH THE RELEVANT TEXT IN THE PASSAGE

Question 1 asks to find something that must be true according to both the Alvarez and the Courtillot theories. Our Passage Map shows us that the Alvarez theory takes all of ¶2 and some of ¶4. That's too much to read through closely. But the Courtillot theory is mentioned only once, in ¶4 lines 22–26. Probably the most efficient way to research this question is to read through those two sentences and then deal with ¶2 answer by answer so we can do focused research.

EXPERT EXCLUSIVE

Remember, success on Inference questions often depends on not throwing away plausible answer choices, even when you haven't proved them to be correct.

Question 2 references lines 16–17, which are in ¶3. Since this is a Logic question, it's best to begin our research with the Passage Map. Here's what our Map has to say about ¶3:

¶3 Initial disagreement, now less doubt

Okay, so the "recent studies in North America" are either part of the initial disagreement or a reason that theories of mass extinction are less doubted now. Already, the word *recent* suggests the latter. But if we weren't confident about that, we could read the context of lines 16–17. The keywords *initially dismissed the theory* [*of mass extinction*] from the sentence before and from the sentence after (*Since these discoveries, doubts about theories of mass extinctions have lessened significantly.*) seal the deal.

STEP 4: MAKE A PREDICTION

Question 1, we know, must be consistent with both theories. Since we researched Courtillot's theory, we can quickly eliminate any answer that disagrees with it.

Question 2 asks *why* the "recent studies in North America" were mentioned. Our research shows us that they provide the evidence that reduces doubt about theories of mass extinction. So an easy prediction would be something like "reasons why theories of mass extinction are doubted less than they used to be."

STEP 5: EVALUATE THE ANSWER CHOICES

Question 1—(A) says that the KT boundary was formed over thousands of years, and that's consistent with Courtillot (line 26). What about Alvarez? Scanning through ¶2 for anything about "KT boundary" and time, we read in lines 9–11 "KT Boundary . . . rapid, massive deposition." The word *rapid* is the only time signal at all, and it hardly fits with *many thousands of years*. Eliminate (A). Perhaps you could eliminate (B) right away if you remembered that both theories are in the "sudden event" camp. But if not, your Passage Map saves the day—*dinosaurs died out gradually over millions of years* fits with *dinosaur records showed a decline lasting millions of years* in ¶3. But your Map shows that to be evidence *against* Alvarez, not in support. So (B) is gone.

Debris saturating the atmosphere is consistent with Cortillot (line 24). What about Alvarez? Well, line 9 says *slow fall of interplanetary debris*. So the *debris* issue is settled. Does it saturate the atmosphere? Not explicitly. But this is an Inference question, and we don't expect to see things explicitly. We do see that there was a *massive deposition* . . . and *massive* would suggest that there's a lot of this stuff, so it's plausible that it saturated the atmosphere. Hmm. Let's leave (C) alone.

> **EXPERT EXCLUSIVE**
> Make sure that you keep the question type in mind! (E) could be the right answer to a Detail question but not to a Logic question.

(D) is the opposite of what Courtillot (as well as Alvarez) is trying to do, so this is a quick Big-Picture elimination. (E) is consistent with Alvarez's reply (lines 26–28). But this is a reply to Courtillot's theory—not his theory itself. So we can't claim that Courtillot would agree, and (E) is eliminated. Since (C) is left standing, it must be right.

Note that we can prove (C) to be the right answer without proving *why* it's right. To do so, we'd not only have to connect all the dots in ¶2, we'd have to tie it all to *mass extinctions* by going back to the details from ¶1. It's much more efficient to throw away (A), (B), (D), and (E).

Question 2—Our predicted answer ("reasons why theories of mass extinction are doubted less than they used to be") leads directly to (D), the correct answer.

(A) sounds nice on its own, but the context has nothing to do with the benefits of field research in a specific way. (B) is the opposite of why those studies are introduced—it is in fact the old belief that these studies dispel. (C) and (E) focus on the details in lines 16–17 themselves—(C) in a distorted way—but not on *why* those details are there.

SUMMARY

The basic principles of Reading Comprehension are the following:

- Look for the Topic and Scope of the passage.
- Get the gist of each paragraph and its structural role in the passage.
- Look for opinions, theories, and points of view—especially the author's.
- Don't obsess over details.

The most common question types are the following:

- Global questions
- Detail questions
- Inference questions
- Logic questions

The Kaplan Method for Reading Comprehension is as follows:

Step 1: Read the passage strategically.

Step 2: Analyze the question stem.

Step 3: Research the relevant text in the passage.

Step 4: Make a prediction.

Step 5: Evaluate the answer choices.

The Reading Comp Practice Quiz begins on the next page. The GMAT will give you three or four questions per passage, drawing those questions from a larger pool of up to six to eight problems. (The selection isn't completely random; the computer considers your current score level and the question types that you've seen so far.)

We've given you all the possible questions for the Quiz Passages so you can see the full range of GMAT questions. But remember that on test day, you'll see only three or four.

Furthermore, remember that on test day, you can't take notes on the computer screen or skip forward and back between questions. So challenge yourself now to not take notes in this book (use scratch paper or a dry erase board) and to do the questions in order.

PRACTICE QUIZ

Directions: The questions in this group are based on the content of a passage. After reading the passage, choose the best answer to each question. Base your answers only according to what is stated or implied in the text.

Questions 1–7 are based on the following passage:

The rich analyses of Fernand Braudel and his fellow *Annales* historians have made significant contributions to historical theory and research. In a departure from traditional
(5) historical approaches, the *Annales* historians assume (as do Marxists) that history cannot be limited to a simple recounting of conscious human actions but must be understood in the context of forces and material conditions that
(10) underlie human behavior. Braudel was the first *Annales* historian to gain widespread support for the idea that history should synthesize data from various social sciences, especially economics, in order to provide a
(15) broader view of human societies over time (although Febvre and Bloch, founders of the *Annales* school, had originated this approach).

Braudel conceived of history as the dynamic interaction of three temporalities. The first of
(20) these, the *événementielle,* involved short-lived dramatic "events," such as battles, revolutions, and the actions of great men, which had preoccupied traditional historians like Carlyle. *Conjonctures* was Braudel's term for larger,
(25) cyclical processes that might last up to half a century. The *longue durée,* a historical wave of great length, was for Braudel the most fascinating of the three temporalities. Here he focused on those aspects of everyday life that
(30) might remain relatively unchanged for

centuries. What people ate, what they wore, their means and routes of travel—for Braudel these things create "structures" that define the limits of potential social change for hundreds
(35) of years at a time.

Braudel's concept of the *longue durée* extended the perspective of historical space as well as time. Until the *Annales* school, historians had taken the juridical political
(40) unit—the nation-state, duchy, or whatever—as their starting point. Yet, when such enormous time spans are considered, geographical features may well have more significance for human populations than
(45) national borders. In his doctoral thesis, a seminal work on the Mediterranean during the reign of Philip II, Braudel treated the geohistory of the entire region as a "structure" that had exerted myriad influences on human
(50) lifeways since the first settlements on the shores of the Mediterranean Sea.

And so the reader is given such arcane information as the list of products that came to Spanish shores from North Africa, the
(55) seasonal routes followed by Mediterranean sheep and their shepherds, and the cities where the best ship timber could be bought.

Braudel has been faulted for the imprecision of his approach. With his Rabelaisian delight
(60) in concrete detail, Braudel vastly extended the realm of relevant phenomena, but this very achievement made it difficult to delimit the boundaries of observation, a task necessary to beginning any social investigation. Further,
(65) Braudel and other *Annales* historians minimize the differences among the social sciences. Nevertheless, the many similarly designed studies aimed at both professional and popular audiences indicate that Braudel

(70) asked significant questions that traditional
historians had overlooked.

1. The primary purpose of the passage is to

   ○ show how Braudel's work changed the
   conception of Mediterranean life held by
   previous historians.

   ○ evaluate Braudel's criticisms of
   traditional and Marxist historiography.

   ○ contrast the perspective of the *longue
   durée* with the actions of major
   historical figures.

   ○ illustrate the relevance of Braudel's
   concepts to other social sciences.

   ○ outline some of Braudel's influential
   conceptions and distinguish them from
   conventional approaches.

2. The author refers to the work of Febvre and
Bloch in order to

   ○ illustrate the limitations of the *Annales*
   tradition of historical investigation.

   ○ suggest the relevance of economics to
   historical investigation.

   ○ debate the need for combining various
   sociological approaches.

   ○ show that previous *Annales* historians
   anticipated Braudel's focus on
   economics.

   ○ demonstrate that historical studies
   provide broad structures necessary for
   economic analysis.

3. According to the passage, all of the following
are aspects of Braudel's approach to history
EXCEPT that he

   ○ attempted to unify the findings of various
   social sciences.

   ○ studied social and economic activities
   that occurred across national
   boundaries.

   ○ pointed out the link between increased
   economic activity and the rise of
   nationalism.

   ○ examined seemingly unexciting aspects
   of everyday life.

   ○ visualized history as involving several
   different time frames.

4. The passage suggests that, compared to
traditional historians, *Annales* historians are

   ○ more interested in other social sciences
   than in history.

   ○ more critical of the achievements of
   famous historical figures.

   ○ more skeptical of the validity of most
   economic research.

   ○ more interested in the underlying
   context of human behavior provided by
   social structure.

   ○ more inclined to be dogmatic in their
   approach to history.

5. The author is critical of Braudel's perspective for which of the following reasons?

   ○ It seeks structures that underlie all forms of social activity.

   ○ It assumes a greater similarity among the social sciences than actually exists.

   ○ It fails to consider the relationship between short-term events and long-term social activity.

   ○ It clearly defines boundaries for social analysis.

   ○ It attributes too much significance to conscious human actions.

6. The passage implies that Braudel would consider which of the following as exemplifying the *longue durée*?

   I. The prominence of certain crops in the diet of a region
   II. The annexation of a province by the victor in a war
   III. A reduction in the population of an area following a disease epidemic

   ○ I only

   ○ III only

   ○ I and II only

   ○ II and III only

   ○ I, II, and III

7. Which of the following statements is most in keeping with the principles of Braudel's work as described in the passage?

   ○ All written history is the history of social elites.

   ○ The most important task of historians is to define the limits of potential social change.

   ○ Those who ignore history are doomed to repeat it.

   ○ People's historical actions are influenced by many factors that they may be unaware of.

   ○ History is too important to be left to historians.

Questions 8–13 are based on the following passage.

In many underdeveloped countries, the state plays an important and increasingly varied role in economic development today. There are four general arguments, all of them related,

(5) for state participation in economic development. First, the entrance requirements in terms of financial capital and capital equipment are very large in certain industries, and the size of these obstacles will serve as

(10) barriers to entry on the part of private investors. One can imagine that these obstacles are imposing in industries such as steel production, automobiles, electronics, and parts of the textile industry. In addition, there

(15) are what Myint calls "technical indivisibilities in social overhead capital." Public utilities, transport, and communications facilities must be in place before industrial development can occur, and they do not lend themselves to

(20) small-scale improvements.

A related argument centers on the demand side of the economy. This economy is seen as fragmented, disconnected, and incapable of using inputs from other parts of the economy.

(25) Consequently, economic activity in one part of the economy does not generate the dynamism in other sectors that is expected in more cohesive economies. Industrialization necessarily involves many different sectors;

(30) economic enterprises will thrive best in an environment in which they draw on inputs from related economic sectors and, in turn, release their own goods for industrial utilization within their own economies.

(35) A third argument concerns the low-level equilibrium trap in which less developed countries find themselves. At subsistence levels, societies consume exactly what they produce. There is no remaining surplus for

(40) reinvestment. As per capita income rises, however, the additional income will not be used for savings and investment. Instead, it will have the effect of increasing the population, which will eat up the surplus and

(45) force the society to its former subsistence position. Fortunately, after a certain point, the rate of population growth will decrease; economic growth will intersect with and eventually outstrip population growth. The

(50) private sector, however, will not be able to provide the one-shot large dose of capital to push economic growth beyond those levels where population increases eat up the incremental advances.

(55) The final argument concerns the relationship between delayed development and the state. Countries wishing to industrialize today have more competitors, and these competitors occupy a more

(60) differentiated industrial terrain than previously. This means that the available

niches in the international system are more limited. For today's industrializers, therefore, the process of industrialization cannot be a

(65) haphazard affair, nor can the pace, content, and direction be left solely to market forces. Part of the reason for a strong state presence, then, relates specifically to the competitive international environment in which modern

(70) countries and firms must operate.

Advanced

8. According to the passage, all of the following are arguments for state economic intervention EXCEPT

  ○ the start-up costs of initial investments are beyond the capacities of many private investors.

  ○ the state must mediate relations between the demand and supply sides of the economy.

  ○ the pace and processes of industrialization are too important to be left solely to market trends.

  ○ the livelihoods and security of workers should not be subject to the variability of industrial trends.

  ○ public amenities are required to facilitate a favorable business environment.

9. Which of the following best states the central point of the passage?

    ○   Without state intervention, many less developed countries will not be able to carry out the interrelated tasks necessary to achieve industrialization.

    ○   Underdeveloped countries face a crisis of overpopulation and a lack of effective demand that cannot be overcome without outside assistance.

    ○   State participation plays a secondary role as compared to private capital investment in the industrialization of underdeveloped countries.

    ○   Less developed countries are trapped in an inescapable cycle of low production and demand.

    ○   State economic planning can ensure the rapid development of nonindustrialized countries' natural resources.

Advanced

10. The author suggests all of the following as appropriate roles for the state in economic development EXCEPT

    ○   safeguarding against the domination of local markets by a single source of capital.

    ○   financing industries with large capital requirements.

    ○   helping to coordinate demand among different economic sectors.

    ○   providing capital inputs sufficient for growth to surpass increases in per capita consumption.

    ○   developing communication and transportation facilities to service industry.

Advanced

11. The author suggests which of the following about the "technical indivisibilities in social overhead capital" (lines 15–16) and the "low-level equilibrium trap" (lines 35–36)?

    ○   The first leads to rapid technological progress; the second creates demand for technologically sophisticated products.

    ○   Both enhance the developmental effects of private sector investment.

    ○   Neither is relevant to formulating a strategy for economic growth.

    ○   The first is a barrier to private investment; the second can attract it.

    ○   The first can prevent development from occurring; the second can negate its effects.

Advanced

12. Which of the following, if true, would cast doubt on the author's argument that state participation is important in launching large-scale industries?

    I.   Coordination of demand among different economic sectors requires a state planning agency.

    II.   Associations of private sector investors can raise large amounts of capital by pooling their resources.

    III. Transportation and communications facilities can be built up through a series of small-scale improvements.

    ○   I only

    ○   II only

    ○   I and II only

    ○   II and III only

    ○   I, II, and III

Advanced

13. According to the passage, the "low-level equilibrium trap" in underdeveloped countries results from

   ○ the tendency for societies to produce more than they can use.

   ○ intervention of the state in economic development.

   ○ the inability of market forces to overcome the effects of population growth.

   ○ the fragmented and disconnected nature of the demand side of the economy.

   ○ one-shot, large doses of capital intended to spur economic growth.

Questions 14–18 are based on the following passage:

The years following the Civil War brought many changes to the Southern states, prompting a large emigration of U.S. citizens to Brazil—9,000 to 40,000 people came, primarily
(5) from the South. In one particular case, this migration of Southerners, many from Alabama and Texas, resulted from direct invitation. Emperor Dom Pedro II of Brazil, in an effort to expand his country, appealed for
(10) colonists from the U.S. South. Dom Pedro II recognized the value these Southerners could have for Brazil in the form of agricultural and educational knowledge. He advertised for citizens from all over the South and even from
(15) some of the Northern states to immigrate to Brazil.

Because they recognized an opportunity to rebuild their lives without yielding their Southern heritage to Northern "improvements"
(20) after the war, many Southerners accepted Dom Pedro's offer. After founding "Vila Americana"

(American Town), one of the most important of the "American colonies" in Brazil, the Southern immigrants did not remain in
(25) isolation. They interacted with and even married local Brazilians and other new colonists.

While becoming integrated into the existing society, these colonists maintained their
(30) distinctive American culture. American industrial technology allowed the colonists to improve farming implements, such as ploughs, rakes, harrows, and hoes, for their fellow Brazilians. Housing also improved with
(35) the introduction of chimneys and gutters. The colonists' emphasis on education and industrial skills contributed to Brazil's success in business; many of the country's public transportation systems were built or run by
(40) American-founded companies. Today, Vila Americana, maintaining this original level of excellence, has the highest education and income levels per capita of any city in Brazil.

14. The primary purpose of the passage is to

   ○ analyze the source of the changes in the lives of Southerners after the Civil War.

   ○ discuss the emigration of U.S. Southerners to Brazil after the Civil War and their benefits to their new country.

   ○ describe how the aftermath of the Civil War changed the lives of all the citizens of the Southern United States.

   ○ demonstrate how Brazil adopted the heritage of the Southern United States and attracted Southerners wanting to revive the antebellum South.

   ○ account for the mass emigration from the United States that took place following the Civil War, particularly from Alabama and Texas.

15. Which of the following does the author suggest about the importance of the emigration of Southerners to Brazil?

   ○ Without the Southern presence, Brazil would never have been settled.

   ○ The Southerners' sole purpose in immigrating was to introduce new inventions to the Brazilians.

   ○ If the Southerners had not emigrated, they would have gone to prison for war crimes.

   ○ Dom Pedro II feared the condition Brazil would be in without the presence of the Americans.

   ○ The Southerners' arrival had a great impact on the development of education and agriculture in Brazil.

16. According to the passage, all of the following statements are correct, EXCEPT

   ○ the Southerners brought their heritage and innovative ideas with them to Brazil.

   ○ many Southerners were looking for a new beginning after the Civil War, independent of Northern interference.

   ○ the influence of the Southerners had a great and lasting effect on Brazil.

   ○ the Southerners fled to Brazil to escape U.S. government policies on farming and education.

   ○ Emperor Dom Pedro II invited Southerners and other U.S. citizens to immigrate to his developing country.

Advanced

17. The author states that Southerners moved to Brazil "because they recognized an opportunity to rebuild their lives without yielding their Southern heritage to Northern 'improvements' after the war" in order to

   ○ explain how fears about losing their traditional culture made Southerners prefer emigration to rebuilding their lives in the United States.

   ○ describe the process by which immigrants from Southern U.S. states replaced native Brazilian culture with their own heritage.

   ○ suggest Dom Pedro II's advertising campaign was designed to tempt Southerners to uproot their lives and move to Brazil.

   ○ illustrate the preference native Brazilians had for the heritage of the Southern United States over the "improvements" Northerners might provide.

   ○ defend the Southerners from the accusation of a traitorous abandonment of their own country by rationalizing their decision to emigrate.

18. The main purpose of paragraph 3 is to

   ○ rationalize for the reader why Dom Pedro specifically requested that Southerners migrate to his country.

   ○ describe the benefits that the Southerners conferred on Brazil in various areas.

   ○ explain the utility of the Southerners' importation of American technology to Brazil's growing agricultural economy.

   ○ elucidate the colonists' process of choosing to colonize the area of Vila Americana because of its rich agricultural history.

   ○ argue that Southerners, because they isolated themselves from other inhabitants, had little impact on Brazilian education and agriculture.

Questions 19–22 are based on the following passage:

Isolated from the rest of the world by circumpolar currents and ice fields, the Dry Valleys of Antarctica never see snowfall. They are the coldest, driest places on earth, yet this
(5) arid, frigid climate supports several delicate ecosystems. Life in these ecosystems consists of relatively few groups of algae, microorganisms, and invertebrates, as well as plants such as lichen and fungi that live beneath the surface
(10) of rocks, where just enough light penetrates for photosynthesis to occur during the short period each year when meltwater is available. This region has proven interesting specifically to scientists researching the possibility of life
(15) on Mars, because the features of the Dry Valleys are strikingly similar to the Martian landscape.

The Dry Valleys' system of lakes provides a particularly interesting area of research. Lake
(20) Hoare boasts a clear ice sun-cover fifteen meters thick that intensifies solar radiation in a way similar to solar panels; summer temperatures in bottom waters can become as high as 25°C, solely from solar heating and
(25) not geothermal heating. This temperature permits huge mats of cyanobacteria to survive and even thrive on the lake floor. Pieces of this mat occasionally break free, floating up to the underside of the icy lake cover to melt through
(30) the ice toward the surface. The intense Antarctic winds, sweeping across the lake's surface, cause the ice to sublimate—turn directly from ice into vapor—rapidly. Such continuous sublimation should eventually
(35) cause the lake to vanish, but a continuous trickle of water from a nearby glacier—melted by the sun—refreshes the water. With a constant source of water, however small, and the heat generated by the solar radiation and
(40) retained by insulation from the thick ice cover, this lake offers an odd paradox: thick ice is responsible for maintaining this lake's liquid state.

The ancient river deltas around the slopes of
(45) Lake Fryxell present one feature typical of all river deltas: sediment thick enough to bury fossil life forms. This very thickness, however, makes a formal scientific search for signs of life impracticable. The floor of Lake Vida, on
(50) the other hand, is covered with discrete piles of sediment up to a meter high that have preserved clear signs of life because rocks lying on the lake's surface, heated by sunlight, melt their way through the thick ice cover. Since
(55) smaller rocks, with a larger surface-area-to-volume ratio, get warmer and sink lower than larger rocks, pieces of gravel penetrate by as much as a meter, forming cracks in the ice that

cause the finest sediment to sink even deeper.
(60) When the lake dries seasonally, the refined
sediment within the ice drops to the lake floor,
leaving a protective layer of gravel on top of
the finer sediment. Dried bacteria in Lake Vida
sediment have been dated back tens of
(65) thousands of years. Some researchers are
hoping that exploration of similar terrain on
Mars may yield similar results.

Advanced

19. According to the passage, thick sediment found in the ancient river deltas of Lake Fryxell

    ○ forms layers of deposits laden with dried bacteria that are tens of thousands of years old.

    ○ masks life forms by continuously depositing new layers on top of older ones.

    ○ makes it unlikely that scientists will search there for traces of life.

    ○ collects liquid water from nearby glaciers warmed by sunlight during the Antarctic summer.

    ○ is devoid of life due to the impenetrable barrier formed by the sediment.

20. The passage is primarily concerned with

    ○ the adaptations of microorganisms that allow them to live in the Dry Valleys' hostile environment.

    ○ the relationship between frozen lakes and glaciers that contributes to the availability of fresh water in the Dry Valleys.

    ○ evidence of past and present life forms in the extreme conditions of Antarctica's Dry Valleys.

    ○ the evolutionary histories of ancient lakes and the clues they hold about life in cold, dry ecosystems.

    ○ the differences and similarities between ancient river deltas and ancient lakes.

21. Based on the information in the passage, scientists looking for signs of life on Mars in conditions similar to those in the Dry Valleys would be most likely to find it in which of the following areas?

    ○ Former river deltas

    ○ Circumpolar ice fields

    ○ Larger rocks

    ○ Former glaciers

    ○ Former lakebeds

22. Based on the information in the passage, mounds of sediment found at the bottom of Lake Vida are refined by which of the following?

  I.   Continual sublimation and ice cover

  II. Large pieces of rock decomposing on the lake floor

  III. Cracks formed in the ice by sinking rocks and gravel

  ○ I only

  ○ I and II

  ○ III only

  ○ II and III

  ○ I, II, and III

Questions 23–27 are based on the following passage:

History has shaped academic medical centers (AMCs) to perform three functions: patient care, research, and teaching. These three missions are now fraught with problems
(5) because the attempt to combine them has led to such inefficiencies as duplication of activities and personnel, inpatient procedures that could and should have been outpatient procedures, and unwieldy administrative
(10) bureaucracies.

One source of inefficiency derives from mixed lines of authority. Clinical chiefs and practitioners in AMCs are typically responsible to the hospital for practice issues
(15) but to the medical school for promotion, marketing, membership in a faculty practice plan, and educational accreditation. Community physicians with privileges at a university hospital add more complications.
(20) They have no official affiliation with the AMC's medical school, but their

cooperation with faculty members is essential for proper patient treatment. The fragmented accountability is heightened by the fact that three
(25) different groups often vie for the loyalty of physicians who conduct research. The medical school may wish to capitalize on the research for its educational value to students; the hospital may desire the state-of-the-art
(30) treatment methods resulting from the research; and the grant administrators may focus on the researchers' humanitarian motives. Communication among these groups is rarely coordinated, and the physicians may
(35) serve whichever group promises the best perks and ignore the rest—which inevitably strains relationships.

Another source of inefficiency is the fact that physicians have obligations to many
(40) different groups: patients, students, faculty members, referring physicians, third-party payers, and staff members, all of whom have varied expectations. Satisfying the interests of one group may alienate others. Patient care
(45) provides a common example. For the benefit of medical students, physicians may order too many tests, prolong patient visits, or encourage experimental studies of a patient. If AMC faculty physicians were more aware of
(50) how much treatments of specific illnesses cost and of how other institutions treat patient conditions, they would be better practitioners, and the educational and clinical care missions of AMCs would both be better served.
(55) A bias toward specialization adds yet more inefficiency. AMCs are viewed as institutions serving the gravest cases in need of the most advanced treatments. The high number of specialty residents and the presence of burn
(60) units, blood banks, and transplant centers validate this belief. Also present at AMCs, though less conspicuous, are facilities for ordinary primary care patients. In fact, many

patients choose to visit an AMC for primary
(65) care because they realize that any necessary
follow-up can occur almost instantaneously.
While AMCs have emphasized cutting-edge
specialty medicine, their more routine medical
services need development and enhancement.
(70)   A final contribution to inefficiency is
organizational complacency. Until recently,
most academic medical centers drew the
public merely by existing. The rising presence,
however, of tertiary hospitals with patient care
(75) as their only goal has immersed AMCs in a
very competitive market. It is only in the past
several years that AMCs have started to
recognize and develop strategies to address
competition.

23. The author's attitude toward the inefficiencies
    at academic medical centers is one of

    ○   reluctant acquiescence.

    ○   strident opposition.

    ○   agonized indecision.

    ○   reasoned criticism.

    ○   enthusiastic support.

24. The author of the passage would most likely
    agree with which of the following statements
    about primary care at AMCs?

    ○   AMCs would make more money if they
        focused mainly on primary care.

    ○   Burn and transplant patients need
        specialty care more than primary care.

    ○   AMCs offer the best primary care for
        most patients.

    ○   AMCs have not tried hard enough to
        publicize their primary care services.

    ○   Inefficiencies at AMCs would be reduced
        if better primary care were offered.

25. The author's primary purpose in this passage
    is to

    ○   discuss the rise and fall of academic
        medical centers.

    ○   explain that multiple lines of authority
        in a medical center create inefficiencies.

    ○   delineate conflicts occurring in
        academic medical facilities.

    ○   examine the differences between
        academic and other health care entities.

    ○   warn that mixed accountabilities result
        in treatment errors.

26. The author implies which of the following
    about faculty physicians at AMCs?

    ○   Most of them lack good business sense.

    ○   They put patients' physical health above
        their hospitals' monetary concerns.

    ○   They sometimes focus on education at
        the expense of patient care.

    ○   They lack official affiliation with the
        medical schools connected to AMCs.

    ○   They choose AMCs because follow-up
        care can be given very quickly.

27. Which of the following would the author
    probably consider a good strategy for
    academic medical centers dealing with
    competition from tertiary hospitals?

    ○   Recruiting physicians away from tertiary
        centers

    ○   Increasing the focus on patient care

    ○   Sending patients to tertiary facilities

    ○   Eliminating specialty care

    ○   Reducing dependence on grant money

Questions 28–31 are based on the following passage:

One of the first attempts to peer into the living human brain was carried out by a neurosurgeon named Wilder Penfield in the 1950s. Penfield opened the skulls of conscious

(5) epileptic patients under local anesthesia and induced a mild electric current into their brains in an attempt to pinpoint the source of seizure activity and then remove that piece of tissue. What he found was even more

(10) remarkable than what he initially set out to do. By stimulating different points on the lower parts of the brain (the temporal lobes), he elicited distinct and vivid memories in his patients. These memories were more precise

(15) than usual memories and incorporated different modalities, such as visual and auditory sense impressions. Penfield's patients reported different types of memories (a moment from childhood, a recollection of a

(20) tune). When the same location in the temporal lobe was stimulated again, the same memory reappeared. Could it be that a physical map of memories exists within our brains?

(25) One might mistakenly conclude from Penfield's experiment that particular memories are stored in specific sites in the brain such that the memory of one's grandmother is stored in one area and the

(30) memory of what one had for dinner is stored in another. While this description is imprecise, the alternative theory, that memory is stored in a unitary superstructure, is also inaccurate. Although it is true that the temporal lobes play

(35) a critical role in memory processes, evidence from brain-imaging studies strongly indicates that memory is divided among a range of distinct but interacting neural systems, each contributing to a unique feature of memory.

(40) One system may be involved to a larger extent in encoding or retrieval, while another may deal with the process of consolidating memory. One specific structure is more active in emotional memory, while others are

(45) employed in working memory, semantic memory, and episodic memory. These multiple memory systems are constantly sharing information and modulating one another.

28. A good title for this passage would be

○ "The Life and Work of Neurosurgeon Wilder Penfield."

○ "The Physical Organization of Memory in the Human Brain."

○ "The Cognitive Functions of the Temporal Lobes."

○ "Historical Progress in the Search for an Epilepsy Cure."

○ "Where Are Childhood Memories Located in the Brain?"

29. Which of the following is mentioned in paragraph 2 with regard to the neural systems of memory?

○ A specific brain structure cannot be involved in more than one aspect of memory.

○ The same neural system is primarily involved in both emotional memory and semantic memory.

○ The lower parts of the brain play a critical role in memory processes.

○ There is a specific brain region that stores the memory of last night's dinner.

○ Epilepsy will affect the storage and retrieval of memories.

Advanced

30. The author uses the phrase "unitary superstructure" to refer to

   ○ the brain as a whole.

   ○ a theory of memory organization preferred by most scientists.

   ○ the cortex of the brain.

   ○ a specific brain region in which all memories are stored.

   ○ the sum of all memory processes, such as encoding, retrieval, and consolidation.

31. All of the following are mentioned in paragraph 1 as part of the surgical procedure Penfield performed on his patients EXCEPT

   ○ Penfield stimulated different points in his patients' temporal lobes.

   ○ Penfield's epileptic patients were not totally anesthetized during the surgery.

   ○ the patients' brains were given small electric shocks during surgery.

   ○ Penfield removed the pieces of tissue responsible for inducing seizures in his patients.

   ○ the patients' skulls were open throughout the surgery.

Questions 32–35 are based on the following passage:

The early 1980s were a time of growing interest in the potential of genetic research. The tedious and painstaking process of analyzing even a short segment of DNA,
(5)   however, posed a problem for scientists until

1983, when Kary Mullis happened upon one of the most important ideas ever discovered in the field of genetics. He helped to develop what would eventually be known as the
(10)   polymerase chain reaction (PCR), the foundation for a quick and easy process to create multiple copies of DNA from a single strand.

Multiple copies of DNA samples are
(15)   necessary for researchers so that they can analyze a DNA sample quickly and with less risk to the original material. To copy a molecule of DNA, its double-helix molecular structure must be unwound into two
(20)   matching halves. Each half is then replicated, and the four resulting segments are reattached to their respective halves, resulting in two identical copies of the complete DNA strand. Mullis's breakthrough was his discovery that naturally occurring
(25)   DNA-copying enzymes known as polymerases could be harnessed to do the job, if pointed to the right stretch of DNA to copy and provided with the right chemical building blocks for making new DNA.
(30)   One complicating factor was the extreme sensitivity of the polymerase enzymes to the heat required to unwind DNA segments. When researchers copied a strand of DNA and then wished to make another copy, a new
(35)   batch of polymerase was needed, since the heat used in the process kept destroying the previous batch. For each single copy of a piece of DNA, then, a technician had to monitor the heating cycle and add new enzymes.
(40)   The discovery of a temperature-resistant polymerase derived from a bacterium that lives in hot springs greatly enhanced the functionality of PCR. This version of the enzyme, able to withstand multiple cycles of
(45)   heating and cooling, could make large numbers of copies from a single strand of DNA with minimal human involvement.

Using the new process, DNA is heated, unwound, replicated, and reassembled over
(50) and over automatically. At each step, the number of copies is doubled, until millions or billions of copies are created. Scientists can now study a piece of DNA without worrying about damaging or destroying it, since
(55) multiple copies are readily available. The PCR process is not wholly error-free, but without this monumental discovery, genetics as we know it today would not exist.

32. The main function of paragraph 3 is to

    ○ examine the need for technicians to be involved in PCR.

    ○ suggest why PCR is not a good method for DNA copying.

    ○ present an alternative to PCR for genetic research.

    ○ explain a problem confronted during the development of PCR.

    ○ identify the complications behind PCR and suggest alternative means.

33. The author of the passage would be most likely to agree with which of the following statements?

    ○ PCR is not error-free but is as close to flawless as it can possibly be.

    ○ PCR was introduced for the sole purpose of making technicians' jobs easier.

    ○ Until PCR, the field of genetics could not exist.

    ○ PCR made the heating of DNA samples less important.

    ○ Natural processes can be harnessed for scientific purposes.

Advanced

34. The author implies that PCR contributed to genetics in all of the following ways EXCEPT for

    ○ allowing for easy multiple copying of a segment of DNA.

    ○ removing scientists' anxiety about destroying DNA samples.

    ○ eliminating altogether the need to add new enzymes during copying.

    ○ streamlining the process of DNA copying.

    ○ making the copying process workable with minimal human involvement.

---

35. The primary purpose of the passage is to

    ○ compare two different methods of copying DNA.

    ○ explain the process of PCR and its invention and evolution.

    ○ describe how Kary Mullis came up with the idea for PCR.

    ○ demonstrate the difficulty of copying DNA.

    ○ explore the role of heat and enzymes in DNA replication.

Questions 36–38 are based on the following passage:

Many sociologists who examined the phenomenon of secrecy considered secrets morally negative because they defined secrets by their content: if concealed information is
(5) negative, it is "secret"; if it is positive or neutral, it is merely "private." Berlin-born philosopher Georg Simmel (1858–1918)

departed from this approach, arguing that a secret is defined not by the kind of

(10) information concealed but by the fact of concealment. A secret is like a box into which any content can be placed; whatever the content, the box, in itself, is morally neutral. Unlike something locked in a box, however, a

(15) secret is not the internal private knowledge of a single person. Simmel saw secrecy as predicated upon a social relationship: use of the word *secret* demands that more than one person know but that others be excluded.

(20) When we receive information, to know that it is secret, we must be told not to tell anyone. Furthermore, knowledge of the existence of a secret is separate from knowledge of its content. By removing the moral bias, Simmel's

(25) framework facilitated objective study of secrets. However, Simmel's discussion of disclosure seems to belie his contention that secrets are morally neutral. For him, inherent in every secret lies the possibility, and the

(30) desire, for revelation—regardless of the consequences. This "attraction of the abyss" gives secrets their "moral badness." Since disclosure of a secret is naughty, and secrecy and disclosure must coexist, the immorality of

(35) disclosure taints the secret itself.

One specific example of research into secrecy is Beryl Bellman's study of the "secret societies" of the West African Kpelle: religious associations, segregated by gender, that all

(40) Kpelle are expected to join. Initiated adults learn restricted information such as the true identities of "spirits," society members wearing masks for ceremonies, who are believed to be supernatural beings. Kpelle

(45) ideology holds that the uninitiated do not know that these spirits are really society members. The initiated may not tell a society's secrets to nonmembers; Kpelle tradition

insists that nonmembers are not allowed to

(50) know. However, Bellman showed that anyone may, in fact, know a society's secrets. The Kpelle word translated as "secret" literally means "you may not speak it." If nonmembers learn secrets, they are restricted

(55) from revealing that they know by penalties ranging from monetary fines to death. Bellman could write about Kpelle societies without violating their rules by focusing not on the content of the secrets but on their

(60) form. Bellman's realization shows that the mechanism of Kpelle secrecy relies on Simmel's model: the importance of keeping of secrets (nondisclosure) as a social act with rules and consequences carries the burden of

(65) morality rather than the personal, internal knowledge of the content of the secret.

36. The "abyss" referred to by Simmel (line 31) is best defined as

○ a deed that is both exciting and dangerous.

○ the ultimate punishment established for telling a secret.

○ the gap between early models of secrecy and his approach.

○ the distance between two people that is bridged by sharing a secret.

○ a feature of the topography in Western Africa.

Advanced

37. Based on the passage, which of the following situations would most clearly violate the rules of a Kpelle secret society?

   ○ A foreign scholar publishes a book about the organization of Kpelle secret societies.

   ○ A woman claims she knows the details of men's initiation rituals.

   ○ A man learns the ritual knowledge of a women's secret society.

   ○ Two women are overheard discussing the identities of their secret society's "spirits."

   ○ A journalist writes about the rules governing secrecy in Kpelle society.

38. From the information in this passage, the author would be most likely to agree with which of the following statements?

   ○ Secrets contain personal information, but lies can be about anything.

   ○ The best social scientists' work must contain no contradictions.

   ○ All Kpelle adults know the secrets of the secret societies.

   ○ Sociologically, how people behave is at least as important as what they know.

   ○ It is impossible to eliminate a moral dimension from the concept of secrets.

Questions 39–44 are based on the following passage:

The study of the outbreak of Severe Acute Respiratory Syndrome (SARS) between late fall 2002 and the summer of 2003 is a fascinating look into how exponentially fast contagious

(5) viruses can spread throughout the world's population if unchecked. Before the virus was officially contained, there were a reported 8,442 confirmed cases of SARS, of which 916 were fatal—a mortality rate of roughly 10 percent. Of all

(10) the SARS-related deaths, however, age seemed to play the most important role: almost 50 percent of the SARS fatalities were over 65 years old.

SARS is a viral infection of the respiratory system caused by a coronavirus known as the

(15) SARS-associated coronavirus (SARS-CoV). Coronaviruses are also believed to be the root of almost all the common colds found in humans. SARS is spread through close contact with an infected person; it's possible to contract

(20) SARS by simply talking in close proximity to an infected person, touching them, or touching a surface contaminated with the respiratory droplets propelled by a sneeze or a cough. Following exposure to SARS-CoV, it usually

(25) takes between 2 to 10 days for symptoms to arise. The first symptoms are comparable to coming down with the flu. One may suffer from fever, headache, muscle pains, shortness of breath, sore throat, and a dry cough. Many

(30) SARS patients eventually develop pneumonia. Of all these symptoms, though, the only one that is universal among all confirmed SARS patients is a very high fever, usually well over 100°F.

(35) The first recorded case of SARS occurred in November 2002 in Foshan City in China's southern province of Guangdong. Analysis conducted by the World Health Organization (WHO) has revealed several groups of

(40) outbreaks in different areas of Guangdong during this time period. Yet curiously, no links have been uncovered among those initial human cases, and they seem to have occurred independently of each other. However,

(45) scientists have discovered the SARS virus in three different animals that were being sold in the live markets of Guangdong at the time, each considered a delicacy in China.

SARS seems to have been spread outside of
(50) the province by a Chinese doctor who treated Guangdong SARS patients and unknowingly became infected himself. The doctor went to Hong Kong to attend a wedding, where he stayed on the ninth floor of the Metropole Hotel.
(55) At the Metropole, he somehow transmitted SARS to 16 other hotel guests, all of whom stayed on the ninth floor. Those infected guests were the original seed that spread the virus to almost 30 countries, with the largest number of cases
(60) found in mainland China, Hong Kong, Taiwan, Singapore, and Canada. Among the original 16 guests was a Chinese-American businessman who transmitted the virus to 20 hospital workers in Singapore. He was then transferred
(65) to a Hong Kong hospital where he died. His suspicious illness and death sparked an investigation by the WHO into SARS, which brought the virus to the world's attention.

After the virus was recognized as a threat to
(70) worldwide health, a global mobilization effort led by the WHO to contain the disease quickly stopped SARS in its tracks. The WHO declared that the virus was officially contained on July 5, 2003. Though the spread of the virus has been
(75) thwarted, it still remains one of the most potentially dangerous viruses in the world. Accordingly, global health authorities are constantly on alert for another possible outbreak.

39. Based on information from the passage, approximately how many people over the age of 65 fatally contracted the SARS virus?

○ 8,400

○ 4,200

○ 900

○ 450

○ 90

40. The discussion in paragraph 2 about how SARS is spread through close contact serves which of the following functions within the passage?

○ It illustrates the need for hospital staff to be well protected against possible infection when dealing with SARS cases.

○ It lists the different possible close-contact scenarios.

○ It demonstrates how easily the virus is spread from person to person.

○ It offers a comparison of SARS to the common cold.

○ It contradicts earlier theories of how the virus is spread.

41. It can be inferred from the passage that

○ the first SARS cases may have occurred by eating or handling infected meat.

○ doctors are very close to discovering a SARS vaccine.

○ the Chinese doctor purposely spread the SARS virus.

○ SARS no longer poses a threat to the global population.

○ the WHO mishandled the SARS outbreak.

| Chapter 6

42. According to the passage, all of the following are true of the Chinese-American businessman EXCEPT that

    ○ he was a guest on the ninth floor of the Metropole Hotel.

    ○ he died in a hospital in Singapore.

    ○ his death sparked a WHO investigation into SARS.

    ○ before he died, he had a very high fever.

    ○ he had been to both Hong Kong and Singapore.

43. The passage provides support for which of the following statements?

    ○ The risk of dying from SARS decreases with age.

    ○ It is impossible to track the origins of an outbreak.

    ○ Coronaviruses are the most deadly strain of virus.

    ○ Males are more susceptible to the SARS virus than females.

    ○ Health care professionals need to be wary of possible SARS infection.

44. Which of the following provides the most appropriate title for the passage?

    ○ "Serial Killer: The Anatomy of the 2003 SARS Outbreak"

    ○ "The Ninth Floor"

    ○ "SARS: An Animal-Human Link?"

    ○ "The Global Impact of the SARS Virus"

    ○ "Conquering SARS"

Questions 45–50 are based on the following passage:

At last count in the year 2004, it was estimated that there were over 800 million mobile phone users worldwide, almost one-eighth of the global population. Underscoring
(5) this dramatic number is a growing suspicion that the radiation emitted by these mobile phones may be dangerous to humans. There is no doubt that the body absorbs varying levels of radiation emitted by cell phones, but the
(10) question is, do these levels pose a health risk?

Mobile phones employ radio waves, more specifically, radiofrequency (RF) energy, to transmit voice data and other information wirelessly between handsets and base
(15) stations. The Food and Drug Administration (FDA) and the Federal Communications Commission (FCC) share the responsibility of making sure every cell phone sold in the United States complies with certain safety
(20) guidelines that limit a person's exposure to RF energy. The amount of RF energy absorbed by a human body when in contact with a cell phone is measured by a unit known as the Specific Absorption Rate (SAR). A phone
(25) deemed "safe" by the FCC must not have a SAR level higher than 1.6 watts per kilogram (1.6 W/kg). Deeming a phone "safe," however, is misleading. The FDA states that though there is "no hard evidence of adverse health
(30) effects [of cell phone use] on the general public," it urges further research into the subject. This statement is vague at best, and rather than answering our question, it brings up a number of others.

(35) This vague stance by the FDA and FCC derives from the fact that most of the research findings on the possible negative effects of cell phone radiation have been controversial. An example of this was a study conducted on rats

(40) in 1995 at the University of Washington in
     Seattle by a research team headed by Henry
     Lai. Lai's team concluded that the exposure of
     rats to RF energy within the FCC cell phone
     SAR limits resulted in DNA breaks in the rats'
(45) brain cells. Such breaks could be linked to
     cancer and brain tumors. With good reason,
     these findings garnered much media
     attention, but they could never be clinically
     replicated, which cast serious doubt upon
(50) them. It is worth noting, however, that one of the
     studies that tried to confirm Lai's findings
     was conducted by a group funded by the cell
     phone manufacturer Motorola.
         The use of cell phones has only recently
(55) become widespread. Regardless of what
     research may indicate, time will offer the true
     answer as to whether cell phones are indeed
     dangerous. Let's hope the outcome of cell phone
     research, unlike that of cigarette research
(60) 50 years ago, does not reach us too late.

45. The author's primary purpose in the passage
    is to

    ○   dispel rumors about the negative side
        effects of cell phone use.

    ○   illustrate how the risks associated with
        using a cell phone outweigh the phone's
        positive uses.

    ○   describe how cell phones transmit voice
        data and other information.

    ○   discuss her personal views on the
        subject of cell phone radiation.

    ○   address the question of whether or not
        cell phone use is unhealthy.

46. It can be inferred from the passage that a phone
    deemed "safe" (line 25) by the FCC would
    actually be better described as

    ○   probably safe.

    ○   possibly safe.

    ○   completely safe.

    ○   somewhat dangerous.

    ○   extremely dangerous.

47. According to the passage, which of the
    following is true?

    ○   Cell phone batteries utilize the power of
        RF energy.

    ○   The FCC would consider a cell phone
        with a SAR level of 1.5 W/kg unsafe.

    ○   Henry Lai concluded that the exposure
        of rats to RF energy could be linked to
        cancer and brain tumors in rats.

    ○   The FDA and FCC believe that further
        cell phone research is unnecessary.

    ○   Smaller cell phones have higher SAR
        ratings.

48. According to information from the passage, it
    can be inferred that which of the following
    devices also emit RF energy?

    ○   A standard wall phone

    ○   A radio broadcast tower

    ○   A DVD player

    ○   A radio speaker

    ○   An Internet router

49. The author most probably notes in lines 50–53 that "one of the studies that tried to confirm Lai's findings was conducted by a group funded by the cell phone manufacturer Motorola" to suggest

    ○ a possible bias on the part of the confirmation group.

    ○ that Lai was a disgruntled ex-employee of Motorola.

    ○ cell phone manufacturers are actively trying to sabotage radiation research.

    ○ that Motorola is looking for alternatives to RF energy.

    ○ Lai's research team lied about its findings.

50. The author draws a comparison between cigarettes and cell phones in the final sentence of the passage in order to

    ○ illustrate a historical precedent.

    ○ demonstrate how quickly a person becomes hooked on his phone.

    ○ display her dislike for both.

    ○ make a point about social etiquette.

    ○ exaggerate the issue to help her illustrate a point.

ANSWERS AND EXPLANATIONS FOLLOW ON THE NEXT PAGE

ANSWERS AND EXPLANATIONS

1. E	11. E	21. E	31. D	41. A
2. D	12. D	22. C	32. D	42. B
3. C	13. C	23. D	33. E	43. E
4. D	14. B	24. E	34. C	44. A
5. B	15. E	25. C	35. B	45. E
6. A	16. D	26. C	36. A	46. B
7. D	17. A	27. B	37. B	47. C
8. D	18. B	28. B	38. D	48. B
9. A	19. C	29. C	39. D	49. A
10. A	20. C	30. D	40. C	50. A

DIAGNOSTIC TOOL

Tally up your score and write down your results below.

Total Correct: _____ out of 50

Percentage Correct: # you got right × 100 ÷ 50: _____

DIAGNOSE YOUR RESULTS

Look back at the questions you got wrong and think about your experience answering them.

STEP 1: FIND THE ROADBLOCKS

Did you struggle to answer some questions? To improve your score, you need to pinpoint exactly what element of these roadblocks tripped you up. To do that, ask yourself these two questions.

1. Did I struggle with the passage?

There are two reasons this might have happened. First, perhaps you got bogged down in the details, needing a long time to read and still not really getting the big picture. If this happened, then you were seduced by the details into "passive reading." Look back at the beginning of the chapter to refresh your memory about the importance of more active, critical reading. Or perhaps you just couldn't distinguish the important parts of the passage from its supporting details. If so, you need more practice identifying keywords. Read the answer explanations to understand how the passages here can be broken down. Either way, Try out Kaplan's *GMAT Verbal Workbook*, which contains strategies that will help you develop the skills you need to read with greater efficiency and comprehension.

2. Did I struggle with the questions?

Again, there are two possibilities here. The first is that you misidentified the question type and so weren't sure what it was really asking. The second is that you understood the question type but weren't sure how to work strategically on it. Go back to the beginning of this chapter and review the question types along with the Kaplan strategies for solving them. And try out Kaplan's *GMAT Verbal Workbook*, which has extensive review of the various question types and lots of practice sets.

STEP 2: FIND THE BLIND SPOTS

Did you answer some questions quickly and confidently—but get them wrong anyway?

When you come across wrong answers like these, you need to figure out what you thought you were doing right, what it turns out you were doing wrong, and why that happened. The best way to do that is to read the answer explanations!

They give you a detailed breakdown of why the correct answer is correct and why all the other answer choices are wrong. This helps to reinforce the Kaplan principles and methods for each question type and helps you figure out what blindsided you so it doesn't happen again. Also, just as with your roadblocks, try to get in as much practice as you can.

STEP 3: REINFORCE YOUR STRENGTHS

Now read through all the answer explanations for the ones you got right. Again, this helps to reinforce the Kaplan principles and methods for each question type, which in turn helps you work more efficiently so you can get the score you want. Keep your skills sharp with more practice.

As soon as you are comfortable with all the GMAT question types and Kaplan methods, complete a full-length practice test under timed conditions. In this way, practice tests serve as milestones; they help you to chart your progress!

If you are aiming for that top score, try out Kaplan's *GMAT 800,* which includes only the toughest GMAT questions and most focused strategies.

For even more practice, you can also try out the GMAT Quiz Bank. You get more than 1,000 questions that you can access 24/7 from any Internet browser, each with comprehensive explanations. You can even customize your quizzes based on question type, content, and difficulty level. Take quizzes in Timed Mode to test your stamina

EXPERT EXCLUSIVE

The Quiz Bank is a great way to practice Reading Comp—since the test is on a computer, this online practice gives you the absolutely best way to get used to the "feel" of GMAT Reading Comprehension.

or in Tutor Mode to see explanations as you work. Best of all, you also get detailed reports to track your progress.

Visit **kaptest.com/GMAT** for more details on the Quiz Bank and for more information on other online and classroom-based options.

Fernand Braudel Passage: Questions 1–7

PASSAGE	ANALYSIS
The **rich analyses** of Fernand Braudel and his fellow *Annales* historians have made **significant contributions** to historical theory and research. In **a departure from traditional** historical **approaches**, the *Annales* **historians assume** . . . **that history cannot be** limited to a simple recounting of conscious human actions **but must be understood** in the context of forces and material conditions that underlie human behavior. Braudel was the first *Annales* historian to gain **widespread support** for the **idea** that history should synthesize data from various social sciences . . . in order to provide a broader view of human societies over time . . .	There's a lot to read in this first paragraph, but the keywords help us to make sense of it. Right away, we get an emphasis keyword and an opinion/idea keyword, so we know that Braudel's contributions are pretty important. They might, in fact, be the Scope. He broke from the traditional approach to broaden the context of historical analysis, including many different social sciences.
Braudel conceived of history as the dynamic interaction of **three** temporalities. The **first** of these, the *événementielle*, . . . *Conjonctures* was . . . The *longue durée* . . . was for Braudel **the most fascinating** of the three temporalities. Here he focused on those aspects of everyday life that might remain relatively unchanged for centuries . . .	The first two words let us know that this paragraph discusses Braudel's ideas in more depth. We don't care about the three "temporalities" (whatever that means) unless we get a question about them. But it's worth noting the emphasis placed on the third one.

Braudel's concept of the *longue durée* extended the perspective of historical space as well as time. **Until the *Annales* school, historians had** . . . **Yet,** . . . geographical features **may well have more significance** . . .

And so the reader is given **such** arcane **information as** . . .

Braudel has been faulted for the imprecision of his approach. . . . **Further** . . . **Nevertheless** . . . **Braudel asked significant questions that traditional historians had overlooked.**

Unsurprisingly, the author gives lots of details about that third "temporality" and, reinforcing the contrast indicated in the first paragraph, its break from traditional approaches to history.

The continuation keyword *and* lets us know that this is right in line with ¶3. *Such information as* lets us know that the info will illustrate those ideas.

Braudel's not perfect, apparently, but the final sentence reminds us of the important new perspective that he brought to the field.

¶1 Braudel & Annales study history in broad context—break from tradition

¶2 Braudel's theory—3 "temporalities"

¶3 Concept of longue durée & its break from tradition

¶4 info related to ⬆

¶5 Braudel's faults; still significant

Topic: Braudel & Annales historians

Scope: Braudel's untraditional approach

Purpose: Describe ⬆

1. E

Primary purpose of the passage signifies this as a Global question. We can go straight to our Passage Map and predict an answer consistent with the Topic, Scope, Purpose, and Structure. In this case, that would be something like "Describe Braudel's untraditional approach to the study of history." That's a great match with (E). The other answers are all too narrow and focus on details. (A) draws on the details in ¶3, (C) draws on details from ¶2, and (D) is based on ¶5. (B) distorts a detail from the passage—Braudel agrees with Marxists (line 6).

EXPERT EXCLUSIVE

Notice that we don't need to understand any French or read much of the detail to understand the big picture of this passage.

2. D

This question asks why the author mentioned a detail, so it is a Logic question. Some Logic questions can be answered right from the Map, but this one focuses on a tiny detail, so let's research the context of that detail as well. Scanning for "Febvre and Bloch," we're led to the parenthetical comment at the end of ¶1. Make sure that you read more than just the comment!

We need the context for it, as provided by the full sentence:

> Braudel was the first *Annales* historian to gain widespread support for the idea that history should synthesize data from various social sciences, especially economics, in order to provide a broader view of human societies over time (although Febvre and Bloch, founders of the *Annales* school, had originated this approach).

Notice the sequence keyword *first* and the contrast keyword *although*. Together, they show us that the Febvre and Bloch came up with the idea before Braudel popularized it. So our prediction addressing the author's reasons for mentioning Febvre and Bloch might be "to show that someone else came up with the ideas before Braudel did." That's consistent only with (D). Notice that (B) and (E) both distort the author's mention of economics. These answers might be tempting if we didn't read the full sentence, since *economics* is mentioned about halfway through. (A) and (C) both draw on the final paragraph, which is not what the question stem addresses.

3. C

Here, you need a detail *not* mentioned in the passage. There's nothing to do here but use your Passage Map and scan the passage looking for the references. It's time consuming but much less time consuming than trying to memorize the entire passage! (A) is mentioned in ¶1 (lines 12–13), (B) in ¶3 (lines 43–45), (D) in ¶2 (lines 29–31), (E) in ¶2 (lines 18–19 . . . you have to determine that "temporalities" means "different time frames," but the descriptions of the terms does that pretty clearly.) (C) distorts the discussion of economic activities, which Braudel considers separate from nationality (lines 43–45).

> **EXPERT EXCLUSIVE**
>
> It's not a coincidence that the support for the right answer is connected to important key words: *"Yet ... geographical features may well have more significance ... than national borders."*

4. D

In this Inference question, correct choice (D) refers to a point made in the opening paragraph. ("[H]istory . . . must be understood in the context of forces and material conditions that underlie human behavior.") (A) is wrong because there's no indication that the *Annales* historians were more interested in other social sciences than in history (they were historians, after all). (B) distorts the detail on which the right answer is based—the *Annales* historians are not critical of the achievements themselves, just critical of the idea that those achievements are all one needs to study in order to understand history. (C) is the exact opposite of what the passage implies—they rely on economic analysis, so it's not likely that they are skeptical of its validity. (E) is wrong because, though it's clear that the *Annales* historians had a dogma of their own, there's no indication that they were any more dogmatic than anyone else.

5. B

This is a Detail question, as it asks for an explicit detail from the passage—in this case, what criticisms the author has of Braudel. Our Passage Map directs our research to the beginning of the last paragraph. Its very first sentence begins "Braudel has been faulted . . . ." But in true GMAT fashion, the right answer does not come from the sentence to which we are sent but from its context. Notice how the key word *further* lets us know that the list of criticisms goes on for three sentences. You'd want to look at all three before going to the answer choices. They are *imprecision, mak[ing] it difficult to delimit boundaries of observation* (whatever that means), and *minimiz[ing] the differences among the social sciences.* It's the last of these that's the basis for the right answer, (B). (A) does present a detail that is in the passage—just not the detail we're looking for. The other answers are all directly contradicted by the passage: (C) by lines 18–19, (D) by lines 62–63, (E) by lines 6–8.

EXPERT EXCLUSIVE

If you are asked about a list of similar details, odds are the answer will come from the last item on the list.

6. A

Our Passage Map tells us that the *longue durée* is discussed both in ¶2 and in ¶3. That's far too much to research all at once, so we'll have to use each Statement in turn as the basis for focused research. We can, however, research the definition of *longue durée*—"a historical wave of great length," and "aspects of everyday life that might remain unchanged for centuries." Since this is an Inference question, we know that we're looking to include Statements that must be true based on the passage but that might not be explicitly in the passage itself. *Diet* in Statement I matches with *what people ate* in line 31, so we can eliminate (B) and (D). Nothing in Statements II or III is consistent with the *longue durée* portions of the passage, and they certainly don't fit with the definition of *longue durée*, so (A) must be correct. (Statement II gives an example of *événmentielle*, and III gives an example of *conjuncture*.)

EXPERT EXCLUSIVE

The most efficient approach to Roman numeral questions is to evaluate the statements one by one, eliminating answers as you go. Had you eliminated (B) and (D) after realizing that Statement I was correct, you'd then only have to realize that Statement II was incorrect to arrive at the right answer. There'd be no need to fret over Statement III at all!

7. D

This isn't a classic Inference question, but we can treat it as one, since we're looking for the statement that *must* be consistent with something from the passage. Braudel's principles are all over this passage, so clearly the best thing to do is go answer by answer. (A) is directly contradicted by lines 28–30. (B), (C), and (E) may present commonly believed ideas, but Braudel never expresses them. (D) accurately states the assumptions underlying Braudel's work (see in particular lines 4–10).

EXPERT EXCLUSIVE

Notice the extreme language in the four wrong answers: *all, most important, doomed,* and *too important*. More sedate language, like *many* and *may*, is more common in correct Inference answers.

EXPERT EXCLUSIVE
You wouldn't need to dissect the arguments even this much. If all you picked up on were the clues to the author's voice in the last paragraph, you could have handled the Global question and had time to do the "open-book" research to answer the others.

State Role in Development Passage: Questions 8–13

PASSAGE	ANALYSIS
In many underdeveloped countries, the state plays an **important** . . . role in economic development today. There are **four general arguments**, all of them related, **for state participation in economic development. First** . . . the *size* of these **obstacles** will serve as **barriers** to entry . . . . **In addition**, . . . they do not lend themselves to *small*-scale improvements.	The author is pretty clear in the second sentence about what the passage will discuss; we're probably going to learn about all four arguments. Without even reading them, we know *why* they're here: to argue in favor of state participation.
	There's a lot of economic jargon in argument #1, but it seems to have something to do with the size of the obstacles.
A related argument . . . **Consequently** . . . Industrialization **necessarily** involves many different sectors; economic enterprises will thrive **best** in an environment in which they draw on inputs from related economic sectors . . .	Here's argument #2. Again with the jargon. But the emphasis keywords *necessarily* and *best* seem to be connected to a need for different sectors.
A third argument concerns the low-level equilibrium trap . . . **Fortunately**, after a certain point, the rate of population growth will decrease . . . . The private sector, **however, will not be able to** . . .	The *what*??? Okay, don't panic. Maybe we don't know what a "low-level equilibrium trap" is, but at least we know that these details are here to explain it.
	Fortunately reveals the author's voice, seeing a decrease in population growth as a good thing. And the author's voice is again revealed, asserting that the private sector can't solve some problem.

The final argument concerns the relationship between delayed development and the state . . . **therefore**, the process of industrialization **cannot** be a haphazard affair, **nor can** the pace, content, and direction **be left solely to market forces.** Part of **the reason for a strong state presence**, then, relates specifically to the competitive international environment . . .

Last argument: something about "delayed development."

The author's voice is all over this paragraph, with *cannot* and *nor can*. Pretty clearly, the author favors state intervention and disagrees that market forces alone can do the job.

¶1 Argument #1—size of obstacles

¶2 Argument #2—many sectors

¶3 Argument #3—low-level equilibrium trap & population

¶4 Argument #4—delayed development/competitive environment

Topic: Underdeveloped countries' economies

Scope: The state's role in the development of ⌐

Purpose: Argue that underdeveloped countries need ⌐

8. D

Here's a good example of why it's helpful to be done with the passage quickly. Some of the answers to this Detail question are pretty tricky. We're looking for a reason *not* given in the passage, which means that the four wrong answers are in there somewhere. *Start-up costs of initial investments* from (A) fits with *entrance requirements in terms of financial capital* in lines 6–7. (B) is trickier. *Demand* is pretty clearly mentioned at the top of ¶2, but what about *supply*? Following are lots of details that might plausibly have something to do with supply. Best to strike (B) out for now, coming back to it if all the others get eliminated as well. (C) mirrors the author's explicit opinion in lines 64–66. Spotting those author's voice keywords would make for quick elimination of this answer choice. (D) talks about *livelihoods and security of workers*, two subjects mentioned nowhere in the passage. Could *public amenities* in (E) mean *public utilities, transport, and communications facilities* from lines 16–17? It's certainly plausible. So (E) should be eliminated as well. Only (D), the correct answer, remains.

> **EXPERT EXCLUSIVE**
>
> You don't need expertise with economics jargon—just sufficient familiarity with common terms like *market forces, start-up costs,* and so forth to allow you to figure out whether answers are plausible.

9. A

The passage as a whole presents reasons state intervention is necessary for the industrialization of many less developed countries. (B) focuses only on ¶2 and ¶3. It also introduces the new idea of outside assistance (*state presence* doesn't mean *foreign presence*). (D) also draws only on those two paragraphs and confuses them to boot. (C) is the opposite of the author's main point, and (E) overstates the case with the extreme words *ensure* and *rapid*.

10. A

You need what's *not* in the passage. (B) and (E) are mentioned in ¶1, (C) in ¶2, and (D) in ¶3. "Safeguarding against the domination of local markets by a single source of capital" is not mentioned.

> **EXPERT EXCLUSIVE**
>
> If you quickly eliminate three answers but struggle trying to go further, it might be best to make a guess. That way you won't fall behind time. If you spend too much time on one answer, you might never get to an easier question afterward, which you'd likely get right.

11. E

Context is critical for any question that references a specific part of the passage, and Inference questions are no exception. Notice how the sentence talking about "technical indivisibilities in social overhead capital" (whatever that means) begins with a nice clear keyword—*in addition*. Whatever this difficult jargon means, it's another example of whatever was discussed in the previous sentence. That sentence lists imposing obstacles. So "technical blah blah blah" must be another obstacle. That eliminates everything but (D) and (E).

Now on to "low-level equilibrium trap." The context here isn't as clear, but at this point our job is simpler—we only need to figure out which of the two remaining answers is supported by the passage. There is no language in ¶3 that fits with attracting investment. But lines 41–46 say "additional income . . . [will] force the society to its former subsistence position." That fits (E) nicely.

12. D

Every now and again you'll see a Weaken question in Reading Comp. Don't panic, as we can deal with them just as we would in a Critical Reasoning question. The author makes four arguments here, and it wouldn't be efficient to try to analyze them all and create four different predictions. It'll be best, as it often is in Roman numeral questions, to go statement by statement.

Statement I fits with the author's main point, so it's hardly reasonable to think that it would weaken any of his arguments. We can eliminate (A), (C), and (E). Note that we now know for sure that Statement II is part of the correct answer. No need to waste your time with it! Statement III directly contradicts the end of ¶1, thus knocking out part of the author's evidence. That would certainly weaken his argument, so (D) is the correct answer. (If you're curious, Statement II contradicts both ¶1 and ¶3.)

13. C

This question is technically a Detail question, but even so it tests your Big-Picture knowledge of the passage, as will many seemingly detail-oriented questions. We know from our Passage Map that we need to look in ¶3 for the answer. Perhaps you read only so much context as the first two sentences of that paragraph. Even so, you could have eliminated (A), which is the exact opposite of the second sentence. It's not likely that state intervention is the problem, as we know from the author's Purpose that he's arguing in favor of such intervention. (B), then, should be eliminated. (D) also is out on big-picture grounds, as it is drawn from the wrong paragraph. (E) seems to be in the paragraph, but read the whole sentence—the author doesn't mention "one-shot, large doses of capital" as a cause of the trap. Rather, it's the private sector's inability to provide those doses that's the culprit. (C), then, is correct.

> **EXPERT EXCLUSIVE**
>
> Even though many of this passage's questions were detail oriented, our work on many of them was greatly aided by our Big-Picture knowledge!

Immigration of Southerners to Brazil Passage: Questions 14–18

PASSAGE

The years following the Civil War brought many changes to the Southern states, prompting a large emigration of U. S. citizens to Brazil . . . primarily from the South. In **one particular case** . . . Emperor Dom Pedro II of Brazil . . . appealed for colonists from the U.S. South. Dom Pedro II **recognized the value** these Southerners could have for Brazil in the form of agricultural and educational knowledge . . .

Because . . . many Southerners **accepted** Dom Pedro's offer. After founding "Vila Americana" (American Town), **one of the most important** of the "American colonies" in Brazil, the Southern immigrants **did not** remain in isolation. They interacted with and even married local Brazilians and other new colonists.

ANALYSIS

The first sentence sets the Topic—the emigration of U.S. Southerners. *In one particular case* is a pretty clear sign of narrowing—perhaps the Scope is their emigration to Brazil.

Note the positive emphasis keyword *value*, drawing our attention not just to the emigration but to its positive effects on Brazil. Odds are we'll read about those effects later.

Details about why Southerners went. Also note the emphasis placed on "Vila Americana" and the contrast between *isolation* and *interacted*.

What about the positive effects?

> **EXPERT EXCLUSIVE**
>
> Notice that even though this passage is about half as long as the "State Role in Development" passage, you need to read almost the same amount. Long passages are full of skippable details; short passages have a denser structure.

... American industrial technology allowed the colonists to **improve** farming implements ... Housing **also improved** ... The colonists' emphasis on education and industrial skills contributed to Brazil's **success** in business ... Today, Vila Americana, maintaining this original level of **excellence**, has the **highest** education and income levels per capita of any city in Brazil.

Ah, here we go. Oodles of positive emphasis keywords. And just as ¶1 predicted, they are associated with agriculture and education!

¶1 Brazil advertises for U.S. Southerners

¶2 Why Southerners came

¶3 Positive effects of emigration—industry, farming, education

Topic: Emigration of U.S. Southerners to Brazil

Scope: The positive effects of ⌐↑

Purpose: Describe ⌐↑

14. B

This Global question is full of classic traps. (B) fits our Topic, Scope, Purpose, and Structure very well, of course. But look at the others—(A), (C), and (E) all draw on details from ¶1, trying to trick you into thinking that the first or second sentence is a "topic sentence." (D) distorts the details from ¶2. Even if "without yielding their Southern heritage" meant "reviv[ing] the antebellum South"—which is too extreme an interpretation—this isn't the overall Purpose of the passage.

15. E

Our Passage Map suggests that the positive effects of the emigration are discussed in ¶3, so the right answer to this Inference question must be based on ideas from that paragraph. A whole paragraph is too much to research beforehand, so we'll go answer by answer. (A) is extreme, since Brazil was already inhabited when the Southerners arrived. (B) is also too extreme, and it does not accurately reflect the reasons that Southerners moved, as stated in the passage in lines 17–20. (C) also misstates their reasons. (D) is too extreme; we know that Dom Pedro thought that the Southerners would bring benefits, but wanting something isn't the same as fearing not getting it. (E) is correct: it reflects statements in ¶3 about the Southerners' influences on Brazilian society.

16. D

According to the passage is a signal of a Detail question. In this case, all four wrong answers will be explicitly in the passage, and the right answer will not be. (D) distorts lines 19–20; the passage tells us nothing about what the "Northern 'improvements'" are—the farming and agriculture information is nowhere in ¶2 at all. (A) and (C) are both supported by ¶3, which talks about the benefits the Southerners brought with them and their lasting effect. (B) is supported by the beginning of ¶2, where the author says that the Southerners "recognized an opportunity to rebuild their lives . . . ." Choice (E) is also incorrect, because the author specifically states that Dom Pedro II advertised for colonists.

> **EXPERT EXCLUSIVE**
>
> Distortions and misrepresentations of details are common GMAT traps.

17. A

Since this asks why the author did something, this is a Logic question. The keyword *because* lets us know that the long, quoted detail is the reason why something happened. To know what, you'd need to read more context from the passage. The full sentence is "Because [quoted detail], many Southerners accepted Dom Pedro's offer." What was Dom Pedro's offer? Again, context is key: the sentence before lets us know that the offer was to emigrate to Brazil. So we could predict an answer to be "It's the reason why U.S. Southerners wanted to move to Brazil." (A) is the only answer that fits well.

(B) distorts the purpose of the detail, which does not describe what the Southerners did upon arrival, just why they went. (It's too extreme in describing those effects, anyway.) (C) is tempting in that the quote directly follows the sentence that mentions Dom Pedro advertising for colonists, but the passage never suggests that the Southerners' desire to be free of Northern influence was suggested by Dom Pedro. (D) is a distortion; Brazilians' preferences are never mentioned in the passage. (E) is outside the scope of the passage and far too extreme.

18. B

The only research needed for this Logic question is to look at your Passage Map, which says that ¶3 focused on "the positive effects of emigration." (B) fits perfectly. (A) is incorrect because Dom Pedro's appeal is the focus of ¶1, not ¶3. (C) is too narrow; only one sentence in ¶3 discusses the technology imported to Brazil. (D) is out of scope, and (E) is the complete opposite of what the author suggests.

> **EXPERT EXCLUSIVE**
>
> If you picked up all those positive emphasis keywords in ¶3, you could answer this question directly from your Passage Map in just a handful of seconds!

EXPERT EXCLUSIVE
Notice how little of the scientific jargon you need to read in order to Map the passage!

Dry Valleys of Antarctica Passage: Questions 19–22

PASSAGE	ANALYSIS
. . . the Dry Valleys of Antarctica . . . They are the **coldest, driest places on earth, yet** this arid, frigid climate **supports** several **delicate** ecosystems. Life in these ecosystems **consists of** . . . This region has proven **interesting** specifically to scientists researching the possibility of life on Mars, **because** . . .	Topic from the first sentence. Next we get a big emphasis phrase followed by emphasis on contrasts. Seems that basically these Valleys are brutal but life still exists there. Plus, lots of details about that life.

A Purpose for all these details. In other words, why the research matters. |
| The Dry Valleys' system of lakes provides a **particularly interesting** area of research . . .. this lake offers an **odd paradox**: thick ice is responsible for maintaining this lake's liquid state. | Looks like we'll get details about the lakes and why they're interesting. No need to read those details closely now that we know why they are here.

The author draws attention to one detail, so it might be worth noting. No sense getting too wrapped up in the other stuff yet—not until a question comes along. |
| . . . Lake Fryxell . . . sediment thick enough to bury fossil **life** forms. This very thickness, **however**, makes a formal scientific search for **signs of life impracticable**. The floor of Lake Vida, **on the other hand** . . . preserved **clear signs of life because** . . . **Since** . . . Some researchers are **hoping** that exploration of similar terrain on Mars may yield similar results. | We're finally talking about "life," which ¶1 told us would be important. Seems the "floor" of Lake Vida is the place to go! We have lots of reasons why that's so. (No need to read them closely now.) We come back to applications for research on Mars. *Since* indicates a reason that researchers hope for applications on Mars. |

¶1 Dry Valleys harsh, but have life

¶2 Details about system of lakes

¶3 Details about fossils and where to find them

Topic: Dry Valleys of Antarctica

Scope: Life in the lakes of ⌐↑

Purpose: Describe phenomena

19. C

The key to all Detail questions is to read for context. The question stem leads us to the first sentence of ¶3, which says that the sediment is "thick enough to bury fossil life forms." But the next sentence says that the thickness "makes a formal scientific search for life impractical." So putting the two sentences together, we might predict the answer thusly: "The sediment may have fossils, but scientists would have a hard time finding them." That fits very nicely with the right answer, (C).

(A) seems tempting but misses the contextual information. It draws on info from the wrong part of the paragraph. (B) is also tempting, but the passage doesn't get nearly this specific about *why* signs of life would be hard to find. (D) draws from ¶2, the wrong part of the passage. (E) is so extreme as to be the opposite of what the passage says—looking for life may be *impractical*, but it is there. So *devoid of life* is not correct.

> **EXPERT EXCLUSIVE**
> Science passages may seem overwhelming if you focus on all the details. The GMAT, however, rewards readers who focus on the author's main interest in these details, not the details themselves.

20. C

Based on our Passage Map, our prediction for this Global question would be something like "describing Dry Valley lakes' ecosystems and how they preserve signs of life." That's a great match with (C). (A) is out of scope, adaptations of organisms are never considered. (B) is too narrow, since it refers to material mentioned only at the end of ¶2. (D) is out of scope; *evolutionary histories* are never discussed, and the *clues about life in cold, dry ecosystems* is a trap for those who thought the passage focused on parallels with Mars. The details referenced in (E) are mentioned only briefly—if you read for structure, you may not even have noticed them!

21. E

There are two ways you could answer this Inference question. If you picked up the focus on life from ¶1 and the keywords in ¶3 that focused on where to find it, you might predict an answer here: "on the floor of lakes." Or perhaps you took the more traditional approach, looking at the detail referenced by the question. That would lead you to the last sentence, which says that scientists would look for "similar terrain." Knowing the value of context, you'd check the previous sentence to see what terrain we're talking about; it's the "Lake Vida sediment." But what kind of terrain is that? Lines

> **EXPERT EXCLUSIVE**
> We usually can't predict the right answer to Inference questions. But every so often, we get a detail-based Inference question that lends itself to predicting. If the GMAT gives you that gift, take advantage of it!

49–52 provide the answer: "The floor of Lake Vida . . . preserved clear signs of life."
(E), which mentions "lakebeds," is the only choice consistent with "floor of a lake." (A)
contradicts ¶3, which says that river deltas are bad places to look. (B), (C) and (D) are
mentioned in the passage but not in connection with what scientists are hoping for.

22. C

EXPERT EXCLUSIVE

Checking whether answer
choices (or statements) are
plausibly consistent with
details is usually *much* easier
than understanding those
details fully on their own.

The detail references in this Inference question lead us to two places.
Mounds of sediment leads us to *piles of sediment* in lines 50–51; *refined* is
mentioned in line 60. So we can expect the right answer to be based on
the dense details in lines 49–63. We could try to read and understand it
all, but it's a lot and it'll be hard to handle if you aren't comfortable with
the science. Far easier to go statement by statement, seeing if the details are
plausibly consistent with the relevant part of the passage.

Statement I—*continuous sublimation*—isn't mentioned at all. (It comes
from line 34, the wrong part of the passage.) That eliminates (A), (B),
and (E). Now you know that Statement III is okay, and you need only check out
Statement II. *Large pieces of rock* may be consistent with *larger rocks* on line 57. But
nowhere does the passage say that those rocks decompose, nor do the large rocks seem
to reach the lake floor. That eliminates (D), leaving (C) the right answer. (Statement
III is consistent with lines 57–58, by the way.)

Academic Medical Center Passage: Questions 23–27

PASSAGE	ANALYSIS
History has shaped academic medical centers (AMCs) to perform three functions: patient care, research, and teaching. These three missions are now **fraught with problems because** the attempt to combine them has led to **such** inefficiencies **as** . . .	Details about AMCs. Don't assume that the first sentence is a "topic sentence," though! Ah, strong negative emphasis. Now we're getting somewhere. *Because* and *such . . . as* let us know that we get some details about what these problems are. Notice the author's voice coming out here, seeming to say, "AMCs have messed up their missions."
One source of inefficiency derives from mixed lines of authority . . . The fragmented accountability is **heightened by the fact that** . . . which **inevitably** strains relationships.	We've got one source of the problem: *mixed lines of authority*. No need to read much more unless we get a question. But we could certainly predict that we'll get more sources!

Another source of inefficiency is the fact that physicians have obligations to many different groups . . . **Satisfying** the interests of one group may **alienate** others. Patient care provides a common **example** . . . If . . . the educational and clinical care missions of AMCs would both be **better served**.

Aha! Source #2—many obligations. Note the contrast set up by *satisfying* and *alienate*. We get an example and a proposed solution.

A bias toward specialization adds **yet more** inefficiency . . . their more routine medical services **need** development and enhancement.

Here's source #3—bias toward specialization. And another proposed fix. (Note how the author's use of *need* reinforces our understanding of her point of view.)

A **final contribution** to inefficiency is organizational complacency. **Until recently** . . . **The rising presence, however** . . .

Source #4—organizational complacency. We get a contrast between past and present.

¶1 AMCs' missions in trouble

¶2 Reason—mixed lines of authority

¶3 Reason—many obligations; proposed solution

¶4 Reason—bias toward specialization; proposed solution

¶5 Reason—organizational complacency

Topic: AMCs' 3 missions

Scope: Inefficiencies hurting

Purpose: Explain the sources of.

23. D

We could say that the author does not approve of the current situation but does not condemn AMCs altogether. (A) is incorrect since the author does not accept the status quo. (B) is extreme—the author's tone is not "strident." (C) is way off: the author is calm and certain of her positions. (E) misses the author's critical attitude toward the problems at AMCs. (D) is correct: the author presents particular criticisms backed up by clearly explained reasons.

EXPERT EXCLUSIVE

Exaggerating criticism, as in (B), is one the GMAT's favorite traps.

24. E

Since this is an Inference question, we need the answer choice that is best supported by what the author says about primary care at AMCs. Inferences are difficult to predict, but our Passage Map should direct us to ¶4, where the author discusses primary care in relation to the bias toward specialization. (A) and (D) are out of scope because neither money nor publicity is discussed in this paragraph. (B) is out of scope; the author does not say enough for us to make a conclusion about the needs of patients. Eliminate (C) as well, because it is not consistent with the main point of the paragraph (bias toward specialization) and we have no information about the quality of primary care outside of AMCs. (E) is correct because it's consistent with last sentence of the paragraph (lines 67–69), which proposes development and enhancement of routine services in AMCs. Given the context of this sentence—in a paragraph that focuses on the inefficiencies added by specialization—it's likely that the author would agree with (E).

25. C

Our Passage Map tells us that the passage discussed the inefficiencies that harm the AMCs' missions. (C) is the only answer choice that captures the author's intention. The challenge was recognizing that *conflicts* and *inefficiencies* meant the same thing in this passage. Perhaps you picked up on "strains relationships" and "alienate" as your clues that this was okay. Or perhaps you said, "Well, it's plausible, I suppose," and selected the right answer by eliminating the other four. (A) is far too broad. (B) focuses only on ¶2, not on the whole passage. (D) is a detail from the last paragraph but not a "concluding sentence." (E) distorts the scope of the passage, which does not discuss treatment errors.

26. C

GUESSING TIP

Answers with definitive, absolute language are much less likely to be correct than answers with qualified language.

Physicians are mentioned throughout the passage, so for this Inference question, there is nothing to do but go through each answer, looking either to eliminate it as clearly wrong or to keep it as plausibly right. (A) distorts the general point of the passage—AMCs may be structured poorly, but that doesn't tell us anything about the business acumen of their physicians. (B) seems tempting, as it plays off of the "obligations to many different groups" that is the focus of ¶3. But the use of "too many" tests, while costly, doesn't necessarily mean that patient's health is being well served. In fact, the very next sentence asserts that if physicians were more aware of cost, then clinical care would improve. Most importantly, note the language difference between (B) and (C). (B) is definitive; (C) is more speculative ("sometimes"). Sure enough, (C) is the answer consistent with lines 44–54, as all these actions are done "for the benefit of medical students." (D) distorts a detail from ¶2, one that discusses community physicians who are not faculty. (E) distorts another detail, one that applies not to physicians but to patients.

27. B

Tertiary hospitals are discussed in ¶5. The passage says that tertiary hospitals are intense competition for AMCs and that they have "patient care as their only goal." The right answer would need to be something that addressed that challenge. (B) does this—if AMCs focused more on patient care, they'd be more competitive. (A) isn't supported, as we aren't told anything about stealing physicians. (C) would assist the tertiary facilities, not the AMCs. (D) distorts ¶4; the bias toward specialized care may be a problem, but the author acknowledges in lines 63–66 that patients often go to AMCs because of the specialty care. (E) distorts criticisms in ¶2; grant administration conflicts may hinder research, but that doesn't mean that they hinder patient care.

Human Brain Passage: Questions 28–31

PASSAGE	ANALYSIS
One of the **first attempts** to peer into the living human brain was carried out by a neurosurgeon named Wilder Penfield . . . What he found was **even more remarkable than** what he initially set out to do. By stimulating different points on the lower parts of the brain (the temporal lobes), he elicited distinct and vivid memories in his patients. These memories were **more precise than usual** memories . . . When the same location in the temporal lobe was stimulated again, the same memory reappeared. **Could it be that a physical map of memories exists within our brains?**	Two very suggestive keywords here. *First* implies that there may be others later; *attempts* opens the possibility that his experiments didn't succeed. We get some details about his experiments, but it's the success or failure of those experiments that should interest us. And the emphasis keywords tell us to focus on his unexpected finding: stimulating certain parts of the brain evoked strong, specific, repeatable memories.
	The author asks a question here, so we should expect the next ¶ to answer it.

One might **mistakenly conclude** from Penfield's experiment that particular memories are stored in specific sites in the brain . . . **While** this description is **imprecise**, the **alternative theory**, that memory is stored in a unitary superstructure, **is also inaccurate.**

The author very clearly *disagrees* with the "specific site" theory that Penfield's work suggests. Hmm . . . what *will* he agree with? Another rejected theory: "unitary superstructure."

Although it is true that the temporal lobes play a **critical** role in memory processes, **evidence** from brain-imaging studies **strongly indicates** that memory is divided among a range of distinct but interacting neural systems, each contributing to a unique feature of memory . . .

Here we go! The author says that "distinct but interacting neural systems" is the right theory. Remember, we don't have to know what that means to know that the author identifies this theory as correct.

¶1 Penfield's brain experiments; unexpected finding about memory

¶2 Memories not in "specific sites" nor in a "unitary superstructure" but are "distinct and interacting."

Topic: The brain

Scope: Where ↑ stores and processes memory

Purpose: Explain why one theory of ↑ is superior to two others.

28. B

A question about a title is a Global question, and it needs a global answer. (A) wrongly focuses on Penfield, who only comes into ¶1. (C) is out of scope, we're focused on memory, not the general question of the temporal lobes and their cognitive functions. (D) and (E) are also too narrow; each tries to trick us into thinking that a detail from ¶1 is a "topic sentence." (B) might at first raise the same suspicion, as it draws most clearly from the final sentence of ¶1, but since that sentence is in the author's voice and sets up the whole of ¶2, (B) is the correct answer. (It's also nicely consistent with the Topic, Scope, and Purpose, as all Global answers must be!)

29. C

"Neural systems of memory" are discussed throughout the whole of ¶2, so the most efficient approach is to go answer by answer, looking for support. (A) is too extreme; lines 43–44 say that "one specific structure is *more* active" in one type of memory than another, but that implies that one structure can be involved in two aspects of memory, just not equally involved. (B) contradicts those same lines, drawing on the list of memories in lines 45–46 as well. "Critical role in memory process" from (C) should have been easy to find, as the key word *critical* should have stood out to you as you read. Lines 34–35 say that it's "the temporal lobes" that are critical. Are they in the lower parts of the brain? Scanning for any other reference to "temporal lobes," we find in line 12 that they are indeed "the lower parts of the brain." So (C) is correct. (D) is explicitly contradicted by lines 25–30. (Here's the importance of reading whole sentences; if you just read the end of the sentence, you'd have thought that (D) was correct.) (E) distorts Penfield's findings. He may have started his research with epileptics, but the passage does not relate memory to epilepsy.

EXPERT EXCLUSIVE

Some of the right answers to the GMAT's most difficult Detail and Inference questions send you on scavenger hunts like (C) does. That's why it's helpful to tell the difference between an answer that you've proved wrong and an answer that you're merely unsure of.

30. D

Here, you simply need to define a phrase as used by the author. A "unitary superstructure" where all memories are stored is mentioned as an alternative theory for an earlier described one: that "particular memories are stored in different sites in the brain." So we can conclude that a memory superstructure will hold all memories in one place. This is a reference to a specific brain region, as (D) indicates. It is not a reference to the brain as a whole, as in (A). The author goes on to say that this superstructure theory is inaccurate; we have no reason to think that this superstructure theory is preferred by most scientists, so (B) is incorrect. (C) is never mentioned in the text. (E) refers to cognitive processes rather than a physical brain region; we have no evidence that this is what the unitary superstructure refers to.

31. D

This Detail question asks us to find what's *not* in ¶1. We'll have to go answer by answer, as we wouldn't want to try to memorize that whole paragraph. Lines 11–12 say that Penfield "stimulat[ed] different points on the lower part of the brain (the temporal lobes) . . . ." That's what is described in (A), so we can rule it out. We're also told that patients were given local, not total, anesthesia, confirming choice (B). And we know that Penfield used a mild electric current on his patients' brains, (C). What about (D)? We know that Penfield's operations were "an attempt to pinpoint the source of seizure activity and then remove that piece of tissue." But the passage never tells us whether he succeeded in achieving this goal. So (D) is the answer. As for (E), we're told in the second sentence that this was the case.

EXPERT EXCLUSIVE

An attempt may not succeed. That which *seems* to be may not actually be. The GMAT makes use of these distinctions quite often, so watch out for them.

DNA Passage: Questions 32–35

PASSAGE	ANALYSIS
The **early 1980s** were a time of growing interest in the potential of genetic research. The **tedious** and **painstaking** process of analyzing even a short segment of DNA, **however, posed a problem** for scientists **until 1983,** when Kary Mullis happened upon **one of the most important ideas ever discovered** in the field of genetics . . . the polymerase chain reaction (PCR), the foundation for a **quick** and **easy** process to create multiple copies of DNA from a single strand.	Okay, the Topic is clear, at least. Analyzing DNA was tough, apparently. Could we ask for stronger emphasis?! This is great! *Quick and easy* contrasts with *tedious and painstaking*.
Multiple copies of DNA samples are **necessary** for researchers . . . To copy a molecule of DNA . . . **Mullis's breakthrough** was his discovery that . . . polymerases could be harnessed **to do the job,** if . . .	We learn why copies are important and how to make them. Ah, the important stuff—what Mullis's breakthrough was: Polymerases (whatever they are) can make copies.
One **complicating** factor was the extreme sensitivity of the polymerase enzymes to the heat required to unwind DNA segments . . .	Heat seems to be a problem, and there are lots of details about why.
The discovery of a **temperature-resistant polymerase** derived from a bacterium that lives in hot springs **greatly enhanced the functionality** of PCR . . . **The PCR process is not wholly error-free, but without this monumental discovery, genetics as we know it today would not exist.**	Ah, looks like we're solving the problem! Again, we couldn't ask for clearer emphasis.

EXPERT EXCLUSIVE

Don't be scared of long passages with lots of jargon. The keywords that will allow you to figure out Structure and Purpose are there, just waiting to help you.

¶1 Analyzing DNA tough until PCR

¶2 Polymerases make multiple copies

¶3 Heat is a problem for polymerase

¶4 Problem solved; PCR not perfect, but still crucial

Topic: Genetic research

Scope: PCR

Purpose: Describe the discovery of PCR & its importance to genetic research.

32. D

Our big-picture reading is all that's necessary to answer this kind of Logic question. Our Passage Map should provide the answer. We said that ¶3 described a problem faced by PCR. That's a perfect match for (D), the right answer. (A) is a trap, based on details from the end of the paragraph that do not represent its main function. (B) is too extreme—just because there were problems doesn't mean that PCR isn't good. In fact, (B) violates the main idea of the whole passage. (C) and (E) are wrong because no alternative method is discussed in this paragraph.

33. E

Since this Inference question refers to no specific part of the passage, our research will have to be done answer by answer. The best prediction we can make is "The right answer *must* be true, based on the passage; I may have to eliminate the four wrong answers in order to find it." (A) is too extreme; the last sentence says PCR is pretty valuable, but that doesn't mean it's "as close to flawless as it can possibly be." (B) is also extreme—making technicians' jobs easier is clearly one of the results of PCR but not its *sole* purpose. And the parade of extreme answer choices continues with (C). Genetics "as we know it today" exists only because of PCR, but that doesn't mean the field of genetics didn't exist before. (D) distorts ¶4; the discovery of "temperature-resistant polymerase" made heating less of a problem, but "temperature-resistant polymerase" and "PCR" are different things. (E) is supported by what the author tells us about Kary Mullis's breakthrough—that it involved harnessing natural enzymes for the purpose of DNA copying and analysis.

> **EXPERT EXCLUSIVE**
> Spotting extreme language is a crucial skill for success on Inference questions.

34. C

The whole passage is about PCR and genetics, so there's no way to research other than answer by answer. We're looking for the one answer that's *not* supported by the passage.

(A), (B), and (E) are supported in the last paragraph. (D) is implied by the fact that less human involvement is necessary; the process is more streamlined than it used to be. With (C), we're told that heat-resistant polymerases can "withstand multiple cycles of heating and cooling" and, thus, "could make large numbers of copies from a single strand of DNA with minimal human involvement," but nowhere does it say that the need to add new enzymes has been eliminated altogether. This answer is too extreme.

35. B

The right answer should match your Passage Map very closely. Looking for an answer like "Describe the discovery of PCR and its importance to genetics research," you might be led to both (B) and (C). But remember that the right answer to a Global question will also be consistent with the overall structure. With ¶2 describing how PCR works, ¶3 discussing a problem with PCR, and ¶4 giving its solution, (B)'s inclusion of "process" and "evolution" is the right answer. (C) is also out of scope because we are never told how Mullis came up with the idea in the first place. (A) is out of scope because we are never told of other methods of copying DNA. (D) and (E) focus on details from ¶1 and ¶3 respectively, not on the passage's primary purpose.

> **EXPERT EXCLUSIVE**
>
> Did this passage scare you at first? Despite its length and technical language, all we needed to get the questions right was the ability to read for the Big Picture and the ability to spot extreme language!

Secrecy Passage: Questions 36–38

PASSAGE

Many sociologists who examined the phenomenon of secrecy **considered** secrets **morally negative because** . . . Georg Simmel . . . **departed from this approach, arguing** that a secret is defined **not** by the kind of information concealed **but** by the fact of concealment . . . Simmel **saw** secrecy as . . . **Furthermore** . . . By removing the moral **bias**, Simmel's framework facilitated **objective** study of secrets. **However**, Simmel's discussion of disclosure seems to **belie his contention** that secrets are **morally neutral** . . . **Since** . . . the **immorality** of disclosure **taints** the secret itself.

One specific example of research into secrecy is Beryl Bellman's study of the "secret societies" of the West African Kpelle . . . Kpelle **ideology holds** . . . Kpelle tradition **insists** . . . Bellman's **realization** shows that the mechanism of Kpelle secrecy **relies on Simmel's model** . . .

ANALYSIS

Secrets are often thought to be negative, plus detail about why.

Simmel disagrees. We get a ton of dense details about his ideas, but the phrases "removing the moral bias" and "objective study" let us know that he viewed secrets as morally neutral. The phrase "his contention that secrets are morally neutral" kind of helps with that, too.

But it seems that the picture is more complicated. Disclosure of a secret is immoral, and that has consequences for the secret itself.

All these details about the Kpelle and their ideology are just one example of secrecy research.

All this stuff is consistent with Simmel, apparently.

¶1 Secrets traditionally thought to be negative; Simmel says secrets themselves neutral, but disclosure immoral.

¶2 An example fitting Simmel's theory.

Topic: Secrecy ←⌐

Scope: Simmel's theories about ⌐⌐

Purpose: Describe ⌐ with an example

36. A

Remember not to consider details on their own but in context. Lines 31–32 clearly imply that "the abyss" is a bad thing. But the sentence before says "inherent in every secret lies the possibility, and the desire, for revelation—regardless of the consequences." And the phrase "*the attraction of* the abyss" fits with that desire very well. Our prediction, then, is that the abyss is something that is fascinating and whose interest outweighs its potential dangers. (A) matches that prediction perfectly. The only other tempting answer is (D), but with no mention of "the consequences," it is insufficient. Notice that (E) uses a definition of the term *abyss*. Watch out for this common wrong-answer trap. You are not looking for the definition you would find in the dictionary; you are looking for the definition as used in the passage.

37. B

Because of the phrase *based on the passage*, this counts as an Inference question—we need the situation that must be a violation of the Kpelle rules, which are detailed in ¶2. It's a lot to read; the rules are mentioned all the way from line 38 to line 60. Best to go answer by answer. (A) is permitted by the rules, as lines 57–60 explicitly say. (B) is the right answer—lines 53–55 say, "if nonmembers learn secrets, they are restricted from revealing that they know," and lines 48–50 say, "Kpelle tradition insists that nonmembers are not allowed to know [secrets]." The situation in (B) violates these rules.

(C) is tempting but explicitly permitted according to lines 50–51: "Anyone may, in fact, know a society's secrets." So the act of learning wouldn't itself be a violation. As long as he doesn't tell anyone, he's following the rules. (D) describes a situation that *might* violate the rules, but that's not enough for the right answer to a GMAT Inference question. We don't know who's overhearing the women in question. If they are overheard by nonmembers, that would be a violation. If only other initiated members could hear them, it would be perfectly permissible. (E) is permitted by the rules since it's fine to talk about the form rather than the content of secrets (lines 57–60).

38. D

As with any Inference question that lacks a specific detail reference, we have no choice but to evaluate each answer one by one, researching the passage for support. (A) distorts the first sentence, in which secrets are not defined by the kind of information but by its moral content. (B) is a "180," an answer that contradicts the passage.

EXPERT EXCLUSIVE

One could have answered this question correctly purely by eliminating answers with extreme language—*anything, must, all,* and *impossible*.

The author points out in lines 26–28 a possible contradiction in Simmel's work, but in 24–26 she says that Simmel "facilitated the objective study of secrets." So clearly some contradictions are permitted within good work. (C) is too extreme. "All Kpelle are expected to join," we read in lines 39–40, but that doesn't mean that all fulfill that expectation. (D), the assertion that how people behave is at least as important as what they know, fits very well with the Kpelle rules. Since it's not knowing a secret that one shouldn't know but rather discussing it that's prohibited, actions clearly count more than knowledge to the Kpelle. The passage says explicitly that this fits Simmel's theory. So (D) is correct. (E) may seem tempting because the author points out that Simmel didn't fully escape the moral dimension of secrets. But that Simmel didn't do it, or even that no one has yet done it, isn't the same as its being impossible to do. (E) is too extreme.

SARS Passage: Questions 39–44

PASSAGE	ANALYSIS
The study of the outbreak of [SARS] between late fall 2002 and the summer of 2003 is a **fascinating** look into how **exponentially** fast contagious viruses can spread throughout the world's population . . . **however**, age seemed to play the **most important** role . . .	The Topic is either SARS itself or the '02–'03 outbreak. Two emphasis keywords draw our attention to the disease's spread.
	Some details on the spread and how deadly SARS can be, especially to the elderly.
SARS is a viral infection of the respiratory system **caused by** . . . SARS is spread through . . . The **first** symptoms are . . . Many SARS patients **eventually** develop . . . the **only** one that is **universal** . . . is a very high fever . . .	Tons of details about SARS. We'll come back here if we have questions about causes or symptoms.
The **first recorded case** of SARS occurred in November 2002 . . . **Analysis** . . . has revealed several groups of outbreaks . . . **Yet curiously**, no links have been uncovered among those **initial** human cases . . . **However**, scientists have discovered the SARS virus in three different animals . . .	Now we're talking about the outbreak. We get some details on where it began and a puzzle about the relationships.

SARS seems to have been **spread** outside of the province by a Chinese doctor . . . The doctor went to Hong Kong . . . he somehow **transmitted** SARS to 16 other hotel guests . . . Those infected guests were the **original seed that spread** the virus to almost 30 countries . . .

A sequence of events that details the spread of SARS.

After the virus was recognized as a **threat** to worldwide health, a global mobilization effort led by the WHO to contain the disease **quickly stopped SARS in its tracks** . . . **Though** the spread of the virus has been thwarted, it **still** remains **one of the most potentially dangerous viruses in the world**. Accordingly, global health authorities are **constantly** on alert for another possible outbreak.

After signifies that the sequence continues.

But now the spread has stopped. SARS is still dangerous, though.

¶1 SARS—age big factor

¶2 Causes & symptoms

¶3 Where outbreak began

¶4 How it spread

¶5 Outbreak stopped; world still on alert

Topic: SARS

Scope: Outbreak of '02–'03

Purpose: Describe the progress of

> **EXPERT EXCLUSIVE**
> Some long passages are just elaborate sequences. In these cases, sequence keywords are the vital ones to find.

39. D

It's easy to get caught up in all the different figures found in this passage, but ¶1 clearly states that of the 916 reported SARS deaths, "almost 50 percent . . . were over 65 years old." Half of approximately 900 is 450, (D). (A) is an approximation of the stated number of total confirmed SARS cases found in line 7. (B) is found by approximating half of the total number of confirmed SARS cases, not the fatalities. (C) is an approximation of the stated number of total SARS fatalities found in line 8. (E) is roughly 10 percent of the SARS fatalities.

EXPERT EXCLUSIVE

Many Logic questions focus on the Big Picture.

40. C

This is one of those seemingly detail-based questions that actually turn out to test your big-picture understanding. The Scope of the passage is the rapid spread of SARS, as first hinted by the emphasis keywords in ¶1. The question stem draws our attention to lines 18–23, which give examples of how easily the virus can be spread person to person (note the emphasis keyword *simply*). So a good prediction would be "It emphasizes just how easy it is to spread SARS." That's consistent with (C).

(A) is certainly true but is not discussed by this passage. (B) summarizes the sentence addressed by the question stem but not its role within the passage as a whole. (D) misconstrues the context of lines 16–18. (E) is incorrect because no earlier theories of SARS transmission are discussed.

41. A

With no specific reference in the question stem to any part of the passage, we'll have to evaluate the answer choices one by one. ¶3 discusses the first SARS cases, so that's where to look for support for (A). The last sentence of that paragraph mentions that the SARS virus was found in several animals, "each considered a delicacy." So exposure to infected meat is supported. But did this cause those first human cases? Sure enough, the answer lies in the context of that sentence. One sentence up, we read that "curiously, no links have been uncovered among those initial human cases." The sentence about the infected animals begins with the keyword *However*. Therefore, the detail about the infected meat *contrasts* with the idea that there's no link to explain how those people became infected—implying that the meat may have been responsible. (A) is correct.

(B) and (C) are incorrect because in the passage there is no mention or suggestion of a possible SARS vaccine or malicious intentions on the part of the Chinese doctor. (D) is directly contradicted by the final sentence. And (E) is contradicted as well: the passage states that shortly after the WHO became aware of the virus, it led a worldwide effort that "quickly stopped SARS in its tracks."

42. B

The Chinese-American businessman is mentioned in line 62. Since four answer choices are mentioned, it is probably most efficient to go answer by answer, researching throughout the context of line 62.

Of all the choices, the only one not supported by facts from the passage is choice (B). For the Chinese-American businessman to be able to transmit "the virus to 20 hospital workers in Singapore," he certainly must have been in a hospital there. However, the very next sentence states that from Singapore, he was "transferred to a Hong Kong hospital where he died."

(A) is incorrect because lines 56–57 point out that all 16 infected guests (one of whom was the businessman) stayed on the ninth floor. (C) is a direct paraphrase of lines 65–67. (D) was the trickiest of the answer choices because the support for it does not come directly from ¶3. However, it can be eliminated because ¶2 points out that the one symptom "universal among all confirmed SARS patients is a very high fever." The businessman was a SARS patient; therefore, he had a high fever. Spotting those emphasis keywords of *only* and *universal* as you read the passage would have gotten you ready for this choice. Lines 63–65, the same that contradict the facts of (A), directly support the facts of (E), so (E) can be eliminated as well.

> **EXPERT EXCLUSIVE**
>
> Take care with EXCEPT questions; after a few answer choices, it's easy to forget that you're looking for what's *not* supported.

43. E

(A) is incorrect, since information on SARS mortality rates in ¶1 demonstrates that the risk of dying from SARS increases with age. (B) is incorrect because, aside from being extreme, it violates the entire sense of the passage, which does trace the origins of an outbreak. (C) is also extreme—coronaviruses may be especially contagious, but there's nothing to suggest that they are the most deadly. And since there's nothing in the passage that discusses whether men or women are more susceptible, (D) is incorrect. Lines 62–64 show that one patient was able to transmit SARS to 20 hospital workers. Add to that the details from lines 18–23, which demonstrate how easily SARS can be spread through close contact, and there's plenty of support for (E).

44. A

Since a title must describe the passage as a whole, this is a Global question. A good prediction based on the Topic, Scope, and Purpose would be something like "A Description of the '02–'03 SARS Outbreak." That's a great fit with (A), the correct answer, which also references how deadly the disease is, a fact stressed throughout the passage.

> **EXPERT EXCLUSIVE**
>
> Author's opinion isn't signaled by the tone of the rhetoric but rather by whether she commits herself to a specific viewpoint.

(B) and (C) focus only on small details. (D) distorts the subject of the last paragraph—the world response—confusing *response* with *impact*. (And even if ¶5 did talk about the world impact, we need an answer that fits the whole passage, not one paragraph.) (E) is explicitly contradicted by the last two sentences of the passage; if SARS "remains one of the most potentially dangerous viruses in the world," it can hardly be said to have been conquered.

Mobile Phone Passage: Questions 45–50

PASSAGE	ANALYSIS
. . . over 800 million mobile phone users . . . Underscoring this **dramatic** number is a **growing suspicion** that the radiation emitted by these mobile phones may be **dangerous** . . . **but the question is**, do these levels pose a health risk?	Once again, emphasis words draw our attention to the Scope—in this case, the radiation emitted by mobile phones.
	If the author asks a question herself, we can be reasonably sure that the passage will address it! What will the answer be?
Mobile phones employ radio waves . . . Deeming a phone "safe," **however, is misleading.** The FDA states that **though** there is "**no hard evidence of adverse health effects** . . . it **urges** further research into the subject. This statement is **vague at best,** and **rather than** answering our question, it brings up a number of others.	Oodles of detail about how mobile phones work.
	Here's the important part, and it's riddled with opinion, emphasis, and contrast keywords. The FDA says, "No risk," but the author thinks that the FDA is ducking the issue.
This **vague** stance . . . **derives from the fact** that most of the research findings on the possible **negative** effects of cell phone radiation have been **controversial**. An **example** of this . . . could be linked to cancer and brain tumors. With **good reason**, these findings garnered much media attention, **but** they could never be clinically replicated, which cast **serious doubt** upon them. It is **worth noting, however**, that one of the studies that tried to **confirm** Lai's findings was conducted by a group funded by the cell phone manufacturer Motorola.	There's a lot to read in this paragraph, as signaled by all these keywords. We learn what the evidence of negative effects is . . .
	. . . and why that evidence is controversial.
	The use of *however* indicates that the author has suspicions about the Motorola-funded study.

Regardless . . . time will offer **the true answer** as to whether cell phones are indeed **dangerous. Let's hope** the outcome . . . does not reach us **too late**.

Despite all of the author's negative emphasis, she does not explicitly say that cell phones are, in fact, dangerous. She certainly uses some negative rhetoric, but there's nothing that commits her to an answer to the question she raised in ¶1.

¶1 Are cell phones dangerous?

¶2 How cell phones work; vague FDA assurance of safety

¶3 Evidence of danger; problems with evidence

¶4 Time will tell

Topic: Cell phones

Scope: Potential danger from radiation from —

Purpose: Discuss

45. E

The author spent the entire passage addressing the question she raised in ¶1. Despite strong language, she never answered the question one way or the other, instead merely pointing out evidence on each side. That rules out (A), (B), and (D). (E) is correct. (C) focuses only on details from ¶2.

46. B

Researching the context of the detail to which this Inference question sends us, and keeping the author's voice in mind, would allow us to predict an answer. The sentence after line 25 says that the term *safe* is "misleading." The author characterizes the FDA's statement as "vague at best," pointing out that "no hard evidence" of danger is different from "safe." So we're looking for the answer that's most consistent with something like "no good evidence of danger." That fits with (B).

(A) is too strong for the author's viewpoint, and (C) is more extreme still (so extreme, in fact, that it winds up contradicting the author's statement that the term *safe* is "misleading"). (D) and (E) are incorrect in the other direction—"no hard evidence" of danger can hardly be construed to mean "dangerous."

EXPERT EXCLUSIVE

Read answer choices carefully. There's a world of difference, for example, between "Henry Lai's team concluded" and "the author concluded"; so too between "unnecessary" and "necessary." Two little letters can change a right answer to a wrong answer!

47. C

The Detail question requires you to go answer by answer, looking for the one choice that's explicitly supported by the passage. (A) distorts lines 11–15, which never mention the battery. (B) is directly contradicted by lines 25–27. (C) leads you to lines 42–46, which tell you what Lai's team concluded. And sure enough, the context of that sentence leads you to "cancer and brain tumors." (C), then, is correct. (D) is directly contradicted by lines 28–31, which say that the FDA "urges further research." And since there is no discussion of different types of phones, (E) is out of scope.

48. B

The language in this question stem fits both Detail and Inference questions. *Inferred* lets us know that the right answer won't be in the text explicitly, but *according to* lets us know that the support itself will be fairly explicit. Only one sentence discusses devices that emit RF energy—lines 11–15. This sentence says that mobile phones use RF "to transmit voice data and other information wirelessly between handsets and base stations." So while we can't predict what specific device the right answer choice will name, we do know that wireless transmission is a key factor. Only (B) must be wireless (that's what *broadcast* implies), so it's our right answer. (A) is out because a "standard" phone uses wires. Radios *receive* RF energy but don't necessarily emit any; radio speakers emit sound. So (D) is wrong. And while DVD players and Internet routers *can* be wireless, they don't *have* to be. So (C) and (E) are out.

EXPERT EXCLUSIVE

Correct answers in Inference questions *must* be true. Answers that *might* be true are wrong.

49. A

Here's another hybrid question—Logic/Inference. What's the *suggested* purpose of the detail? As we research, we see that the contrast keyword *however* implies that the study in question ran counter to the idea from the previous sentence, which tells us that there are serious doubts about "these findings." What findings? Lai's, which suggest that cell phones could be dangerous. So the fact that Motorola funded a confirmation study lends doubt to the idea that said study undercut Lai's. Our prediction is something like "a potential problem in the confirmation study."

That leads us to (A) and to (C). But (C) is too extreme to fit with this passage— "possible bias" is a much better fit for the GMAT than "actively trying to sabotage." So (A) is correct.

(B) distorts the connection between Lai and the confirmation study. (D) might be true, but we are not told anything about *why* Motorola funded the study, only what effects that funding might have had. Lai's results might not have been confirmed, but it's too extreme to say that he was lying, so (E) is incorrect.

50. A

This Logic question asks the purpose of the last sentence. The previous sentence reflects the point of the paragraph—that even though current research isn't conclusive, time will reveal whether cell phones are dangerous. The cigarette essentially reminds us that once before, there was a product that everyone said was safe but turned out not to be. In other words, the author is illustrating her point with precedent. (A) is correct.

> **EXPERT EXCLUSIVE**
>
> You may see one or two unusual question types on test day, so make sure you understand what the question is asking before solving it.

(B) distorts the purpose of the comparison—the author is concerned with cancer, not addictive behavior. (C) is too extreme; certainly the author uses some negative emphasis, but she ultimately doesn't give any opinion other than "the issue isn't settled yet." (D), like (B) distorts the author's scope; while there is social etiquette for cell phones and for cigarettes, the author does not discuss it. (E) is tempting, but "exaggerate" is too extreme; we ourselves may not think that cell phones are as dangerous as cigarettes, but our own ideas can get us in trouble—there's no support *in the passage* for the idea that this is an exaggeration.

CHAPTER 7: QUANTITATIVE SECTION STRATEGIES AND PRACTICE

- What the Quantitative Section Tests
- Quantitative Analysis
- How to Manage the Quantitative Section
- How the Quantitative Section Is Scored

A little less than half of the GMAT multiple-choice questions are Quantitative (math) questions. You'll have 75 minutes to answer 37 math questions in two formats: Problem Solving and Data Sufficiency. These two formats are mingled throughout the Quantitative section, so you never know what's coming next. Here's what you can expect to see.

Quantitative Question Type	Approximate Number of Questions
Problem Solving	22
Data Sufficiency	15
Total:	37 questions

WHAT THE QUANTITATIVE SECTION TESTS

Of course, the GMAT tests your math skills. So you will have to use knowledge that you might not have thought much about for a few years. And even if you use math all the time, it's probably been a while since you couldn't use a calculator or computer. So getting some oil into the math gears is definitely a crucial part of your prep.

EXPERT EXCLUSIVE

The GMAT only covers math that U.S. students usually see during or before their first two years of high school. No trigonometry, no advanced algebra, no calculus.

But the range of math topics tested is actually fairly limited. The same concepts are tested again and again in remarkably similar ways.

Arithmetic is the most commonly tested topic in GMAT math, covering about half of all the questions. **Algebra** is second, covering about one-quarter of the questions. **Geometry** questions account for less than one-sixth of all GMAT math questions. The other questions relate to a variety of less frequently tested topics, such as graphs and logic.

The good news is that if you're comfortable with arithmetic and algebra, you've already taken a big step toward doing well on the GMAT. Don't worry if you haven't done math in school for a long time. You're using it all the time in daily life; every time you leave a 15 percent tip, you're practicing one of your most important GMAT math skills—percents. So we've included a Math Skills Refresher in Part Six that shows you exactly what concepts are being tested on the GMAT.

QUANTITATIVE ANALYSIS

Most of the math tests you've taken before—even other standardized tests like the SAT and the ACT—ask questions in a fairly straightforward way. You know pretty quickly how you should solve the problem, and the only thing holding you back is how quickly or accurately you can do the math.

But the GMAT is a little different. Often the most difficult part of a GMAT Quantitative problem is figuring out what math skills to use in the first place! In fact, the GMAT's hardest Quant problems are about 95 percent analysis, 5 percent calculation. You'll have to do the following:

- Understand complicated or awkward phrasing.
- Process information presented in an illogical order.
- Analyze incomplete information.
- Simplify complicated information.

> **EXPERT EXCLUSIVE**
>
> The harder the problem, the more analysis you need to do *before* you use your math skills.

In the next few chapters, we'll show you how to approach Quant problems strategically so you can do the analysis that will lead you to efficient solutions, correct answers, and a high score.

But first, let's look at some techniques for managing the whole section.

HOW TO MANAGE THE QUANTITATIVE SECTION

The best way to attack the computer-adaptive GMAT is to exploit the way it determines your score. Here's what you're dealing with:

- **Penalties:** If you run out of time at the end of the section, you get a penalty that's about twice what you'd have received if you got all those answers wrong. *And* there's an extra penalty for long strings of wrong answers at the end.

- **No review:** There is no going back to check your work. You cannot go back to double-check your earlier answers or skip past a question that's puzzling to try it again later. So if you finish early, you won't be able to use that remaining time.
- **Difficulty level adjustment:** Questions get harder or easier, depending on your performance. Hard questions raise your score more when you get them right and hurt your score less when you get them wrong. Easier questions are the opposite—getting them right helps your score less, and getting them wrong hurts your score more.

What you do *before* the test will make the real difference. Obviously, the best of both worlds is being able to get the early questions mostly right, while taking less than *two minutes per question on average* so that you have a little extra time to think about those harder questions later on. To achieve that goal, you need to do three things:

> **EXPERT EXCLUSIVE**
>
> Solving quickly doesn't mean rushing! Rushing = wrong answer! Rather, solving quickly means taking an approach that's faster to execute than the "straight math"–estimating instead of calculating, for example, or picking actual numbers to replace the variables.

(1) **Know your math basics cold:** Don't waste valuable time sweating over adding fractions, reverse-FOILing quadratic equations, or using the rate formula. When you do math, you want to feel right at home. The math skills review in this book will show you exactly what math skills and concepts you can expect to encounter on test day.

(2) **Look for shortcuts:** Most GMAT problems have many possible solutions. So the test makers deliberately build in shortcuts and "back doors" to reward critical thinkers with extra time. We'll show you how to find them!

(3) **Practice, practice, practice:** Do lots of practice problems so that you get as familiar as possible with the GMAT's most common analytical puzzles. That way you can handle them quickly (and correctly!) when you see them on test day. We've got tons in the upcoming chapters.

If you do this, you'll do more than just set yourself up to manage the section well. You'll also set a solid foundation for the section—a level of question difficulty that you will always get right. That way, if you struggle on a few hard questions and go down to the midrange questions, that's OK! Because you'll get all of them right, which will send you right back up to the high-value hard questions again.

Also, during the test, do your best not to fall behind early on. Don't rush, but don't linger. Those first 5 questions shouldn't take more than 10 minutes total, and the first 10 questions shouldn't take more than 20 minutes. If you notice that you are falling behind, try to solve some questions more quickly (or if you're stuck, make strategic guesses) to catch up.

EXPERT EXCLUSIVE

Since missing hard questions doesn't hurt your score very much but not finishing definitely does, making a few guesses on the hardest questions so that you can finish on time may well earn you your highest possible score.

STRATEGIC GUESSING

Occasionally, you'll find that you have to make a guess, but don't guess at random. Narrowing down the answer choices first is imperative! Otherwise, your odds of getting the right answer will be pretty slim. Follow this plan when you guess:

(1) **Avoid answer choices that make you suspicious.** You can get rid of these without doing any work on the problem! These answer choices just look wrong, or they conform to common wrong-answer types. For example, if only one of the answer choices in a Problem Solving question is negative, chances are that it will be incorrect.

(2) **Eliminate answer choices you know are wrong.** You can often identify wrong answer choices after a little calculation. For instance, on Data Sufficiency questions, you can eliminate at least two answer choices by determining the sufficiency of just one statement.

(3) **Choose one of the remaining answer choices.** By choosing from fewer options, your chances of getting the question right go way up. You definitely want those odds!

EXPERT EXCLUSIVE

It's hard to judge the true difficulty level of a question. A question that seems easy to you may simply be playing to your personal strengths and be very difficult for many other test takers. So treat every question as if it counts!

EXPERIMENTAL QUESTIONS

Some questions on the test are experimental. These questions are not factored into your score. They are questions that the GMAC is evaluating for possible use on future tests. To get good data, the test makers have to test each question against the whole range of test takers—that is, high and low scorers. Therefore, you could be on your way to an 800 and suddenly come across a question that feels out of line with how you think you are doing.

Don't panic! Just do your best and keep on going. The difficulty level of the experimental questions you see has little to do with how you're currently scoring. And remember, there is no way for you to know for sure whether a question is experimental or not, so treat every question as if it were scored.

HOW THE QUANTITATIVE SECTION IS SCORED

The Quantitative section of the GMAT is quite different from the math sections of most paper-and-pencil tests. The major difference between the test formats is that the CAT adapts to your performance. Each test taker is given a different mix of questions depending on how well he is doing on the test. The questions get harder or easier depending on whether the current question is answered correctly or not. Your score is not directly determined by how many questions you get right but by how hard the questions you get right are.

When you start a section, the computer

- assumes you have an average score (500); and
- gives you a medium-difficulty question. About half of the people who take the test will get this question right, and half will get it wrong. What happens next depends on whether you answer the question correctly.

As you answer questions correctly,

- your score goes up; and
- you are given a slightly harder question.

As you answer questions incorrectly,

- your score goes down; and
- you are given a slightly easier questions.

> **EXPERT EXCLUSIVE**
> At the printing of this book, the 50th percentile on the Quant section was a raw score of 39 out of 51.

> **EXPERT EXCLUSIVE**
> If you're struggling at the end, feeling like you're missing half the questions, don't panic! It's OK. In fact, it's what's supposed to happen.

CHAPTER 8: **PROBLEM SOLVING**

- Question Format and Structure
- The Basic Principles of Problem Solving
- The Kaplan Method for Problem Solving

Problem Solving questions test basic math skills and an understanding of some elementary mathematical concepts—ones most U.S. students have learned by 10th grade. Most importantly, they test the ability to reason quantitatively.

If business schools wanted to know how much math you knew, they could easily look at your college transcript to see what math classes you took and how you fared in them. So why require the GMAT? Because they want to look at something else. In business school, you will be given *a lot* of information, especially in case studies. One of the biggest challenges you'll face will be figuring out how to think about all that information—how it fits together, what deductions you can make from it, and how it pertains to business challenges.

So the Quantitative section presents you with microcosms of that task—mathematical puzzles in which the data is often presented in a confusing or misleading way, demanding that you first figure out how you can solve the puzzles before beginning any calculations. Hence the name "Problem Solving" instead of just "Math."

The more difficult questions rarely involve math that is much more difficult than the math used in intermediate-range questions. Rather, the task of analyzing the problem to figure out what math to use gets harder.

Happily, the format of the questions is simple enough: a standard multiple-choice question with five answer choices. To answer a question, select the choice that correctly answers the question.

QUESTION FORMAT AND STRUCTURE

The instructions for the Problem Solving questions look like this:

> **Directions:** Solve the problems and choose the best answer.
>
> **Note:** Unless otherwise indicated, the figures accompanying questions have been drawn as accurately as possible and may be used as sources of information for answering the questions.
>
> All figures lie in a plane except where noted.
>
> All numbers used are real numbers.

 **GO ONLINE**

Your downloadable study sheet summarizes many key math principles and strategies.

There are about 22 Problem Solving questions on each GMAT Quantitative section. The directions indicate that some diagrams on the GMAT are drawn to scale, which means that you can use them to estimate measurements and size relationships. Other diagrams are labeled "Not drawn to scale," so you can't eyeball them. In fact, when a diagram says "Not drawn to scale," working past the confusing picture is often the key to the problem.

The directions also let you know that you won't have to deal with imaginary numbers, such as $\sqrt{-1}$, and that you'll be dealing with flat figures, such as squares and circles, unless a particular question says otherwise.

THE BASIC PRINCIPLES OF PROBLEM SOLVING

By adopting a systematic approach to Problem Solving, you will have a clear, concise method for thinking through your way to a response. You won't waste time by attacking a question in a tentative or haphazard manner, nor will you get stuck doing inefficient math. A systematic approach will ensure that you find the most efficient solution to the problem and that you make as few careless and unnecessary errors as possible.

ANALYZE AND SIMPLIFY BEFORE SOLVING

The biggest mistake test takers make on GMAT Problem Solving is doing the math right after reading the problem (or even more dangerously, *while* reading the problem). Problem Solving questions are written to be confusing, and the approach that the question might seem to be talking you into is usually not the most efficient. Consider this problem:

> At a certain diner, Joe ordered 3 doughnuts and a cup of coffee and was charged $2.25. Stella ordered 2 doughnuts and a cup of coffee and was charged $1.70. What is the price of 2 doughnuts?
>
> ○ $0.55
>
> ○ $1.00
>
> ○ $1.10
>
> ○ $1.30
>
> ○ $1.80

Someone who started doing math right away might have immediately jotted down something like $J = 3d + c$, thereby making the problem a lot tougher by introducing a variable, J, that really doesn't need to be part of the solution. Someone else might slavishly use x and y instead of d and c, making her job harder, as a part of her brain that could be used to solve the problem will be taken up remembering whether x stood for doughnuts or coffee.

EXPERT EXCLUSIVE

Time invested in analysis usually pays off in a much more efficient solution and in less time spent on the question overall.

However, someone who analyzes the question before getting into math might say, "Hang on a sec . . . those orders are very similar . . . in fact, they are different by only one doughnut! So the price of a doughnut could be calculated just by subtracting the prices of the orders!" And while that first person is wasting time writing out $S = 2d + c$, this person has almost completely solved the problem.

Here's another example of the benefit of analysis and simplification:

> What is the product of all the possible values of x if
>
> $$x^2(x+2) + 7x(x+2) + 6(x+2) = 0?$$
>
> ○ −29
>
> ○ −12
>
> ○ 12
>
> ○ 29
>
> ○ 168

Doing math before any analysis, we'd distribute the multiplication and get $x^3 + 9x^2 + 20x + 12 = 0$. Yecch. Not simple.

But if we analyze first, we'd say, "If I distribute, I'll get some nasty-looking cubic equation. There's got to be an easier way. If only all those $(x + 2)$s were gone, I'd have a normal quadratic, and those aren't so bad. Hey! That's it! I can "get rid of" those $(x + 2)$s by factoring them out!" And then we are on our way to solving:

$$x^2(x + 2) + 7x(x + 2) + 6(x + 2) = 0$$

Factor: $(x + 2)(x^2 + 7x + 6) = 0$ ⟵——— much simpler

Reverse-FOIL: $(x + 2)(x + 6)(x + 1) = 0$

Solve for x: $x = -2$ or -6 or -1

Multiply: $-2 \times -6 \times -1 = -12$

Focus on What's Asked

Go back to the problem with the doughnuts and the coffee. Did you spot the trap? The question doesn't ask for the price of a doughnut but rather for the price of *two* doughnuts. Sure enough, one of the answer choices gives the cost of only one.

Focusing on what's asked will also help you to choose an efficient approach. Consider this question:

> **EXPERT EXCLUSIVE**
>
> In this question, answer choices (A) and (D) are the value of the individual variables. Right answers to the wrong questions are the most common wrong answer type in Problem Solving.

If $4x + y = 8$ and $y - 3x = 7$, then what is the value of $x + 2y$?

○ $\dfrac{1}{7}$

○ 3

○ 15

○ $\dfrac{52}{7}$

○ $\dfrac{60}{7}$

We might just rush into solving for x and y and then plugging them in, but let's focus on what we're asked for: not x or y individually but rather $x + 2y$. How could we solve for *that*? Well, one equation has $4x$ and the other $-3x$. Together, that's x. Each has one y, so together that's $2y$. Aha! We just add the equations together!

We'll just rearrange $y - 3x = 7$ to $-3x + y = 7$ so things line up nicely.

Combine equations:
$$\begin{array}{r} 4x + y = 8 \\ +[-3x + y = 7] \\ \hline x + 2y = 15 \end{array}$$

Look how quick that was! And all because we focused on the question.

Consider Alternative Approaches

We just saw three questions that were all solved easiest in a manner other than the math that might first occur to us. We added equations in the $x + 2y$ problem, factored instead of multiplied in the $(x + 2)$ problem, and if we picked up on the potential shortcut to the diner problem, then we'd subtract equations:

$$
\begin{array}{r}
(3d + 1c = 2.25) \\
-[2d + 1c = 1.70] \\
\hline
d \quad\;\; = 0.55 \\
2d \quad\;\; = 1.10
\end{array}
$$

The lesson: It pays to *think* about what you're doing before diving into math. Most problems can be solved many different ways, some easy and some not so easy. The GMAT writes the questions in such a way that the first approaches that occur to us are usually of the not-so-easy variety. So keep turning the problem over in your mind until you find an approach that will work. Trust your intuition—if you're thinking of a solution and say to yourself, "Ucch, this feels way too hard," then look for a different approach. If you say, "Oh, yeah! I can definitely solve this way," then you've got a good approach.

> **EXPERT EXCLUSIVE**
>
> *Easy* is a relative term. What's not easy to some may be easy for you and vice versa.

Here's how someone who trusts their intuition might approach a very hard question, considering different approaches until finding one that works:

$$
\begin{array}{r}
AB \\
+\; BA \\
\hline
187
\end{array}
$$

In the addition problem above, *A* and *B* represent digits in two different two-digit numbers. What is the sum of *A* and *B*?

- ○ 9
- ○ 13
- ○ 15
- ○ 17
- ○ 23

> **EXPERT EXCLUSIVE**
>
> Being able to solve for an expression without being able to solve for individual variables is a common GMAT pattern.

"Well. Hmm. I'm really not sure how to begin approaching this one. First of all, what does 'A and B represent digits in two different two-digit numbers' even *mean*? Let's see . . . I know that a digit is any of the integers 0 through 9 and that a two-digit number is something like 42, or 11. Oh, I get it! *AB* is a two-digit number with *A* in the tens place and *B* in the units place. If *A* is 3 and *B* is 5, then *AB* is 35.

"Alright, now I know what I'm looking at. How do I solve? I could just experiment with different possibilities, plugging different combinations of digits in until I get *AB* + *BA* = 187. But since there are 10 digits, there'd be something like 100 different possible combinations. I really don't want to do that.

"There's got to be some other way to solve. Maybe this is one of those questions where I can solve for the expression I'm asked about without figuring out the individual variables. Alright . . . 'sum of A and B' . . . that's $A + B$. Where am I going to get $A + B$ from? Let me look back at the question stem . . . Hey! I see $A + B$:

$$\begin{array}{r} AB \\ + BA \\ \hline 187 \end{array}$$

EXPERT EXCLUSIVE

Notice the high ratio of analysis to math needed to solve this problem. That's the hallmark of the most difficult GMAT problems.

"So the answer is the sum of the digits in the tens place. Is the answer 18? Well, for one thing, 18 doesn't seem to be an answer choice. For another thing, who's to say that this $A + B$ in the tens column isn't getting any spillover from the $B + A$ in the units column? So the answer might be 18, but might be less. Ugh. This won't work, either. Oh well, at least I know that answer (E) is too large, since the answer is either 18 or something less.

"Hey . . . wait a second . . .. $B + A$? That's the same as $A + B$. So the answer is also the sum of the digits in the units places:

$$\begin{array}{r} A\,|B \\ + B\,|A \\ \hline 18\,|7 \end{array}$$

"So the units digit of the answer has to be 7. Let me look at the answers . . . AHA!!! Only (D) has a 7 in the units place. So the answer has to be (D)! Awesome. I am just crushing this test!"

Notice this test taker isn't put off by the challenging presentation of the problem, even though she isn't sure at first how she's going to solve it. Notice how she separates what she understands from what she doesn't, so she doesn't feel overwhelmed. Notice too how she keeps turning over possible approaches, rejecting them the minute they get too hard to follow or seem not to be working. She uses what she knows about the GMAT to help her, and she looks everywhere for clues to the solution—both in the question stem and in the answer choices.

That's the attitude to develop, the attitude that all great test takers share: that there must be a straightforward way to solve and there's no need to panic if it isn't found right away. And even if she doesn't find the algebra-based solution that her high school math teacher would have wanted, she gets the right answer and controls the test.

Of course, most alternative approaches don't take that much work to find. But they all involve staying open to approaches that might not occur to you immediately. Two such approaches are so straightforward, can eliminate so much math, and can be used so often that they deserve special mention. These two are Picking Numbers and Backsolving.

Picking Numbers

Picking Numbers is a powerful alternative to solving problems by brute force. Rather than trying to work with unknown variables, you pick concrete values for the variables. In essence, you're transforming algebra or abstract math rules into basic arithmetic, a much simpler task! Pick Numbers to stand in for the variables or unknowns.

How does Picking Numbers work?

- Pick **permissible** numbers; some problems have explicit rules like "x is odd." Other problems have implicit rules. For example, if a word problem says, "Betty is five years older than Tim," don't pick $b = -2$ and $t = -7$; they just wouldn't make any sense in the problem.

- Pick **manageable** numbers. Some numbers are simply easier to work with than others. $d = 2$ will probably be a more successful choice than will $d = 492\sqrt{\pi}$, for example. The problems themselves will tell you what's manageable. For instance, $d = 2$ wouldn't be a great pick if an answer choice were $\dfrac{d}{12}$. (The numbers 12, 24, or even 120 would be much better in that case because they are all divisible by 12.)

- Approach the problem as basic arithmetic instead of algebra or number properties.

- Test every answer choice—sometimes certain numbers will yield a "false positive" in which a wrong answer looks right. If you get more than one "right answer," just pick a new set of numbers. The truly correct answer must work for all permissible numbers.

> **EXPERT EXCLUSIVE**
>
> Say "permissible and manageable" to yourself every time you Pick Numbers so you don't make the problem more difficult than it needs to be.

Contrary to popular myth, it's just fine to pick 0 or 1. True, the special properties of 0 and 1 do sometimes cause "false positives." But so do other numbers. And the GMAT sometimes writes questions based on those special properties, so if you aren't considering 0 and 1, you won't get the right answer to those questions. Furthermore, they are the most manageable numbers in all of math. Imagine Picking Numbers for the following problem with anything other than $b = 0$ or $b = 1$:

$$7^b + 7^b + 7^b + 7^b + 7^b + 7^b + 7^b =$$

- ○ 7^b
- ○ 7^{b+1}
- ○ 7^{7b}
- ○ 8^b
- ○ 49^b

The occasional inconvenience of repicking numbers is far outweighed by the advantages that 0 and 1 provide.

Picking $b = 1$:

$$= 7^b + 7^b + 7^b + 7^b + 7^b + 7^b + 7^b$$
$$= 7^1 + 7^1 + 7^1 + 7^1 + 7^1 + 7^1 + 7^1$$
$$= 7 + 7 + 7 + 7 + 7 + 7 + 7$$
$$= 49$$

Plugging $b = 1$ into the answer choices yields

(A) 7

(B) 49

(C) 7^7—Whatever that is, it's a lot bigger than 49.

(D) 8

(E) 49

So we need to pick a new number. Let's try $b = 0$.

$$= 7^b + 7^b + 7^b + 7^b + 7^b + 7^b + 7^b$$
$$= 7^0 + 7^0 + 7^0 + 7^0 + 7^0 + 7^0 + 7^0$$
$$= 1 + 1 + 1 + 1 + 1 + 1 + 1$$
$$= 7$$

Plugging $b = 0$ into (B) and (E), the two possible answers, yields

(B) 7

(E) 1

The answer is (B).

> **EXPERT EXCLUSIVE**
>
> The advice to avoid 0 and 1 is among the most commonly offered bad advice out there. Though 0 and 1 have properties that can complicate some problems, those same properties let these numbers radically simplify others. Don't be scared out of using two of the most powerful and manageable numbers in all of math!

There are four signals that Picking Numbers will be a possible approach to the problem:

(1) Asked for a Fraction of an Unknown Whole

(2) Variable(s) in the Answer Choices

(3) Multiple Variables in the Question Stem

(4) Asked for What "Could Be," "Must Be," "Cannot Be," etc.

These aren't in any particular order. You'll see many instances of each case on test day. We'll start with the first.

Asked for a Fraction of an Unknown Whole

In this case, pick a number for the total and walk through the arithmetic of the problem. Look in the question stem and the answer choices for clues about what the most manageable number might be.

Example: Carol spends $\frac{1}{4}$ of her savings on a stereo and $\frac{1}{3}$ less than she spent on the stereo for a television. What fraction of her savings did she spend on the stereo and television?

- ○ $\frac{1}{4}$
- ○ $\frac{2}{7}$
- ○ $\frac{5}{12}$
- ○ $\frac{1}{2}$
- ○ $\frac{7}{12}$

> **EXPERT EXCLUSIVE**
>
> Lowest common denominators of fractions in the question stem are good choices for numbers to pick. So are numbers that appear frequently as denominators in the answer choices.

In this case, the common denominator is 12, so let the number 12 represent Carol's total savings (12 dollars). That means she spends $\frac{1}{4} \times 12$ dollars, or 3 dollars, on her stereo, and $\frac{2}{3} \times 3$ dollars, or 2 dollars, on her television. That comes out to be $3 + 2 = 5$ dollars; that's how much she spent on the stereo and television combined. You're asked what *fraction* of her savings she spent. Because her total savings is 12 dollars, she spent $\frac{5}{12}$ of her savings; (C) is correct. Notice how picking a common denominator for the variable (Carol's savings) made it easy to convert each of the fractions $\left(\frac{1}{4} \text{ and } \frac{2}{3} \times \frac{1}{4} \text{ of her savings} \right)$ to a simple number.

A tricky part of this question is understanding how to determine the price of the television. The television does not cost $\frac{1}{3}$ of her savings. It costs $\frac{1}{3}$ *less* than the stereo; that is, it costs $\frac{2}{3}$ as much as the stereo.

> **CAUTION**
>
> Read carefully. The GMAT will often switch the basis of fractions midway through a problem.

By the way, some of these answers could have been eliminated quickly through basic logic. (A) is too small; the stereo alone costs $\frac{1}{4}$ of her savings. (D) and (E) are too large. The television costs *less* than the stereo, so the two together must cost less than $2 \times \frac{1}{4}$, or half, of Carol's savings. We'll look more at using logic to eliminate answers in a few pages.

A subcategory of this case is when the answers are given in percents.

Example: The manufacturer of Sleep-Ez mattresses is offering a 10% discount on the price of its king-size mattress. Some retailers are offering additional discounts. If a retailer offers an additional 20% discount, then what is the total discount available at that retailer?

- ○ 10%
- ○ 25%
- ○ 28%
- ○ 30%
- ○ 35%

Since the answers are in percents, let's pick the price of the mattress to be $100. (Remember, realism is irrelevant—only permissibility and manageability matter!) The manufacturer offers a 10% discount: 10% of $100 is $10. So now the mattress costs $90.

> **EXPERT EXCLUSIVE**
>
> When the answers are in percents, 100 will almost always be the most manageable number to pick.

Then the retailer offers an additional 20% discount. Since the price has fallen to $90, a 20% discount is now a reduction of $18. The final price of the mattress is $90 − $18, or $72.

The mattress has been reduced to $72 from an original price of $100. That's a $28 reduction. Since we started with $100, $28 is 28% of the original. Choice (C) is correct.

Variable(s) in the Answer Choices

Whenever the answer choices use variables, you should consider Picking Numbers. Make sure that you test each answer choice, just in case.

Example: If $a > 1$, which of the following is equal to $\dfrac{2a+6}{a^2+2a-3}$?

- ○ a
- ○ $a + 3$
- ○ $\dfrac{2}{a-1}$
- ○ $\dfrac{2a}{a-3}$
- ○ $\dfrac{a-1}{2}$

The question says that $a > 1$, so the easiest permissible number will probably be 2. Then $\dfrac{2(2)+6}{2^2+2(2)-3} = \dfrac{4+6}{4+4-3} = \dfrac{10}{5} = 2$. Now let's substitute 2 for a in each answer choice, looking for choices that equal 2 when $a = 2$. We will eliminate choices that do not equal 2 when $a = 2$. Choice (A): $a = 2$. Choice (A) is possibly correct. Choice (B): $a + 3 = 2 + 3 = 5$. This is not 2. Discard. Choice (C): $\dfrac{2}{a-1} = \dfrac{2}{2-1} = \dfrac{2}{1} = 2$. Possibly correct. Choice (D): $\dfrac{2a}{a-3} = \dfrac{2(2)}{2-3} = \dfrac{4}{-1} = -4$. This is not 2. Discard. Choice (E): $\dfrac{a-1}{2} = \dfrac{2-1}{2} = \dfrac{1}{2}$. This is not 2. Discard.

We're down to (A) and (C). When more than one answer choice remains, we must pick another number. Try $a = 3$. Then $\dfrac{2(3)+6}{3^2+2(3)-3} = \dfrac{6+6}{9+6-3} = \dfrac{12}{12} = 1$. Now let's work with the remaining answer choices. Choice (A): $a = 3$. This is not 1. Discard. Now that all four incorrect answer choices have been eliminated, we know that (C) must be correct. Let's check to see if it equals 1 when $a = 3$. Choice (C): $\dfrac{2}{a-1} = \dfrac{2}{3-1} = \dfrac{2}{2} = 1$. Choice (C) does equal 1 when $a = 3$.

A subcategory of this situation is the Word Problem. The test maker is very good at writing confusing word problems. Picking Numbers can resolve a lot of that confusion. The key to Picking Numbers in word problems is to reread the question stem after you've picked numbers, substituting the numbers in place of the variables.

EXPERT EXCLUSIVE
Picking Numbers makes word problems much easier to comprehend.

Example: A car rental company charges for mileage as follows:

x dollars per mile for the first n miles and $x + 1$ dollars per mile for each mile over n miles. How much will the mileage charge be, in dollars, for a journey of d miles, where $d > n$?

○ $d(x + 1) - n$

○ $xn + d$

○ $xn + d(x + 1)$

○ $x(n + d) - d$

○ $(x + 1)(d - n)$

Suppose that you pick $x = 4$, $n = 3$, and $d = 5$. Now the problem would read like this:

A car rental company charges for mileage as follows:
$4 per mile for each of the first 3 miles and $5 per mile for each mile over 3 miles. How much will the mileage charge be, in dollars, for a journey of 5 miles?

All of a sudden, the problem has gotten much more straightforward! The first 3 miles are charged at $4/mile. So that's $4 + $4 + $4, or $12. There are 2 miles remaining, and each one costs $5. So that's $5 + $5, a total of $10. If the first 3 miles cost $12 and the next 2 cost $10, then the total charge is $12 + $10, which is $22.

> **EXPERT EXCLUSIVE**
>
> Picking Numbers one by one, rather than all at once, can help you to pick permissible numbers. Usually it's best to start with the variable that appears most often.

Plugging $x = 4$, $n = 3$, and $d = 5$ into our answer choices, we get

(A) $5(4 + 1) - 3 = 22$

(B) $4 \times 3 + 5 = 17$

(C) $4 \times 3 + 5(4 + 1) = 37$

(D) $4(3 + 5) - 5 = 27$

(E) $(4 + 1)(5 - 3) = 10$

Only (A) yields the desired number, so (A) is the answer. No need for algebra at all.

Multiple Variables in the Question Stem

If a question presents you with multiple unknowns, you can pick numbers even when there are no variables in the answer choices.

Example: If $\dfrac{c-a}{c-b}=2$, then $\dfrac{5b-5a}{c-a}=$

○ 0.5

○ 1

○ 1.5

○ 2

○ 2.5

EXPERT EXCLUSIVE

Even if you can do the math-based solution, Pick Numbers or Backsolve if that's faster. You'll want to use that time to solve harder questions.

Let's start with a manageable number for c but one that's big enough to leave some "wiggle room" to pick numbers for a and b. $c=8$ seems like a good starting point. That gives us

$$\frac{8-a}{8-b}=2$$

If we pick $a=2$, then we have

$$\frac{8-2}{8-b}=\frac{6}{8-b}=2$$

So $8-b$ will have to equal 3. That means $b=5$.

Now all we have to do is plug $c=8$, $a=2$, and $b=5$ into the question:

$$\frac{5b-5a}{c-a}=\frac{(5\times5)-(5\times2)}{8-2}=\frac{25-10}{6}=\frac{15}{6}=\frac{5}{2}=2.5$$

What's the algebraic solution? Who cares! With Picking Numbers we got the answer quickly and easily. On test day, that's exactly what we want.

Asked for What "Could Be," "Must Be," "Cannot Be," etc.

This is a slightly different style of question, usually based not on algebra or arithmetic but rather on the properties of the numbers themselves. Some of these questions can be very abstract, so Picking Numbers really helps—just as with word problems, making a Number Properties question concrete helps us to understand it.

EXPERT EXCLUSIVE

When the phrase "which of the following" appears in a Problem Solving question, the answer is slightly more likely to be (D) or (E) than (A), (B), or (C). Note: This is only true for Problem Solving in the Quantitative section, not for Verbal.

Example: If a and b are odd integers, which of the following must be an even integer?

○ $a(b-2)$

○ $ab+4$

○ $(a+2)(b-4)$

○ $3a+5b$

○ $a(a+6)$

You can run through the answer choices quite quickly using the Picking Numbers strategy. Try $a = 1$, $b = 3$. Only (D), $3 + 15 = 18$, is even.

Another approach that works well for many "must be"/"could be" problems is to pick different numbers for each answer choice, looking to eliminate the wrong answers. The principle of focusing on what's asked is particularly important here, as you need a clear idea of what you're looking for in a wrong answer.

EXPERT EXCLUSIVE

Roman Numeral questions are rare but can be big time wasters if you don't work strategically. Evaluate statements one at a time, eliminating answer choices as you go. Usually you should start with the statement that appears most frequently in the answer choices.

Example: If x and y are distinct factors of 24, then which of the following CANNOT be a factor of 24?

I. $(x + y)^2$

II. $x^2 - y^2$

III. $xy + y^2$

○ I only

○ I and II

○ II and III

○ II only

○ III only

The question asks us to figure out which statement or statements can never be a factor of 24. That means we can eliminate a statement if it could ever possibly be a factor of 24. If we pick some numbers that don't yield a factor of 24, all that means is that the statement *might* be part of the right answer. But if we pick numbers that do yield a factor of 24, we know that any answer with that statement can be eliminated. It'll be much more straightforward, then, to prove answers wrong rather than to prove them right.

Since the question involves factors of 24, it'll be a good idea to list them out:

$$1, 2, 3, 4, 6, 8, 12, 24$$

EXPERT EXCLUSIVE

When a question deals with a small set of specific numbers, write them down. You'll find keeping track of the options to be much easier.

Statement II appears three times, so if we can eliminate it, we'll be down to two answers right away. Squaring something large like 24 or 12 is going to produce a really big number, not a factor of 24. So let's go smaller: $x = 4$ and $y = 2$, perhaps. Then $x^2 - y^2$ would equal $16 - 4$, or 12. 12 is a factor of 24, so we can eliminate any answer containing Statement II. That leaves only (A) and (E).

Let's look at statement III next. Not only are we squaring and multiplying, but we're also adding . . . this number is going to get big fast. To keep it in our target range, let's pick the smallest numbers on our list, $x = 1$ and $y = 2$. Then $xy + y^2$ would equal $1(2) + 4$, or 6. That's a factor of 24, so (E) is eliminated. We know that (A) is the right answer without ever having to evaluate statement I.

Backsolving

Backsolving is just like Picking Numbers, except instead of coming up with the number yourself, you use the numbers in the answer choices. You'll literally work backwards through the problem, looking for the answer that agrees with the information in the question stem. This is a good approach whenever the task of plugging in an answer to the question would allow you to confirm its details in a straightforward way.

You want to Backsolve systematically, not randomly. Start with either (B) or (D). If the one you pick isn't correct, you'll often be able to figure out whether you need to try a number that's larger or one that's smaller. Since the answers will be in ascending or descending order, you'll be able to eliminate several answers at once.

Backsolving can save you a great deal of time. It is also an exceptional approach when you have no idea how to begin a problem.

Example: Ron begins reading a book at 4:30 PM and reads at a steady pace of 30 pages per hour. Michelle begins reading a copy of the same book at 6:00 PM. If Michelle started 5 pages behind the page that Ron started on and reads at an average pace of 50 pages per hour, at what time would Ron and Michelle be reading the same page?

- ○ 7:00 PM
- ○ 7:30 PM
- ○ 7:45 PM
- ○ 8:00 PM
- ○ 8:30 PM

We could perhaps set up a complex system of equations to solve this problem. But we'd actually need six separate equations to solve it! Even if you knew exactly what those equations would be and how to go through them, that's not a very efficient approach. So let's Backsolve. We'll pick an answer and see whether Michelle and Ron are on the same page at that time. There's no compelling reason to prefer one choice to another. So just quickly choose (B) or (D).

EXPERT EXCLUSIVE

If you know an answer is right by process of elimination, don't waste time confirming it. You already know that it's right—trust your analysis and move on to the next problem with more time on the clock.

Let's say we choose (D). On what page is Ron at 8:00 PM? He started reading at 4:30 PM, so he's been reading for 3.5 hours. His pace is 30 pages per hour. So he's read 30 × 3.5, or 105 pages. Since Michelle started 5 pages behind, she'd need to read 110 pages to be at the same place. Did she? Well, she's been reading since 6:00 PM, so she's read for 2 hours. At 50 pages per hour, she's read 100 pages. That's 10 short of what she needs. So (D) is not the right answer.

Since she's reading faster than Ron, she'll catch up to him with more time. So they'll be on the same page sometime after 8:00 PM. Only one answer fits the bill—choice (E). It must be correct.

That's why you should select either (B) or (D): 20 percent of the time, you'll have picked the right answer. Another 20 percent of the time, you'll know the right answer by process of elimination without ever having to test another choice!

Sometimes you may have to test more than one, though. Stick to (B) or (D), and you'll save valuable time and worry.

Example: A crate of apples contains 1 bruised apple for every 30 apples in the crate. Three out of every 4 bruised apples are considered not fit to sell, and every apple that is not fit to sell is bruised. If there are 12 apples not fit to sell in the crate, how many apples are there in the crate?

- ○ 270
- ○ 360
- ○ 480
- ○ 600
- ○ 840

Start Backsolving with choice (B). Suppose that there are 360 apples in the crate. Then $\frac{360}{30}$ apples, or 12 apples, are bruised. Then $\frac{3}{4}$ of 12 apples, or 9 apples, are unsaleable. This is too few unsaleable apples. So (B) is too small.

The answer must be larger than 360, so (A) and (B) are eliminated. Regardless of what we might suspect the answer to be, we should next test (D). If (D) is not right, we'll know whether it's too large (in which case (C) would be correct) or too small (in which case (E) would be correct). No matter what, we'll only have to test one choice.

Using (D), we'll suppose that there are 600 apples in the crate. Then $\frac{600}{30}$ apples, or 20 apples, are bruised. Of those 20, $\frac{3}{4}$, or 15, are unsaleable. That's too many. So (D) and (E) are out, proving that (C) is correct.

Backsolving works for more than just word problems. You can use it whenever only one variable appears in the question stem.

Example: What is the value of x if $\frac{x+1}{x-3}-\frac{x+2}{x-4}=0$?

- ○ −2
- ○ −1
- ○ 0
- ○ 1
- ○ 2

Since (D) looks easier to work with than (B), let's start with that.

$\frac{1+1}{1-3}-\frac{1+2}{1-4}=\frac{2}{-2}-\frac{3}{-3}=-1-(-1)=0$. Bingo!

DON'T BE AFRAID TO GUESS

A well-placed guess can sometimes be the best thing you can do on a problem. Because of the severe penalty exacted on those who fail to finish, you need to stay on a steady pace. If you fall behind, it's a very good idea to guess on the hardest problems. That way you'll get back lost time instead of falling further behind. And while you shouldn't be afraid to guess, you *should* be afraid to rush! The GMAT builds in twists and writes problems in complicated ways; rushing almost always leads to a misperception of the problem. The test makers build wrong answers based on the most common misperceptions. So rushing through a problem virtually guarantees a wrong answer. Far better to guess.

Sometimes you just have no idea how to approach a problem—instead of throwing away three or four minutes getting frustrated, make a guess. If you didn't know how to approach the problem, you weren't likely to choose the right answer, and you can use the time to solve other problems.

Lastly, there are some problems that are *best* solved using guessing techniques. The two keys to good guessing are (1) elimination of likely wrong answers by using your knowledge of the problem and of the GMAT's tendencies and (2) maintaining your "Big-Picture" focus—remembering that your performance on the section as a whole matters much more than your performance on two

EXPERT EXCLUSIVE

It can be very frustrating to chase your tail for five minutes on a tough problem, and that frustration will make it difficult for you to think critically on the next few problems. Good guessing can prevent that, saving you from several wrong answers in a row.

or three questions. Better to make a guess in one minute and be done with a hard problem than spend six minutes before guessing; the extra time will pay off.

There are six guessing strategies that you can apply to Problem Solving:

(1) Use Logic

(2) Estimate the Answer

(3) Eliminate Numbers from the Question Stem

(4) Eliminate the Oddball

(5) Eliminate Uncritical Solutions

(6) On "Which of the Following" Questions, Favor (D) and (E)

You won't be able to use all of these strategies on every problem. But if you run through the "checklist" and eliminate what you can, you'll make your best possible guess in the least possible amount of time. Let's look at the strategies.

Use Logic

Some answers are simply logically impossible. By analyzing and simplifying before attempting to solve, you may know enough about the problem to eliminate many answers. Consider this problem:

> A container holding 12 ounces of a solution that is 1 part alcohol to 2 parts water is added to a container holding 8 ounces of a solution that is 1 part alcohol to 3 parts water. What is the ratio of alcohol to water in the resulting solution?
>
> ○ 2:5
>
> ○ 3:7
>
> ○ 3:5
>
> ○ 4:7
>
> ○ 7:3

EXPERT EXCLUSIVE

Roman Numeral questions are good candidates for logic-based guessing. If you can evaluate only one statement, you can still logically eliminate several answers.

It seems a challenging problem at first glance. But the simplified version of the problem is that we're adding a 1:2 solution to a 1:3 solution. So logically, the right answer has to be between 1:3 (or ⅓, or 0.333 . . .) and 1:2 (or ½, or 0.5). (A) and (B) are both in that range, but all the others are above 1:2. So you can make a guess—with 50 percent odds of being right—analyzing the problem logically.

Point of information: The answer is (B). The 12-ounce solution has 4 oz alcohol and 8 oz water. The 8 oz solution has 2 oz alcohol and 6 oz water. Add the amounts of alcohol and water to get 6 oz alcohol and 14 oz water for a ratio of 3:7 alcohol to water.

Estimate the Answer

The GMAT asks some questions that are intended to be solved via estimation.

Example: The product of all positive even numbers less than or equal to 20 is closest to which of the following?

  ○ 10^6

  ○ 10^7

  ○ 10^8

  ○ 10^9

  ○ 10^{10}

If you had a calculator on the Quant section, you could quickly figure out that the product in question is 3,715,891,200. But with no calculator, what on earth can be done? The keys to the solution are the word *closest* and the big spread of values in the answer choices—each is 10 times the nearest value. This problem has "estimate" written all over it.

Let's jot down the numbers in question:

$$2 \times 4 \times 6 \times 8 \times 10 \times 12 \times 14 \times 16 \times 18 \times 20$$

Now, how to estimate these values? Since each answer is a power of 10, we should estimate each value in a way that easily relates to 10:

> **EXPERT EXCLUSIVE**
>
> When a question stem includes a word like *approximately*, that's a clear signal that estimation is the best approach you can take.

$$2 \times 4 \times 6 \times 8 \times 10 \times 12 \times 14 \times 16 \times 18 \times 20$$

$$2 \times 4 \times 6 \times 10 \times 10 \times 10 \times 10 \times 20 \times 20 \times 20$$

What about the small ones? Well, $2 \times 4 \times 6 = 48$, which is very close to 50.

$$50 \times 10 \times 10 \times 10 \times 10 \times 20 \times 20 \times 20$$

Continuing to look for tens:

$$(5 \times 10) \times 10 \times 10 \times 10 \times 10 \times (2 \times 10) \times (2 \times 10) \times (2 \times 10)$$

EXPERT EXCLUSIVE

The hardest questions are the ones you'll be most likely to need to guess on—and are also the ones that will hurt your score the *least* when you get them wrong. So don't be afraid to guess!

That's eight 10s, one 5, and three 2s:

$$2 \times 2 \times 2 \times 5 \times 10^8$$

$$(2 \times 2) \times (2 \times 5) \times 10^8$$

$$4 \times 10 \times 10^8$$

$$4 \times 10^9$$

That's closer to 10^9 than to 10^{10}, so (D) is the correct answer. No calculator needed, just the willingness to estimate!

Eliminate Numbers from the Question Stem

The test makers lay psychological traps as well as mathematical ones, and this guessing principle helps you to stay out of them. It's part of human psychology to deal with being lost by looking for familiar things. When we get lost in a problem, we tend to grab hold of familiar numbers . . . such as those we've just seen in the question stem. The GMAT doesn't like to reward people who get lost with right answers, so these numbers tend to be wrong.

Eliminate the Oddball

EXPERT EXCLUSIVE

Don't panic if you solve with math, Picking Numbers, or Backsolving and discover the answer to be an oddball or a number repeated from the question stem. Very occasionally, they will be right. But that shouldn't deter you from eliminating them when guessing. The odds of them being wrong are very high.

This is psychology again. Our eyes are attracted to difference. (Next time you watch a movie or a TV show, notice how often no one else is dressed in the same color as the main character—it's a subtle trick to keep your attention where the director wants it.) Random guessers, then, will be attracted to uniqueness. As the GMAT does not like to reward random guessing, the "oddballs" should be eliminated.

A word of warning about this technique: The GMAT also uses a little reverse psychology. The test makers know that people tend to be afraid of answers that seem *too* out of line with the others. These outlying values, then, will sometimes be *correct*. What Kaplan means by an "oddball," then, is *not* a number that's notably bigger or smaller but an answer choice that is structurally unique—the only fraction or the only negative number, for example.

Look at these five answer choices:

- $\sqrt{2}$
- 2
- 4
- 16
- 2,056

The answer 2,056 is *not* an oddball and should not be eliminated. But $\sqrt{2}$ is and should be.

Eliminate Uncritical Solutions

Because the GMAT is a test of critical thinking, answers that you'd get just by mashing numbers together are usually wrong. Consider this problem:

> A bag holds 2 red marbles and 3 green marbles. If you removed two randomly selected marbles from the bag, without replacement, what is the probability that both would be red?

- ○ $\dfrac{1}{10}$
- ○ $\dfrac{1}{5}$
- ○ $\dfrac{3}{10}$
- ○ $\dfrac{2}{5}$
- ○ $\dfrac{1}{2}$

> It's true that we want two of the five marbles in the bag. But GMAT questions usually require a little more math than just that, so $\dfrac{2}{5}$ isn't likely to be correct. (In fact, it's the odds of getting *one* red marble when selecting one; the probability of getting two red when selecting two is actually $\dfrac{1}{10}$.)

On "Which of the Following" Questions, Favor (D) and (E)

When Problem Solving questions include the phrase "which of the following," the answer is about 60 percent likely to be either (D) or (E). So if you haven't eliminated both of them for other reasons, the odds are in your favor if you select one of those two choices.

Keep Your Eyes Open

Believe it or not, there are some GMAT problems for which a guessing strategy—most notably Logic or Estimation—is the best approach you could take. Remember that the test makers aren't trying to judge your math skills alone; they are also testing your ability to find efficient solutions to problems. Every so often, they give you a set of answers with only one possible answer!

Example: If a bicyclist in motion increases his speed by 20% and then increases his speed by another 15%, what percent of the original speed is the total increase in speed?

- ○ 20%
- ○ 35%
- ○ 38%
- ○ 65%
- ○ 135%

> **EXPERT EXCLUSIVE**
>
> Make sure to look at the answer choices before you choose your approach. Otherwise, you might not realize that you can estimate.

It's true that we could pick the original speed to be 100, but thinking logically about the question and the answers, we can do better here. The speed goes up 20% and then up another 15%. That 15% increase is being applied not to the original speed but to the speed after the first increase. If it were 15% of the original, then the total increase would be 20% + 15% = 35% (that's the "uncritical solution"). But since the second increase is a little more, the total increase will be a little more than 35%. Only one answer, (C), fits the bill. So (C) must be correct!

If applied strategically, guessing will be a great tool for you on test day. It will help keep you out of time management trouble, help you to feel confident and in charge of the test, and occasionally reward you with a very quick right answer.

THE KAPLAN METHOD FOR PROBLEM SOLVING

Now that you've got a grip on the basic principles of Problem Solving, let's look at how to attack the questions you'll see on the test.

STEP 1. ANALYZE THE QUESTION

> **EXPERT EXCLUSIVE**
>
> Don't start to solve too soon. Analyze and simplify first, and you'll be several steps ahead of the competition.

Begin your analysis of the problem by getting an overview. If it's a word problem, what's the basic situation? Or is this an algebra problem? An overlapping sets problem? A permutations problem? Getting a basic idea of what's going on will help you to organize your thinking.

If there's anything that can be quickly simplified, do so . . . but don't start solving yet. For example, if a question stem gave you the classic quadratic $x^2 - y^2 = 64$, it would be fine to rewrite it immediately as $(x + y)(x - y) = 64$. But you wouldn't want to start solving for values; doing so would likely cause you to miss an important aspect of the problem or to overlook an efficient alternative solution.

Also, make sure to glance at the answer choices. Can they help you choose an approach? If they are variable expressions, you can pick numbers. If they are widely spread, you can estimate. Perhaps they will trigger an important insight for you.

STEP 2. STATE THE TASK

Before you choose your approach, make sure you know what you're solving for. The most common wrong answer trap in Problem Solving is the right answer—but to the wrong question. And perhaps you won't have to do as much work as you might think—you may be able to solve for what you need without calculating the value of every single variable involved in the problem.

STEP 3. APPROACH STRATEGICALLY

The operative word here is *strategically*. Resist the temptation to hammer away at the problem, hoping for something to work. Analyze the problem to find the most straightforward approach that allows you to make sense of the problem.

There is rarely a "right approach." Choose the easiest for you given the current problem. Broadly speaking, there are three basic approaches.

Approach 1: A Kaplan Strategy

Frequently there will be a more efficient "side door" approach to the math for those who analyze the problem carefully. Consider Picking Numbers or Backsolving. These approaches can simplify some tough problems and should always be on your mind as possible alternatives.

Approach 2: Straightforward Math

Sometimes simply doing the math is the most efficient approach. But remember, only do math that feels *straightforward*. To be sure, the hardest problems will make you sweat during the *analysis*, but you should never find yourself doing very complicated math.

Remember, the only thing that matters is that you select the correct answer. There is no human GMAT grader out there who's going to give you extra points for working out a math problem the hard way!

> **EXPERT EXCLUSIVE**
> Pay attention to that little voice in your head that says, "Yuck! I don't want to solve the problem this way–too hard!" It's an important signal that the approach you're considering isn't straightforward enough.

Approach 3: Guess Strategically

If you notice that estimation or simple logic will get you the answer, use those guessing techniques. They will often be faster than doing the math. If you have spent 60–90 seconds analyzing the problem and still haven't found a straightforward solution, make a guess. You only have an average of two minutes per problem, so you need to keep moving.

And if you have fallen behind pace, you need to guess strategically to get back on track. Hunt actively for good guessing situations and guess quickly on them (within 20–30 seconds). Don't wait until you fall so far behind that you are forced into random guesses or forced to guess on questions that you could otherwise have easily solved. And don't try to make up time by rushing!

STEP 4. CONFIRM YOUR ANSWER

You aren't able to go back after the section to check your work, so you need to build that into your work on each problem. The most efficient way to do this is to reread the question stem. If you notice a wrinkle to the problem that you missed earlier, you should redo the problem (if you have time) or change your answer. If you got everything the first time, move on to the next problem with confidence.

Now, try the Kaplan Method for Problem Solving on the following example:

> If $w > x > y > z$ on the number line, y is halfway between x
> and z, and x is halfway between w and z, then $\dfrac{y - x}{y - w} =$
>
> ◯ $\dfrac{1}{4}$
>
> ◯ $\dfrac{1}{3}$
>
> ◯ $\dfrac{1}{2}$
>
> ◯ $\dfrac{3}{4}$
>
> ◯ 1

Step 1: Analyze the Question

There's a very complicated relationship among four variables. Since there are multiple variables in the problem, Picking Numbers is a possible approach. The answer choices are all numbers, so we won't have to test each answer choice—we'd just plug numbers into the question. Since the phrase *number line* appears, we may want to consider drawing a number line to help us visualize the situation:

Step 2: State the Task

We have to evaluate a rather complicated fraction: $\dfrac{y - x}{y - w}$.

Step 3: Approach Strategically

The math seems like it would be very, very annoying. We'd have to translate the rules about what's halfway between what into equations. Picking Numbers, on the other hand, will be much more straightforward.

The rules are pretty complicated, so let's pick numbers one at a time. x and z each appear twice in the rules, so starting with those two numbers would seem to make sense.

Let's go with $z = 1$ and $x = 3$ to leave room for y.

y is halfway between 3 and 1, so $y = 2$.

x, or 3, is halfway between w and 1, so $w = 5$.

Nothing to do now but plug in these numbers:
$$\frac{y-x}{y-w} = \frac{2-3}{2-5} = \frac{-1}{-3} = \frac{1}{3}$$
Answer (B). Not too bad, thanks to Picking Numbers.

Step 4: Confirm Your Answer

Let's see . . . did we understand all those rules? "y is halfway between x and z." Check. "x is halfway between w and z." Check. Another potential error would have been to make w the smallest variable instead of the largest. (Notice how the question stem puts w on the left, even though it belongs on the right-hand side of the number line?) That's something else we could catch in this step.

SUMMARY

The Basic Principles for Problem Solving are the following:

- Analyze and simplify before solving.
- Focus on what's asked.
- Consider alternative approaches.
- Don't be afraid to guess.

The Kaplan Method for Problem Solving is as follows:

Step 1:   Analyze the question.

Step 2:   State the task.

Step 3:   Approach strategically.

Step 4:   Confirm your answer.

PRACTICE QUIZ

Directions: Solve the problems and choose the best answer.

1. $7.38 + 10.075 =$

   ○ 10.813

   ○ 17.113

   ○ 17.355

   ○ 17.383

   ○ 17.455

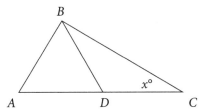

2. In the diagram above, if $AB = AD = BD = DC$, then $x =$

   ○ 30

   ○ 35

   ○ 40

   ○ 45

   ○ 60

3. If $2x - 4y = -2$ and $3x - 2y = 3$, then $2y + x =$

   ○ $\dfrac{3}{2}$

   ○ 2

   ○ $3\dfrac{1}{2}$

   ○ 5

   ○ $5\dfrac{1}{2}$

4. Joan spends 20 percent of her income on taxes and 20 percent of the remainder on rent. What percent of her income does she spend on rent?

   ○ 8%

   ○ 10%

   ○ 16%

   ○ 20%

   ○ 24%

5. An overnight courier service charges $5.00 for the first 2 ounces of a package and $0.75 for each additional ounce. If there is a 6 percent sales tax added to these charges, how much does it cost to send a 6-ounce package?

   ○ $4.24

   ○ $8.00

   ○ $8.48

   ○ $9.28

   ○ $10.60

6. If $\dfrac{3M}{2N} = 0.125$, what is the value of N in terms of M?

   ○ $\dfrac{M}{8}$

   ○ $\dfrac{8}{M}$

   ○ $4M$

   ○ $8M$

   ○ $12M$

7. Company *C* sells a line of 25 products with an average retail price of \$1,200. If none of these products sells for less than \$420 and exactly 10 of the products sell for less than \$1,000, what is the greatest possible selling price of the most expensive product?

   ○ \$2,600

   ○ \$3,900

   ○ \$7,800

   ○ \$11,800

   ○ \$18,200

8. If $\frac{n}{2}$ is an even integer, what is the remainder when *n* is divided by 4?

   ○ 0

   ○ 1

   ○ 2

   ○ 3

   ○ 4

9. A certain industrial loom weaves 0.128 meters of cloth every second. Approximately how many seconds will it take for the loom to weave 25 meters of cloth?

   ○ 178

   ○ 195

   ○ 204

   ○ 488

   ○ 512

10. If $a - b = \dfrac{a^2 - b^2}{b^2 - a^2}$ and $b^2 - a^2 \neq 0$, then $b - a =$

    ○ −1

    ○ 0

    ○ 1

    ○ 2

    ○ It cannot be determined from the information given.

11. If a sequence of consecutive integers of increasing value has a sum of 63 and a first term of 6, how many integers are in the sequence?

    ○ 11

    ○ 10

    ○ 9

    ○ 8

    ○ 7

12. A cube of white styrofoam is painted red and then cut parallel to a pair of parallel sides to form two rectangular solids of equal volume. What percent of the surface area of each of the new solids is not painted red?

    ○ 15%

    ○ $16\frac{2}{3}\%$

    ○ 20%

    ○ 25%

    ○ $33\frac{1}{3}\%$

13. Ann and Bob drive separately to a meeting. Ann's average driving speed is greater than Bob's average driving speed by one-third of Bob's average driving speed, and Ann drives twice as many miles as Bob. What is the ratio of the number of hours Ann spends driving to the meeting to the number of hours Bob spends driving to the meeting?

    ○ 8:3

    ○ 3:2

    ○ 4:3

    ○ 2:3

    ○ 3:8

14. If $0 < p < 1$, which of the following has the least value?

    ○ $\dfrac{1}{p^2}$

    ○ $\dfrac{1}{\sqrt{p}}$

    ○ $\dfrac{1}{p^2+1}$

    ○ $\dfrac{1}{\sqrt{p+1}}$

    ○ $\dfrac{1}{(p+1)^2}$

15. In a certain game, each player scores either 2 points or 5 points. If n players score 2 points and m players score 5 points, and the total number of points scored is 50, what is the least possible positive difference between n and m?

    ○ 1

    ○ 3

    ○ 5

    ○ 7

    ○ 9

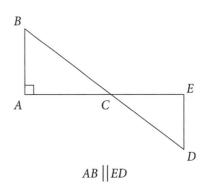

$AB \parallel ED$

Note: Figure not drawn to scale.

16. In the figure above, $ED = 1$, $CD = 2$, and $AE = 6\sqrt{3}$. What is the perimeter of $\triangle ABC$?

    ○ $3\sqrt{3}$

    ○ $10 + 5\sqrt{3}$

    ○ $10\sqrt{3}$

    ○ $15 + 5\sqrt{3}$

    ○ $25\sqrt{3}$

17. James's library contains only reference, biography, and fiction books in the ratio of 1:2:7, respectively. If James's library contains 30 books, how many biographies does he own?

    ○ 2

    ○ 3

    ○ 4

    ○ 6

    ○ 10

18. Which of the following fractions is smaller than $\frac{2}{5}$?

    ○ $\frac{7}{16}$

    ○ $\frac{4}{11}$

    ○ $\frac{3}{7}$

    ○ $\frac{4}{9}$

    ○ $\frac{9}{20}$

19. A sink contains exactly 12 liters of water. If water is drained from the sink until it holds exactly 6 liters of water less than the quantity drained away, how many liters of water were drained away?

    ○ 2

    ○ 3

    ○ 4.5

    ○ 6

    ○ 9

20. In a certain state, a person may inherit up to $4,000 tax-free. Any amount in excess of $10,000 is taxed at a rate of 8 percent, and any amount between $4,000 and $10,000 is taxed at a rate of 5 percent. If Tony inherits $11,500, how much tax will he have to pay?

    ○ $210

    ○ $270

    ○ $300

    ○ $420

    ○ $510

21. The amount of gas in a gas storage tank is halved by draining 15 gallons of gas from it. If p gallons of gas are then added to the tank, how many gallons of gas are there in the storage tank?

    ○ $15 + p$

    ○ $30 - p$

    ○ $30 + p$

    ○ $2p - 30$

    ○ $p - 15$

Advanced

22. Machine A can process 6,000 envelopes in 3 hours. Machines B and C working together but independently can process the same number of envelopes in $2\frac{2}{5}$ hours. If machines A and C working together but independently process 3,000 envelopes in 1 hour, then how many hours would it take machine B to process 12,000 envelopes?

    ○   2

    ○   3

    ○   4

    ○   6

    ○   8

---

x% on time
43% up to 15 minutes delayed
17% 15–30 minutes delayed
12% 30–60 minutes delayed
3% more than 60 minutes delayed

23. The chart above describes departures from a certain airport on a certain day. If 1,200 flights were delayed, how many flights departed on time?

    ○   250

    ○   300

    ○   350

    ○   400

    ○   900

24. Cheese, bologna, and peanut butter sandwiches were made for a picnic in a ratio of 11 to 7 to 18. If a total of 216 sandwiches were made, how many bologna sandwiches were made?

    ○   15

    ○   30

    ○   38

    ○   42

    ○   48

25. If a rectangle with width 49.872 inches and length 30.64 inches has an area that is 15 times the area of a certain square, which of the following is the closest approximation to the length, in inches, of a side of that square?

    ○ 5

    ○ 10

    ○ 15

    ○ 20

    ○ 25

26. If $y = -(4 - 5)$, then $y =$

    ○ −2

    ○ −1

    ○ 0

    ○ 1

    ○ 2

27. If a store purchases a sweater for a wholesale price of $36 and then sells the sweater at a retail price of $50, what is the approximate percent increase in the price?

    ○ 18%

    ○ 24%

    ○ 33%

    ○ 34%

    ○ 39%

28. What is the ratio of $\dfrac{31}{18}$ to the product $13\left(\dfrac{31}{18}\right)$?

    ○ $\dfrac{1}{18}$

    ○ $\dfrac{1}{13}$

    ○ $\dfrac{13}{18}$

    ○ $\dfrac{18}{13}$

    ○ 31

Advanced

29. Four different prime numbers, each less than 20, are multiplied together. What is the greatest possible result?

    ○ 21,879

    ○ 28,728

    ○ 40,755

    ○ 46,189

    ○ 49,742

Advanced

30. A baseball card collector has 1,100 cards that are in mint condition and 400 cards that are not. Of those cards in mint condition, 60% are rookie cards. If 740 of the cards in his collection are not rookie cards, then how many cards in the collection are rookie cards that are not in mint condition?

    ○ 100

    ○ 300

    ○ 440

    ○ 760

    ○ 1,500

31. $\dfrac{5.005}{2.002} =$

    ○ 2.05

    ○ 2.50025

    ○ 2.502

    ○ 2.5025

    ○ 2.5

32. How many different subsets of the set {10, 14, 17, 24} contain an odd number of elements?

    ○ 3

    ○ 6

    ○ 8

    ○ 10

    ○ 12

Advanced

---

33. Of the students at North State University, 1/6 are math majors, and 2/5 do not study a foreign language. If 60% of the math majors also study a foreign language, then what is the ratio of non-math majors who study a foreign language to those who do not?

    ○ 2:5

    ○ 2:3

    ○ 5:6

    ○ 6:5

    ○ 3:2

34. Which of the following must equal zero for all real numbers x?

    I. $x^3 - x^2$

    II. x^0

    III. x^1

    ○ None

    ○ I only

    ○ II only

    ○ I and II only

    ○ II and III only

35. The population of City A is three times the population of City B. Together, Cities A and B have twice the population of City C. What is the ratio of the population of City C to the population of City B?

    ○ 1:4

    ○ 1:2

    ○ 2:1

    ○ 3:1

    ○ 4:1

36. If the fraction $\dfrac{m}{n}$ is negative, which of the following CANNOT be true?

    ○ $\dfrac{n}{m} > \dfrac{m}{n}$

    ○ $mn < 0$

    ○ $n - m > 0$

    ○ $mn^3 > 0$

    ○ $m - n > 0$

37. The speed of a train pulling out of a station is given by the equation $s = t^2 + t$, where s is the speed in kilometers per hour and t is the time in seconds from when the train starts moving. The equation holds for all situations where $0 \le t \le 4$. In kilometers per hour, what is the positive difference in the speed of the train 4 seconds after it starts moving compared to the speed 2 seconds after it starts moving?

   ○ 0

   ○ 6

   ○ 14

   ○ 20

   ○ 38

38. If Lisa walks t blocks in 3 minutes, how many minutes will it take her to walk s blocks at the same rate?

   ○ $\dfrac{s}{3t}$

   ○ $\dfrac{3s}{t}$

   ○ $\dfrac{3}{st}$

   ○ $\dfrac{3t}{s}$

   ○ $\dfrac{t}{3s}$

Advanced

39. A chemist has 10 liters of a solution that is 10 percent nitric acid by volume. He wants to dilute the solution to 4 percent strength by adding water. How many liters of water must he add?

   ○ 15

   ○ 18

   ○ 20

   ○ 25

   ○ 26

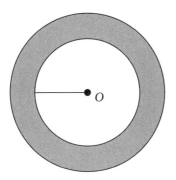

40. In the figure above, a circular swimming pool (the unshaded area) is surrounded by a circular walkway (the shaded area). Both the circular swimming pool and the entire circular region consisting of the swimming pool and the walkway have the center O. If the radius of the swimming pool is 10 meters and the width of the walkway is 5 meters, how many square meters greater than the surface area of the swimming pool is the area of the walkway?

○ 25π

○ 50π

○ 100π

○ 125π

○ 225π

41. Molly purchased Brand A binders at $8.00 apiece and Brand B binders at $5.60 apiece. If she bought a total of 12 binders for $84.00, how many Brand A binders did she buy?

○ 2

○ 5

○ 6

○ 7

○ 10

Advanced

42. A photo is being taken of Central High School's nine-member wrestling team. The team will stand in two rows, with the five shortest in the front row. The coach is also in the picture, in the middle of the back row. One of the taller boys is known to misbehave; to keep him from disrupting the photo session, he is placed next to the coach. How many possible arrangements of people are there for the photo?

○ 24

○ 30

○ 720

○ 1,440

○ 2,880

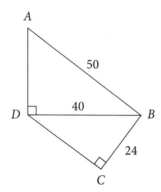

43. What is the perimeter of quadrilateral *ABCD* above?

    ○ 106

    ○ 114

    ○ 120

    ○ 127

    ○ 136

44. A local farmer grows wheat on land he rents for a fixed cost of $200,000 per year. The variable cost of growing one bushel of wheat is $10. In a certain year, the farmer grows and sells 50,000 bushels of wheat and makes a profit of $150,000, after paying the fixed cost to rent the land. If every bushel sold for the same price, what was the selling price, in dollars, of a bushel of wheat?

    ○ 3

    ○ 7

    ○ 11

    ○ 13

    ○ 17

45. In a rectangular coordinate system, triangle *ABC* is drawn so that one side of the triangle connects two points on the *y*-axis, $A(0, 2)$ and $B(0, -4)$. If point *C* has coordinates $(c, 0)$, where $c > 0$, and the area of *ABC* is 21, then $c =$

    ○ $\dfrac{7}{3}$

    ○ 7

    ○ $\sqrt{53}$

    ○ $\sqrt{65}$

    ○ 21

Advanced

46. A drawer has six loose blue socks and six loose white socks. If four socks are removed from the drawer at random and without replacement, what is the probability that one pair of each color was selected?

    ○ $\dfrac{2}{33}$

    ○ $\dfrac{5}{66}$

    ○ $\dfrac{5}{33}$

    ○ $\dfrac{5}{11}$

    ○ $\dfrac{1}{2}$

Advanced

47. If $x + y = 2$ and $x^2 - xy - 10 - 2y^2 = 0$, what does $x - 2y$ equal?

    ○ 0

    ○ 1

    ○ 2

    ○ 5

    ○ 10

48. The average speed of a certain train was measured every 6 minutes and was found to have increased by 3 miles per hour during each successive 6-minute interval after the first interval. If in the third 6-minute interval, its speed was 24 miles per hour, how many miles did the train travel in the first 6-minute interval?

    ○ 0.6

    ○ 1.2

    ○ 1.8

    ○ 2.4

    ○ 3.0

Advanced

49 If the product of the integers a, b, c, and d is 546 and if $1 < a < b < c < d$, what is the value of $b + c$?

    ○ 273

    ○ 185

    ○ 21

    ○ 10

    ○ 4

Advanced

50. In a certain laboratory, chemicals are identified by a color-coding system. There are 20 different chemicals. Each is coded with either a single color or a unique two-color combination. If the order of colors in the pairs doesn't matter, what is the minimum number of different colors needed to code all 20 chemicals with either a single color or a unique pair of colors?

    ○ 5

    ○ 6

    ○ 7

    ○ 20

    ○ 40

ANSWERS AND EXPLANATIONS

1. E	11. E	21. A	31. E	41. D
2. A	12. D	22. E	32. C	42. D
3. D	13. B	23. D	33. E	43. E
4. C	14. E	24. D	34. A	44. E
5. C	15. B	25. B	35. C	45. B
6. E	16. D	26. D	36. D	46. D
7. D	17. D	27. E	37. C	47. D
8. A	18. B	28. B	38. B	48. C
9. B	19. E	29. D	39. A	49. D
10. C	20. D	30. A	40. A	50. B

DIAGNOSTIC TOOL

Tally up your score and write down your results below.

Total Correct: _____ out of 50

Percentage Correct: # you got right × 100 ÷ 50: _____

DIAGNOSE YOUR RESULTS

Look back at the questions you got wrong and think about your experience answering them.

Step 1: Find the Roadblocks

Did you struggle to answer some questions? To improve your score, you need to pinpoint exactly what element of these roadblocks tripped you up. To do that, ask yourself these two questions.

1. Did I not know the math?

Maybe you didn't understand a term or piece of math jargon, like *consecutive*. Maybe you forgot a formula, like the area of a triangle or how to solve combinations. Or maybe math just isn't your thing. Try out Kaplan's *GMAT Math Foundations*, which contains a review of all the fundamental math concepts tested on the GMAT using a back-to-basics, tutor-led approach, as well as practice drills to build speed and accuracy.

You still may have been able to solve by using an alternative approach. Go back over the section on Picking Numbers and Backsolving and read the answer explanations.

2. Did I know the math but still struggle to solve the problem?

That's a sign of rushing into a solution before fully analyzing the problem. The harder the problem, the more analysis is required to find an efficient solution. Go back over the Basic Principles of Problem Solving and read the answer explanations.

Step 2: Find the Blind Spots

Did you answer some questions quickly and confidently but get them wrong anyway?

When you come across wrong answers like these, you need to figure out what you thought you were doing right, what it turns out you were doing wrong, and why that happened. The best way to do that is to read the answer explanations!

You probably misread an important part of the question stem. Did you reread each question stem after solving? Or perhaps you made a careless error in your math. Did you choose the most straightforward approach possible? The harder the approach, the greater the likelihood of making a mistake. Also, just as with your roadblocks, try to get in as much practice as you can.

> **EXPERT EXCLUSIVE**
> Did you pass up opportunities to solve easily by Picking Numbers or Backsolving? The GMAT doesn't care *how* you solve, only whether you select the right answer!

Step 3: Reinforce Your Strengths

Now read through all the answer explanations for the ones you got right. Again, this helps to reinforce the Kaplan principles and methods, which in turn helps you work more efficiently so you can get the score you want. Keep your skills sharp with more practice.

As soon as you are comfortable with all the GMAT question types and Kaplan methods, complete a full-length practice test under timed conditions. In this way, practice tests serve as milestones.

If you are aiming for that top score, try out Kaplan's *GMAT 800*, which includes only the toughest GMAT questions and most focused strategies.

For even more practice, you can also try out the GMAT Quiz Bank! You get more than 1,000 questions that you can access 24/7 from any Internet browser, each with comprehensive explanations. You can even customize your quizzes based on question type, content, and difficulty level. Take quizzes in Timed Mode to test your stamina or in Tutor Mode to see explanations as you work. Best of all, you also get detailed reports to track your progress.

Visit **kaptest.com/GMAT** for more details on our Quiz Bank and for more information on our other online and classroom-based options.

EXPERT EXCLUSIVE

Even on basic arithmetic questions, the GMAT builds in opportunities to save time via alternative approaches.

1. E

It doesn't get any more straightforward than this, but you still need to work carefully and avoid careless errors. For example, (A) is what you'd get if you didn't line up the decimals. There's also an opportunity to do very little arithmetic by applying a little logic: 7.38 + 10.075 must be greater than 7.38 + 10, which is 17.38 . . . so any answer below that number can go. That eliminates (A), (B), and (C). Furthermore, the answer has to be 0.075 greater than 17.38 . . . choice (D)—17.383—is only 0.003 greater, so it too can go. (E) must be correct, as it is the only answer choice left!

EXPERT EXCLUSIVE

To solve multiple-shape questions, look at what information about one shape tells you about another. For example, the fact that triangle *ABD* is equilateral tells you something about the measure of angle *BDC*.

2. A

This question tests two common shapes: equilateral triangles and isosceles triangles. The key to this question, as in most Geometry questions, is to put what the text of the question stem tells you about the shape into the picture so that you can visualize the relationships clearly. Four lines are of equal length:

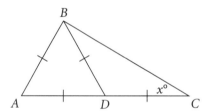

Because all the sides of triangle *ABD* are equal, its angles must all be 60°. And because *DC* = *BD*, the measure of angle *DBC* is the same as that of angle *DCB*:

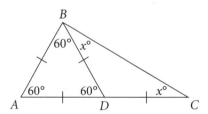

Now we could solve for *x* if we knew the measure of angle *BDC*; since the sum of the angles in a triangle is 180°, we can set up this equation: $180° = BDC + 2x°$. Can we figure *BDC* out? Absolutely. Supplementary angles add up to 180°. Since angle *BDA* is 60°, angle $BDC = 180° - 60° = 120°$.

$$180° = BDC + 2x°$$

Substitute *BDC*: $\qquad 180° = 120° + 2x°$

Subtract 120°: $\qquad 60° = 2x°$

Divide by 2: $\qquad 30° = x°$

3. D

This question showcases the importance of focusing on what's asked and looking for alternative approaches. Sure, we could use one equation to solve for one variable in terms of the other, substitute into the second equation, and thus solve for one variable. Then we'd substitute that value in to solve for the other variable. Then, knowing the values of x and y, we'd plug them into $2y + x$ and get the answer. But that's a lot of steps, and there's a faster way.

EXPERT EXCLUSIVE
The GMAT likes to reward test takers who look for clever combinations of equations.

We are asked not for x and y themselves but for $2y + x$. Is there a way to find it directly, without finding x and y first? If we subtract the first equation from the second, we get—on the left side—exactly the expression that we are asked the value of:

$$3x - 2y = 3$$
$$- [2x - 4y = -2]$$
$$\overline{x + 2y = 5}$$

Although the order of x and y is reversed from the expression in the question, the left side of the last equation is what we are looking for. Choice (D) it is.

4. C

If Joan spends 20 percent of her income on taxes, then the remainder is 80 percent of her income, which is $0.8x$. If she spends 20 percent of this remaining 80 percent on rent, she spends

$$0.2(0.8x) = 0.16x$$

Because $0.16x$ is 16 percent of x, 16 percent of her income goes to rent.

This is also a great Picking Numbers problem, as is any with percents as answer choices. If she has income of $100, then she spends $20 on taxes, leaving $80. And 20% of 80 is $0.2(80) = 16$. And here's why we pick 100 . . . 16 is 16% of 100.

This is also a great guessing question. Since we take 20% of the income away for taxes *before* Joan pays her rent, she pays 20% of less than her total income. So that must be close to, but a little less than, 20% of that income. Answer (C) is the only one that fits the bill.

5. C

There are two rate charges—one for anything up to 2 ounces and a second for each ounce above 2 ounces. On top of that, a tax is applied. So to calculate the full charge, we need to (1) take the initial charge, (2) figure out the number of ounces above 2, (3) figure out the charge for those extra ounces, (4) add the charges, then (5) figure the tax.

EXPERT EXCLUSIVE
When solving word problems, make sure that you understand the basic situation and plan your approach before you start doing any math.

EXPERT EXCLUSIVE

Learn the common decimal-fraction equivalencies. They'll give you opportunities to simplify your arithmetic.

First 2 ounces:	$5.00
Amount above:	6 ounces − 2 ounces = 4 ounces
4 ounces @ $0.75/ounce:	$4 \times \$\dfrac{3}{4} = \$3.00$
Pretax total:	$5.00 + $3.00 = $8.00
Add 6% tax:	$8.00 + 0.06($8.00)
	$8.00 + $0.48
	$8.48

6. E

We want to isolate N. Fractions are often easier to deal with than decimals: $0.125 = \dfrac{1}{8}$.

$$\frac{3M}{2N} = \frac{1}{8}$$

Cross multiply: $\qquad 8 \times 3M = 1 \times 2N$

$$24M = 2N$$

Divide by 2: $\qquad 12M = N$

EXPERT EXCLUSIVE

When asked to solve for the greatest one thing could be, you'll likely have to find the *least* something else can be. If solving for the least one thing could be, you'll probably need to find the greatest of something else.

You also could have Picked Numbers. Given that one answer is $\dfrac{M}{8}$, $M = 8$ would be a good choice.

7. D

Since the 25 products sell at an average of $1,200, to buy one of each, we'd have to spend $25 \times \$1,200 = \$30,000$. We want to find the greatest possible selling price of the most expensive product. The way to maximize this price is to minimize the prices of the other 24 products. Ten of these products sell for less than $1,000, but all sell for at least $420. This means that (in trying to minimize the price of 24 items) we can have 10 sell at $420. That leaves 14 more that sell for $1,000 or more. So in order to keep minimizing, we'll price these at $1,000. That means that, out of the $30,000 we know it will take at least $10(\$420) + 14(\$1,000) = \$18,200$ to purchase the 24 other items. The final, most expensive item can thus cost as much as $\$30,000 - \$18,200 = \$11,800$.

8. A

EXPERT EXCLUSIVE

You don't always have to Pick Numbers for variables directly. When the question stem tells you something about an expression (such as $\dfrac{n}{2}$), you'll be guaranteed to find a permissible number for the variable by picking a permissible value for the expression.

Whenever you see a remainder question, you should Pick Numbers. The abstract math is, well, abstract. *Really* abstract. But look at how straightforward Picking Numbers is in remainder questions:

$\dfrac{n}{2}$ is an even integer, so let's pick $\dfrac{n}{2} = 2$. That means $n = 4$.

Then 4 divided by 4 is 1, with a remainder of 0. (A) is the answer.

9. B

Though 0.128 is a strange number, that word *approximately* should catch our eye as we first read over the question stem. That's a clear signal that Estimation will be a great approach to the problem.

We're asked for the approximate number of seconds needed to weave 25 meters of cloth at a rate of 0.128 meters every second. We could set up a proportion, but this is what that math would be:

$$\frac{25 \text{ meters}}{y \text{ seconds}} = \frac{0.128 \text{ meters}}{1 \text{ second}}$$

We would eventually wind up with $\dfrac{25}{0.128}$, and that would be a pain. So let's estimate.

An easy place to start will be 100 seconds, since that will just move the decimal point. In 100 seconds, the loom will weave 12.8 meters. That's close to half of what we want. In 200 seconds, the loom would weave $12.8 \times 2 = 25.6$ meters. That's very close to, but just above, what we want. So the right number of seconds will be just under 200. Sure enough, only one answer meets that criterion. (B) is correct.

And we never have to calculate $25 \div 0.128 = 195.3125$ to figure it out!

10. C

$x - y = -(y - x)$ is an important idea for the GMAT. It is most commonly used to re-express answer choices, but here it shows up in the question stem: $a^2 - b^2 = -(b^2 - a^2)$. Notice also that the given equation involves $a - b$, but we're solving for $b - a$, which we can also express as $-(a - b)$.

$$a - b = \frac{a^2 - b^2}{b^2 - a^2}$$

$a^2 - b^2 = -(b^2 - a^2)$:
$$a - b = \frac{-(b^2 - a^2)}{(b^2 - a^2)}$$

Cancel common factors:
$$a - b = \frac{-1}{1}$$
$$a - b = -1$$

Multiply by -1:
$$-(a - b) = -(-1)$$
$$b - a = 1$$

11. E

The answer choices let us know that the biggest this sequence could be is 11 numbers. That's not so many that we couldn't just start adding them by hand, stopping when we reach 63:

$$6 + 7 = 13$$
$$13 + 8 = 21$$

EXPERT EXCLUSIVE

Often listing out possibilities and sequences by hand is faster than figuring out the math on the spot. Only in very hard problems is it unrealistic to list things out in under two minutes.

$$21 + 9 = 30$$
$$30 + 10 = 40$$
$$40 + 11 = 51$$
$$51 + 12 = 63$$

When we count the number of terms in the sequence from 6 to 12, we count 7 integers in total.

This would also have been a good Backsolving problem. Say you started with (D) and tested a sequence of 8 integers:

$$6 + 7 + 8 + 9 + 10 + 11 + 12 + 13$$

Using the formula for adding long strings of consecutive numbers,

$$\text{sum} = \frac{\text{first} + \text{last}}{2} \times (\#\text{ of terms})$$

$$\text{sum} = \frac{6+13}{2} \times 8$$

$$\text{sum} = \frac{6+13}{1} \times 4$$

$$\text{sum} = 19 \times 4$$

$$\text{sum} = 76$$

EXPERT EXCLUSIVE

Notice that the number of terms in a sequence that runs from integer x to integer y is *not* $y - x$ but rather $y - x + 1$. Many counting-based GMAT problems are based on this.

We needed the sum to be 63, so we clearly have too many numbers. That leaves (E) as the only possible answer.

12. D

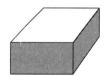

In the figure above, meant to represent one of the two half cubes, the three unseen sides (the back, bottom, and left side) are also shaded. It's the top—the surface that used to be "inside" the cube—that's still white. Let's count up the surfaces, calling a full cube face (a face on the original cube) 1 unit. Then let's find the areas of the faces of the half cube.

We have the bottom and top here, which makes 2 square units. Each of the other four faces has an area of half a square unit, so that's $4 \times \frac{1}{2}$, or another 2 square units. The total surface area of the cube, then, is $2 + 2 = 4$ square units. One whole cube face (the top), which has an area of 1 square unit, is still white, so $\frac{1}{4}$, or 25 percent, of the surface area is not red.

13. B

With multiple unknowns (the two speeds, two distances, and two times), this is a great Picking Numbers problem. Since Ann drives $\frac{1}{3}$ faster than Bob, let's pick a number for Bob that's a multiple of 3. Why not 3? Let's say that Bob drives 3 miles per hour. Then Ann drives $\frac{1}{3}$ faster, or 4 miles per hour. Now, the other information we have to consider is how far each travels. Ann drives twice as far as Bob. Let's pick 12 as the number of miles she drives (it's a multiple of both 3 and 4, the numbers we've already chosen—that's usually a good idea). If Ann drives 12 miles, then Bob drives 6 miles. So now how much time will each spend driving? Ann will drive 12 miles at 4 miles per hour:

$$4 \text{ miles per hour} \times A \text{ hours} = 12 \text{ miles}$$
$$4A = 12$$
$$A = 3$$

Bob will drive for 6 miles at 3 miles per hour:

$$3 \text{ miles per hour} \times B \text{ hours} = 6 \text{ miles}$$
$$3B = 6$$
$$B = 2$$

So the ratio of the amount of time that Ann will drive to amount of time that Bob will drive is 3:2.

Notice that answer choice (D) is simply the ratio reversed. Be careful to note exactly what you are looking for! You would solve for answer choice (A) if you multiplied the distance by the speed instead of dividing. Answer choice (E) is simply the reverse of (A).

14. E

Since there are variables in the answer choices, Picking Numbers is a workable approach.

EXPERT EXCLUSIVE
It's perfectly OK to switch approaches partway through a problem if you sense that doing so will be easier.

Before you start your solution, remember to consider the question. We're looking for the answer choice with the least value. And look at those answers . . . all fractions with the same numerator (1). Fractions with the same numerator are smaller if the denominator is bigger (because that denominator is getting divided into more pieces). So we can re-express the question thusly: Which has the *largest denominator*?

Our answer choices will have us both squaring and taking the square root of our fraction p. So we want to build this fraction out of a numerator and denominator that are small (so the numbers don't get unwieldy when squared) and perfect squares (so we can easily take a square root). The two numbers that fit the best are 1 and 4. So p will equal $\frac{1}{4}$.

(A)'s denominator is now $\left(\frac{1}{4}\right)^2$, which is $\frac{1}{16}$. (B)'s denominator is $\sqrt{\frac{1}{4}}$, or $\frac{1}{2}$. (B)'s denominator is considerably larger. (C)'s denominator is $1\frac{1}{16}$, which is much larger still. So far (C) is the winner.

(D) is hard to compare to (C) directly, so move on to something easier . . . a comparison of (C) to (E). (E)'s denominator is $\left(\frac{5}{4}\right)^2$, or $\frac{25}{16}$, or $1\frac{9}{16}$. That's bigger than (C).

Now we have to compare (D) to (E). Notice that the expressions are very similar. (D) takes the square root of $p + 1$, whereas (E) squares it. $p + 1$ is $\frac{5}{4}$, which is bigger than 1. Squaring a number greater than 1 produces a larger result; taking the square root of a number greater than 1 produces a smaller result. So (E) has the largest denominator and, therefore, is the least of the answer choices.

15. B

> **EXPERT EXCLUSIVE**
>
> Sometimes the only approach that will occur to you is trial and error. As long as the number of possibilities is reasonably small and you've analyzed the problem so that you aren't working randomly, it's a fine approach. The only important thing is that you get the right answer in a reasonable length of time!

Here's a great example of a question that rewards you if you are in the habit of analyzing before you do math. After all, what math can you do? But look at how it flows if you follow the Kaplan method.

Studying the question stem, we see that players are restricted to scoring either 2 or 5 points and that the sum of all the points is 50. We're asked to find the least possible difference between n and m, which is to say that we need to get the number of 2-point scorers as close as possible to the number of 5-point scorers. How to approach this? Hmm . . . no straightforward math is occurring to us. What strategy could we use? With multiple variables, we can Pick Numbers.

Let's start off with a nice clear set and give all 50 points to the 5-point players. So $m = 10$ and $n = 0$. Clearly, a difference of 10 is possible. But is it the *least* possible difference? Well, no. For one thing, 10 is not an answer choice! So let's change these numbers. But what to? What about one lower; could $m = 9$? That would be 45 points, leaving 5. But players who score only 2 points can't combine for 5. So $m = 9$ is not permissible. How about $m = 8$? That's 40 points, leaving 10. The 10 points can be scored by the other players, if $n = 5$. That's a difference of $8 - 5 = 3$, which is an answer choice.

But (B) isn't the smallest answer choice given, so we have to keep going. Let's try $m = 6$, as we discovered that odd values of m won't be permissible. That's 30 points, leaving 20. In that case, $n = 10$. The difference is now $10 - 6 = 4$. We're not getting smaller numbers at this point but bigger ones. So (B) is as small as we can get.

Are there ways of "math-ing" the answer? Well, yes. There are. But they all require great big "Eureka!" moments. And if one of those approaches occurs to you, that's great. But since the GMAT is adaptive and will get harder and harder the better you do, it's vital that you are comfortable working your way through questions even when you aren't getting "Eureka!" moments. Following the Kaplan method and our Basic Principles of Problem Solving will not only help those moments to come, they will also get you through the problem efficiently when those moments don't.

16. D

The key is to recognize similar triangles. If *AB* is parallel to *ED*, then the alternate interior angles are equal: angle *ABC* is equal to angle *CDE,* and right angle *BAC* is equal to angle *CED*. Angle *BCA* is a vertical angle with *ECD*, so the two of them are equal. Once we see that the triangles are similar, we know that the ratio between their corresponding sides is the same for all three pairs of sides. That, in turn, tells us that the same ratio will hold for their perimeters (which are, after all, just the sums of the sides).

> **EXPERT EXCLUSIVE**
>
> Similar triangles are the key to some of the GMAT's hardest triangle questions.

We could use the Pythagorean theorem to determine the length of *CE*, but since triangle *CED* is a right triangle with a leg that measures 1 and a hypotenuse that measures 2, triangle *CED* must be a 30-60-90 special right triangle. That makes *CE* equal $\sqrt{3}$. Now if *CE* plus *AC* is $6\sqrt{3}$ and *CE* alone is just $\sqrt{3}$, then *AC* must be $5\sqrt{3}$. *AC* is the side corresponding to *CE*. Since *AC* is 5 times the length of *CE*, the perimeter of triangle *BAC* is 5 times that of triangle *CED*. Triangle *CED* has a perimeter of $1 + 2 + \sqrt{3}$, or $3 + \sqrt{3}$. Five times this is $15 + 5\sqrt{3}$.

17. D

Since a ratio gives relative size rather than absolute size, we need to figure out what number, multiplied by the ratio, will give us the actual number of each type of book. Of course, we're only concerned with one type of book—biographies. If we call the unknown number *x*, we can create an algebraic equation. The expression $1x + 2x + 7x$ is equal to the total number of books, which we've been told is 30. Therefore, $x + 2x + 7x = 30$; $10x = 30$; $x = 3$. So James owns $2(3) = 6$ biographies.

As a savvy Kaplan test taker, you might have solved this even more quickly by noticing that the parts of the ratio (1, 2, and 7) add up to 10. So for every 10 books, there must be 1 reference, 2 biographies, and 7 fiction books. Since there are 30 books, which is 3×10, we can find the actual number of any type of book by multiplying that part of the ratio by 3.

18. B

We're asked to find the one fraction that is smaller than $\frac{2}{5}$. The answers give us fractions of many different denominators. Converting them all into common

EXPERT EXCLUSIVE

The GMAT uses elevenths with surprising frequency: $\frac{1}{11}=$ 0.090909… ; $\frac{2}{11}=$ 0.181818…; $\frac{3}{11}=0.272727…$; and so on. The repeating decimal is the numerator times 9. (Incidentally, the repeating decimal of the ninths is the numerator times 11: $\frac{1}{9}=$ 0.111111…; $\frac{2}{9}=0.222222…$; and so on. How cool is that?)

denominators is possible but annoying. Look for a way to compare quickly. If you know the common fraction-decimal equivalencies, you can evaluate a few of them: $\frac{2}{5}=0.4$, so the right answer will be less than that; $\frac{4}{11}=$ 0.363636 . . ., which is clearly less than 0.4, so (B) is correct.

If you didn't know the equivalencies, you'd have needed other ways to compare. One way is to compare fractions to benchmark values. For example, $\frac{2}{5}=\frac{4}{10}$, so it is $\frac{1}{10}$ less than $\frac{1}{2}$. (A) is $\frac{1}{16}$ less than $\frac{1}{2}$, (C) is $\frac{1}{14}$ less than $\frac{1}{2}$, (D) is $\frac{1}{18}$ less than $\frac{1}{2}$, and (E) is $\frac{1}{20}$ less than $\frac{1}{2}$. They are all "less small" than $\frac{2}{5}$, so (B) must be the right answer.

19. E

The key to this somewhat confusing word problem is to concentrate on what the question asks for: the quantity of water drained away, which we'll call x. We're told that x liters of water are drained away and $x-6$ liters are left. So x (the number of liters taken away) plus $x-6$ (the number of liters left) equals 12 (total liters originally in the sink). Therefore, $x+(x-6)=12$, $x+x-6=12$, $2x-6=12$, $2x=18$, and $x=9$. Note that wrong answer choice (B) is the liters of water left.

EXPERT EXCLUSIVE

Expect GMAT word problems to be confusing at first. Read carefully and don't start solving until you understand the situation described.

We can also use Backsolving here. Start with (B). If 3 liters were drained, then $12-3=9$ liters remain. The amount of water remaining is not 6 liters less than the amount of water drained away. Choice (B) is too small. We can eliminate (A) and (B). Next move on to (D). If 6 liters were drained, then $12-6=6$ liters remain. The amount of water remaining is not 6 liters less than the amount of water drained away. (D) is too small. Choice (E) must be correct.

20. D

The trick here is being careful about what quantity is taxed at what rate. Since Tony pays 8% of everything over $10,000, he pays that rate on $11,500 - $10,000 = $1,500. His first $4,000 isn't taxed, so he pays 5% of $10,000 - $4,000 = $6,000. Now it's just straightforward calculation: 8% of $1,500 is $0.08 \times \$1,500 = 8 \times \$15 = \$120$; 5% of $6,000 is $0.05 \times \$6,000 = 5 \times \$60 = \$300$. Add the two together, and we've got his total tax: $120 + $300 = $420. *In percent word problems, always make sure you're taking the proper percent of the proper quantity.*

21. A

The key is interpreting the first sentence, which tells you how many gallons of gas are left in the tank after 15 gallons are drained. Since draining 15 gallons cuts the amount of gas in half, there must originally have been 2×15, or 30, gallons in the tank. After the 15 gallons are drained away, there are 15 gallons left. Since p gallons are added to the 15 gallons left in the tank, the number of gallons at the end is $15 + p$.

If you were confused by the first sentence and couldn't deduce the amount of gas left in the tank, you could still logically eliminate all the answers but (A) and (C). Since the problem says that p gallons are *added*, the right answer has to be something-or-other *plus p*.

22. E

We're asked for the time it takes machine B to process 12,000 envelopes. We'll need to be careful about the size of the job, as the data are for different-sized jobs. Machines B and C together can process 6,000 envelopes in $2\frac{2}{5}$ (or $\frac{12}{5}$) hours. The combined work equation, then, is $\frac{BC}{B+C}=\frac{12}{5}$ for 6,000 envelopes. So we could solve for B if we knew how long C took by itself. To know that, we'll use the fact that machines A and C together take 1 hour for 3,000 envelopes, or 2 hours for 6,000. So $\frac{AC}{A+C}=2$. Since machine A takes 3 hours for 6,000, that's $\frac{3C}{3+C}=2$. So $3C=6+2C$. That means $C=6$. Plugging that back into $\frac{BC}{B+C}=\frac{12}{5}$, we get $\frac{6B}{B+6}=\frac{12}{5}$. Cross multiplying gives $30B=12B+72$. Subtract $12B$ from each side to get $18B=72$, or $B=4$. But since that was only for 6,000 envelopes, we need to double that to 8 hours for 12,000 envelopes.

23. D

The chart tells us what percent of the flights were late, and the text tells us what number of flights were late (the number of flights that the percentage represents). We have to figure out the number of flights that were *not* late (that were on time). We calculate 43% + 17% + 12% + 3% = 75% of the flights were late. That's a nice, neat percentage, representing $\frac{3}{4}$. So $\frac{3}{4}$ of the flights were late, which means $\frac{1}{4}$ of the flights were on time. That makes the calculation very easy: 1,200 flights were late, which is equal to $\frac{3}{4}$ of all the flights. Call the total number of flights F. Then, since 1,200 flights is equal to $\frac{3}{4}$ of all the flights, we can write the equation $\frac{3}{4}F=1,200$. Solve for F:

$$\frac{3}{4}F=1,200$$
$$3F=1,200(4)$$
$$3F=4,800$$
$$F=\frac{4,800}{3}=1,600$$

The total number of flights is 1,600. We know that $\frac{1}{4}$ of all the flights were on time. So the number of flights that were on time is $\frac{1}{4}F=\frac{1}{4}(1,600)=400$.

EXPERT EXCLUSIVE

Keep looking for opportunities to solve for what you're asked for without calculating the value of every variable. You'll save valuable time.

When the GMAT gives you numbers this big, there is often a shortcut in the arithmetic. And there is one here. Stay focused on what's asked. If delayed flights are $\frac{3}{4}$ of all flights, then on-time flights are $\frac{1}{4}$. So the number of delayed flights is three times that of on-time flights: $\frac{1,200}{3} = 400$.

24. D

EXPERT EXCLUSIVE

Check the answers before beginning work on a ratio question. You can use this "multiple shortcut" with surprising frequency.

There's a shortcut to solving this one. We're told that cheese, bologna, and peanut butter sandwiches are made in the ratio of 11 to 7 to 18. Every time they make 11 cheese sandwiches, they also have to make 7 bologna and 18 peanut butter sandwiches. So there must be $11x$ cheese sandwiches (and we don't know what x is at this point), $7x$ bologna sandwiches, and $18x$ peanut butter sandwiches. How many bologna sandwiches were made? Well, the number of bologna sandwiches must be some multiple of 7. Only choice (D), 42, is a multiple of 7.

If you didn't notice that, you'd have solved the problem algebraically, which is also pretty simple. If you add $11x$ (the number of cheese sandwiches), $7x$ (the number of bologna sandwiches), and $18x$ (the number of peanut butter sandwiches), you get 216 sandwiches. In other words: $11x + 7x + 18x = 216$; $36x = 216$; $x = 6$. So there were $7(6) = 42$ bologna sandwiches.

25. B

EXPERT EXCLUSIVE

Don't be intimidated by scary-looking numbers like 49.872 … the test makers know that you don't have a calculator, so these numbers are good indications that you can estimate.

Follow the question carefully. We're ultimately interested in the length of a side of "a certain square." We've been given a clue: the square's area is $\frac{1}{15}$ the area of a rectangle measuring 49.872 by 30.64. Fortunately, we've been told we need only the "approximate" length of a side, so we can work with approximates throughout. The area of the rectangle, then, is approximately 50×30, or 1,500. The area of the square will be approximately $\frac{1}{15}$ of that, or 100. The length of the side of a square is always the positive square root of the area (side $\times$ side = area), so this square has sides of approximately 10 inches.

26. D

To solve this equation, we need to follow the order of operations and simplify the expression inside the parentheses first. Since $4 - 5 = -1$, we can restate the original equation as $y = -(-1)$, or $y = 1$. Choice (D) is correct.

27. E

We can calculate a percent increase by dividing the increase in price by the original price. The price went from \$36 to \$50, so the increase is $50 - 36 = 14$. The original value was \$36, so the fractional increase is $\frac{14}{36}$, or $\frac{7}{18}$.

To convert a fraction (or decimal) to a percent, multiply that fraction (or decimal) by 100. So $\frac{7}{18} = \frac{7}{18} \times 100 = \frac{7}{9} \times 50 = \frac{350}{9}$ = approximately 38.89%. This is closest to choice (E).

28. B

Ratios are just another way of expressing fractions. Therefore, the ratio $\frac{31}{18} : 13\left(\frac{31}{18}\right)$ is the same as the fraction $\dfrac{\left(\frac{31}{18}\right)}{13\left(\frac{31}{18}\right)}$. The term $\frac{31}{18}$ cancels, leaving us with just $\frac{1}{13}$, which is (B).

29. D

To find the greatest product, we could multiply the greatest four primes less than 20. Do you suspect that to be far too much work? That's great GMAT instinct. Since a prime has no factors other than 1 and itself, $19 \times 17 \times 13 \times 11$ cannot have any other prime factors. So we can eliminate any answer that's a multiple of a smaller prime. (B) and (E) are clearly multiples of 2, and (C) is clearly a multiple of 5. Testing for multiples of 3 is fairly straightforward—the digits must sum to a multiple of 3. The digits of (A) sum to 27, so (A) is a multiple of 3. (D), as the only answer not eliminated, must be correct.

30. A

These overlapping set problems are often best solved by organizing the data into a chart:

	rookie	not rookie	Total
mint	0.6(1,100)=660		1,100
not mint			400
Total		740	

Then you can just add or subtract as needed to fill in the other spots until you arrive at your answer:

	rookie	not rookie	Total
mint	660	440	1,100
not mint	100	300	400
Total	760	740	1,500

He has 100 rookie cards that are not in mint condition: answer (A).

EXPERT EXCLUSIVE

Look at the expressions or "chunks" before you get carried away calculating values; the GMAT gives you opportunities to avoid much of the worst math.

EXPERT EXCLUSIVE

You'll need to have the first primes memorized: 2, 3, 5, 7, 11, 13, 17, 19. Knowing a few more (like 23, 29, 31, 37, and 41) can't hurt either.

EXPERT EXCLUSIVE

Common factors are the key to some of the GMAT's most puzzling arithmetic questions.

31. E

When we see what appears to be a lengthy arithmetic problem, we should look for ways to simplify the work. When fractions are involved, think about factoring the numerator and denominator, looking for terms that will cancel out.

In this case, $5.005 = 5 \times 1.001$, and $2.002 = 2 \times 1.001$. So we can rewrite the original fraction as $\dfrac{5.005}{2.002} = \dfrac{5(1.001)}{2(1.001)} = \dfrac{5}{2} = 2.5$. Choice (E) is correct.

32. C

A subset of an original set is any set that contains one or more elements of the original set but no elements of any other set. So {10, 14} is a subset of the original set in this problem, but {5, 10, 14} is not because 5 was not in the original set.

We need to determine the number of subsets that have an odd number of elements. So for this four-member set, we need to determine the number of subsets that have one or three elements.

There are 4 subsets that contain exactly one element: {10}, {14}, {17}, and {24}.

To find the number of three-element subsets, we can think of this as a combinations problem. The order of the elements is not important—the set {10, 14, 17} is the same as the set {10, 17, 14}—so the question becomes, How many ways are there to choose 3 elements from a set of 4, when order doesn't matter?

The combinations formula is $\dfrac{n!}{k!(n-k)!}$, where n is the number of elements in the original set and k is the number of elements in the subset. Here $n = 4$ and $k = 3$, so the number of combinations is $\dfrac{4!}{3!(4-3)!} = \dfrac{4 \times 3 \times 2 \times 1}{(3 \times 2 \times 1)(1)} = 4$. So, there are 4 one-element subsets and 4 three-element subsets, for a total of 8 subsets with an odd number of elements.

EXPERT EXCLUSIVE

When counting combinations, make sure to count systematically so you don't miss any.

Instead of using the combinations formula, we could also have listed all the subsets of {10, 14, 17, 24} that contain three elements:

{10, 14, 17}

{10, 14, 24}

{10, 17, 24}

{14, 17, 24}

So when you also consider the 4 subsets with one element, there are 8 subsets of {10, 14, 17, 24} that contain an odd number of elements.

33. E

It's probably easiest to Pick Numbers so that this problem becomes much simpler. Since we have to find 1/6 of the students and we are asked to find a percentage, 600 is a very safe number to pick for the total number of students. That means there are 100 math majors, 60 of whom study a foreign language, and there are 240 students who do not study a foreign language. Now let's put this data into the overlapping sets chart:

	math	non-math	Total
foreign lang.	60		
no foreign lang.			240
Total	100		600

Now it's a simple matter of addition and subtraction to fill the rest of the spots:

	math	non-math	Total
foreign lang.	60	300	360
no foreign lang.	40	200	240
Total	100	500	600

The ratio of non-math majors who study a foreign language to those who do not is 300:200, or 3:2.

34. A

For a Roman Numeral problem, we want to find the statement that appears in the most choices and work with it first; if we can eliminate it, we can quickly reduce the number of possible choices.

Here, statement II shows up three times, so let's start there. By definition, any nonzero number raised to the exponent zero is equal to 1, so x^0 cannot equal zero. Thus, we can eliminate (C), (D), and (E). Based on the remaining choices, we can see that either statement I must equal zero or none of the statements must equal zero.

Our next step is to evaluate statement I. Let's Pick Numbers. If x is 1, then $x^3 - x^2$ is $1 - 1 = 0$. But if we try $x = 2$, we find that $x^3 - x^2 = 2^3 - 2^2 = 8 - 4 = 4$. So this statement might be equal to zero, but it doesn't have to be. We can eliminate (B). In fact, none of the statements has to be zero, so (A) is correct.

35. C

Let a be the population of City A, let b be the population of City B, and let c be the population of City C. Since a is three times larger than b, $a = 3b$, and the population of A and B together is $3b + b$, or $4b$.

Furthermore, since the population of A and B together is twice the population of C, we can write the equation $4b = 2c$, or $c = 2b$. Dividing both sides by b gives $\frac{c}{b} = 2$, so the ratio of c to b is 2:1.

EXPERT EXCLUSIVE

Who cares that most cities have a population greater than 3? It's *permissibility* and *manageability* that matter, not realism.

Alternatively, we could solve this problem by Picking Numbers. For City A, pick any small number easily divisible by 3; in fact, picking 3 will work well. If the population of A is 3, then the population of B must be 1, and their combined population must be 4. Since C's population is half that of A and B together, it must be 2. Thus the ratio of C to B is 2:1.

36. D

This is a number properties question, so Picking Numbers will work. Since m divided by n must be negative, one of the two numbers m or n must be negative, and the other must be positive. So we'll test two pairs of numbers: $m = 3$, $n = -1$ and $m = -3$, $n = 1$. Because the question asks, "Which of the following . . . ," we'll start with choice (E).

(E): Using the first pair of values, $m - n = 3 - (-1) = 4$. That's greater than zero, so (E) could be true; there is no need to test the second pair. We can eliminate (E).

Testing (D), we find

$$(3)(-1)^3 = (3)(-1) < 0, \text{ and } (-3)(1)^3 = (-3)(1) < 0$$

Both pairs give values less than zero, so (D) is not true in either case. (D) looks good, but on a "cannot"/"must" problem, we need to make sure we didn't get a false positive. This can be confirmed either by testing the other choices or by recognizing that since one and only one of the two numbers must be negative, and any negative number cubed will still be negative, mn^3 will either involve multiplying a positive m times a negative n^3 or a negative m times a positive n^3 and, therefore, the product mn^3 could never be positive.

37. C

Like many GMAT word problems, the initial presentation is a little confusing. Don't try to comprehend everything all at once. When you read the question stem the first time, focus on understanding the basic situation. Here, we're given a formula for figuring out the speed of a train at any given time. We're asked for the difference between the speed at 4 seconds and the speed at 2 seconds.

To answer this question, all we need to do is use the formula we're given to calculate the speeds, then subtract.

Speed formula: $\qquad\qquad s = t^2 + t$

Solve for $t = 4$ seconds: $\qquad s = 4^2 + 4 = 16 + 4 = 20$

Solve for $t = 2$ seconds: $s = 2^2 + 2 = 4 + 2 = 6$

Difference: $20 - 6 = 14$

38. B

Let's use the formula Distance = Speed $\times$ Time. In this case, we want to find the time required to walk s blocks, so let's divide both sides of the formula by Speed to get $\dfrac{\text{Distance}}{\text{Speed}} = \text{Time}$. We are told that the distance is s blocks, so we just need to find Lisa's speed.

If we go back to the distance formula and divide both sides by Time, we see that $\text{Speed} = \dfrac{\text{Distance}}{\text{Time}}$. Lisa walked t blocks in 3 minutes, so her speed is $\dfrac{t \text{ blocks}}{3 \text{ minutes}} = \dfrac{t}{3}$ blocks per minute. So $\dfrac{\text{Distance}}{\text{Speed}} = \dfrac{s \text{ Blocks}}{\frac{t}{3} \text{ blocks per minute}} = (s)\left(\dfrac{3}{t}\right) = \dfrac{3s}{t}$ minutes. Choice (B) is correct.

Sound complicated? Picking Numbers makes fast work of this problem. Let's pick a manageable number of blocks to walk in 3 minutes: 3 blocks in 3 minutes sounds pretty straightforward, so $t = 3$. Now we'll let s equal 2. The question then is "If Lisa can walk 3 blocks in 3 minutes, how many minutes does it take her to walk 2 blocks?" 3 blocks in 3 minutes is 1 block per minute; 2 blocks will take 2 minutes.

> **EXPERT EXCLUSIVE**
>
> On test day, don't try to show off your "math smarts"; show off your "GMAT smarts" instead. If Picking Numbers is easier, Pick Numbers.

Plug $t = 3$ and $s = 2$ into the answer choices. Only (B) yields the number we want, 2. So (B) is correct.

39. A

In "changing mixture" problems, the first thing to identify is which components change and which stay the same. In this case, water is being added, so its volume, as well as that of the total mixture, is changing; however, nitric acid is neither added nor removed, so that volume is constant.

We can calculate the volume of that original nitric acid content with a simple equation—multiply the volume by the percent concentration.

$(\text{Volume}_1)(\text{Concentration}_1) = \text{Acid}_1$

The exact same formula applies to the new solution that we'll have after more water is added.

$(\text{Volume}_2)(\text{Concentration}_2) = \text{Acid}_2$

But the amount of acid is unchanged between mixtures! Thus, we can set the two expressions equal to each other:

$$(\text{Volume}_1)(\text{Concentration}_1) = \text{Acid}_1 = \text{Acid}_2 = (\text{Volume}_2)(\text{Concentration}_2)$$

$$(\text{Volume}_1)(\text{Concentration}_1) = (\text{Volume}_2)(\text{Concentration}_2)$$

Plugging in the values from the question stem, we get this:

$$(10\%)(10) = (4\%)(V_2)$$
$$\frac{10}{100} \times 10 = \frac{4}{100}V_2$$
$$\frac{\cancel{100}}{4} \times \frac{10}{\cancel{100}} \times 10 = V_2$$
$$V_2 = 25$$

Note that choice (D) is a trap answer for those who stop too soon; this question is asking how much water was *added*, not what the final volume was! Since we started with 10 liters of liquid and ended with 25, we added 15 liters of water, and (A) is correct.

40. A

> **EXPERT EXCLUSIVE**
>
> Complex "shaded area" shapes are just the sum or the difference of other, simpler shapes.

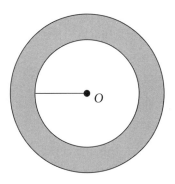

Read carefully. We're not asked for the area of the pool or the walkway but for the difference between them. So we will need the area of each, and then we'll subtract. Let's take the area of the pool first. The area of a circle with a radius r is πr^2, and we know that the pool has a radius of 10 meters. Thus, the area of the circular swimming pool is $\pi(10)^2 = \pi(100) = 100\pi$.

Since the pool has a radius of 10 meters and the walkway is 5 meters wide, the radius of the region consisting of the circular swimming pool together with the walkway is $10 + 5 = 15$ meters. Therefore, the area of this circular region is $\pi(15)^2 = \pi(225) = 225\pi$. We now subtract the area of the pool from this area to find the area of the walkway. We find that $225\pi - 100\pi$, or 125π, is the area of the walkway.

Now we need the difference between the area of the walkway and the area of the pool, which is $125\pi - 100\pi$, or 25π. So (A) is correct.

Be careful to avoid the trap answers. Choice (C) is the area of the pool; choice (D) is the area of the walkway; choice (E) is the area of the entire circular region.

41. D

This classic word problem illustrates the importance of studying the question stem and answer choices, as well as determining what's asked, before starting to work on the problem. It's tempting to write down $a = 8.00$ and $b = 5.60$, because we're given price first. But we aren't asked for price! We're asked for the number of Brand A binders. So those two equations will make our life quite complicated, as we'd now need two new variables for the number of binders.

By determining what we're asked before we start solving, though, we know to let a equal the number of Brand A binders and to let b equal the number of Brand B binders. For the number of binders purchased, we have $a + b = 12$, and for the amount spent, we have $\$8a + \$5.60b = \$84$.

To use combination to solve the equations, we need one of the variables to have the same coefficient in both equations so that it will cancel out. If we multiply the first equation by 8, we get $8a + 8b = 96$.

So we can write the two equations as follows:

$$8a + 8b = 96$$
$$8a + 5.60b = 84$$

If we subtract the bottom equation from the top one, we get $(8a - 8a) + (8b - 5.60b) = 96 - 84$, or $2.4b = 12$. If we divide both sides by 2.4, we are left with $b = 5$. Thus, Molly must have purchased $12 - b = 12 - 5 = 7$ Brand A binders. Choice (D) is the correct answer.

This is also a great Backsolving opportunity. Let's say you started with (B). That means Molly would have bought 5 Brand A binders at $8 apiece and $12 - 5 = 7$ Brand B binders at $5.60 apiece. That's $5 \times \$8 = \$40.00$ for the Brand A binders and $7 \times \$5.60 = \$39.20$ for the Brand B binders. We get $\$40.00 + \$39.20 = \$79.20$, which is less than she actually spent. She needs more of the expensive Brand A binders, so (A) and (B) are eliminated.

In (D), she buys 7 Brand A binders at $8 apiece and $12 - 7 = 5$ Brand B binders at $5.60 apiece. That's $7 \times \$8 = \$56.00$ for the Brand A binders, and $5 \times \$5.60 = \$28.00$ for the Brand B binders. We add $\$56.00 + \$28.00 = \$84.00$, which is exactly what we're looking for. Answer (D) is correct.

EXPERT EXCLUSIVE

Most permutation and combination questions require some careful analysis before calculations can be done.

42. D

Because the question asks how many *arrangements* are possible, we know that the order in which the guests are seated matters and, therefore, that we're dealing with a *permutation* problem.

As with most upper-level GMAT permutations problems, the standard formulas are tough to apply. It's often best to draw a picture (the numbers that go in the blanks will be multiplied together):

Back: ___ × ___ × ___ × ___ × ___

Front: ___ × ___ × ___ × ___ × ___

Then write in the possible number of choices for each space. The front row is clear, as there are no restrictions. Any of the five shortest could be on the left; once one is selected, any of the four remaining may follow him; once two are placed, any of the remaining three may be placed; and so forth. The middle spot of the back row has only one possibility, the coach:

Back: ___ × ___ × _1_ × ___ × ___

Front: _5_ × _4_ × _3_ × _2_ × _1_

But what about the rest of the back row? It's unclear how many options we have for the two spots adjacent to the coach. Theoretically, any of the four tall players could go on his right, but then we wouldn't know how many possibilities would be left for the spot on his left—if the one misbehaving player was on his right, any of the remaining three could be there. But if not, then there'd be only one choice possible—he'd have to go on the left. (Notice, though, that we know the answer has to be something larger than $5 \times 4 \times 3 \times 2 \times 1 \times 1 = 120$, which eliminates two answer choices.)

So start with the two spots you *are* sure about—the ones on the outside of the back row. There are three possible selections for the left-most spot (any of the three tall, well-behaved players); there would then be two possible choices remaining for the right-most spot:

Back: _3_ × ___ × _1_ × ___ × _2_

Front: _5_ × _4_ × _3_ × _2_ × _1_

Now things are clearer. There are two choices remaining for the spot on the left of the coach (either the misbehaving player or the last well-behaved one); once one is selected, there will only be one possibility for the final spot:

Back: _3_ × _2_ × _1_ × _1_ × _2_

Front: _5_ × _4_ × _3_ × _2_ × _1_

So, the number of arrangements is $3 \times 2 \times 1 \times 1 \times 2 \times 5 \times 4 \times 3 \times 2 \times 1 =$ $12 \times 120 = 1,440$.

43. E

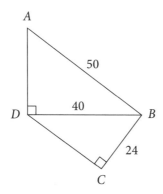

> **EXPERT EXCLUSIVE**
>
> Look for Pythagorean triples and the other special right triangles whenever the GMAT gives you a triangle problem. Finding them will save you a lot of time compared to using the Pythagorean theorem.

The perimeter of a quadrilateral is the sum of the lengths of its sides. For *ABCD*, the perimeter is $AB + BC + CD + DA$. From the figure, we know that $AB = 50$ and $BC = 24$. So we need to find the lengths of *CD* and *DA*.

To find the length of *DA*, let's consider right triangle *ABD*. This triangle is a multiple of the 3-4-5 right triangle, with each member of the 3:4:5 ratio multiplied by 10. Since $BD = 40 = 4 \times 10$ and $AB = 50 = 5 \times 10$, *DA* must have a length of $3 \times 10 = 30$.

Now let's consider right triangle *BCD*. This triangle is also a multiple of the 3-4-5 right triangle. However, in this triangle, each member of the 3:4:5 ratio is multiplied by 8. Since $BC = 24 = 3 \times 8$ and $BD = 40 = 5 \times 8$, *CD* must have a length of $4 \times 8 = 32$.

Now we have the lengths of all the sides of quadrilateral *ABCD*: $AB = 50$, $BC = 24$, $CD = 32$, and $DA = 30$. So the perimeter of quadrilateral *ABCD* is

$$AB + BC + CD + DA = 50 + 24 + 32 + 30 = 136$$

44. E

Studying the question stem and the answer choices would allow you to make some quick eliminations with no calculation at all. We're told that the farmer makes a profit selling his wheat and that his costs include $10 per bushel. To make a profit, he would have to sell each bushel for more than $10 apiece. Otherwise, he'd lose money on every bushel sold! So (A) and (B) can be thrown away immediately.

Backsolving is a very straightforward approach to this problem. Let's start with (D), especially since (B) has already been eliminated. The 50,000 bushels sold for $13 each give $650,000 of revenue. The farmer's costs are $10 per bushel, or $500,000, plus $200,000 rent. That's a total of $700,000. So selling wheat at $13/bushel still loses the farmer money. (E), as the only number larger than 13, must be correct.

Algebraically, if p = selling price per bushel in dollars and Profit = Revenue – Fixed Cost – Variable Cost, the following equation can be written: $150{,}000 = 50{,}000p - 200{,}000 - (50{,}000 \times 10)$. Solving this for p will result in $850{,}000 = 50{,}000p$, or $p = 17$.

45. B

No picture is given in the question stem, but that's no reason not to draw one yourself.

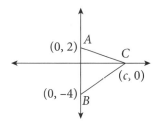

For triangle ABC, let's call the side that lies on the y-axis between $A(0,2)$ and $B(0,-4)$ the base of the triangle.

Since the distance between these two points is 6, we can say that the base of the triangle is 6 units in length. Because the base lies along the y-axis, the height will therefore be the distance from the y-axis to the third point, $C(c, 0)$. Since c represents the distance from the y-axis to point C, finding the height will give us the value of c, because c is positive.

Now we use the formula for the area of a triangle, $\frac{1}{2}$(base)(height). In this case, the base is 6 and the area is 21.

$$\frac{1}{2} \text{ base (height)} = \text{area}$$

Substitute values and variables:

$$\frac{1}{2}6(c) = 21$$
$$3(c) = 21$$
$$c = 7$$

The answer is (B).

46. D

There are several ways to calculate this probability, but two are the most efficient. One is to count desired outcomes and possible outcomes separately, using the combinations formula rather than fractions:

# of possible outcomes = any 4 socks selected from the total 12. Order of selection wouldn't matter (we've got the same 4 socks, no matter which was drawn first), so that's

$$12C4 = \frac{12!}{4!\,8!} = \frac{12 \times 11 \times 10 \times 9 \times 8 \times 7 \times 6 \times 5 \times 4 \times 3 \times 2 \times 1}{4 \times 3 \times 2 \times 1 \, 8 \times 7 \times 6 \times 5 \times 4 \times 3 \times 2 \times 1} = \frac{12 \times 11 \times 10 \times 9}{4 \times 3 \times 2 \times 1} = 11 \times 5 \times 9$$

(Since we hope that common factors will cancel out later, we'll leave the number like this, rather than figuring out the product.)

# of desired outcomes = any 2 of the 6 blue socks and any 2 of the 6 white socks. That's 6C2 and 6C2. Since *and* becomes *multiply*, we have 6C2 × 6C2 =

$$(6C2)^2 = \left(\frac{6 \times 5 \times 4 \times 3 \times 2 \times 1}{2 \times 1 \times 4 \times 3 \times 2 \times 1}\right)^2 = \left(\frac{6 \times 5}{2 \times 1}\right)^2 = 15^2 = 15 \times 15$$

(Again, we're hoping factors will cancel out.)

$$\text{Probability} = \frac{\text{\# of desired outcomes}}{\text{\# of possible outcomes}} = \frac{15 \times 15}{11 \times 5 \times 9} = \frac{5}{11}$$

Another approach is to calculate the probability for exactly one desired outcome and multiply that by the number of ways that outcome could be achieved:

One desired outcome is BBWW. Since there are 6 of each sock and no replacement is made between draws, the probability for that outcome is this:

$$\text{BBWW} = \frac{6}{12} \times \frac{5}{11} \times \frac{6}{10} \times \frac{5}{9} = \frac{1}{2} \times \frac{5}{11} \times \frac{3}{5} \times \frac{5}{9} = \frac{5}{66}$$

The number of ways that BBWW could be arranged is $\frac{4!}{2!\,2!} = 6$.

(You could have thought of this either as 4C2 or as the "rearranged letters" calculation.)

Then $\frac{5}{66} \times 6 = \frac{5}{11}$.

Either way, (D) is the answer. (A) is the probability of drawing all socks of the same color; (B) is the possibility of one particular outcome of the desired six.

47. D

We have two equations and two variables, but because the second equation is not linear, we can't solve directly for x and y. Instead, since the second equation is a quadratic equation, we should think about factoring.

If we add 10 to both sides of the second equation, we get $x^2 - xy - 2y^2 = 10$. Now the left side looks like a quadratic expression that we can factor with reverse FOIL. Since we could get the x^2 term by multiplying x and x, we know both factors will contain x. Next we need to determine what two factors multiplied together will give us $-2y^2$. We need either $-2y$ and y or $2y$ and $-y$. Since the coefficient of the xy term is negative, we should choose $-2y$ and y, because the sum of the outer and inner products will give us $-xy$. Thus, the factorization of $x^2 - xy - 2y^2$ is $(x + y)(x - 2y)$.

EXPERT EXCLUSIVE

If you're puzzled about how to approach a question with a quadratic, reverse-FOIL it. Odds are the problem will be greatly simplified.

EXPERT EXCLUSIVE

When you're asked for the value of an expression, you can often solve for that expression directly. Don't waste time solving for all the variables individually if you don't have to.

Now, notice that both factors of $x^2 - xy - 2y^2$ appear in the question stem. We are told that $x + y = 2$, and we are asked to find the value of $x - 2y$.

We can find the value of $x - 2y$ if we return to the quadratic equation. We know that $(x + y)(x - 2y) = 10$. Since $x + y = 2$, we can replace $(x + y)$ with 2, giving us $2(x - 2y) = 10$, or $(x - 2y) = 5$. So (D) is correct.

Did you get to $2(x - 2y) = 10$ and then go further to $2x - 4y = 10$ or to $x = 5 + 2y$? If so, you lost sight of what was asked. You may find it helpful to write down what's asked on your scratch paper so it's always in your line of sight.

48. C

We need to find the distance traveled in the first 6-minute interval. Because Distance = Rate × Time and we already know that the time is 6 minutes, all we need to do is find the train's speed (its rate) during the first interval in order to find the distance.

EXPERT EXCLUSIVE

The most efficient solution is often found by starting with what you're asked and working backwards, instead of writing down equations based on the first part of the question stem.

We are given that the train's average speed increased by 3 miles per hour during each interval. During the third interval, its average speed was 24 miles per hour. So in the second interval, its speed must have been $24 - 3 = 21$. Similarly, its speed in the first interval must have been $21 - 3 = 18$ miles per hour.

Now we have time (6 minutes) and speed (18 miles per hour). But the time is in minutes and the speed is in miles per hour. We can't calculate the distance unless we convert the time to hours or the speed to miles per minute. An hour has 60 minutes, so 6 minutes is $\frac{6}{60} = \frac{1}{10}$ of an hour. Therefore, the distance is $\frac{1}{10}$ hours × 18 miles per hour = $\frac{18}{10} = 1.8$ miles. So (C) is correct.

49. D

The stem gives us one equation, $abcd = 546$, and asks us to find $b + c$. There is no way to solve directly for b and c, but we know they must be factors of 546, so let's start by factoring 546. Since it's even, one factor must be 2, so $546 = (273)(2)$. Now factor 273 by dividing it by 3: $273 = (91)(3)$. Now factor 91; its factors are 13 and 7. Putting this all together, the factors of 546 are 2, 3, 7, and 13. All of these are prime, so 546 cannot be factored any further.

EXPERT EXCLUSIVE

Many GMAT problems are based on prime factors. If you don't know how to begin thinking about a number, especially a big one, find its prime factors. The problem will likely become simpler.

Now go back to the equation we were given: $abcd = 546$. Since the prime factors of 546 are 2, 3, 7, and 13, it must be the case that $(2)(3)(7)(13) = abcd$. Since we are told that $1 < a < b < c < d$, it must also be the case that

b and c are the middle 2 factors. Thus, $b = 3$ and $c = 7$. So $b + c = 10$, and (D) is correct.

50. B

Because the order of colors in the pairs doesn't matter, the number of two-color codes that can be made will be the number of ways one can select two colors from the total number of colors; that is, the number of combinations of two colors that can be created.

Since we're asked for the minimum possible number of colors, we'll have to Backsolve a little differently. If we test (B) and discover that 6 colors are enough to code all 20 chemicals, that wouldn't prove that 5 isn't also enough. So we'll have to start with (A). If 5 is enough, (A) is the right answer because there's nothing smaller. If 5 isn't enough, we'll test (B) and on up if necessary.

If we have 5 colors, there are 5 possible single-color codes. (If you wanted to calculate 5C5, you could, but it's faster just using common sense.) As for the two-color codes, we need to calculate 5C2. That's $\dfrac{5!}{2!(5-2)!} = \dfrac{5!}{2!3!} = \dfrac{5 \times 4 \times 3 \times 2 \times 1}{2 \times 1 \times 3 \times 2 \times 1} = 10$. So the total of one- and two-color codes is $5 + 10 = 15$. That's not enough, so we'll try (B).

If we have 6 colors, there are 6 possible single-color codes. For the number of two-color codes, we need to calculate 6C2. That's $\dfrac{6!}{2!(6-2)!} = \dfrac{6!}{2!4!} = \dfrac{6 \times 5 \times 4 \times 3 \times 2 \times 1}{2 \times 1 \times 4 \times 3 \times 2 \times 1} = 15$. So the total of one- and two-color codes is $6 + 15 = 21$. That's enough for our 20 chemicals, so (B) is correct.

If guessing on this problem, we could have eliminated (D) and (E). Because some chemicals will use pairs of colors, there is no need to have as many colors as chemicals, (D) or more colors than chemicals, (E).

CHAPTER 9: **DATA SUFFICIENCY**

- Question Format and Structure
- The Basic Principles of Data Sufficiency
- The Kaplan Method for Data Sufficiency
- Guessing in Data Sufficiency

Data Sufficiency is just a fancy name for a skill that you use all of the time, one that's actually very important in business. The basic idea is to determine when you have enough information to make a decision or solve a problem. The big difference between Data Sufficiency on the GMAT and most of the "data sufficiency" problems you come across in real life is that the GMAT problems are concerned solely with math facts and relationships.

Let's say you want to know whether a particular manager is doing a good job in her department. If you were informed that her department spent $50,000 more than it took in this year, would you be justified in saying that she was doing a bad job? Of course not—there could be all kinds of factors causing the loss that were beyond her control. For instance, the department might have spent $250,000 more than it took in last year when she wasn't in charge, so she could be making great improvements, even though the department is still losing money.

Data Sufficiency questions measure your ability to recognize what information is relevant to a problem and to determine at what point there is sufficient information to solve the problem. The questions are accompanied by some initial information and two Statements, labeled (1) and (2). You must decide whether the Statements provide enough data to allow you to answer the question.

 GO ONLINE

Many people struggle with Data Sufficiency at first because of the unfamiliarity of the format. It's vital that you practice as much as you can. Work through the questions online so that on test day you are as comfortable as you can be.

QUESTION FORMAT AND STRUCTURE

The instructions for the Data Sufficiency section on the GMAT look like this:

Directions: In each of the problems, a question is followed by two statements containing certain data. You are to determine whether the data provided by the statements are sufficient to answer the question. Choose the correct answer based upon the statements' data, your knowledge of mathematics, and your familiarity with everyday facts (such as the number of minutes in an hour or cents in a dollar). You must indicate whether

○ Statement (1) ALONE is sufficient, but statement (2) is not sufficient.

○ Statement (2) ALONE is sufficient, but statement (1) is not sufficient.

○ BOTH statements TOGETHER are sufficient, but NEITHER statement ALONE is sufficient.

○ EACH statement ALONE is sufficient.

○ Statements (1) and (2) TOGETHER are NOT sufficient.

Note: Diagrams accompanying problems agree with information given in the question but may not agree with additional information given in statements (1) and (2).

All numbers used are real numbers.

These directions may seem confusing at first, but they become clear with use. Let's walk through a simple problem:

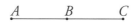

> **EXPERT EXCLUSIVE**
> Assume that diagrams in Data Sufficiency are *not* drawn to scale.

What is the length of segment *AC* ?

(1) *B* is the midpoint of *AC*.

(2) *AB* = 5.

We know that there is a line *AC* with point *B* somewhere in between *A* and *C*. We're asked to figure out the length of *AC*.

Statement (1) tells you that *B* is the midpoint of *AC*, so *AB* = *BC* and *AC* = 2*AB* = 2*BC*. Since Statement (1) does not give a value for *AB* or *BC*, you cannot answer the question using Statement (1) alone. Statement (2) says that *AB* = 5. Since Statement (2) does not give you a value for *BC*, the question cannot be answered by Statement (2) alone. Using both Statements together, you can find a value for both *AB* and *BC*; therefore you can find *AC*, and the answer to the question is choice (C).

THE BASIC PRINCIPLES OF DATA SUFFICIENCY

KNOW THE DATA SUFFICIENCY ANSWER CHOICES COLD

The directions and answer choices for Data Sufficiency questions never change. Become familiar with them now so you can save time and minimize errors when you actually take the test.

Let's take another look at the five answer choices:

> ○ Statement (1) ALONE is sufficient, but statement (2) is not sufficient.
>
> ○ Statement (2) ALONE is sufficient, but statement (1) is not sufficient.
>
> ○ BOTH statements TOGETHER are sufficient, but NEITHER statement ALONE is sufficient.
>
> ○ EACH statement ALONE is sufficient.
>
> ○ Statements (1) and (2) TOGETHER are NOT sufficient.

> **EXPERT EXCLUSIVE**
>
> Note that three answers—(A), (B), and (D)—depend on evaluating the Statements separately. Don't let one Statement pollute your thinking about the other.

At Kaplan, we use the acronym **1-2-TEN** when thinking of the answers.

1—Only Statement **(1)** is sufficient.

2—Only Statement **(2)** is sufficient.

T—You must put the Statements **together** for them to be sufficient.

E—**Either** Statement is sufficient.

N—**Neither** separately nor together are the Statements sufficient.

Knowing these choices cold will help you quickly narrow down your answer and will aid you in guessing.

> If Statement (1) is sufficient, the answer could only be (A) or (D). *Eliminate (B), (C), and (E).*
>
> If Statement (1) is insufficient, the answer could only be (B), (C), or (E). *Eliminate (A) and (D).*
>
> If Statement (2) is sufficient, the answer could only be (B) or (D). *Eliminate (A), (C), and (E).*
>
> If Statement (2) is insufficient, the answer could only be (A), (C), or (E). *Eliminate (B) and (D).*

You also want to avoid a common mistake on Data Sufficiency: answering (C) when the answer is actually (A), (B), or (D). If either Statement by itself is sufficient, then of course the two Statements together will be sufficient as well. But (C) is correct *only* when each Statement alone is insufficient.

KNOW THE TWO TYPES OF DATA SUFFICIENCY QUESTIONS

There are two broad types of Data Sufficiency questions, and they play by slightly different rules. The two types are Value questions and Yes/No questions.

Value Questions

A Value question will ask you for the exact value of something. If a Statement narrows the possibilities down to exactly one number, then it is sufficient. Otherwise, not.

Example:

What is the value of x?

(1) $x^2 - 7x + 6 = 0$

(2) $5x = 30$

Statement (1) can be reverse-FOILed to $(x - 1)(x - 6) = 0$, which means that there are two possible values for x, either 1 or 6. That makes Statement (1) insufficient.

Statement (2) has only one possible result, $x = 6$. So it is sufficient.

Since Statement (1) is insufficient and Statement (2) is sufficient by itself, the answer is (B).

But it's not always a variable that the question will ask you to find a value for. Some questions ask for the value of an expression.

Example:

What is the value of $4n - 5m$?

(1) $\dfrac{n}{5} = \dfrac{m}{4}$

(2) $n = 25$

> **CAUTION**
>
> The GMAT asks questions that can be answered without knowing the values of all the variables. Don't rush to assume that you need the value of all the variables—just the value of what's asked.

Notice that the question asks for the value not of n and m individually but of $4n - 5m$ itself. If we cross multiply the equation in Statement (1), we get $4n = 5m$. Subtract $5m$ from each side, and we get $4n - 5m = 0$. So while we don't have a value for n or m, we have a value for what we need: $4n - 5m$. Statement (1) is sufficient.

Statement (2) gives us one variable but not the other. It is insufficient, and the answer is (A).

The GMAT defines sufficiency in a Value question to be an actual number. An expression isn't sufficient.

Example:

What is the value of y?

(1) $3y = 21$

(2) $2x + y = 18$

Statement (1) gives $y = 7$. That's sufficient. But Statement (2) only gives us $y = 18 - 2x$. Even though we can get "$y =$", what y is equal to isn't a number. So Statement (2) is insufficient. The answer is (A).

Yes/No Questions

About one-third of the Data Sufficiency questions that you'll see on test day don't ask a question that demands a numerical response but rather a yes-or-no response. For example:

Is z even?

The question doesn't really care whether z is 2, 4, 6, 8, or 800. Just whether it's even—yes or no.

A Statement is sufficient if it answers the question, regardless of what the answer is. In other words, if a Statement answers the question "definitely yes," then that Statement is sufficient. So is a Statement that answers the question "definitely no."

EXPERT EXCLUSIVE
No is as sufficient as *yes*. It's *maybe* that's insufficient.

Example:

Is $4 + \dfrac{n}{6}$ an integer?

(1) n is a multiple of 3.

(2) n divided by 6 has a remainder of 0.

Since 4 is already an integer, the question depends on whether $\dfrac{n}{6}$ is an integer, which is to say it depends on whether n is a multiple of 6.

Statement (1) tells us that n is a multiple of 3. Some multiples of 3 are also multiples of 6 (6, 12, 18, etc.). But some are not (3, 9, 15, etc.). So Statement (1) only gives us an answer of "maybe" and is therefore insufficient.

Statement (2) tells us $\frac{n}{6}$ is an integer. Regardless of which multiple of 6 n equals—6, 12, 18, 66, or 660—we always get a "yes." That's sufficient. The answer is (B).

But what if Statement (2) said this instead:

> (2) n divided by 6 has a remainder of 3.

Now Statement (2) tells us $\frac{n}{6}$ is definitely *not* an integer. So regardless of what number n might be—3, 9, 15, 63, or 663—our answer is "definitely no." Because it's a *definite answer*, this version of Statement (2) is also sufficient, and the answer is still (B)!

EXPERT EXCLUSIVE

Every so often, a Statement will be redundant with information given in the question stem or will simply be a known mathematical fact, like the formula for the area of a circle. Those Statements are always insufficient.

THE STATEMENTS ARE ALWAYS TRUE

The Statements are new pieces of data about the problem and are always true. A common mistake among test takers is to try to verify a Statement. Also, sometimes it's tempting to reverse the question and the Statements. That won't lead to the right answer either.

Example:

> If x is an integer, and $0 < x < 4$, is x prime?
>
> (1) $x > 1$.
>
> (2) x is even.

According to the question stem, x could be 1, 2, or 3. We know that 2 and 3 are prime but 1 is not. Let's look at Statement (1). Knowing that x is greater than 1 rules out 1, leaving only 2 and 3 as possible values of x. We don't yet know which it is, but that's okay—both 2 and 3 are prime, so we have an answer: "definitely yes." Sufficient.

A common error would be to say of Statement (2), "It's not sufficient because not all the primes in the question are even." But we aren't asked whether every possible value that might answer "yes" is consistent with the Statement. Rather, we're asked whether every value consistent with the Statement answers the question the same way. What we should say is this: "Of the possible numbers—1, 2, and 3—only one of them is even. Now I know that x is 2; 2 is prime, so the Statement gives me a definite yes. Sufficient." The answer is (D).

The fact that the Statements are always true has an important corollary that will help you catch careless errors: the Statements will never contradict each other. True, they won't always be sufficient, but they'll never be mutually exclusive. If you think two Statements are disagreeing with each other, you should recheck your work, because you have made an error.

Example:

What is the value of t?

(1) $t^2 = t$

(2) $t + 6 = 6$

This is a straightforward Value question for which we need a value of t. Let's say that you made an error in your analysis of Statement (1) and thought that t had to equal 1. You'd think that Statement (1) was sufficient.

Then you'd look at Statement (2). Simplifying, we'd learn that t equals 0. That's also sufficient. So you'd think that the answer would be (D). But the Statements contradict each other:

(1) $t = 1$

(2) $t = 0$

That isn't possible. So you'd know to go back and recheck your work. "Statement (2) pretty obviously says that $t = 0$," you might say, "so I'll recheck my work on Statement (1). Is 1 the only number that equals itself when squared? What about the 0 from Statement (2) . . . let's see . . . oh, of course! $0^2 = 0 \times 0 = 0$. So Statement (1) actually permits *two* values and is insufficient."

(1) $t = 0$ or 1

(2) $t = 0$

The correct answer is (B), not (D).

IT'S ALL ABOUT THE QUESTION STEM

The most common error committed by test takers on Data Sufficiency questions is to rush past the question and dive into the Statements, doing a whole bunch of math. You wouldn't want that in a conversation:

You: Excuse me, sir, could you give me directions to th—

Unhelpful person: Oh yeah, yeah, yeah. Go left and make a right at the third light.

EXPERT EXCLUSIVE

If you understand the Data Sufficiency directions and answer choices but still often get wrong answers, odds are that you aren't spending enough time with the question stem.

Obviously, this guy has no business giving you an answer because he doesn't know your question yet. Similarly, we shouldn't rush through the question stem. For one thing, there's a huge difference between a Value question and a Yes/No question. Let's take a look at an identical pair of Statements:

(1) $x^3 = x$	(1) $x^3 = x$
(2) $x^2 = x$	(2) $x^2 = x$

Here's how they evaluate:

(1) $x = -1, 0,$ or 1	(1) $x = -1, 0,$ or 1
(2) $x = 0$ or 1	(2) $x = 0$ or 1

But we still have no idea what the answers are without knowing the questions:

What is the value of x?	Is $x < -1$?
(1) $x = -1, 0,$ or 1	(1) $x = -1, 0,$ or 1
(2) $x = 0$ or 1	(2) $x = 0$ or 1

For the left-hand question, Statement (1) is insufficient because there are three possible values of x. Statement (2) is also insufficient because there are two possible values. Even when the Statements are considered together, x might be either 0 or 1. That's two values, which is insufficient for a Value question. Answer (E).

But the right-hand question is a Yes/No question, asking whether x is less than −1. Let's look at Statement (1). Is $-1 < -1$? No. Is $0 < -1$? No. Is $1 < -1$? No. Always no: sufficient. Same for Statement (2); either value answers no, so it's sufficient as well. Answer (D).

That's as different as two answers can be, and it had *nothing* to do with the Statements. It's all about the question stem!

EXPERT EXCLUSIVE

If you have an opportunity to simplify the question stem, do so. The Statements will become much easier to evaluate.

But we want to look for more than just whether the question is a Value or a Yes/No question. You saw how Problem Solving questions get much easier with some analysis and simplification before an approach is chosen. So too with Data Sufficiency.

Example:

If $w \neq x$, $w \neq z$, and $x \neq y$, is $\dfrac{(x-y)^3(w-z)^3}{(w-z)^2(x-y)(w-x)^2} > 0$?

(1) $x > y$

(2) $w > z$

Wow. What a scary question stem. But take a closer look at that fraction. There are a lot of shared terms. Using the laws of exponents, we can cancel the $(w - z)^2$ and the $(x - y)$ in the denominator:

If $w \neq x$, $w \neq z$, and $x \neq y$, is $\dfrac{(x - y)^{3\text{-}1}(w - z)^{3-2}}{\cancel{(w-z)^2}\ \cancel{(x-y)}(w - x)^2} > 0$? or,

That changes the question to this:

If $w \neq x$, $w \neq z$, and $x \neq y$, is $\dfrac{(x - y)^2(w - z)}{(w - x)^2} > 0$?

Better already. We can simplify further by thinking logically about the question. We aren't asked for the value of anything, just whether this complicated fraction is positive. What could we say about that already? Well, for one thing, we know that a squared term cannot be negative. So there's no way that $(x - y)^2$ or $(w - x)^2$ is negative. In fact, since $w \neq x$ and $x \neq y$, they can't be zero, either. So those two terms are both positive, which is the only thing that matters to the question. We can simplify the question even further, to this:

Is $\dfrac{(\text{Positive})(w - z)}{(\text{Positive})} > 0$?

Since multiplying and/or dividing $(w - z)$ by anything positive will not change its sign, we have this:

Is $(w - z) > 0$?

Now *that's* a simple question! Look at how much easier the Statements have become to evaluate:

(1) $x > y$

(2) $w > z$

Statement (1) is totally irrelevant to whether $w - z > 0$. Insufficient.

Statement (2) tells us that w is bigger than z, so $w - z$ must be positive. (Subtract z from both sides of the inequality, and you get $w - z > 0$.) That's a "definite yes." Sufficient. Answer (B).

The more analysis and simplification you do with the question stem, the easier dealing with the Statements will be.

THINK ABOUT SUFFICIENCY, NOT CALCULATION

Get into the habit of thinking about what's needed for *sufficiency*, rather than doing arithmetic calculations. One of the ways that the GMAT makes a Data Sufficiency question harder is to make the numbers scarier. But if you aren't worrying about arithmetic, you won't be fazed by this.

EXPERT EXCLUSIVE

Logical deductions are as important as algebra to the process of simplification.

Example:

If $x > 0$, what is the value of x?

(1) $x > 5$

(2) $40 - x^2 = 4$

For a Value question, we need one value of x. The question stem tells us that x is positive but nothing else. Statement (1) is insufficient, as there are plenty of numbers greater than 5.

Statement (2) could be calculated to produce a value for x^2, and then we could calculate x. But actually doing so is a waste of time. Far better to realize that squared terms yield one positive value and one negative value. Since the question stem says that x must be positive, we'd eliminate the negative possibility, leaving only one value . . . exactly what we need for sufficiency. Answer (B).

Might not seem like a big deal with these numbers, but what if you got this Statement instead?

(2) $497\pi - 18\sqrt[4]{29}x^2 = 29.7\pi$

If you realized that the x^2 would yield one positive value and one negative and that the negative was disallowed by the question stem, meaning that there was only one possible answer, you'd know that this Statement is also sufficient and wouldn't need to work any harder with this one than with the "easier" one.

The "*N*-Variables, *N*-Equations" Rule

EXPERT EXCLUSIVE

For the *n*-variable, *n*-equations rule to count, the equations must be linear (no exponents) and distinct (different).
$x + y = 7$ and $2x + 2y = 14$ are *not* distinct, as the second is just double the first.

Perhaps one of the most powerful tools to evaluate sufficiency is the *n*-variables, *n*-equations rule. If you have the same number of distinct, linear equations as you do variables, you are guaranteed to be able to solve for all of the variables. If there are two variables, you need two equations to solve for all the values. If you have three variables, you need three equations. If you have four variables, you need four equations.

Example:

A coffee cart made $2,400 in revenue. If a large cup of coffee costs twice as much as a small cup, the cart sold 950 large cups, and it sold nothing besides the two sizes, then how many small cups of coffee did it sell?

(1) A large cup of coffee costs $2.

(2) If the cart had sold 20% fewer small cups, its revenue would have been reduced by $4\frac{1}{6}$%.

There are four factors that affect this problem—(1) the price of a small cup, (2) the price of a large cup, (3) the number of small cups sold, and (4) the number of large cups sold. That's four variables, so four distinct, linear equations would guarantee that we could solve for anything. How many do we have already? Well, something-or-other equals $2,400 (that's one), there's a relationship between the prices (that's two), and we get the number of large cups (that's three). With three equations for four variables, *any new equation* will be sufficient (as long as it doesn't introduce a new variable).

Statement (1) is a new equation and is sufficient. Statement (2) is a more complicated equation, and it would be annoying to calculate. But it is still a new equation, and it is therefore sufficient. Answer (D).

Imagine how much time it would take to work through these equations. Using the *n*-variable, *n*-equations rule, it need take no longer than a minute.

One word of caution, though . . . having the same number of equations guarantees sufficiency, but having fewer does *not* guarantee insufficiency. The GMAT will set up equations so that you can sometimes solve for what's asked even though you can't solve for everything.

Example:

A fruit stand sells apples, pears, and oranges. If oranges cost $0.50 each, then what is the cost of 5 oranges, 4 apples, and 3 pears?

(1) The cost of 1 apple is $0.30.

(2) The cost of 8 apples and 6 pears is $3.90.

There are three variables in this problem (the cost of an orange, the cost of an apple, and the cost of a pear), so three equations could solve for everything. We're given one (the exact price of an orange). So two more equations will guarantee sufficiency. But we should keep our eyes open for a way to answer our question with less. Since we already know the price of an orange, the only thing we'd need to answer our question is the price of 4 apples and 3 pears.

Statement (1) is insufficient, as we still do not know anything about the price of a pear. Statement (2) is only one equation, but if we divided it by 2, we'd get the cost of 4 apples and 3 pears, exactly what we need. Sufficient. Answer (B).

Proportions

Another common way to get sufficiency without all the values is to ask questions based on proportions (ratios, percents, averages, rates/speed, etc). The goal of the following exercise is to get you to think about what kind of information can be sufficient to answer a question, even though you can't calculate for the value of every variable. Read the question and each statement below, asking yourself whether it gives you enough information to answer. Don't bother trying to come up with the actual value!

> What was the percent increase in profits for Company X between 1991 and 1993?

Do the following Statements provide sufficient information?

1. The company earned 20 percent less profit in 1991 than in 1993.

2. The average annual profit between 1991 and 1993 was 12.5% higher than the profit in 1991.

3. The average of the annual profits of 1991 and 1993 was 12.5% higher than the profit in 1991.

4. In 1991, the profit was $4.5 million less than in 1993.

Statement 1 is sufficient. We could "reverse" the math and figure out percent increase from the given decrease. Let the 1993 profit equal P_{1993} and the 1991 profit equal P_{1991}. The Statement can be translated to $P_{1991} = 0.8 \, (P_{1993})$, which is $P_{1991} = \frac{4}{5}(P_{1993})$. That means $P_{1993} = \frac{5}{4} P_{1991} = 1.25 \, (P_{1991})$. That's 125% of 1991, or a 25% increase.

> **EXPERT EXCLUSIVE**
>
> Don't waste time doing needless math. As soon as you know that you'll get the relationship you're looking for, stop!

Statement 2 is insufficient because we don't know what the profit in 1992 was and it is included in the calculation.

Statement 3 is sufficient because you are given a proportional relationship between the two years' profits $\left(\dfrac{P_{1991} + P_{1993}}{2} = 1.125(P_{1991}) \right)$.

The question asks us for a proportional relationship, so this is what we need!

Statement 4 is insufficient because there is no total; we don't know what percentage $4.5 million represents.

 KAPLAN STRATEGY

The Basic Principles of Data Sufficiency are the following:

- Know the Data Sufficiency answer choices cold.
- Know the two types of Data Sufficiency questions.
- The Statements are always true.
- It's all about the question stem.
- Think about sufficiency, not calculation.

THE KAPLAN METHOD FOR DATA SUFFICIENCY

This is the essential systematic approach to mastering Data Sufficiency. Use this approach for every Data Sufficiency question. It will allow you to answer questions quickly and will guarantee that you avoid the common GMAT mistake of subconsciously combining the Statements instead of using them separately.

STEP 1: FOCUS ON THE QUESTION STEM

There are three things to think about in this step:

- **Value or Yes/No?**

  Which question type is this? The rules for sufficiency are a little different. If you treat a Yes/No question as if it were a Value question, you probably won't get the right answer!

- **Simplify.**

  If the question can be reduced to a simpler form, either through math or through logic, do so!

- **What's needed?**

  What kind of information would get you the answer to the question? The more you think about what information would be sufficient, the better able you'll be to evaluate the Statements.

Don't rush through this step, even for seemingly simple questions. The more you glean from the question stem, the easier it will be to find the right answer.

STEP 2: EVALUATE EACH STATEMENT SEPARATELY

Since the answer choices depend on considering each Statement alone, don't let the information from one carry over into the other. Start with the Statement that you feel will be easier to evaluate. That way you'll be more confident. There's no need to start with Statement (1) unless you want to! Remember that each Statement is true. Don't waste time verifying the Statement; just evaluate whether this new information lets you answer the question.

As you evaluate the two Statements, use your noteboard to keep track of which answer choices you have ruled out as incorrect. Remember:

- If (1) is sufficient, eliminate (B), (C), and (E).
- If (1) is insufficient, eliminate (A) and (D).
- If (2) is sufficient, eliminate (A), (C), and (E).
- If (2) is insufficient, eliminate (B) and (D).

STEP 3: EVALUATE THE STATEMENTS TOGETHER ONLY IF NECESSARY

You only need to consider the Statements together if each is insufficient on its own. When you evaluate the Statements together, keep in mind that each Statement is true.

> **EXPERT EXCLUSIVE**
>
> Of Data Sufficiency questions, 60 percent never require Step 3.

So a value would have to be permitted by *both* Statements to make it through Step 3. Let's look at some basic examples.

Example 1:

What is the value of x?

(1) $x = -1, 0,$ or 1

(2) $x = 0$ or 1

We need one value for x to answer the question. Statement (1) presents three values, and Statement (2) presents two. So we need to consider the Statements together. Both 0 and 1 are permitted in each Statement. So together the Statements yield two values and are insufficient. Answer (E).

Example 2:

What is the value of x?

(1) $x = -1, 0,$ or 1

(2) $x = 1, 2,$ or 3

We need one value for x to answer the question. Statement (1) presents three values, as does Statement (2). So we need to consider the Statements together. Only $x = 1$ is permitted by both. So together the Statements yield one value and are sufficient. Answer (C).

Example 3:

What is the value of x?

(1) $x < 1$

(2) $x = 0$ or 1

We need one value for x to answer the question. Statement (1) presents an infinite range of values, and Statement (2) presents exactly two values. So we need to consider the Statements together. Statement (2) rules out every possible value except 0 and 1. Statement (1) rules out 1. Together, the only permitted value is 0. Sufficient. Answer (C).

Example 4:

Is x prime?

(1) $x < 4$

(2) $x > 1$

This is a Yes/No question, so we don't really care what x is, only whether we can definitively answer the question. Statement (1) permits some prime numbers (like 2 and 3) but permits nonprime numbers (like 1) as well. Statement (2) also permits primes (like 2 and 3) and nonprimes (like 4). So we need to evaluate these Statements together. We could put the two together like this: $1 < x < 4$. So it looks like x could only be 2 or 3 and must be prime, right?

Ahh, we just fell for a trap! *We weren't told that* x *is an integer!* Sure, x could be 2 or 3 . . . but 2.5 is also permitted and isn't prime. So the Statements together only say, "Maybe x is prime, and maybe it isn't." Insufficient. Answer (E).

> **EXPERT EXCLUSIVE**
> What a question stem doesn't tell you is just as important as what it does—variables only have to be integers if the question stem says explicitly that they are.

Here's how Kaplan's Method for Data Sufficiency works in practice with several questions.

Team X won 40 basketball games. What percent of its basketball games did Team X win?

(1) Team X played the same number of basketball games as Team Y.

(2) Team Y won 45 games, representing 62.5 percent of the basketball games it played.

○ Statement (1) ALONE is sufficient, but statement (2) is not sufficient.

○ Statement (2) ALONE is sufficient, but statement (1) is not sufficient.

○ BOTH statements TOGETHER are sufficient, but NEITHER statement ALONE is sufficient.

○ EACH statement ALONE is sufficient.

○ Statements (1) and (2) TOGETHER are NOT sufficient.

> **EXPERT EXCLUSIVE**
>
> Jotting down formulas involved in a problem can help you focus on the different pieces of data that you'll need.

Step 1: Focus on the Question Stem

- **Value or Yes/No?** This is a value question, so we need exactly one possible winning percentage.
- **Simplify.** Not much simplification to be done on this one, unless you feel shaky when it comes to percentages. In that case, you might jot down something like $\frac{\text{wins}}{\text{games}} = ?$ to keep track of the different parts of the problem.
- **What's needed?** Since we know how many games Team X won, we only need to know how many they played to know the winning percentage.

Step 2: Evaluate Each Statement Separately

Pick the statement that seems easiest. We can often get in a rut looking at Statement (1) first, so let's start with (2). This tells us how many games Team Y won and would allow us to calculate the number it played. (Don't actually do the calculation—just know that it could be done!) But what does Team Y have to do with anything? Insufficient. We can eliminate (B) and (D).

> **EXPERT EXCLUSIVE**
>
> Don't try to do everything in your head. Jotting down what you learn from each statement . . .
>
> (1) #games X = #games Y
>
> (2) #games Y
>
> . . . will make it easier to evaluate the statements together.

Now we look at Statement (1) alone. We would know what we need—the number of games Team X played— only if we knew how many Team Y played. True, we learned how many in Statement (2). But we have to evaluate each Statement *separately*, as if the other one didn't exist. Just by itself, Statement (1) is insufficient, and we can eliminate (A) as well.

Step 3: Evaluate the Statements Together Only If Necessary

Since (1) and (2) are each insufficient, we need to consider the two together. Statement (1) tells us that if we got the number of games that Team Y played, we could answer our question. Statement (2) allows us to calculate that number. So when taken together, we could calculate what we need. (Don't actually carry out that calculation!) Sufficient. Answer (C).

Let's look at another example, one that showcases the importance of Step 1 even for seemingly simple questions.

If $2b - 2a^2 = 18$, what is the value of b ?

(1) $a^2 = 1,156$

(2) $a > 0$

○ Statement (1) ALONE is sufficient, but statement (2) is not sufficient.

○ Statement (2) ALONE is sufficient, but statement (1) is not sufficient.

○ BOTH statements TOGETHER are sufficient, but NEITHER statement ALONE is sufficient.

○ EACH statement ALONE is sufficient.

○ Statements (1) and (2) TOGETHER are NOT sufficient.

Step 1: Focus on the Question Stem

- **Value or Yes/No?** Value. We need one exact value.
- **Simplify.** The equation we're given is pretty simple. There's only one other variable in the problem, so we might be able to get away without simplifying here. Still, it wouldn't hurt to write down $b = 9 + a^2$.
- **What's needed?** It's tempting to think that we need a value for a. And sure, that would work. But take a closer look at that equation. The other term isn't a:

$$b = 9 + a^2$$

We need a value for a^2, not a.

> **EXPERT EXCLUSIVE**
>
> Most short DS questions have traps that we'll fall into if we don't think carefully. "Short = Sneaky" is a good rule of thumb.

Step 2: Evaluate Each Statement Separately

Statement (1) gives us exactly what we need: a value for a^2. Sufficient. Eliminate (B), (C), and (E).

Statement (2) hardly tells us the exact value of anything. Insufficient. Eliminate (D).

The correct answer is (A).

Step 3: Evaluate the Statements Together Only if Necessary

Not necessary here. Notice the trap, though. If we thought we needed the value of a, we would have needed to put the Statements together.

Short questions are often trickier than they might at first appear. Long ones, however, are often easier than we might think at first glance. Don't get intimidated by the length. Just take things one piece at a time, look for ways to simplify the problem and stay focused on exactly what information you'd need to solve the problem.

> A certain company produces exactly three products, X, Y, and Z. In 1990, what was the total income for the company from the sale of its products?
>
> (1) In 1990, the company sold 8,000 units of product X, 10,000 units of product Y, and 16,000 units of product Z.
>
> (2) In 1990, the company charged $28 per unit for product X and twice as much for product Z.
>
> ○ Statement (1) ALONE is sufficient, but statement (2) is not sufficient.
>
> ○ Statement (2) ALONE is sufficient, but statement (1) is not sufficient.
>
> ○ BOTH statements TOGETHER are sufficient, but NEITHER statement ALONE is sufficient.
>
> ○ EACH statement ALONE is sufficient.
>
> ○ Statements (1) and (2) TOGETHER are NOT sufficient.

Step 1: Focus on the Question Stem

- **Value or Yes/No?** Value. We need one exact value for the income.
- **Simplify.** We aren't given much to simplify here, other than the fact that there are three products.
- **What's needed?** Total income of X, Y, and Z.

Step 2: Evaluate Each Statement Separately

Statement (1) gives us units sold for each but nothing about revenue. Insufficient. Eliminate (A) and (D).

Statement (2) gives us the revenue per unit for X and Z but nothing for Y and nothing about how much is sold. Insufficient. Eliminate (B) as well.

Step 3: Evaluate the Statements Together Only If Necessary

Since both Statements are insufficient, we have to look at them together. We get everything we need for X and for Z, but we still don't know what the company charges for Y. Insufficient. Answer (E).

Note that focusing on exactly what you needed to answer the question—the total income from all three products—allowed you to avoid wasting time calculating the profits for X and Z. You knew that without Y, such calculations were fruitless. You can avoid calculations (on a math test no less!) by determining exactly what information you need to solve the problem. Then you can recognize straight off when you have that necessary information. When you use the Kaplan Method for Data Sufficiency and take an overview of the problem at the beginning (Step 1), you save yourself unnecessary labor.

> A number of bacteria were placed in a petri dish at 5:00 AM.
> If the number of bacteria in the petri dish grew for 5 days, by
> doubling every 12 hours, how many bacteria were in the petri
> dish at 5:00 PM on the third day?
>
> (1) From 5:00 AM to 5:00 PM on the second day, the number of
>   bacteria increased by 100 percent.
>
> (2) 20 bacteria were placed in the petri dish at 5:00 AM the first day.
>
> ○ Statement (1) ALONE is sufficient, but statement (2) is not sufficient.
>
> ○ Statement (2) ALONE is sufficient, but statement (1) is not sufficient.
>
> ○ BOTH statements TOGETHER are sufficient, but NEITHER
>   statement ALONE is sufficient.
>
> ○ EACH statement ALONE is sufficient.
>
> ○ Statements (1) and (2) TOGETHER are NOT sufficient.

Step 1: Focus on the Question Stem

- **Value or Yes/No?** Value. We need an exact number of bacteria.
- **Simplify.** No math to simplify here, but let's make sure that we understand the situation. We start with some unknown number of bacteria, which doubles every 12 hours for 5 days.
- **What's needed?** Since we're told the formula for how these bacteria grow, the number of bacteria at *any stage* would give us what we need. If we got the number at the beginning, we'd need to double 5 times. If we got the number at 5 PM on day 4, we'd divide by 2 twice.

Step 2: Evaluate Each Statement Separately

A quick glance at the Statements shows us that Statement (2) gives us exactly what we're looking for—an exact number of bacteria at a specific time. There's no need to waste time doing calculations; we know that they *could* be done, and that's all that matters. Sufficient. Eliminate (A), (C), and (E).

Statement (1) just reiterates the formula about how the bacteria grow. That's not new information and so can't be sufficient.

The correct answer is (B); Step 3 is unnecessary.

> **EXPERT EXCLUSIVE**
>
> In multiple-figure problems, you need to pass information from one figure to the next.

As you'll see in the next example, geometry also shows up on Data Sufficiency. Be very careful with any diagrams you are given! Things may not be what they seem. Try the problem below.

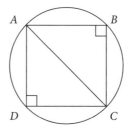

If points *A*, *B*, *C*, and *D* are points on the circumference of the circle in the figure above, what is the area of *ABCD* ?

(1) The radius of the circle is $\dfrac{\sqrt{2}}{2}$.

(2) *ABCD* is a square.

○ Statement (1) ALONE is sufficient, but statement (2) is not sufficient.

○ Statement (2) ALONE is sufficient, but statement (1) is not sufficient.

○ BOTH statements TOGETHER are sufficient, but NEITHER statement ALONE is sufficient.

○ EACH statement ALONE is sufficient.

○ Statements (1) and (2) TOGETHER are NOT sufficient.

Step 1: Focus on the Question Stem

- **Value or Yes/No?** Value. We need an exact area.
- **Simplify.** For geometry, simplifying means adding information to the picture. Since angle *B* is a right angle, *AC* is the circle's diameter. (We also could have

gotten that from angle *D*.) But what we don't know is as important. We don't know anything about the angles at *A* and *C*. They *could* be right angles, as they appear to be. But they don't *have* to be. We could slide either *B* and/or *D* along the circumference, as long as we kept them right angles:

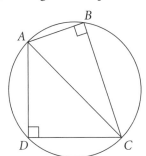

> **EXCLUSIVE**
> Geometry-based DS questions test your ability to reimagine the shape based on the available facts.

- **What's needed?** There are two ways we could know the area of *ABCD*. One way is to know the area of the two right triangles (*ABC* and *ADC*), then add them together. For that, we'd need to know the length of each leg—*AD*, *CD*, *AB*, and *BC*. The other way is to confirm that *ABCD* is the square that it seems to be and get the length of one side. And if *ABCD* is a square, then the square's diagonal would also be the circle's diameter; we could get the side length from the radius.

Step 2: Evaluate Each Statement Separately

Statement (1) gives us the radius, which in turn gives us the diameter, which in turn gives us the hypotenuse of each triangle. But we have no information about angles *A* or *C*, so by itself, (1) is insufficient. Eliminate (A) and (D).

Statement (2) confirms that *ABCD* is in fact a square. But with no measurements of anything, we don't know any lengths, so we don't know the area. Insufficient. Eliminate (B).

Step 3: Evaluate the Statements Together Only If Necessary

Together we've got what we need . . . (1) gives us enough to find *AC*. (2) tells us that *AB* = *BC* = *AD* = *CD*. That means that both triangles are isosceles right triangles, so we can use the 45-45-90 triangle ratio to solve for the lengths, which we'd then use to get the area. Of course, *don't calculate* any of that! Sufficient. Answer (C).

If you drew a complete blank on the geometry in this problem, don't worry. Geometry is a fairly small part of the GMAT and should never become your top priority. Moreover, you could have eliminated some answer choices even if you knew almost nothing about squares and circles. You might have been baffled by (1), but look at (2). No numbers! There are no numbers in the stimulus either, so (2) can't possibly be sufficient to

> **EXCLUSIVE**
> Diagrams in Data Sufficiency may not be drawn to scale, so don't assume anything just by the way they look.

provide a number for the area. So you could eliminate (B) and (D), which leaves you with a one-in-three chance of guessing correctly.

Now let's look at an example of a common Data Sufficiency trap.

What is the value of x?

(1) $x^2 - 9 = 16$

(2) $3x(x - 5) = 0$

○ Statement (1) ALONE is sufficient, but statement (2) is not sufficient.

○ Statement (2) ALONE is sufficient, but statement (1) is not sufficient.

○ BOTH statements TOGETHER are sufficient, but NEITHER statement ALONE is sufficient.

○ EACH statement ALONE is sufficient.

○ Statements (1) and (2) TOGETHER are NOT sufficient.

Step 1: Focus on the Question Stem

- **Value or Yes/No?** Value. We need one exact value for x.
- **Simplify.** We aren't given anything to simplify. But we know that short DS questions can be tricky, so we'll be on the lookout for traps.
- **What's needed?** We're unlikely to get something as easy as the direct value of x, but we may get an equation we can use to calculate it.

Step 2: Evaluate Each Statement Separately

Statement (1) gives us a value for x^2, so it's tempting to think that we'd get a value for x. But be careful! Don't forget that when a term is squared, we *get a positive answer regardless of whether the original value was positive or negative*. So unless $x^2 = 0$ (which it doesn't here), there will be two possible values for x—one positive and one negative. Insufficient. Eliminate (A) and (D).

There's no need to distribute the multiplication in Statement (2); since it is equal to zero, we can calculate the possible values of x. The expression $3x(x - 5) = 0$ would be true if $x = 0$ or if $x = 5$. That's one value too many. Insufficient. Eliminate (B).

Step 3: Evaluate the Statements Together Only If Necessary

If you calculated the possible values for x in Statement (1), you'd be looking at this:

(1) $x = 5$ or -5

(2) $x = 0$ or 5

EXPERT EXCLUSIVE

If you see a squared term in DS, beware! The trap will be assuming that the underlying value is positive. Remember that it could be negative as well. The numbers 1 and 0 and fractions also behave in special ways when squared.

Only $x = 5$ is permitted in both, so only one value remains. Sufficient.

Or perhaps you didn't calculate values for Statement (1), moving on to (2) as soon as you realized that (1) would yield two values. In that case, you can plug the permitted values in Statement (2) back into Statement (1):

$$x^2 - 9 = 16$$

$$x = 0 \text{ or } 5$$

$$0^2 - 9 = 16 \quad \text{or} \quad 5^2 - 9 = 16$$

$$-9 \neq 16 \quad \text{or} \quad 16 = 16$$

Since -9 is not 16, $x = 0$ is not permitted by Statement (1). Only $x = 5$ is, so we're down to one value. Sufficient. Answer (C).

If Picking Numbers in Step 3, you'll need to pick numbers that are permitted by both statements.

> If z is an integer, what is the units digit of z^3?
>
> (1) z is a multiple of 5.
>
> (2) $\sqrt{z}$ is an integer.
>
> ○ Statement (1) ALONE is sufficient, but statement (2) is not sufficient.
>
> ○ Statement (2) ALONE is sufficient, but statement (1) is not sufficient.
>
> ○ BOTH statements TOGETHER are sufficient, but NEITHER statement ALONE is sufficient.
>
> ○ EACH statement ALONE is sufficient.
>
> ○ Statements (1) and (2) TOGETHER are NOT sufficient.

Step 1: Focus on the Question Stem

- **Value or Yes/No?** Value. But we don't need a value for z or even for z^3. We need a value for its units digit.
- **Simplify.** There is a way to simplify units-digit questions. But let's pretend for a minute that you don't know it.
- **What's needed?** If you aren't sure what you need, you'll have to Pick Numbers.

EXPERT EXCLUSIVE

You always need to try at least two sets of numbers when Picking Numbers in Data Sufficiency. Try to use the second set to prove that the Statement is insufficient.

EXPERT EXCLUSIVE

You have to square integers so often on the GMAT that you should have the first 16 "perfect squares" memorized for test day: from $0^2 = 0$ to $15^2 = 225$.

Step 2: Evaluate Each Statement Separately

Statement (1) tells us that z is a multiple of 5. We're going to be cubing, so let's not pick $z = 65$ or something complicated like that. $z = 10$ will be easy to cube, so let's start there: 10^3 is 1,000, the units digit of which is 0.

But that doesn't mean the units digit is *guaranteed* to be 0. We only know that it *could* be 0. To know for sure, we want to try a different number. If we can prove that the units digit of z^3 could be something else, we can prove Statement (1) insufficient.

Let's try the simplest of all multiples of 5: $z = 5$. Then $z^3 = 125$. Now the units digit is 5. So clearly at least two values are permitted; Statement (1) is insufficient. Eliminate (A) and (D).

Statement (2) tells us that z is a "perfect square"—a number whose square root is an integer. So z could be 0, 1, 4, 9, 16, 25, 36, and so on. Of all of these, $z = 1$ has got to be the easiest. In this case, $z^3 = 1$ as well, so the units digit is 1. If we try $z = 4$, then $z^3 = 64$, and the units digit is 4. Again, at least two values are possible, so Statement (2) is insufficient. Eliminate (B).

EXPERT EXCLUSIVE

When multiplying, adding, or subtracting, the units digit of the answer is affected only by the units digit of the numbers multiplied, added, or subtracted.

Step 3: Evaluate the Statements Together Only If Necessary

Now we have to find a number that's both a perfect square and a multiple of 5. If you don't know the perfect squares, you'll have to do some trial and error. If you do know them, you can quickly list them out until you find two:

0, 1, 4, 9, 16, **25**, 36, 49, 64, 81, **100** . . .

If $z = 100$, it's easy enough to cube: $100^3 = 1,000,000$. The units digit is 0.

If $z = 25$, it's a little tougher to cube: $25^3 = 15,625$. The units digit is 5.

Two values are still possible, so the answer is (E).

"Wait a minute!" you say. "That arithmetic was way too annoying to be the most efficient solution!" You're absolutely right, you crafty Kaplan student, you. Let's take a brief break from Data Sufficiency strategy to show how it could have been easier.

For one thing, **don't be afraid of zero.** Zero is a multiple of every number. So $z = 0$ would have been a perfectly permissible substitute for $z = 10$ and $z = 100$.

But that wasn't the awful one: 25^3 is the calculation you're looking to avoid. The key to making this easier is to notice when you are focusing on the question that you care only about units digits. When multiplying, only the units digits matter to the units digit of the answer. Observe the long-form multiplication:

25	$\overset{2}{25}$
$\times\,25$	$\times\,25$
Start with $5 \times 5 \ldots$	5 The next is $(5 \times 2) + 2$, but that answer goes in the *tens place*.

And so it will go with all the calculations from here on; they'll be in the tens place or above, leaving the 5 in the units place untouched. So if we are asked about the units place, our math can look like this:

25^3:	$25 \times 25 \times 25$
Look at the first multiplication:	$(25 \times 25) \times 25$
Only the units digits matter:	(blah 5 × blah 5) × (blah 5)
$5 \times 5 = 25$(blah 5):	(blah 5) × (blah 5)
Only the units digit matters:	5

In fact, that's the simplification that we could have done right from the beginning.

Let's get back to Data Sufficiency strategy.

Here's another question that will showcase the value of simplifying the question stem.

> If *x* and *y* are prime numbers, is $y(x - 3)$ odd?
>
> (1) $x > 10$
>
> (2) $y < 3$
>
> ○ Statement (1) ALONE is sufficient, but statement (2) is not sufficient.
>
> ○ Statement (2) ALONE is sufficient, but statement (1) is not sufficient.
>
> ○ BOTH statements TOGETHER are sufficient, but NEITHER statement ALONE is sufficient.
>
> ○ EACH statement ALONE is sufficient.
>
> ○ Statements (1) and (2) TOGETHER are NOT sufficient.

Step 1: Focus on the Question Stem

- **Value or Yes/No?** Yes/No. If $y(x - 3)$ is definitely odd, sufficient. If $y(x - 3)$ is definitely even, sufficient. If we can't say, insufficient.

EXPERT EXCLUSIVE

If you need to meet multiple conditions to answer yes, failing to meet even one of them will guarantee a no.

- **Simplify.** We can use the rules of odds and evens to simplify this. The only way to multiply and get an odd answer is to multiply odd × odd. So the question can be simplified to "Is y odd *and* $(x - 3)$ odd?"

Using the rules of primes, we can even go further. Since 2 is the only even prime number, the only way for y to be odd is for y to *not* be 2. And the only way for $(x - 3)$ to be odd is for x to be 2 (since only even − odd = odd).

So here's the completely simplified form of the question: "Is $x = 2$ *and* $y \neq 2$?"

- **What's needed?** We can say "definitely yes" if $x = 2$ *and* $y \neq 2$. We can say "definitely no" if *either* $x \neq 2$ *or* $y = 2$.

EXPERT EXCLUSIVE

Let the question guide you when picking your numbers. If the question is about primes, it will almost certainly be about whether a variable is 2, as 2 is the smallest of the primes and the only one that is even. (If the question stem also says "even" or "odd," then it's almost guaranteed to be about 2.)

Step 2: Evaluate Each Statement Separately

Simplifying questions routinely pays off in fast analysis. Statement (1) says that $x > 10$. Clearly, x can't be 2. So we can say "definitely no." Sufficient. Statement (2) says that $y < 3$. The question stem says that y is prime. The only prime number smaller than 3 is 2. Again we can say "definitely no." Sufficient. Answer (D).

Had you not simplified fully, you could Pick Numbers. For Statement (1), you must pick x to be a prime above 10. $x = 11$ is a good choice. y can be any prime, so let's pick $y = 3$. Plugging these values into $y(x - 3)$, we get $3(11 - 3) = 3(8) = 24$, which is not odd.

We have to pick a second set of numbers. Since this question is about primes and odds, chances are that the question will revolve around whether or not something is 2, the only even prime. (Indeed, our simplification showed this to be the case.) x can't be 2, so we'll pick $x = 13$. y could be, though, so we'll pick $y = 2$. Now $y(x - 3) = 2(13 - 3) = 2(10) = 20$, which is also not odd. Looks like we'll get a "no" all the time. Sufficient. Eliminate (B), (C), and (E).

Here's Picking Numbers for Statement (2). y must equal 2, but x could be any prime at all. Let's start with $x = 3$. Now $y(x - 3) = 2(3 - 3) = 2(0) = 0$, which is even.

The second set of numbers for Statement (2) must still have $y = 2$. x wasn't 2 before, so let's make it 2 now. So, $y(x - 3) = 2(2 - 3) = 2(-1) = -2$, which is even.

We seem to get "even" every time. So the answer is "definitely no." Sufficient. Answer (D).

Let's wrap up our investigation into the Kaplan Method for Data Sufficiency by walking through another Yes/No problem that sets up an important trap to watch out for when Picking Numbers.

Is the product of x, y, and z equal to 1?

(1) $x + y + z = 3$.

(2) x, y, and z are each greater than 0.

○ Statement (1) ALONE is sufficient, but statement (2) is not sufficient.

○ Statement (2) ALONE is sufficient, but statement (1) is not sufficient.

○ BOTH statements TOGETHER are sufficient, but NEITHER statement ALONE is sufficient.

○ EACH statement ALONE is sufficient.

○ Statements (1) and (2) TOGETHER are NOT sufficient.

Step 1: Focus on the Question Stem

- **Value or Yes/No?** Yes/No. If $xyz = 1$, then the answer is yes. If $xyz \neq 1$, then the answer is no. Either would be sufficient.
- **Simplify.** The question already seems as simple as can be.
- **What's needed?** It's often worth thinking about how you could get the yes or no that you're looking for. x, y, and z all equaling 1 would give you a yes. But is it the only way? This question is short and, therefore, tricky.

  Remember that unless otherwise noted, the variables do not have to be integers. $x = 100$, $y = 0.1$, and $z = 0.1$ would also get a yes!

Step 2: Evaluate Each Statement Separately

Picking Numbers for Statement (1), we can readily see how to get a yes: $x = 1$, $y = 1$, and $z = 1$. Can we Pick Numbers in such a way that the sum is 3 but the product is not 1? Not if we only consider positive integers. But if we consider different kinds of numbers, we can easily find some. Zero doesn't alter a sum but forces a product to be 0. So $x = 3$, $y = 0$, and $z = 0$ will give us our no. Since we can get both a yes and a no, Statement (1) is insufficient. Eliminate (A) and (D).

Statement (2) rules out the possibility of using 0 but not the possibility of using fractions or decimals. So $x = 1$, $y = 1$, and $z = 1$ is also permissible here, but so is something like $x = 100$, $y = 100$, and $z = 100$. So xyz could equal 1, but it could also equal 1,000,000. So we can get both a yes and a no here as well. Insufficient. Eliminate (B).

> **EXPERT EXCLUSIVE**
>
> The special properties of 0, 1, and fractions make these numbers great candidates for Picking Numbers in Data Sufficiency. Some questions cannot be answered correctly if you don't consider them!

Step 3: Evaluate the Statements Together Only If Necessary

Since both Statements are insufficient, we need to consider them together. Can we pick numbers that add to 3 and are all positive? Again, $x = 1$, $y = 1$, and $z = 1$ makes the cut. Can we think of numbers that *don't* multiply to 1 that also are consistent with the Statements? Once again, we have to expand our thinking to include other kinds of numbers. Fractions and decimals make things bigger when added but smaller when multiplied. $x = 2.8$, $y = 0.1$, and $z = 0.1$ fits the bill. They are all positive and add to 3. Their product is $2.8(0.1)(0.1) = 0.028 \ldots$ so we can get a yes, but we can get a no as well. Insufficient. Answer (E).

GUESSING IN DATA SUFFICIENCY

When you run into a real horror-show question, like the following, don't forget to use a sound Data Sufficiency guessing strategy. That means skipping a Statement that looks too daunting and trying to eliminate some answer choices by looking at the easier Statement. Try your hand at the tough question below. Don't try to solve it; instead, see if you can narrow down the possibilities quickly.

EXPERT EXCLUSIVE

Because the test is adaptive, even the strongest test takers will see questions on which they'll need to guess.

What was the maximum temperature in City A on Saturday, May 14?

(1) The average (arithmetic mean) of the maximum daily temperatures in City A from Sunday, May 8, to Saturday, May 14 was 72°, which was 2° less than the average (arithmetic mean) of the maximum daily temperatures in City A from Monday, May 9, to Friday, May 13.

(2) The maximum temperature on Saturday, May 14, was 5° greater than the maximum temperature in City A on Sunday, May 8.

○ Statement (1) ALONE is sufficient, but statement (2) is not sufficient.

○ Statement (2) ALONE is sufficient, but statement (1) is not sufficient.

○ BOTH statements TOGETHER are sufficient, but NEITHER statement ALONE is sufficient.

○ EACH statement ALONE is sufficient.

○ Statements (1) and (2) TOGETHER are NOT sufficient.

Even on a difficult question, you can still use the Kaplan Method for Data Sufficiency.

Step 1: Focus on the Question Stem

- **Value or Yes/No?** Value. We need an exact maximum temperature.
- **Simplify.** The question doesn't give any information that can be simplified.
- **What's needed?** We haven't hit the hard part yet—we need exactly one possible maximum temperature.

Step 2: Evaluate Each Statement Separately

Statement (1) is where the misery begins. Skip it and go to Statement (2); it's much easier.

Statement (2) tells us that what we're looking for is 5 degrees more than the temperature on some other day. Without that other day, we don't have the value we need. Insufficient. We can eliminate (B) and (D) and give ourselves a one-in-three chance to get the right answer.

Perhaps you feel comfortable evaluating Statement (1). Perhaps you don't. It mentions the day we're interested in, so it might be sufficient. But it mentions a lot of other days as well.

Let's pretend for a moment that you aren't sure how to evaluate Statement (1). A common line of thought is "I'm not sure what to do, so it must not be sufficient." The GMAT doesn't reward that mentality! So complicated or hard-to-evaluate statements are more likely to be sufficient than insufficient. Avoid (E) and lean toward (A), unless you have a logical reason to suspect that (1) alone is insufficient. (C) is the right answer to this particular problem.

Don't let this one leave you with a bad taste in your mouth. You're unlikely to run into anything as horrible as Statement (1) on test day. The point of this exercise is to show you that even if you do hit something this bad, you're still in control. You work the odds, you look for the strategic approach, and you increase your likelihood of picking up a point.

Here's the solution. Working with Statement (1), if the average maximum temperature from May 8 to May 14 was 72°, then the sum of the maximum temperatures of those days is $7 \times 72 = 504°$. If the average maximum temperature from May 9 to May 13 was 72 + 2, or 74°, then the sum of the maximum temperatures of those days was $5 \times 74 = 370°$.

> **EXPERT EXCLUSIVE**
>
> Statements about proportions (averages, percents, ratios, rates/speeds, etc.) are often more sufficient than they first appear.

The difference between those numbers is just the sum of the maximum temperature on May 8, which we'll call x, and the maximum temperature on May 14, which we'll call y (since these two days were left out of the second time period). So $x + y = 504 - 370 = 134$. But Statement (2) tells us that $y - x = 5$. We have the two different linear equations $x + y = 134$ and $y - x = 5$. These equations lead to a single value for y, so the Statements taken together are sufficient.

EXPERT EXCLUSIVE

Don't always start with Statement (1). Start with the easier of the two. If you can figure out one Statement, you'll considerably improve the odds of guessing correctly.

This example demonstrates how guessing can be more practical for some questions. By looking at only one Statement, you can narrow down the possibilities to two or three choices. This can be a great help, particularly on difficult problems for which you think you might have to guess. But you must be sure you know the rules absolutely cold by test day.

- If Statement (1) is sufficient, eliminate (B), (C), and (E). The answer must be (A) or (D).
- If Statement (2) is sufficient, eliminate (A), (C), and (E). The answer must be (B) or (D).
- If Statement (1) is insufficient, eliminate (A) and (D). The answer must be (B), (C), or (E).
- If Statement (2) is insufficient, eliminate (B) and (D). The answer must be (A), (C), or (E).

SUMMARY

The Basic Principles of Data Sufficiency are the following:

- Know the Data Sufficiency answer choices cold.
- Know the two types of Data Sufficiency questions.
- The Statements are always true.
- It's all about the question stem.
- Think about sufficiency, not calculation.

The Kaplan Method for Data Sufficiency is as follows:

Step 1: Focus on the question stem.
  - Value or Yes/No?
  - Simplify.
  - What's needed?

Step 2: Evaluate each Statement separately.
  - Start with the easier Statement.

Step 3: Evaluate the Statements together only if necessary.
  - Perform this step only if both Statements are insufficient alone.

Data Sufficiency Guessing Principles:

- Evaluate the easier Statement if you can and eliminate answer choices.
- Hard-to-understand Statements are likely to be sufficient.

PRACTICE QUIZ

Directions: In each of the problems, a question is followed by two statements containing certain data. You are to determine whether the data provided by the statements are sufficient to answer the question. Choose the correct answer based upon the statements' data, your knowledge of mathematics, and your familiarity with everyday facts (such as the number of minutes in an hour or cents in a dollar). You must indicate whether

- ○ Statement (1) ALONE is sufficient, but statement (2) is not sufficient.

- ○ Statement (2) ALONE is sufficient, but statement (1) is not sufficient.

- ○ BOTH statements TOGETHER are sufficient, but NEITHER statement ALONE is sufficient.

- ○ EACH statement ALONE is sufficient.

- ○ Statements (1) and (2) TOGETHER are NOT sufficient.

Note: Diagrams accompanying problems agree with information given in the questions, but they may not agree with additional information given in statements (1) and (2).

All numbers used are real numbers.

1. What is the ratio of the discounted price of an item to the list price?

   (1) The discounted price is $4 less than the list price.

   (2) The discounted price is 20 percent less than the list price.

   ○ Statement (1) ALONE is sufficient, but statement (2) is not sufficient.

   ○ Statement (2) ALONE is sufficient, but statement (1) is not sufficient.

   ○ BOTH statements TOGETHER are sufficient, but NEITHER statement ALONE is sufficient.

   ○ EACH statement ALONE is sufficient.

   ○ Statements (1) and (2) TOGETHER are NOT sufficient.

2. Does $x = y$?

   (1) $x^2 - y^2 = 0$

   (2) $(x - y)^2 = 0$

   ○ Statement (1) ALONE is sufficient, but statement (2) is not sufficient.

   ○ Statement (2) ALONE is sufficient, but statement (1) is not sufficient.

   ○ BOTH statements TOGETHER are sufficient, but NEITHER statement ALONE is sufficient.

   ○ EACH statement ALONE is sufficient.

   ○ Statements (1) and (2) TOGETHER are NOT sufficient.

3. Does rectangle A have a greater perimeter than rectangle B ?

   (1) The length of a side of rectangle A is twice the length of a side of rectangle B.

   (2) The area of rectangle A is twice the area of rectangle B.

   ○ Statement (1) ALONE is sufficient, but statement (2) is not sufficient.

   ○ Statement (2) ALONE is sufficient, but statement (1) is not sufficient.

   ○ BOTH statements TOGETHER are sufficient, but NEITHER statement ALONE is sufficient.

   ○ EACH statement ALONE is sufficient.

   ○ Statements (1) and (2) TOGETHER are NOT sufficient.

4. How many students scored less than the average (arithmetic mean) of the class on a test?

    (1) The average (arithmetic mean) of the class was 83.

    (2) Fourteen students scored above the average (arithmetic mean) of the class.

    ○   Statement (1) ALONE is sufficient, but statement (2) is not sufficient.

    ○   Statement (2) ALONE is sufficient, but statement (1) is not sufficient.

    ○   BOTH statements TOGETHER are sufficient, but NEITHER statement ALONE is sufficient.

    ○   EACH statement ALONE is sufficient.

    ○   Statements (1) and (2) TOGETHER are NOT sufficient.

5. If $ab < ac$, which is greater, b or c?

    (1) $a < 0$

    (2) $c < 0$

    ○   Statement (1) ALONE is sufficient, but statement (2) is not sufficient.

    ○   Statement (2) ALONE is sufficient, but statement (1) is not sufficient.

    ○   BOTH statements TOGETHER are sufficient, but NEITHER statement ALONE is sufficient.

    ○   EACH statement ALONE is sufficient.

    ○   Statements (1) and (2) TOGETHER are NOT sufficient.

6. If p, q, and r are even numbers and $2 < p < q < r$, what is the value of q?

    (1) $r < 10$

    (2) $p < 6$

    ○   Statement (1) ALONE is sufficient, but statement (2) is not sufficient.

    ○   Statement (2) ALONE is sufficient, but statement (1) is not sufficient.

    ○   BOTH statements TOGETHER are sufficient, but NEITHER statement ALONE is sufficient.

    ○   EACH statement ALONE is sufficient.

    ○   Statements (1) and (2) TOGETHER are NOT sufficient.

7. If there are 250 words on each page, how many pages can Michael read in an hour?

   (1) There are 25 ten-word lines on each page, and there is nothing else on each page.

   (2) Michael can read 300 words per minute.

   ○ Statement (1) ALONE is sufficient, but statement (2) is not sufficient.

   ○ Statement (2) ALONE is sufficient, but statement (1) is not sufficient.

   ○ BOTH statements TOGETHER are sufficient, but NEITHER statement ALONE is sufficient.

   ○ EACH statement ALONE is sufficient.

   ○ Statements (1) and (2) TOGETHER are NOT sufficient.

8. Is $m > n$?

   (1) $\dfrac{3}{7} < m < \dfrac{5}{7}$

   (2) $\dfrac{2}{7} < n < \dfrac{4}{7}$

   ○ Statement (1) ALONE is sufficient, but statement (2) is not sufficient.

   ○ Statement (2) ALONE is sufficient, but statement (1) is not sufficient.

   ○ BOTH statements TOGETHER are sufficient, but NEITHER statement ALONE is sufficient.

   ○ EACH statement ALONE is sufficient.

   ○ Statements (1) and (2) TOGETHER are NOT sufficient.

9. What is the value of $a^4 - b^4$?

   (1) $a^2 + b^2 = 0$

   (2) $b = a$

   ○ Statement (1) ALONE is sufficient, but statement (2) is not sufficient.

   ○ Statement (2) ALONE is sufficient, but statement (1) is not sufficient.

   ○ BOTH statements TOGETHER are sufficient, but NEITHER statement ALONE is sufficient.

   ○ EACH statement ALONE is sufficient.

   ○ Statements (1) and (2) TOGETHER are NOT sufficient.

10. If *R* is an integer, is *R* evenly divisible by 3?

    (1) 2*R* is evenly divisible by 3.

    (2) 3*R* is evenly divisible by 3.

    ○ Statement (1) ALONE is sufficient, but statement (2) is not sufficient.

    ○ Statement (2) ALONE is sufficient, but statement (1) is not sufficient.

    ○ BOTH statements TOGETHER are sufficient, but NEITHER statement ALONE is sufficient.

    ○ EACH statement ALONE is sufficient.

    ○ Statements (1) and (2) TOGETHER are NOT sufficient.

11. Susan flipped a fair coin *N* times. What fraction of the flips came up heads?

    (1) $N = 24$

    (2) The number of flips that came up tails was $\frac{3}{8}N$.

    ○ Statement (1) ALONE is sufficient, but statement (2) is not sufficient.

    ○ Statement (2) ALONE is sufficient, but statement (1) is not sufficient.

    ○ BOTH statements TOGETHER are sufficient, but NEITHER statement ALONE is sufficient.

    ○ EACH statement ALONE is sufficient.

    ○ Statements (1) and (2) TOGETHER are NOT sufficient.

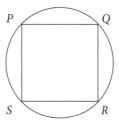

12. If the vertices of quadrilateral *PQRS* above lie on the circumference of a circle, is *PQRS* a square?

    (1) Side *PS* is equal in length to a radius of the circle.

    (2) The degree measure of minor arc *QR* is 45°.

    ○ Statement (1) ALONE is sufficient, but statement (2) is not sufficient.

    ○ Statement (2) ALONE is sufficient, but statement (1) is not sufficient.

    ○ BOTH statements TOGETHER are sufficient, but NEITHER statement ALONE is sufficient.

    ○ EACH statement ALONE is sufficient.

    ○ Statements (1) and (2) TOGETHER are NOT sufficient.

13. If he did not stop along the way, what speed did Bill average on his 3-hour trip?

    (1) He traveled a total of 120 miles.

    (2) He traveled half the distance at 30 miles per hour and half the distance at 60 miles per hour.

    ○ Statement (1) ALONE is sufficient, but statement (2) is not sufficient.

    ○ Statement (2) ALONE is sufficient, but statement (1) is not sufficient.

    ○ BOTH statements TOGETHER are sufficient, but NEITHER statement ALONE is sufficient.

    ○ EACH statement ALONE is sufficient.

    ○ Statements (1) and (2) TOGETHER are NOT sufficient.

14. What is the value of $\dfrac{x+z}{x-y}$?

    (1) $x + z = 3$

    (2) $y + z = 2$

    ○ Statement (1) ALONE is sufficient, but statement (2) is not sufficient.

    ○ Statement (2) ALONE is sufficient, but statement (1) is not sufficient.

    ○ BOTH statements TOGETHER are sufficient, but NEITHER statement ALONE is sufficient.

    ○ EACH statement ALONE is sufficient.

    ○ Statements (1) and (2) TOGETHER are NOT sufficient.

15. If x is a positive integer less than 10 and $x + 2$ is a prime number, what is the value of x?

    (1) $x + 3$ is the square of an integer.

    (2) $x + 7$ is the cube of an integer.

    ○ Statement (1) ALONE is sufficient, but statement (2) is not sufficient.

    ○ Statement (2) ALONE is sufficient, but statement (1) is not sufficient.

    ○ BOTH statements TOGETHER are sufficient, but NEITHER statement ALONE is sufficient.

    ○ EACH statement ALONE is sufficient.

    ○ Statements (1) and (2) TOGETHER are NOT sufficient.

16. On a certain construction crew, each crew member has exactly one job, and there are 3 carpenters for every 2 painters. What percent of the entire crew is carpenters or painters?

    (1) Eighteen percent of the crew are carpenters.

    (2) Twelve percent of the crew are painters.

    ○ Statement (1) ALONE is sufficient, but statement (2) is not sufficient.

    ○ Statement (2) ALONE is sufficient, but statement (1) is not sufficient.

    ○ BOTH statements TOGETHER are sufficient, but NEITHER statement ALONE is sufficient.

    ○ EACH statement ALONE is sufficient.

    ○ Statements (1) and (2) TOGETHER are NOT sufficient.

17. A rectangular aquarium provides 36 square centimeters of water surface area per fish. How many fish are there in the aquarium?

    (1) The edges of the aquarium have lengths of 60, 42, and 30 centimeters.

    (2) The aquarium is filled to a depth of 40 centimeters.

    ○ Statement (1) ALONE is sufficient, but statement (2) is not sufficient.

    ○ Statement (2) ALONE is sufficient, but statement (1) is not sufficient.

    ○ BOTH statements TOGETHER are sufficient, but NEITHER statement ALONE is sufficient.

    ○ EACH statement ALONE is sufficient.

    ○ Statements (1) and (2) TOGETHER are NOT sufficient.

18. At Consolidated Foundries, for a resolution to become policy, a quorum of at least half the 20 directors must pass the resolution by at least a two-thirds majority. At a meeting of the board of directors, did resolution X pass or fail?

    (1) Ten directors voted for resolution X.

    (2) Seven directors voted against resolution X.

    ○ Statement (1) ALONE is sufficient, but statement (2) is not sufficient.

    ○ Statement (2) ALONE is sufficient, but statement (1) is not sufficient.

    ○ BOTH statements TOGETHER are sufficient, but NEITHER statement ALONE is sufficient.

    ○ EACH statement ALONE is sufficient.

    ○ Statements (1) and (2) TOGETHER are NOT sufficient.

19. Is $x + y$ positive?

    (1) $x - y$ is positive.

    (2) $y - x$ is negative.

    ○ Statement (1) ALONE is sufficient, but statement (2) is not sufficient.

    ○ Statement (2) ALONE is sufficient, but statement (1) is not sufficient.

    ○ BOTH statements TOGETHER are sufficient, but NEITHER statement ALONE is sufficient.

    ○ EACH statement ALONE is sufficient.

    ○ Statements (1) and (2) TOGETHER are NOT sufficient.

Advanced

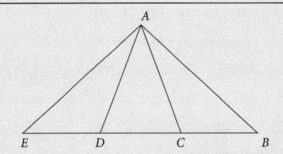

20. In the figure above, segments AD and AC divide $\angle EAB$ into three nonoverlapping angles that are equal in measure. Are AE and AB equal in length?

    (1) $AD = AC$

    (2) $AC = CB$

    ○ Statement (1) ALONE is sufficient, but statement (2) is not sufficient.

    ○ Statement (2) ALONE is sufficient, but statement (1) is not sufficient.

    ○ BOTH statements TOGETHER are sufficient, but NEITHER statement ALONE is sufficient.

    ○ EACH statement ALONE is sufficient.

    ○ Statements (1) and (2) TOGETHER are NOT sufficient.

21. If x and y are positive, x is what percent of y ?

    (1) $x = \dfrac{1}{16}$

    (2) $x = 4y$

    ○ Statement (1) ALONE is sufficient, but statement (2) is not sufficient.

    ○ Statement (2) ALONE is sufficient, but statement (1) is not sufficient.

    ○ BOTH statements TOGETHER are sufficient, but NEITHER statement ALONE is sufficient.

    ○ EACH statement ALONE is sufficient.

    ○ Statements (1) and (2) TOGETHER are NOT sufficient.

22. A shopper bought a tie and a belt during a sale. Originally, the tie cost more than the belt. Which item did he buy at the greater dollar discount?

    (1) He bought the tie at a 20 percent discount.

    (2) He bought the belt at a 25 percent discount.

    ○ Statement (1) ALONE is sufficient, but statement (2) is not sufficient.

    ○ Statement (2) ALONE is sufficient, but statement (1) is not sufficient.

    ○ BOTH statements TOGETHER are sufficient, but NEITHER statement ALONE is sufficient.

    ○ EACH statement ALONE is sufficient.

    ○ Statements (1) and (2) TOGETHER are NOT sufficient.

23. Joyce has a recipe for a batch of brownies and a recipe for a coffee cake. How many cups of flour does her recipe for a batch of brownies require?

    (1) When Joyce bakes a batch of brownies and a coffee cake following her recipes, she uses a total of $4\dfrac{1}{2}$ cups of flour.

    (2) When Joyce bakes 2 batches of brownies and 3 coffee cakes following her recipes, she uses a total of 11 cups of flour.

    ○ Statement (1) ALONE is sufficient, but statement (2) is not sufficient.

    ○ Statement (2) ALONE is sufficient, but statement (1) is not sufficient.

    ○ BOTH statements TOGETHER are sufficient, but NEITHER statement ALONE is sufficient.

    ○ EACH statement ALONE is sufficient.

    ○ Statements (1) and (2) TOGETHER are NOT sufficient.

24. Calvin has a collection of 116 cassettes, compact discs, and vinyl records, with more vinyl records than any other medium. If the number of compact discs in his collection is four times as large as the difference between the number of records and the number of cassettes, then how many compact discs does he have?

(1) If he buys 10 more cassettes, he will have 58 cassettes.

(2) He has three times as many cassettes as compact discs.

○ Statement (1) ALONE is sufficient, but statement (2) is not sufficient.

○ Statement (2) ALONE is sufficient, but statement (1) is not sufficient.

○ BOTH statements TOGETHER are sufficient, but NEITHER statement ALONE is sufficient.

○ EACH statement ALONE is sufficient.

○ Statements (1) and (2) TOGETHER are NOT sufficient.

Advanced

25. Is the volume of sphere A greater than the volume of sphere B?

(1) The radius of sphere A is 17% larger than the radius of sphere B.

(2) A cube circumscribed in sphere A would have a greater volume than a cube circumscribed in sphere B.

○ Statement (1) ALONE is sufficient, but statement (2) is not sufficient.

○ Statement (2) ALONE is sufficient, but statement (1) is not sufficient.

○ BOTH statements TOGETHER are sufficient, but NEITHER statement ALONE is sufficient.

○ EACH statement ALONE is sufficient.

○ Statements (1) and (2) TOGETHER are NOT sufficient.

Advanced

26. If m is a positive integer, is m^3 an odd integer?

(1) m is an even integer.

(2) $\sqrt{m}$ is an even integer.

○ Statement (1) ALONE is sufficient, but statement (2) is not sufficient.

○ Statement (2) ALONE is sufficient, but statement (1) is not sufficient.

○ BOTH statements TOGETHER are sufficient, but NEITHER statement ALONE is sufficient.

○ EACH statement ALONE is sufficient.

○ Statements (1) and (2) TOGETHER are NOT sufficient.

Advanced

27. Is p positive?

    (1) The square of p is positive.

    (2) $|p| - p$ is positive.

    ○   Statement (1) ALONE is sufficient, but statement (2) is not sufficient.

    ○   Statement (2) ALONE is sufficient, but statement (1) is not sufficient.

    ○   BOTH statements TOGETHER are sufficient, but NEITHER statement ALONE is sufficient.

    ○   EACH statement ALONE is sufficient.

    ○   Statements (1) and (2) TOGETHER are NOT sufficient.

28. There are two lines at an airline ticket counter. The first line contains exactly 20 people, 2 of whom are flying to Taipei. What percent of the people in the second line are flying to Taipei?

    (1) There are twice as many people flying to Taipei in the second line as in the first line.

    (2) The total number of people in both lines is 36, and the total number of people in both lines who are flying to Taipei is 6.

    ○   Statement (1) ALONE is sufficient, but statement (2) is not sufficient.

    ○   Statement (2) ALONE is sufficient, but statement (1) is not sufficient.

    ○   BOTH statements TOGETHER are sufficient, but NEITHER statement ALONE is sufficient.

    ○   EACH statement ALONE is sufficient.

    ○   Statements (1) and (2) TOGETHER are NOT sufficient.

29. What is the value of m if $m = \dfrac{4c}{5d}$ and d is not equal to zero?

    (1) $c = 10d$

    (2) $c = 2$

    ○   Statement (1) ALONE is sufficient, but statement (2) is not sufficient.

    ○   Statement (2) ALONE is sufficient, but statement (1) is not sufficient.

    ○   BOTH statements TOGETHER are sufficient, but NEITHER statement ALONE is sufficient.

    ○   EACH statement ALONE is sufficient.

    ○   Statements (1) and (2) TOGETHER are NOT sufficient.

30. What is the value of $2x - y$?

    (1) $x + y = 12$

    (2) $x - y = 4$

    ○ Statement (1) ALONE is sufficient, but statement (2) is not sufficient.

    ○ Statement (2) ALONE is sufficient, but statement (1) is not sufficient.

    ○ BOTH statements TOGETHER are sufficient, but NEITHER statement ALONE is sufficient.

    ○ EACH statement ALONE is sufficient.

    ○ Statements (1) and (2) TOGETHER are NOT sufficient.

31. Are at least 20 percent of the people in City H who are at least 30 years old bilingual?

    (1) In City H, 25 percent of the bilingual population is at least 30 years old.

    (2) In City H, of the population at least 30 years old, 18 percent of the women and 17 percent of the men are bilingual.

    ○ Statement (1) ALONE is sufficient, but statement (2) is not sufficient.

    ○ Statement (2) ALONE is sufficient, but statement (1) is not sufficient.

    ○ BOTH statements TOGETHER are sufficient, but NEITHER statement ALONE is sufficient.

    ○ EACH statement ALONE is sufficient.

    ○ Statements (1) and (2) TOGETHER are NOT sufficient.

32. What is the value of the product DE?

    (1) $ABCD > 0$

    (2) $BCDE = 0$

    ○ Statement (1) ALONE is sufficient, but statement (2) is not sufficient.

    ○ Statement (2) ALONE is sufficient, but statement (1) is not sufficient.

    ○ BOTH statements TOGETHER are sufficient, but NEITHER statement ALONE is sufficient.

    ○ EACH statement ALONE is sufficient.

    ○ Statements (1) and (2) TOGETHER are NOT sufficient.

33. What is the value of x?

    (1) $2x^2 = 18$

    (2) $3(x + 2y) = 6y - x + 12$

    ○ Statement (1) ALONE is sufficient, but statement (2) is not sufficient.

    ○ Statement (2) ALONE is sufficient, but statement (1) is not sufficient.

    ○ BOTH statements TOGETHER are sufficient, but NEITHER statement ALONE is sufficient.

    ○ EACH statement ALONE is sufficient.

    ○ Statements (1) and (2) TOGETHER are NOT sufficient.

34. Of the members of a marching band, what percentage are boys who play trombone?

    (1) Thirty percent of the members of the band play trombone.

    (2) Sixty percent of the members of the band are boys.

    ○ Statement (1) ALONE is sufficient, but statement (2) is not sufficient.

    ○ Statement (2) ALONE is sufficient, but statement (1) is not sufficient.

    ○ BOTH statements TOGETHER are sufficient, but NEITHER statement ALONE is sufficient.

    ○ EACH statement ALONE is sufficient.

    ○ Statements (1) and (2) TOGETHER are NOT sufficient.

Advanced

35. If m and n are both positive, what is the value of $m\sqrt{n}$?

    (1) $\dfrac{mn}{\sqrt{n}} = 10$

    (2) $\dfrac{m^2 n}{2} = 50$

    ○ Statement (1) ALONE is sufficient, but statement (2) is not sufficient.

    ○ Statement (2) ALONE is sufficient, but statement (1) is not sufficient.

    ○ BOTH statements TOGETHER are sufficient, but NEITHER statement ALONE is sufficient.

    ○ EACH statement ALONE is sufficient.

    ○ Statements (1) and (2) TOGETHER are NOT sufficient.

36. At a certain restaurant, the total price for one hamburger and one drink is $3.50. How much does one drink cost?

    (1) If the price of the drink were half of its present price, the price of a drink would be one-fifth of the price of a hamburger.

    (2) The cost of one hamburger and two drinks is $4.50.

    ○ Statement (1) ALONE is sufficient, but statement (2) is not sufficient.

    ○ Statement (2) ALONE is sufficient, but statement (1) is not sufficient.

    ○ BOTH statements TOGETHER are sufficient, but NEITHER statement ALONE is sufficient.

    ○ EACH statement ALONE is sufficient.

    ○ Statements (1) and (2) TOGETHER are NOT sufficient.

37. The price per share of stock A increased by 25 percent during the same period of time that the price per share of stock B decreased by 25 percent. The original price per share of stock A was what percent of the original price per share of stock B?

    (1) The increased price per share of stock A was equal to the decreased price per share of stock B.

    (2) The increase in the price per share of stock A was $\frac{3}{20}$ of the original price per share of stock B.

    ○ Statement (1) ALONE is sufficient, but statement (2) is not sufficient.

    ○ Statement (2) ALONE is sufficient, but statement (1) is not sufficient.

    ○ BOTH statements TOGETHER are sufficient, but NEITHER statement ALONE is sufficient.

    ○ EACH statement ALONE is sufficient.

    ○ Statements (1) and (2) TOGETHER are NOT sufficient.

38. A bag of coins contains only nickels, dimes, and quarters. There are 38 coins in all. What is the total value of all the coins in the bag?

    (1) Quarters account for half the value of the coins in the bag.

    (2) The value of all the dimes equals the value of all the nickels.

    ○ Statement (1) ALONE is sufficient, but statement (2) is not sufficient.

    ○ Statement (2) ALONE is sufficient, but statement (1) is not sufficient.

    ○ BOTH statements TOGETHER are sufficient, but NEITHER statement ALONE is sufficient.

    ○ EACH statement ALONE is sufficient.

    ○ Statements (1) and (2) TOGETHER are NOT sufficient.

39. Is the integer x a multiple of 5?

    (1) x divided by 3 leaves a remainder of 2.

    (2) x divided by 4 leaves no remainder.

    ○ Statement (1) ALONE is sufficient, but statement (2) is not sufficient.

    ○ Statement (2) ALONE is sufficient, but statement (1) is not sufficient.

    ○ BOTH statements TOGETHER are sufficient, but NEITHER statement ALONE is sufficient.

    ○ EACH statement ALONE is sufficient.

    ○ Statements (1) and (2) TOGETHER are NOT sufficient.

40. Megacorp International spent a total of $90,000,000 on television, magazine, and billboard advertising combined. How much of the total was spent on television advertising?

    (1) The total spending for billboard and magazine advertising was 20% less than the amount spent on television advertising.

    (2) The company spent 50% more on magazine advertising than on billboard advertising.

    ○ Statement (1) ALONE is sufficient, but statement (2) is not sufficient.

    ○ Statement (2) ALONE is sufficient, but statement (1) is not sufficient.

    ○ BOTH statements TOGETHER are sufficient, but NEITHER statement ALONE is sufficient.

    ○ EACH statement ALONE is sufficient.

    ○ Statements (1) and (2) TOGETHER are NOT sufficient.

41. The integer x is even, and the integer y is odd. Is the integer z odd?

    (1) $xyz + 1$ is odd.

    (2) $xy + xz + yz$ is even.

    ○ Statement (1) ALONE is sufficient, but statement (2) is not sufficient.

    ○ Statement (2) ALONE is sufficient, but statement (1) is not sufficient.

    ○ BOTH statements TOGETHER are sufficient, but NEITHER statement ALONE is sufficient.

    ○ EACH statement ALONE is sufficient.

    ○ Statements (1) and (2) TOGETHER are NOT sufficient.

42. What is the area of the floor in Dan's rectangular bedroom that will not be covered by a particular rectangular rug?

    (1) The area of the floor in Dan's bedroom is 300 square feet.

    (2) After the rug is placed in Dan's room, there will be a 24-inch strip of exposed floor between the rug and the wall along all sides of the rug.

    ○ Statement (1) ALONE is sufficient, but statement (2) is not sufficient.

    ○ Statement (2) ALONE is sufficient, but statement (1) is not sufficient.

    ○ BOTH statements TOGETHER are sufficient, but NEITHER statement ALONE is sufficient.

    ○ EACH statement ALONE is sufficient.

    ○ Statements (1) and (2) TOGETHER are NOT sufficient.

Advanced

43. If z is an integer, is z prime?

    (1) $15! < z$

    (2) $17! + 2 \leq z \leq 17! + 17$

    ○ Statement (1) ALONE is sufficient, but statement (2) is not sufficient.

    ○ Statement (2) ALONE is sufficient, but statement (1) is not sufficient.

    ○ BOTH statements TOGETHER are sufficient, but NEITHER statement ALONE is sufficient.

    ○ EACH statement ALONE is sufficient.

    ○ Statements (1) and (2) TOGETHER are NOT sufficient.

Advanced

44. A right triangle has sides of lengths A and $2B$ and hypotenuse of length $A + B$. What is the perimeter?

    (1) $A = 3$

    (2) $A = \dfrac{3B}{2}$

    ○ Statement (1) ALONE is sufficient, but statement (2) is not sufficient.

    ○ Statement (2) ALONE is sufficient, but statement (1) is not sufficient.

    ○ BOTH statements TOGETHER are sufficient, but NEITHER statement ALONE is sufficient.

    ○ EACH statement ALONE is sufficient.

    ○ Statements (1) and (2) TOGETHER are NOT sufficient.

Advanced

45. If x is positive, is x prime?

    (1) x^3 has exactly four distinct positive integer factors.

    (2) $x^2 - x - 6 = 0$

    ○ Statement (1) ALONE is sufficient, but statement (2) is not sufficient.

    ○ Statement (2) ALONE is sufficient, but statement (1) is not sufficient.

    ○ BOTH statements TOGETHER are sufficient, but NEITHER statement ALONE is sufficient.

    ○ EACH statement ALONE is sufficient.

    ○ Statements (1) and (2) TOGETHER are NOT sufficient.

Advanced

46. If x is not equal to zero, is $\dfrac{1}{x} > 1$?

    (1) $\dfrac{y}{x} > y$

    (2) $x^3 > x^2$

    ○ Statement (1) ALONE is sufficient, but statement (2) is not sufficient.

    ○ Statement (2) ALONE is sufficient, but statement (1) is not sufficient.

    ○ BOTH statements TOGETHER are sufficient, but NEITHER statement ALONE is sufficient.

    ○ EACH statement ALONE is sufficient.

    ○ Statements (1) and (2) TOGETHER are NOT sufficient.

47. At the beginning of last year, a car dealership had 150 cars in stock, which the dealership had purchased for $20,000 each. During the same year, the dealership made only one purchase of cars. What is the total amount spent by the dealership on the cars it had in stock at the end of last year?

    (1) Last year, the dealership purchased 50 cars for $18,000 each.

    (2) Last year, the total revenue from the sale of cars was $180,000.

    ○ Statement (1) ALONE is sufficient, but statement (2) is not sufficient.

    ○ Statement (2) ALONE is sufficient, but statement (1) is not sufficient.

    ○ BOTH statements TOGETHER are sufficient, but NEITHER statement ALONE is sufficient.

    ○ EACH statement ALONE is sufficient.

    ○ Statements (1) and (2) TOGETHER are NOT sufficient.

48. What is the minimum number of rectangular shipping boxes Company L will need in order to ship 120 products, all of which are rectangular solids with exactly the same dimensions?

    (1) The dimensions of each product are 3 inches in length, 4 inches in depth, and 6 inches in height.

    (2) Each shipping box is a cube with an edge of length one foot.

    ○ Statement (1) ALONE is sufficient, but statement (2) is not sufficient.

    ○ Statement (2) ALONE is sufficient, but statement (1) is not sufficient.

    ○ BOTH statements TOGETHER are sufficient, but NEITHER statement ALONE is sufficient.

    ○ EACH statement ALONE is sufficient.

    ○ Statements (1) and (2) TOGETHER are NOT sufficient.

49. If set Z has a median of 19, what is the range of set Z?

    (1) $Z = \{18, 28, 11, x, 15, y\}$

    (2) The average (arithmetic mean) of the members of set Z is 20.

    ○ Statement (1) ALONE is sufficient, but statement (2) is not sufficient.

    ○ Statement (2) ALONE is sufficient, but statement (1) is not sufficient.

    ○ BOTH statements TOGETHER are sufficient, but NEITHER statement ALONE is sufficient.

    ○ EACH statement ALONE is sufficient.

    ○ Statements (1) and (2) TOGETHER are NOT sufficient.

Advanced

50. If each of a, b, and c is positive and $a = 5b + 7c$, what is the value of $\frac{a}{b}$?

    (1) $2b + 5c = 50$

    (2) $3b - 5c = 0$

    ○ Statement (1) ALONE is sufficient, but statement (2) is not sufficient.

    ○ Statement (2) ALONE is sufficient, but statement (1) is not sufficient.

    ○ BOTH statements TOGETHER are sufficient, but NEITHER statement ALONE is sufficient.

    ○ EACH statement ALONE is sufficient.

    ○ Statements (1) and (2) TOGETHER are NOT sufficient.

ANSWERS AND EXPLANATIONS FOLLOW ON THE NEXT PAGE

ANSWERS AND EXPLANATIONS

1. B	11. B	21. B	31. B	41. B
2. B	12. D	22. E	32. C	42. E
3. C	13. D	23. C	33. B	43. B
4. E	14. C	24. D	34. E	44. A
5. A	15. D	25. D	35. D	45. B
6. A	16. D	26. D	36. D	46. B
7. B	17. E	27. B	37. D	47. E
8. E	18. B	28. B	38. C	48. C
9. D	19. E	29. A	39. E	49. C
10. A	20. A	30. C	40. A	50. B

DIAGNOSTIC TOOL

Tally up your score and write down your results below.

Total Correct: _____ out of 50

Percentage Correct: # you got right × 100 ÷ 50: _____

DIAGNOSE YOUR RESULTS

Look back at the questions you got wrong and think back on your experience answering them.

Step 1: Find the Roadblocks

Did you struggle to answer some questions? To improve your score, you need to pinpoint exactly what element of these roadblocks tripped you up. To do that, ask yourself these three questions.

1. Did I not know the math?

Maybe you've forgotten how to figure out the area of a triangle or what PEMDAS stands for. Or maybe math just isn't your thing.

If you know you need to brush up on your math skills, try out the Kaplan's *GMAT Math Workbook*, which contains focused review of all the fundamental math concepts tested on the GMAT, as well as practice exercises to build speed and accuracy.

2. Was it the question type that threw me off?

Then you need to become more comfortable with it! Data Sufficiency questions have a unique format that you need to master so it doesn't slow you down on test day. If this question's format was a problem for you, go back to the beginning of this chapter and review the Kaplan principles and method for Data Sufficiency questions. Make sure you understand the principles and how to apply the method. These strategies will help to improve your speed and efficiency on test day.

Also, get as much practice as you can so that you grow more at ease with this question type format. For even more practice, try out Kaplan's *GMAT Math Workbook,* which includes practice sets for this question type.

3. Did I know the math but struggle to evaluate the Statements?

If this is the case, then you probably didn't focus enough on the question stem. Perhaps you didn't simplify or weren't sure what you needed to answer the question. Read the answer explanation, which will show you how you could have dealt with the question stem more efficiently.

> **EXPERT EXCLUSIVE**
>
> "Blind spots" on Data Sufficiency are usually the result of falling into a trap. Take a close look at your blind spots and figure out what the trap was so that you stay out of it on test day.

Another possibility is that you weren't sure what numbers to pick. The answer explanations will help here, too. But nothing develops that skill like practice. Try out Kaplan's *GMAT Math Workbook,* which has more practice sets.

Step 2: Find the Blind Spots

Did you answer some questions quickly and confidently but get them wrong anyway?

When you come across wrong answers like these, you need to figure out what you thought you were doing right, what it turns out you were doing wrong, and why that happened. The best way to do that is to read the answer explanations!

They give you a detailed breakdown of why the correct answer is correct and why all the other answer choices are wrong. This helps to reinforce the Kaplan principles and methods for each question type and helps you figure out what blindsided you so it doesn't happen again. Also, just as with your roadblocks, try to get in as much practice as you can.

Step 3: Reinforce Your Strengths

Now read through all the answer explanations for the ones you got right. Again, this helps to reinforce the Kaplan principles and methods, which in turn helps you work more efficiently so you can get the score you want. Keep your skills sharp with more practice.

As soon as you are comfortable with all the GMAT question types and Kaplan methods, complete a full-length practice test under timed conditions. In this way, practice tests serve as milestones; they help you to chart your progress! So don't save them all for the final weeks.

If you are aiming for that top score, try out Kaplan's *GMAT 800,* which includes only the toughest GMAT questions and most focused strategies.

For even more practice, you can also try out the GMAT Quiz Bank! You get more than 1,000 questions that you can access 24/7 from any Internet browser, each with comprehensive explanations. You can even customize your quizzes based on question type, content, and difficulty level. Take quizzes in Timed Mode to test your stamina or in Tutor Mode to see explanations as you work. Best of all, you also get detailed reports to track your progress.

Visit **kaptest.com/GMAT** for more details on our Quiz Bank and for more information on our other online and classroom-based options.

1. B

We need a ratio, or any proportional relationship, between the two prices.

(1) *Insufficient.* Merely knowing that there is a $4 difference won't suffice. The list price could be $40, making the ratio 36:40, which is 9:10. Or the list price could be $10, making the ratio 3:5.

(2) *Sufficient.* Knowing the percentage difference, as opposed to the actual dollar difference, allows us to determine the ratio. The ratio of a quantity 20 percent less than another quantity to that other quantity is 8:10, or 4:5.

2. B

We want know whether x equals y. Since this is a Yes/No question, a Statement will be sufficient if it allows us to answer "definitely yes" or "definitely no." To answer the question, we may need to rearrange equations so that x and y are on opposite sides of the equal sign.

> **EXPERT EXCLUSIVE**
>
> The presence of a squared variable is a sign of a trap. Don't forget that the underlying variable could have a negative value!

(1) *Insufficient.* There's a common trap here, one you need to learn for test day. It may look as though the two variables are equal, but they aren't necessarily. All the Statement tells us is that x^2 is equal to y^2. That doesn't mean that x equals y, because one could be negative and the other positive. Suppose x equals 2; y could also equal 2, or it could equal −2.

(2) *Sufficient.* The only way for $(x-y)^2$ to equal zero is if $(x-y)$ itself is zero:

$$x - y = 0$$

Add y to both sides: $x = y$

That's exactly what we're looking for.

3. C

This Yes/No question asks you to compare perimeters (recall that the perimeter is the sum of the sides). It's tempting to think that we need to know the sides of the rectangles, but quite often, it's possible to answer a Yes/No question without values. All we need to do is be able to *compare* the perimeters. It's also important to remember that a no answer could come from the perimeters being equal.

(1) *Insufficient.* Read carefully—it doesn't say, "The length of *A* is twice the length of *B*, and the width of *A* is twice the width of *B*." If it did, it surely would be sufficient. It just says that "a side" of *A* is twice "a side" of *B*. We don't know anything about the other side.

Picking Numbers will make this clear. Perhaps rectangle *B* is 5 by 10. Rectangle *A* has to have a side that's twice a side of *B*. Let's double the 5 side of *B*. So rectangle *A* is 10 by *something*. That *something* could be *anything*. It could, in fact, be 5 . . . rectangle *A* would be 10 × 5 and equivalent to *B*, in which case *A*'s perimeter would not be greater. Or *A* could be 10 × 100, in which case its perimeter would be much greater. Since we can get both a no and a yes, the Statement is insufficient.

(2) *Insufficient.* This one is tricky. The key, though, is to envision a very long, thin rectangle for *B*. If it is 50 by 1, its perimeter is greater than that of a rectangle *A* that is 10 by 10, even though *B*'s area is only half that of *A*. The answer then would be no. It's easy to see how the answer could be yes, as it's not hard to envision *A* as having a greater perimeter in addition to its greater area. Picking rectangle *B* to be 3 by 4 and rectangle *A* to be 4 by 6 is just one example.

> **EXPERT EXCLUSIVE**
> Extreme possibilities are often very helpful when Picking Numbers in Data Sufficiency.

Since neither Statement is sufficient on its own, we need to evaluate them together. So not only is Rectangle *A*'s area twice that of Rectangle *B*, but one of its sides is twice as long as one of *B*'s sides. Since area is length × width, rectangle *A* and *B* must have one side length in common. If you "see" that logically, that's fantastic; you get to save some time. But you could figure it out with algebra:

> **EXPERT EXCLUSIVE**
> You don't have to pick all the values at once. Start with one and figure out what other values would be permissible.

One side of *A* is double one side of *B*:	$l_A = 2l_B$
Area of *A* is double area of *B*:	$l_A w_A = 2(l_B w_B)$
Substitute:	$2l_B w_A = 2l_B w_B$
Divide both sides by $2l_B$:	$w_A = w_B$

Since one side of *A* equals one side of *B*, those sides' contributions to the perimeters will be equal. But the other side of *A* will be longer than the corresponding side of *B*, so its contribution to the perimeter will be greater. Therefore, *A*'s perimeter must be greater.

Or use Picking Numbers:

> *B* is 5 by 10, so its area must be 50. *A*'s area must be 100. One of *A*'s sides must be twice one of *B*'s sides. So *A* might have a side length of $10 \times 2 = 20$. If *A*'s area is 100 and one side is 20, the other side must be $100 \div 20 = 5$. So *A* would be 5 by 20. Perimeter of *A* is 50, and perimeter of B is 30.

> But perhaps we double the *other* side of *B*. Perhaps *A* has a side length of $5 \times 2 = 10$. If *A*'s area is 100 and one side is 10, the other side must be $100 \div 10 = 10$. So *A* would be 10 by 10. Perimeter of *A* is 40, and perimeter of *B* is 30.

> *A* is always greater, so we have a "definitely yes."

No matter which approach we take, the answer is (C).

4. E

This value question is fairly straightforward—we need the exact number of students who scored below the average. Keep in mind that we don't need the scores themselves, just how many were under the average.

(1) *Insufficient.* Knowing what the average is tells us nothing about *how many* scored below it.

(2) *Insufficient.* Since we don't know the total number of students, we can't use the number above the average to calculate the number below. (A harder version of this statement would tell you the total number of students—you still wouldn't know how many scored below the average because you still wouldn't know how many scores *equal* the average.)

We have to combine the Statements. Since Statement (1) was totally irrelevant, it doesn't add anything to Statement (2). Still insufficient. Answer (E).

5. A

EXPERT EXCLUSIVE

Correct answers to DS inequality questions often depend upon the effect of negative numbers.

This is essentially a Yes/No question; the only difference is that instead of asking for a "definite yes" or a "definite no," it's asking for "definitely *b*" or "definitely *c*." The important feature is that we need a *definite* answer. In this way, it is just like a Yes/No question.

The question stem has some given information that can be simplified. So before we think about what we need to answer the question, let's simplify:

$$ab < ac$$

Divide both sides by *a*:   PROBLEM! We don't know if *a* is positive or negative!

One of the GMAT's favorite algebra tricks is the fact that when you divide an inequality by a negative number, the inequality sign reverses direction. In Data Sufficiency, that means keeping track of two possibilities. Split your work along two columns:

	a is positive	*a* is negative
Divide both sides by *a*:	$b < c$	$b > c$

So what we need is to know whether *a* is positive or negative. Know that, and we know the answer.

(1) *Sufficient.* This is exactly what we need. If $a < 0$, then *b* is definitely greater.

(2) *Insufficient.* The sign of *c* is irrelevant to what we need.

6. A

We know that all three variables are even numbers greater than 2 and that *q* is greater than *p* but less than *r*. These could be consecutive even integers (2, 4, 6, 8), but they don't have to be. It's hard to tell what you need to answer the question. It's unlikely that the GMAT would just give us the value of *q* directly. We'll probably have to calculate it or deduce it from the Statements.

(1) *Sufficient.* *r* could be 8, in which case *q* would have to be 6 (and *p* would have to be 4). If *r* were anything smaller (like 6), then we couldn't find permissible even numbers for both *q* and *p*. So *r* must be 8. Therefore, *q* must be 6.

> **EXPERT EXCLUSIVE**
> DS questions will try to trap you into thinking about only one possible set of values.

(2) *Insufficient.* If *p* is less than 6, it can only be 4. Sure, that's consistent with consecutive numbers, so *q* could be 6. But that doesn't mean that the numbers *have* to be consecutive. *q* could be any even number 6 or above . . . 8, 10, even 2,000,000!

7. B

To find the number of pages per hour that Michael reads, we need a rate. Most helpful would be words per hour, but in fact, any rate will do—words per day, year, etc.

(1) *Insufficient.* This tells us merely how the words are arranged on the page. It provides no information about Michael's reading speed.

(2) *Sufficient.* This is a rate, exactly what we wanted. Since we know that he reads 300 words per minute and the question told us there are 250 words per page, we can compute how many pages he reads per hour. On test day, you wouldn't bother doing this computation. For the record, it's

$$\frac{300 \text{ (words/min)} \times 60 \text{(min/hour)}}{250 \text{ (words/page)}} = 72 \text{ (pages/hour)}$$

8. E

Other than the fact that this is a Yes/No question, there's not much to pull out of this stem.

(1) *Insufficient.* Spend no time thinking about this. Since n is never mentioned, the statement cannot be sufficient.

(2) *Insufficient.* Same principle here. We get a range of values for n but are told nothing about m.

In combining the two Statements, we want to see whether we can have m greater than n and also have m not greater than n. If we can, the answer is (E); if we can't, it's (C). Certainly m can be greater. It could be just less than $\frac{5}{7}$ and thus greater than the entire range of values for n. The question then becomes: Can n be greater than or equal to m? Yes, n could be just a hair less than $\frac{4}{7}$, with m being just a hair more than $\frac{3}{7}$. (With $\frac{10}{21}$ for m and $\frac{11}{21}$ for n, both Statements are true, and $n > m$.) The answer is (E).

A number line can help you to visualize the ranges:

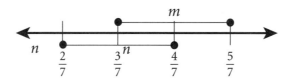

Clearly, there are possible values of m that are greater than possible values of n and vice versa.

9. D

Knowing the values of a and b would be nice, but all we need is to know the difference between a^4 and b^4. It's also worth noting that $a^4 - b^4$ is a classic quadratic:
$$a^4 - b^4 = (a^2 + b^2)(a^2 - b^2).$$

> **EXPERT EXCLUSIVE**
>
> You don't have to know the value of each variable in order to know the value of an expression.

(1) *Sufficient.* Had we noted the classic quadratic, we'd substitute $a^2 + b^2 = 0$ into $a^4 - b^4 = (a^2 + b^2)(a^2 - b^2)$ to get $a^4 - b^4 = (0)(a^2 - b^2)$. Since 0 times anything is 0, $a^4 - b^4 = 0$.

Alternately, we could realize that since a squared term can never be negative, the only way that $a^2 + b^2 = 0$ is possible is if both a and b equal 0.

(2) *Sufficient.* If the variables are equal, then their values when raised to the fourth power are equal, and $a^4 - b^4 = 0$.

10. A

To be "evenly divisible by 3" is to be a multiple of 3. So this Yes/No question asks whether R is a multiple of 3.

(1) *Sufficient.* We are told "$2R$ is evenly divisible by 3," which means that $\frac{2R}{3}$ is an integer. For that to be the case, the 3 in the denominator would have to be cancelled by a factor of 3 in the numerator. 2 does not have a factor of 3, so the factor of 3 *must* come from R. If R has a factor of 3, it is definitely a multiple of 3.

Perhaps you'd prefer to Pick Numbers. To guarantee that you pick a permissible number, pick for $2R$ instead of just R. Let's pick $2R = 6$. Then $R = 3$, which answers our question with a yes. If we try $2R = 9$, we get $R = 4.5$, but the question stem says that R is an integer, so we have to throw this number away and try again. Let's test $2R = 12$. Then $R = 6$, which is also a multiple of 3. No matter what we try, the only permitted values are multiples of 3.

(2) *Insufficient.* Similar reasoning is at work here. We are told "$3R$ is evenly divisible by 3," which means that $\frac{3R}{3}$ is an integer. The 3 in the numerator cancels the denominator. So R is an integer . . . any integer at all. It could be a multiple of 3, sure. But it doesn't have to be.

Again, we could use Picking Numbers. If $3R = 6$, then $R = 2$. If $3R = 9$, then $R = 3$. R may be a multiple of 3, but doesn't have to be.

11. B

We're asked for the value of $\frac{\text{\# of heads}}{\text{\# of flips}}$. Since the number of flips is N, we could also say that we want $\frac{\text{\# of heads}}{N}$. It's important to remember when asked for the value of an expression (especially a proportion, like a fraction or a ratio) that we don't need the value of each separate variable—just the expression itself.

(1) *Insufficient.* This tells us how many coin tosses there were but leaves us clueless as to how many came up heads. (Note that you cannot infer that 12 of the tosses were heads just because the coin is described as "fair." Although a fair coin tends to come up heads half the time, in any given series of flips, the number of times it comes up heads can vary significantly.)

(2) *Sufficient.* By telling us what fraction came up tails, this Statement tells us what fraction came up heads. Since only heads or tails are possible, and since $\frac{3}{8}$ were tails, the remaining $\frac{5}{8}$ were heads.

EXPERT EXCLUSIVE

If you pick a number that isn't permitted by either the Statement or the given information of the stem, that number cannot be considered. It's *not* a no! It's just . . . gone.

EXPERT EXCLUSIVE

If the two Statements are very similar, the subtle difference between them is probably very important.

EXPERT EXCLUSIVE

When a question asks for the value of a proportion, a Statement with proportional information is often sufficient.

12. D

PQRS is described only as a quadrilateral, which means only that it has four sides, not that any side has to be the same length as another. We want to know whether or not it's also a square, meaning that all four sides are the same length. Notice how Data Sufficiency diagrams can be misleading. *PQRS* could look quite different from what's depicted. It could look like this:

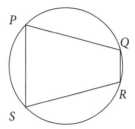

(1) *Sufficient.* If *PS* is equal to the radius, the quadrilateral cannot be a square. Imagine if it were a square:

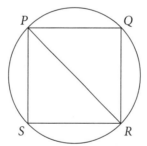

EXPERT EXCLUSIVE

The special right triangles are powerful tools and show up in some unexpected ways.

If *PQRS* were a square, all the sides would be equal. That would mean that *PS* = *SR* = radius. And *PSR* would be an isosceles right triangle, making *PR* the diameter. The diameter is radius × 2. But the hypotenuse of an isosceles right triangle is side × $\sqrt{2}$. Since the side is the same length as the radius and the hypotenuse is the same as the diameter, we have a circle with a diameter of radius × $\sqrt{2}$. That's not possible. Therefore, *PQRS* definitely cannot be a square.

(2) *Sufficient.* For *PQRS* to be a square, the degree measure of all four minor arcs (*PQ*, *QR*, *RS*, and *SP*) must be one quarter of the circle. Since every circle is 360°, the degree measure of each of the arcs would have to be 90°. Since minor arc *QR* is 45°, *PQRS* isn't a square.

13. D

We want Bill's average rate. The rate formula is *Distance = Rate × Time*. We know the time (3 hours), so merely finding out the distance he traveled would be sufficient.

(1) *Sufficient.* Exactly as hoped for. With the distance known, we could plug it into the rate formula and compute Bill's rate. We won't, however, because all we need to know is that we could solve for the rate; doing so would waste valuable time.

(2) *Sufficient.* If he covered the same distance at 30 mph as he did at 60 mph, he must have been traveling at 30 mph for twice as long as he was at 60 mph. Given that he traveled for 3 hours, he traveled at 30 mph for 2 hours and 60 mph for 1 hour. That comes to 120 miles total distance, and again we can solve for the rate.

If you weren't confident about that evaluation, you could use the chart that Kaplan recommends for multi-leg rate calculations:

	Rate	Time	Distance
part 1 of trip			
part 2 of trip			
entire trip			

Plug in the data from the question stem and Statement (2):

	Rate	Time	Distance
part 1 of trip	30		d/2
part 2 of trip	60		d/2
entire trip		3	

Now fill in the Total Distance and the two empty Time boxes (since $R \times T = D$, $T = D/R$):

	Rate	Time	Distance
part 1 of trip	30	d/60	d/2
part 2 of trip	60	d/120	d/2
entire trip		3	d

At this point, we could add $\dfrac{d}{60} + \dfrac{d}{120} = 3$ to solve for the total distance, which is what we need for sufficiency. We wouldn't actually want to do the calculation, of course.

14. C

Although the value of all three variables would, of course, give us the answer, we want to assume that the GMAT will give us the value of the expression we're asked for without the value of all the individual variables. So we're looking for values for the numerator $x + z$ and the denominator $x - y$ themselves or even a value for the fraction as a whole.

EXPERT EXCLUSIVE

Adding or subtracting equations often produces fast solutions to GMAT problems.

(1) *Insufficient.* This supplies the numerator, but as we have no idea what the value of the denominator is, we cannot evaluate the fraction.

(2) *Insufficient.* We cannot determine the value of either part of the fraction.

Since we know the value of the numerator from Statement (1), combining the two is just a matter of trying to determine the value of the denominator, $x - y$. As it turns out, we can do this. Statement (2) can be rewritten as $z = 2 - y$. Substituting that value for z into Statement (1) yields $x + 2 - y = 3$. Subtracting 2 from both sides yields $x - y = 1$. We now have a value for the denominator as well as the numerator, so we can find the value of the fraction.

You could also solve by subtracting one equation from another:

$$\begin{aligned} x + z &= 3 \\ -[y + z] &= 2 \\ \hline x - y &= 1 \end{aligned}$$

You could even Pick Numbers:

> Since z appears twice, start there. Let's say $z = 1$. That means $x + 1 = 3$, so $x = 2$. And $y + 1 = 2$, so $y = 1$. Plugging those numbers into our question, we get $\dfrac{x + z}{x - y} = \dfrac{2 + 1}{2 - 1} = \dfrac{3}{1} = 3$.
>
> Now try a second set to see whether we get the same result. Let's try a different kind of number for z . . . $z = -3$, say. That means $x - 3 = 3$, so $x = 6$. And $y - 3 = 2$, so $y = 5$. Plugging those numbers into our question, we get $\dfrac{x + z}{x - y} = \dfrac{6 - 3}{6 - 5} = \dfrac{3}{1} = 3$.
>
> You get 3 no matter what you try. Sufficient.

15. D

The information in this question stem could definitely use some simplifying. Because the list of possible values is fairly small, it's a good use of time to write them all out. That way you won't miss any or get confused.

x is a positive integer less than 10:	1, 2, 3, 4, 5, 6, 7, 8, 9
$x + 2$:	3, 4, 5, 6, 7, 8, 9, 10, 11
$x + 2$ is prime:	3, 5, 7, 11
possible values of x:	1, 3, 5, 9

So we are given four possible values of x, {1, 3, 5, 9}, and we are asked whether we can narrow this list down to just one value.

(1) *Sufficient.* Just plug in the values above: 1 + 3 = 4; 3 + 3 = 6; 5 + 3 = 8; 9 + 3 = 12. Only 4 is the square of an integer, so we know the value of *x*.

(2) *Sufficient.* Just plug in the values again: 1 + 7 = 8; 3 + 7 = 10; 5 + 7 = 12; 9 + 7 = 16. Only 8 is the cube of an integer, so again we know the value of *x*.

16. D

We want to know what percent of the crew is made up of carpenters and painters together. Because we're given the ratio of carpenters to painters, if we're told how many there are of either, we can compute the total of both. We'd still need to know, though, how many people are in the crew, because there could be people in the crew who are not carpenters or painters. Another way to solve this, and a way that's much more likely on a Data Sufficiency question, is to get a proportional relationship between the total crew and either the carpenters or the painters. Since we're only asked for a proportion $\left(\dfrac{\text{carpenters} + \text{painters}}{\text{total crew}} \right)$, a proportion is all we really need.

(1) *Sufficient.* This is essentially a ratio between carpenters and the whole crew. For every 100 members of the crew, there are 18 carpenters. From the question itself, we can determine that 12% of the whole crew are painters (this comes from the 3:2 ratio), so the percent of the whole crew who are carpenters or painters is (18% + 12% = 30%).

(2) *Sufficient.* Same idea, just the other way around. If 12 percent are painters, then 18 percent are carpenters (from the 3:2 ratio again), so 30 percent are either carpenters or painters.

17. E

We're given a proportion between water surface area and fish. So to calculate the number of fish, we need the water surface area of the aquarium. Notice we don't need the regular surface area (for which we'd need measurements of length, width, and height) but the *water* surface area. An aquarium has glass on five sides and exposed water on only one . . . the top. So the water surface area is just the area of the top of the aquarium, which is defined only by length times width. (Height would be needed for volume, but that isn't part of the proportion we're given.) Therefore, we need the value of length × width of the aquarium.

(1) *Insufficient.* We know the dimensions of the tank . . . but not which measurement corresponds to which side. Length × width could be 60 × 42, 60 × 30, or 42 × 30. The Statement is enough to calculate the aquarium's *entire* surface area; we just don't know which face is the one with exposed water. It's a trap for anyone who doesn't focus on the question and realize that we need *water* surface area.

(2) *Insufficient.* We know the height of the water but not its length or width, which is what we need for the surface area.

Even combined, we don't have enough data. If the aquarium is filled to a depth of 40 centimeters, we can rule out 30 as the height of the aquarium. But the height could still be 42 or 60. So the length × width could still be 60 × 30 or 42 × 30. Without an exact value, the Statements are still insufficient.

> **EXPERT EXCLUSIVE**
>
> The more you analyze the question stem, the easier the Statements will be to evaluate.

18. B

The rules say that a resolution must be passed by at least two-thirds of half of the 20 directors. Half of 20 is 10, and two-thirds of that is $6\frac{2}{3}$. Since we can't have fractional directors, we're left with 7—the absolute minimum number of directors required to pass a resolution. Of course, if more directors are voting, more votes are needed to pass the resolution. Twenty directors voting, for example, would require 14 votes in favor.

(1) *Insufficient.* Ten votes might or might not pass a resolution, depending on how many directors vote. If only 10 vote, it passes; if 20 vote, it doesn't.

(2) *Sufficient.* Seven votes against means that even if all 20 directors vote, a $\frac{2}{3}$ majority is impossible. The resolution doesn't pass.

19. E

The brevity of this question is a big red flag that something tricky is going on. What hints do we see that might let us know what the trick is? Well, since the terms *positive* and *negative* show up, it probably has something to do with the difference between the two kinds of numbers. If we Pick Numbers, let's not fall into the trap of assuming that everything has to be positive.

> **EXPERT EXCLUSIVE**
>
> Be careful when plugging a negative number into subtraction. If *y* is negative, then *x* – *y* results in adding a positive number to *x*.

(1) *Insufficient.* Pick 10 for *x* and 5 for *y*. This satisfies the Statement and would allow us to answer yes to the question. We can't stop here, though; we have to try different values to see if we can answer the question no.

Since we know negative numbers will be the issue, let's use −5 and −10. Since $x - y$ still has to be positive, we'll need to pick $x = -5$ and $y = -10$. Now the answer to our question is no; $-5 + -10$ is not positive.

(2) *Insufficient.* We can use the same values here. $x = 10$ and $y = 5$ are permitted by this Statement, as are $x = -5$ and $y = -10$. The former set answers our question yes, and the latter answers it no.

Since the same two sets of numbers are permissible in each Statement, combining the Statements doesn't change anything. We can still have a yes and a no. (By the way, kudos if you noticed that since $(x - y) = -(y - x)$, Statements (1) and (2) are, in fact, identical.)

20. A

We're asked whether *AE* and *AB* are equal. If they are equal, then *ABE* would be an isosceles triangle, and angle *AEB* would equal angle *ABE*. So that's what we need—to know if those two angles are equal. But let's see if we can simplify our question any, based on what we're given. We know that angles *EAD*, *DAC*, and *CAB* are equal. What does that tell us about the two angles we need?

Looking at triangles *EAD* and *CAB*, realizing that they have one pair of equal angles already, we can see that if angles *ADE* and *ACB* are equal, then so will be the angles we need—*AED* and *ABC*.

(1) *Sufficient*. This tells us that the middle triangle (*ACD*) is isosceles. The angles facing the two equal sides are, therefore, equal (these are angles *ACD* and *ADC*). Since these angles are equal, their supplementary angles (*ADE* and *ACB*) are also equal. Since those two supplementary angles are equal, the third and final angles (*AED* and *ABC*) in the two outside triangles must also be equal. Looking at the whole figure then, we see that triangle *ABE* is isosceles. Therefore, *AE* is equal to *AB*.

(2) *Insufficient*. This allows us to conclude that angles *CAB* and *CBA* are equal, but that's of no help. We learn nothing more about triangle *ADE*, so we cannot answer the question.

21. B

From the stem, x and y are positive. We want to know the percent of y that x is. A percent is just a proportion. So we need the proportional relationship between x and y, which is to say that we're looking for $\frac{x}{y}$.

(1) *Insufficient*. The value of x has been given, but the value of y has not, and thus the desired percent cannot be found.

(2) *Sufficient*. Dividing each side by y gives us $\frac{x}{y} = 4$. That's exactly what we're looking for.

22. E

From the stem, we can see that we want to compare the number of dollars discounted from the price of the tie with the number of dollars discounted from the price of the belt. Notice that we need to compare dollars to dollars, not percent to percent—though of course, information that outright stated that one discount was a greater dollar amount would also be sufficient.

(1) *Insufficient*. Only information about the tie is given. We know nothing about the belt. Eliminate (A) and (D).

(2) *Insufficient*. Only information about the belt is given. We know nothing about the tie. Eliminate (B).

In combination: We now know that the percentage discount for the belt was larger than that for the tie. If the belt originally cost more, or even the same, that would guarantee a larger dollar discount on the belt. But since the tie originally cost more, we can't say for sure which item had the larger dollar discount.

Picking Numbers will make this clear: Let's say the belt's original cost is $100, so it was discounted by $25. If the tie's original cost were $200, then it would be discounted by $40; the tie would have the larger dollar discount. But if the tie's original cost were $110, then it would be discounted by $22; then the belt would have the larger dollar discount. Choose (E).

23. C

The simplest way to look at most word problems is to count variables and equations. There are two variables in this problem—the amount of flour used in the brownie recipe and in the coffee cake recipe. (We'll call them b and c.) We need b. We are given no equations at all, so two distinct equations will be sufficient.

(1) *Insufficient.* One batch of brownies (b) and one coffee cake (c) together require 4.5 cups of flour. We get one equation, $b + c = 4.5$, with two variables. We can't solve for either variable. Eliminate (A) and (D).

(2) *Insufficient.* Same story. Two batches of brownies and three coffee cakes together require 11 cups of flour. Therefore, $2b + 3c = 11$. We can't solve the problem for either variable. Eliminate (B).

In combination, since the equations are different, and since there are only two variables, we can solve for the values of the variables. Remember, you can solve for a variable if you have as many different linear equations as you have variables in the equations. Choose (C).

EXPERT EXCLUSIVE

The *n*-variables, *n*-equations rule is a big time saver.

24. D

Since Calvin has a collection of 116 items, the number of cassettes (c) plus the number of discs (d) plus the number of vinyl records (v) equals 116: $c + d + v = 116$. The other statement is much harder to translate. But since we know it must be able to be translated into an equation *somehow*, we can say with confidence that we have two equations and three variables. We need only one more equation (as long as it is different) to be able to solve for everything. [In case you're curious, the second equation is $d = 4(v - c)$.]

(1) *Sufficient.* Here's a new equation: $c + 10 = 58$. No need to work through the math. We know that three different equations will let us solve for all three variables.

(2) *Sufficient.* Same story: $c = 3d$. This is another different equation, so we can solve for d. Choose (D).

25. D

Since this is a Yes/No question, we don't have to find the exact volumes, just the differences between them. Since we don't have to calculate, it doesn't matter if we don't know the formula for volume of a sphere—since the only measurement that could affect the volume of a sphere is its radius, we just care which radius is bigger.

(1) *Sufficient.* Clearly the radius of *A* is bigger, so its volume must be bigger. No need to calculate anything.

(2) *Sufficient.* Don't be intimidated by the complex calculations you'd need to set up equations. Since this is Data Sufficiency, we rarely have to work through equations. Since there must be *some* kind of relationship between the volume of a sphere and the volume of an inscribed cube, the fact that the cube in *A* is bigger than the cube in *B* lets us know that the volume of sphere *A* is larger.

26. D

Because $m^3 = m \times m \times m$, m^3 will be odd if *m* is odd, and m^3 will be even if *m* is even. Thus, the question is really asking if *m* is odd.

(1) *Sufficient.* Statement (1) says that *m* is even, so it can't be odd. Thus, Statement (1) is sufficient to answer no to the question. Eliminate (B), (C), and (E).

> **EXPERT EXCLUSIVE**
>
> Remember, "definitely no" is sufficient. It's "maybe" that's insufficient.

(2) *Sufficient.* In Statement (2), if the positive square root of *m* is an even integer, then *m* must be the product of two even integers. Therefore, *m* must be even. So *m* is *not* odd; the answer to the question is no. (D) is correct.

Picking Numbers would have been a good way to evaluate this Statement, too. Let $\sqrt{m} = 2$. That means *m* is 4. Then pick $\sqrt{m} = 4$. That means *m* is 16. We get an even number in any case, so our answer to the question is a clear no.

27. B

This is a Yes/No question, so the answer must be always yes or always no in order to have sufficiency.

(1) *Insufficient.* Statement (1) tells us that the square of *p* is positive, or $p^2 > 0$. This means that *p* could be positive or negative; when we square either a positive or a negative, we always get a positive. The only thing we really learn from Statement (1) is that *p* is not 0. So we can't answer the question definitively. Statement (1) is insufficient; eliminate (A) and (D).

(2) *Sufficient.* If *p* were positive, then $|p|$ would be equal to *p*. Therefore, $|p| - p$ would equal $p - p$, which of course is 0. But we're told that $|p| - p$ is positive, not 0. Since the Statements are always correct, this means that *p* cannot possibly be positive. Since the answer is "definitely no," the Statement is sufficient. Choose (B).

28. B

To find the percentage of people in the second line flying to Taipei, we need to know how many people are in the second line and how many of them are flying to Taipei. The stem gives us information only about the first line, so let's go on to the Statements.

(1) *Insufficient.* Statement (1) tells us that four people in the second line are flying to Taipei but gives us no information about how many people are in this line, so the Statement is insufficient. Eliminate (A) and (D).

(2) *Sufficient.* Since there are 36 people in the two lines combined and there are 20 people in the first line, there must be $36 - 20 = 16$ people in the second line. Similarly, 6 people in total are flying to Taipei and 2 of them are in the first line, so 4 of them must be in the second line. So Statement (2) tells us how many people are in the second line and how many of them are flying to Taipei; therefore, it is sufficient. Choice (B) is correct.

The *n*-variables, *n*-equations rule makes quick work of Statement (2). You need the value of two variables, and the second Statement provides you with two equations (separated by *and*).

29. A

The stem gives us one equation, $m = \dfrac{4c}{5d}$, and asks us to find a value for m. It's tempting to think that we need to find the values of c and d—and of course that would give us the answer—but we should be on the lookout for a way to find the value of $\dfrac{4c}{5d}$ directly.

Since $\dfrac{4c}{5d} = \dfrac{4}{5} \times \dfrac{c}{d}$, all we really need is $\dfrac{c}{d}$.

(1) *Sufficient.* Divide both sides by d, and we have $\dfrac{c}{d} = 10$. That's exactly the value we need.

> **EXPERT EXCLUSIVE**
>
> Don't get caught up doing calculations. The values of coefficients (e.g., the 4 and the 5) rarely matter in Data Sufficiency.

If you hadn't fully simplified the question, you could still successfully evaluate this Statement by substituting $10d$ for c:

$$m = \frac{4c}{5d} = \frac{4(10d)}{5d} = \frac{4(10d)^2}{5d} = 8$$

Picking Numbers would be a good, straightforward approach as well:

$c = 10d$ . . . Pick $d = 2$ and $c = 20$. Now substitute:

$$m = \frac{4c}{5d} = \frac{4(20)}{5(2)} = \frac{4(2)(10)}{10} = 8$$

Trying a second set, $d = -2$ and $c = -20$:

$$m = \frac{4c}{5d} = \frac{4(-20)}{5(-2)} = \frac{-4(2)(10)}{-10} = 8$$

Same value each time . . . sufficient.

(2) *Insufficient.* This tells us that $c = 2$ but says nothing about d, $\dfrac{c}{d}$, or $\dfrac{4c}{5d}$. Thus, it is insufficient. If you thought you had to solve for both c and d individually, you might have thought you needed this Statement together with Statement (1) for sufficiency.

30. C

Although finding the values of *x* and *y* will definitely give us sufficiency, we won't need the individual values if we can find a value for the expression $2x - y$. So we'll be looking either for information on *x* and *y* or on the expression $2x - y$.

(1) *Insufficient*. This gives us one equation with two variables, so we have no way to solve for *x* and *y*. We also can't rearrange the equation to isolate the expression $2x - y$, so Statement (1) is insufficient. Eliminate (A) and (D).

(2) *Insufficient*. We have basically the same story. With only one equation, we can't solve for *x* and *y*, and the equation also cannot be solved for $2x - y$. So Statement (2) is also insufficient. Eliminate (B).

When we combine the Statements, we have two distinct linear equations and two variables, so we can solve for *x* and *y*. (C) is the correct choice.

31. B

Since this is a Yes/No question, we don't need to find the exact percentage of people 30 and over who are bilingual. We only need to know for sure whether the number is at least 20 percent.

(1) *Insufficient*. This Statement gives us the wrong proportion. Picking some simple numbers shows us why. Let's say that City H has only 4 bilingual people—1 is at least 30 years old. If there were only 2 people in the whole city over 30, then 50% of them would be bilingual! But if there were 10 people over 30, only 10% of them would be bilingual. Eliminate (A) and (D).

> **EXPERT EXCLUSIVE**
> When different mixtures or proportions get added, the sum is bounded by the highest and lowest proportion. Here, the final percentage of the population that is bilingual must be between 18 and 17 percent.

(2) *Sufficient*. Statement (2) tells us that the percentage of women 30 and over who are bilingual is less than 20 percent and that the percentage of men 30 and over who are bilingual is also less than 20 percent. Since neither group is at least 20 percent bilingual, the total population (women and men) of people 30 and over must be less than 20 percent bilingual. Thus, we can definitely say that the answer to the question is "always no." Statement (2) is sufficient, and (B) is correct.

32. C

We don't get much information from the question stem other than the fact that we are looking for the values of *D* and *E* or their product, so let's go right to the Statements.

(1) *Insufficient*. Since the product *ABCD* is greater than zero, we know that none of these four variables can be equal to zero. So *D* isn't zero, but we don't know anything about *E* or the product *DE*, so Statement (1) is insufficient. We can eliminate (A) and (D).

> **EXPERT EXCLUSIVE**
> Many DS question must be solved by logical deductions rather than calculations or algebra.

(2) *Insufficient.* Since the product *BCDE* is equal to zero, at least one of these four variables must be zero, but that's as far as we can go with this Statement. It does not give us the value of *DE*, so it is also insufficient.

Taking the Statements together, we know from Statement (1) that *A, B, C,* and *D* are all *not* equal to zero and from Statement (2) that at least one of *B, C, D,* and *E* must be equal to zero. So *E* must be zero, and the product *DE* must also be zero. The two Statements together are sufficient, and (C) is correct.

33. B

We are given no information about *x* in the stem, so we'll have to go right to the Statements to find the value of *x*.

(1) *Insufficient.* Sure, we know that $x^2 = 9$. But *x* could be either 3 or −3.

EXPERT EXCLUSIVE

Always simplify when you can. You're bound to find something important.

(2) *Sufficient.* This Statement appears at first to be one equation with two variables, which wouldn't be solvable. But there are *x*'s and *y*'s in several places, so we can simplify the equation. First, expand the left side by multiplying out the 3. That gives you $3x + 6y = 6y − x + 12$. If we subtract 6*y* from each side, we've got $3x = −x + 12$. Adding *x* to each side gives us $4x = 12$, or $x = 3$. (B) is correct.

34. E

The number of boys who play trombone, together with the number in the band, would be sufficient to answer this question. But since we're asked for a percentage, we should be alert to the possibility of getting the proportion we need directly, *without* the actual numbers.

And if you recognized this as an overlapping sets problem, it might have served you well to jot down the chart we recommend for such situations:

	boys	girls	Total
play trombone			
don't play trombone			
Total			

(1) *Insufficient.* Statement (1) tells us only that 30 percent of the people in the band play trombone. It doesn't tell us how many band members there are or how many band members are boys who play trombone. Nor does it tell us what percent of all the band members are boys who play trombone. Statement (1) is insufficient. Eliminate (A) and (D).

(2) *Insufficient.* Statement (2) tells us that 60 percent of the members of the band are boys. It doesn't tell us what percent or fraction of the boys play trombone. So Statement (2) is insufficient. Eliminate (B).

Taking the Statements together, we know that 30 percent of the members of the band play trombone and that 60 percent of the members of the band are boys. Yet we have no information about what percent or fraction of the 30 percent of the band members who play trombone are boys, and we have no information about what percent or fraction of the 60 percent of the band members who are boys play trombone. The Statements taken together are insufficient.

If you weren't sure, the chart would have helped you to realize this:

	boys	girls	Total
play trombone			30%
don't play trombone			
Total	60%		100%

We can deduce this . . .

	boys	girls	Total
play trombone			30%
don't play trombone			70%
Total	60%	40%	100%

. . . but that's as far as we can go. Insufficient. Answer (E).

35. D

For sufficiency, we need to find either the values for m and n or the value of $m\sqrt{n}$ itself.

> **EXPERT EXCLUSIVE**
>
> No need to be intimidated by radicals. To get rid of them with math, square both sides of the equation. To get rid of the math entirely, Pick Numbers.

You may want to simplify the question to get rid of the radical. Since we want $m\sqrt{n}$ = value, we could square both sides to get m^2n = value^2. The fact that we cannot tell from a squared term whether the underlying value is negative or positive doesn't matter here, as we are told by the question stem that m and n are both positive.

There's a lot that would answer our question: $m\sqrt{n}$, m^2n, or m and n themselves.

(1) *Sufficient.* With only one equation, we cannot solve for m and n individually. So let's see whether we can solve for $m\sqrt{n}$ or m^2n. There are many possible ways to do the math. Here's one:

$$\frac{mn}{\sqrt{n}} = 10$$

Multiply both sides by $\sqrt{n}$: $\qquad\qquad mn = 10\sqrt{n}$

EXPERT EXCLUSIVE

Picking Numbers often has more steps than math. But if you feel uncomfortable with the math, Picking Numbers will be more comfortable and, therefore, both faster and safer.

Square both sides: $m^2 n^2 = 100n$

Divide both sides by n: $m^2 n = 100$

Here's another:

$$\frac{mn}{\sqrt{n}} = 10$$

Multiply fraction by $\dfrac{\sqrt{n}}{\sqrt{n}}$: $\dfrac{mn}{\sqrt{n}} \times \dfrac{\sqrt{n}}{\sqrt{n}} = 10$

$\sqrt{n} \times \sqrt{n} = n$: $\dfrac{mn\sqrt{n}}{n} = 10$

Cancel the n's: $m\sqrt{n} = 10$

Either way, we get something we need. Sufficient.

We also could have Picked Numbers. Since n appears twice, let's start by picking a value for n. $n = 4$ should be nice and straightforward.

$n = 4$:
$$\frac{mn}{\sqrt{n}} = 10$$
$$\frac{m(4)}{\sqrt{4}} = 10$$
$$\frac{4m}{2} = 10$$
$$2m = 10$$
$$m = 5$$

Plugging $n = 4$ and $m = 5$ into the question: $m\sqrt{n} =$

$5(2) = 10$

Now we need to try another set. The number 1 has unique properties—it's the only positive number that is unchanged by the square root operation—so let's pick $n = 1$ and see if that changes the outcome:

$n = 1$:
$$\frac{mn}{\sqrt{n}} = 10$$
$$\frac{m(1)}{\sqrt{1}} = 10$$
$$\frac{1m}{1} = 10$$
$$m = 10$$

Plugging $n = 1$ and $m = 10$ into the question: $m\sqrt{n} =$

$10(1) = 10$

We get the same outcome either way. Sufficient.

(2) *Sufficient*. Multiplying each side by 2 gives us a value for m^2n, one of the expressions that will give us the answer. Again, we could have Picked Numbers. It would be easier to pick a number for m first in this Statement, as we are squaring it.

$$\frac{m^2n}{2} = 50$$

$m = 2$:

$$\frac{4n}{2} = 50$$

Cancel common factors:

$$2n = 50$$

Divide by 2:

$$n = 25$$

Plugging $n = 25$ and $m = 2$ into the question:

$$m\sqrt{n} =$$

$$2(5) = 10$$

Now for a second set. As before, we'll take advantage of the special properties of 1 to maximize our chances of finding a different answer and proving the Statement insufficient:

$$\frac{m^2n}{2} = 50$$

$m = 1$:

$$\frac{1n}{2} = 50$$

Multiply by 2:

$$n = 100$$

Plugging $n = 100$ and $m = 1$ into the question:

$$m\sqrt{n} =$$

$$1(10) = 10$$

Same value. Sufficient. Answer (D).

36. D

This is the sort of DS question in which the n-variable, n-equation rule is easiest to use. With two variables (the price of a drink and the price of a hamburger) and one equation (something equals $3.50), we need only one more equation to solve, as long as no new variable is introduced.

(1) *Sufficient*. It's a complicated translation, but we don't need to make it. There's no new variable, and an equation can be derived from this Statement. Sufficient.

(2) *Sufficient*. Same deal here. It's a new equation, so we know we can solve the problem. No need to waste time going through the calculations.

37. D

Percents are just another way of expressing fractions; if we know one, we know the other. So we can think of the question stem as "The original price per share of stock A was what *fraction* of the original price per share of stock B ?"

Let a represent the original per share of stock A and let b represent the original per share of stock B. To answer the question, we need to find the fraction $\frac{a}{b}$. In other words, dividing a by b tells us what fraction of b is represented by a.

(1) *Sufficient.* Statement (1) says that (a plus 25% of a) is equal to (b minus 25% of b). Expressing this as an equation, we have $a + 0.25a = b - 0.25b$. This is one equation with two unknowns. While we cannot solve this equation for the values of either a or b, sometimes one equation with two variables can be solved for an expression containing both variables. Here, we have $a + 0.25a = b - 0.25b$, which is equivalent to $1.25a = 0.75b$.

Dividing by b gives us $\frac{1.25a}{b} = 0.75$, and then dividing by 1.25 gives us $\frac{a}{b} = \frac{0.75}{1.25}$. There is no need to simplify any further. We have found the fraction we were looking for. Statement (1) is sufficient. Eliminate (B), (C), and (E).

(2) *Sufficient.* Statement (2) says that $0.25a = \left(\frac{3}{20}\right)b$. The fraction $\frac{3}{20}$ is equivalent to 0.15, so we have $0.25a = 0.15b$, or $\frac{0.25a}{b} = 0.15$. Dividing by 0.25, we get $\frac{a}{b} = \frac{0.15}{0.25}$. There is no need to simplify further. As with Statement (1), finding the fraction is enough to show sufficiency. Both Statements alone are sufficient, so (D) is correct.

Notice that Statement (1) and Statement (2) both gave us the same value for $\frac{a}{b}$, as they must:
$$\frac{0.75}{1.25} = \frac{(0.15)(5)}{(0.25)(5)} = \frac{0.15}{0.25}$$

> **EXPERT EXCLUSIVE**
>
> The only time you need to translate English into math is if you suspect either that one of the equations gives you what you want directly or that one of the equations is not distinct.

38. C

There are three types of coins in the bag, but we don't know how many of any kind there are, so we have three variables: the number of quarters, the number of dimes, and the number of nickels.

To figure out how much money is in the bag, we'll need the actual number of each kind of coin. One way to get this would be to have three equations for our three variables. Since the total of all coins equals 38, two more equations will be sufficient.

(1) *Insufficient.* Pick Numbers; we could have 8 quarters ($2.00) with 20 nickels and 10 dimes ($2.00) or we could have 6 quarters ($1.50), 30 nickels and 0 dimes ($1.50)

(2) *Insufficient.* No information is provided about the number of quarters.

Together, though, we would have a total of three distinct equations. That's what we need. Sufficient. Answer (C).

Note that for Statements (1) and (2), we cannot just say, "Oh, too few equations—insufficient," because we cannot have fractional numbers of coins. Although a system of two equations with three variables will have an infinite number of algebraic solutions, it may have only one *integer* solution. For instance, if the stem told us there there were exactly four coins, Statement (1) would then become sufficient: the *only* way to have four coins with half of their value in quarters is with one quarter, two dimes, and one nickel!

39. E

This is a Yes/No question, so either "always yes" or "always no" is required for sufficiency. When working with multiples and remainders, Picking Numbers is a good strategy. We'll use the Statements to determine what numbers we can pick for x.

> **EXPERT EXCLUSIVE**
>
> Listing out different possibilities makes short work of some otherwise very abstract problems.

(1) *Insufficient*. If x divided by 3 leaves a remainder of 2, then x must be 2 greater than some multiple of 3. The multiples of 3 are 3, 6, 9, 12, 15, 18, etc., so x could be 5, 8, 11, 14, 17, 20, and so on. Some of these possible values of x are multiples of 5 (for example, 5 and 20), but others (8, 11, etc.) are not. So we cannot definitively answer the question, meaning that (1) is insufficient. Eliminate (A) and (D).

(2) *Insufficient*. Approach Statement (2) in the same way. If there is no remainder when x is divided by 4, then x is a multiple of 4, such as 4, 8, 12, 16, 20, and so on. Once again, x might or might not be a multiple of 5, so (2) is also insufficient. Eliminate (B).

Now look at the Statements together. We need to consider only those numbers that appear in both of our sets. There are two ways we could have sufficiency: either every number that appears in both sets *is* a multiple of 5 (sufficient-yes), or every number that appears in both sets is *not* a multiple of 5 (sufficient-no). The first two numbers that appear in both sets are 8 and 20. If $x = 8$, x is not a multiple of 5, but if $x = 20$, x is a multiple of 5. We still can't answer the question. Even when taken together, the Statements are insufficient.

40. A

Let's use the variables t, m, and b to represent the amounts, in dollars, spent on television, magazine, and billboard advertising, respectively. So then $t + m + b = 90$ million. As we evaluate the Statements, we will be looking for information that would allow us to solve this equation for the value of t, the amount spent on television advertising.

> **EXPERT EXCLUSIVE**
>
> It's worth taking the time to translate equations if you suspect that the question has a trap for the unwary.

(1) *Sufficient*. It's tempting just to say, "We need two more equations, and this is only one," and be done with it. But notice that this equation has an expression, "total spending for billboard and magazine advertising," that is the same as one from the question stem: "magazine and billboard advertising combined." There's a chance that

these expressions might cancel each other out, giving us sufficiency with fewer equations than we suspected. Let's check. Statement (1) tells us that magazine and billboard advertising was 20 percent less than television advertising. In other words, magazine and billboard advertising was equal to 80 percent of television advertising. Stated as an equation, we have $m + b = 80\%$ of t, or $m + b = 0.80t$. So we can replace $m + b$ in our original equation with $0.80t$. This gives us $t + 0.80t = \$90$ million. We could certainly solve this for t, so Statement (1) must be sufficient. We can eliminate (B), (C), and (E).

(2) *Insufficient.* Statement (2) tells us only that $m = 1.50b$. Replacing m in our original equation gives us $t + 1.50b + b = \$90$ million. We still have two variables and only one equation, so we can't solve for t. Thus, Statement (2) is insufficient.

41. B

This is a Yes/No question involving odds and evens. We can apply the odd/even rules, such as odd $\times$ odd = odd, or we can Pick Numbers.

(1) *Insufficient.* Statement (1) tells us that $xyz + 1$ is odd. Only an even number plus 1 will yield an odd number. So xyz must be even. We know from the stem that x is even, y is odd, and z is an integer, so for xyz we have an even integer $\times$ an odd integer $\times$ an integer = an even integer. Since the product already includes one even number (x), the result must be even whether z is odd or even.

Let $x = 2$ and $y = 3$. So $xyz = (2)(3)z = 6z$, which will be even regardless of the value of z, because the product of any even integer and any integer will always be even. If $z = 1$, $6z = 6$, which is even. If $z = 2$, $6z = 12$, which is also even. So we can't determine if z is odd or even. Statement (1) is insufficient; eliminate (A) and (D).

(2) *Sufficient.* In Statement (2), we'll keep in mind the same rule that any integer times an even integer is even. We know x is even, so xy and xz are both even. Thus, we have even + even + yz = even. An even plus an even will be even, so we can simplify the situation to even + yz = even. So yz must be even, because the sum of two even numbers will be even, but the sum of an even and an odd will be odd.

Now, if yz must be even and we know from the stem that y is odd, then z itself must be even. In other words, we now know that z is *never* odd, so Statement (2) is sufficient. Based on Statement (2), the answer to the question is no. Choice (B) is correct.

42. E

To know the area of Dan's room that is *not* covered, we'll need the area of his room and the area of the rug. Subtracting one from the other would give us the answer.

> **EXPERT EXCLUSIVE**
>
> Draw pictures if you have a tough time visualizing geometry-based questions.

(1) *Insufficient.* To solve, we'll need to know the dimensions of Dan's room and the rug itself. Statement (1) tells us the total area of Dan's room but nothing about the size of the rug, so it is insufficient. Eliminate (A) and (D).

(2) *Insufficient*. Statement (2) tells us how wide the exposed area is, but without also knowing the length and width of the room or the rug, we cannot calculate the uncovered area. So Statement (2) is also insufficient. Eliminate (B).

Statements (1) and (2): Now we know the area of the room and the width of the exposed space, but because many different room dimensions could result in an area of 300 square feet, the Statements together are insufficient.

Pick Numbers to confirm this. Suppose the room is 30 × 10. Since 24 inches is 2 feet, 2 feet will be exposed on all sides, so the dimensions of the rug must be 30 − 2 − 2 = 26 and 10 − 2 − 2 = 6. The area of the rug is 26 × 6 = 156 square feet, so the exposed area is 300 − 156 = 144 square feet.

But the room could also be 20 × 15 (among other possibilities). In this case, the rug would be 16 × 11 with an area of 176. The exposed area would be 300 − 176 = 124 square feet.

Since there is more than one possible value for the exposed area, the Statements taken together are insufficient. Choice (E) is correct.

43. B

For *z* to be prime, it can have no factors other than 1 and itself. There's not much more to the question than this.

(1) *Insufficient*. No matter what 15! equals (and we definitely shouldn't calculate it!!), there must be *some* prime numbers that are greater. And, of course, plenty of the numbers larger than 15! are nonprime. (Each of the even numbers, for example, would have a factor of 2.)

(2) *Sufficient*. It's hard to wrap your head around a number like 17! + 2, but when dealing with super-large numbers, writing out their factorization can be helpful:

$$17! + 2 = (17 \times 16 \times 15 \times 14 \times 13 \times 12 \times 11 \times 10 \times 9 \times 8 \times 7 \times 6 \times 5 \times 4 \times 3 \times 2 \times 1) + 2$$

For 17! + 2 to be prime, it can have no factors other than 1 and 17! + 2 itself. So can we find a factor to pull out of 17! + 2? We sure can! Since 2 is common to 17! and 2, it can be factored out:

$$17! + 2 = 2 \times (17 \times 16 \times 15 \times 14 \times 13 \times 12 \times 11 \times 10 \times 9 \times 8 \times 7 \times 6 \times 5 \times 4 \times 3 \times 1 \times 1 + 1)$$

Therefore, 17! + 2 is clearly a multiple of 2 and, thus, is not prime. We can do the same thing with 17! + 3:

$$17! + 3 = (17 \times 16 \times 15 \times 14 \times 13 \times 12 \times 11 \times 10 \times 9 \times 8 \times 7 \times 6 \times 5 \times 4 \times 3 \times 2 \times 1) + 3$$

$17! + 3 = 3 \times (17 \times 16 \times 15 \times 14 \times 13 \times 12 \times 11 \times 10 \times 9 \times 8 \times 7 \times 6 \times 5 \times 4 \times 1 \times 2 \times 1 + 1)$

Therefore, $17! + 3$ is clearly a multiple of 3 and, thus, is not prime. The same logic applies all the way up to $17! + 17$. There's not a prime number in the bunch, so the answer is "definitely no."

44. A

The perimeter of the triangle is the sum of the lengths of the sides, or $A + 2B + (A + B)$. To find a value for the perimeter, we need to find values for A and B. To do so, we'll need some equations involving these two variables. The fact that the problem concerns a right triangle is a clue that we should use the Pythagorean theorem to set up an equation involving A and B.

> **EXPERT EXCLUSIVE**
>
> Always do the math with quadratics. As they may have two solutions, the *n*-variable, *n*-equations rule doesn't necessarily apply to them.

The Pythagorean theorem tells us that for any right triangle, $x^2 + y^2 = z^2$, where x and y are the legs and z is the hypotenuse. So replacing these variables with the ones from the problem, we have $A^2 + (2B)^2 = (A + B)^2$.

FOIL: $\qquad\qquad\qquad\qquad\qquad\qquad A^2 + (2B)^2 = A^2 + 2AB + B^2$

Subtract A^2 from each side: $\qquad\qquad\qquad (2B)^2 = 2AB + B^2$

$\qquad\qquad\qquad\qquad\qquad\qquad\qquad\qquad 4B^2 = 2AB + B^2$

Subtract B^2 from each side: $\qquad\qquad\qquad 3B^2 = 2AB$

Divide each side by B: $\qquad\qquad\qquad\qquad 3B = 2A$

> **EXPERT EXCLUSIVE**
>
> The GMAT hides important aspects of problems in fractions, so always clear the denominators when doing algebra.

Despite its being a quadratic, it wound up simplifying to one linear equation. So any other linear equation will allow us to solve for A and B.

(1) *Sufficient.* We could substitute into $3B = 2A$ and solve for both variables.

(2) *Insufficient.* Multiply both sides by 2 to clear the fraction in $A = \dfrac{3B}{2}$, and we get $3B = 2A$, exactly what the question stem told us. Since this is not a new equation, it adds nothing.

45. B

We have a Yes/No question, so we'll need to know if x is always prime or never prime. When working with primes, keep in mind that 2 is the smallest prime number and the only even prime. Other than that, all we know from the stem is that $x > 0$, so let's evaluate the Statements.

(1) *Insufficient.* Can we find any prime values for x such that x^3 has four distinct factors? If $x = 2$, which is prime, then $x^3 = 2^3 = 8$, which has four distinct factors (1, 2, 4, and 8). So it's *possible* that x is prime. But does it have to be prime? Let's consider other positive numbers with four distinct factors. The smallest such number is 6 (its factors are 1, 2, 3, and 6), so suppose $x^3 = 6$. In this case, $x = \sqrt[3]{6}$, which is not even an

integer, much less a prime number. So we've found both prime and nonprime values for *x* that make (1) true. Therefore, (1) is insufficient to determine whether or not *x* is prime. Eliminate (A) and (D).

(2) *Sufficient.* In this case, we can solve the equation to find possible values for *x*. Factor the left side using reverse FOIL to get $(x - 3)(x + 2) = 0$. The equation has one negative root and one positive root, meaning that there are two possible values for *x*, one negative and one positive. The stem tells us that *x* must be positive, so there is actually only one possible value of *x*. Since we could find exactly one value for *x*, we can answer the question definitively; if we know what *x* is, we know whether or not it is prime. Statement (2) is sufficient.

46. B

The question seems straightforward, but we should always simplify fractions by clearing the denominator:

$$\text{Is } \frac{1}{x} > 1 ?$$

Multiply by *x*:

If *x* is positive	If *x* is negative
Is $1 > x$?	Is $1 < x$?

"Hey . . . wait a sec," you say. "Negative numbers can't be greater than 1!" You're absolutely right. What we've just discovered, essentially, is that any negative value will answer the question with a no. The only numbers that will answer the question yes are positive numbers less than 1. So we can simplify the question thusly: Is $0 < x < 1$?

(1) *Insufficient.* We can eliminate *y* by dividing both sides by *y*, but since we don't know if *y* is positive or negative, we have to consider both cases. If it is positive, we get $\frac{1}{x} > 1$, but if *y* is negative, we get $\frac{1}{x} < 1$. So we cannot answer the question definitively, meaning that Statement (1) is insufficient. Eliminate (A) and (D).

(2) *Sufficient.* For Statement (2), we know from the stem that *x* is not 0. So x^2 is positive. Dividing both sides of the inequality $x^3 > x^2$ by x^2, we have $x > 1$. So we will never have $0 < x < 1$, meaning that the answer to the question is no. Statement (2) is sufficient, and (B) is correct.

47. E

We're asked for the amount spent on all the cars in stock at the end of the year. We're told the value of the stock on hand at the beginning of the year. We're also told that the dealership made one additional purchase, but we aren't told its value. We also aren't told the value of any cars sold over the year. So we need two pieces of information: the value of the purchased cars and the value of the sold cars.

EXPERT EXCLUSIVE

Sometimes a Statement will help you to see a possibility that you didn't consider before.

(1) *Insufficient.* Statement (1) tells us about cars purchased during the year but gives us no information about how many were sold. Thus, we can't determine how many were in stock at the end of the year. Statement (1) is insufficient. Eliminate (A) and (D).

(2) *Insufficient.* Statement (2) tells us only how much money the dealership received from the sale of cars. Since we don't know how much each car sold for, we can't determine the number of cars sold or the number in stock at the end of the year. Thus, Statement (2) is insufficient, and we can eliminate (B). We could also have determined that this Statement is insufficient because it does not give us any information about how many cars were purchased or how much was spent on them.

Did you at first think that Statement (1) was sufficient? If so, Statement (2) could have reminded you that sold cars are part of this scenario.

Combining the Statements, there still is no information about the number of cars the dealership had in stock at the end of last year or the amount spent on each of these cars in stock at the end of the year. The Statements taken together are insufficient.

48. C

We need to know how many products will fit inside one shipping box. If we have this number, we can divide the total number of products (120) by the number per shipping box to find out how many shipping boxes are needed. So as we evaluate the Statements, we'll need to know the dimensions and volume of both the products and the shipping boxes; only with that information will we be able to determine how many products can fit in one shipping box.

(1) *Insufficient.* Statement (1) gives us the dimensions of each product, from which we could calculate the volume if we multiplied the dimensions together. But without any information about the dimensions of the shipping boxes, Statement (1) is insufficient. Eliminate (A) and (D).

(2) *Insufficient.* Statement (2) tells us that the volume of the shipping boxes is one cubic foot. Since the boxes are cubes, their dimensions must be 1 foot by 1 foot by 1 foot. But without any information about the products, Statement (2) is also insufficient. Eliminate (B).

When we combine the Statements, we see that we have everything we need. Statement (1) tells us the dimensions and, therefore, the volume of each product; Statement (2) gives us the dimensions and volume of the shipping boxes. This is sufficient to answer the question, so (C) is correct. There is no need to do the actual calculations.

49. C

The range of a set is the difference between the largest and smallest values in the set. From the stem, we know that the median, or middle value, is 19 but nothing about the largest and smallest values, so let's go on to the Statements.

EXPERT EXCLUSIVE

The GMAT will only give you sets out of order. Always rearrange them in ascending (or descending) order.

(1) *Insufficient.* Let's first put the known elements of the set in ascending order. Excluding x and y, the set is {11, 15, 18, 28}. Since the median is 19 and there is an even number of terms, the average of the two middle terms must be 19. There are already two numbers less than 18, so if either x or y is less than 18, then 18 becomes the fourth term in the set. If that happens, the median would be the average of 18 and some number less than 18—so the median could never be 19. Therefore, neither x nor y can be less than 18.

Given that 18 must be the third term in the set, it must also be the case that either x or y (or both) must be 20 for the median to be 19. So let's say that $x = 20$; now the set, excluding y, is {11, 15, 18, 20, 28}. But where does y fit in? All we can say is that y must be 20 or more. If y is 20, the range is $28 - 11 = 17$. But y could also be the largest value. If y is 30, the range is $30 - 11 = 19$. We can't determine a single value for the range based on Statement (1), so the Statement is insufficient.

(2) *Insufficient.* There is no definite relationship between the mean and the median. The set could be {18, 19, 23}, but it also could be {17, 19, 24}. Both sets have a median of 19 and a mean of 20, but the range of the first set is $23 - 18 = 5$ and the range of the second set is $24 - 17 = 7$. In fact, we could write many sets that have a median of 19 and a mean of 20, each with a different range. So Statement (2) is insufficient.

Statements (1) and (2) together: From Statement (1), we know the set has 6 elements and that either x or y must be 20. From (2), we know that the average is 20. For a set of 6 elements with an average of 20, the sum of the numbers must be $6 \times 20 = 120$ (the average formula tells us that the sum of the terms of the set equals the average of the terms in the set times the number of terms in the set).

So it must be the case that $11 + 15 + 18 + 28 + x + y = 120$, or $x + y = 48$. Since we know that either x or y must be equal to 20, let's say that $x = 20$. We have $20 + y = 48$, or $y = 28$. Thus, the set is {11, 15, 18, 20, 28, 28}. The range must be $28 - 17 = 11$, so the Statements together are sufficient. (C) is correct.

50. B

The equation that we're given seems fairly straightforward. But we're asked not for the value of a but for the value of $\frac{a}{b}$. So let's see what this equation tells us about $\frac{a}{b}$.

$$a = 5b + 7c$$

Divide both sides by b to create $\frac{a}{b}$:
$$\frac{a}{b} = \frac{5b + 7c}{b}$$

Split the fraction:
$$\frac{a}{b} = \frac{5b}{b} + \frac{7c}{b}$$

Cancel the b's:
$$\frac{a}{b} = 5 + \frac{7c}{b}$$

So we can answer our question if we learn the value of $\frac{c}{b}$.

(1) *Insufficient.* Statement (1) gives us the equation $2b + 5c = 50$. We cannot solve the two equations $a = 5b + 7c$ and $2b + 5c = 50$ with three variables for the values of any of a, b, and c. Furthermore, we cannot solve these two equations for the value of $\frac{a}{b}$, and we cannot solve these two equations for the value of $\frac{c}{b}$. Statement (1) is insufficient. We can eliminate choices (A) and (D).

We can also show that Statement (1) is insufficient by Picking Numbers. The values $b = 10$ and $c = 6$ satisfy the equation $2b + 5c = 50$ of Statement (1). From the equation $a = 5b + 7c$ of the question stem, we find that when $b = 10$ and $c = 6$, $a = 92$. In this case, $\frac{a}{b} = \frac{92}{10} = \frac{46}{5}$.

The values $b = 20$ and $c = 2$ also satisfy the equation $2b + 5c = 50$ of Statement (1). From the equation $a = 5b + 7c$ of the question stem, we find that when $b = 20$ and $c = 2$, $a = 114$. In this case, $\frac{a}{b} = \frac{114}{20} = \frac{57}{10}$. So different values for $\frac{a}{b}$ are possible. Again, Statement (1) is insufficient.

(2) *Sufficient.* Statement (2) says that $3b - 5c = 0$. Adding $5c$ to both sides of this equation, we have $3b = 5c$. Dividing both sides of this equation by 5, we have $\frac{3b}{5} = c$. Dividing both sides of this equation by b, we have $\frac{3}{5} = \frac{c}{b}$. Thus, $\frac{c}{b} = \frac{3}{5}$. We have the value of $\frac{c}{b}$. We can find the value of $\frac{a}{b}$. It is not actually necessary to find the value of $\frac{a}{b}$ by substituting $\frac{3}{5}$ for $\frac{c}{b}$ in the equation $\frac{a}{b} = 5 + 7\left(\frac{c}{b}\right)$. Knowing that we could is enough. Statement (2) is sufficient. Choice (B) is correct.

CHAPTER 10: **WORD PROBLEMS**

- The Basic Principles of Word Problems
- Word Problems in Problem Solving
- Common Word Problem Categories
- Word Problems in Data Sufficiency

Word problems appear throughout the Quantitative section. GMAT word problems can be particularly tricky. Odds are that you find them trickier than you remember word problems being in school. There's a reason for this: the GMAT writes them differently! So we're going to dedicate a separate section to them.

EXPERT EXCLUSIVE

If you are struggling to understand a portion of a word problem, that's a sign that you're trying to digest too much information at once. Break up the problem into smaller pieces.

These word problems test three skills that are important for business school success: (1) arranging chaotic data into logical patterns, (2) quantifying relationships, and (3) goal-oriented thinking. The sort of word problems that you saw in elementary school through high school all went more or less like this: "A, B, C, D, E. What's F?" But GMAT word problems tend to go like this: "B, E, F, C, A. What's D?" And a Data Sufficiency problem would be: "B, C, E, A. What's F?" while hiding D in a Statement.

Often the most frustrating aspect of word problems is the odd way in which information is presented. Don't get frustrated. Just break down the information into small pieces and take things one step at a time. Say you see this sentence: "There are twice as many dollars in George's wallet as the amount that is five dollars less than the amount in Bill's wallet." Instead of trying to translate it into math all in one go, approach it piecemeal:

"Okay," we'll say, "let's call the amount in George's wallet G and the amount in Bill's wallet B. Now, it seems that G is not compared to B but to 5 dollars less than B. That would mean $(B - 5)$. G is twice as large as $(B - 5)$. That means G is bigger. So if I am to set them *equal* to each other, I'll have to multiply $(B - 5)$ by two. $G = 2(B - 5)$ is the equation."

If we had tried to translate it in the order it's written, we might wind up with something like $2G = 5 - B$, and you can be sure that there'd be a wrong answer choice waiting to take advantage of that. So think carefully before you translate.

That's the hard part in word problems—taking the English sentences and extracting the math from them. The actual math in word problems tends to be the easiest part! The following translation table should help you start dealing with English-to-Math translation.

> **EXPERT EXCLUSIVE**
>
> Don't automatically choose *x* and *y* for everything. Pick letters (or groups of letters) that will be clear at a glance.

Word Problems Translation Table

English	Math
Equals, is, was, will be, has, costs, adds up to, the same as, as much as	=
Times, of, multiplied by, product of, twice, double, by	×
Divided by, per, out of, each, ratio	÷
Plus, added to, and, sum, combined	+
Minus, subtracted from, smaller than, less than, fewer, decreased by, difference between	−
A number, how much, how many, what	x, n, etc.

THE BASIC PRINCIPLES OF WORD PROBLEMS

BEFORE PLUNGING INTO MATH, READ OVER THE ENTIRE PROBLEM AND GAIN A GENERAL UNDERSTANDING OF THE SITUATION

> **EXPERT EXCLUSIVE**
>
> Paraphrasing the situation before you do any math provides a nice self-diagnosis: if you can't paraphrase the situation, you won't know how to put the math together.

Word problems are frequently written so that the math you might do at the beginning winds up being an inefficient path to the solution. Focus first on getting a basic overview of the situation—a paraphrase, basically. Consider this problem:

> Bill received three fewer presents for his birthday than did John, who received half the number of presents as Betty and Sue averaged. If Sue received as many as John and Betty put together, and Bill and John together received one more than did Betty, then how many presents did Bill receive?

If you started doing math right away, it would be very easy to write this equation: $B - 3 = J$. But that would be a mistranslation. Bill needs to receive fewer presents than John; to be equal, we'd need to take the 3 away from John: $B = J - 3$. And even if you got that right, diving into math sets you up for trouble. Why? Because if you are focusing on translating instead of understanding, your next equation would be: $J = \frac{1}{2}\frac{B+S}{2}$.

Did you notice the problem? The GMAT has given you a scenario with two people whose names begin with *B*. If you don't differentiate between Bill and Betty in your scratchwork, you'll be lost.

The best way to start this problem would be to say, "All right . . . there are four people and a bunch of equations relating the number of presents they received. And I need to be careful—there are two *B* names."

"Bill received three fewer presents for his birthday than did John." $B_{ill} = J - 3$

"John received half the number of presents as Betty and Sue averaged." $J = \dfrac{1}{2} \dfrac{B_{etty} + S}{2}$

"Sue received as many as John and Betty put together." $S = J + B_{etty}$

"Bill and John together received one more than did Betty." $B_{ill} + J = B_{etty} + 1$

ALWAYS KEEP TRACK OF EXACTLY WHAT YOU'RE AFTER

To solve word problems efficiently, it helps to make sure you know exactly what the question is asking. Efficient solutions to complicated word problems begin by working backwards, focusing on what you need in order to answer the question—as you have already seen with Step 2 of the Kaplan Method for Problem Solving and Step 1 of the Kaplan Method for Data Sufficiency.

> **EXPERT EXCLUSIVE**
>
> Once you've made sense of what you're looking for, scan through the problem for information that pertains to it. That information usually *won't* be the first thing in the question stem.

Example: Brand X Soda Co. pays *f* dollars per liter for its syrup. If Brand X soda is made by mixing 4 parts soda water to 1 part syrup and is sold for *z* dollars per liter, what is Brand X Soda Co.'s profit on *m* liters of soda, assuming that soda water costs *a* dollars per liter?

There are an awful lot of variables floating around this problem. But if you stay focused on what you're after, you'll know how to put them together. We're asked to solve for "profit." What is profit? Well, profit is revenue minus costs. So the first thing we write down, before any variables, should be

$$\boxed{\text{revenue} - \text{costs}}$$

This way, we can break the problem into discrete chunks and approach each one on its own, instead of trying to solve everything all at once. Let's start with revenue. Scan through the problem looking for information pertaining to revenue. We first get stuff about cost and composition of soda, which is irrelevant to revenue. Then we learn that soda is sold for *z* dollars per liter. We next read that we want the profit (and therefore the revenue) for *m* liters. At *z* dollars per liter, *m* liters will bring in a revenue of *mz*.

$$\boxed{mz - \text{costs}}$$

Now we focus on the cost of soda. Hmm. We see cost of syrup and cost of soda water, which has the word *soda* in it but isn't soda. No cost of soda. That's weird. The only other thing we learn about soda is that it is 4 parts soda water to 1 part syrup. Oh! Soda is made of syrup and soda water, so the costs of those things will give us the cost of soda!

$$mz - m(\text{cost of soda water} + \text{cost of syrup})$$

We get a ratio of water:syrup :: 4:1. Thus, 4 liters of soda water would cost $4a$, and 1 liter of syrup would cost f. That's $4a + f$ for 5 liters total. We've been using "cost per liter" up till now, not "cost per 5 liters," so let's not switch things around now. If 5 liters of soda cost $4a + f$, 1 liter of soda costs $\frac{4a + f}{5}$. With m liters, our total costs are $m\left(\frac{4a + f}{5}\right)$.

$$mz - m\left(\frac{4a + f}{5}\right)$$

Odds are that the GMAT would then factor out the common m:

$$m\left(z - \frac{4a + f}{5}\right)$$

Keeping track of what we're after allows us to think critically about the mess of information that most word problems provide.

LEARN TO RECOGNIZE THE DIFFERENT TYPES OF PROBLEMS AND WHAT YOU SHOULD DO FOR EACH

Some word problems involve straightforward algebraic translation, such as the one we just did. Others may require organizing the data in different ways. Overlapping Sets questions, for example, require careful tracking of information, as do some Rate problems. You already looked at some of these, and we'll touch on them again in a bit.

As you do more and more practice problems, you'll begin to get a sense of what "category" a word problem falls into. Not only should you learn for each type the fundamental approaches that work for you, you should also pay attention to which types you handle very well and which you struggle with. What approaches work best for you? On test day, it will really help you out if you know after only 10–15 seconds what approach you will take or whether you want to guess.

WORD PROBLEMS IN PROBLEM SOLVING

Let's get a quick refresher on Kaplan's Method for Problem Solving and look at how to apply it to word problems.

Step 1: Analyze the question.
Step 2: State the task.
Step 3: Approach strategically.
Step 4: Confirm your answer.

STEP 1: ANALYZE THE QUESTION

It's critical that you do no math at this stage. This step is roughly equivalent to our first basic principle for word problems—gaining a general understanding of the situation before diving into math. Get a general paraphrase of the problem (no numbers or formulas; they'll get you going into math). If you can "categorize" the problem in this step, that will help you gain control of the problem too.

> **EXPERT EXCLUSIVE**
> There is no "right way" to solve word problems. Take the approach that you feel will identify the right answer most easily.

STEP 2: STATE THE TASK

This is the second basic principle in action. The question stem is frequently written in a confusing manner, and you won't really know how to think about the information until you know what you're looking for.

STEP 3: APPROACH STRATEGICALLY

Make sure that you follow an approach that feels straightforward. It's unlikely that you can understand the problem better by doing a whole bunch of math. Understanding has to precede math.

> **EXPERT EXCLUSIVE**
> If you haven't been able to get a handle on an approach after 60 seconds or so, you should consider making a strategic guess.

(a) **Kaplan strategy.** Picking Numbers or Backsolving are frequently faster than math, as they cut through much of the algebra. And if you cannot quite figure out what math to do, these approaches may make the problem understandable. By turning unknowns into actual values, you'll have made the problem concrete.

(b) **Straightforward math.** If you can see the math setup clearly, by all means do the math. But if the math doesn't feel straightforward, that's a big warning to take a different approach.

(c) **Strategic guess.** If you cannot find a straightforward math approach and you are unsure of how you could Pick Numbers or Backsolve, make an educated guess. Invest your valuable time in a problem that you are more likely to get right. But stay open to the possibility that a guessing strategy—particularly Estimation or Logic—might actually be the most efficient solution!

STEP 4: CONFIRM YOUR ANSWER

Since the GMAT writes deliberately confusing word problems, it's possible that you missed a wrinkle. Read the question stem over before clicking "next." If you accounted for all of the information, move on in confidence. If you notice that you missed something, you know your answer is wrong. You should then decide, *based on how much time you have left*, whether to resolve the problem or make a guess.

Let's look at a sample word problem, going through the Kaplan method and focusing on each step.

> Jacob is now 12 years younger than Michael. If in 9 years Michael will be twice as old as Jacob, how old will Jacob be in 4 years?
>
> ○   3
> ○   7
> ○   15
> ○   21
> ○   25

Step 1: Analyze the Question

Instead of translating to math straight away, we get an overview: two people, Jacob and Michael, with some complex relationships between their ages. The answers are just numbers, which suggests that Backsolving may be a possible approach.

Step 2: State the Task

We're solving for Jacob's age in 4 years, not Jacob's age now. J is Jacob's age, and we want $J + 4$. There's likely to be a trap answer based on this. We could use this for guessing—odds are the right answer is 4 more than another answer choice.

Step 3: Approach Strategically

Based on the way the GMAT writes common *wrong* answer choices, we know the right answer is likely to be either (B) or (E), since they are each 4 more than another choice. So if we were falling behind on time, this would be a good guessing opportunity. But let's say that we have time to solve.

Backsolving: The answer choice clearly relates to information in the question stem, so this is a great Backsolving problem. We've already identified (B) as a likely answer, so we'll start with that. If Jacob will be 7 in 4 years, he is 3 now. The first sentence of the question says that Jacob is now 12 years younger than Michael. That would make Michael 15 years old.

The next sentence is about how old they'll be in 9 years. Then Jacob will be $3 + 9 = 12$, and Michael will be $15 + 9 = 24$. The question stem says that Michael should then be twice as old as Jacob. If they are 24 and 12 respectively, that's true. All the information in the question stem fits with (B), so it is correct.

Straightforward Math: Let's look at the English-to-Math translation:

Jacob's age	is now	Michael's age	(but) 12 years younger
J	$=$	M	-12

In this case, we switched the order of the sentence as we translated it from English to Math. The phrase "12 years younger than Michael" became "Michael's age (but) 12 years younger."

Sometimes the order of the terms in English will differ slightly from the order in math. If you get confused, pick some sample values. If Michael is 15 years old, then Jacob is 12 years younger, or 3. Therefore, $J = M - 12$. To continue, here's the rest of the translation:

Michael	in 9 years	will be	twice as old as Jacob
M	$+9$	$=$	$2(J + 9)$

Notice that Jacob's age became $J + 9$? That's because the whole relationship is set nine years in the future. It's important to adjust expressions appropriately based on the situation.

So we know that $J = M - 12$ and $M + 9 = 2(J + 9)$. The question asks for $J + 4$. Solve for J by substituting.

$$J = M - 12$$
$$J + 12 = M$$

$$M + 9 = 2(J + 9)$$
$$(J + 12) + 9 = 2J + 18$$
$$J + 21 = 2J + 18$$
$$J + 3 = 2J$$
$$3 = J$$
$$7 = J + 4$$

Remember that we're looking for $J + 4$, not J, so (B) is correct.

Another way to solve this problem is by combining the equations. When you have two equations, you can add or subtract them from one another just as though they were

EXPERT EXCLUSIVE

Think carefully before writing equations. Comparisons rarely translate straight from left to right.

EXPERT EXCLUSIVE

Age-based problems often involve difficult combinations of addition and multiplication. Picking Numbers and Back-solving are usually much safer than algebra.

regular numbers. You just have to set it up right, with like variables directly above one another.

$$M + 9 = 2J + 18$$
$$-[M - 12 = J]$$
$$21 = J + 18$$
$$3 = J$$
$$7 = J + 4$$

Step 4: Confirm Your Answer

Let's see . . . did we catch all the wrinkles in the problem? Did we notice that the second sentence is about what's true in nine years? Yep. Did we answer Jacob's age four years from now instead of his age today? Yep. Okay, then we're moving on!

Did you notice that the Backsolving solution was much quicker than the math solution? It's often the case that Picking Numbers and Backsolving are easier than math. Yet because we are trained to do math in school, we can sometimes forget to consider those approaches. So we're going to focus on them now before going on to talk about some common word problem categories.

PICKING NUMBERS

Picking Numbers is a good approach whenever there are multiple variables or variables in the answer choices or when you are asked for a fraction of an unknown whole. It's a good alternative approach if the math isn't occurring to you. In many cases, it is superior to math, even when the math does occur to you. The bottom line is, if you can see yourself solving the problem by plugging in numbers, go ahead and solve that way. Make sure that you pick numbers that are easy to use and that fit any restrictions in the problem.

Here are a few guidelines for when to plug in numbers and what numbers you should try:

> **EXPERT EXCLUSIVE**
>
> The number 0 is often not logically permitted in the situation described in word problems. The number 1 can sometimes be dangerous, as it increases the likelihood of a "false positive." But 1 is an easy number to use, so don't shy away from it if you want to use it.

- In problems involving percents in the answer choices, a good number to start with is often 100, because it is so easy to find a percent of 100.
- In problems with two or more fractions, try using the least common denominator of the fractions involved.
- Picking Numbers is almost always the fastest way to do problems about remainders.
- When the problem and its answer choices are all expressed in terms of variables such as x or y, you can avoid algebra by simply making up values for x and y. When you plug in numbers for the variables and do the arithmetic involved, you will get another number as a result. Take the numbers you used for x and y and plug them into the variables in the

answer choices—assuming only one choice results in the same number as in the problem, that choice is the answer.

Let's take a look at Picking Numbers in action.

> The value of a certain antique car increased by 30 percent from 1986 to 1990 and then decreased by 20 percent from 1990 to 1994. The car's value in 1994 was what percent of its value in 1986?
>
> ○ 90%
>
> ○ 100%
>
> ○ 104%
>
> ○ 110%
>
> ○ 124%

GO ONLINE

Practice Picking Numbers each month with your new quiz.

Let's say the car was originally worth $100 in 1986. It increases by 30% of $100, or $30, which means it was worth $130 in 1990. Then it decreases 20%: $0.20 \times 130 = 26$. So it decreased by $26. Therefore, it was worth $104 in 1994. The car was worth $104, which is 104% of $100. The answer is (C).

Try each of the next two word problems on your own, using the strategy of Picking Numbers. Feel free to refer to the bullet-point guidelines for Picking Numbers. After you've worked through each question, consult the Kaplan solution.

> At an international dinner, $\frac{1}{5}$ of the attendees were from South America. If the number of North Americans at the dinner was $\frac{2}{3}$ greater than the number of South Americans, what fraction of people at the dinner were from neither South America nor North America?
>
> ○ $\frac{1}{5}$
>
> ○ $\frac{2}{5}$
>
> ○ $\frac{7}{15}$
>
> ○ $\frac{8}{15}$
>
> ○ $\frac{2}{3}$

You should notice immediately that the problem contains two fractions: $\frac{1}{5}$ and $\frac{2}{3}$. The least common denominator is 15, so let's say the total number of people at the dinner was 15. That means we have 3 South Americans in the room. We also have North Americans numbering two-thirds more than that, or $3 + \frac{2}{3}(3)$, which is 5. So there were 8 people from South America or North America, which means 7 people were not from either place. So $\frac{7}{15}$ of the people in the room were from neither South America nor North America. The correct answer, therefore, is (C).

Here's another Picking Numbers example.

> If the price of item X increased by 20% and then by a further 20%, what percent of the original price is the increase in price?
>
> ○ 24%
>
> ○ 40%
>
> ○ 44%
>
> ○ 66%
>
> ○ 140%

Let's say the price was originally $100. It increases by 20% of $100 (which is $20), so now the price is $120. The price then increases by 20% of $120 $\left(\frac{1}{5} \times \$120 = \$24\right)$, which means an increase of $24. So the price is now $144, or 44% more than the original price of $100. The correct answer, therefore, is (C).

BACKSOLVING

You will remember that in Backsolving, you plug in the answer choices and see which one works. You won't have to try all the choices, as you'll be able to eliminate several choices at once. Start either with (B) or with (D). If the one you pick is the right answer, great! If not, you'll usually be able to figure out whether you need a larger or smaller number. As the answer choices are arranged in ascending or descending order, you can quickly eliminate other choices.

Follow along as we Backsolve through this word problem:

EXPERT EXCLUSIVE

With practice, Backsolving will be just as fast as, if not faster than, "traditional" solutions.

> An insurance company provides coverage for a certain dental procedure according to the following rules: the policy pays 80% of the first $1,200 of cost and 50% of the cost above $1,200. If a patient had to pay $490 of the cost for this procedure himself, how much did the procedure cost?
>
> ○ $1,200
>
> ○ $1,300
>
> ○ $1,500
>
> ○ $1,600
>
> ○ $1,700

Because the policy pays 80% of the first $1,200 of cost, the patient must pay 20% of $1,200. One-fifth of $1,200 is $240.

Let's try (B). If the procedure cost $1,300, then the patient pays $240 + 50% of $100. Then $240 + $50 = $290, which is too small. Eliminate (A) and (B).

We need a larger number, so try (D). If the procedure cost $1,600, then the patient pays $240 plus 50% of $400, which is $240 + $200, totaling $440—too small. The answer must be (E).

COMMON WORD PROBLEM CATEGORIES

The GMAT repeats some kinds of word problems with great regularity. Learn a few tips for dealing with them, and many GMAT word problems will start to feel predictable and, therefore, manageable if not downright reassuring.

These are also discussed in the Math Skills Refresher Appendix. If you've already gone through that portion of this book, let this serve as a reminder of things to look for on test day. If you haven't, then do so after these pages.

RATE PROBLEMS

Two kinds of rate problems show up most frequently: you are given a rate that you must convert, or you are given more than one rate.

Converting Rates

The most common is a problem that gives you a rate that you must then convert. Follow along with this example:

> If José does GMAT word problems at a constant rate of 2 problems every 5 minutes, how many seconds will it take him to do *N* problems?
>
> ○ $\dfrac{2}{5}N$
>
> ○ $2N$
>
> ○ $\dfrac{5}{2}N$
>
> ○ $24N$
>
> ○ $150N$

There are two common ways of doing rate problems: algebraically and by plugging in numbers. Let's try both for the problem above.

EXPERT EXCLUSIVE

The most common rate is speed. But a rate is any Quantity A *per* Quantity B.

$$\text{Rate} = \frac{\text{Quantity A}}{\text{Quantity B}}.$$

Algebraic Solution: Let's call the number of seconds that we've been asked to find T. The first hurdle that we need to clear in this problem is that we're given a rate in minutes but asked to calculate the number of seconds. Let's change the rate we're given to seconds so we can get that aspect of the problem out of the way. There are 60 seconds to a minute. So we need to change the rate:

$$\frac{2 \text{ problems}}{5 \text{ minutes}} \times \frac{1 \text{ minute}}{60 \text{ seconds}} = \frac{2 \text{ problems}}{300 \text{ seconds}} = \frac{1 \text{ problem}}{150 \text{ seconds}}$$

Since the rates are the same, N and T will be in the same proportion as the rate we are given. So we can set up this equation:

$$\frac{1}{150} = \frac{N}{T}$$

GO ONLINE

Use your online study sheet to review math facts and formulas.

Now cross multiply to solve for T: $T = 150N$. The answer is (E).

Picking Numbers Solution: Let's say that $N = 2$. That means José does exactly 2 problems every 5 minutes, or 300 seconds (5×60 seconds = 300 seconds). Now look for the answer choices that yield 300 when $N = 2$. The only one that does is (E), so that must be the answer.

More Than One Rate

The second-most common rate problem has more than one rate. If your paraphrase of the question stem is anything like "First this guy moves at one speed, then at another," then you're dealing with a multiple rate problem. There is frequently a lot of information to deal with. And if we tried to solve it algebraically, we'd need at least six distinct equations. (And if there were three speeds, we'd need *nine!*)

EXPERT EXCLUSIVE

Charts are excellent ways to keep track of complicated problems.

Instead, organize the data with this chart:

	Rate	Time	Distance
part 1 of trip			
part 2 of trip			
entire trip			

Since Rate × Time = Distance, the boxes of this chart multiply across. Since the distance of the first part of the trip plus the distance of the second part equals the total distance, the Distance column adds down. Same for Time. But not for Rate. If you need to calculate the speed for the entire trip, use the Average Speed formula:

$$\text{Average speed} = \frac{\text{Total distance}}{\text{Total time}}$$

Let's go through a sample problem, and you'll see how the chart helps you.

A powerboat crosses a lake at 18 miles per hour and returns at 12 miles per hour. If the time taken turning the boat around was negligible and it returns by the same route, then what was the boat's average speed for the round trip, in miles per hour?

When you notice that it's a "two-part trip" problem, jot down the chart:

	Rate	Time	Distance
part 1 of trip			
part 2 of trip			
entire trip			

Now fill in the data given by the problem:

	Rate	Time	Distance
part 1 of trip	18		
part 2 of trip	12		
entire trip			

Now what? We clearly have to get some information about either the time or the distance to be able to solve for much of anything. The only other piece of information we have is that the boat travelled the same route both times. That means the distance must have been the same. We could use the variable D, but the math will get fairly complicated if we do. Let's keep it simple and Pick Numbers. A number that's a multiple both of 18 and of 12 will make the math work out nicely, so let's say the lake was 36 miles across:

	Rate	Time	Distance
part 1 of trip	18		36
part 2 of trip	12		36
entire trip			

Now we can solve for the times and the total distance:

	Rate	Time	Distance
part 1 of trip	18	2	36
part 2 of trip	12	3	36
entire trip			72

And finally for total time:

	Rate	Time	Distance
part 1 of trip	18	2	36
part 2 of trip	12	3	36
entire trip		5	72

Now we have what we need to solve for average rate. It's $\frac{\text{total distance}}{\text{total time}} = \frac{72}{5} = 14.4$ mph.

EXPERT EXCLUSIVE
On the GMAT, the average of two rates will *never* be the simple average of the two numbers.

EXPERT EXCLUSIVE
When doing two-rate problems, Pick Numbers or Backsolve whenever you can; the problems are complicated enough without us making them deliberately harder for ourselves!

WORK PROBLEMS

Word problems that involve multiple people or machines working together to complete a task are fairly common. To calculate for the total time needed for everyone working together to finish the job, use this formula:

> The reciprocal of the time it takes everyone working together =
> the sum of the reciprocals of the times it would take each
> working individually. (The reciprocal of A is $\frac{1}{A}$.)

Let's look at a seemingly complicated work problem and see how the formula makes things much easier.

EXPERT EXCLUSIVE

If there are only two people working together, use a slightly different form of the same calculation:

Total Time $= \dfrac{AB}{A+B}$

(A and B are the times it takes the two people working alone to finish the job.) By solving for the total time directly instead of for its reciprocal, you'll avoid a common trap.

Working together, John, David, and Roger require $2\frac{1}{4}$ hours to complete a certain task, if each of them works at his respective constant rate. If John alone can complete the task in $4\frac{1}{2}$ hours and David alone can complete the task in 9 hours, how many hours would it take Roger to complete the task, working alone?

- ○ $2\frac{1}{3}$
- ○ $4\frac{1}{2}$
- ○ $6\frac{3}{4}$
- ○ 9
- ○ 12

Work Equation: Here's the solution, employing the work equation.

$$\frac{1}{T} = \frac{1}{J} + \frac{1}{D} + \frac{1}{R}$$

$$\frac{1}{2.25} = \frac{1}{4.5} + \frac{1}{9} + \frac{1}{R}$$

$$\frac{4}{9} = \frac{2}{9} + \frac{1}{9} + \frac{1}{R}$$

$$\frac{1}{9} = \frac{1}{R}$$

$$R = 9$$

Hour-by-Hour Approach: An alternative approach to this kind of problem that some find intuitive and quick is to break down the work on an hour-by-hour basis. Take David first. By himself, he could do the entire task in 9 hours. Therefore, during every single hour that the guys work together, David will be doing $\frac{1}{9}$ of the task ($\frac{1}{9}$ is just the reciprocal of 9). In the second hour, he'll do another $\frac{1}{9}$. And in that extra $\frac{1}{4}$ hour, he'll do $\frac{1}{36}$ of the task. Add them up: David will be doing $\frac{1}{9} + \frac{1}{9} + \frac{1}{36} = \frac{9}{36} = \frac{1}{4}$ of the entire task during the period in question.

EXPERT EXCLUSIVE
Some harder work problems involve tasks left undone. In those cases, you'd need to use this hour-by-hour approach.

How about John? He's much faster than David. Working alone, he could do the entire task in $4\frac{1}{2}$ hours (or $\frac{9}{2}$). So during each hour he works, he'll do the reciprocal of $\frac{9}{2}$ (or $\frac{2}{9}$) of the task. Multiply that $\frac{2}{9}$ of a task per hour by the $2\frac{1}{4}$ hours the guys work, and you see that John himself will account for $\frac{2}{9} \times \frac{9}{4}$ or $\frac{1}{2}$ the task.

With David and John accounting for $\frac{1}{4}$ and $\frac{1}{2}$ of the task respectively, that leaves exactly $\frac{1}{4}$ of the task to be performed by Roger. You can either see that this means that Roger and David work at the same rate—so it'll take Roger 9 hours, too—or just divide $2\frac{1}{4}$ hours by $\frac{1}{4}$ task to get 9 hours per task, choice (D).

Note that even where Backsolving helps, it does not absolve you of thoroughly understanding the question. You must understand what's being asked before you can apply Backsolving.

OVERLAPPING SETS

This is one of the GMAT's trickier setups for word problems. But by organizing the data well, you can handle these questions. You are dealing with an Overlapping Sets problem whenever it presents a group that is divided into two nonexclusive (i.e., potentially overlapping) subgroups.

EXPERT EXCLUSIVE
Take your time setting up the chart so that the groups overlap. Once set up, the chart will do much of the hard work for you!

> A group of 25 children went to the circus, 60% of whom liked the clowns. If the number of boys who liked the clowns was three more than the number who didn't, and the number of boys was one larger than the number of girls, then how many girls did not like the clowns?

EXPERT EXCLUSIVE
The harder the overlapping sets question, the more likely it is to involve proportions.

In your overview of the problem, you can see that there are some complex relationships going on; you shouldn't try to understand them all at once. But notice that there are two ways in which students can be classified: boy or girl, liked or didn't like the clowns. That makes this an Overlapping Sets problem.

The Math Skills Refresher Appendix to this book discusses three different ways of solving overlapping sets, and you'll be well served to practice each. But the one that offers the most flexibility, shows the most detail, and is therefore frequently the safest to use if you struggle with this question type is this chart:

	in Group 1	not in Group 1	Total
in Group 2			
not In Group 2			
Total			

In this problem, the two groupings are boy or girl and likes clowns or doesn't like clowns. So here's the chart we'd use for this problem:

	likes clowns	doesn't like	Total
boys			
girls			
Total			

Now enter the information from the question stem:

	likes clowns	doesn't like	Total
boys	$x + 3$	x	$g + 1$
girls		?	g
Total	60% of 25		25

Two calculations can be done right away: 60% of 25 = (0.6)(25) = 15. Also, $(g + 1) + g = 25$. That means $2g + 1 = 25$, so $2g = 24$ and $g = 12$.

	likes clowns	doesn't like	Total
boys	$x + 3$	x	13
girls		?	12
Total	15		25

The next two calculations suggested by the chart are the total number of people who don't like clowns, $25 - 15 = 10$, and the value of x, $(x + 3) + x = 13$ or $2x + 3 = 13$. That means $2x = 10$, or $x = 5$.

	likes clowns	doesn't like	Total
boys	8	5	13
girls		?	12
Total	15	10	25

Now we know the answer to our question . . . the number of girls who didn't like the clowns is $10 - 5$, or 5. We can fill in the girls who like clowns too, just for fun.

	likes clowns	doesn't like	Total
boys	8	5	13
girls	7	5	12
Total	15	10	25

Because this chart shows all nine possible data points in these problems, it allows you to answer any question that might be asked. Fraction of girls who liked the clowns? It's $\frac{7}{12}$. Percentage of students who didn't like the clowns that were boys? It's 50%. Ratio of girls who liked the clowns to boys who didn't? It's 7:5.

When Overlapping Sets questions involve proportions, be very clear about what the basis of the proportion is. For example, the number of boys who didn't like the clowns could be described as 20% (of the students), 50% (of the students who didn't like clowns), or 100% (as large as the number of girls who didn't like the clowns).

WORD PROBLEMS IN DATA SUFFICIENCY

> **EXPERT EXCLUSIVE**
> Writing down the formula used may help you focus on what you need.

Data Sufficiency word problems are a little different from other types of word problems. They often require very little calculation, and if you attack them without thinking first, you will nearly always waste time and end up crunching numbers.

If a Data Sufficiency word problem is based on some kind of formula, such as the area of a circle, ask yourself what kind of information would give you the area of a circle. Then, if Statement (1) tells you the circle's circumference, don't calculate! It is sufficient to know that you could have calculated. Your motto should be "Think—don't crunch!"

Here's how Kaplan's Method for Data Sufficiency relates to word problems.

STEP 1: FOCUS ON THE QUESTION STEM

The simplest way to look at word problems is to count variables and equations. If the Statements give you enough distinct equations, you are guaranteed sufficiency.

> **EXPERT EXCLUSIVE**
> DS word problems involving proportions (rates, percentages, etc.) frequently have Statements that are sufficient to answer the question without giving you enough info for *all* the variables.

If you need two or more equations to know everything, then be on the lookout for an equation that would give you what's asked without giving you the value of all the variables.

It is usually not necessary to translate the English into math, but you should do so if you suspect that the question has a "trick" to it—either equations that are not distinct or equations that give you what you need without giving you *all* the variables.

STEP 2: EVALUATE THE STATEMENTS SEPARATELY

> **EXPERT EXCLUSIVE**
> A complicated Statement may be more sufficient than it first appears.

If you have the same number of equations as you have variables, there is no need to do any translation or calculation whatsoever. You know that the Statement is sufficient.

If you have fewer equations, don't immediately rule the Statement insufficient. It's possible, especially in a proportions- or rates-based question, that the Statement gives you the answer. You may want to translate the Statement into equations.

STEP 3: EVALUATE THE STATEMENTS TOGETHER ONLY IF NECESSARY

Keep the same principles in mind as you do in Step 2. If you have the same number of distinct equations as variables, you know that you can solve. If not, see whether you can answer the question regardless. But don't get caught doing too much calculation. The instant that you know whether you'll be able to answer the question, select the appropriate answer choice—(C) or (E).

Let's put these strategies into practice. Try the two problems below. Try to conceptualize what you need without actually solving for it. Keep the relevant formulas in mind and ask yourself, "What do I need?" and, "What kind of Statement would give it to me?"

If there are 32 guests at a party, what is the average (arithmetic mean) age of the guests?

(1) The sum of the ages of the guests is 1,536 years.
(2) The youngest guest, Tracy, is 24 years old, and the oldest guest, Pat, is 68 years old.

○ Statement (1) by itself is sufficient to answer the question, but statement (2) by itself is not.

○ Statement (2) by itself is sufficient to answer the question, but statement (1) by itself is not.

○ Statements (1) and (2) taken together are sufficient to answer the question, even though neither statement by itself is sufficient.

○ Either statement by itself is sufficient to answer the question.

○ Statements (1) and (2) taken together are not sufficient to answer the question, requiring more data pertaining to the problem.

> **EXPERT EXCLUSIVE**
>
> Think about the average formula. Do you *really* need the age of each guest?

Remember the average formula:

$$\text{Average} = \frac{\text{Sum of the terms}}{\text{Number of terms}} = \frac{\text{Sum}}{32}$$

So we just need the sum to calculate the average. Does either of the Statements give us the sum? Yes, Statement (1) does. Statement (2) does not give us the sum; there's no way to figure it out from the range in (2) because the guests in between can be of all sorts of ages. So the answer is (A).

Here's a second example.

> A rectangle has length y feet and width z feet. What is its area in square feet?
>
> (1) z is the reciprocal of y.
> (2) The fence around the perimeter of the rectangle is 720 feet.
>
> ○ Statement (1) by itself is sufficient to answer the question, but statement (2) by itself is not.
>
> ○ Statement (2) by itself is sufficient to answer the question, but statement (1) by itself is not.
>
> ○ Statements (1) and (2) taken together are sufficient to answer the question, even though neither statement by itself is sufficient.
>
> ○ Either statement by itself is sufficient to answer the question.
>
> ○ Statements (1) and (2) taken together are not sufficient to answer the question, requiring more data pertaining to the problem.

First recall the formula for the area of a rectangle: Area = length × width.

Here you might want to draw a picture of a rectangle with the length and width labeled y and z respectively.

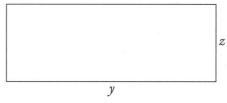

This would be a hard problem, but if you focus on what you need to know, you're less likely to be fooled. We need the area of this rectangle, which is length × width or, in this case, $y \times z$. We need a number. Would Statement (1) give us a number? It's not clear at first glance, so let's test it: $z = \dfrac{1}{y}$, so $y \times z = y \times \dfrac{1}{y} = 1$. The area must be 1, and Statement (1) is sufficient. How about Statement (2)? It gives us the perimeter. But this doesn't give us $y \times z$. It tells us that $2(y + z) = 720$, or $y + z = 360$. But this doesn't tell us the individual values of y and z or the product of y and z, so this Statement is insufficient. (A) is correct.

> **EXPERT EXCLUSIVE**
>
> If asked to find an expression (such as yz), you can often get the answer with fewer equations than variables.

Now let's look at a word problem not based on a common formula.

Jessica has an investment portfolio of stocks and bonds. If she sells half her stocks, how many stocks and bonds will she be left with?

(1) If she were to buy six more stocks, she would have twice as many stocks as bonds.

(2) If she were to triple the number of her bonds, she would have three less than twice the number of her stocks.

○ Statement (1) by itself is sufficient to answer the question, but statement (2) by itself is not.

○ Statement (2) by itself is sufficient to answer the question, but statement (1) by itself is not.

○ Statements (1) and (2) taken together are sufficient to answer the question, even though neither statement by itself is sufficient.

○ Either statement by itself is sufficient to answer the question.

○ Statements (1) and (2) taken together are not sufficient to answer the question, requiring more data pertaining to the problem.

We get one equation in Statement (1) and another equation in Statement (2). You need both equations to answer the question, so you need both Statements. The answer is (C). Thus, you solve a difficult problem in under 30 seconds, and the time you save can help you get another question right.

Try to apply these techniques as best you can on the Practice Test. Use the Math Skills Refresher Appendix to brush up on any basic concepts that are troubling you.

SUMMARY

The Basic Principles of Word Problems are the following:

- Before plunging into math, read over the entire problem and gain a general understanding of the situation.
- Always keep track of exactly what you're after.
- Learn to recognize the different types of problems and what you should do for each.

CHAPTER 11: ANALYTICAL WRITING ASSESSMENT (AWA) STRATEGIES AND PRACTICE

- Essay Format and Structure
- The Basic Principles of Analytical Writing
- How the AWA Is Scored
- The Kaplan Method for Analytical Writing
- Breakdown: Analysis of an Argument
- Breakdown: Analysis of an Issue
- GMAT Style Checklist

The AWA is the first task on the GMAT. After you are situated at your computer workstation, you will be presented with the two essay assignments: an *Argument* essay and an *Issue* essay. You will have 30 minutes to complete each.

For both essays, you will have to analyze a given topic and then type your essay into a simple word processing program. It allows you to do only basic functions:

> **EXPERT EXCLUSIVE**
> One or two spelling errors or a few minor grammar errors will not lower your score. But many spelling errors can hurt your score, as can an error serious enough to impair your intended meaning.

- Insert text.
- Delete text.
- Cut and paste.
- Undo the previous action.
- Scroll up and down on the screen.

Spell check and grammar check functions are not available in the program, so you will have to check those things carefully yourself.

Thirty minutes is not enough time to produce the same kind of essay you'd write for a college class. Nor is it enough time to do a lot of trial and error as you type. It is, however, enough time to write a "strong first draft" if you plan it carefully, and that's what the essay graders are looking for.

The Argument essay always comes first, the Issue essay second. After the essays, you'll get an 8-minute break before the Quant section begins.

EXPERT EXCLUSIVE

The tutorial is a good opportunity to make sure that your keyboard and mouse are in good working order. If you need to change seats, it is far better to discover this before the timed sections begin.

ESSAY FORMAT AND STRUCTURE

At the start of the AWA, you'll be given a brief tutorial on how to use the word processor. If you are concerned that you do not type very fast, you should spend some time practicing with full-page text documents between now and test day.

ANALYSIS OF AN ARGUMENT ESSAY

The first assignment is the Argument essay. Your task is to assess the logic and use of evidence in an argument. It doesn't matter whether you agree or disagree with the argument's conclusion. Rather, you need to explain the ways in which the author has failed to fully support that conclusion.

Let's take a look at a sample prompt:

> The following appeared in a memo from the CEO of Hula Burger, a chain of hamburger restaurants.
>
> "Officials in the film industry report that over 60% of the films released last year targeted an age 8–12 audience. Moreover, sales data indicate that, nationally, hamburgers are the favorite food among this age group. Since a branch store of Whiz Vid Video Store opened in town last year, hamburger sales at our restaurant next door have been higher than at any other restaurant in our chain. Because the rental of movies seems to stimulate hamburger sales, the best way to increase our profits is to open new Hula Burger restaurants right nearby every Whiz Vid Video Store."
>
> Discuss how well reasoned you find this argument. In your discussion, be sure to analyze the line of reasoning and the use of evidence in the argument. For example, you may need to consider what questionable assumptions underlie the thinking and what alternative explanations or counterexamples might weaken the conclusion. You can also discuss what sort of evidence would strengthen or refute the argument, what changes in the argument would make it more logically sound, and what, if anything, would help you better evaluate its conclusion.

Where are the holes in the argument? In what ways does it fail to be completely convincing? Why might the plan fail? Not only do you have to identify its major weaknesses, you must also explain them.

ANALYSIS OF AN ISSUE ESSAY

For the Issue essay, you will be given a statement that expresses an opinion (sometimes two) about something. Your task is to communicate your views on the issue. Whether you agree or disagree with the opinion given in the essay prompt is irrelevant—there is no "right answer." What matters is how well you support your view.

> **EXPERT EXCLUSIVE**
> The issue will be broad and two sided by design. That way, there are no "right answers" or "wrong answers." Still, you must stake out a position.

Here's a sample Issue prompt:

> "Everyone in the country over the age of 12 should be required to perform a minimum amount of public service. Such a required contribution would not only help society as a whole, but it would also add to the individual's character."

> Discuss the extent to which you agree or disagree with the opinion stated above. Support your views with reasons and/or examples from your own experience, observations, or reading.

Although you must take a side (Should everyone—even children—be required to perform public service? Or not?), it doesn't matter which side you take. What matters is whether your argument is convincing. Can you come up with good reasons why your side is correct and explain your reasoning with relevant examples?

THE BASIC PRINCIPLES OF ANALYTICAL WRITING

You aren't just being evaluated on the strength of your ideas. Your score will also depend on how well you express them. If your writing style isn't clear, your ideas won't come across, no matter how brilliant they are.

Good essay writing isn't just grammatically correct. It is also clear and concise. The following principles will help you express your ideas in good GMAT style.

 READ MORE

Turn to the Editorials or Op–Ed page of your local newspaper. There should be some good examples of clear, concise language.

YOUR CONTROL OF LANGUAGE IS IMPORTANT

Writing that is grammatical, concise, direct, and persuasive displays the "superior control of language" (as the test maker terms it) that earns top GMAT Analytical Writing scores. To achieve effective GMAT style in your essays, you should pay attention to the following points.

Grammar

Your writing must follow the same general rules of standard written English that are tested by Sentence Correction questions. If you're not confident of your mastery of grammar, review the Sentence Correction section.

Diction

Diction means word choice. Do you use the words *affect* and *effect* correctly? What about *its* and *it's*, *there* and *their*, *precede* and *proceed*, *principal* and *principle*, and *whose* and *who's*?

Syntax

Syntax refers to sentence structure. Do you construct your sentences so that your ideas are clear and understandable? Do you vary your sentence structure?

KEEP THINGS SIMPLE

EXPERT EXCLUSIVE

Sentence fragments are not acceptable, nor are informal structures such as bullet points or numerical enumeration (i.e., "(1)" instead of "first").

Perhaps the single most important thing to bear in mind when writing a GMAT essay is to keep everything simple. This rule applies to word choice, sentence structure, and organization. If you obsess about how to spell an unusual word, you can lose your way. The more complicated your sentences are, the more likely they'll be plagued by errors. The more complex your organization gets, the more likely your argument will get bogged down in convoluted sentences that obscure your point.

Keep in mind that simple does not mean *simplistic*. A clear, straightforward approach can still be sophisticated and convey perceptive insights.

MINOR GRAMMATICAL FLAWS WON'T HARM YOUR SCORE

EXPERT EXCLUSIVE

The essay graders know that you only have 30 minutes and are not expecting the kind of writing that would be in a doctoral dissertation. Think of writing a memo or a business letter–clarity and concision trump an "educated tone."

Many test takers mistakenly believe they'll lose points over a few mechanical errors. That's not the case. GMAT essays should be final first drafts. This means that a couple of misplaced commas, misspellings, or other minor glitches aren't going to affect your score. Occasional mistakes of this type are acceptable. In fact, according to the scoring rubric, a top-scoring essay may well have a few minor grammatical flaws.

But if your essays are littered with misspellings and grammar mistakes, the graders may conclude that you have a serious communication problem.

So be concise, forceful, and correct. An effective essay wastes no words; makes its point in a clear, direct way; and conforms to the generally accepted rules of grammar and form.

USE A LOGICAL STRUCTURE

Good essays have a straightforward, linear structure. The problem is that we rarely think in a straightforward, linear way. That's why it's so important to plan your response before you begin typing. If you write *while* planning, your essay will likely loop back on itself, contain redundancies, or fail to follow through on what it sets up.

Logical structure consists of three things:

(1) *Paragraph unity.* Paragraph unity means each paragraph discusses one thing and all the discussion of that one thing happens in that paragraph. Let's say that you're responding to the issue essay example we just saw and one of your points was that involuntary service might build resentment instead of character. The next paragraph should move on to another idea—perhaps something about the appropriateness of forcing a 12-year-old into work. If, in the middle of that next paragraph, you went back to your resentment point, you'd be violating paragraph unity.

(2) *Train of thought.* This is similar to paragraph unity, but it applies to the whole essay. It's awkward to keep jumping back and forth between the different sides of an issue, for example. Lay out the support for one side fully, then address the other. Don't write another paragraph about a topic you've already discussed.

> **EXPERT EXCLUSIVE**
>
> In the Issue essay, be clear from the first paragraph what your position is. The most common flow error is waiting until the end of the essay to do so.

(3) *Flow.* The basic idea of flow is that you should deliver on what you promise and not radically change the subject. If your intro says that you will mention reasons why Hula burgers might be less popular among the 8- to 12-year-old demographic than regular hamburgers are, you need to make sure that you actually do so. Similarly, avoid suddenly expanding the scope of the essay in the last sentence.

> **♟ KAPLAN STRATEGY**
>
> The Basic Principles for success in Analytical Writing are the following:
>
> - Your control of language is important.
> - Keep things simple.
> - Minor grammatical flaws won't harm your score.
> - Use a logical structure.

HOW THE AWA IS SCORED

Your essays will be graded on a scale from 0 to 6 (highest). You'll get one score, which will be an average of the scores that you receive for each of the two essays, rounded up to the nearest half point. Your essay will be graded by a human grader as well as a computerized essay grader (the IntelliMetric™ System). The two grade completely independently of each other—IntelliMetric™ isn't told the human's score, nor is the human told the computer's. If the two scores are identical, then that's your score.

EXPERT EXCLUSIVE

IntelliMetric™ and the human grader agree on the same grade about 55 percent of the time and agree on identical or adjacent grades 97 percent of the time. (Only 3 percent of essays need rereading.) These figures are equivalent to how often two trained human graders agree!

If the scores differ by one point, those scores are averaged. If they disagree by more than one point, a second human will grade the essay to resolve any differences.

IntelliMetric™ was designed to make the same judgments that a good human grader would. In fact, part of the Graduate Management Admission Council's (GMAC's) argument for the validity of IntelliMetric™ is that its performance is indistinguishable from a human's. Still, you should remember that it is *not* a human and write accordingly.

Before you begin to write, outline your essay. Good organization always counted, and now it's more important than ever.

IntelliMetric's™ grading algorithm was designed using 400 officially graded essays for each prompt. That's a huge sample of responses, so don't worry about whether IM will understand your points—it's highly likely that someone out of those 400 responses had a similar idea. Computers are not good judges of humor or creativity. (The human judges don't reward those either. The standard is business writing, and you really shouldn't be making smart-alecky remarks in, say, an email to a CEO.)

The length of your essay is not a factor; the computer does not count the number of words in your response.

Use transitional phrases like *first*, *therefore*, *since*, and *for example* so that the computer can recognize structured arguments.

Though the IntelliMetric™ doesn't grade spelling per se, it could give you a lower score if it can't understand you or thinks you used the wrong words.

EXPERT EXCLUSIVE

Since scoring discrepancies are resolved by human graders, you needn't worry about the computer not recognizing the validity of your examples.

Here's what your essay will be graded on:

- *Quality of your reasoning*. For the Issue essay, how compelling were your reasons? On the Argument essay, did you discover the major weaknesses of the argument?
- *Organization*. Does your essay have good paragraph unity, structure, and flow?
- *Development*. It's not enough simply to assert good points. Do you explain them well? How relevant are the examples you provide?
- *Writing*. The GMAC calls this "control of the elements of standard written English." How well do you express your ideas?

Now let's take a more in-depth look at the scoring scale so you get a sense of what to aim for.

- **6: Outstanding.** Essays that earn the top score must be insightful, well developed, logically organized, and skillfully written. Among the words that the test maker uses to describe a 6 essay are *cogent*, *clear*, *effective*, and *insightful*.

- **5: Strong.** A 5 essay is well developed and well written but may not be as compellingly argued as a 6. There may also be more frequent or more serious writing errors than in a 6. The test maker describes a 5 as *generally thoughtful*, *sensible*, and *good*.

- **4: Adequate.** The important elements of the argument or issue are addressed but not explained robustly. The organization is good, but ideas may not be connected well. The writing may have some flaws but is generally acceptable. The test maker calls a 4 *competent*, *adequate*, *satisfactory*, and *reasonably clear*.

- **3: Limited.** A 3 response misses important elements of the Issue or Argument, has little or no development of its ideas, and doesn't clearly express its meaning. The test maker uses these words to describe a 3: *plainly flawed*, *tangential*, *irrelevant*, and *not clear*.

- **2: Seriously Flawed.** An essay scoring a 2 has some serious problems. It may not use any examples whatsoever or support its ideas in any way. Its writing will have many errors that interfere with the meaning of the sentences. An Issue essay that scores a 2 may well not develop a position on the issue, and an Argument essay that scores a 2 may be written like an Issue essay—substituting your own ideas for objective analysis. Here's how a 2 is described: *unclear*, *disorganized*, and *has serious and frequent problems*.

- **1: Fundamentally Deficient.** These are rare. A 1 score is reserved for essays that provide little to no evidence of the ability to understand or analyze an issue or to develop ideas in any way. A 1 essay will have so many writing errors that the essay may be unintelligible. The test maker describes a 1 as *incoherent* and having *severe and persistent errors*.

- **0: No Score.** 0s aren't worse than 1s per se. They signify an attempt to avoid addressing the prompt at all, either by writing only random or repeating characters or by copying the prompt. You could also score a 0 by not writing in English or by addressing a completely different topic.

- **NR: Blank.** Speaks for itself. This is what you get if you write no essay at all. Some schools will not consider your GMAT score if your essay receives an NR. By skipping the essay, you give yourself an unfair advantage—everyone else wrote essays for an hour *before* the Quant and Verbal sections!

EXPERT EXCLUSIVE

Notice that a 6 need not be "perfect," just very good.

EXPERT EXCLUSIVE

Notice the change in language between 4 and 3? The essay grading is almost pass/fail in nature: There's a clear line between 1–3 (bad) and 4–6 (good).

EXPERT EXCLUSIVE

Violate the essay directions, either by not taking a position on an Issue or by taking one in an Argument, and you risk scoring a 2.

THE KAPLAN METHOD FOR ANALYTICAL WRITING

Here's the deal: You have a limited amount of time to show the business school admissions people that you can think logically and express yourself in clearly written English. They don't care how many syllables you can cram into a sentence or how fancy your phrases are. They care that you're making sense. Whatever you do, don't hide beneath a lot of hefty words and abstractions. Make sure that everything you say is clearly written and relevant to the topic. Get in there, state your main points, back them up, and get out.

STEP 1: TAKE APART THE ISSUE/ARGUMENT

- Read it through to get a sense of the scope of the matter.
- In the Argument essay, identify the author's conclusion and the evidence used to support it.
- In the Issue essay, paraphrase both sides of the issue to define the two opinions clearly.

You can take about 2 minutes on this step.

EXPERT EXCLUSIVE

Step 2 of the Kaplan method is very much like paraphrasing Weakeners and Strengtheners for a Critical Reasoning question.

STEP 2: SELECT THE POINTS YOU WILL MAKE

- In the "Analysis of an Argument" essay, identify all the important gaps between the evidence and the conclusion. Think of how you'll explain or illustrate those gaps and under what circumstances the author's assumptions would not hold true. Also, think about how the author could remedy these weaknesses.
- In the "Analysis of an Issue" essay, think of the arguments and examples for *both* sides and decide which side you will support or the exact extent to which you agree with the stated position.

Step 2 should take about 5 minutes.

EXPERT EXCLUSIVE

You can't afford to "save your best for last" on a timed essay.

STEP 3: ORGANIZE

- Outline your essay.
- Lead with your best arguments.
- Think about how the essay as a whole will flow.

If you decide on basic templates for your two essays before test day, this step will take less than 1 minute.

STEP 4: WRITE YOUR ESSAY

- Be direct.
- Use paragraph breaks to make your essay easier to read.

- Use transitions to link related ideas; they will help your writing flow.
- Finish strongly.

You can afford no more than 20 minutes of typing. The other 10 minutes should be dedicated to planning and correcting.

STEP 5: PROOFREAD YOUR WORK

- Save enough time to read through the entire essay—2 minutes as a minimum.
- Fix any spelling, grammar, syntax, or diction errors.
- Add any needed keywords to improve the flow of your ideas.
- Don't add any new ideas or change the structure of your essay. There just isn't time.

> **EXPERT EXCLUSIVE**
>
> By planning your response before you type, you'll find it much easier to write because you won't be worrying about what to say—just focusing on how to say it.

As explained before, the two essay types you'll write—Argument and Issue—require generally similar tasks. You must analyze a subject, take an informed position, and explain that position in writing. The two essay types, however, require different specific tasks.

BREAKDOWN: ANALYSIS OF AN ARGUMENT

The stimulus and question stem of an Analysis of an Argument topic should look something like this:

> "The problem of poorly trained teachers that has plagued the state public school system is bound to become a good deal less serious in the future. The state has initiated comprehensive guidelines that oblige state teachers to complete a number of required credits in education and educational psychology at the graduate level before being certified."
>
> Explain how logically persuasive you find this argument. In discussing your viewpoint, analyze the argument's line of reasoning and its use of evidence. Also explain what, if anything, would make the argument more valid and convincing or help you to better evaluate its conclusion.

> **EXPERT EXCLUSIVE**
>
> Become familiar with the Argument essay directions beforehand so you don't waste valuable time reading them on test day.

THE STIMULUS

Analysis of an Argument topics that present an argument will probably remind you of Critical Reasoning questions. The basic idea is similar. Just as in Critical Reasoning, the writer tries to persuade you of something—her conclusion—by citing some evidence. So look for these two basic components of an argument: a conclusion and supporting evidence. You should read the arguments in the Analysis of an Argument topics in much the same way you read Critical Reasoning questions; be on the lookout for assumptions—the ways the writer makes the leap from evidence to conclusion.

EXPERT EXCLUSIVE

Note that you are asked to discuss whether the argument is "persuasive," not whether its conclusion is "correct."

The Question Stem

The question stem instructs you to decide how convincing you find the argument, explain why, and discuss what might improve the argument. Unlike the Issue essay, there's a right answer here: the argument always has some problems. You want to focus your efforts on finding them, explaining them, and fixing them.

Exactly what are you being asked to do here?

Explain how logically persuasive you find this argument. In discussing your viewpoint, analyze the argument's line of reasoning and its use of evidence.

Translation: Critique the argument. Discuss the ways in which it is not convincing: How and why might the evidence not fully support the conclusion?

Also explain what, if anything, would make the argument more valid and convincing or help you to better evaluate its conclusion.

Translation: Spot weak links in the argument and offer constructive modifications that would strengthen them.

Let's use the Kaplan Method for Analytical Writing on the Analysis of an Argument topic we saw before:

"The problem of poorly trained teachers that has plagued the state public school system is bound to become a good deal less serious in the future. The state has initiated comprehensive guidelines that oblige state teachers to complete a number of required credits in education and educational psychology at the graduate level before being certified."

Explain how logically persuasive you find this argument. In discussing your viewpoint, analyze the argument's line of reasoning and its use of evidence. Also explain what, if anything, would make the argument more valid and convincing or help you to better evaluate its conclusion.

1. Take Apart the Argument

First, identify the conclusion—the point the argument's trying to make. Here, the conclusion is this:

The problem of poorly trained teachers that has plagued the state public school system is bound to become a good deal less serious in the future.

Next, identify the evidence—the basis for the conclusion. Here, the evidence is the following:

> The state has initiated comprehensive guidelines that oblige state teachers to complete a number of required credits in education and educational psychology at the graduate level before being certified.

Finally, sum up the argument in your own words:

> The problem of badly trained teachers will become less serious because they'll be getting better training.

EXPERT EXCLUSIVE

If you aren't able to put the argument in your own words, you don't yet understand it well enough to analyze it sufficiently. Don't rush this step; you can afford a full two minutes if you need it.

2. Select the Points You Will Make

Now that you've found the conclusion and evidence, think about what assumptions the author is making or any reasoning flaws she commits. Also, think about any unaddressed questions that you feel would be relevant.

- She assumes that the courses will improve teachers' classroom performance.
- What about bad teachers who are already certified? Would they also be required to retrain?
- Have currently bad teachers already had this training?
- Will this have any unintended negative consequences?

EXPERT EXCLUSIVE

You don't need to make your notes in complete sentences. Just write enough to remind yourself of the point you're going to make when you type the essay.

You also will need to explain how these assumptions could be false or how the questions reveal weaknesses in the author's argument. Add to your notes:

- She assumes that the courses will improve teachers' classroom performance. What if the problem is cultural? Or if it's a language barrier? Or if the teacher doesn't know the subject?
- What about bad teachers who are already certified? Would they also be required to retrain? If not, those bad teachers would still be in the system.
- Have currently bad teachers already had this training? If so, this fact demonstrates that this training won't solve the problems.
- Will this have any unintended negative consequences? What does this training cost? If the state has to pay for it, will that mean less money available to the classroom? If teachers have to pay for it, then will good teachers leave the system?

Then think about evidence that would make the argument stronger or more logically sound.

- Evidence verifying that the training will make teachers better
- Evidence that currently bad teachers have not already received this training and that they either will soon receive it or will be removed from the classroom
- Evidence that the cost of the training is not prohibitive

 GO ONLINE

Practice responding to the AWA prompts on your online syllabus. Work on a computer, but to mimic test conditions, don't use the automatic spell check or grammar check.

3. Organize

Look over the notes you've jotted down. Select the strongest point to be first, the next-strongest to be second, and so on. Two criteria determine whether a point is strong. One is how well you can explain it. If, for example, you aren't sure how to explain potential negative consequences of an expensive training program, you should use that idea last—if at all. The other is how severe a problem the weakness poses to the argument's persuasiveness. If the training doesn't work, for example, the argument is in serious trouble!

Then decide how you'll arrange your points. There are several valid ways to organize an essay. You can discuss all of the problems and then move on to all of the needed solutions. Or you can discuss one problem and its solution, then move on to the next.

The following is an example of the latter approach:

¶ restate argument (conc: solve problem of poorly trained teachers; ev: courses in educational psychology)

¶ assumes courses = better performance. Culture? Language? Subject matter? Need ev. of relevance.

¶ assumes current bad teachers not already trained. If they have, training doesn't work. Need ev. of no training.

¶ assumes bad teachers will go if not trained. If not, will be bad until they retire. Need everyone to be trained or leave.

¶ assumes not too $. If too $, can cause problems. Need ev. of low $.

> **EXPERT EXCLUSIVE**
>
> You may not have time to use all your points. Leaving your weakest for last means that if you run short on time, you'll leave out your weakest point instead of your best.

4. Write Your Essay

Begin typing or writing your essay now. Keep in mind the basic principles of writing that we discussed earlier.

Keep your writing simple and clear. Choose words that you know how to use well. Avoid the temptation to make your writing "sound smarter" with overly complicated sentences or vocabulary that feels awkward.

Keep your eye on the clock and make sure that you don't run out of time to proofread. If you need to, leave out your last point or two. (Make sure that you include at least two points.) Let's pretend that the writer of the following essay had only four minutes left on the clock after the fourth paragraph. She wisely chooses neither to rush through her final paragraph nor to skip proofreading. Instead, she leaves out her point about cost.

The writer concludes that the present problem of poorly trained teachers will become less severe in the future because of required credits in education and psychology. However, the conclusion relies on assumptions for which there is no clear evidence.

The writer assumes that the required courses will make better teachers. In fact, the courses might be entirely irrelevant to the teachers' failings. If, for example, the prevalent problem is cultural and linguistic gaps between teacher and student, graduate-level courses that do not address these specific issues probably won't do much good. The courses also would not be heplful for a teacher who did not know their subject matter. The argument that the courses will improve teachers would be strengthened if the writer provided evidence that the training will be relevant to the problems.

In addition, the writer assumes that currently poor teachers have not already had this training. In fact, the writer doesn't mention whether or not some or all of the poor teachers have had similar training. The argument would be strengthened considerably if the writer provided evidence that currently poor teachers have not had training comparable to the new requirements.

Finally, the writer assumes that poor teachers currently working will either stop teaching in the future or will have received training. The writer provides no evidence, though, to indicate that this is the case. As the argument stands, it's highly possible that only brand-new teachers will be receiving the training and the bright future to which the writer refers is decades away. Only if the writer provides evidence that all teachers in the system will receive training—and will then change there teaching methods accordingly—does the argument hold.

> **EXPERT EXCLUSIVE**
> Three well-written points will score better than four poorly written ones. Two well-written points will score better than three poorly written ones.

5. Proofread Your Work

Save a few minutes to go back over your essay and catch any obvious errors. Look over the essay above. It has at least four grammar errors and is missing at least one keyword. By leaving herself ample proofreading time, our author will be able to find them.

- ¶1—no errors
- ¶2
  - Add a keyword to the beginning of the paragraph. Since it is the first assumption discussed, "The writer assumes . . ." should be changed to "First, the writer assumes. . . ."

EXPERT EXCLUSIVE

They and *their* are often used as a gender-neutral singular in informal English. But that use violates the rules of the formal "standard" English that the GMAT requires.

- The second-to-last sentence has some trouble: "The courses also would not be heplful for a teacher who did not know their subject matter." For one thing, "heplful" should be "helpful". For another "a teacher" is singular, but "their" is plural. Let's change "a teacher" to "teachers."
- ¶3—no errors
- ¶4
  - There's an awkward phrase about halfway through: "only brand-new teachers will be receiving the training." There's no need for anything but simple future tense: "only brand-new teachers will receive the training."
- In the last sentence, "there teaching methods" should be "their teaching methods."

The best way to improve your writing and proofreading skills is practice. Write some practice essays using the prompts provided by the test maker at **mba.com** or in the *Official Guide to GMAT Review*. These prompts—from the pool from which the computer selects students' essay problems—are the actual ones that the GMAT tests.

BREAKDOWN: ANALYSIS OF AN ISSUE

EXPERT EXCLUSIVE

The issue will have good arguments on each side. But note that the essay prompt forces you to choose one over the other.

The stimulus and question stem of an Analysis of an Issue topic will look something like this:

> Many assert that individuals allowed to work flexible schedules at home will be both more productive and happier than colleagues working under more traditional arrangements. But others assert that the close supervision of an office workplace is necessary to ensure productivity and quality control and to maintain morale.
>
> Which argument do you find more compelling, the case for flexible work conditions or the opposing viewpoint? Explain your position using relevant reasons or examples drawn from your own experience, observations, or reading.

THE STIMULUS

In this example, the stimulus consists of a few sentences that discuss two points of view on a general issue. Sometimes the stimulus is a single sentence. You don't need prior knowledge of any specific subject matter to discuss the issue.

The first sentence or two introduce the general issue and express one point of view. Sometimes, a keyword—here, it's the word *but*—will signal the introduction of the contrasting point of view. In other cases, the contrasting viewpoint will not be explicitly stated. In those cases, you must deduce what that opposing view is.

THE QUESTION STEM

The stem asks you which of the two viewpoints you find more convincing and instructs you to explain your position using reasons or examples. Though the specific wording will vary for each question, the basic task will be essentially the same.

Exactly what are you being asked to do here?

> Which argument do you find more compelling, the case for flexible work conditions or the opposing viewpoint?

Translation: There are two conflicting viewpoints here. Take one side or the other.

> Explain your position using relevant reasons or examples drawn from your own experience, observations, or reading.

Translation: Argue your position, using specific examples. Support your points with evidence.

Not all issue topics will look exactly like our example. Some may present only a sentence in which the two conflicting viewpoints are not specified, as in this instance:

> Allowing individuals to work flexible schedules is an idea that makes sense.

Notice how this is just a reworking of our original topic. Here, the two viewpoints are implicit, so your task includes a little digging: What are the two viewpoints? From here, your basic task is the same. Explain what the issue is and make a case for one opinion on that issue.

Now let's use the Kaplan Method for Analytical Writing on this Analysis of an Issue topic:

> Many assert that individuals allowed to work flexible schedules at home will be both more productive and happier than colleagues working under more traditional arrangements. But others assert that the close supervision of an office workplace is necessary to ensure productivity and quality control and to maintain morale.

> Which argument do you find more compelling, the case for flexible work conditions or the opposing viewpoint? Explain your position using relevant reasons or examples drawn from your own experience, observations, or reading.

> **EXPERT EXCLUSIVE**
>
> The essay graders are looking for explanations, not assertions. Just saying that something is true isn't good enough—you need to show *why* it's true.

1. Take Apart the Issue

This prompt gave us two opinions on an issue, though some prompts will only give us one. Regardless of how the Issue prompt is written, we should begin by summarizing *both* sides of the debate. Here, we can paraphrase the two sides as "Flexible schedules make workers happier and more productive," versus "Traditional, supervised workplaces make people happier and more productive."

2. Select the Points You Will Make

So which side do you take? Remember, this isn't about showing the admissions people what your politics are—it's about showing you can formulate an argument and write it down. Think through the pros and cons of each side and choose the side for which you have more relevant things to say. For this topic, that process might go something like this.

Arguments for flexible schedules:

- People feel more valued, work better.
- Fewer absences.
- People feel happier if they don't have to commute.

Arguments for traditional workplace:

- People less likely to waste time if boss is there.
- People need to feel part of a team.
- More quality control possible.
- More resources available.

> **EXPERT EXCLUSIVE**
>
> Think of *reasons*, not just examples. The test maker is very clear that readers are looking for several different reasons in support of your position, not several examples illustrating only one reason.

You should add to your list of reasons any support or examples you can think of.

Arguments for flexible schedules:

- People feel more valued, work better—???
- Fewer absences—can work from home if sick.
- People feel happier if they don't have to commute—ex: LA commute.

Arguments for traditional workplace:

- People less likely to waste time if boss is there.
- People need to feel part of a team—isolation vs. friendship.
- More quality control possible—boss can check in on work.
- More resources available—technical & staff.

In this example, the writer could think of more supporting details for the reasons on the "traditional workplace" side, so that is the viewpoint she will argue. It would have been great if she knew of a business that had abandoned telecommuting in favor of a traditional office environment; she could have used that as a good illustration of her reasoning. But even without that, she can write a strong essay.

Her final step is to plan a rebuttal of the opposing side: difficult commutes can be eased in other ways, such as by staggered work schedules and subsidized mass transit costs.

> **EXPERT EXCLUSIVE**
>
> The best way to demonstrate to the essay grader that you considered the issue carefully is to address arguments from both sides while being clear about which side you're on.

3. Organize

Your first paragraph should always restate the issue. A common mistake is to present only your own side, but strong authors will define both positions clearly. Once the debate has been framed, then you can define the position you hold—and therefore, implicitly, the position you disagree with.

Now it's time to arrange your points in order. It's best to start with your most compelling point. If you need to drop a point for time, let it be your weakest. Finish by addressing and rebutting an argument from the other side.

Here's how this author might organize her points. Noting that "the boss" showed up in two different points, she rolls those two points into one. That way she avoids seeming redundant.

¶ frame the issue—home versus office. Happier & more productive at office.

¶ team spirit—friendships vs. isolation

¶ more resources = higher productivity. Technical & staff resources.

¶ boss can supervise—less wasted time, more quality control

¶ OTHER SIDE: home = no painful commute. REBUTTAL: staggered shifts; share mass transit cost

4. Write Your Essay

Remember that your main goal is to communicate your ideas clearly. Don't try to impress the grader with academic-sounding rhetoric. It's also wise to avoid strident rhetoric—let the quality of your ideas do the convincing.

Keep your eye on the clock and make sure that you don't run out of time to proofread. If you need to, drop one of your supporting arguments. You need at least two supporting arguments, and you need to address the other side.

Here's how this essay might be written:

Many companies face the decision to either allow employees flexible work schedules or to maintain traditional work environments. I will show that workers are happier and more productive in a traditional office environment.

A main reason that people are happier in traditional offices is the team spirit and personal satisfaction that come from working in a group. People who spend their workday at home are more likely to feel isolated from the company and divorced from the final product. Additionally, people who work in an office environment are also more likely to form close friendships with co-workers than those who are rarely in the office, which fosters greater happiness and stability within the company.

The bottom line for businesses is, of course, productivity, and there are several reasons why the traditional workplace promotes greater productivity than work at home. One reason is the increased resources the workplace provides. An office space is more likely to have better technical resources than a home work space. Also, the company staff provides problem-solving resources to which a home worker would not have direct access.

EXPERT EXCLUSIVE

That there is no real-world example is made up for by how well the points are explained. It's the logic of your supporting arguments that counts, not the number of examples you can think of.

Traditional work space is far better from a managerial standpoint, as well. An office environment makes for easier supervision and quality control. Managers can make sure employees aren't wasting time or doing shoddy work. Also, a manager can more quickly spot and fix problems if they are occurring in the office, increasing productivity significantly.

Working from home does have its benefits, of course. Rush-hour traffic can make for a very difficult commute, whereas those who work from home need not commute at all. However, there are ways that an employer can address those concerns without giving up the benefits that a traditional workplace provides. For example, the cost of mass transit could be partially reimbursed, which would not only save employees the stress of driving in rush hour but would also improve morale. Also, work shifts can be staggered, allowing some employees to periodically avoid rush hour altogether. All in all, it is clear that there are greater advantages to the traditional work environment. The traditional office space allows for workers to be happier and more productive than those who work at home.

5. Proofread Your Work

Be sure to save at least two minutes to check your writing. Read through the sample essay above, looking for writing that could be improved. There are five style errors and two grammar errors:

- ¶1
  - Use of the first person is often weak style. "I will show . . ." could be changed to "A close examination of the issue reveals . . ."
- ¶2
  - This sentence has plenty of errors:
    - Additionally, people who work in an office environment are also more likely to form close friendships with co-workers than those who are rarely in the office, which fosters greater happiness and stability within the company.

EXPERT EXCLUSIVE
It's often easier and faster to rewrite awkward sentences in a later proofreading step than to try to write each sentence perfectly the first time.

  "Additionally" and "also" are redundant. "Office environment" is also redundant—an office *is* an environment. The comparison is slightly off—"more *likely to form* . . . than *those who*." It's better to compare action to action. And let's see if we can avoid saying "office" twice in the same sentence. There's a modification error at the end—the use of "which" means that we are describing the word immediately before the comma, but the author meant not to describe "office" but "the forming of close friendships."

    - Additionally, people who work in an office are more likely to form close friendships with co-workers than are those who work from home, an occurrence that fosters greater happiness and stability within the company.
- ¶3—No errors.
- ¶4—No errors.
- ¶5
  - "Work from home" comes just a little bit after "working from home." Vary word choice a little. Replace "those who work from home" with "those with home offices."

GMAT STYLE CHECKLIST

- **Be concise:**
  - Cut out words, phrases, and sentences that don't add any information or serve a purpose.
  - Watch out for repetitive phrases such as "refer back" or "serious crisis."
  - Don't use conjunctions to join sentences that would be more effective as separate sentences.

EXPERT EXCLUSIVE
Two short or midlength sentences can often be more effective than one very long sentence.

- **Be forceful:**
  - Avoid jargon and pompous language; it won't impress anybody. For example, "a waste of time and money" is better than "a pointless expenditure of temporal and financial resources."
  - Avoid clichés and overused terms or phrases (for example, "beyond the shadow of a doubt").
  - Don't be vague. Avoid generalizations and abstractions when more specific words would be clearer.
  - Don't use weak sentence openings. Be wary of sentences that begin with "there is" or "there are." For example, "There are some ways that this sentence is awkward," should be rewritten as "This sentence is awkward in some ways."
  - Don't refer to yourself needlessly. Avoid pointless phrases like "in my personal opinion"; even phrases such as "I agree" or "I think" are considered stylistically weak.
  - Don't be monotonous: vary sentence length and style.
  - Use transitions to connect sentences and make your essay easy to follow.
- **Be correct:**
  - Stick to the rules of standard written English.

SUMMARY

The Basic Principles of Analytical Writing are the following:

- Your control of language is important.
- Keep things simple.
- Minor grammatical flaws won't harm your score.
- Use a logical structure.

The Kaplan Method for Analytical Writing is as follows:

Step 1: Take apart the issue/argument.

Step 2: Select the points you will make.

Step 3: Organize.

Step 4: Write your essay.

Step 5: Proofread your work.

PRACTICE ESSAYS

Directions: Write an essay on each of the topics below. The writing should be concise, forceful, and grammatically correct. After you have finished, proofread to catch any errors. Allow yourself 30 minutes to complete each essay.

ARGUMENT ESSAY

The following appeared in a memo from the regional manager of Luxe Spa, a chain of high-end salons.

"Over 75% of households in Parksboro have Jacuzzi bathtubs. In addition, the average family income in Parksboro is 50% higher than the national average, and a local store reports record-high sales of the most costly brands of hair and body care products. With so much being spent on personal care, Parksboro will be a profitable location for a new Luxe Spa—a salon that offers premium services at prices that are above average."

Discuss how well reasoned you find this argument. In your discussion, be sure to analyze the line of reasoning and the use of evidence in the argument. For example, you may need to consider what questionable assumptions underlie the thinking and what alternative explanations or counterexamples might weaken the conclusion. You can also discuss what sort of evidence would strengthen or refute the argument, what changes in the argument would make it more logically sound, and what, if anything, would help you better evaluate its conclusion.

> **EXPERT EXCLUSIVE**
>
> Practice writing under timed conditions so that you get a feel for how much you can afford to write while still being able to proofread.

ISSUE ESSAY

"The invention of the Internet has created more problems than it has solved. Most people would have a higher quality of life had the Internet never been invented."

From your perspective, is this an accurate observation? Why or why not? Explain, using reasons and/or examples from your experience, observations, and reading.

After writing out your essays, compare them to the sample responses that follow. Don't focus on their length, as word count is not part of the grading rubric. Rather, focus on how logical the structures are and how each essay makes its points in a clear and straightforward style.

ARGUMENT ESSAY

Though it might seem at first glance that the regional manager of Luxe Spa has good reasons for suggesting that Parksboro would be a profitable place for a new spa, a closer examination of the arguments presented reveals numerous examples of leaps of faith, poor reasoning, and ill-defined terminology. In order to better support her claim, the manager would need to show a correlation between the figures she cites in reference to Parksboro's residents and a willingness to spend money at a spa with high prices.

EXPERT EXCLUSIVE

Notice that the essayist focuses on how the evidence *might not* support the conclusion instead of trying to prove that it *does not*.

EXPERT EXCLUSIVE

This essay would be stronger if it pointed out how a small population might not be enough to support a spa. But a 6 essay can have a few minor errors.

The manager quotes specific statistics about the percentage of residents with Jacuzzis and the average income in Parksboro. She then uses these figures as evidence to support her argument. However, neither of these statistics as presented does much to bolster her claim. Just because 75% of homes have Jacuzzis doesn't mean those homeowners are more likely to go to a pricey spa. For instance, the presence of Jacuzzis in their houses may indicate a preference for pampering themselves at home. Parksboro could also be a planned development in the suburbs where all the houses are designed with Jacuzzis. If this is the case, than the mere ownership of a certain kind of bathtub should hardly be taken as a clear indication of a person's inclination to go to a spa. In addition, the fact that Parksboro's average family income is 50% higher than the national average is not enough on its own to predict the success or failure of a spa in the region. Parksboro may have a very small population, for instance, or a small number of wealthy people counterbalanced by a number of medium- to low-income families. We simply cannot tell from the information provided. In addition, the failure of the manager to provide the national average family income for comparison makes it unclear if earning 50% more would allow for a luxurious lifestyle or not.

The mention of a local store's record-high sales of expensive personal care items similarly provides scant evidence to support the manager's assertions. We are given no indication of what constitutes "record-high" sales for this particular store or what "most costly" means in this context. Perhaps this store usually sells very few personal care products and had one unusual month. Even if this one store sold a high volume of hair- and body-care products, it may not be representative of the Parksboro market as a whole. And perhaps "most costly" refers only to the most costly brands available in Parksboro, not to the most costly brands nationwide. The manager needs to provide much more specific information about residents' spending habits in order to provide compelling evidence that personal care ranks high among their priorities.

To make the case that Parksboro would be a profitable location for Luxe Spa, the regional manager should try to show that people there have a surplus of income and a tendency to spend it on indulging in spa treatments. Although an attempt is made to make this very argument, the lack of supporting information provided weakens rather than strengthens the memo. Information such as whether there are other high-end spas in the area and the presence of tourism in the town could also have been introduced as reinforcement. As it stands, Luxe Spa would be ill-advised to open a location in Parksboro based solely on the evidence provided here.

ISSUE ESSAY

The emergence of the Internet in the 1990s fundamentally changed the way people exchange information. With this dynamic web of technology, people across the world are immediately connected to information—and each other—through the quick click of a button, and normal business operations for major corporations were radically altered. It's true that this industry has had a bumpy beginning—for instance, its spectacular economic meltdown in the late nineties and the advent of file sharing are just a few of the issues raised by the Internet. But while the Internet has created more than its fair share of moral and financial issues for today's consumer, it's unreasonable to assume that the Internet has produced more problems than benefits.

> **EXPERT EXCLUSIVE**
> Note how clearly the essayist showed both that he carefully considered both sides and which one he chose.

As with any new technology, the Internet opened up infinite avenues allowing businesses to streamline operations. Delivery of information is instantaneous. Communication by email eliminates high phone and paper costs and contributes to overall efficiency, saving time that would have been spent mailing documents or holding a long conversation on the phone. Web-enabling transactions—whether buying products for a major corporation or downloading an application to a university—can cut costs in the millions of dollars. A recent article in the magazine *Fast Company* tells how Jonathan Ayers, CEO of Carrier Corp. (the world's largest manufacturer of air conditioners), used the Web to cut costs of over $100 million. In short, the Internet allows companies to execute business quicker and cheaper, which leads to customer satisfaction—and profitability.

> **EXPERT EXCLUSIVE**
> Note how the example is used to illustrate the larger point about streamlined operations.

One of the larger challenges posed by the Internet has to do with intellectual property and copyrighting. Napster was the first to realize a major benefit of the Internet: file sharing. Started in a dorm room, the company's software enabled users to swap digitized music files—for free. Eventually, the software put a significant dent in music sales, becoming a constant worry for music executives and artists alike. However, this isn't the first time the entertainment industry has faced this concern; VHS and audio tape recorders posed the same threat in the seventies and eighties. Companies like Napster and LimeWire simply pushed the entertainment industry to find creative solutions to the copyright issues—creating jobs as they solved the problem. For instance, Apple's iTunes, an online music store where each song costs $0.99, made $70 million in its first year.

EXPERT EXCLUSIVE

It's not necessary to spend this much text rebutting the opposing side's arguments. It doesn't hurt, of course, but it's not required.

The economy certainly suffered a great deal in 1999 and 2000, as the world saw the fast-rising dot-com industry implode, causing a depression that was exacerbated by the tragic events of 9/11. The implosion was not due to the technology of the Internet; rather, it was due to distorted, impractical attitudes and unsound business decisions. Wealth was concentrated in shares of stock that were unrealistically inflated, and as long as the stock prices were high, analysts, investors, and even federal regulators took a lax attitude towards business models and company practices. Therefore, the dot-com bust can be attributed to a lapse in human judgment rather than the existence of the Internet.

Finally, the consumer benefits of the Internet can't be ignored. Small businesses are better able to promote themselves and can introduce their products to a far-reaching audience of consumers. The Internet has simplified and improved things like travel reservations, communication, and customer service. For example, customers of shipping companies like FedEx or UPS are now able to track packages online, rather than making a phone call that eventually leads to a ten-minute wait on hold.

The very definition of *technology* is the application of scientific knowledge in industry or business. A new idea begets other new ideas, and along with them comes a period of adjustment, both for industries and for society. The introduction of the Internet opened up a new world of communication, allowing for business to advance, just as the invention of the car, electricity, and the printing press did for past generations. To eschew new technology because of some of its negative characteristics is to deny the progression of society.

Integrated Reasoning

CHAPTER PREVIEW

Integrated Reasoning

Integrated Reasoning is a new section of the GMAT that will appear in June 2012. Since announcing the new section, GMAC, the organization that owns and administers the GMAT, has released details about the new section's form and content. In this chapter, Kaplan offers practice questions and test-taking strategies based on the information available from GMAC at the time of this book's publication (January 2012).

SECTION FORMAT AND STRUCTURE

THE FORM AND CONTENT OF THE INTEGRATED REASONING SECTION

Integrated Reasoning questions are intended to resemble the types of problems students will encounter in business school and in business and management careers. These questions focus on test takers' ability to solve complex problems using data from multiple sources in a variety of formats.

You will be asked to analyze different types of data (presented in graphs, tables, and passages, among other formats), synthesize data in verbal and graphical formats, and evaluate outcomes and tradeoffs. Some of the data will be in interactive formats, such as spreadsheets. You may need to sort data within columns to determine the answer or click on multiple tabbed pages to view additional information.

There will be 12 questions in the Integrated Reasoning section, and some questions may include multiple parts. For example, a single graph, discussion, or chart may be used as the basis for several parts of one question, and each question may measure a different skill set.

The Integrated Reasoning section will contain four new question types:

- **Graphics Interpretation** questions test your ability to interpret graphs and graphical images.
- **Multi-Source Reasoning** questions test your ability to synthesize data on multiple tabbed pages.
- **Table Analysis** questions ask you to analyze a sortable table or spreadsheet.
- **Two-Part Analysis** questions ask you to answer questions that have two components.

In this chapter, you will find two examples of each type of question set. You can find additional sample questions in your online companion, where your first full-length practice test contains an Integrated Reasoning section complete with answers and explanations. GMAC's sample questions are located at **gmac.com/nextgen**.

Because the questions in the Integrated Reasoning section will vary greatly in form and content, flexibility will be key to success. Since Integrated Reasoning questions draw on many of the same skills you need for the Verbal and Quantitative sections, thorough practice with GMAT questions of all types is the best way to prepare for Integrated Reasoning.

THE LENGTH AND NAVIGATION OF THE INTEGRATED REASONING SECTION

The new Integrated Reasoning section will be 30 minutes long, equal in length to the Analysis of an Issue essay it replaces. The total length of the exam will remain approximately four hours, including two optional breaks.

Navigation on the Integrated Reasoning section, as on the rest of the GMAT, will move forward only. You may not skip questions and go back to them later, and you may not return to questions you have already answered. If you are unsure of the answer, you will need to take your best guess and keep going.

Unlike the Quantitative and Verbal sections of the GMAT, the Integrated Reasoning section will not be computer adaptive. Your performance on one question will not determine the difficulty of the one that follows.

DIFFERENCES IN THE USER INTERFACE

The Integrated Reasoning section will look very different from the rest of the GMAT. Because hands-on experience is the best way to learn the user interface, it is recommended that you practice with these question types in your online companion and at **gmac.com/nextgen**.

In the Integrated Reasoning section, you will see question formats other than multiple-choice. You may be required to select your answer from drop-down menus and true/false options. The new formats are simple and easy to use but will look very different from the multiple-choice questions used in the Quantitative and Verbal sections and will in some respects require different techniques.

You will also need to understand how to navigate through spreadsheets and tabbed pages. For Table Analysis questions, you will be presented with a table of data that can be sorted by using a drop-down menu. Pay close attention to how the drop-down menu operates and make sure to consider all your sorting options. Multi-Source Reasoning questions will require you to integrate information from several tabbed pages.

You will have the use of an onscreen calculator for the Integrated Reasoning section *only*. You will not be allowed to bring your own calculator into the exam. The calculator will perform basic functions and can be accessed by clicking an icon on the screen. A calculator screen will then pop up over the question. Use caution when accessing the calculator. You run the risk of entering information incorrectly, resulting in a wrong answer; moreover, rounding and estimation are often much faster than the time-consuming process of entering multiple large numbers. Use the calculator only when necessary.

THE INTEGRATED REASONING QUESTION TYPES

Now that you have an idea of what to expect in the Integrated Reasoning section, let's look at each of the four question types.

GRAPHICS INTERPRETATION

Graphics Interpretation questions test your ability to interpret and analyze data presented visually in graphs or graphical images. For each question, you are likely to see a graph with accompanying text and several questions.

As with a Reading Comprehension passage, you do not need to absorb every bit of information on the graph to answer the questions. What you *do* need to do is get the gist of the graph and what it contains so that you can efficiently find the information you need. You will then read the question stem, view the answer choices, and use the information in the graph to select the correct answer.

The test maker has provided sample Graphics Interpretation questions featuring scatter plots. The examples in this chapter also feature scatter plots. However, you should prepare yourself to see other types of graphs or graphical images on the test. The test maker's sample questions also included answer choices presented in the form of a drop-down menu. From the menu, test takers must select the number, word, or phrase that accurately completes a statement based on the information in the graph. Here, for ease of reading, the answer choices are presented in multiple-choice format.

Let's take a look at some Graphics Interpretation questions.

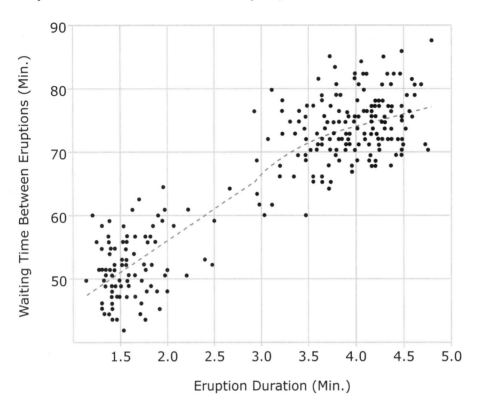

Eruptions of the Old Faithful Geyser, Yellowstone National Park

The graph above is a scatter plot with each point representing the duration of an eruption of Old Faithful, a geyser in Yellowstone National Park, and the time in minutes until the following eruption occurred. The dotted line represents a regression line. For each blank, select the answer choice that correctly completes the statement according to the information in the graph.

1. The relationship between the duration of eruptions and the waiting time between eruptions is _____.

   ○ linear and positive
   ○ nonlinear and positive
   ○ linear and negative
   ○ nonlinear and negative

2. The graph suggests that Old Faithful has _____ of eruption.

   ○ one type
   ○ two distinct types
   ○ more than two distinct types

3. For an eruption of less than two minutes, the maximum recorded wait time is _____ the minimum recorded wait time of an eruption of more than four minutes.

   ○ greater than
   ○ equal to
   ○ less than

Get the Gist of the Graph

Your first step with a question of this type should be to read the paragraph that accompanies the graph. This text is important; it will give an overview of the information the graph contains and how it is presented. On test day, you'll want to take a moment to paraphrase the content of this paragraph to confirm your understanding; the paragraph tells you that the graph shows the behavior of a single geyser, Old Faithful. The graph presents two types of information: how long the eruptions of Old Faithful last and how long it then takes before the next eruption happens. Each point on the graph represents an eruption.

Next, look at the graph itself. Get a bird's-eye view of the graph by reading the title and the labels of the axes and notice how the information from the paragraph is represented in the graph. Here, you'll notice that the duration, or length, of the eruption is measured against the waiting time that follows it before the next eruption. Now look at the units of measurement that correspond to each axis and determine whether the scales are similar. In this case, both axes are measured in minutes, but the scales are very different: The x-axis is measured in 0.5-minute increments, while the y-axis is measured in 10-minute increments. Furthermore, the x-axis starts at 1.0 and ends at 5.0, while the y-axis starts at 40 and goes to 90. Then notice if there are any specific features mentioned in the accompanying paragraph that you see represented on the graph, such as a regression line.

The final step before answering the questions is to look at the data to see if they fall into a general pattern. On this scatter plot, most of the data points separate into two distinct groups. With a pattern this clear, you can anticipate that this observation will be key to answering one or more of the accompanying questions. Making these observations before analyzing the questions will help you answer each question more effectively.

Answer the Questions

Question 1: First, read and paraphrase the question. It asks about the relationship between the duration of eruptions and the waiting time between eruptions, which means that you are looking for a pattern in how the data points are arrayed on the graph. Before attempting to predict an answer, scan the answer choices. Here, you see the words "linear," "nonlinear," "positive," and "negative," which indicate that the pattern may take the shape and slope of a line. The regression line will help you here. There is more than one type of regression line, and in this case, the exact type of regression line has not been specified. You should know, however, that a regression line, whether it's calculated by the least-squares method or a less common method, represents the shift of the points as a whole. The regression line slopes upward—meaning the waiting time gets longer as the explosion duration gets longer. This is a positive relationship—both variables tend to increase and decrease together—so you can narrow the answer down to choices (A) and (B). Next you need to determine whether the relationship is linear or nonlinear by looking at the shape of the regression line. You'll notice that the regression "line" isn't really a line, because its slope changes as the amounts of time get longer. Since the relationship isn't linear through the entire data set, the answer is choice (B).

Question 2: This question might seem a little tricky at first, since the way it's worded might make you think you need to know something qualitative about the types of eruptions the geyser experiences—perhaps something about their magnitude or geological characteristics. But the GMAT will never require you to have outside knowledge beyond high school math and general knowledge of grammar and logic. All the information you need to answer this question is contained in the graph. Begin by paraphrasing the question for yourself: Does Old Faithful have one, two, or more than two distinct types of eruption? As you noticed before, the data points separate themselves into two main clusters. There are a few stray data points scattered outside these clusters, but their number is not significant. Therfore, you can infer from the graph that Old Faithful has two types of eruptions, choice (B).

Question 3: For this question, you need to examine the data in the graph more closely. This statement contains a comparison between two data points: the maximum wait time for an eruption that lasts less than two minutes and the minimum wait time for an eruption that lasts more than four minutes. Note that you're asked to compare the wait times of these two points—that's their height along the *y*-axis. So this question asks you to find these two points and compare their heights. The first point is the highest point to the left of the two-minute line on the *x*-axis, which looks to be just below 65 on the *y*-axis. Now find the second point, the lowest point to the right of the four-minute line on the *x*-axis. The lowest point to the right of that line appears to be just below the 70-minute mark on the *y*-axis. The first point is therefore lower than the second, so you would choose "less than," choice (C).

We've discussed how, before attacking any Graphics Interpretation question, you need to understand what the graph contains and how it is constructed. You can then target your research to answer each question correctly and efficiently. Try using these techniques on the next set of questions.

Public Elementary and High Schools, by State: 2008–2009

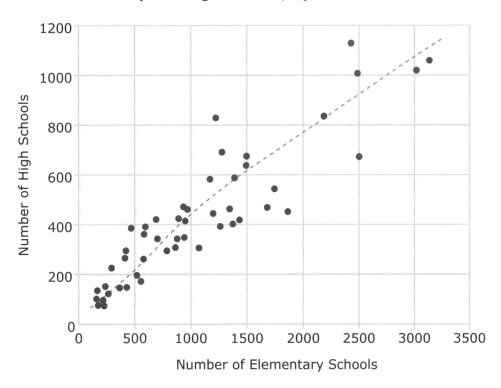

The graph above is a scatter plot with 49 points. The 49 points represent the number of elementary and high schools in 48 U.S. states and the District of Columbia (the number of schools in California and Texas is too large to appear on a graph of this scale). The dotted line represents a regression line. For each blank, select the answer choice that correctly completes the statement according to the information in the graph.

1. The slope of the regression line is _____.

   ○ greater than 1
   ○ approximately 1
   ○ less than 1

2. Approximately _____ percent of the states (including the District of Columbia) represented in the graph have fewer than 500 elementary schools.

   ○ 10
   ○ 25
   ○ 50
   ○ 75
   ○ 90

3. Approximately _____ percent of the states (including the District of Columbia) represented in the graph have fewer than 500 high schools.

○ 10
○ 25
○ 50
○ 75
○ 90

4. The point corresponding to the greatest total number of schools also corresponds to the greatest number of _____.

○ elementary schools
○ high schools
○ both high schools and elementary schools

Get the Gist of the Graph

First, familiarize yourself with the text that describes the graph. It tells you that each data point represents a state (or the District of Columbia) and that each state is plotted on the graph according to the number of elementary and high schools it contains.

Now take a look at the graph to get the big picture. You see that elementary schools are plotted along the x-axis and high schools along the y-axis. In this case, both axes begin at zero, but again the scales of the two axes are different. The axis for elementary schools increases in increments of 500, while the axis for high schools moves up more slowly, in increments of 200. Looking at the points with these increments in mind, you can see that the states generally have more elementary schools than high schools. Again, you see a pattern in the graph; the data points and the regression line trend upward. That pattern makes sense—states that have more kids or higher populations are generally going to need more schools of both types.

Answer the Questions

Question 1: First read the question; then glance at the answer choices. Again, as a Kaplan-trained test taker, you'll see how important it is to look at the answer choices before predicting an answer; this important step will save you time on test day. You'll notice that your only choices are a slope greater than, equal to, or less than 1. Think about what it means for a line to have a slope of 1. It rises at the same rate that it moves to the right. A line with a slope of 1 usually makes a 45-degree angle with the x- and y-axes. The line on this graph looks to be about 45 degrees, so does it have a slope of 1? If you said "no," you just avoided an important trap in this question. A line with a slope of 1 makes a 45-degree angle with the x- and y-axes only when the scales of both axes are the same. But here, the scales are not the same; the numbers on the y-axis move upward much more slowly than the numbers on the x-axis. Remember the formula for the slope of a line:

$$\text{Slope} = \frac{\text{Change in } y}{\text{Change in } x} \text{, or to put it another way, Slope} = \frac{\text{Rise}}{\text{Run}}$$

On this graph, the change in y is a lot less than the corresponding change in x. So the slope will be less than 1. You can test this out quickly using some approximate points from the graph. The regression line is close to the points (500, 200) and (1,000, 400). As the line moves up by 200, it moves to the right by 500. Plugging these points into the slope formula above, you get $\frac{400-200}{1000-500}$, which reduces to $\frac{2}{5}$, a positive fraction less than 1. Choice (C) is correct.

Question 2: This question asks about elementary schools only, so focus on the *x*-axis and count the number of points that fall to the left of the 500 mark on that axis. This number appears to be about 13 points. (The exact number does not matter, as the question is asking for an approximate percentage.) Since you want to know what percentage these states represent out of all the states on the graph, you can set up a fraction: 13 over the total number of data points, which the paragraph accompanying the graph tells you is 49. Using estimation, $\frac{13}{49} \approx \frac{13}{50}$, which when converted to a percentage is equal to 26 percent. The closest answer is choice (B).

Question 3: This question looks similar to the previous question, except it is asking about high schools, which are measured on the *y*-axis. This time, you need to estimate the percentage of schools that are below 500 on the *y*-axis. Rather than counting up all the points below 500, which would be a time-consuming task, count the points *above* 500, find the percentage that those points represent, and subtract that percentage from 100. In this case, you have about 13 points above 500, representing approximately 25 percent of the total (you might recall this same calculation from the previous question). Subtracting this percentage from 100 percent leaves you with 75 percent, or choice (D).

Question 4: Read the question and notice that you are looking for a particular point: the state with the greatest total number of schools. There are two points in the upper right portion of the graph that look like they could be the answer: the point highest on the *y*-axis and the point farthest to the right on the *x*-axis. Also, recall that that the axes are scaled differently and the increments on the *x*-axis increase much more quickly than those on the *y*-axis. The point farthest to the right, then, will have the greatest number of schools. The state represented by this point has the greatest total number of elementary schools, but it does not have the greatest number of high schools. The answer is choice (A).

MULTI-SOURCE REASONING

As its name suggests, Multi-Source Reasoning tests your ability to take information from multiple sources and synthesize it to answer questions. On the GMAT, the information will likely be presented on multiple tabs. You will have to click through the tabs to find the information you need. The data can be in the form of text, charts, or tables and may be presented in a combination of all three.

The information on the tabs may seem overwhelming, so you'll need to approach it similarly to how you approach Reading Comprehension. Get the gist of what the tabs contain and take brief notes highlighting the main points of each tab. Don't try to absorb all of the information at first, but make sure you scan all of the information on each tab so that you'll know where to find it when you answer the questions.

Based on the sample questions released by the test maker at the time of publication, the tabbed pages will be on the left side of the screen, and the questions will be on the right. There may be more than one page of questions, in which case you will click on the Next button to advance to the next page of questions. You can get hands-on experience with tabbed pages in your online companion. Take a few minutes to become familiar with the navigation of this section. Doing so will save you valuable time when answering the questions.

Tab #1 | Tab #2 | Tab #3

Racket City, Australia, is home to a variety of professional sports teams of various degrees of success and national acclaim. Table 1 breaks down the three types of revenue earned from January to June 2010 by Racket City's four major sports teams. Table 2 focuses on the monthly revenue earned from January to June 2010 by Racket City's rugby team, the Racket City Rockets.

Tab #1 | Tab #2 | Tab #3

Table 1: Racket City Sports Team Revenues

January–June 2010

Team	Revenue (in millions of Australian dollars)		
	Venue Revenue	Media Revenue	Other Revenue
Rugby	50.9	75.3	34.9
Australian Rules Football	28.5	31.0	43.7
Soccer	41.4	22.3	17.8
Cricket	9.0	10.2	10.9

Tab #1 | Tab #2 | Tab #3

Table 2: Racket City Rockets Rugby Team Revenues

January–June 2010

Month	Revenue (in millions of Australian dollars)		
	Venue Revenue	Media Revenue	Other Revenue
January	1.1	8.4	2.7
February	11.7	15.6	5.2
March	10.3	18.2	9.1
April	8.2	16.9	8.5
May	14.6	11.9	5.5
June	5.0	4.3	3.9

1. Consider the two months in which the Rockets had the highest media revenues. Use the information from those two months to evaluate whether the following statements can be inferred from the data given. Choose *Yes* if the statement can be accurately inferred; otherwise choose *No*.

Yes	No	
○	○	The Rockets' total media revenue during those two months accounted for more than one-half of the Rockets' total media revenue from January to June 2010.
○	○	The Rockets' average monthly venue revenue during those two months was greater than the January–June 2010 total venue revenue of the Racket City cricket team.
○	○	The Rockets' total revenue during those two months was greater than the January–June 2010 total revenue of the Racket City soccer team.
○	○	From the first of those two months to the second, the Rockets' total revenue decreased by more than 10 percent.

2. During how many months of the January–June 2010 period did the Rockets' total monthly revenue exceed 25 percent of the Australian rules football team's total revenue from January to June 2010?

   ○ 1
   ○ 2
   ○ 3
   ○ 4
   ○ 5

Get the Gist of the Tabbed Pages

We approached Graphics Interpretation by first getting a general sense of how the graph works. Similarly, you need to know what is on each tabbed page before you begin answering Multi-Source Reasoning questions. Take brief notes on the content of each tab as you examine it. On the first tab, the text informs you that you are about to see two tables of information about Australian sports teams. More specifically, the first table will show the revenue of four sports teams in Racket City, and the second table will focus on one of the teams, the Racket City Rockets rugby team, in more detail.

Next, move to the second tab. Here, you are given a table with revenue, in millions of Australian dollars, split among three categories: venue, media, and other. Since there is no total revenue column, you can assume that the "other" category catches all other revenue not caught in the venue and media categories. Thus, by adding the three columns together, you will get the total revenue for each row. Also note that the table shows revenue over a six-month period—January to June—and the rugby team is the highest in every revenue category.

Switch to the third tab to view another table. This one also shows revenue in millions of Australian dollars broken up into the same three categories. It covers the same six-month period. However, rather than compare the revenues earned by different sports teams to one another, this table compares the revenues earned in different months by the same team, the Rockets rugby team.

Answer the Questions

Question 1: When you see a question with multiple parts, be sure to read the introductory sentences carefully. Here, they tell you that you are considering only the two months in which the Rockets rugby team had the highest media revenues. Before reading any further, go back to Tab 3, which shows the Rockets' monthly revenue. The highest media revenues appear in March and April. While you are reading the rest of the prompt, you are *only* concerned with March and April. For each statement you see, you will choose "Yes" or "No" to indicate whether the statement can be accurately inferred from the information in the tabbed pages.

Question 1a: The rugby team's total media revenue in March and April was 18.2 + 16.9 = 35.1 million dollars. Your task is to determine whether that amount is more than half of the total media revenue from January to June, a six-month period. This is a good time to refer to your notes about what's on each tabbed page. On Tab 2, Table 1 shows the rugby team's total media revenue for those six months: 75.3 million dollars. Subtract the March and April revenue from that amount, and you get 75.3 − 35.1 = 40.2 million dollars. Thus, the March and April revenue is less than half, making the answer to this question "No."

You could also approach this question by recognizing that in order for 35.1 million to be more than half of the amount, the other four months must sum to less than 35.1 million. Adding the other four months together, you get 8.4 + 15.6 + 11.9 + 4.3 = 40.2 million dollars, and your answer would again be "No."

In answering this question, you might have noticed something important about these two tables. Both cover the same span of months, so the total of each column of Table 2 is equal to the value of the corresponding column for the rugby team in Table 1. Knowing the way these two tables are related may be of use throughout the remaining questions.

Question 1b: You see that you will need to determine the Rockets' average venue revenue during March and April. To calculate the answer, you need to add the two months together and divide by 2. However, before diving into calculations, finish reading the question. It asks you to determine whether that figure is greater than the total venue revenue of the cricket team for the entire six-month period. You will need to consult both tables to answer this question. Starting with Table 1, you see that the venue revenue of the cricket team is listed at 9.0 million dollars. Make a note of this and go to Table 2, where you can determine the average of March and April. Remember: Your task is to determine whether the average is greater than 9 million. Always look for shortcuts; if both months were higher than 9 million, there would be no need to calculate the average. But in this case, both of the numbers are not higher than 9, so you still need to average them. However, before you launch into calculations, try a more strategic approach. Recall that when you want the average of only two terms, the average will be the point exactly halfway between the two terms. The number 9 is exactly halfway between 8 and 10, but since 8.2 and 10.3 are both slightly higher than 8 and 10, respectively, that means the average of the two terms must be greater than 9. Using this line of reasoning, you can save yourself valuable time and mental energy by answering the question "Yes" without actually calculating the exact average. Of course, you can always determine the answer by performing the calculation: $\frac{10.3 + 8.2}{2} = \frac{18.5}{2} = 9.25$ million dollars. The answer to the question is still "Yes."

Question 1c: This question asks you to compare the rugby team's total revenue for March and April with the soccer team's total revenue for January through June. Again, you need to consult both tables. Start with Table 2 and locate the rows for March and April. Next, add all three columns across to get the total for each month:

Calculate March:	10.3 + 18.2 + 9.1 = 37.6
Calculate April:	8.2 + 16.9 + 8.5 = 33.6
Combine the two:	37.6 + 33.6 = 71.2

Next, you need to use Table 1 to calculate the total revenue for the soccer team to determine whether it is less than 71.2 million:

Calculate soccer:	41.4 + 22.3 + 17.8 = 81.5

The Rockets' total revenue for those two months was not greater than the total revenue for the soccer team from January to June, so the answer is "No."

Question 1d: Start by translating the statement: From March to April, the Rockets' total revenue decreased by more than 10 percent. You just calculated the total revenue for March and April in the last problem, so if you've written your scratch work legibly, there is no need to recalculate. Your task is to determine whether the total revenue decreases by more than 10 percent. As with almost all math problems (both here and in the Quantitative section), there is more than one way to solve. Straightforward math yields: $\frac{37.6 - 33.6}{37.6} = \frac{4}{37.6} \approx 0.10638$, or about 10.64 percent, which is greater than 10 percent. However, notice that you could approach the question more strategically by first figuring out 10 percent of the total March revenues, or 10 percent of 37.6 million, which is 3.76 million. Now look to see whether the difference between the total revenues in March and April is more than 3.76 million. Subtracting 33.6 from 37.6, you get an even 4 million dollars. You've just used a more efficient way to determine that the total revenue decreased by more than 10 percent. The answer to the question is "Yes."

Question 2: This question asks you to calculate each month of the Rockets' total revenue and compare it to 25 percent of the football team's total revenue for the entire six-month period. That's a lot of information, so take it one step at a time. Start with Table 1 and calculate 25 percent of the football team's total revenue:

Calculate total football revenue:	28.5 + 31.0 + 43.7 = 103.2
Multiply by 25 percent:	103.2 × 0.25 = 25.8

Next, go to Table 2 and determine whether the total revenue of the rugby team for each month is greater than 25.8 million. Start with January. Remember to estimate whenever possible to save yourself time. Without doing any calculation, you can see that January's total revenue is far too low. February's total revenue is a close call, so add the different types of revenue together: 11.7 + 15.6 + 5.2 = 32.5 million. That's higher than 25.8 million, so February's total revenue is greater than 25 percent of the football team's revenue. You already know from your work on the previous question that the revenue totals for March and April are well above 25.8 million (and if you didn't remember this fact, you could quickly estimate the totals), so the tally is up to three months with revenue totals greater than 25.8 million. You can likely tell by estimation that May's total revenue is also greater than 25.8 million, but the addition proves it: 14.6 + 11.9 + 5.5 = 32.0 million. You're now up to four months that exceed 25.8 million. You can tell by looking at June's revenue that the numbers are far too low, making the total number of months 4, answer choice (D).

You've learned from working through this set of Multi-Source Reasoning questions that it's crucial to get the gist of each tabbed page and take brief notes highlighting the main points before attempting to answer any questions. Now try applying these techniques to the next set of Multi-Source Reasoning questions.

Email #1 | Email #2 | Email #3

*Email from **project manager** to financial officer*

August 3, 9:43 a.m.

Did all three bids arrive on time last night? We need to minimize delays on construction, so if the contractors have submitted their estimates and our research team has compiled reports on the contractors' histories, we should make a decision on which firm to hire by the end of the day.

Email #1 | Email #2 | Email #3

*Email from **financial officer** in response to the project manager's August 3, 9:43 a.m. email*

August 3, 10:12 a.m.

Appaloosa Construction sent us a bid of $1.35 million. Its bid is the highest of the three, but its track record is spotless; none of the past 10 major projects it has worked on has gone over budget by more than 4%. Breton Construction did manage to underbid them— its representative claims that it can do the project for $1.25 million. However, in the past two years, Breton oversaw two different projects that went over budget by a full 25%. If our project were to exceed Breton's estimate by a comparable percentage, we would run out of funds before completion. Finally, Campolina Construction presented a $1.1 million plan, and its track record is as good as Appaloosa's. Unfortunately, although Appaloosa and Breton can both start tomorrow, Campolina would be unable to begin work until August 25, so we cannot accept Campolina's low bid.

Email #1 | Email #2 | Email #3

*Email from **project manager** in response to the financial officer's August 3, 10:12 a.m. email*

August 3, 10:38 a.m.

Even though Breton's work could potentially cost less than either of the other two, that savings does not justify the risk of being unable to complete the project. But as far as Campolina is concerned, you're not considering the actual cost of a delay. It's true that we are losing money at a constant rate each day we don't start building. But even after factoring in the losses of waiting until August 25, the estimated cost of working with Campolina still ends up $50,000 below Appaloosa's bid.

1. Consider each of the following statements. Does the information in the three emails support the inferences as stated? Choose *Yes* if the statement can be accurately inferred; otherwise choose *No*.

Yes	No	
○	○	The total budget for the project is between $1.4 million and $1.5 million.
○	○	The project manager and the financial officer agree in their evaluation of Appaloosa's bid.
○	○	In making their decision, the project manager and the financial officer considered how much time the contractors would spend on construction.
○	○	The project manager and the financial officer disagree about the best choice of contractors for completing the project.
○	○	The project manager is willing to wait a few days before deciding on Campolina's bid.

2. The amount of money lost each day that construction is delayed is closest to

- ○ $2,500
- ○ $10,000
- ○ $20,000
- ○ $55,000
- ○ $65,000

Get the Gist of the Tabbed Pages

First, look through the tabbed pages and notice the basics: You have three emails, sent minutes apart, between a project manager and a financial officer. Use your Reading Comprehension Passage Mapping skills to create a brief synopsis of each email in your scratch work:

Email 1—project manager to financial officer:

- Asking about the bids
- Start construction as soon as possible
- Make a decision by the end of the day

Email 2—financial officer to project manager:

- Appaloosa—$1.35 million—great track record
- Breton—$1.25 million—usually over budget—would run out of funds before completion
- Campolina—$1.1 million—can't begin work until August 25—can't accept

Think strategically here: Although the financial officer never draws an explicit conclusion about which company should be hired, his opinion is clear. Breton would cause the company to run out of money for the project, and Campolina's delayed start date is unacceptable, so the financial officer must be in favor of Appaloosa.

Email 3—project manager to financial officer:

- Breton—not worth the risk
- Reminder about the cost of delay
- Campolina is still cheaper, even with the delay

It is not necessary to jot down all of the figures and calculations from the email. Just as with Reading Comprehension, if you need the details, they will be there for you to refer to later.

Answer the Questions

Question 1: Notice that you have another set of yes/no questions. As always, you'll want to read the introductory sentences very carefully. Your task is to consider whether the inferences in the questions are supported by the information in the three emails. Critical Reasoning skills will help you here; you must use *only* the evidence in the three emails to determine your answers.

Question 1a: This question asks whether the budget falls within a range, so your task is to find the budget within these emails. Notice that the specific amount of the budget is never stated. The only mention of a budget, or rather of exceeding a budget, is in the second email where the financial officer discusses Breton. This email states that Breton bid $1.25 million, and if this bid is exceeded by 25 percent, the project will go over budget. Remember, to calculate $1.25 million increased by 25 percent, you can't just add the two numbers together: $1.5 million is a trap for test takers who add $1.25 million + $0.25 million. The actual number is $1.25 million × 125% ≈ $1.56 million. The budget falls outside of the given range, making the answer "No." Note that the actual budget *could* fall within the range. For instance, the budget could be $1.49 million, in which case $1.56 million would go over budget. However, since costs of $1.56 million would also break the bank of a $1.52 million budget, there is no way to tell for sure that the budget is less than $1.5 million; the answer is still "No."

Question 1b: This question refers to Appaloosa's bid and the opinions of the two writers. Look back at your notes: The financial officer is in favor of accepting Appaloosa's bid, while the project manager is in favor of accepting Campolina's instead. The two do not agree on their assessment of Appaloosa's bid, making the answer to this question "No."

Question 1c: Read carefully here. Time is discussed, but it is discussed in reference to when the construction can begin, not how long it will take. There isn't any reference to the length of construction in your notes, and if you glance through the three emails, there isn't any information there either. The answer is "No."

Question 1d: This question is very similar to the one asking about Appaloosa's bid. This time, the question is asking whether the two people disagree about the best contractor to hire. The answer to this question, as seen in your notes on the emails, is "Yes." The project manager thinks Campolina is the best choice, and the financial officer is in favor of Appaloosa.

Question 1e: The wording of this statement is tricky, so answer it by doing some careful research in the emails. Here, the question asks whether the project manager is willing to wait a few days to decide. Glance at your notes to find relevant keywords: "decide" is mentioned in the first email, and "delay," or waiting, is mentioned in the third. Going to the first email, you see that the project manager wanted to reach a decision by the end of the day. This seems to contradict the inference given in the question, but don't stop just yet. Check the third email to see whether the project manager changed her mind. In the third email, the project manager discusses waiting, stating that it might be acceptable to wait to begin construction with Campolina—but there is nothing in this email about waiting to make a decision. Thus, you cannot infer that the project manager is willing to wait a few days, and the answer here is "No."

Question 2: By now, you can expect that you'll need to find information in multiple emails to answer this question. Looking at your notes, you see that the delay costs are discussed in the third email. The email states that a constant amount is lost every day that construction is delayed. From the second email, you find that the other two companies can start the next day, August 4, but Campolina can't start until August 25, a delay of 21 days. Next, use the information given to determine how much money is lost in those 21 days.

The third email says that even with the delay, Campolina would cost $50,000 less than Appaloosa's $1.35 million bid, or $1.3 million. That means the cost caused by the delay would be $1.3 million − $1.1 million, or $200,000. To determine the cost per day, calculate $\frac{\$200,000}{21} \approx \$9,524$. However, since the question asks for the number that's "closest to" the amount lost per day, you can save time by estimating. Round 21 to 20 and calculate much more easily that $200,000 divided by 20 is $10,000, or answer choice (B).

TABLE ANALYSIS

Table Analysis questions measure your ability to interpret and analyze information presented in a sortable table similar to a spreadsheet. You will likely see a table, a paragraph of text that describes it, and several questions. The questions may have a variety of answer choice formats. In the sample questions available at the time of this book's publication, the test maker used a true/false format; however, it is possible that other question formats may be used.

Directly above the table, you will see a Sort button that, when clicked, opens a drop-down menu of options that correspond to the column headers in the table. When you select a category from the drop-down menu, the entire chart will be sorted in order based on the category you select. If the information in that column is numerical, it will be sorted from lowest to highest. If the information in that column is text, it will be sorted in alphabetical order. In this book, a working Sort button is obviously not an option, so use the column headings to determine how the tables can be sorted. While working through the questions in this book, decide how you would sort the information before answering each question. To gain experience sorting tables in the test interface, use your online companion.

The key to understanding the table will be the paragraph of text that accompanies it. Read this first to get a general overview of the table's content. Then look at the table itself, paying special attention to the table headings and the drop-down menu.

Now let's look at some Table Analysis questions.

Total Fall Enrollment in Private Degree-Granting Institutions: 2008

Sort By [Select... ▾]

| | Undergraduate | | | | | Postbaccalaureate | | |
| | 4-year | | 2-year | | | | | |
	Total	Not-for-profit	For-profit	Not-for-profit	For-profit	Total	Not-for-profit	For-profit
United States	**3,774,521**	**2,501,181**	**942,306**	**35,351**	**295,683**	**1,356,140**	**1,124,987**	**231,153**
Alabama	58,558	23,229	34,000	0	1,329	7,343	4,128	3,215
Arizona	291,869	3,539	275,530	0	12,800	81,066	4,507	76,559
California	264,775	136,304	76,356	2,375	49,740	147,979	129,522	18,457
Colorado	69,460	18,375	40,733	165	10,187	20,507	13,586	6,921
District of Columbia	71,465	37,967	33,498	0	0	49,061	36,575	12,486
Florida	206,477	106,089	79,732	152	20,504	56,629	48,067	8,562
Georgia	76,356	47,701	23,670	1,057	3,928	23,757	17,940	5,817
Illinois	200,263	134,075	56,676	1,126	8,386	98,568	86,235	12,333
Indiana	88,896	68,677	13,020	495	6,704	16,110	15,652	458
Iowa	113,385	45,397	67,601	151	236	16,487	10,919	5,568
Massachusetts	173,897	166,873	2,800	1,737	2,487	97,339	97,203	136
Michigan	101,252	93,562	4,649	0	3,041	23,507	22,870	637
Minnesota	78,855	50,793	25,723	106	2,233	75,567	21,232	54,335
Missouri	117,735	95,299	12,510	2,275	7,651	49,937	49,298	639
New York	390,435	341,205	24,241	6,575	18,414	168,531	166,449	2,082
North Carolina	75,228	68,524	4,635	572	1,497	18,773	18,039	734
Ohio	146,395	107,277	7,044	1,272	30,802	31,669	30,621	1,048
Pennsylvania	251,369	195,359	17,783	7,492	30,735	83,943	83,372	571
Tennessee	75,283	54,023	8,373	278	12,609	18,187	17,097	1,090
Texas	127,359	92,495	12,935	867	21,062	36,657	33,996	2,661
Virginia	90,439	59,959	24,416	0	6,064	27,236	24,789	2,447

The table above gives the 2008 enrollment in private degree-granting institutions for the 20 states with the highest total enrollment, as well as for the District of Columbia. These statistics do not include state-funded and federally funded public institutions. The data include both for-profit and not-for-profit institutions; enrollment for both of these categories is provided in addition to the total enrollment.

1. Consider the following statements about enrollment in these states (including the District of Columbia). For each statement, indicate whether the statement is *True* or *False*, based on the information provided in the table.

True	False	
○	○	The state with the largest number of students enrolled in for-profit four-year undergraduate programs has the smallest number of students enrolled in not-for-profit four-year undergraduate programs.
○	○	Combined, the two states with the lowest nonzero enrollment in for-profit two-year undergraduate programs have more students enrolled in not-for-profit than in for-profit programs.
○	○	The state with the median number of students enrolled in not-for-profit four-year undergraduate programs also has the median number of students enrolled in not-for-profit two-year undergraduate programs.
○	○	More than half of the students enrolled in degree-granting programs in Minnesota attend for-profit schools.

2. The state with the median number of postbaccalaureate enrollments has approximately how many more students enrolled in not-for-profit postbaccalaureate programs than in for-profit ones?

- ○ 24,000
- ○ 29,500
- ○ 31,500
- ○ 34,000
- ○ 45,000

Get the Gist of the Table

As with Graphics Interpretation questions, your first step should be to read the text accompanying the table. Here, the text explains that the table shows the private school enrollment numbers for various states, as well as for the District of Columbia, in 2008. It also tells you that the table distinguishes between for-profit and not-for-profit institutions.

Next, look at the table itself and read the column headings. The private institutions are split into two main categories, undergraduate and postbaccalaureate, which are further broken down into for-profit and not-for-profit schools. The undergraduate schools are also divided into two- and four-year programs. Total enrollment numbers for undergraduate and postbaccalaureate programs are also provided. This is a lot of information, and you will need to pay attention to how it is organized in order to answer the questions.

Answer the Questions

Question 1a: Many Table Analysis questions ask you to compare pieces of information. Take each question one piece at a time. For this question, you first need to find the state with the largest enrollment in for-profit four-year undergraduate schools. Look at your table and find the column that contains that information. Here, it's easy to see that Arizona has the highest enrollment, with 275,530 students. If you weren't able to see that at a glance, you can sort the table by the for-profit four-year undergraduate column. Now that you have the first piece of information, it's time to find the second. You now know that you're looking for information about Arizona. Sort the table by the not-for-profit four-year undergraduate column, and you'll see that Arizona is by far the lowest, at 3,539 students. Arizona, the state with the largest for-profit four-year undergraduate enrollment, does in fact have the smallest not-for-profit four-year undergraduate enrollment, so the answer is "True."

Question 1b: Notice the keyword "combined" in the question. This means that you will find more than one number and add them together. You are looking for the two states with the lowest nonzero enrollment in for-profit two-year undergraduate colleges. First, sort the table by for-profit two-year undergraduate colleges:

Sort By [Undergraduate 2-year For-profit | ▼]

		Undergraduate				Postbaccalaureate		
		4-year		**2-year**				
	Total	Not-for-profit	For-profit	Not-for-profit	For-profit	Total	Not-for-profit	For-profit
United States	**3,774,521**	**2,501,181**	**942,306**	**35,351**	**295,683**	**1,356,140**	**1,124,987**	**231,153**
District of Columbia	71,465	37,967	33,498	0	0	49,061	36,575	12,486
Iowa	113,385	45,397	67,601	151	236	16,487	10,919	5,568
Alabama	58,558	23,229	34,000	0	1,329	7,343	4,128	3,215
North Carolina	75,228	68,524	4,635	572	1,497	18,773	18,039	734
Minnesota	78,855	50,793	25,723	106	2,233	75,567	21,232	54,335
Massachusetts	173,897	166,873	2,800	1,737	2,487	97,339	97,203	136
Michigan	101,252	93,562	4,649	0	3,041	23,507	22,870	637
Georgia	76,356	47,701	23,670	1,057	3,928	23,757	17,940	5,817
Virginia	90,439	59,959	24,416	0	6,064	27,236	24,789	2,447
Indiana	88,896	68,677	13,020	495	6,704	16,110	15,652	458
Missouri	117,735	95,299	12,510	2,275	7,651	49,937	49,298	639
Illinois	200,263	134,075	56,676	1,126	8,386	98,568	86,235	12,333
Colorado	69,460	18,375	40,733	165	10,187	20,507	13,586	6,921
Tennessee	75,283	54,023	8,373	278	12,609	18,187	17,097	1,090
Arizona	291,869	3,539	275,530	0	12,800	81,066	4,507	76,559
New York	390,435	341,205	24,241	6,575	18,414	168,531	166,449	2,082
Florida	206,477	106,089	79,732	152	20,504	56,629	48,067	8,562
Texas	127,359	92,495	12,935	867	21,062	36,657	33,996	2,661
Pennsylvania	251,369	195,359	17,783	7,492	30,735	83,943	83,372	571
Ohio	146,395	107,277	7,044	1,272	30,802	31,669	30,621	1,048
California	264,775	136,304	76,356	2,375	49,740	147,979	129,522	18,457

The two lowest nonzero enrollment states are Iowa and Alabama. Now that you've identified the two relevant states, determine what the question is asking: Do these states have more students enrolled in not-for-profit than in for-profit programs? In the table, each state has three categories of for-profit and three categories of not-for-profit schools, so you will need to do some calculations.

First, calculate the not-for-profit enrollments in each state. Use your onscreen calculator:

Iowa: 45,397 + 151 + 10,919 = 56,467

Alabama: 23,229 + 0 + 4,128 = 27,357

Then, add the two totals together:

Combined: 56,467 + 27,357 = 83,824 students

Next, calculate the for-profit enrollments:

Iowa: 67,601 + 236 + 5,568 = 73,405

Alabama: 34,000 + 1,329 + 3,215 = 38,544

Combined: 73,405 + 38,544 = 111,949 students

There are more students enrolled in for-profit institutions than in not-for-profit institutions, making the answer to this question "False." However, the calculation process uses up precious time, and it is easy to introduce errors when you are entering so many numbers into the calculator.

Approaching strategically can save you time. You can accurately estimate the answer just by looking at the four-year undergraduate institutions. In Iowa, the for-profit enrollment exceeds the not-for-profit enrollment by about 22,000 students. In Alabama, the difference is about 11,000, leading to a combined difference of about 33,000 in favor of the for-profit side. The two-year undergraduate institutions also have more for-profit students, so the trend continues. On the postbaccalaureate side, there are more enrollments in not-for-profit schools, but given how small the numbers are, there is no way they will balance out the 33,000-student difference you already calculated. Through strategic estimation, you can determine which category has more students in much less time than it would take to calculate precisely.

Question 1c: Here, you are asked again to compare two pieces of information. By now, you should be zeroing in on the keywords in the statement that will tell you how to sort the table. In this case, you are looking for the "not-for-profit four-year undergraduate" column and the "not-for-profit two-year undergraduate" column. Also notice the keyword "median," which appears twice. You need to sort two columns and compare the median numbers. The median number of each set will appear exactly in the middle of the set when all the terms are placed in ascending or descending order. You won't be able to eyeball the median number, so get ready to use the Sort function. First, sort by not-for-profit four-year undergraduate institutions:

Sort By (Undergraduate 4-year Not-for-profit | ▼)

		Undergraduate				Postbaccalaureate		
		4-year		2-year				
	Total	Not-for-profit	For-profit	Not-for-profit	For-profit	Total	Not-for-profit	For-profit
United States	**3,774,521**	**2,501,181**	**942,306**	**35,351**	**295,683**	**1,356,140**	**1,124,987**	**231,153**
Arizona	291,869	3,539	275,530	0	12,800	81,066	4,507	76,559
Colorado	69,460	18,375	40,733	165	10,187	20,507	13,586	6,921
Alabama	58,558	23,229	34,000	0	1,329	7,343	4,128	3,215
District of Columbia	71,465	37,967	33,498	0	0	49,061	36,575	12,486
Iowa	113,385	45,397	67,601	151	236	16,487	10,919	5,568
Georgia	76,356	47,701	23,670	1,057	3,928	23,757	17,940	5,817
Minnesota	78,855	50,793	25,723	106	2,233	75,567	21,232	54,335
Tennessee	75,283	54,023	8,373	278	12,609	18,187	17,097	1,090
Virginia	90,439	59,959	24,416	0	6,064	27,236	24,789	2,447
North Carolina	75,228	68,524	4,635	572	1,497	18,773	18,039	734
Indiana	88,896	68,677	13,020	495	6,704	16,110	15,652	458
Texas	127,359	92,495	12,935	867	21,062	36,657	33,996	2,661
Michigan	101,252	93,562	4,649	0	3,041	23,507	22,870	637
Missouri	117,735	95,299	12,510	2,275	7,651	49,937	49,298	639
Florida	206,477	106,089	79,732	152	20,504	56,629	48,067	8,562
Ohio	146,395	107,277	7,044	1,272	30,802	31,669	30,621	1,048
Illinois	200,263	134,075	56,676	1,126	8,386	98,568	86,235	12,333
California	264,775	136,304	76,356	2,375	49,740	147,979	129,522	18,457
Massachusetts	173,897	166,873	2,800	1,737	2,487	97,339	97,203	136
Pennsylvania	251,369	195,359	17,783	7,492	30,735	83,943	83,372	571
New York	390,435	341,205	24,241	6,575	18,414	168,531	166,449	2,082

There are 21 states in this table, so you will be looking for the 11th state. To calculate which line you're looking for in a table with an odd number of lines, you can always use the following formula: Median $= \frac{\text{Total} - 1}{2} + 1$.

In this example, $\frac{21-1}{2} + 1 = 10 + 1 = 11$. According to the sorted chart, the 11th state is Indiana. Once you know to focus on Indiana, sort the table by not-for-profit two-year undergraduate institutions:

Sort By [Undergraduate 2-year Not-for-profit | ▼]

| | Undergraduate | | | | | Postbaccalaureate | | |
| | 4-year | | 2-year | | | | | |
	Total	Not-for-profit	For-profit	Not-for-profit	For-profit	Total	Not-for-profit	For-profit
United States	**3,774,521**	**2,501,181**	**942,306**	**35,351**	**295,683**	**1,356,140**	**1,124,987**	**231,153**
Arizona	291,869	3,539	275,530	0	12,800	81,066	4,507	76,559
Michigan	101,252	93,562	4,649	0	3,041	23,507	22,870	637
Virginia	90,439	59,959	24,416	0	6,064	27,236	24,789	2,447
District of Columbia	71,465	37,967	33,498	0	0	49,061	36,575	12,486
Alabama	58,558	23,229	34,000	0	1,329	7,343	4,128	3,215
Minnesota	78,855	50,793	25,723	106	2,233	75,567	21,232	54,335
Iowa	113,385	45,397	67,601	151	236	16,487	10,919	5,568
Florida	206,477	106,089	79,732	152	20,504	56,629	48,067	8,562
Colorado	69,460	18,375	40,733	165	10,187	20,507	13,586	6,921
Tennessee	75,283	54,023	8,373	278	12,609	18,187	17,097	1,090
Indiana	88,896	68,677	13,020	495	6,704	16,110	15,652	458
North Carolina	75,228	68,524	4,635	572	1,497	18,773	18,039	734
Texas	127,359	92,495	12,935	867	21,062	36,657	33,996	2,661
Georgia	76,356	47,701	23,670	1,057	3,928	23,757	17,940	5,817
Illinois	200,263	134,075	56,676	1,126	8,386	98,568	86,235	12,333
Ohio	146,395	107,277	7,044	1,272	30,802	31,669	30,621	1,048
Massachusetts	173,897	166,873	2,800	1,737	2,487	97,339	97,203	136
Missouri	117,735	95,299	12,510	2,275	7,651	49,937	49,298	639
California	264,775	136,304	76,356	2,375	49,740	147,979	129,522	18,457
New York	390,435	341,205	24,241	6,575	18,414	168,531	166,449	2,082
Pennsylvania	251,369	195,359	17,783	7,492	30,735	83,943	83,372	571

Again, Indiana is the median (the 11th state), so the answer to this question is "True."

Question 1d: For this question, you'll be looking for information about Minnesota. Specifically, you'll need to find the number of students in that state who attend for-profit schools and then determine whether that number is more than half of Minnesota's total enrollment.

Again, approach strategically here—rather than add all the numbers, do some comparisons. In the four-year undergraduate programs, there are approximately 25,000 more students in not-for-profit schools. Look next at the two-year undergraduate enrollments. These numbers are probably too low to significantly affect the total, so turn your attention to the postbaccalaureate column: Here there are approximately 33,000 more students enrolled in for-profit schools. Because 33,000 is significantly higher than 25,000, you know that there are more students enrolled in the for-profit schools, making the answer to this question "True."

Of course, if you have time to check your work, straight math works here, as well:

For-profit: $25{,}723 + 2{,}233 + 54{,}335 = 82{,}291$

Not-for-profit: $50{,}793 + 106 + 21{,}232 = 72{,}131$

More than half the enrollments in Minnesota are in for-profit institutions, confirming our answer of "True."

Question 2: Here, you first need to find the state with the median number of postbaccalaureate programs. Begin by sorting the "Total" column in this category:

Sort By [Postbaccalaureate Total | ▼]

| | Undergraduate | | | | | Postbaccalaureate | | |
| | **4-year** | | **2-year** | | | | | |
	Total	Not-for-profit	For-profit	Not-for-profit	For-profit	Total	Not-for-profit	For-profit
United States	**3,774,521**	**2,501,181**	**942,306**	**35,351**	**295,683**	**1,356,140**	**1,124,987**	**231,153**
Alabama	58,558	23,229	34,000	0	1,329	7,343	4,128	3,215
Indiana	88,896	68,677	13,020	495	6,704	16,110	15,652	458
Iowa	113,385	45,397	67,601	151	236	16,487	10,919	5,568
Tennessee	75,283	54,023	8,373	278	12,609	18,187	17,097	1,090
North Carolina	75,228	68,524	4,635	572	1,497	18,773	18,039	734
Colorado	69,460	18,375	40,733	165	10,187	20,507	13,586	6,921
Michigan	101,252	93,562	4,649	0	3,041	23,507	22,870	637
Georgia	76,356	47,701	23,670	1,057	3,928	23,757	17,940	5,817
Virginia	90,439	59,959	24,416	0	6,064	27,236	24,789	2,447
Ohio	146,395	107,277	7,044	1,272	30,802	31,669	30,621	1,048
Texas	127,359	92,495	12,935	867	21,062	36,657	33,996	2,661
District of Columbia	71,465	37,967	33,498	0	0	49,061	36,575	12,486
Missouri	117,735	95,299	12,510	2,275	7,651	49,937	49,298	639
Florida	206,477	106,089	79,732	152	20,504	56,629	48,067	8,562
Minnesota	78,855	50,793	25,723	106	2,233	75,567	21,232	54,335
Arizona	291,869	3,539	275,530	0	12,800	81,066	4,507	76,559
Pennsylvania	251,369	195,359	17,783	7,492	30,735	83,943	83,372	571
Massachusetts	173,897	166,873	2,800	1,737	2,487	97,339	97,203	136
Illinois	200,263	134,075	56,676	1,126	8,386	98,568	86,235	12,333
California	264,775	136,304	76,356	2,375	49,740	147,979	129,522	18,457
New York	390,435	341,205	24,241	6,575	18,414	168,531	166,449	2,082

The median state here is Texas. The question asks you to find the difference in enrollments between for-profit and not-for-profit postbaccalaureate institutions in Texas. Additionally, the question is asking for an approximate value, so you can round when calculating the answer. Look at the not-for-profit and for-profit columns in the postbaccalaureate category. Texas has approximately 34,000 students enrolled in not-for-profit postbaccalaureate programs and 2,500 enrolled in for-profit postbaccalaureate programs. That is an approximate difference of 31,500 students. The correct answer is (C).

Remember, for success in Table Analysis, you need to understand what information the table contains and how it is organized before attacking the questions. Pay close attention to the column headings and use the Sort function whenever possible, especially when finding the median. Apply this strategic approach to the next set of Table Analysis questions.

Household Size: Occupied Housing Units by State, 2010 Census

Sort By (Select...   ▾)

	1-person households	2-person households	3-person households	4-person households	5-person households	6-person households	7-or-more-person households	Total households
Connecticut	373,648	443,095	226,658	197,116	84,916	29,348	16,306	1,371,087
Maine	159,533	213,695	84,340	64,010	23,840	7,854	3,947	557,219
Massachusetts	732,263	813,166	417,216	353,676	150,842	51,409	28,503	2,547,075
New Hampshire	133,057	188,923	85,046	70,835	27,365	9,286	4,461	518,973
Vermont	72,233	96,889	39,695	31,210	11,107	3,480	1,828	256,442

The above data is drawn from 2010 census data for New England (excluding Rhode Island, whose data is not available). The table provides the total number of households in each state and the distribution of households of various sizes within each state.

1. Based on the information in the table above, the population of Vermont is approximately

   ○ 194,000
   ○ 256,000
   ○ 440,000
   ○ 510,000
   ○ 600,000

2. Consider the following statements about these states. For each statement, evaluate whether that statement is *True* or *False*, according to the information in the table.

True	False	
○	○	New Hampshire has the largest percent difference between the number of two-person households and the number of three-person households.
○	○	The median household size of all households in the five states combined is two people.
○	○	Of the seven categories of household size, Maine has the median number of households in exactly three.
○	○	In each of the seven categories of household size, Massachusetts has more households than the next highest two states combined.

Get the Gist of the Table

When the tables have fewer rows of information, don't expect the questions to be easier—you will likely have to do as much calculation as you do for tables with many rows, if not more. Begin as always by reading the paragraph of text that accompanies the table. It tells you that the table provides data about the number of households and the size of those households in several New England states.

Now look at the table itself. Note the column headings, which are broken down into households of seven different sizes, plus the total number of households, for each of the five states. Take note of the outliers in the data sets; a quick glance at the "Total" column shows you that Massachusetts has an overwhelmingly large number of households compared to the other states.

Answer the Questions

Question 1: This question asks for the approximate population of Vermont, but be careful: The answer is *not* 256,000, the approximate number in the "Total" column. The GMAT is very unlikely to ask you a question that can be answered with a number directly from the table. In this case, 256,000 is the approximate number of households, not the approximate number of people. To determine population, you must multiply the number of households by the number of people in each household. The calculation works out like this:

$$1(72,233) + 2(96,889) + 3(39,695) + 4(31,210) + 5(11,107) + 6(3,480) + 7(1,828) =$$

$$72,233 + 193,778 + 119,085 + 124,840 + 55,535 + 20,880 + 12,796 =$$

$$599,147$$

This is approximately 600,000, answer choice (E). To simplify the process, you could choose instead to round the numbers to the nearest thousand before multiplying and adding them. Looking at the answer choices, you'll see they are spaced widely enough to make this a safe strategy.

Note that here you multiplied the number in the category "7-or-more" simply by 7; in reality, there are likely some households with more than seven members, but since the number of households in this "7-or-more" category is so small compared to those in the other categories, the difference isn't likely to matter much. Rounding up, you get a total somewhere near 600,000, choice (E).

Question 2a: Here, you are presented with another series of true/false statements. The first one asks you to find the percent difference between two-person and three-person households in New Hampshire and compare that to the percent difference between two-person and three-person households in each other state. Recall that percent difference can be calculated by finding the difference between the two numbers and then dividing that difference by the original. For New Hampshire, that is $\frac{188,923 - 85,046}{188,923} = 0.5498$, or approximately 55 percent. In order for New Hampshire to be the largest, all other states must have a smaller percent difference.

You've got four more states, so think strategically. New Hampshire has more than a 50 percent difference, so if you can determine that a given state has less than a 50 percent difference, there is no need to do the actual calculation for that state. In this way, you know that you can eliminate Connecticut and Massachusetts, since you can look at them and see that there's slightly less than a 50 percent difference (the three-person-household number is slightly more than half of the two-person-household number in each state). To prove this statement false, you only need to find one state that has a difference larger than 55 percent. Let's start with Maine: $\frac{213{,}695 - 84{,}340}{213{,}695} = 0.6053$, or approximately 60 percent. Maine has a higher percentage difference, making this statement "False."

Question 2b: Now you're being asked to determine the median household size for all states combined. To do this, first sum up the total number of households for all five states (the far right column). The total number of households in all five states is 1,371,087 + 557,219 + 2,547,075 + 518,973 + 256,442 = 5,250,796. That means that if you were to place all these households in order according to their size, the median household would be roughly the $\frac{5{,}250{,}796}{2}$ = 2,625,398th household. The household size of the 2,625,398th household is therefore the median household size. To determine the household size of that particular household, you must add the number of households together until you reach the 2,625,398th household. You can start at either end of the table since you are trying to find the middle number. In this case, the bigger numbers are for the smaller households, so it will be quicker to start on the left with the one-person households:

$$373{,}648 + 159{,}533 + 732{,}263 + 133{,}057 + 72{,}233 = 1{,}470{,}734$$

You haven't reached the 2,625,398th house yet, so keep going with the two-person households. This time, you need to add all of the two-person households to the total number of one-person households that you calculated:

$$1{,}470{,}734 + 443{,}095 + 213{,}695 + 813{,}166 + 188{,}923 + 96{,}889 = 3{,}226{,}502$$

Now you have passed the 2,625,398th mark, so the median household must fall somewhere in the group of two-person households. Therefore, you can mark this statement as "True."

Note that you ended up leaping past the median household by more than half a million households. That suggests that the exact numbers didn't matter; when you see a similar problem on test day, you can round to the nearest thousand, or even to the nearest ten thousand, to save time.

Question 2c: This is another question about medians. You need to find the median number for each of the seven categories and determine whether Maine has the median for exactly three of them. It's time to use the Sort function again.

1-person households:

Sort By [1-person households | ▼]

	1-person households	2-person households	3-person households	4-person households	5-person households	6-person households	7-or-more-person households	Total households
Vermont	72,233	96,889	39,695	31,210	11,107	3,480	1,828	256,442
New Hampshire	133,057	188,923	85,046	70,835	27,365	9,286	4,461	518,973
Maine	159,533	213,695	84,340	64,010	23,840	7,854	3,947	557,219
Connecticut	373,648	443,095	226,658	197,116	84,916	29,348	16,306	1,371,087
Massachusetts	732,263	813,166	417,216	353,676	150,842	51,409	28,503	2,547,075

Maine is the median for one-person households. That's one instance so far.

2-person households:

Sort By [2-person households ▾]

	1-person households	2-person households	3-person households	4-person households	5-person households	6-person households	7-or-more-person households	Total households
Vermont	72,233	96,889	39,695	31,210	11,107	3,480	1,828	256,442
New Hampshire	133,057	188,923	85,046	70,835	27,365	9,286	4,461	518,973
Maine	159,533	213,695	84,340	64,010	23,840	7,854	3,947	557,219
Connecticut	373,648	443,095	226,658	197,116	84,916	29,348	16,306	1,371,087
Massachusetts	732,263	813,166	417,216	353,676	150,842	51,409	28,503	2,547,075

Maine is again the median; that makes two instances.

3-person households:

Sort By [3-person households ▾]

	1-person households	2-person households	3-person households	4-person households	5-person households	6-person households	7-or-more-person households	Total households
Vermont	72,233	96,889	39,695	31,210	11,107	3,480	1,828	256,442
Maine	159,533	213,695	84,340	64,010	23,840	7,854	3,947	557,219
New Hampshire	133,057	188,923	85,046	70,835	27,365	9,286	4,461	518,973
Connecticut	373,648	443,095	226,658	197,116	84,916	29,348	16,306	1,371,087
Massachusetts	732,263	813,166	417,216	353,676	150,842	51,409	28,503	2,547,075

New Hampshire is the median; keep going.

4-person households:

Sort By [4-person households ▾]

	1-person households	2-person households	3-person households	4-person households	5-person households	6-person households	7-or-more-person households	Total households
Vermont	72,233	96,889	39,695	31,210	11,107	3,480	1,828	256,442
Maine	159,533	213,695	84,340	64,010	23,840	7,854	3,947	557,219
New Hampshire	133,057	188,923	85,046	70,835	27,365	9,286	4,461	518,973
Connecticut	373,648	443,095	226,658	197,116	84,916	29,348	16,306	1,371,087
Massachusetts	732,263	813,166	417,216	353,676	150,842	51,409	28,503	2,547,075

New Hampshire again; not what you're looking for.

5-person households:

Sort By [5-person households ▾]

	1-person households	2-person households	3-person households	4-person households	5-person households	6-person households	7-or-more-person households	Total households
Vermont	72,233	96,889	39,695	31,210	11,107	3,480	1,828	256,442
Maine	159,533	213,695	84,340	64,010	23,840	7,854	3,947	557,219
New Hampshire	133,057	188,923	85,046	70,835	27,365	9,286	4,461	518,973
Connecticut	373,648	443,095	226,658	197,116	84,916	29,348	16,306	1,371,087
Massachusetts	732,263	813,166	417,216	353,676	150,842	51,409	28,503	2,547,075

Still New Hampshire.

6-person households:

Sort By [6-person households ▾]

	1-person households	2-person households	3-person households	4-person households	5-person households	6-person households	7-or-more-person households	Total households
Vermont	72,233	96,889	39,695	31,210	11,107	3,480	1,828	256,442
Maine	159,533	213,695	84,340	64,010	23,840	7,854	3,947	557,219
New Hampshire	133,057	188,923	85,046	70,835	27,365	9,286	4,461	518,973
Connecticut	373,648	443,095	226,658	197,116	84,916	29,348	16,306	1,371,087
Massachusetts	732,263	813,166	417,216	353,676	150,842	51,409	28,503	2,547,075

New Hampshire is the median frequently in this table. There's only one more chance to find a third instance of Maine being the median.

7-or-more-person households:

Sort By [7-or-more-person households ▾]

	1-person households	2-person households	3-person households	4-person households	5-person households	6-person households	7-or-more-person households	Total households
Vermont	72,233	96,889	39,695	31,210	11,107	3,480	1,828	256,442
Maine	159,533	213,695	84,340	64,010	23,840	7,854	3,947	557,219
New Hampshire	133,057	188,923	85,046	70,835	27,365	9,286	4,461	518,973
Connecticut	373,648	443,095	226,658	197,116	84,916	29,348	16,306	1,371,087
Massachusetts	732,263	813,166	417,216	353,676	150,842	51,409	28,503	2,547,075

No luck. The median is once again New Hampshire.

Maine is the median in exactly two of the seven categories, making the answer to this statement "False."

Question 2d: From your first glance at the table, you noticed that Massachusetts has by far the largest total number of households. So you can guess that Massachusetts might be the greatest in every subcategory. You can sort the tables as before to determine the rankings of the states in each column. For each one, you need to determine whether the number of households in Massachusetts is greater than the second-highest state plus third-highest state. Perform the calculation for each household-size category and, where possible, use approximation instead of calculation:

1-person households: Is 732,263 > 373,648 + 159,533? Yes

2-person households: Is 813,166 > 443,095 + 213,695? Yes

3-person households: Is 417,216 > 226,658 + 85,046? Yes

4-person households: Is 353,676 > 197,116 + 70,835? Yes

5-person households: Is 150,842 > 84,916 + 27,365? Yes

6-person households: Is 51,409 > 29,348 + 9,286? Yes

7-or-more-person households: Is 28,503 > 16,306 + 4,461? Yes

Since Massachusetts is higher than the next highest two states combined in each category, the answer here is "True." Note that you did not need to perform the exact calculations for any of those comparisons; once you identified the correct values to compare, you could estimate the sum of the second-highest state plus the third-highest state and see that in each case, it is less than the number of households in Massachusetts.

Two-Part Analysis

Simply put, Two-Part Analysis will involve questions that have solutions in two parts. In the samples released by the test maker, the Two-Part Analysis questions consisted of a few lines of text and instructions to select numbers in a table based on the given information.

It is likely that you will need to set up an algebraic equation to solve Two-Part Analysis questions. You'll want to begin by first reading the text and identifying the two unknowns. Then, you'll create an equation that relates the two values or variables, for example, x and y. Once you've set up your equation, you can start plugging in answer choices from the table until you find two corresponding values that work together.

Two-Part Analysis can be hard to visualize, so let's take a look at some questions to see how this all works.

1. At University X there are 146 students who are taking economics and 97 students who are taking history.

   In the table below, pick two numbers that are consistent with the information that is given. In the first column, select the row that shows the number of students at University X who are taking at least one of economics and history, and in the second column, select the row that shows the number of students at University X who are taking both economics and history.

Taking at Least One of Economics and History	Taking Both Economics and History	Possible Answers
○	○	78
○	○	83
○	○	104
○	○	154
○	○	160
○	○	164

Get the Gist of the Information

The text in Two-Part Analysis questions is likely to be brief, so read it thoroughly before doing anything else. Here, you are given information about students at University X: the number of students who are taking economics, 146, and the number of students who are taking history, 97. The question asks you to find two numbers: first, the number of students taking at least one of these two subjects and, second, the number of students taking both.

Answer the Questions

Start by solving for the number of students taking at least one subject. The most efficient way to determine this number is to think critically. If you add together the numbers of students taking each subject, you get: 146 + 97 = 243. However, you know from the question stem that some students are taking both; if you rely on simple addition, you end up counting those students twice. Instead, set up an equation that relates the number of students in *at least* one subject, a, to the number of students in *both*, b.

Initial formula: # in at least one = # in Group 1 + # in Group 2 − # in both

Fill in what you know: $a = 146 + 97 - b$

Simplify: $a = 243 - b$

Before you start plugging in the answer choices to find two values that satisfy this equation, think critically: Which number will be bigger? In this case, it has to be a, because all of the students who are taking both, b, must be accounted for in the number of students who are taking at least one, a. With that in mind, move to the answer choices.

Because your equation is $a = 243 - b$, start by plugging b into the equation to determine if there is a corresponding value for a in the chart. b must be the smaller of the two numbers, so start testing at the top of the column with $b = 78$. Your equation is now $a = 243 - 78 = 165$. Do you see 165 in the possible answer choices? Nope. The closest they get is 164, so this is not the correct answer.

Once you know that 78 is not a possible answer for b, move on to 83. Plugging it into the formula, you have $a = 243 - 83 = 160$. Do you see 160 among the possible answer choices? Yes. This question format always has a single solution, so you don't need to test any further answer choices. You have your answer: $a = 160$ and $b = 83$.

Before submitting your answers, make sure that you enter each of your choices in the correct column. It would be unfortunate to do all of the work correctly, get the correct answers, and then not receive credit simply because you selected the numbers in the opposite columns. Look back at your scratch work and remember that a represents the number of students in at least one subject and b represents the number of students in both subjects. You can now be sure that 160 belongs in the first column and 83 belongs in the second column.

Take what you've learned about solving for unknowns by using the given information to set up an equation and apply it to the next Two-Part Analysis question.

2. When car P travels at a constant speed of x miles per hour for 84 minutes, and car Q travels at an average speed of y miles per hour for 168 minutes, car P travels 21 miles more than car Q.

   In the table below, select a value for x and a value for y that together are consistent with the given information. In the first column, select the row that corresponds to the value of x, and in the second column, select the row that corresponds to the value of y.

Value of x	Value of y	Possible Answers
○	○	8
○	○	14
○	○	17
○	○	29
○	○	42
○	○	49

Get the Gist of the Information

When reading the information, remember that your goal is to use it to create an equation that relates the two unknowns, x and y. The text gives information about two cars and states one definitive relationship between them: Car P travels 21 more miles than car Q. That is enough to indicate that your equation will focus on distance traveled. Go back to the beginning of the question stem to determine what you can about the distance the two cars travel.

Answer the Questions

Since the time traveled is given in terms of minutes, and speed in terms of miles per hour, you need to convert to get all of the times expressed in the same units.

$$\text{Car } P \text{ time traveled} = 84 \text{ minutes} \times \left(\frac{1 \text{ hour}}{60 \text{ minutes}} \right) = 1.4 \text{ hours}$$

$$\text{Car } Q \text{ time traveled} = 168 \text{ minutes} \times \left(\frac{1 \text{ hour}}{60 \text{ minutes}} \right) = 2.8 \text{ hours}$$

Since *distance = speed × time*, the distance each car traveled, in terms of x and y, is as follows:

$$\text{Car } P \text{ distance traveled} = \left(\frac{x \text{ miles}}{\text{hour}} \right) \times 1.4 \text{ hours} = 1.4x \text{ miles}$$

$$\text{Car } Q \text{ distance traveled} = \left(\frac{y \text{ miles}}{\text{hour}} \right) \times 2.8 \text{ hours} = 2.8y \text{ miles}$$

Once you have determined the distance traveled by each car, use the information that car P travels 21 miles farther to set up the following equation: $1.4x = 2.8y + 21$. Before moving to the answer choices, be sure to get one variable entirely by itself. In this case, you can divide both sides by 1.4 to get $x = 2y + 15$. You can now plug possible values for y into this equation to see what value for x would result.

To simplify the process of plugging in answer choices, first determine which value is going to be bigger. Since all of the answer choices are positive (as they would have to be, since they represent the speed a car travels), you know that x must be greater than y. This makes sense when you think back to the logic of the problem, which specifies that car P travels a greater distance than car Q in a shorter amount of time.

Use the possible answer choices to start testing for y. As before, since you are starting with the smaller value, y, you will start plugging in numbers from the top of the list and work down. Start with $y = 8$. Substituting into the equation, you get $x = 2(8) + 15 = 31$. Since 31 is not an option in the table, you know that 8 is not the value of y. Next, try $y = 14$. In this case, the calculation would be $x = 2(14) + 15 = 43$. Again, 43 is not one of the available choices, so keep going. If $y = 17$, then $x = 2(17) + 15 = 49$. Since 49 is among the answer choices, it must be the value for x. Again, be very careful when filling in the answer choices. Your answers are $x = 49$ and $y = 17$.

CONCLUSION

As you've seen from the examples in this chapter, Integrated Reasoning questions will measure many of the same skills that you use for the Quantitative and Verbal sections of the test, such as paraphrasing information, finding keywords, determining whether an inference is supported, and using estimation instead of calculation. Regular review of the questions in this chapter, as well as the Integrated Reasoning section on your first practice test in the online companion, will help you get the best score you possibly can on Integrated Reasoning. For more information about the Integrated Reasoning section, go to **testchange.com**, Kaplan's GMAT Test Change Information Center, which will be updated regularly as the debut of the new GMAT approaches.

CHAPTER 12: TAKE CONTROL OF THE TEST

In the earlier parts of this book, we looked at the content covered by the various sections of the GMAT. Then we discussed the test expertise you'll need to move through the sections. Now we turn to the often overlooked topic of test mentality; that is, how to get into peak mental condition for the GMAT.

DEVELOP GOOD MENTAL CONDITIONING

Frame of mind has a lot to do with success. Here's what's involved in developing the best frame of mind for the GMAT.

TEST AWARENESS

To do your best on the GMAT, you must always keep in mind that the test is unlike other tests that you've taken, both in terms of content and in terms of the scoring system. If you took a test in high school or college and got a quarter of the questions wrong, you'd probably receive a pretty lousy grade. But due to the adaptive nature of the GMAT, missing only a quarter of the questions would give you a very high score. The test is designed to push test takers to their limits, so people rarely get every question right. In fact, you can get a handful of questions wrong and still score in the top 1 percent.

In other words, don't let what you consider to be a subpar performance on a handful of questions ruin your performance on the rest. A couple of missed questions won't, by themselves, spoil your score. But if you allow the frustration of those questions to unnerve you, your emotions can snowball out of control, ruining your performance on other questions or on the section as a whole. That kind of thing could potentially do serious damage to your score. Missing a few points won't do you in, but losing your head will.

> **EXPERT EXCLUSIVE**
>
> The questions that you are likely to struggle on most will be the hardest ones—the ones that hurt your score *least* to miss.

The test is designed to find your limits, so it should be challenging. If you feel you've done poorly on a section, don't sweat it. The point is, you must remain calm and collected. Simply do your best on each section, and once a section is over, forget about it and move on.

EXPERT EXCLUSIVE

Don't freak out if a question seems "too easy." It might be experimental. Or perhaps you are just well prepared, have great strategies, and are beating the test! Do your best, get it right, and move on in confidence.

EXPERT EXCLUSIVE

Essays add an hour to the test. You *must* include the essays on your practice tests if you want to develop the proper stamina.

Moreover, don't try to guess which questions are unscored (we're referring to the experimental questions). This practice has gotten countless test takers into trouble. They convince themselves that a certain question is the one that doesn't count and then don't take it seriously. You cannot know which questions are experimental, so treat each one as if it counts. That way, you're covered no matter what.

Stamina

The GMAT is a grueling experience, and some test takers simply run out of gas when they reach the final questions. To avoid this, you must prepare by taking several practice tests in the week or two before the test so that on test day, two 75-minute sections plus two essays will seem like a breeze—at least not a hurricane.

Your online companion includes full-length CATs for just this purpose. If you finish all of the tests included with this book, another option is to download GMAC's Powerprep software, which contains full-length exams and is available free from **mba.com**. The one drawback to the software is that it recycles questions from the *Official Guide to the GMAT Review*, GMAC's own test-prep book, and these questions come from previously administered GMATs. However the CATs on the software should give you a good indication of your score range.

Confidence

Confidence in your ability leads to quick, sure answers and a sense of confidence that translates into more points. Confidence feeds on itself, and unfortunately, so does self-doubt. If you lack confidence, you end up reading sentences and answer choices two, three, or four times to the point where you confuse yourself and get off track. This ruins your timing, which only perpetuates a downward spiral.

If you subscribe to a controlled GMAT mindset, however, you'll gear your practice toward taking control of the test. And when you have achieved that goal—armed with the principles, techniques, strategies, and approaches explained in this book—you'll be ready to face the GMAT with supreme confidence.

The Right Attitude

Those who approach the GMAT as an obstacle and who rail against the necessity of taking it usually don't fare as well as those who see the GMAT as an opportunity. Those who look forward to doing battle with the GMAT—or, at least, who enjoy the opportunity to distinguish themselves from the rest of the applicant pack—tend to score better than do those who resent or dread it.

Take our word for it: attitude adjustment is a proven test-taking technique. Here are a few steps you can take to make sure you develop the right GMAT attitude:

- Look at the GMAT as a challenge but try not to obsess over it; you certainly don't want to psyche yourself out of the game.
- Remember that, yes, the GMAT is obviously important, but contrary to popular belief, this one test will not single-handedly determine the outcome of your life.
- Try to have fun with the test. Learning how to match your wits against those of the test makers can be a very satisfying experience, and the reading and thinking skills you'll acquire will benefit you in business school, as well as in your future career.
- Remember that you're more prepared than most people. You've trained with Kaplan. You have the tools you need, plus the ability to use those tools.

MANAGE STRESS

The countdown has begun. Your date with the test is looming on the horizon. Anxiety is on the rise. The butterflies in your stomach have gone ballistic, and your thinking is getting cloudy. Maybe you think you won't be ready. Maybe you already know your stuff, but you're going into panic mode anyway. Don't freak! It's possible to tame that anxiety and stress—before and during the test.

Remember, some stress is normal and good. Anxiety is a motivation to study. The adrenaline that gets pumped into your bloodstream when you're stressed helps you stay alert and think more clearly. But if you feel that the tension is so great that it's preventing you from using your study time effectively, here are some things you can do to get it under control.

TAKE CONTROL

Lack of control is a prime cause of stress. Research shows that if you don't have a sense of control over what's happening in your life, you can easily end up feeling helpless and hopeless. Try to identify the sources of the stress you feel. Which ones can you do something about? Can you find ways to reduce the stress you're feeling from any of these sources?

> **EXPERT EXCLUSIVE**
>
> Don't know where to begin? Writing down a list of your stressors can help you to get a handle on things.

FOCUS ON YOUR STRENGTHS

Make a list of areas of strength you have that will help you do well on the test. We all have strengths, and recognizing your own is like having reserves of solid gold at Fort Knox. You'll be able to draw on your reserves as you need them, helping you solve difficult questions, maintain confidence, and keep test stress and anxiety at a distance. And every time you recognize a new area of strength, solve a challenging problem, or score well on a practice test, you'll increase your reserves.

IMAGINE YOURSELF SUCCEEDING

Close your eyes and imagine yourself in a relaxing situation. Breathe easily and naturally. Now think of a real-life situation in which you did well on an assignment. Focus on this success. Now turn your thoughts to the GMAT and keep your thoughts and feelings in line with that successful experience. Don't make comparisons between them; just imagine yourself taking the upcoming test with the same feelings of confidence and relaxed control.

SET REALISTIC GOALS

Facing your problem areas gives you some distinct advantages. What do you want to accomplish in the time remaining? Make a list of realistic goals. You can't help feeling more confident when you know you're actively improving your chances of earning a higher test score.

EXERCISE YOUR FRUSTRATIONS AWAY

Whether it's jogging, biking, push-ups, or a pickup basketball game, physical exercise will stimulate your mind and body and improve your ability to think and concentrate. A surprising number of students fall out of the habit of regular exercise, ironically because they're spending so much time prepping for exams. A little physical exertion will help you to keep your mind and body in sync and to sleep better at night.

EXPERT EXCLUSIVE
You can't bring food or drink into the testing room. But you can keep something in your locker to recharge you between sections.

EAT WELL

Good nutrition will help you focus and think clearly. Eat plenty of fruits and vegetables; low-fat protein such as fish, skinless poultry, beans, and legumes; and whole grains such as brown rice, whole-wheat bread, and pastas. Don't eat a lot of sugary and high-fat snacks or salty foods.

SLEEP WELL

Every GMAT problem requires careful critical thinking. And that's the first mental skill to go away when we are sleep deprived. Get a full night's sleep as often as you can during your preparation, especially as test day approaches.

KEEP BREATHING

Conscious attention to breathing is an excellent way to manage stress while you're taking the test. Most of the people who get into trouble during tests take shallow breaths; they breathe using only their upper chests and shoulder muscles and may even hold their breath for long periods of time. Conversely, those test takers who breathe deeply in a slow, relaxed manner are likely to be in better control during the session.

STRETCH

If you find yourself getting spaced out or burned out as you're studying or taking the test, stop for a brief moment and stretch. Even though you'll be pausing for a moment, it's a moment well spent. Stretching will help to refresh you and refocus your thoughts.

PREPARE THE WEEK BEFORE THE EXAM

Is it starting to feel like your whole life is a buildup to the GMAT? You've known about it for years, worried about it for months, and now spent at least a few weeks in solid preparation for it. As the test gets closer, you may find your anxiety is on the rise. You shouldn't worry. After the preparation you've received from this book, you're in good shape for the day of the test. To calm any pretest jitters you may have, though, let's go over a few strategies for the couple of days before the test.

THE WEEK BEFORE THE TEST

In the week or so leading up to test day, you should do the following:

- Visit the testing center if you can. Sometimes seeing the actual room where your test will be administered and taking notice of little things—such as the kind of desk you'll be working on, whether the room is likely to be hot or cold, etc.—may help to calm your nerves. And if you've never been to the test center, visiting beforehand is a good way to ensure that you don't get lost on test day. If you can go on the same day of the week and at the same time of day as your actual test, so much the better; you'll be able to scope out traffic patterns and parking. Remember, you must be on time—the computers at the test centers are booked all day long.

- Practice working on test material, preferably a full-length test, at the same time of day that your test is scheduled for as if it were the real test day.

- Time yourself accurately so you don't feel as though you are rushing on test day.

- Evaluate thoroughly where you stand. Use the time remaining before the test to shore up your weak points, rereading the appropriate sections of this book. But make sure not to neglect your strong areas; after all, this is where you'll rack up most of your points.

THE DAY BEFORE THE TEST

Try to avoid doing intensive studying the day before the test. There's little you can do to help yourself at this late date, and you may just wind up exhausting yourself and burning out. Our advice is to review a few key concepts, get together everything you'll need for test day, and then take the

> **EXPERT EXCLUSIVE**
>
> Stretching is especially important during the Verbal section—it's easy to spend a long time just staring at the screen, tiring your eyes. Taking them away from the screen for a few seconds helps a great deal.

> **EXPERT EXCLUSIVE**
>
> Cramming won't work! It can induce test-taking burnout. On the day before the test, just relax and store energy.

⬆ GO ONLINE

Download your online Study Sheet and bring it with you for review as you travel to the test center.

night off entirely. Go to see a movie, rent a video, or watch some TV. Try not to think too much about the test.

THE DAY OF THE TEST

Leave early, giving yourself plenty of time. Read something to warm up your brain; you don't want the GMAT to be the first written material your brain tries to assimilate that day. Dress in layers for maximum comfort. That way, you'll be able to adjust to the testing room's temperature. In traveling to the test center, leave yourself enough time for traffic or mass transit delays.

Be ready for a long day. Total testing time, remember, is three and a half hours. When you add the administrative paperwork before and after, and the two 8-minute breaks, you're looking at an experience of four hours or more.

Here are some other last-minute reminders to help guide your work on test day:

EXPERT EXCLUSIVE

Getting super-hard problems in the middle is a great sign! It means that you got most of the early problems right and are in the highest-value question set with much of the test still to come. You're on your way to a great score!

- Read each question stem carefully and reread it before making your final selection.
- Don't get bogged down in the middle of any section. You may find later questions more to your liking. So don't freak. Eliminate answer choices, guess, and move on.
- Don't fall behind early. Even if you get most of the first 10 questions right, you'll wind up rushing yourself into enough errors that you cancel out your early success. Keep a steady pace throughout the test and finish each section strong, avoiding the penalty for not completing all the questions.
- Don't bother trying to figure out which questions are unscored. It can't help you, and you might very well be wrong. Instead, just determine to do your best on every question.
- Confidence is key. Accentuate the positives and don't dwell on the negatives! Your attitude and outlook are crucial to your performance on test day.
- During the exam, try not to think about how you're scoring. It's like a baseball player who's thinking about the crowd's cheers and the sportswriters and his contract as he steps up to the plate: there's no surer way to strike out. Instead, focus on the question-by-question task of picking an answer choice. The correct answer is there. You don't have to come up with it; it's sitting right there in front of you!

CANCELLATION AND MULTIPLE SCORES POLICY

Unlike many things in life, the GMAT allows you a second chance. If you finish the test feeling that you've not done as well as you can, you always have the option to cancel your score—before you see the score, of course. Immediately after you complete the test—but before you view your scores—a message will appear, asking if you want to cancel your scores. You cannot cancel your scores after they are displayed or reported to you.

Canceling a test means that it won't be scored. It will just appear on your score report as a canceled test. No one will know how well or poorly you really did—not even you.

If you cancel your scores,

- they cannot be reinstated.
- you will not receive a refund for the test.
- a score cancellation notice will be sent to you and the schools you selected as score recipients.
- the score cancellation will remain a part of your permanent record and will be reported on all future score reports.

If you do not cancel your scores,

- you can choose to see and print a copy of your unofficial scores for the multiple-choice sections of the GMAT.
- an official score report, including the scores for the AWA, will be available online and sent to your designated schools 20 days after you take the test.

When deciding whether to cancel your score, a good rule of thumb is to make an honest assessment of whether you'll do better on the next test. Wishful thinking doesn't count; you need to have a valid reason to believe that the next time will be different. Remember, no test experience is going to be perfect, and the test is designed to find the limits of your ability. Two legitimate reasons to cancel your test are illness and personal circumstances that cause you to perform unusually poorly on that particular day. Also, if you feel that you didn't prepare sufficiently, then it may be advisable to cancel your score and approach your test preparation a little more seriously the next time.

But keep in mind that test takers historically underestimate their performance, especially immediately following the test. They tend to forget about all of the things that went right and focus on everything that went wrong. So unless your performance is terribly marred by unforeseen circumstances, don't cancel your test. Just remember, cancellations are permanent. Once you hit that button, you can't change your mind.

If you take more than one test without canceling, then the three most recent scores will show up on each score report, so the business schools will see them all. Most business schools count only your highest GMAT score, but a few may average your scores. Check with individual schools for their policies on multiple scores.

> **EXPERT EXCLUSIVE**
> After all the hard work you've done preparing for and taking the GMAT, make sure you celebrate afterward—and start thinking about all of the great times you'll be having at the business school of your choice!

> **EXPERT EXCLUSIVE**
> Because the test is adaptive, you are practically guaranteed to feel as if you struggled on it. That doesn't mean that you did badly! Only cancel your scores if you know objectively that you couldn't have been at your best—you're sick, you didn't sleep the night before, etc.

## Part Three

GETTING INTO BUSINESS SCHOOL

CHAPTER 13: WHERE AND WHEN TO APPLY

When considering where to apply to business school, ask yourself two questions:

(1) What schools should I consider, regardless of my chances?

(2) Of those schools, where can I realistically get in?

CONSIDERING WHERE TO APPLY

The decision about where to go to business school should not be taken lightly. It will determine your daily life for the next several years and will influence your academic and career paths for years to come. Many people let a professor or mentor or rankings in popular magazines influence their choice of school—only to find out that the school was a wrong choice for their personal needs. So by putting in some work today, you'll be ensured a happy business school choice tomorrow. Let's look at some of the factors that you'll need to consider.

OVERALL REPUTATION

Each year, several publications release rankings of business schools. You should start by reviewing these rankings, because they'll provide a frame of reference for how different schools are regarded in the marketplace.

Don't place too much stock in the rankings, though you should consider a program's overall reputation. The better your school is regarded in the marketplace, the better your job prospects are likely to be upon graduation. You will notice that there is a general correlation between schools' rankings and starting salaries.

Find out which programs are highly regarded in the areas that interest you. Which schools are viewed as responsive to students' changing needs, and which schools are seen as less responsive? What schools are "hot"? How have they earned that designation?

TEACHING METHODS

Business school professors teach using the case method, lectures, or, in most cases, a combination of both. Everyone learns differently, so select a school with a teaching environment that allows you to thrive.

A lecture-based classroom is, in all likelihood, what you experienced as an undergraduate. The professor provides information, and interaction between the students and the professor, or among the students, is controlled and generally limited. In a case-method environment, on the other hand, the professor doesn't lecture but rather facilitates an open dialogue with the students by asking probing questions and giving students most of the "air time."

Each class revolves around actual business situations, and students are cast in the role of decision maker. You could be given the facts about a struggling business, for instance, and then placed in charge of developing a plan for business improvement. The case method is particularly popular at programs that specialize in teaching general management. Harvard Business School and Virginia's Darden School are two of the better-known schools that use the case method as their principal teaching tool.

Is one teaching method inherently better than the other? That depends on you. Some students prefer the more controlled, structured environment of traditional lectures. Others thrive on the case method, in which a less formal, no-holds-barred, open forum encourages many viewpoints but provides no single answer.

Another issue to keep in mind is that in a case-method classroom, as much as half of your grade will be based on class participation. If you are someone who needs no encouragement to air your views, you'll have no problem. If, however, you think you'd be less than eager to participate in this type of forum, you should seriously consider whether it would be the right environment for you.

Most programs enhance the value of your educational experience by exposing you to real-world situations where possible. For example, many schools will encourage students to undertake a field study in their second year. Business simulations, computer-based programs that enable you to test your decision-making skills, are also a popular teaching tool.

CLASS AND SECTION SIZE

Class size and structure are two factors that will have a significant impact on your business school experience. Some students prefer the intimacy of a smaller class and the opportunity to get to know everyone. Others prefer the energy of a larger class and the increased resources and facilities that it can support.

Many programs divide the class into sections, also known as cohorts, and have students take all or most of their first-year classes with that same group. In fact, at some schools, section members actually stay in the same classroom, and the professors rotate among rooms.

There are several advantages to the section concept. By working with the same classmates day after day, you build a camaraderie borne out of a shared, often intense, first-year experience. You get to know each other in a way that is not possible in a more traditional classroom structure. More likely than not, you'll forge lasting relationships with your section mates. The downside of the section system is that you have less exposure to classmates who are not in your section. Organized club activities, however, enable you to meet other students outside the classroom who share your interests.

SCHOOL LOCATION

The two key questions that you should consider regarding a school's location are these: How will it affect the overall quality of your business school experience, and how will it affect your employability? Some students prefer an urban setting. Others prefer a more rustic environment. Some want their business school to be part of the overall university campus; others would like a separate campus.

Geography may be an important criterion for you. Perhaps you're constrained by a spouse's job. Or perhaps you know where you want to live after graduation. You won't be limited in where you can find a job if you graduate from a school that has a national reputation, but if you attend a school with more of a regional name, be sure that it is highly regarded in that area.

CURRICULUM

To maximize the value of your business school experience, be sure that a school's curriculum matches up with your own interests. If your primary interest is general management, then seek out those programs whose strengths include general management.

The top-tier schools tend to be strong in all areas, but even the elite programs are viewed as having particular specialties. For example, Kellogg is thought to be especially strong for marketing, Wharton for finance, and Harvard for general management. Of course, many Harvard MBAs pursue finance careers; Wharton grads, marketing; and Kellogg grads, general management. You should, nevertheless, familiarize yourself with the general marketplace perceptions about the programs you're considering. It will help you think more clearly about the selection process.

FACULTY

The quality of a school's faculty is important and is reflected in each program's reputation. An important question to ask, though, is, Will you get to take classes with a school's star professors? With the proliferation of executive education programs, top teachers at many highly ranked schools are sometimes assigned to teach executive education students instead of MBAs. If one of your prime motivations in attending a certain program is to take classes from specific professors, make sure that you will have that opportunity.

COMPETITIVENESS

By its nature, and by the nature of the students it attracts, business school fosters a competitive environment. But business is also about cooperation—working together toward a common goal. Many schools have addressed this tension by introducing team-based learning into their curricula.

Some schools have reputations for fostering an intense environment, whereas others are considered more supportive. Try not to base your perceptions about the academic environment at various schools on the schools' reputations alone. Sit in on first-year classes to assess the dynamics. Ask yourself: Do the students work well together? Do they support each other? Do they treat each other with respect, even when they disagree? Does the professor facilitate a positive learning atmosphere? Find out about each school's grading system. When a program grades on a forced curve, some students feel motivated, and others feel unwanted pressure. How do you think you'd react to it?

When you visit a school, talk to students to learn how they feel about the environment. You'll probably get a variety of viewpoints, but there's no better way to get a feel for what a school is like, what the students are like, and how you will fit in there.

PLACEMENT

When you get right down to it, the main purpose of attending business school is to enhance your career prospects, both short- and long-term. Look into each school's placement records to find out the following:

- How many companies recruit on campus?
- What kinds of companies recruit on campus?
- What percentage of the class has job offers by graduation?
- What is the breakdown of jobs by industry?
- What is the average starting salary?

Try not to overemphasize the significance of average starting salary when you evaluate programs. Though there is a correlation between the top-ranked schools and starting salaries, other factors determine your starting salary and your overall attractiveness to prospective employers. Some recruiters place a high value on your pre–business school experience. Others care more about your B-school academic record.

Moreover, some industries—notably management consulting and investment banking—pay at the high end of the spectrum. So the salary statistics of schools that send a high percentage of students into these fields are skewed upward.

If you enroll in a traditional two-year program, learn about summer job opportunities between your first and second year. For one thing, the money will be helpful. For another, your summer position can give you firsthand experience in a new job or industry that you can leverage when you graduate. Many summer jobs ultimately lead to full-time offers. Plus, a substantive summer experience will make you a more attractive job candidate for prospective employers.

Finally, don't just look at the first jobs that a school's graduates take. Where are they in 5, 10, and even 25 years? Your career is more like a marathon than a sprint. So take the long view. A strong indicator of a school's strength is the accomplishments of its alumni.

CLASS PROFILE

Because much of your learning will come from your classmates, especially in case-method classes, consider the makeup of your class. A school with a geographically, professionally, and ethnically diverse student body will expose you to far more viewpoints than will a school with a more homogeneous group.

To get a feel for the class profile of a particular school, look at these readily available statistics:

- Undergraduate areas of study
- Percentage of international students
- Percentage of women
- Percentage of minorities
- Percentage of married students
- Average years of work experience
- Types of companies for which students worked
- Average age and age range of entering students

Let's look at average age. Over the past few decades, students attending business school have been getting older. Currently, the average age of the entering student is approximately 27 at many of the top schools. But the average is a little misleading because it consists of many 26-year-olds and significantly fewer 30-, 40-, and 50-year-olds who skew the average upward. So if you're an older applicant, ask yourself how you will fit in with a predominantly younger group of students. For many, the fit is terrific. For others, the transition is tougher.

NETWORKING

Forging relationships—with your section mates, your classmates, and, in a larger sense, all the alumni—is a big part of the business school experience. One of the things that you'll take with you when you graduate, aside from an education, a diploma, and debt, is that network. And whether you thrive on networking or consider it a four-letter word, it's a necessity. At some point, it may help you advance your career, land a piece of business, or perhaps even finance a new venture.

Many programs have large, organized networks that you can access. This is a strong selling point for those schools. As with any other single factor, don't make networking potential your sole criterion but do keep it in mind as you evaluate programs.

WORKLOAD

Think about how hard you are prepared to work. It's generally true that the more effort you put in, the more you'll gain, but some programs really pile it on first-year students. That can limit the amount of time and energy that you'll have left to devote to outside activities.

For students with families, the first year of B-school requires not just a sacrifice of income but of time that you can spend with your spouse or children. Don't underestimate how all-encompassing your first year will be. At some point, this can be a strain on even the strongest relationships. Fortunately, the second year tends to be more manageable.

If you enroll in a part-time program, the time constraints may be even more severe because you have to handle the rigors of your course load on top of your job.

QUALITY OF LIFE

Your business school experience will extend far beyond your classroom learning, particularly for full-time students. Find out as much as you can about the schools that interest you. What kind of city life is available nearby? What kind of recreational facilities are offered? Regardless of your interests, your ability to maintain balance in your life in the face of a rigorous academic challenge will help you keep a healthy outlook.

Housing is another quality-of-life issue to consider. Is campus housing available? Is off-campus housing convenient? Is it affordable? Where do most of the students live?

Quality of life is also an important consideration for spouses and significant others, especially if school requires a move to a new city. When the first year takes over your life, your spouse may feel left out. Find out what kind of groups and activities there are for partners. For example, are there any services to help your spouse find employment?

FULL-TIME VERSUS PART-TIME

In a full-time program, you can focus your energy on your studies to maximize your learning. You're also likely to meet more people and forge closer relationships with your classmates. Many programs are oriented toward the full-time student, though they may offer part-time programs. A part-time schedule may also make it difficult for you to take classes with the best professors.

There are, however, many compelling reasons to attend business school part-time. The most obvious reason is that you are working full-time. Perhaps your employer will help subsidize you if you continue working. Or perhaps you don't want to abandon the career track that you're on.

Though some prospective employers may place more value on an MBA earned full-time, others recognize and respect the commitment required to complete an MBA part-time. If you decide to attend business school part-time, the good news is that there are many fine programs from which to choose.

MBA VERSUS EXECUTIVE EDUCATION

For most applicants with two, three, or four years of work experience, executive education is not a feasible option because they don't have enough experience. But if you are a middle manager or a small-business owner with a need for functional training, executive education programs may be worth exploring.

Executive education programs, a growing area for many business schools, essentially bring together individuals with similar educational needs and provide a focused, intensive learning experience. For example, middle managers with 10 to 15 years experience may attend a 12-week, full-time program to study such core subjects as marketing, finance, operations, and management accounting. It's sort of a mini MBA.

If the MBA is important for you as a credential, be aware that executive education programs generally do not award MBAs. But if your organization will be sponsoring you and you plan to stay there, this may be an invaluable career opportunity that you don't want to pass up.

If you are looking for training in very specific areas, then perhaps much of an MBA program's curriculum would not be of interest to you, and executive education would make more sense. So although executive education is not a substitute for an MBA, you may find it worth considering.

CONSIDERING WHERE YOU CAN GET IN

Now that you've developed a list of schools that meet your needs, you should take an objective look at your chances of getting into them.

ASSESS YOUR CHANCES

A good way to get a sense of how business schools will perceive you is to make up a fact sheet with your GMAT scores (or projected scores), your GPA, and your work experience. Outside activities will contribute to the overall "score" that admissions officers will use to evaluate you, but let's stick with the raw data for now.

The next step is to find a current source of information about B-school programs. Several guides are published every year that provide data about acceptance rates for given years, median GPA, and GMAT scores. The school of your dreams may not care very much about your GPA, but it might be very interested in your GMAT score. Make sure you find out what your target school prioritizes in its search for worthy applicants.

One of the best ways to gauge whether you're in contention for a certain program is to compare your numbers to its. You don't need to hit the nail on the head. *Median* means "average," so some applicants do better or worse than the GMAT score or GPA cited. And remember those other factors—most importantly, your work experience—that add up to make you a desirable applicant. Comparing numbers is merely a good way to get a preliminary estimate of your compatibility with the schools of your choice.

PICK "SAFE" SCHOOLS

Now that you have some idea of where you fall in the applicant pool, you can begin to make decisions about your application strategy. Some students waste their time and money with a scattergun approach, shooting off applications to a host of schools.

No matter what your circumstances, choose at least one school that is likely to accept you. It should be one that fits your academic goals and your economic circumstances. If your GMAT scores and GPA are well above a school's median scores and you don't anticipate any problems with other parts of your record or application, you've probably found a safe school.

PICK "WISHFUL THINKING" SCHOOLS

Reach high and apply to one or two very competitive programs. You may be surprised! Some people underestimate their potential and apply only to "sure thing" schools. It would be disappointing if you were to end up at one of those schools and discover that it didn't provide the rigorous training you wanted.

DECIDING WHEN TO APPLY

With business school applications on the rise again, the issue of when to apply for admission has become very important. There are perfect times to begin and end the application process. You should begin a year before you plan to enter school. Find out the following essential dates as early as possible and incorporate them into your own personal application schedule:

- Standardized test registration deadlines
- Transcript deadlines (Some schools send out transcripts only on particular dates.)
- Letters of recommendation deadlines
- Application deadlines (Submit your application as early as possible to ensure that you get a fair and comprehensive review.)
- Financial aid forms deadlines (Federal/state programs, universities, and independent sources of aid all have definite deadlines.)

SETTING UP AN APPLICATION SCHEDULE

The following seasonal schedule is organized to help you understand how to proceed through the admissions process.

Summer

- Request applications from schools. If they're not available yet, ask for last year's so you can get a feel for the questions you'll have to answer.
- Write drafts for your essays and talk them over with others.
- Browse through business school catalogs and collect information on different grants and loans. Create your own B-school financial aid library.
- Consider registering for the GMAT in the fall. This will give you plenty of time to submit your scores with your application.
- Research your options for test preparation. Take the test included in this book to give yourself a good idea of where you stand with regard to the GMAT.

Early Fall

- Ask for recommendations. Make sure that your recommenders know enough about you to write a meaningful letter. Once your recommenders have agreed to write a recommendation, let them know when deadlines will be so you can avoid any timing conflicts.

Late Fall

- Take the GMAT.
- Request applications from schools, if you haven't already done so.
- Request institutional, state, and federal financial aid materials from school aid offices.
- Request information on independent grants and loans.
- Order transcripts from your undergraduate (and any graduate) institution(s).

Winter

- Fill out applications. Submit them as early as possible.
- Fill out financial aid applications. Submit these early as well.
- Make sure your recommendation writers have the appropriate forms and directions for mailing. Remind them of deadline dates.

Spring

- Sit back and relax. Most schools indicate how long they will take to inform you of their decision. This is also a crucial time to solidify your financial plans as you begin to receive offers of aid (with any luck).

The timing described here is rough, and you needn't follow it exactly. The most important thing is to know the strict deadlines well in advance so that you'll be able to give your application plenty of quality time.

USEFUL BUSINESS SCHOOL RESOURCES

Here are some resources you should find helpful in your quest for business school information.

MBA FORUMS

These MBA school fairs, sponsored by the GMAC each year, are a wonderful resource and an excellent way to browse the programs. Representatives of more than 75 graduate management schools from the United States and abroad are on hand to answer questions. The schedule typically includes Forums in New York, Chicago, San Francisco, Los Angeles, and Washington, D.C., among other cities.

Web: **mba.com/mba/schoolsandprograms**

GRADUATE MANAGEMENT ADMISSION SEARCH SERVICE

A free service, the GMASS makes your name available to schools whose specifications for applicants match your profile, as per your GMAT registration information. This automatic service will send you mailings from schools about their MBA programs, admissions procedures, and financial aid.

Web: **gmass.org**

MBA PROGRAM INFORMATION

The MBA Program Information Site is an international business school site containing a database with details on 2,500 MBA programs from 1,290 business schools and universities in 123 countries, as well as advice pages for the prospective candidate.

Web: **mbainfo.com**

OFFICIAL GMAT WEBSITE

This site includes links to business schools on the Web, a school search engine, and information about the GMAT. You can also register online for the GMAT here.

Web: **mba.com**

MBA DEPOT

This site provides an open line of communication between students and alumni to share experiences and resources for B-school.

Web: **mbadepot.com**

eSTUDENTLOAN

This free site provides information about and online applications for student loans. You can instantly compare loans that match your specific needs.

Web: **estudentloan.com**

FINAID

This site has everything you ever wanted to know about financial aid, including free scholarship and fellowship search services and descriptions of financial aid sources. Sponsored by the National Association of Student Financial Aid Administrators.

Web: **finaid.org**

SUMMARY

When considering where to apply, evaluate the following:

- Overall reputation
- Teaching methods
- Class and section size
- School location
- Curriculum
- Faculty
- Competitiveness
- Placement
- Class profile
- Networking
- Workload
- Quality of life
- Full-time versus part-time
- MBA versus executive education

When considering where you can get in, look at these sections:

- Assess Your Chances
- Pick "Safe" Schools
- Pick "Wishful Thinking" Schools

CHAPTER 14: **HOW TO APPLY**

Your first step is to access the application forms online from the various schools that you've selected. Once you begin the applications, you'll notice one thing quickly: no two applications are exactly alike. Some ask you to write one essay or personal statement, and others may ask for three or more. Some have very detailed forms requiring extensive background information; others are satisfied with your name and address and little else.

Despite these differences, most applications follow a general pattern with variations on the same kinds of questions. So read this section with the understanding that, although not all of it is relevant to every application, these guidelines will be valuable for just about any business school application that you'll encounter.

HOW SCHOOLS EVALUATE APPLICANTS

Each business school has its own admissions policies and practices, but all programs evaluate your application on a range of objective and subjective criteria. Regardless of which schools you are pursuing, understanding how admissions officers judge your candidacy can give you a leg up on the competition.

Generally, all admissions officers use the application process to measure your intellectual abilities, management skills, and personal characteristics. When you submit your application, admissions officers will evaluate the total package. Most admissions officers look for reasons to admit candidates, not for reasons to reject them. Your challenge, therefore, is to distinguish yourself positively from the other candidates.

INTELLECTUAL ABILITY

To assess your intellectual ability, admissions officers look at two key factors: your academic record and your GMAT score.

Academic Record

Your GPA is important, but it's just part of the picture. Admissions officers will consider the reputation of your undergraduate institution and the difficulty of your courses. Admissions officers are well aware that comparing GPAs from different schools and even different majors from the same school is like comparing apples and oranges. So they'll look closely at your transcript. Do your grades show an upward trend? How did you perform in your major? How did you fare in calculus and other quantitative courses?

Admissions officers focus primarily on your undergraduate performance, but they will consider graduate studies and nondegree coursework that you have completed. Be sure to submit those transcripts.

If you have a poor academic record, it will be tougher to get into a top school but by no means impossible. Your challenge is to find other ways to demonstrate your intellectual horsepower. A high GMAT score, intelligently written essays, and recommendations that highlight your analytical abilities will help. If your record does not show any evidence of quantitative skills, you should consider taking courses in accounting and statistics to demonstrate your aptitude.

GMAT Score

An integral part of the admissions process at virtually all schools, the GMAT measures general verbal and quantitative skills and is designed to predict academic success in the first year of a graduate business school program.

When admissions officers review your GMAT score, they'll look primarily at your overall score. However, they'll also look at your various subscores, particularly if they have any questions about your abilities in either area. If you've taken the GMAT more than once, schools will generally credit you with your highest score, though some may average the scores or take the most recent.

Used by itself, the GMAT may not be a great predictor of academic performance, but it is the single best one available. The GMAT does not measure your intelligence, nor does it measure the likelihood of your success in business. As with any standardized test, by preparing properly for the GMAT, you can boost your score significantly.

Through June 2012, the GMAT will contain two essay sections, dubbed the "Analytical Writing Assessment" (AWA). The essays you type into the computer are graded on a 1 to 6 scale and sent to the schools you designate along with your traditional 200–800 score. The AWA is designed to provide schools with information about your communications skills that is not otherwise captured in the GMAT.

Essentially, the AWA is another tool that schools can use to evaluate you. Although it won't reduce the importance of the essays on your applications, it may alter the number of essays a school asks you to write. Business schools have recognized that the AWA provides you with an opportunity to demonstrate your ability to think critically and communicate complex ideas in a very limited time period. For that reason, admissions officers may be as interested in reading your writing samples as they are in relying solely on your GMAT score.

Even though the AWA is scored separately from the multiple-choice sections, you should prepare for it with the same intensity that you put into preparing for the rest of the GMAT. Outstanding writing samples can help you stand out from the crowd. Conversely, seriously flawed essays can reduce your admissions chances.

MANAGEMENT SKILLS

To evaluate your management skills, admissions officers look at work experience and other relevant activities. That does not mean that you need to have managed people to be an impressive candidate. Perhaps you've managed projects, resources, or portfolios. Each of these can provide an excellent forum for you to demonstrate evidence of your management aptitude.

You can communicate some of your management abilities through the straightforward "data" part of your application. Be sure to describe your job responsibilities. Don't list your title and assume that an admissions officer knows what you do or the level of your responsibilities. This is especially important if your job is nontraditional for an aspiring MBA.

Admissions officers will look at your overall career record. How have you progressed? Have you been an outstanding performer? What do your recommendation writers say about your performance? Have you progressed to increasingly higher levels of responsibility? If you have limited work experience, you will not be expected to match the accomplishments of an applicant with 10 years of experience, but you will be expected to demonstrate your abilities.

The essays also provide an opportunity to demonstrate your management aptitude. Many essay questions specifically ask you to discuss your professional experiences and how you handled different situations. With thoughtful, well-written essays, you can highlight your management strengths for admissions officers.

Extracurricular activities and community involvement also present opportunities for you to highlight your skills. For younger applicants, college activities play a more significant role than for more seasoned applicants. Your activities say a lot about who you are and what's important to you. Were you a campus leader? Did your activities require discipline and commitment? Did you work with a team? What did you learn from your involvement?

Active community involvement provides a way for you to demonstrate your management skills and to impress admissions officers with your personal character. In fact, many applications ask directly about community activities. If you are contemplating getting involved in your community, here's a chance to do something worthwhile and enhance your application in the process.

PERSONAL CHARACTERISTICS

The third, and most subjective, criterion on which schools evaluate you is your personal characteristics. Admissions officers judge you in this area primarily through your essays, recommendations, and personal interview (if applicable). Although different schools emphasize different qualities, most seek candidates who demonstrate leadership, maturity, integrity, responsibility, and teamwork.

The more competitive schools place special emphasis on these criteria because they have many qualified applicants for each available spot in the class. In fact, the top-tier programs generally require numerous essays so that they can get a complete feeling for each applicant's personal qualities.

WHO REVIEWS YOUR APPLICATION?

At most schools, the board includes professional admissions officers. And at some schools, second-year students and/or alumni play a role in reviewing applications and interviewing candidates.

Admissions officers are not always representative of the group of students they admit. Many boards contain a high percentage of women and minorities. Board members recognize the importance of diversity in the classroom and in many cases have a mandate to increase it. Although some admissions officers have had management training and business experience, many have not. They tend to be people oriented and have strong interpersonal skills. They want to get to "know" you through your application, and they are partial to well-written essays.

WHAT DECISIONS ARE MADE

Upon reviewing your application, the admissions board may make any number of decisions, including the following:

- *Admit:* Congratulations, you're in. But read the letter carefully. The board may recommend or, in some cases, require you to do some preparatory coursework to ensure that your quantitative or language skills are up to speed.

- *Reject:* At the top schools, there are far more qualified applicants than there are spaces in the class. Even though you were rejected, you can reapply at a later date. However, if you are considering reapplying, you need to understand why you were rejected and whether you have a reasonable chance of being admitted the next time around. Some schools will speak with you about your application, but they often wait for the end of the admissions season, by which time you may have accepted another offer.

- *Deferred admit:* This decision is reserved for when the admissions board considers you a strong candidate but believes you would benefit from an additional year or two of work experience before attending. Because most applicants now have at least two years' experience before applying to school, deferred admission is not as common as it once was.

- *Reject with encouragement to reapply:* This isn't just a polite rejection. One step down from a deferred admit, it's a way for a school to say, "We like you, and we think with more experience you'd be a strong candidate."

- *Hold over until the next decision period:* Sometimes the admissions board isn't comfortable making a decision by the scheduled reply date. Perhaps you're right on the borderline, and the board wants to see how you stack up against the next group of applicants. In this case, all you can do is wait, but frequently the result is positive.

- *Waiting list:* Schools use the waiting list—the educational equivalent of purgatory—to manage class size. The good news is that you wouldn't be on the list if you weren't considered a strong candidate. The bad news is there is no way to know with certainty whether you'll be accepted. Be aware, though, that schools do tend to look kindly upon wait-listed candidates who reapply in a subsequent year.

- *Request for an interview:* Schools at which an interview is not required may request that you interview prior to their making a final decision. Your application may have raised some specific issues that you can address in an interview, or perhaps the board feels your essays did not give them a complete enough picture to render a decision. Look at this as a positive opportunity to strengthen your case.

PREPARING YOUR APPLICATION

There are no magic formulas that automatically admit you to, or reject you from, the school of your choice. Rather, your application is like a jigsaw puzzle. Each component— GPA, GMAT score, professional experience, school activities, recommendations—is a different piece of the puzzle.

Outstanding work experience and personal characteristics may enable you to overcome a mediocre academic record. Conversely, outstanding academic credentials will not ensure your admission to a top-tier school if you do not demonstrate strong management skills and solid personal character. Your challenge in preparing your application is to convince the admissions board that all of the pieces in your background fit together to form a substantial and unique whole.

YOUR APPLICATION AS A MARKETING TOOL

When it comes to applying to business school, you are the product. Your application is your marketing document. Marketing yourself doesn't mean that you should lie or even embellish; it just means that you need to make a tight presentation of the facts. Everything in your application should add up to a coherent whole and underscore the fact that you are not only qualified to be in the class but that you should be in it.

Many application forms have a certain tone, one that's comforting and accepting. "Why would you like to come to our school?" they seem to be asking. They do want an answer to that question, but what's even more important—the subtext for the whole application process—is a bigger question: "Why should we accept you?" This is the question that your application will answer. And with some effective marketing strategies, your answer will be clear, concise, coherent, and strong.

So how do you portray an image? First of all, it should fit; it should be natural. Don't bother to try to sell yourself as something you're not. It'll be uncomfortable for you, and it probably won't work.

Besides, part of what readers do when they evaluate your application is form an image of you from the various parts of your application. Your job is to help them, not hinder them.

MAXIMIZING THE VARIOUS PARTS OF YOUR APPLICATION

Let's look at how you should approach the specific parts of the application.

THE ESSAY

Your essays are a critical part of your application. The situations you choose to write about and the manner in which you present them can have a major bearing on the strength of your candidacy.

Writing an effective essay requires serious self-examination and sound strategic planning. What major personal and professional events have shaped you? What accomplishments best demonstrate your management abilities? Admissions officers are interested in getting to know you as a complete person. The topic and perspective you choose sends a clear signal about what's important to you and what your values are.

Common Essay Questions

Every application is unique, but most will include essay questions that fall into one of several basic types. Here are the six kinds of questions you can expect to see:

1. **Describe (1, 2, or 3) significant accomplishments and discuss why you view them as such.**

Here, the admissions board is looking to get a sense of what you consider important. The events you choose to write about say a lot about you, as do the reasons you consider them significant.

2. **Why are you pursuing an MBA? Where do you hope to be 5 years from now? 10 years?**

Admissions officers want to see that you've thought through the reasons for going to business school. Although they don't expect you necessarily to map out your entire career path, they will look for you to demonstrate forward thinking.

3. **What are your strengths and weaknesses?**

Answer truthfully. Don't settle for pat responses. When discussing your strengths, you may want to include a brief example of an experience that highlights your strengths, if length permits. Writing about weaknesses can be tricky. The board is looking for evidence of self-awareness and maturity, but be careful about raising red flags. Describing a weakness that's really a strength ("I'm so honest that . . . " or "I'm so committed to my employees that . . . ") is a safe approach, but it doesn't provide much insight and it may turn off some admissions officers.

4. **Describe an ethical dilemma you have faced and discuss how you handled it.**

With this question, admissions officers will evaluate not just your ethical "compass" but also your thoughtfulness, maturity, and integrity. What's most important is that you demonstrate your ability to exercise responsible judgment and learn from difficult personal circumstances.

5. **Is there anything else you would like the admissions board to know about you?**

If your undergraduate performance is the weak link of your application, or if there's a gap in your employment record that is likely to raise a red flag, now is the time to discuss it. But don't be defensive. Discussing the hardships you have faced in a straightforward, nondefensive manner can help you turn a potential pitfall into a strength on your application.

6. **If you could effect one change at your current job, what would it be?**

Admissions officers recognize that many (especially younger) applicants have not yet reached levels to make fundamental changes at work. This question lets you flex your brain power in talking about changes you'd like to see. It reveals how knowledgeable you are about business in general and your business in particular. It also provides clues about how you think. For example, do you think about big-picture issues, or do you focus on the details?

General Essay Tips

Once you have established your topic, you now need to start writing. Keep the following things in mind:

- **Length:** Schools are pretty specific about how long they want your essays to be. Adhere to their guidelines.
- **Spelling/typos/grammar:** Remember, your application is your marketing document. What would you think of a product that's promoted with sloppy materials containing typos, spelling errors, and grammatical mistakes?
- **Write in the active voice:** Candidates who write well have an advantage in the application process because they can state their case in a concise, compelling manner.
- **Tone:** On the one hand, tout your achievements and present yourself as a poised, self-confident applicant. On the other hand, arrogance and self-importance do not go over well with admissions officers.
- **Creative approach:** Admissions officers who review thousands of essays every year may consider your approach gimmicky or simply find it distracting. Remember, your challenge is to stand out in the applicant pool in a positive way. Don't let your creativity obscure the substance of your application.

Making Your Essay Distinctive

One of the first mistakes that some applicants make is in thinking that "thorough" and "comprehensive" are sufficient qualities for their essays. They try to include as much information as possible, without regard for length limitations or strategic intent. Application readers dread reading these bloated essays. So how do you decide what to include?

Unless asked for them, don't dwell on your weak points. One of the best ways to be distinctive is to sell your image briefly and accurately, including real-life examples to back up your points.

Distinctive essays answer the questions that admissions officers think about while reading essays: What's different about this applicant? Why should we pick this applicant over others? Authentic enthusiasm can be a plus, and writing about parts of your life or career that are interesting and relevant help grab a reader's attention.

THE INTERVIEW

Because communication skills are such an integral part of effective management, many B-schools include personal interviews as part of the admissions process.

- **Review your application.** If you've submitted your application prior to the interview, your interviewer is likely to use it as a guide and may ask specific questions about it. Be sure you remember what you wrote.

- **Be ready to provide examples and specifics.** Professionally trained interviewers are more likely to ask you about specific situations than they are to ask broad, open-ended questions. Here are a few situations an interviewer may ask you to discuss: "Tell me about a recent accomplishment." "Discuss a recent situation in which you demonstrated leadership." "Give me an example of a situation in which you overcame difficult circumstances." You do not need to "script" or overrehearse your responses, but you should go into the interview confident that you can field any question.

- **Be open and honest.** Don't struggle to think of "right" answers. The only right answers are those that are right for you.

- **Ask questions.** The interview is as much an opportunity for you to learn about the school as for the school to learn about you. Good questions demonstrate your knowledge about a particular program and your thoughtfulness about the entire process.

- **Follow proper business decorum.** Be on time, dress appropriately, and follow up with thank-you letters. Treat the process as you would a job interview, which in many respects it is.

- **Watch your nonverbal cues.** Nonverbal communication is much more important than people realize. Maintain eye contact, keep good posture, sustain positive energy, and avoid nervous fidgeting. It will help you come across as confident, poised, and mature.

- **Be courteous to the administrative staff.** These people are colleagues of the board members, and how you treat them can have an impact, either positive or negative.

- **Relax and have fun.** Interviews are naturally stressful. But by being well prepared, you can enhance your prospects for admission, learn about the school, and enjoy yourself in the process.

THE RECOMMENDATIONS

Choose recommenders who can write meaningfully about your strengths. One of the more common mistakes is to sacrifice an insightful recommendation from someone who knows you well for a generic recommendation from a celebrity or alum. Admissions officers are not impressed by famous names. Good choices for recommenders include current and past supervisors, professors, academic and nonacademic advisers, and people you work with in community activities.

If a school requests an academic recommendation but you are not able to provide one, try to identify someone who can discuss your intellectual attributes, particularly if your academic record is not your strength. Similarly, if requesting a recommendation from your employer would create an awkward situation, look for someone else who can comment on your management skills. Your recommendations are not likely to make or break your application, but they will confirm your strengths and, in some cases, help you overcome perceived weaknesses in your application.

If you wish to submit an extra recommendation, it's generally not a problem. Most schools will include the letter in your file, and those that don't will not penalize you for it. You should, however, send a note explaining why you have requested an additional recommendation so it does not appear that you can't follow instructions.

Asking for Recommendations

There are two fundamental rules of requesting recommendations:

Rule 1: Ask early.

Rule 2: Ask nicely.

Once your recommenders have agreed, let them know about deadlines well in advance to avoid potential scheduling conflicts. The more time they have, the better the job they'll do recommending you. As for asking nicely, you should let the person know you think highly of his or her opinion and you'd be happy and honored if he or she would consider writing you a letter of recommendation.

BEFORE YOU SUBMIT YOUR APPLICATION . . .

When your essays are complete and you are finalizing your applications, take two more steps to ensure that your applications are as strong as they can be.

1. Reread the essay in the context of your entire application. Does the total package make sense? Does it represent you favorably? Is everything consistent? Have you demonstrated your intellectual ability, management skills, and personal characteristics? Most important, do you feel good about the application? You wouldn't want to be rejected on the basis of an application that you don't believe represents the real you.

2. Ask someone whose opinion you respect to review your application. An impartial person is sure to pick up spelling or grammatical errors that you've overlooked. Maybe you have left out something important. In addition, because

your application is an intensely personal document that requires significant self-examination, you may not be able to remain objective. Someone who knows you and can be frank will tell you whether your application has "captured" you most favorably.

Some schools prohibit you from using any outside help on your application. A last-minute once-over from a friend or family member is probably within reason, but you may want to ask the school directly what is permissible.

A SPECIAL NOTE FOR INTERNATIONAL STUDENTS

The MBA has become a degree of choice for people around the globe. If you are not from the United States but are considering attending a graduate management program at a university in the United States, here is what you'll need to get started.

- If English is not your first language, you will probably need to take the Test of English as a Foreign Language (TOEFL) or show some other evidence that you are proficient in English. If you graduated from an English-speaking college, you may not need to take the TOEFL.
- You will need to take the GMAT. Some graduate business programs may require you to take the GRE (Graduate Record Examination) as well or accept it in place of the GMAT.
- You will need to obtain an I-20 Certificate of Eligibility from the school you plan to attend if you intend to apply for an F-1 Student Visa to study in the United States.

KAPLAN ENGLISH PROGRAMS*

If you need more help with the complex process of business school admissions, assistance preparing for the TOEFL or GMAT, or help improving your English skills in general, you may be interested in Kaplan's programs for international students.

Visit **kaplaninternational.com** for more details.

*Kaplan is authorized under federal law to enroll nonimmigrant alien students. Kaplan is accredited by ACCET (Accrediting Council for Continuing Education and Training).

## Part Four

PRACTICE TEST

HOW TO TAKE THIS TEST

Before taking this practice test, find a quiet place where you can work uninterrupted for four hours or so. Make sure you have a comfortable desk and several No. 2 pencils.

This is a full-length practice test. It is not adaptive, and you will not get a 200–800 score. However, this test will give you an opportunity to practice your Kaplan methods and strategies, as well as a chance to try your endurance on a 3½-hour test.

It's best if you have a computer with a word processor available to type your essays (remember to turn off the automatic spell-check). Nonetheless, we have provided paper to handwrite your essays if a computer is not available. This practice test includes two scored multiple-choice sections and two Analytical Writing sections. Use the answer grid that follows to record your multiple-choice answers.

Once you start the practice test, don't stop until you've gone through all four sections. Remember, you can review any question within a section, but you may not go back or forward to a different section.

You'll find the answer key and explanations following the test.

Good luck!

GMAT PRACTICE TEST ANSWER SHEET

Remove (or photocopy) the answer sheet and use it to complete the practice test.

Quantitative

1. Ⓐ Ⓑ Ⓒ Ⓓ Ⓔ	11 Ⓐ Ⓑ Ⓒ Ⓓ Ⓔ	21. Ⓐ Ⓑ Ⓒ Ⓓ Ⓔ	31. Ⓐ Ⓑ Ⓒ Ⓓ Ⓔ
2. Ⓐ Ⓑ Ⓒ Ⓓ Ⓔ	12. Ⓐ Ⓑ Ⓒ Ⓓ Ⓔ	22. Ⓐ Ⓑ Ⓒ Ⓓ Ⓔ	32. Ⓐ Ⓑ Ⓒ Ⓓ Ⓔ
3. Ⓐ Ⓑ Ⓒ Ⓓ Ⓔ	13. Ⓐ Ⓑ Ⓒ Ⓓ Ⓔ	23. Ⓐ Ⓑ Ⓒ Ⓓ Ⓔ	33. Ⓐ Ⓑ Ⓒ Ⓓ Ⓔ
4. Ⓐ Ⓑ Ⓒ Ⓓ Ⓔ	14. Ⓐ Ⓑ Ⓒ Ⓓ Ⓔ	24. Ⓐ Ⓑ Ⓒ Ⓓ Ⓔ	34. Ⓐ Ⓑ Ⓒ Ⓓ Ⓔ
5. Ⓐ Ⓑ Ⓒ Ⓓ Ⓔ	15. Ⓐ Ⓑ Ⓒ Ⓓ Ⓔ	25. Ⓐ Ⓑ Ⓒ Ⓓ Ⓔ	35. Ⓐ Ⓑ Ⓒ Ⓓ Ⓔ
6. Ⓐ Ⓑ Ⓒ Ⓓ Ⓔ	16. Ⓐ Ⓑ Ⓒ Ⓓ Ⓔ	26. Ⓐ Ⓑ Ⓒ Ⓓ Ⓔ	36. Ⓐ Ⓑ Ⓒ Ⓓ Ⓔ
7. Ⓐ Ⓑ Ⓒ Ⓓ Ⓔ	17. Ⓐ Ⓑ Ⓒ Ⓓ Ⓔ	27. Ⓐ Ⓑ Ⓒ Ⓓ Ⓔ	37. Ⓐ Ⓑ Ⓒ Ⓓ Ⓔ
8. Ⓐ Ⓑ Ⓒ Ⓓ Ⓔ	18. Ⓐ Ⓑ Ⓒ Ⓓ Ⓔ	28. Ⓐ Ⓑ Ⓒ Ⓓ Ⓔ	
9. Ⓐ Ⓑ Ⓒ Ⓓ Ⓔ	19. Ⓐ Ⓑ Ⓒ Ⓓ Ⓔ	29. Ⓐ Ⓑ Ⓒ Ⓓ Ⓔ	
10. Ⓐ Ⓑ Ⓒ Ⓓ Ⓔ	20. Ⓐ Ⓑ Ⓒ Ⓓ Ⓔ	30. Ⓐ Ⓑ Ⓒ Ⓓ Ⓔ	

right in Quantitative

wrong in Quantitative

Verbal

1. Ⓐ Ⓑ Ⓒ Ⓓ Ⓔ	12 Ⓐ Ⓑ Ⓒ Ⓓ Ⓔ	23. Ⓐ Ⓑ Ⓒ Ⓓ Ⓔ	34. Ⓐ Ⓑ Ⓒ Ⓓ Ⓔ
2. Ⓐ Ⓑ Ⓒ Ⓓ Ⓔ	13. Ⓐ Ⓑ Ⓒ Ⓓ Ⓔ	24. Ⓐ Ⓑ Ⓒ Ⓓ Ⓔ	35. Ⓐ Ⓑ Ⓒ Ⓓ Ⓔ
3. Ⓐ Ⓑ Ⓒ Ⓓ Ⓔ	14. Ⓐ Ⓑ Ⓒ Ⓓ Ⓔ	25. Ⓐ Ⓑ Ⓒ Ⓓ Ⓔ	36. Ⓐ Ⓑ Ⓒ Ⓓ Ⓔ
4. Ⓐ Ⓑ Ⓒ Ⓓ Ⓔ	15. Ⓐ Ⓑ Ⓒ Ⓓ Ⓔ	26. Ⓐ Ⓑ Ⓒ Ⓓ Ⓔ	37. Ⓐ Ⓑ Ⓒ Ⓓ Ⓔ
5. Ⓐ Ⓑ Ⓒ Ⓓ Ⓔ	16. Ⓐ Ⓑ Ⓒ Ⓓ Ⓔ	27. Ⓐ Ⓑ Ⓒ Ⓓ Ⓔ	38. Ⓐ Ⓑ Ⓒ Ⓓ Ⓔ
6. Ⓐ Ⓑ Ⓒ Ⓓ Ⓔ	17. Ⓐ Ⓑ Ⓒ Ⓓ Ⓔ	28. Ⓐ Ⓑ Ⓒ Ⓓ Ⓔ	39. Ⓐ Ⓑ Ⓒ Ⓓ Ⓔ
7. Ⓐ Ⓑ Ⓒ Ⓓ Ⓔ	18. Ⓐ Ⓑ Ⓒ Ⓓ Ⓔ	29. Ⓐ Ⓑ Ⓒ Ⓓ Ⓔ	40. Ⓐ Ⓑ Ⓒ Ⓓ Ⓔ
8. Ⓐ Ⓑ Ⓒ Ⓓ Ⓔ	19. Ⓐ Ⓑ Ⓒ Ⓓ Ⓔ	30. Ⓐ Ⓑ Ⓒ Ⓓ Ⓔ	41. Ⓐ Ⓑ Ⓒ Ⓓ Ⓔ
9. Ⓐ Ⓑ Ⓒ Ⓓ Ⓔ	20. Ⓐ Ⓑ Ⓒ Ⓓ Ⓔ	31. Ⓐ Ⓑ Ⓒ Ⓓ Ⓔ	
10. Ⓐ Ⓑ Ⓒ Ⓓ Ⓔ	21. Ⓐ Ⓑ Ⓒ Ⓓ Ⓔ	32. Ⓐ Ⓑ Ⓒ Ⓓ Ⓔ	
11. Ⓐ Ⓑ Ⓒ Ⓓ Ⓔ	22. Ⓐ Ⓑ Ⓒ Ⓓ Ⓔ	33. Ⓐ Ⓑ Ⓒ Ⓓ Ⓔ	

right in Verbal

wrong in Verbal

Analysis of an Argument Essay
Time—30 minutes

Directions: Provide a critique of the argument below. Focus on one or all of the following, depending upon your considered opinion of the argument: questionable assumptions underlying the reasoning, alternative explanations or evidence that would weaken the reasoning, and/or additional information that would support or weaken the argument. Read the statement below and the directions that follow it. Write your final response on the pages provided. Allow yourself 30 minutes to plan and write your response.

The following appeared in the advertising literature of Travelshack.com, an online travel magazine and vacation resort catalogue.

"Your vacation resort can ill afford not to publicize its offerings on Travelshack.com. Our readership has more than doubled in the past year alone and is dominated by savvy consumers with large disposable incomes. Witness the experience of Snowbert Ski Lodge. Since it began advertising itself on our website a year ago, it has regularly been booked to capacity, and its annual profits have increased more than threefold from the previous year."

Explain how logically persuasive you find this argument. In discussing your viewpoint, analyze the argument's line of reasoning and its use of evidence. Also explain what, if anything, would make the argument more valid and convincing or help you to better evaluate its conclusion.

GO ON TO THE NEXT PAGE

Use this space to write your essay: (Note: You will have to type your essay on the GMAT CAT.)

_____

_____

_____

_____

_____

_____

_____

_____

_____

_____

_____

_____

_____

_____

_____

_____

_____

_____

_____

IF YOU FINISH BEFORE TIME IS CALLED, YOU MAY CHECK YOUR WORK ON
THIS SECTION ONLY. DO NOT TURN TO ANY OTHER SECTION IN THE TEST.

STOP

Analysis of an Issue Essay
Time—30 minutes

Directions: Analyze and present your point of view on the issue described below. There is no "right" point of view. In developing your point of view, you should consider the issue from a number of different viewpoints. Read the statement below and the directions that follow it. Write your final response on the page provided. Allow yourself 30 minutes to plan and write your response.

"Some people argue that those who do not send their children to public schools should not have to fund these schools through taxes, since neither parents nor children benefit from these schools. They ignore the fact that everyone benefits from the strong economy that a well-educated populace generates."

Which argument do you find more compelling, the case for forcing everyone to fund public schools or the opposing viewpoint? Explain your position using relevant reasons or examples taken from your own experience, observations, or reading.

GO ON TO THE NEXT PAGE

Use this space to write your essay: (Note: You will have to type your essay on the GMAT CAT.)

IF YOU FINISH BEFORE TIME IS CALLED, YOU MAY CHECK YOUR WORK ON THIS SECTION ONLY. DO NOT TURN TO ANY OTHER SECTION IN THE TEST.

STOP

Quantitative Section
Time—75 minutes, 37 questions

Problem Solving Directions: Solve the problems and choose the best answer.

Data Sufficiency Directions: In each of the problems, a question is followed by two statements containing certain data. You are to determine whether the data provided by the statements are sufficient to answer the question. Choose the correct answer based upon the statements' data, your knowledge of mathematics, and your familiarity with everyday facts (such as the number of minutes in an hour or cents in a dollar).

Note: Unless otherwise indicated, the figures accompanying questions have been drawn as accurately as possible and may be used as sources of information for answering the questions. All figures lie in a plane except where noted. All numbers used are real numbers.

- ○ Statement (1) by itself is sufficient to answer the question, but statement (2) by itself is not;

- ○ Statement (2) by itself is sufficient to answer the question, but statement (1) by itself is not;

- ○ Statements (1) and (2) taken together are sufficient to answer the question, even though neither statement by itself is sufficient;

- ○ Either statement by itself is sufficient to answer the question;

- ○ Statements (1) and (2) taken together are not sufficient to answer the question, requiring more data pertaining to the problem.

Note: Diagrams accompanying problems agree with information given in the questions, but they may not agree with additional information given in Statements (1) and (2).

Example:

$$A \qquad B \qquad C$$

What is the length of segment AC?
(1) B is the midpoint of AC.
(2) $AB = 5$

Explanation: Statement (1) tells you that B is the midpoint of AC, so $AB = BC$ and $AC = 2AB = 2BC$. Since Statement (1) does not give a value for AB or BC, you cannot answer the question using Statement (1) alone. Statement (2) says that $AB = 5$. Since Statement (2) does not give you a value for BC, the question cannot be answered by Statement (2) alone. Using both statements together, you can find a value for both AB and BC; therefore, you can find AC, so the answer to the problem is choice (C).

GO ON TO THE NEXT PAGE ▷

1. The price of copper rose by 25 percent and then fell by 20 percent. The price after these changes was

   ○ 20 percent greater than the original price.

   ○ 5 percent greater than the original price.

   ○ the same as the original price.

   ○ 5 percent less than the original price.

   ○ 15 percent less than the original price.

2. If Sidney is taller than Roger, Roger is taller than Vernon, and Billy is taller than both Roger and Felix, then which of the following statements must be true?

   ○ Felix is shorter than Roger.

   ○ Sidney is taller than Billy.

   ○ Roger is shorter than Felix.

   ○ Sidney is taller than Felix.

   ○ Billy is taller than Vernon.

3. If $-\dfrac{3}{4}x + 3y - \dfrac{1}{2} = \dfrac{3}{2}y - \dfrac{1}{4}x$, what is the value of x?

   (1) $y^2 = 4$

   (2) $y = 2$

   ○ Statement (1) by itself is sufficient to answer the question, but statement (2) by itself is not.

   ○ Statement (2) by itself is sufficient to answer the question, but statement (1) by itself is not.

   ○ Statements (1) and (2) taken together are sufficient to answer the question, even though neither statement by itself is sufficient.

   ○ Either statement by itself is sufficient to answer the question.

   ○ Statements (1) and (2) taken together are not sufficient to answer the question, requiring more data pertaining to the problem.

GO ON TO THE NEXT PAGE

4. To meet a government requirement, a bottler must test 5 percent of its spring water and 10 percent of its sparkling water for purity. If a customer ordered 120 cases of spring water and 80 cases of sparkling water, what percent of all the cases must the bottler test before it can send the water out?

   ○ 6.5%

   ○ 7.0%

   ○ 7.5%

   ○ 8.0%

   ○ 8.5%

5. If $xy > 0$, which of the following CANNOT be true?

   ○ $x > 0$

   ○ $y < 0$

   ○ $x + y < 0$

   ○ $\dfrac{x}{y} < 0$

   ○ $\dfrac{x}{y} > 0$

6. What is the value of a if $3^{3a + 4} = 9^a$?

   ○ -4

   ○ -2

   ○ -1

   ○ 1

   ○ 4

Class	Average Age	No. of Students
A	15 years	6
B	16 years	12

7. Is the standard deviation of ages of students in class A greater than the standard deviation of the age of students in class B?

   (1) The difference between the ages of any two students in class A is always more than 1 year.

   (2) No student in class B is more than 6 months older than any other student.

   ○ Statement (1) by itself is sufficient to answer the question, but statement (2) by itself is not.

   ○ Statement (2) by itself is sufficient to answer the question, but statement (1) by itself is not.

   ○ Statements (1) and (2) taken together are sufficient to answer the question, even though neither statement by itself is sufficient.

   ○ Either statement by itself is sufficient to answer the question.

   ○ Statements (1) and (2) taken together are not sufficient to answer the question, requiring more data pertaining to the problem.

GO ON TO THE NEXT PAGE ⇨

8. A list contains 11 consecutive integers. If x is the smallest integer on the list, what is the greatest integer on the list?

   (1) If x is the smallest integer on the list, then $(x + 72)^{\frac{1}{3}} = 4$.

   (2) If x is the smallest integer on the list, then $\dfrac{1}{64} = x^{-2}$.

   ○ Statement (1) by itself is sufficient to answer the question, but statement (2) by itself is not.

   ○ Statement (2) by itself is sufficient to answer the question, but statement (1) by itself is not.

   ○ Statements (1) and (2) taken together are sufficient to answer the question, even though neither statement by itself is sufficient.

   ○ Either statement by itself is sufficient to answer the question.

   ○ Statements (1) and (2) taken together are not sufficient to answer the question, requiring more data pertaining to the problem.

9. The average (arithmetic mean) of $3a + 4$ and another number is $2a$. What is the average of the other number and a?

   ○ $2a$

   ○ $a - 4$

   ○ $a - 2$

   ○ $a + 2$

   ○ $a + 4$

10. Tom reads at an average rate of 30 pages per hour, while Jan reads at an average rate of 40 pages per hour. If Tom starts reading a novel at 4:30, and Jan begins reading an identical copy of the same book at 5:20, at what time will they be reading the same page?

    ○ 9:30

    ○ 9:00

    ○ 8:40

    ○ 7:50

    ○ 7:00

11. Todd's construction company is capable of building 40 houses a year. Todd's brother Mike also owns a construction company. How long does it take the two companies together to build 64 houses?

    (1) Mike's construction company is capable of building houses twice as fast as Todd's company does.

    (2) Mike's construction company is capable of building 20 houses every three months.

    ○ Statement (1) by itself is sufficient to answer the question, but statement (2) by itself is not.

    ○ Statement (2) by itself is sufficient to answer the question, but statement (1) by itself is not.

    ○ Statements (1) and (2) taken together are sufficient to answer the question, even though neither statement by itself is sufficient.

    ○ Either statement by itself is sufficient to answer the question.

    ○ Statements (1) and (2) taken together are not sufficient to answer the question, requiring more data pertaining to the problem.

12. How many multiples of 3 are there among the integers 15 through 105 inclusive?

    ○ 30
    ○ 31
    ○ 32
    ○ 33
    ○ 34

13. If x is a prime number, what is the value of x?

    (1) $x < 15$

    (2) $(x - 2)$ is a multiple of 5.

    ○ Statement (1) by itself is sufficient to answer the question, but statement (2) by itself is not.

    ○ Statement (2) by itself is sufficient to answer the question, but statement (1) by itself is not.

    ○ Statements (1) and (2) taken together are sufficient to answer the question, even though neither statement by itself is sufficient.

    ○ Either statement by itself is sufficient to answer the question.

    ○ Statements (1) and (2) taken together are not sufficient to answer the question, requiring more data pertaining to the problem.

GO ON TO THE NEXT PAGE

14. Steve gets on the elevator at the 11th floor of a building and rides up at a rate of 57 floors per minute. At the same time, Joyce gets on an elevator on the 51st floor of the same building and rides down at a rate of 63 floors per minute. If they continue traveling at these rates, at which floor will their paths cross?

   ○ 19

   ○ 28

   ○ 30

   ○ 32

   ○ 44

15. George takes 8 hours to copy a 50-page manuscript, while Sonya can copy the same manuscript in 6 hours. How many hours would it take them to copy a 100-page manuscript, if they worked together?

   ○ $6\frac{6}{7}$

   ○ 9

   ○ $9\frac{5}{7}$

   ○ $10\frac{2}{3}$

   ○ 14

16. For the equation $x^2 + 2x + m = 5$, where m is a constant, 3 is one solution for x. What is the other solution?

   ○ −5

   ○ −2

   ○ −1

   ○ 3

   ○ 5

17. If both 5^2 and 3^3 are factors of $n \times 2^5 \times 6^2 \times 7^3$, what is the smallest possible positive value of n?

   ○ 25

   ○ 27

   ○ 45

   ○ 75

   ○ 125

18. If a rectangle has length a and width b, what is its area?

   (1) $2a = \dfrac{15}{b}$

   (2) $a = 2b - 2$

   ○ Statement (1) by itself is sufficient to answer the question, but statement (2) by itself is not.

   ○ Statement (2) by itself is sufficient to answer the question, but statement (1) by itself is not.

   ○ Statements (1) and (2) taken together are sufficient to answer the question, even though neither statement by itself is sufficient.

   ○ Either statement by itself is sufficient to answer the question.

   ○ Statements (1) and (2) taken together are not sufficient to answer the question, requiring more data pertaining to the problem.

GO ON TO THE NEXT PAGE

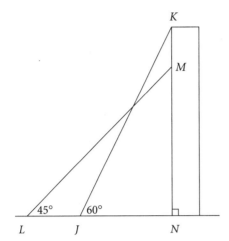

19. In the figure above, line segments *JK* and *LM* represent two positions of the same board leaning against the side *KN* of a wall. The length of *KN* is how much greater than the length of *MN*?

    (1) The length of *LN* is $\sqrt{2}$ meters.

    (2) The length of *JN* is 1 meter.

    ○ Statement (1) by itself is sufficient to answer the question, but statement (2) by itself is not.

    ○ Statement (2) by itself is sufficient to answer the question, but statement (1) by itself is not.

    ○ Statements (1) and (2) taken together are sufficient to answer the question, even though neither statement by itself is sufficient.

    ○ Either statement by itself is sufficient to answer the question.

    ○ Statements (1) and (2) taken together are not sufficient to answer the question, requiring more data pertaining to the problem.

20. How many different ways can 2 students be seated in a row of 4 desks so that there is always at least one empty desk between the students?

    ○ 2

    ○ 3

    ○ 4

    ○ 6

    ○ 12

21. What is the ratio of men to women enrolled in a certain class?

    (1) The number of women enrolled in the class is 3 less than half the number of men enrolled.

    (2) The number of women enrolled in the class is $\frac{2}{5}$ of the number of men enrolled.

    ○ Statement (1) by itself is sufficient to answer the question, but statement (2) by itself is not.

    ○ Statement (2) by itself is sufficient to answer the question, but statement (1) by itself is not.

    ○ Statements (1) and (2) taken together are sufficient to answer the question, even though neither statement by itself is sufficient.

    ○ Either statement by itself is sufficient to answer the question.

    ○ Statements (1) and (2) taken together are not sufficient to answer the question, requiring more data pertaining to the problem.

GO ON TO THE NEXT PAGE ⇨

22. A clothing supplier stores 800 coats in a warehouse, of which 15 percent are full-length coats. If 500 of the shorter-length coats are removed from the warehouse, what percent of the remaining coats are full length?

   ○ 5.62%

   ○ 9.37%

   ○ 35%

   ○ 40%

   ○ 48%

23. Are the integers q, r, and s consecutive?

   (1) The average (arithmetic mean) of q, r, and s is r.

   (2) $r - q = s - r$

   ○ Statement (1) by itself is sufficient to answer the question, but statement (2) by itself is not.

   ○ Statement (2) by itself is sufficient to answer the question, but statement (1) by itself is not.

   ○ Statements (1) and (2) taken together are sufficient to answer the question, even though neither statement by itself is sufficient.

   ○ Either statement by itself is sufficient to answer the question.

   ○ Statements (1) and (2) taken together are not sufficient to answer the question, requiring more data pertaining to the problem.

24. For a certain performance at a concert hall, a total of 2,350 tickets were sold in the orchestra, first mezzanine, and second mezzanine. How many orchestra tickets were sold?

   (1) The number of first mezzanine tickets sold was one-half the number of second mezzanine tickets sold.

   (2) The total number of first and second mezzanine tickets sold was 50 percent greater than the number of orchestra tickets sold.

   ○ Statement (1) by itself is sufficient to answer the question, but statement (2) by itself is not.

   ○ Statement (2) by itself is sufficient to answer the question, but statement (1) by itself is not.

   ○ Statements (1) and (2) taken together are sufficient to answer the question, even though neither statement by itself is sufficient.

   ○ Either statement by itself is sufficient to answer the question.

   ○ Statements (1) and (2) taken together are not sufficient to answer the question, requiring more data pertaining to the problem.

GO ON TO THE NEXT PAGE

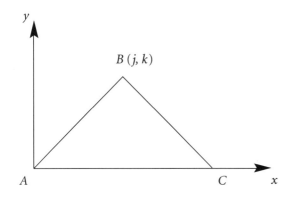

25. If the area of the triangle above is 8, what are the coordinates of point C?

   ○ $(0, 2jk)$

   ○ $(j^2 + k^2, 0)$

   ○ $\left(\dfrac{8}{k}, 0\right)$

   ○ $\left(0, \dfrac{16}{j}\right)$

   ○ $\left(\dfrac{16}{k}, 0\right)$

26. If the probability of rain on any given day in City X is 50 percent, what is the probability that it rains on exactly 3 days in a 5-day period?

   ○ $\dfrac{8}{125}$

   ○ $\dfrac{2}{25}$

   ○ $\dfrac{5}{16}$

   ○ $\dfrac{8}{25}$

   ○ $\dfrac{3}{4}$

27. A recipe for soda requires w liters of water for every liter of syrup. If soda is made according to this recipe using m liters of syrup and sold for j dollars a liter, what will be the gross profit if syrup costs k dollars a liter and water costs nothing?

   ○ $m(w + j - k)$

   ○ $jm\left(\dfrac{1}{w} + 1\right)$

   ○ $m(jw - k)$

   ○ $(j - k)m$

   ○ $jm(1 + w) - km$

28. A certain car dealership has two locations. Last month, an average (arithmetic mean) of 11 cars per salesperson was sold at location A, and an average of 16 cars per salesperson was sold at location B. What was the average number of cars sold per salesperson at this dealership last month?

    (1) Last month, the number of salespeople at location A was 3 times the number of salespeople at location B.

    (2) Last month, the total number of cars sold at location A was 132, and the total number of cars sold at location B was 64.

    ○ Statement (1) by itself is sufficient to answer the question, but statement (2) by itself is not.

    ○ Statement (2) by itself is sufficient to answer the question, but statement (1) by itself is not.

    ○ Statements (1) and (2) taken together are sufficient to answer the question, even though neither statement by itself is sufficient.

    ○ Either statement by itself is sufficient to answer the question.

    ○ Statements (1) and (2) taken together are not sufficient to answer the question, requiring more data pertaining to the problem.

29. If an "anglet" is defined as 1 percent of 1 degree, then how many anglets are there in a circle?

    ○ 0.36

    ○ 3.6

    ○ 360

    ○ 3,600

    ○ 36,000

GO ON TO THE NEXT PAGE

30. In a certain telephone poll, 600 people were asked whether they were in favor of, against, or undecided on a certain bill being debated in the legislature. How many of the people polled were in favor of the bill?

    (1) The number of people who were in favor of the bill was 200 greater than the number of people who were against it.

    (2) Two hundred people were undecided, which was twice as many as the number who were against the bill.

    ○ Statement (1) by itself is sufficient to answer the question, but statement (2) by itself is not.

    ○ Statement (2) by itself is sufficient to answer the question, but statement (1) by itself is not.

    ○ Statements (1) and (2) taken together are sufficient to answer the question, even though neither statement by itself is sufficient.

    ○ Either statement by itself is sufficient to answer the question.

    ○ Statements (1) and (2) taken together are not sufficient to answer the question, requiring more data pertaining to the problem.

31. A number of bricks were purchased to build a fireplace at a cost of 40 cents each, but only $\frac{3}{4}$ of them were needed. If the unused 190 bricks were returned and their cost refunded, what was the cost of the bricks used to make the fireplace?

    ○ $76

    ○ $228

    ○ $304

    ○ $414

    ○ $570

32. If x is a number such that $-2 \le x \le 2$, which of the following has the largest possible absolute value?

    ○ $3x - 1$

    ○ $x^2 + 1$

    ○ $3 - x$

    ○ $x - 3$

    ○ $x^2 - x$

GO ON TO THE NEXT PAGE

33. What is the smallest value of x for which
$$\left(\frac{12}{x} + 36\right)(4 - x^2) = 0?$$

   ○ -3

   ○ -2

   ○ $-\dfrac{1}{2}$

   ○ $-\dfrac{1}{4}$

   ○ 2

34. What is the value of b?

   (1) $2a - b = 3$

   (2) $a = b - (1 - a)$

   ○ Statement (1) by itself is sufficient to answer the question, but statement (2) by itself is not.

   ○ Statement (2) by itself is sufficient to answer the question, but statement (1) by itself is not.

   ○ Statements (1) and (2) taken together are sufficient to answer the question, even though neither statement by itself is sufficient.

   ○ Either statement by itself is sufficient to answer the question.

   ○ Statements (1) and (2) taken together are not sufficient to answer the question, requiring more data pertaining to the problem.

35. Which of the following is greater than 1,000.01?

   ○ 0.00001×10^8

   ○ 0.0101×10^4

   ○ 1.1×10^2

   ○ 1.00001×10^3

   ○ 0.00010001×10^7

GO ON TO THE NEXT PAGE

36. If $a \neq b$, what is the value of $a + b$?

    (1) $\dfrac{a^2 - b^2}{a - b} = 6$

    (2) $(a + b)^2 = 36$

    ○ Statement (1) by itself is sufficient to answer the question, but statement (2) by itself is not.

    ○ Statement (2) by itself is sufficient to answer the question, but statement (1) by itself is not.

    ○ Statements (1) and (2) taken together are sufficient to answer the question, even though neither statement by itself is sufficient.

    ○ Either statement by itself is sufficient to answer the question.

    ○ Statements (1) and (2) taken together are not sufficient to answer the question, requiring more data pertaining to the problem.

37. If $2^{2m+1} = 2^{n+2}$, what is the value of $m + n$?

    (1) $2^{3n-1} = 256$

    (2) $2^{m+2n} = 256$

    ○ Statement (1) by itself is sufficient to answer the question, but statement (2) by itself is not.

    ○ Statement (2) by itself is sufficient to answer the question, but statement (1) by itself is not.

    ○ Statements (1) and (2) taken together are sufficient to answer the question, even though neither statement by itself is sufficient.

    ○ Either statement by itself is sufficient to answer the question.

    ○ Statements (1) and (2) taken together are not sufficient to answer the question, requiring more data pertaining to the problem.

STOP

Verbal Section
Time—75 minutes, 41 questions

Reading Comprehension Directions: Each passage will be followed by questions relating to that passage. After reading through the passage, choose the best response to each question and mark it on your answer sheet. Base your answers on information that is either stated or implied in the passage and not on your own knowledge. You may refer to the passage while answering the questions.

Sentence Correction Directions: These questions consist of sentences that are either partly or entirely underlined. Below each sentence are five versions of the underlined portion of the sentence. The first of these, choice (A), duplicates the original version. The four other versions revise the underlined portion of the sentence. Read the sentence and the five choices carefully and select the best version. If the original seems better than any of the revisions, select choice (A). If not, choose one of the revisions.

These questions test your recognition of correct grammatical usage and your sense of clear and economical writing. Choose answers according to the norms of standard written English for grammar, word choice, and sentence construction. Your selected answer should express the intended meaning of the original sentence as clearly and precisely as possible, while avoiding ambiguous, awkward, or unnecessarily wordy constructions.

Critical Reasoning Directions: Select the best answer for each question.

GO ON TO THE NEXT PAGE

1. According to a recent study, advertisements in medical journals often contain misleading information about the effectiveness and safety of new prescription drugs. The medical researchers who wrote the study concluded that the advertisements could result in doctors prescribing inappropriate drugs to their patients.

   The researchers' conclusion would be most strengthened if which of the following were true?

   ○ Advertisements for new prescription drugs are an important source of revenue for medical journals.

   ○ Editors of medical journals are often unable to evaluate the claims made in advertisements for new prescription drugs.

   ○ Doctors rely on the advertisements as a source of information about new prescription drugs.

   ○ Advertisements for new prescription drugs are typically less accurate than medical journal articles evaluating those same drugs.

   ○ The Food and Drug Administration, the government agency responsible for drug regulation, reviews advertisements for new drugs before the ads have been printed.

2. Uninformed about students' experience in urban classrooms, critics often condemn schools' performance as gauged by <u>an index, such as standardized test scores, that are called objective and can be quantified and overlook less measurable progress, such as that</u> in higher-level reasoning.

   ○ an index, such as standardized test scores, that are called objective and can be quantified and overlook less measurable progress, such as that

   ○ an index, such as standardized test scores, that are called objective and can be quantified and overlook less measurable progress, such as what is made

   ○ an index, such as standardized test scores, that is called objective and can be quantified and overlook less measurable progress, such as what is made

   ○ a so-called objective index, such as standardized test scores, that can be quantified and overlook less measurable progress, such as what is made

   ○ a so-called objective index, such as standardized test scores, that can be quantified and overlook less measurable progress, such as that

GO ON TO THE NEXT PAGE

3. A common social problem in the workplace occurs <u>when workers accept supervisory positions, and it causes them to lose</u> the trust of their former coworkers.

- ○ when workers accept supervisory positions, and it causes them to lose

- ○ by a worker accepting supervisory positions, which causes him to lose

- ○ when workers accept supervisory positions and so lose

- ○ when a worker who accepts a supervisory position, thereby losing

- ○ if a worker accepts a supervisory position, he would lose

Questions 4–7 refer to the following passage.

An important feature of the labor market in recent years has been the increasing participation of women, particularly married women. Many analysts suggest, however, that
(5) women comprise a secondary labor market where rates of pay and promotion prospects are inferior to those available to men. The principal reason is that women have, or are assumed to have, domestic responsibilities
(10) that compete with paid employment. Such domestic responsibilities are strongly influenced by social values, which require women to give priority to home and family over paid employment.
(15) The difficulties that women face in the labor market and in their ability to reach senior positions in organizations are accentuated with the arrival of children. In order to become full-time employees, women with children must
(20) overcome the problems of finding good, affordable child care and the psychological barriers of workplace marginality. Some

women balance domestic and workplace commitments by working part-time. However,
(25) part-time work is a precarious form of employment. Women part-timers are often the first laid off in a difficult economy. These workers are often referred to as the "reserve army" of female labor.
(30) One researcher has found that approximately 80 percent of women in their twenties who have children remain at home. Such women who later return to work represent another sector of the workforce facing difficulties. When the
(35) typical houseworker returns to the labor market, she is unsure of herself in her new environment. This doubt is accentuated by her recent immersion in housework, a very private form of work. Without recent employment experience,
(40) these women confront a restricted range of opportunities and will almost certainly be offered low-status jobs with poor prospects.

Even women professionals who interrupt their careers to have children experience
(45) difficulties. Their technical skills may become rusty or obsolete, important networks of business contacts are broken, and their delayed return to work may mean that they are likely to come up for promotion well after
(50) the age that would be otherwise normal. Consequently, women, even those of high ability, may find themselves blocked in the lower echelons of an organization, overlooked, or even "invisible" to senior
(55) management.

GO ON TO THE NEXT PAGE ➔

4. The author of the passage is primarily concerned with

    ○ advocating changes in employers' practices towards women with children.

    ○ examining some of the reasons women rarely reach the higher echelons of paid labor.

    ○ describing the psychological consequences for women of working outside the home.

    ○ taking issue with those who believe women should not work outside the home.

    ○ analyzing the contribution of women to industry and business.

5. The passage provides information to support which of the following statements about women workers?

    ○ It is the responsibility of employers to provide child care accommodations for women workers with children.

    ○ Women in high-status positions are easily able to integrate career and children.

    ○ Conditions for working mothers are much better today than they were 20 years ago.

    ○ The decision to work outside the home is often the source of considerable anxiety for women with children.

    ○ With the expense of child care, it is often not profitable for women with children to work.

6. The author's discussion of women professionals in the last paragraph serves to

    ○ show that the difficulties of integrating careers and motherhood can be overcome.

    ○ indicate that even women of higher status are not exempt from the difficulties of integrating careers and children.

    ○ defend changes in the policies of employers towards working mothers.

    ○ modify a hypothesis regarding the increased labor force participation of women.

    ○ point out the lack of opportunities for women in business.

7. According to the passage, men generally receive higher salaries and have a better chance of being promoted because women

    ○ tend to work in industries that rely almost exclusively on part-time labor.

    ○ lack the technical and managerial experience of their male counterparts.

    ○ have responsibilities outside of the workplace that demand considerable attention.

    ○ are the first to be laid off when the economy grows at a very slow pace.

    ○ suffer discrimination in the male-dominated corporate environment.

GO ON TO THE NEXT PAGE ▷

8. A state legislator argues that her state's ban on casino gambling is inconsistent and impractical, since other forms of gambling such as bingo and the state lottery are legal. She claims that, instead of vainly attempting to enforce the ban, the legislature should simply legalize all gambling and to do so would also have the positive effect of reducing the crime rate.

Which of the following, if true, most seriously weakens the legislator's argument above?

○ Since many people enjoy the thrill of participating in illegal practices, legalizing gambling would probably cause a decline rather than an increase in this activity.

○ Because prosecutors rarely seek prison terms for illegal gamblers, legalizing gambling would not result in a significant savings of money.

○ Long-term studies have shown that the number of people who participate in the lottery is higher now than it was when the lottery was prohibited.

○ Legalizing gambling would entice gamblers from states where it is still banned, and many of them are involved in other illegal activities such as drug smuggling.

○ Many people who participate in illegal gambling claim that they would risk their money on the stock market if they had more disposable income.

9. A researcher studying cats discovered that during the dream state of sleep, the cerebral cortex of a cat's brain fires messages to its body as rapidly as it does during wakefulness. In an effort to determine why the sleeping cat's body does not respond to the messages being fired by the brain, the researcher removed a cluster of neurons from a sleeping cat's brain stem, the part of the brain that connects the cerebral cortex to the spinal cord. After he had done so, the still sleeping cat got up, pounced as if it were chasing a mouse, and arched its back.

Which of the following, if true, taken together with the information above, best supports the conclusion that the sleeping cat was acting out its dreams?

○ The neurons that were removed from the brain stem normally serve to trigger the dream state of sleep and the rapid brain activity that accompanies it.

○ The cerebral cortex is able to receive and transmit sensory information even when the brain is in a sleeping state.

○ The neurons that were removed from the brain stem are normally responsible for transmitting messages from the cerebral cortex.

○ The neurons that were removed from the brain stem normally prevent messages fired by the cerebral cortex during sleep from being received by the spinal cord.

○ The types of brain waves produced by the cerebral cortex during sleep have distinctly different properties from those produced during a wakeful state.

GO ON TO THE NEXT PAGE ⟶

10. Glaciologists studying the melting Alpine glacier believe that a recently found frozen corpse, <u>apparently that of a shepherd who is thought to have lived</u> about 4,600 years ago, was preserved uncrushed by snow and ice because of the body's unique topographical position.

    ○ apparently that of a shepherd who is thought to have lived

    ○ that of a shepherd, apparently, who was thought to live

    ○ that of an apparent shepherd who was thought to live

    ○ that of a shepherd who is thought of as apparently living

    ○ that of a shepherd who was apparently thought to live

11. In contrast to Walt Whitman, <u>Ezra Pound considered that late 19th-century American poetry is not a distinct formal repertoire informed by its own ideology and is</u> essentially an outgrowth of the British poetic tradition.

    ○ Ezra Pound considered that late 19th-century American poetry is not a distinct formal repertoire informed by its own ideology and is

    ○ Ezra Pound considered late 19th-century American poetry not as a distinct formal repertoire informed by its own ideology but

    ○ Ezra Pound considered late 19th-century American poetry not a distinct formal repertoire informed by its own ideology but

    ○ it was considered by Ezra Pound that late 19th-century American poetry is not a distinct formal repertoire informed by its own ideology but

    ○ late 19th-century American poetry was considered by Ezra Pound not to be a distinct formal repertoire informed by its own ideology and is

GO ON TO THE NEXT PAGE ⟩

Questions 12–14 refer to the following passage.

A 1973 Supreme Court decision and related Senate hearings focused congressional criticism on the 1966 Freedom of Information Act. Its unconditional exemption of any
(5) material stamped "classified"—i.e., containing information considered relevant to national security—forced the Court to uphold non-disclosure in *EPA v. Mink*. Justice Potter Stewart explained that the Act provided "no
(10) means to question a decision to stamp a document 'secret.'" Senate witnesses testified that the wording of certain articles in the Act permitted bureaucrats to discourage requests for newsworthy documents.
(15) In response, a House committee drafted HR 12471, proposing several amendments to the Act. A provision was reworded to ensure release of documents to any applicant providing a "reasonable description"—exact
(20) titles and numbers were no longer to be mandatory. The courts were empowered to review classified documents and rule on their status. The Senate companion bill, S 2543, included these provisions as well as others:
(25) standardization of search and copy fees, sanctions against noncompliant federal employees, and a provision for nonexempt portions of a classified document to be released.
(30) The Justice and Defense departments objected to the changes as "costly, burdensome, and inflexible." They argued that the time limits imposed on response "might actually hamper access to
(35) information." The Pentagon asserted that judicial review of exemptions could pose a threat to national security. President Ford, upon taking office in August 1974, concurred.
HR 12471 passed in March 1974; S 2543 was
(40) approved in May after the adoption of further

amendments to reduce the number of unconditional exemptions granted in 1966. The Hart Amendment, for instance, mandated disclosure of law enforcement records, unless
(45) their release would interfere with a trial or investigation, invade personal privacy, or disclose an informer's identity. This amendment provoked another presidential objection: millions of pages of FBI records
(50) would be subject to public scrutiny, unless each individual section were proven exempt.
Before submitting the legislation to Ford, a joint conference of both houses amalgamated the two versions of the bill, while making
(55) further changes to incorporate Ford's criticisms. The administration of disciplinary sanctions was transferred from the courts to the executive branch; provisions were included to accord due weight to
(60) departmental expertise in the evaluation of "classified" exemptions. The identity of confidential sources was in all cases to be protected. Ford nevertheless vetoed the bill, but the veto was overridden by a two-thirds vote in
(65) both houses.

GO ON TO THE NEXT PAGE ⟩

12. According to the passage, the Justice and Defense departments opposed the proposed revision of the Freedom of Information Act on the grounds that it

    ○ was an attempt to block public access to information.

    ○ would violate national security agreements.

    ○ would pose administrative problems.

    ○ was an attempt to curtail their own departmental power.

    ○ would weaken the president's authority.

13. Which of the following statements, if true, supports the assertion that "judicial review of exemptions could pose a threat to national security" (lines 36–37)?

    ○ Judges lack the expertise to evaluate the significance of military intelligence records.

    ○ Many of the documents that are presently stamped "classified" contain information that is inaccurate or outdated.

    ○ It would be time consuming and expensive for judges to review millions of pages of classified records.

    ○ Some judges are likely to rule on exemptions in accordance with vested interests of political action groups.

    ○ The practice of judicial review of exemptions will succeed only if it meets with presidential approval.

14. Which of the following statements is in accordance with President Ford's position on disclosure of FBI records?

    ○ FBI records should be exempt from the provisions of the Freedom of Information Act.

    ○ FBI records should only be withheld from release if such release constitutes a threat to national security.

    ○ It would be too expensive and time consuming to identify exempt sections of FBI records.

    ○ Protection of the identity of confidential sources is more important than the protection of personal privacy or investigative secrecy.

    ○ FBI records should not be reviewed section by section before being released to the public.

15. Local reporters investigating the labor dispute reported that only half of the workers in the plant were covered by the union health plan; at least as much as a hundred and more others had not any health insurance whatsoever.

    ○ at least as much as a hundred and more others had not any

    ○ at least as much as more than a hundred others had no

    ○ more than a hundred others had not any

    ○ more than a hundred others had no

    ○ there was at least a hundred or more others without any

GO ON TO THE NEXT PAGE ⇨

16. According to a commonly held archaeological theory, the Neanderthals of Europe, an archaic version of *Homo sapiens*, competed with and were eventually replaced by modern humans with little or no interbreeding between the two populations. A rival theory, developed more recently, suggests that Neanderthals were more similar to modern humans than previously supposed—that, in fact, modern humans evolved from them and from other archaic versions of *Homo sapiens*.

    Evidence that would strongly support the more recent theory concerning the relationship between Neanderthals and modern humans would be

    ○ DNA analyses indicating that modern humans appeared in Africa 200,000 years ago, before migrating to Europe and other continents.

    ○ archaeological evidence that Neanderthals and modern humans developed similar cultures, shared stone tools, and performed similar burial rituals.

    ○ skulls of early modern humans in central Europe that exhibit a bone near the mandibular nerve that is a typical Neanderthal characteristic.

    ○ evidence that the stone tools of Neanderthals remained unchanged for thousands of years, while the tools of modern humans in Europe were more specialized.

    ○ biological evidence that Neanderthals had unique physical traits that enabled them to survive Ice Age temperatures in Europe.

17. Archaeologists have shown that ingesting lead in drinking water was a significant health hazard for the ancient Romans, <u>like that of modern Americans.</u>

    ○ like that of modern Americans.

    ○ as that for modern Americans.

    ○ just as modern Americans do.

    ○ as do modern Americans.

    ○ as it is for modern Americans.

GO ON TO THE NEXT PAGE ▷

18. Born Nathan Weinstein in New York City on October 17, 1903, <u>Nathanael West's first novel, *The Dream Life of Balso Snell* was written during a stay in Paris and published when the author</u> was twenty-eight.

    ○ Nathanael West's first novel, *The Dream Life of Balso Snell* was written during a stay in Paris and published when the author

    ○ Nathanael West's first novel, *The Dream Life of Balso Snell*, written while he was staying in Paris, was published when the author

    ○ Nathanael West's *The Dream Life of Balso Snell*, his first novel, was written while the author was staying in Paris and published when he

    ○ Nathanael West wrote his first novel, *The Dream Life of Balso Snell*, during a stay in Paris and published it when he

    ○ when Nathanael West was staying in Paris, he wrote his first novel, *The Dream Life of Balso Snell*, publishing it when he

19. Aggressive fertility treatments are not responsible for the rise in the incidence of twin births. Rather, this increase can be attributed to the fact that women are waiting longer to become mothers. Statistically, women over 35 are more likely to conceive twins, and these women comprise a greater percentage of women giving birth than ever before.

    The argument above is flawed in that it ignores the possibility that

    ○ many women over 35 who give birth to twins are not first-time mothers.

    ○ women over 35 are not the only women who give birth to twins.

    ○ the correlation between fertility treatments and the increased incidence of multiple births may be a coincidence.

    ○ on average, women over 35 are no more likely to conceive identical twins than other women are.

    ○ women over 35 are more likely to resort to the sorts of fertility treatments that tend to yield twin births.

GO ON TO THE NEXT PAGE

Questions 20–23 refer to the following passage.

Modern methods of predicting earthquakes recognize that quakes, far from being geologic anomalies, are part of the periodic accumulation and discharge of seismic energy.
(5)   As continents receive the horizontal thrust of seafloor plates, crustal strains develop. Accumulation of strain can take anywhere from 100 years in certain coastal locations to over a millennium in some inland regions
(10)   before a critical point is reached and a rupture occurs. In both areas, the buildup of strain is accompanied by long- and short-range precursory phenomena that are crucial to earthquake prediction.
(15)   Quakes along active faults—like those along the Pacific coasts—are usually frequent; scientists designate such areas as quake-prone. However, when the time interval between quakes is great, as in inland regions, locating
(20)   active faults is only a beginning. Geological scars of past subsidence, cracks, and offsets are useful in determining potential quake locations, as are seismicity gaps, areas where no small quakes have been recorded.
(25)   Seismologists may also consult the historical record. Primary sources range from eyewitness accounts of ancient quakes to recent official documentation of quake-related damage.
(30)   Once the perimeters of a quake-prone zone are established, a network of base stations can monitor precursory phenomena. Stations must extend over a wide area yet be placed at measured intervals to obtain precise readings.
(35)   Changes in geochemical readings (electric currents, radon concentrations) and in groundwater levels, as well as the occurrence of microearthquakes, are valuable precursors. Crustal movements—tilting, rising, and
(40)   expansion or contraction of the ground

surface—can be read through triangulation and leveling surveys taken over the course of decades. Theoretically, if an area's critical strain is known—the magnitude of strain
(45)   necessary to produce a rupture—subtracting the measured accumulated crustal strain from the critical strain will indicate a time frame for an impending quake.
    Violent tilting and foreshocks are among
(50)   phenomena classified as short-term precursors. Many are still being identified as new quakes occur. Such precursors are valuable since their appearance can permit prediction of a quake to within hours of the
(55)   primary rupture. Here, too, historical documents are useful. Seismologists recognized the liquefaction of sand as a precursor after a 1964 quake in Japan.

20. According to the passage, a major difference between coastal regions and inland regions is that in coastal regions

   ○   crustal strain does not occur.

   ○   earthquakes are less numerous.

   ○   critical points are reached more quickly.

   ○   precursory phenomena are seldom observed.

   ○   seafloor plate action is less powerful.

GO ON TO THE NEXT PAGE ⟩

21. The primary purpose of the passage is to

   ○ clarify the way in which earthquakes develop in inland locations.

   ○ show that earthquakes are a result of the normal accumulation and discharge of seismic energy.

   ○ discuss the accumulation of crustal strain in coastal regions.

   ○ argue that precursory phenomena should be disregarded in attempts at quake prediction.

   ○ describe methods of earthquake prediction and explain the importance of precursory phenomena.

22. The primary function of the third paragraph is to

   ○ explain the relationship between accumulated and critical strain.

   ○ describe the use of precise intervals in establishing networks of base stations.

   ○ summarize the differences between earthquakes in coastal and inland regions.

   ○ outline some of the methods used by seismologists to predict earthquakes.

   ○ suggest that critical strain is not spread evenly along most major fault lines.

23. According to the passage, knowledge of an area's critical strain can help seismologists

   ○ estimate the date of a future earthquake.

   ○ calculate the severity of an initial rupture.

   ○ measure the seismic force along a fault.

   ○ revise the distances between base stations.

   ○ predict the rate of future crustal movement.

GO ON TO THE NEXT PAGE

24. Until the federal government began providing low-cost flood insurance to coastal property owners, construction along beaches was limited by owners' fears that their property would be washed away. Since the insurance was made available, however, beachfront construction has boomed, and land erosion has increased at a dangerous rate.

    Which of the following, if feasible, offers the best prospects for the federal government to put a stop to the problem of land erosion along beaches?

    ○ Prohibiting beachfront property owners from embellishing or adding to existing buildings

    ○ Utilizing computer science techniques to obtain detailed information on the extent and rapidity of land erosion along beaches

    ○ Enacting building codes requiring new beachfront structures in flood-threatened areas to be elevated above the high-water level of a storm

    ○ Compensating beachfront property owners for moving to a new location off the coast while canceling flood insurance benefits for any new or remaining beachfront construction

    ○ Requiring beachfront property owners receiving flood insurance coverage to adopt construction standards that will protect their buildings from inundation

25. In commercial garment construction, one advantage of serging over single-needle sewing is that the seam allowance is overcast as the seam is sewn <u>instead of</u> a separate process requiring deeper seam allowances.

    ○ instead of

    ○ rather than in

    ○ in contrast with

    ○ as opposed to

    ○ as against being done in

GO ON TO THE NEXT PAGE ⇨

26. People with Williams syndrome, a rare mental disorder, are often highly articulate and sensitive. Not uncommonly, they are gifted in music and possess rich vocabularies. Yet these same people, because of their lack of ability in basic arithmetic and difficulty distinguishing left from right, are misleadingly labeled mentally retarded. As evaluated by conventional means, such as IQ tests, their intelligence is no higher than that of people with Down syndrome, despite the fact that people with Down syndrome have uniformly limited cognitive abilities and show no specialized aptitudes.

The author is arguing that

- ○ conventional methods of measuring intelligence, such as IQ tests, are inadequate for evaluating the capabilities of people with certain mental disorders, such as Williams syndrome.

- ○ people with Down syndrome usually have less verbal and musical ability but more mathematical and spatial ability than do people with Williams syndrome.

- ○ conventional methods of measuring intelligence tend to consider basic mathematical and spatial ability to be more important than verbal and musical skills.

- ○ people with Williams syndrome are only rarely given the opportunity to develop their unique musical and verbal abilities.

- ○ people with Williams syndrome need greater encouragement if they are to develop their mathematical spatial skills.

27. When the nineteenth-century German bacteriologist Robert Koch identified a particular bacterium as responsible for cholera, Max von Pettenkoffer, a physician, expressed his skepticism by voluntarily drinking an entire bottle of the allegedly responsible bacteria. Although von Pettenkoffer took his failure to come down with the disease as a refutation of Koch's hypothesis that cholera was caused by bacteria, Koch argued that von Pettenkoffer had been protected by his own stomach acid. The acid secreted by the stomach, Koch explained, kills most ingested bacteria.

Which of the following, if true, provides the most evidence to support Koch's counterargument?

- ○ Peptic ulcers, often associated with excessive secretions of stomach acid, are common in certain areas characterized by high rates of cholera.

- ○ As von Pettenkoffer later admitted that he had previously had cholera, it is probable that he had developed antibodies that protected him from a second attack.

- ○ Cholera is endemic in areas in which poor sanitation results in high concentrations of cholera bacteria in drinking water.

- ○ Although stomach acid kills most ingested bacteria, large numbers of *E. coli* bacteria nonetheless manage to make their way to the lower intestine of the digestive tract.

- ○ Cholera bacteria ingested with bicarbonate of soda, a neutralizer of stomach acid, is more likely to result in cholera than if the bacteria are ingested alone.

GO ON TO THE NEXT PAGE ⟹

28. The Limón Dance Company believes that, since the death of José Limón in 1972, <u>they have and will continue to perpetuate the shared artistic vision of Limón and his mentor and collaborator Doris Humphrey,</u> who both choreographed works in the company's active repertory.

   ○ they have and will continue to perpetuate the shared artistic vision of Limón and his mentor and collaborator Doris Humphrey,

   ○ they have and will continue to perpetuate Limón and his mentor and collaborator Doris Humphrey's shared artistic vision,

   ○ it has and will continue to perpetuate the shared artistic vision of Limón and his mentor and collaborator Doris Humphrey,

   ○ it has perpetuated and will continue perpetuating the artistic vision that Limón and his mentor and collaborator Doris Humphrey shared,

   ○ it has continued to perpetuate the shared artistic vision of Limón and his mentor and collaborator Doris Humphrey,

29. Agencies studying discrimination in housing have experimentally proved that minority clients are often discouraged as prospective buyers of residential real estate and <u>the antidiscrimination legislation of recent decades were only mitigating, rather than abolishing, inequity in housing practices.</u>

   ○ the antidiscrimination legislation of recent decades were only mitigating, rather than abolishing, inequity in housing practices

   ○ in recent decades, the antidiscrimination legislation only mitigated, rather than abolishing, inequity in housing practices

   ○ that antidiscrimination legislation of recent decades has only mitigated, rather than abolished, inequity in housing practices

   ○ that, in recent decades, antidiscrimination legislation has only mitigated, rather than abolishing, housing practices' inequity

   ○ that recent decades' antidiscrimination legislation only were mitigating, rather than abolishing, housing practices' inequity

GO ON TO THE NEXT PAGE ▷

30. Citing the legal precedent set by asbestos exposure cases, a state judge agreed to combine a series of workplace disability cases involving repetitive stress injuries to the hands and wrists. The judge's decision to consolidate hundreds of suits by data entry workers, word processors, newspaper employees, and other workers who use computers into one case is likely to prove detrimental for the computer-manufacturing companies being sued, notwithstanding the defense's argument that the cases should not be combined because of the different individuals and workplaces involved.

Which of the following, if true, casts the most serious doubt on the validity of the judge's decision to consolidate the cases?

○ Unlike asbestos exposure cases, in which the allegedly liable product is the same in each situation, the type and quality of the allegedly liable office equipment is different in each case

○ The fact that consolidation will accelerate the legal process may prove advantageous for the defense, as it limits the number of witnesses who can testify for the plaintiffs

○ One of the most common causes of repetitive stress injuries is companies' failure to allow their employees adequate rest time from using computer keyboards

○ Whereas exposure to asbestos often leads to fatal forms of cancer, repetitive stress injury typically results in personal discomfort and only rarely in unemployability

○ The issue of responsibility for repetitive stress injury cannot be resolved without first addressing the question of its existence as an actual medical condition.

31. Each of William Kennedy's novels in the "Albany Trilogy"—*Ironweed*, *Legs*, and *Billy Phelan's Greatest Game*—are set in the area around Albany, New York, a region whose history also suggested some details of the novel's plots.

○ Each of William Kennedy's novels in the "Albany Trilogy"—*Ironweed*, *Legs*, and *Billy Phelan's Greatest Game*—are set in the area around Albany, New York,

○ *Ironweed*, *Legs*, and *Billy Phelan's Greatest Game*—each of them novels in William Kennedy's "Albany Trilogy"—are set in the area around Albany, New York,

○ William Kennedy's "Albany Trilogy" novels—*Ironweed*, *Legs*, and *Billy Phelan's Greatest Game*—are all set in the area around Albany, New York,

○ Novels by William Kennedy—*Ironweed*, *Legs*, and *Billy Phelan's Greatest Game*—each one of the "Albany Trilogy" novels, is set in the area around Albany, New York,

○ Novels by William Kennedy—*Ironweed*, *Legs*, and *Billy Phelan's Greatest Game*—every one of the "Albany Trilogy" novels are set in the area around Albany, New York,

GO ON TO THE NEXT PAGE

32. Between 1977 and 1989, the percentage of income paid to federal taxes by the richest 1 percent of Americans decreased from 40 percent to 25 percent. By the end of that same period, however, the richest 1 percent of Americans were paying a larger proportion of all federal tax revenues, growing from 12.7 percent in 1977 to 16.2 percent in 1989.

Which of the following, if true, contributes most to an explanation of the discrepancy described above?

○ Between 1977 and 1989, the Internal Revenue Service increased the percentage of its staff members responsible for audits and tax collection.

○ Between 1977 and 1989, the before-tax income of the richest 1 percent of Americans increased by over 75 percent when adjusted for inflation.

○ Between 1977 and 1989, many of the richest 1 percent of Americans shifted their investments from taxable to untaxable assets.

○ Between 1977 and 1989, the tax rate paid by middle-income Americans was reduced, but several tax loopholes were eliminated.

○ Between 1977 and 1989, the amount of federal taxes paid by the richest 1 percent of Americans increased by $45 billion, while the amount paid by all Americans rose by $50 billion.

Questions 33–35 refer to the following passage.

Contamination is the unintended presence of harmful substances or organisms in food. While it is true that recent scientific advances have resulted in safer foods, better methods of
(5) preservation, and improved storage practices, it is still necessary to guard against the practices that can increase the likelihood of food contamination. Because food-borne illness poses a potentially serious threat to
(10) public health, preventing contamination of safe food needs to be a prime objective of every food service manager. Furthermore, a food service manager must possess accurate information on the different hazards
(15) associated with the contamination of food in the event that a food-borne illness crisis does arise. A full understanding of the biological, chemical, and physical hazards allows the food service manager to implement the control
(20) measures necessary to minimize the health risks associated with food and, thus, to decrease the possibility of contamination.

The most serious risk associated with food is the biological hazard. Biological hazards are
(25) dangers to food from pathogenic (disease-causing) microorganisms, such as bacteria, viruses, parasites, and fungi, and from toxins that occur in certain plants and fish. When biological hazards result in food-borne
(30) illnesses, these illnesses are generally classified as either infections or intoxications. A food-borne infection is a disease that results from eating food containing living harmful microorganisms. One of the most frequently
(35) reported diseases of this type is salmonellosis, which results from the consumption of food contaminated with live pathogenic *Salmonella*.

GO ON TO THE NEXT PAGE ▷

The other major form of biologically induced
(40) food-borne illness is intoxication,
which results when toxins, or poisons, from
bacterial or mold growth are present in
ingested food and cause illness in the host (the
human body). These toxins are generally
(45) odorless and tasteless and are capable of
causing disease even after the microorganisms
have been killed. *Staphylococcus* food
intoxication is one of the most common types
of food-borne illness reported in the United
(50) States.

33. Which of the following best expresses the
main idea of the passage?

○ Despite recent scientific advances,
food-borne illness continues to present
a serious risk to public health.

○ Although chemical and physical
hazards can cause a food-borne illness,
biological hazards pose the most serious
risk of food contamination.

○ Knowledge of contamination sources is
essential for a food service manager to
safely operate a food establishment.

○ Biological, chemical, and physical
hazards represent the main sources of
food contamination.

○ The illnesses caused by the
contamination of food by biological
hazards take the form of either a
food-borne infection or a food-borne
intoxication.

34. The author of the passage would most
likely agree that a food service manager's
comprehension of the nature of potential
food hazards is

○ crucial to the safety of a food service
operation.

○ necessarily limited due to the
complexity of contamination sources.

○ the primary factor in an employer's
decision to hire that manager.

○ utilized exclusively for the prevention of
food-borne illness.

○ vitally important but nearly impossible
to attain.

35. According to the passage, pathogenic
microorganisms

○ are the most common form of biological
hazard.

○ can only trigger a food-borne illness
when alive.

○ are toxins that occur in certain plants
and fish.

○ include life forms such as bacteria and
parasites.

○ are difficult to detect because they are
odorless and tasteless.

GO ON TO THE NEXT PAGE

36. Still employing the system of binomial nomenclature devised in the 18th century by Linnaeus, new technology enables modern-day biological taxonomists to not only classify species but to sort their evolutionary relationships by an approach that analyzes the sequences of DNA.

    ○ new technology enables modern-day biological taxonomists to not only classify species but to sort

    ○ modern-day biological taxonomists using new technology can not only classify species but also sort

    ○ using new technology enables modern-day biological taxonomists to not only classify species but they also sort

    ○ using new technology not only in classifying species modern-day biological taxonomists are enabled to also sort them for

    ○ when modern-day biological taxonomists are enabled by new technology, not only do they classify species, they also can sort

37. American executives, unlike their Japanese counterparts, have pressure to show high profits in each quarterly report, with little thought given to long-term goals.

    ○ have pressure to show

    ○ are under pressure to show

    ○ are under pressure of showing

    ○ are pressured toward showing

    ○ have pressure that they should show

38. The impact of the 1930s crisis on the different regions of Country X varied depending on the relationship of each region's economy to the international marketplace, with Region A most drastically affected. Interestingly, demand in foreign markets for Region A's tropical crops was only slightly affected by the drop in income levels after 1929; the same was true of foreign demand for the temperate-zone basic foodstuffs produced by Region B. However, Region B was better able to survive the crisis because it could adjust the supply of its crops. Since Region A could not, its economy was devastated by the slight decrease in foreign demand.

    Which one of the following provides the most reasonable explanation for the fact that Region A's economy was more drastically affected by the slight decrease in demand than was Region B's?

GO ON TO THE NEXT PAGE

○ Tropical crops like those produced by Region A usually command higher prices on the world market than do basic foodstuffs like those produced by Region B.

○ Region B's economy was dependent on annual crops, the supply of which is easily adjusted because the plants are renewed each year, in contrast to the perennial crops grown in Region A.

○ Because tropical goods are generally bought by more affluent consumers, demand for these products rarely declines even when overall income levels drop.

○ The temperate-zone basic foodstuffs produced in Region B directly competed with similar crops produced by the countries that imported Region B's goods.

○ Because Region B's economy was dependent on the export of basic foodstuffs, there was only a slight decline in demand for its goods even after income levels dropped.

39. In the late 19th century, <u>when Vassar was a small, recently founded women's college, founding professor and astronomer Maria Mitchell taught as many Astronomy majors in a given year as there are today, when</u> Vassar is a much larger, coeducational college.

○ when Vassar was a small, recently founded women's college, founding professor and astronomer Maria Mitchell taught as many Astronomy majors in a given year as there are today, when

○ when Vassar was a small, recently founded women's college, in a given year, founding professor and astronomer Maria Mitchell taught just as many Astronomy majors as there are in a given year today, when

○ while Vassar was a small, recently founded women's college, founding professor and astronomer Maria Mitchell taught a number of Astronomy majors in a given year such as there are today, when

○ while Vassar was a small, recently founded women's college, founding professor and astronomer Maria Mitchell taught such a number of Astronomy majors in a given year as are there today, whereas

○ when Vassar was a small, recently founded women's college, founding professor and astronomer Maria Mitchell taught a number of Astronomy majors just as large in a given year as the number that is there today, while

GO ON TO THE NEXT PAGE

40. The work of short fiction writer Charles Chesnutt reflects characteristic interests of his contemporary "local colorists" <u>as much as the intellectual ferment and historical reassessments of Black American culture during the late 19th century.</u>

    ○ as much as the intellectual ferment and historical reassessments of Black American culture during the late 19th century.

    ○ as much as it did the intellectual ferment in, and historical reassessments of, Black American culture in the late 19th century.

    ○ as much as it had reflected, during the late 19th century, the intellectual ferment and historical reassessments of Black American culture.

    ○ as much as it was reflective and characteristic of the intellectual ferment and historical reassessments of late 19th century Black American culture.

    ○ as much as it does the intellectual ferment and historical reassessments of late-19th-century Black American culture.

41. Just as the various languages contributing to English broaden and enrich its expressive range with words as diverse as the Arabic *simoon,* the Greek *zephyr,* and the Native American *chinook,* <u>so the many musical traditions coexisting in U.S. culture create unlimited possibilities for the fusion of musical styles.</u>

    ○ so the many musical traditions coexisting in U.S. culture create unlimited possibilities for the fusion of musical styles.

    ○ similarly, the coexistence of many musical traditions in U.S. culture create unlimited possibilities in the fusing of musical styles.

    ○ the many musical traditions coexisting in U.S. culture are creating unlimited possibilities in musical styles' fusion.

    ○ in the same way, possibilities for the fusion of musical styles are unlimited, owing to the many musical traditions that coexist in U.S. culture.

    ○ so it is in U.S. culture, where the many coexistent musical traditions make it possible that unlimited fusion of musical styles may be created.

STOP

## Part Five

PRACTICE TEST ANSWERS AND EXPLANATIONS

PRACTICE TEST
ANSWER KEY

QUANTITATIVE			
1. C		20. D	
2. E		21. B	
3. B		22. D	
4. B		23. E	
5. D		24. B	
6. A		25. E	
7. C		26. C	
8. A		27. E	
9. C		28. D	
10. D		29. E	
11. D		30. B	
12. B		31. B	
13. E		32. A	
14. C		33. B	
15. A		34. B	
16. A		35. E	
17. D		36. A	
18. A		37. D	
19. D			

VERBAL			
1. C		22. D	
2. E		23. A	
3. C		24. D	
4. B		25. B	
5. D		26. A	
6. B		27. E	
7. C		28. E	
8. D		29. C	
9. D		30. A	
10. A		31. C	
11. C		32. B	
12. C		33. C	
13. A		34. A	
14. A		35. D	
15. D		36. B	
16. C		37. B	
17. E		38. B	
18. D		39. A	
19. E		40. E	
20. C		41. A	
21. E			

QUANTITATIVE SECTION EXPLANATIONS

1. C

Here we have a percent problem with no numbers. One thing you know: You can't simply subtract the percents to get "25% minus 20% equals a 5% increase," because the percents are of different wholes. The percent decrease is a percentage of the new, increased amount, not a percentage of the original amount. The best way to solve problems like this is to use a concrete number. Since we're dealing with percents, the number to start with is 100. (Don't worry about whether 100 is a "realistic" number in the context of the problem; we just need a convenient number to tell us how big the final amount is relative to the starting amount.) Say the price of copper starts at $100. Because 25% of $100 is $25, if the price of copper increases by 25%, it rises by $25 to $125. Now the price decreases by 20%. Because 20% is $\frac{1}{5}$, the price drops by $\frac{125}{5}$, or $25. So the price drops to $100. That's the original price, so the answer is (C).

2. E

This problem is just a matter of keeping the information straight. The easiest way to do this is to make a scratchwork chart, putting one person's initial above another when the first person is known to be taller. The trick is to make sure you don't unwittingly imply a relationship in heights when none is stated, so draw your chart very carefully. Sidney is known to be taller than Roger, so Sidney's initial goes above Roger's. Roger is taller than Vernon, so Vernon goes below Roger (and Sidney). Billy is taller than Roger, so he goes above Roger. But who is taller: Sidney or Billy? We have no way of knowing, so we'll put Billy next to Sidney. Billy is also taller than Felix, so we put Felix underneath Billy. However, we have no idea of Felix's height in relation to anyone else's, so we should put Felix off to the side. Your chart might look something like this:

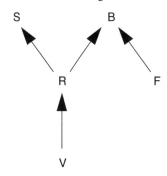

Now try the answer choices. As we just said, we only know Felix's height in relation to Billy, so (A) and (C) are out. (B) isn't necessarily true either: Both Sidney and Billy are taller than Roger, but we don't know who is taller than the other. That kills (D), too: Though Sidney and Billy are both taller than Roger, we can't conclude that Sidney is also taller than Felix simply because Billy is. (E) is left by process of elimination. Just to check, Billy is taller than Roger and Roger is taller than Vernon, so Billy does indeed have to be taller than Vernon.

3. B

Our first instinct might be to do a bunch of math on the complicated equation. But with only two variables, we just need the value of one to solve for the other. Since we are asked for x, we need a value for y. There's no need to do any calculation.

(1) Insufficient: y may equal 2, but it may also equal -2. Since y could have two values, x could have two values as well. Be careful of squared variables—the GMAT often tests the concept that they may have negative as well as positive solutions.

(2) Sufficient: The value of y is given, so the value of x can be determined. The Statement is sufficient.

4. B

We are asked to find the percentage of all cases that must be tested. The total number of cases is 120 + 80 = 200. For the spring water, the bottler must test 0.05(120) = 6 cases, and for the sparking water, he must test 0.1(80) = 8 cases. The total number of cases to be tested for the spring and sparkling water combined is 6 + 8 = 14, which is $\frac{14}{200} = \frac{7}{100} = 7\%$ of all cases.

5. D

The GMAT rewards those who think critically about the information in the question stem, not those who just do a bunch of math and leave it at that. $xy > 0$ cannot be simplified mathematically, but there is something that can be deduced from it—that x and y must have the same sign. Either both are positive or both are negative.

We are asked to find the answer choice that could never be true under any circumstances. Since the question stem gives us information about positives and negatives, those are the circumstances that we'll use in analyzing the answer choices. If x and y are both positive, (A) and (E) are true. If x and y are both negative, (B), (C), and (E) are true. That leaves only (D), which must always be false. A fraction can only be negative if the numerator and denominator (x and y here) have different signs.

It would also be possible to solve this problem by Picking Numbers. It would be very important to keep the question in mind and not stop at the first false answer choice, as you'd only know that it *could* be false, not that it *must* be.

6. A

The first thing we know when we see a problem like this is that it doesn't require advanced exponential computation. The GMAT isn't about testing difficult computation; it tests whether

we understand the basic rules of manipulating exponents. We can only apply those rules if the expressions have the same base. The equation can be rewritten: $(3)^{(3a+4)} = (3^2)^a$. When we raise a power to an exponent, we multiply the exponents: $(3^2)^a = (3)^{2a}$. So the equation is $(3)^{(3a+4)} = (3)^{2a}$. Since both sides of the equation have the same base, 3, we can set the two exponents equal: $3a + 4 = 2a$. The rest is simple algebra: $3a + 4 = 2a$, $a + 4 = 0$, and $a = -4$.

7. C

To determine the standard deviation for a set of numbers, you need to know how the numbers are spread out within the set. Since the table (stem) gives us the averages and the number of students, we need information about how spread out the students are in Class A and Class B to solve.

(1) Insufficient: This Statement gives you information about how spread out Class A is but offers you no information about Class B.

(2) Insufficient: This Statement gives you information about how spread out Class B is but offers you no information about Class A.

In combination: The Statements are sufficient since Statement (1) gives information about the standard deviation of Class A and (2) gives information about the standard deviation for Class B. Although you cannot determine the exact standard deviations of either class, you can see that Class B has a much narrower distribution of members than Class A, and from this, you could determine that Class A would have a greater standard deviation than Class B. Choice (C) is the correct answer.

8. A

Since the numbers are consecutive, we only need know any value, along with its place on the list, to be able to determine the entire list—largest value included.

(1) Sufficient: We're given one variable and one equation for the smallest integer on the list. That means we could solve for the smallest integer and add 10 to find the greatest integer. Remember, an exponent of 1/3 is equivalent to a cube root, which will only have one solution—we don't need to get caught up in the math here.

(2) Insufficient: If $\frac{1}{64} = x^{-2}$, then $\frac{1}{64} = \frac{1}{x^2}$ and $x^2 = 64$.

So $x = 8$ or $x = -8$.

There are two different possibilities for the smallest integer on the list, so there must be two different possibilities for the greatest integer on the list. Statement (2) is insufficient.

9. C

We're told that the average of $3a + 4$ and another number, which we'll call x, is $2a$. That means $\frac{(3a+4)+x}{2} = 2a$. We can solve for x in terms of a:

Original equation: $\frac{(3a+4)+a}{2} = 2a$

Multiply both sides by 2: $(3a + 4) + x = 4a$

Subtract 4 from both sides: $3a + x = 4a - 4$

Subtract $3a$ from both sides: $x = a - 4$

We are asked not to find x, although wrong answer (B) awaits us if we lose sight of that. Rather, we are asked to solve for the average of x and a.

Average of x and a: $\frac{x+a}{2}$

Substitute $x = a - 4$: $\frac{a-4+a}{2}$

Combine like terms: $\frac{2a-4}{2}$

Cancel the 2: $a - 2$

You could also have solved this by Picking a Number for a, such as 2. Then, $3a + 4$ is 10, and the average of 10 and the unknown number x is $2a$, or 4. So $\frac{10+x}{2} = 4$, $10 + x = 8$, and $x = -2$. The average of x and a, therefore, is just the average of -2 and 2, which is $\frac{2+(-2)}{2}$, or 0. So look at the answer choices for the ones that equal 0 when $a = 2$. The only one that fits is (C), $a - 2$.

10. D

We're told to figure out when Jan will catch up with Tom. Jan reads at the rate of 40 pages per hour, and Tom reads at the rate of 30 pages per hour. Tom starts reading 50 minutes ahead of Jan. Since 50 minutes is $\frac{5}{6}$ of an hour, by the time Jan starts reading at 5:20, Tom has already read $\frac{5}{6} \times 30 = 25$ pages. You might have saved yourself some work by noticing that Jan gains 10 pages an hour on Tom, since she reads 10 pages an hour faster. Since he's got a head start of 25 pages at 5:20, it should take her $\frac{25\text{(pages)}}{10\text{(pages/hour)}} = 2.5$ (hours) for her to catch him.

You can also work out the problem algebraically. The number of pages Jan has read at any given time after 5:20 is $40x$, where x is the time in hours from 5:20. At 6:20 she's read 40 pages, at 7:20 she's read 80 pages, etc. The number of pages that Tom has read at any time after 5:20 is $25 + 30x$. We want to know when these quantities will be equal; that is, when $25 + 30x = 40x$.

Solving for x, we get $25 = 40x - 30x$, $25 = 10x$, $2\frac{1}{2} = x$.

So it takes $2\frac{1}{2}$ hours for Jan to catch Tom. Since Jan started at 5:20, this means she will catch Tom at precisely 7:50.

This is also a very good Backsolving question. See where each is at a given time. If they are on the same page, that's the right answer. Let's say we started with (B). At 9:00, Tom will have been reading for 4½ hours at 30 pages per hour. That's 4.5(30) = 135 pages. Jan will have been reading for 3⅔ hours at 40 pages per hour. That's $\frac{11}{3}(40)=146\frac{2}{3}$ pages. Jan is ahead of Tom, so we need an earlier time. Eliminate (A) and (B), then test (D). At 7:50, Tom will have been reading for 3⅓ hours at 30 pages per hour. That's $\frac{10}{3}(30)=$ 100 pages. Jan will have been reading for 2½ hours at 40 pages, for a total of 2.5(40) = 100 pages. They're on the same page. (D) is correct.

11. D

The only thing we'd need to figure out how long it would take to build 64 houses is the speed with which each company builds houses. This being Data Sufficiency, we wouldn't bother with the calculation. We're already given the rate at which Mike's company builds, so all we need is Todd's company's rate.

(1) Sufficient: This allows us to get Mike's time from Todd's time, which we already know.

(2) Sufficient: Mike's rate is exactly what we're looking for.

12. B

It wouldn't be too ridiculously time consuming just to list out all the multiples of 3 in question (15, 18, 21, 24, 27, . . . 102, 105) and then count them. We have 2 minutes per question, and it would take about that long—perhaps less—to solve the problem that way. The key would be beginning that solution quickly and not wasting 90 seconds looking for a faster way.

If you happen to see the faster way, then of course that's a great solution. As with many hard GMAT questions, the solution involves factoring. Since these numbers are all multiples of 3, they can all be re-expressed as 3 × something:

15 = 3 × 5; 18 = 3 × 6; 21 = 3 × 7; 24 = 3 × 8; . . .
102 = 3 × 34; 105 = 3 × 35.

So counting the multiples of 3 in the list of 15 through 105 is exactly the same as counting the number 5 through 35. Now 35 − 5 = 30, but don't forget to add 1 to that result. (Counting 1 through 10, there are not 10 − 1 = 9 numbers but 9 + 1 = 10 numbers.) The answer is 31.

13. E

All we know is that x is a prime number. We want enough information to determine which prime number x is. Our method, then, is to try to find more than one prime that fits with whatever information we're given. If we can, the information is insufficient; if we can't—if we can find only one prime that fits with the information—then the information is sufficient.

(1) Insufficient: If $x < 15$, x could be 2, 3, 5, 7, 11, or 13. Eliminate (A) and (D).

(2) Insufficient: If $(x − 2)$ is a multiple of 5, then x is 2 more than a multiple of 5. So the question is: Can we find more than one prime number that is 2 more than a multiple of five? Yes. Multiples of 5 are 0, 5, 10, 15, 20, and so on. Two more than 5 is 7—a prime number. While 2 more than 10 is 12, which isn't a prime number, 2 more than 15 is 17, which is prime. Eliminate (B).

In combination: Statement 1 narrowed down the possible values of x to 2, 3, 5, 7, 11, and 13. Remember that 0 is a multiple of 5 as well. So both 2 and 7 are 2 more than a multiple of 5, so we cannot find a single answer to the question using both Statements. Choose (E).

14. C

Steve travels at 57 floors per minute and Joyce at 63 floors per minute. So they are decreasing the number of floors between them at a rate of 57 + 63, or 120 floors per minute. This is 2 floors per second. Since they start out 40 floors apart, it'll take them $\frac{40}{2}$ or 20 seconds to meet. After 20 seconds, which is $\frac{1}{3}$ of a minute, Steve will have moved $57 \times \frac{1}{3}$ or 19 floors, and he will be on the 30th floor, the same floor Joyce will be on after 20 seconds.

If you were pressed for time or had trouble finding a straightforward solution, you could have Estimated the answer. If they were traveling at the same speed, they'd meet right in the middle—floor 31. But Joyce is traveling a little bit faster, so they'll meet a little below floor 31. Eliminate (D) and (E). (A) should go too; as their speeds are very close, they'll meet *near* floor 31. Choose between (B) and (C). With only a 6-floor-per-minute difference between speeds that are about 10 times that, the speeds are *almost* identical. (C), closer to the middle, is the safer guess.

15. A

In 8 hours, George will have copied 50 pages, and Sonya will have copied more than 50 pages (since she needs only 6 hours to do 50 pages). That means that in 8 hours, the two of them together can copy more than 100 pages. But all the answer choices except (A) are longer than 8 hours, so (A) must be correct.

This problem could also be solved by calculating.

George takes 8 hours to do a 50-page manuscript, so each hour, he copies $\frac{50}{8} = 6\frac{1}{4}$ pages. Each hour, Sonya copies $\frac{50}{6} = 8\frac{1}{3}$ pages. Working together, in 1 hour they would copy

$6\frac{1}{4} + 8\frac{1}{3}$ or $14\frac{7}{12}$ pages. Divide that number into 100 (the number of pages we want copied), and we'll have the number of hours needed. The solution is $6\frac{6}{7}$.

16. A

Because we know that 3 is a solution, we can plug it into the equation. Thus, $3^2 + 2(3) + m = 5$, $9 + 6 + m = 5$, $15 + m = 5$, and $m = -10$. We can now rewrite the equation as $x^2 + 2x - 10 = 5$, or $x^2 + 2x - 15 = 0$. Factoring the left side of this equation, we see that $(x + 5)(x - 3) = 0$, which has the solutions -5 and 3. Therefore, $x = -5$ is the other solution.

17. D

The correct approach here is not to multiply out the numbers but to factor the large number completely. Since 5^2 and 3^3 are both factors of the larger number, that means that they can be completely divided out of that larger number. In other words, there must be two factors of 5 and three factors of 3 in that large number. Any 5s or 3s that can't be factored out of $2^5 \times 6^2 \times 7^3$ will have to be factors of n. So completing the prime factorization, we get $n \times 2^5 \times 2^2 \times 3^2 \times 7^3$. We can combine the 2s: $n \times 2^7 \times 3^2 \times 7^3$. The only common factors so far are two 3s. That means that the two 5s and the remaining 3 must all be factors of n for the two 5s and three 3s to be factors of the entire product. The smallest number that has two 5s and one 3 as factors is $5 \times 5 \times 3$, or 75.

18. A

The formula for the area of a rectangle is area = length $\times$ width. So here we have area = $a \times b$. Since we are only asked for the rectangle's area, rather than its length and width, we can answer the question without actually determining a or b. All we really need is the product of a and b. (After all, a rectangle with area 6 could have sides of 3 and 2 or sides of 6 and 1. Either way, it has an area of 6.)

(1) Sufficient: While we cannot solve the equation for either variable, we can find the product of the two variables. We multiply both sides by b. This gives us $2ab = 15$. Now we can divide both sides by 2 and get a value for ab. Eliminate (B), (C), and (E).

(2) Insufficient: We cannot solve this single equation for either variable, nor can we find the value of ab from it. Choose (A).

19. D

LMN is a 45°-45°-90° triangle, so the lengths of its sides are related by the ratio $x : x : x\sqrt{2}$. Likewise, JKN is a 30°-60°-90° triangle, so the lengths of its sides are related by the ratio $x : x\sqrt{3} : 2x$. For both of these triangles, learning the length of any side enables us to calculate the lengths of the other two sides. In addition, both triangles are formed by leaning the same board against a wall, so $LM = JK$. So learning the length of any side of either triangle enables us to find all the other 5 side lengths for both triangles—the other 2 side lengths of that triangle and also all 3 side lengths of the other triangle.

(1) Sufficient: It gives exactly what we need— one side of one of the triangles.

(2) Sufficient: A different side, but any will do. Remember, there's no need to do the calculation.

20. D

The numbers involved here are very small, so we can count out the answer fairly quickly, without having to worry about how to calculate with math. The key to this question, as to any question for which we choose to write out possibilities, is to work systematically so we don't overlook anything.

Let's draw four dashes for the desks and call the students A and B. Now we'll draw all the possibilities:

A ___ B ___
A ___ ___ B
___ A ___ B

The question doesn't say who comes first, so redraw with B in the front (or perhaps you realized that it would be the same number as with A in the front):

B ___ A ___
B ___ ___ A
___ B ___ A

That's a total of 6 possible arrangements.

21. B

We need the ratio of men to women. We need to keep in mind that we are only solving for the proportion $\frac{\text{men}}{\text{women}}$, not for the actual numbers of each. So we need a proportion and will keep our eyes open for one.

(1) Insufficient: The phrase *3 less than* ruins it. Otherwise we'd have a 1:2 ratio of women to men, giving us a 2:1 ratio of men to women. But with the *3 less than* thrown in, we cannot derive a ratio. Ratios are comparisons by division or multiplication, using a common divisor or multiple; less than is a comparison by addition or subtraction. We can't get the former from the latter. To demonstrate by Picking Numbers, if there are 9 people in the class, we get 8 men and 1 woman—an 8:1 ratio. But if there are 12 people in the class, we get 10 men and 2 women—a 5:1 ratio. Eliminate (A) and (D).

(2) Sufficient: $\frac{2}{5}$ is a comparison by division; it is a ratio.

There are 2 women for every 5 men—or a 5:2 ratio of men to women. Choose (B).

22. D

The warehouse has two kinds of coats in it: full-length and shorter coats. Initially 15 percent of the coats are full-length, but then a number of the short coats are removed. We're asked to calculate what percent of the remaining coats are full-length. The key to this question is first to calculate the number of full-length coats. At first, there are 800 coats in the warehouse; if 15 percent of these are full-length, then $\frac{15}{100} \times 800 = 15 \times 8 = 120$ coats are full-length.

Then 500 short coats are removed. So that makes 300 coats in total remaining. There are still 120 full-length coats in the warehouse. What percentage of 300 does 120 represent? $\frac{120}{300} = \frac{40}{100} = 40$ percent.

Incidentally, since only shorter coats are removed, the proportion of full-length coats must be rising. By using logic, you could have eliminated (A) and (B) immediately.

23. E

We are dealing with three integers, q, r, and s. We need to determine either that they cannot be consecutive or must be consecutive. Anything else is insufficient.

(1) Insufficient: This tells you that q, r, and s are evenly spaced and that r is the middle term, but the terms could be 1, 2, 3; or 0, 5, 10; or myriad other options. Eliminate (A) and (D).

(2) Insufficient: Again, from this Statement, all we can determine is that we are dealing with evenly spaced integers, but we do not know whether they are consecutive or spaced further apart. We also could have picked numbers here (since r appears twice, it's easiest to start with r). The same numbers

you used in Statement (1) would work here as well. $q = 1$, $r = 2$, and $s = 3$ are all permissible, as are $q = 0$, $r = 5$, and $s = 10$. Eliminate (B).

In combination: Since each Statement gave the same information about integers q, r, and s, the Statements in combination are insufficient as well. Choice (E).

24. B

A good beginning to any Data Sufficiency word problem is to count variables and equations. There are three variables here and only one equation. We know, therefore, that any two new equations would tell us everything. But we also know the GMAT and know that it likes to give us sufficiency with less than we might think. We're asked for the number of orchestra tickets sold and given an equation representing the sum of all the sections. We can rethink this equation as 2,350 = orchestra + (sum of the other sections). So if we know that sum, we'll also be able to answer the question.

(1) Insufficient: This gives us a ratio between the other two sections. But ratios alone tell us nothing about actual values. Eliminate (A) and (D).

(2) Sufficient: This Statement gives an equation relating orchestra tickets to the sum of the other sections. We can rewrite the given equation as 2,350 = orchestra + (1.5 × orchestra) and solve for what we're asked for: the number of orchestra tickets sold.

25. E

To solve this, you need to know the formula for the area of a triangle, and you need to understand the basics of coordinate geometry. First, you should notice that point C is on the x-axis. That means C has a y-coordinate of 0, which allows you to eliminate (A) and (D). Even if you couldn't figure out how to do any more, this would considerably improve your odds of guessing the correct answer.

In general, any time you are told the area of a triangle, you should suspect that the formula for the area ($\frac{1}{2}$ base × height = area) will come into play. We can use this formula to find the x-coordinate of C. Notice that the segment AC is a base of the triangle. Since this segment lies entirely along the x-axis and since A is at the origin (with an x-coordinate of 0), the length of the segment is exactly the x-coordinate of C. So if we find the length of the base AC, we'll have C's x-coordinate. The y-coordinate of the apex B is k, so the distance of B above the x-axis is k. Since the base lies along the x-axis, that means the height of the triangle is k. Now we have enough to fill in our equation: $\frac{1}{2}$ base × height = area. We know that $\frac{1}{2} b \times k = 8$, where b, the base, is equal to the x-coordinate of C.

We get

$$(b)(k) = 16; b = \frac{16}{k}$$

The coordinates of C are $\left(\frac{16}{k}, 0\right)$. The answer is (E).

26. C

Use the probability formula:

$$\text{Probability} = \frac{\text{Desired \# of outcomes}}{\text{Possible \# of outcomes}}$$

First, determine the number of possible outcomes of rain for City X over a 5-day period. There are two possibilities for each day—rain or no rain—so the total number of possible outcomes would be $2 \times 2 \times 2 \times 2 \times 2 = 32$.

Next, determine the desired outcomes. One approach is to list the ways in which you could get rain on exactly 3 days. They are as follows:

RRRNN, RRNRN, RRNNR, RNRRN, RNRNR, RNNRR, NRRRN, NRRNR, NRNRR, NNRRR

There are 10 desired outcomes in all, and a systematic run-through of the possibilities should account for them all. There are other ways to count the ways in which we could have gotten rain on 3 days out of 5. Perhaps you recognized this as a combinations question: We are choosing 3 days to have rain. That's $_5C_3$, or

$$\frac{5!}{3!(5-3)!} = \frac{5!}{3!2!} = \frac{5 \times 4 \times 3 \times 2 \times 1}{3 \times 2 \times 1 \times 2 \times 1} = 10$$

Or perhaps you conceptualized this as a "rearranging letters" problem (discussed in chapter 8). The number of ways to rearrange RRRNN is also $\frac{5!}{3!2!}$, or 10. So the probability is $\frac{10}{32} = \frac{5}{16}$, and choice (C) is the correct answer.

27. E

The question asks for the gross profit: That's the cost of the soda minus the cost of the syrup used in making the soda. The cost of the syrup is km, the cost per liter times the number of liters of syrup. The cost of the soda is j (the price per liter) times the number of liters of soda. The number of liters of soda is just the number of liters of syrup, m, plus the number of liters of water, which is mw, since the recipe requires w liters of water for every liter of soda. Therefore, the cost of the soda is $j(m + mw)$. That makes the gross profit $j(m + mw) - km$. The answer is not expressed in exactly this form; finding it depends on your ability to use the distributive law in algebraic expressions. Recognizing (E) as the answer is just a matter of seeing that $jm(1 + w) = j(m + mw)$.

Alternatively, you could do this question by Picking Numbers. Remember, you still have to figure out how to do the substitution in order to get the right number for the gross profit. Pick small numbers for the variables. Say $w = 2$, $m = 4$, $j = 3$, and $k = 5$. Then we have 4 liters of syrup; that costs $4k = 20$ dollars. We have $4w = 8$ liters of water; that makes $8 + 4 = 12$ liters of soda. The total cost of the soda is $12j = 36$ dollars. So the profit is $36 - 20 = 16$ dollars. The correct answer choice should result in 16 if we plug in all the above values for w, m, j, and k. The only choice that works out is (E).

Remember: sometimes when you Pick Numbers, you'll find that more than one choice gives the right answer; in those cases, you have to try to narrow it down again with a new set of values.

28. D

We want the average. This Statement has two less equations than the number of variables—a warning sign that something sneaky might be going on. So let's do a little translation. We're solving for $\dfrac{\text{cars}}{\text{salespeople}}$. That's $\dfrac{11a + 16b}{a + b}$, where a is the number of salespeople at location A and b is the number of salespeople at location B. Any information that allows us to evaluate this expression will be sufficient.

(1) Sufficient: Here we get an equation that allows us to express each of a and b in terms of the other. Since a is $3b$, we can substitute $3b$ for a in our original expression and solve for the average.

$$\frac{11a + 16b}{a + b} = \frac{11(3b) + 16b}{3b + b}$$

$$= \frac{33b + 16b}{4b} = \frac{49b}{4b} = \frac{49}{4}$$

The instant you realize that the b's are all going to cancel out, you should stop calculating and note this Statement as sufficient.

(2) Sufficient: Here we get the total number of cars sold at each of A and B. This allows us to determine the number of salespeople at each location, which we've symbolized as a and b. With values for a and b, we can find the value of the expression $\dfrac{11a + 16b}{a + b}$ and thus determine the average. Choose (D).

29. E

If an "anglet" is 1 percent of a degree, then there are 100 anglets in each degree. Since there are 360 degrees in a circle, there are 100×360, or 36,000, anglets in a circle.

30. B

You know that 600 people were polled, and you know that they voted either in one of three categories: in favor, against, or undecided. In terms of equations and variables, we have 1 equation and 3 unknowns: $F + A + U = 600$.

(1) Insufficient: Gives you information about those who were in favor and those who were against, but since we are given no information on those undecided, the Statement is insufficient.

(2) Sufficient: Gives you the number undecided and an equation from which you can find the number against the bill. Once these two values are determined, you can find the number of those in favor. Choice (B) is the correct answer.

31. B

We're looking for the cost of the bricks that were actually used to make the fireplace. To find that, we need to know how many bricks were used and what each brick costs. Since $\dfrac{3}{4}$ of the bricks were used, $\dfrac{1}{4}$ of the bricks weren't used. That unused quarter of the total amounted to 190 bricks. That means that number of bricks that were used, $\dfrac{3}{4}$

of the total, amounted to 3×190, or 570 bricks. Each brick cost 40 cents, so the total cost of the bricks that were used must have been $0.40 \times 570 = 228$ dollars.

32. A

This problem asks for the expression with the greatest possible absolute value, so we have to remember to consider negative values; problems like this are often set up to trip those who assume the answer must be a positive number. The only way to solve this is to try each choice. Since x can be any number from -2 to 2 inclusive and we're looking for the greatest possible absolute value, it makes sense to plug these two extreme values of x into each choice. For each choice, then, the largest possible absolute value will result either from giving x the value of 2 or from giving x the value of -2.

In (A), $3x - 1$ is 5 when $x = 2$ and -7 when $x = -2$. In (B), $x^2 + 1$ is 5 when $x = 2$ and also when $x = -2$. In (C), $3 - x$ is 1 when $x = 2$ and 5 when $x = -2$. In (D), $x - 3$ is -1 when $x = 2$ and -5 when $x = -2$. In (E), $x^2 - x$ is 2 when $x = 2$ and 6 when $x = -2$. Out of these possible values for the expressions, -7 has the largest absolute value, so (A) is the answer.

33. B

Don't make the mistake of multiplying out the parentheses—that would be too time consuming and complicated. We're presented with two quantities that have a product of zero. Therefore, at least one of the two quantities must have a value of zero. So the question is really asking: What's the smallest value of x that will make one of these parenthetical expressions equal zero?

You can save yourself further time by checking the second expression first (as it is easier to work with). Suppose $x^2 - 4 = 0$. Then $x^2 = 4$, and x can be 2 or -2. That immediately narrows down the choices to (A) and (B), since -2 is already smaller than (C), (D), and (E). You can then check (A) directly by seeing whether $\frac{12}{x} + 36$ is 0 when $x = -3$: $\frac{12}{-3} + 36$ equals $(-4) + 36$, which equals 32, which is definitely not 0. So (A) can't be the answer, and we're left with only (B). Alternatively, you could have checked for any other possible values of x by setting $\frac{12}{x} + 36$ equal to 0 and solving: $\frac{12}{x} + 36 = 0$; $\frac{12}{x} = -36$; $-36x = 12$; $x = \frac{12}{-36}$; $x = -\frac{1}{3}$. You'd still have discovered that -2 is the smallest value of x, but it's a more time-consuming method.

34. B

We need b. Nothing more to it than that.

(1) Insufficient: This is one equation with two variables. We cannot solve for either variable. Eliminate (A) and (D).

(2) Sufficient: The equation hasn't been simplified, and that should set off alarm bells. It looks to be insoluble: one equation, two variables. Yet the variable a occurs twice. When we simplify, by removing the parentheses, we get $a = b - 1 + a$. Subtracting a from each side, we have $0 = b - 1$. This can be solved for b. Choose (B).

35. E

To solve this problem, we need to restate each answer choice as a simple number by multiplying out the powers of 10. To multiply by a positive power of 10, move the decimal point to the right the same number of places as the exponent of 10. So to simplify (A), take 0.00001 and move the decimal point 8 places to the right. After 5 places, we have 1.0; 3 more places gives us 1,000. We want a number greater than 1,000.01, so we move on. Moving the decimal 4 places to the right in (B) only gives us 101. (C) becomes 110. (D) converts to 1,000.01 exactly. Therefore, we know (E) is right without figuring it out (as a matter of fact, it converts to 1,000.1).

36. A

We want information about the values a and b or about the value of their sum. We keep in mind that neither a nor b is necessarily positive or an integer.

(1) Sufficient: The numerator is the difference of two squares. This is a common expression on the GMAT, and we know instantly that it factors into $(a + b)$ times $(a - b)$. Canceling the $(a - b)$ from both the numerator and denominator, we're left with the value of $a + b$. Eliminate (B), (C), and (E).

(2) Insufficient: There's a common GMAT trap here. You might have been inclined to remove the exponent from the left side of the equation to get a value for $a + b$. However, we cannot find the value of $a + b$ simply by knowing that $(a + b)^2 = 36$ because both 6 and −6 squared result in 36. Choose (A).

37. D

As with the previous question, we want information about the sum of two variables. Unlike in the previous question, though, we get useful information. If the two expressions are equal and if the bases are equal, then the exponents have to be equal (2 taken to some power can only equal 2 to that power). So we start out knowing that $(2m + 1) = (n + 2)$. One equation, two variables.

Any new equation will be sufficient (as long as it introduces no new variables).

(1) Sufficient: It's a new equation. Just what we needed. Don't let the fact that the variable is in the exponent throw you. We'd figure

out what power of 2 equals 256 (turns out to be 2^8). We'd then set the exponents equal to each other and have an equation with which we could solve for n. We could then solve for m and add them together for the answer. This Statement is sufficient so we eliminate (B), (C), and (E).

(2) Sufficient: Similar situation here. It's a second, different equation with the same two variables found in the equation as in the question stem, so we can solve for the values of the variables. Thus, we can determine their sum. Choose (D).

VERBAL SECTION EXPLANATIONS

1. C

In question 1, we're asked to strengthen the researchers' alarming conclusion that the misinformation they've discovered in journal advertisements could lead doctors to misprescribe drugs. This argument works only if we assume that the information in the ads influences the doctors in some way. Since the best way to strengthen an argument is to confirm the truth of an assumption, we're looking for the answer that says something like, "Yes, doctors are influenced by information in the ads." According to (C), doctors use the ads as a resource for information about new prescription drugs. So (C) is correct.

(A) indicates the ads are important to publishers as a source of revenue but does nothing to show that the ads are important to doctors, let alone that they can affect doctors' prescriptions.

(B) and (D) support the notion that the ads are or can be misleading: (B) tells us that journal editors often can't tell whether an ad is deceptive, and (D) tells us that ads are usually less accurate than articles evaluating the drugs. But we already know that the ads contain misleading information, so these choices add nothing. On the GMAT, correct Strengthen/Weaken answers *never* address the evidence but rather the link between that evidence and the conclusion. (E) weakens the argument by suggesting that a government agency is watching out for potentially harmful, misleading claims.

2. E

The beginning of the underlined part should be "an index … that is called objective," not "an index … that are called objective." If you catch an obvious error like this, quickly scan the other choices for versions that repeat it. That knocks out (B). (Remember you don't need to reread (A); it's the same as the original, and we already know that's wrong.) Now we are left with (C), (D), and (E). The crucial difference here is between the wordy phrase "progress, such as what is made"—in (C) and (D)—and (E)'s "progress such as that". (E)'s wording is preferable because it is shorter. (C)'s and (D)'s "what is made" is unnecessary to make the proper reference to "progress."

Also note the 3-2 split between "that are/is called objective" and "so-called objective." This is an important GMAT style point—as long as the meaning is unchanged, the phrase with fewer words is preferable. (This is true for essays as well, by the way!)

3. C

Perhaps you noticed the poor usage of the pronoun *it* in the sentence as written. *It* is meant to refer to "workers accept[ing] supervisory positions." But that's an *action*, not a *thing*.

Therefore *it* is incorrect. Eliminate (A). All of the other answers focus instead on the cause-and-effect dynamic. Among them, (B) is wordiest and could be eliminated on those grounds.

Scanning the beginning of the choices, we see a 3-1-1 split among *when*, *by*, and *if*. Your ear probably recognizes "a problem occurs when" or "a problem occurs if" as correct usage and "a problem occurs by" as awkward. Eliminate (B). There's another split between "workers" and "a worker." The end of the sentence says "their," so clearly we need the plural. Eliminate (B)—if you hadn't done so already—as well as (D) and (E).

By this point, you've eliminated everything but (C), so you know that (C) is correct. On test day, you'd select it and move on. Just two more things for you to focus on for your prep. First, read (D) closely. Notice how it sounds okay on its own, but by including the word *who*, the answer choice puts the verb *accepts* into a subordinate clause. As a result, the sentence has no main verb. This is a sneaky trick the GMAT will use from time to time. Secondly, most people don't say things like "and so lose" in everyday speech. Sometimes the GMAT uses construction that is correct according to the rules of standard English but sounds a little "stuffy" for common usage. Don't eliminate an answer just because you think, "I would never say it that way."

Passage 1—Women in the Labor Market

PASSAGE	ANALYSIS
An **important** feature of the labor market in recent years has been the increasing participation of women . . . Many analysts **suggest, however,** that women comprise a **secondary** labor market where rates of pay and promotion prospects are **inferior** to those available to men. The **principal reason** is that women have, or are **assumed** to have, domestic responsibilities . . .	The topic is clear right at the start—women in the labor market.
	Women don't seem to be paid or promoted as much, and domestic responsibilities seem to take the blame. (Note the "assumed," though . . . that opens the door for the author to put the blame somewhere else later.)
The **difficulties** that women face in the labor market . . . are **accentuated** with the arrival of children. . . . Some women balance domestic and workplace commitments by working part-time. **However,** part-time work is a **precarious** form of employment . . .	Children don't help much. And part-time work is not a good solution. Note how the "distancing" word choices of ¶1 ("analysts suggest" and "assumed") are gone. We are now looking at the author's own viewpoint.
. . . Such women who later return to work represent **another** sector of the workforce facing **difficulties.** . . . these women confront a **restricted** range of opportunities and **will almost certainly** be offered **low-status** jobs with **poor** prospects.	Lots of detail here, but the keywords at the end of the paragraph make it clear: Women who return to work don't get good offers.
Even women professionals who interrupt their careers to have children experience difficulties. . . . **Consequently,** women, even those of **high ability,** may find themselves **blocked** in the **lower** echelons of an organization, **overlooked,** or even **"invisible"** to senior management.	Women professionals have it no better. (Note all the negative emphasis words at the end of the paragraph.)

¶**1** Women face inferior job prospects—domestic responsibilities blamed

¶**2** Children make things tough; part-time work precarious

¶**3** No good prospects on return to work

¶**4** High-ability professionals struggle too

Topic: Women in the labor market

Scope: Difficulties faced by ⌐↑ ←⌐

Purpose: Explain the causes behind ___⌐

4. B

The right answer to Global questions must reflect the passage's Topic, Scope, Purpose, and overall point of view. Our prediction for the answer would be something like "Explain the difficulties faced by women in the labor market." (B) is the only choice that fits.

(A) incorrectly broadens the scope to employers' practices in general, whereas the author is concerned only with pay and promotion. Besides, the author restricts himself to discussing the current state of affairs; he doesn't advocate anything.

(C) takes a detail in paragraphs 2 and 3 and wrongly blows it up into the author's primary concern.

(D) and (E) are completely off the topic, and contrary to what (D) says, the author doesn't take issue with others' views.

5. D

Lines 18–21 suggest that it is up to working women themselves, not employers (A), to make child care arrangements. We might anticipate that the author of this passage would agree with (A), but no support for this position is actually given. That's an important aspect of GMAT Inference questions—the right answer isn't just *probably* true but *definitely* true.

(B) is a 180° trap. Paragraph 4 says that women in high-status positions, such as professionals, face problems advancing their careers while caring for their children.

The passage doesn't compare conditions for today's working mothers with those that existed 20 years ago, so eliminate (C).

Answer (D) is based on lines 34–36, which say, "When the typical homemaker returns to the labor market, she is unsure of herself in her new environment." (D) is correct.

Although lines 19–21 imply that reasonably priced child care can be difficult to find, (E), the passage doesn't go so far as to suggest that the expense of child care often makes it unprofitable for mothers to work.

6. B

The gist of paragraph 4 is that even women of high ability and status—professionals—face career problems if they decide to have children.

(A) is a 180° trap. The point of paragraph 4 is to explain that even the most able women may *not* be able to "overcome" the difficulties "of integrating career and motherhood."

Paragraph 4 does not address labor policies (C) or increasing female participation in the labor force (D). Moreover, the author doesn't ever "defend changes" or "modify a hypothesis."

(E) is too vague. Paragraph 4 draws a definite link between career opportunities and children: It's not about a general lack of career opportunities for women.

7. C

The question sends us to the second sentence of paragraph 1, which discusses "pay and promotion prospects … inferior to those available to men." Context is key for detail-oriented questions. The very next sentence blames the disparity on "domestic responsibilities." That fits only with (C).

The passage states that some women work part-time (lines 22–24), not that women in general tend to get work in industries that rely on part-time labor (A).

Paragraph 4 indicates that *some* women—those who took time off to raise children—can lack technical skills. But (B) suggests that *all* women lack those skills. Furthermore, paragraph 4 is not the part of the passage addressed by the question stem.

According to lines 26–27, part-time women, not women in general (as choice (D) says), are likely to be laid off in an economic slowdown. Besides, this fact has nothing to do with inferior pay and promotion rates.

(E) is beyond the scope of the passage: The author doesn't discuss general workplace discrimination against women.

8. D

The legislator claims that legalizing gambling would reduce crime. Her evidence is that some gambling—namely bingo and the lottery—is already legal, and she suggests that the ban is somehow not working anyway. Whenever the GMAT asks us to weaken a plan or a proposal, look for an answer that explains why the proposal will fail even though the evidence is correct. In this case, that means we are looking for an answer that explains that legalizing gambling *won't* reduce crime (may even increase it), even though bingo and the lottery are already legal.

(D) fits the bill—it shows that legal gambling would attract other illegal activity.

(A) comes close but misses the point. It explains why the crime rate wouldn't drop by as much as the legislator might predict. But it's too focused on the effects of legalization on gambling. The right answer must focus on crime. Same for (C)—we're not that interested in whether gambling will increase or decrease. As for (B), the legislator never gave "significant savings" as a reason for revoking the ban, so the news that there won't be any such savings doesn't hurt her. It's not at all clear what effect, if any, (E) has on her proposal. That alone is good enough reason to discard it.

9. D

The Kaplan strategy of looking at the question stem before tackling the stimulus really pays off with question 9. We're given the conclusion—that the cat in question is acting out its dreams. We'll be looking for the researchers' evidence, and to answer the question, we'll be thinking along the lines of adding to this evidence so as to further support the conclusion (in other words, we're looking for the assumption). Realizing all of this, before we even read the stimulus, makes its story and our lives easier.

Before neuron removal, we're told, the dreaming cat's cortex fires messages, but the cat doesn't respond. After neuron removal, the dreaming cat gets up and jumps around. We then jump to the conclusion that the cat is acting out its dreams. There are two missing pieces here. One is the connection between "dreams" and the "messages" in the cerebral cortex. Another puzzling aspect of this argument is how *removing* a connection between the cerebral cortex and the spinal cord would help a message get through to the body. (D) addresses the latter hole in the argument—it establishes that the neurons prevented the cerebral cortex's messages from reaching the spinal cord during sleep. Therefore, the removal of the neurons allowed, for the first time, messages to reach the spinal cord while the cat slept. This makes it more plausible that when the cat rose and pounced, it was responding to those messages—acting out its dreams.

(A) is ambiguous and unhelpful. If the cat wasn't already dreaming when the neurons were removed, then their removal would presumably prevent the cat from dreaming (since they trigger the dream state); in that case, it couldn't have been acting out its dreams. If the cat was already in a dream state when the neurons were removed, then we have no idea about the effect of removing the neurons. (B) adds nothing to the information in the stimulus. We already know that the cerebral cortex is busy during sleep. If (C) were true, there would be no messages, and therefore no dreams, coming from the cerebral cortex after the neurons were removed, so the cat couldn't be acting out its dreams. Be careful: On Strengthen/Weaken questions, the test makers commonly present choices that have the opposite effect of the one they ask for. (E) is irrelevant, as "brain waves" (*a new term—be wary*) don't matter. We're interested in how brain messages (dreams) travel; specifically, what stops them from being acted on during the sleeping state.

10. A

From a quick scan of the answers, you see the main difference is between choices that use *is* and choices that use *was*. Now, use logic. Pay attention to the time clue *recently*. The shepherd's body was only recently found, so it wouldn't make sense to put the discussion of "How long ago did he live?" in the past. *Is,* in (A) and (D), must be correct. It's also important to be able to recognize and quickly eliminate illogical choices like (D). (D)'s wording doesn't really make sense. If the dead person is "thought of as apparently living," he wouldn't be a corpse.

11. C

The answers use *considered* in different ways. The proper use of *considered* is to leave it alone—no prepositions at all. Eliminate (A) and (D), which use *that*; (B), which uses *as*; and (E), which uses *to be*. That one split alone can answer the question for us!

On test day, that's enough. Since you're prepping, though, it's helpful in a review to consider all the errors so you can be ready for anything when you take the GMAT. There's a clear difference among the answers—some begin with *Ezra Pound*, others with something else. A person could be "in contrast to Walt Whitman," but neither a consideration (D) nor poetry (E) could be.

There's also a difference at the end of the answer choices—a 3-2 split between "but" and "and is." Since the sentence says that American poetry is "*not* something," the appropriate connector should say "*but* something else." Eliminate (A) and (E). Lastly, (D) and (E) say "considered by Ezra Pound," a passive construction that the GMAT does not prefer.

Passage 2—Freedom of Information Act

PASSAGE	ANALYSIS
A 1973 Supreme Court decision and related Senate hearings focused congressional **criticism** on the 1966 Freedom of Information Act. . . .	A whole lot of detail about the Freedom of Information Act. We learn that Congress didn't like it.
In **response**, a House committee drafted HR 12471, **proposing** several amendments to the Act. . . . The Senate companion bill, S 2543, included these provisions as well as others . . .	Congress responds by proposing some laws. Don't worry about what those laws are until you get a question about them!
The Justice and Defense departments **objected** . . . They **argued** that . . . The Pentagon **asserted** that judicial review of exemptions could pose a **threat** to national security. President Ford, upon taking office in August 1974, **concurred**.	Now the executive branch gets in the game. Seems that it didn't like the changes.
HR 12471 **passed** in March 1974; S 2543 was **approved** in May after the adoption of further amendments . . . The Hart Amendment, **for instance** . . . This amendment **provoked** another presidential **objection** . . .	The laws were passed anyway, and the president was not thrilled.
Before submitting the legislation to Ford, a joint conference of both houses amalgamated the two versions of the bill, while making further changes to **incorporate Ford's criticisms** . . . Ford **nevertheless vetoed** the bill but was **overridden** by a two-thirds vote in both houses.	Congress tried to compromise with the president, but he still vetoed the bill. It passed anyway, however.

¶1 F.I.A. criticized by Congress

¶2 Congress proposes new laws

¶3 President doesn't like proposed changes

¶4 Laws pass anyway

¶5 Compromise rejected; law passes

Topic: Freedom of Information Act

Scope: Changes to ⬏ ⬅

Purpose: Describe the history of _____

12. C

Lines 31–32 say that the Justice and Defense departments objected to revision as "costly, burdensome, and inflexible." They opposed revision, in other words, for administrative reasons.

According to lines 34–35, the Justice and Defense departments argued that changes "might actually hamper access to information." But they did not go so far as to suggest that the revision was an attempt to limit public access to information (A).

Although the Pentagon thought that revision might pose national security problems, it didn't argue that changes violated specific national security agreements (B).

(D) and (E) are beyond the scope: Neither the Justice nor the Defense department protested revision on the grounds that it would weaken either its power or presidential authority.

13. A

The Pentagon doesn't offer much justification for its assertion that judicial review would cause national security problems. We know that the president agreed but don't learn why. We need an answer that explains the connection between judges and national security dangers. (A) does this; if judges don't have the necessary expertise, they might release information that would endanger national security.

(B) and (C) don't explain the danger posed by judicial review. (D) seems tempting, but no explicit link is drawn between political interests and security concerns. (Compare that to the use of "military intelligence" in (A).) Same problem with (E)—there's no reason given to think that presidential approval necessarily has anything to do with national security. Perhaps the president would disapprove for other reasons.

14. A

Lines 47–51 indicate that Ford was opposed to the release of FBI records. He didn't want them to be open to public scrutiny.

(B) and (E)—180° choices—wrongly suggest that Ford was open to the idea of a release of FBI records.

(C) is incorrect. Based on lines 49–51, we can infer that Ford perceived barriers to exemption of individual FBI records, but we can't assume that expense was one of these barriers.

There is no hint in the passage that Ford believed it was more important to protect confidential sources than personal privacy or investigative secrecy (D). Paragraph 4 tells us that all three are protected by the Hart amendment, but no distinction like (D)'s is drawn.

15. D

Here's a great example of how concision is rewarded on the GMAT. All the answer choices mean the exact same thing, and (D) conveys this meaning in the fewest words.

If you weren't confident enough that (D) was both correct and concise, you could also eliminate the answer choices one by one. (A) and (B) both say "as much . . . as a hundred," which should be *as many* because *a hundred* is countable. (C) and (E) have "not any" and "without any," phrases that are synonymous— and thus redundant—with *whatsoever* in the non-underlined portion.

16. C

We're asked to support the more recent theory. The old theory says that modern humans simply outcompeted Neanderthals and that there was little to no interbreeding. The new theory says that modern humans evolved from

Neanderthals. To support the new theory, we'd need evidence that is consistent with that theory but inconsistent with the other. The difference involves ancestry. To reject the old theory in favor of the new, we'll look for an answer that suggests that modern humans are the descendants of Neanderthals. We'd reject anything that said the two groups had nothing to do with each other.

(C) fits with what we're looking for—evidence that modern humans came from Neanderthals.

(A) and (D) are 180s—they support the old theory, not the new one. (E) is also not what we want, as it calls Neanderthals "unique." (B) may be tempting, but it uses cultural evidence. The argument is focused on the biological relationship.

17. E

Whenever you see a sentence with the word *like*, remember that it must compare the same type of things, using language that is parallel. Ingesting lead "was a significant health hazard for the ancient Romans," just as it "is for modern Americans." Only (E) exhibits the required parallel structure. (C) and (D) would be parallel with "ancient Romans ingested lead." (A) and (B) leave out the needed verb.

A brief note: the word "like" is only used to compare two nouns. Since our comparison is between two clauses, *ingesting lead . . . was . . .* and *it is*, we needed to use "as," as seen in the other four answer choices.

18. D

When an introductory phrase is set off by a comma, make sure it logically refers to what follows. It's not Nathanael West's first novel or "when Nathanael West staying in Paris" that was

"born Nathan Weinstein." It's Nathanael West himself, so (D) is right.

19. E

The argument might seem sensible at first glance, saying that age of the mother is the cause of twin births, not fertility treatments. Happily, we read the question stem first and know to be on the lookout for something overlooked. What if there is a connection between a mother's age and fertility treatments? If older women tend to receive fertility treatments more often, then those treatments could be responsible for twin births. (If you like to look at things structurally, the argument says, "X didn't cause Y. W caused Y." But if W caused X first, then X could well be the cause of Y.)

(E) gives us exactly what we'd predict.

(A) and (D) introduce irrelevant considerations. The author's argument is that fertility drugs aren't responsible for the increase in twins. It doesn't matter that, as (A) says, many of these older women aren't first-time mothers. Nor does it matter that, as (D) says, these older women are no more likely to produce *identical* twins. As for (B), the author's point was simply that women over 35 are more likely to have twins than are younger women; her argument doesn't require that only women over 35 bear twins. (C) is wrong: Since the author argues that the drugs are not responsible for the increased incidence of twins, she must believe, rather than overlook, the idea that any correlation between drugs and the increase of twin births is coincidental.

Passage 3—Predicting Earthquakes

PASSAGE	ANALYSIS
Modern methods of predicting earthquakes **recognize** that quakes, **far from** being geologic anomalies, are part of the periodic . . . long- and short-range precursory phenomena that are **crucial** to earthquake prediction.	Yecch. Lots of detail. But stay focused on the big picture: Quakes aren't anomalies but part of a cycle. There are long- and short-range phenomena that allow quakes to be predicted.
Quakes along active faults . . . are usually frequent . . . **However** . . . locating active faults is **only a beginning** [painful detail] are **useful** in determining potential quake locations, as are [more detail]. **Seismologists may also** [again, detail].	Lots of ways to predict quake locations.
Once the perimeters of a quake-prone zone are established, a network of base stations can monitor precursory phenomena. . . . [some sciencey stuff] are **valuable precursors** . . . **Theoretically**, if an area's critical strain is known . . . [painful detail] will indicate a time frame for an impending quake.	Steering clear of the ridiculous detail, we see *why* it's here: predicting a quake's time frame.
Violent tilting and foreshocks are among phenomena classified as short-term precursors . . . Such precursors are **valuable since** . . .	Short-term precursors.

¶1 Quakes are predictable

¶2 Predicting where

¶3 Predicting when

¶4 Short-term precursors

Topic: Predicting earthquakes

Scope: Precursors useful in ⬆

Purpose: Describe ⬆

20. C

Paragraph 1 contrasts coastal regions, where crustal strains build rapidly, with inland regions, where strains build more slowly. (C) paraphrases that distinction.

(A) flatly contradicts the passage—the first paragraph states that crustal strain is great in coastal regions. (B) contradicts the passage—quakes are less numerous in *inland* areas. (D) also contradicts the passage—you can infer that in coastal areas, which experience frequent quakes, precursory phenomena must be common. (E) contradicts the passage—paragraph 1 indicates that coastal regions confront thrusting sea floor plates.

21. E

Choice (E) encompasses the passage's Topic and Scope plus the content of all four paragraphs—the importance of precursors.

(A) is too narrow—the passage says little about earthquakes in inland areas. (B) mentions introductory information in paragraph 1. It neglects the passage's topic—methods of earthquake prediction. (C) has the same problem as (A)—it's too narrow. Coastal regions are only part of the picture in this passage. (D) is also too narrow, and it's inconsistent with the passage. Precursory phenomena are key to earthquake prediction.

22. D

Paragraph 3 lists a lot of details that are useful for predicting when an earthquake will strike. That fits very nicely with (D).

(A) and (B) are the sorts of answers we can fall for if our reading becomes too detail oriented. They both represent details in ¶3 but not the main function of the paragraph. (C) addresses details in ¶1 and ¶2. The paragraph never

suggests "that critical strain is not spread evenly along most major fault lines," (E).

23. A

"Strain" is mentioned in ¶1, but the question asks about "critical strain," which is discussed only at the end of ¶3. There, we read "critical strain will indicate a time frame for an impending quake." That fits perfectly with (A).

There is nothing anywhere about calculating "the severity of an initial rupture" (B). It's unclear what the term *seismic force* means, so (C) is no good. (D) refers to an unrelated detail from the beginning of the paragraph. (E) is tempting because "crustal movement" is discussed in the context, but it is ultimately wrong because it leaves out the idea of predicting a time frame for the next earthquake.

24. D

In question 24, the federal government provided low-cost flood insurance to coastal property owners. Unfortunately, this caused a new problem—the resulting boom in coastal construction has led to dangerous land erosion. In GMAT Critical Reasoning, the first task in solving a problem is to identify correctly the cause of the problem. The cause here is construction, both existing and expected construction. Since beachfront construction caused the erosion, a good solution would be to put an end to this construction. (D) would likely accomplish this. Not only does it discourage new construction by canceling flood insurance benefits, but it may well facilitate removal of some of the existing dwellings by compensating residents who relocate.

(A) may prevent the construction of property additions, but it wouldn't do anything to halt the boom in the construction of new buildings or to get rid of existing buildings. As for (B), we already know that the erosion rate is "dangerous"; that's why we're looking for a choice that suggests a solution. Conducting further study isn't a solution. (C) sounds like a good plan for preventing flood damage to new buildings. We are asked, however, to prevent erosion, and we're given no reason to think that elevating houses will do so. (E) makes the same mistake. (E) would protect the buildings from flood damage, but the problem we're to address is that of protecting the beaches from erosion.

25. B

This sentence draws a comparison between two processes for overcasting a seam allowance: "the seam allowance is overcast *as* the seam is sewn... ." We need a preposition that properly expresses the contrast between overcasting allowances *as* the garment is being sewn and overcasting allowances *in* a separate process from sewing. That eliminates (A), (C), and (D), which fail to make the proper comparison because they lack the preposition *in* at the end.

(E) is far too wordy, using five words to do what (B) does in three; in addition, *as against* isn't an idiomatically correct usage.

26. A

The author says that conventional methods of measuring intelligence, such as IQ tests, classify people with Williams syndrome as mentally retarded, on a par with Down syndrome sufferers, because they're poor at math and can't tell left from right. He calls this label "misleading," pointing out that people with Williams syndrome are often gifted in other areas, such as language and music, whereas Down syndrome sufferers have limited abilities in all areas. His point in telling us this is that the conventional tests don't do a good job of evaluating the people with Williams syndrome, since they miss the gifts that these people have.

That's (A): his argument is that conventional intelligence tests can't accurately measure people with disorders like Williams syndrome.

(B) may or may not be true (it's not stated by the author), but it's not the author's main point. He compares the two syndromes to make another point about the failure of conventional intelligence tests. (C) is closer, but when you're asked for the author's point, be careful not to be misled by choices that simply restate a part of the author's argument. The author seems to imply (C), but this isn't what he's trying to prove. It's merely a piece of his argument, something that he implies on the way to making his point about the failure of intelligence tests to measure people with Williams syndrome. (D) discusses what might happen when people with Williams syndrome are diagnosed as mentally retarded, but the author's focus is on the mislabeling itself, not on its possible results. Like (C), (D) seems reasonably inferable from the argument but isn't the point of the argument. As for (E), the author never suggests that the mathematical and spatial skills of people with Williams syndrome either can or should be developed.

27. E

After reading the stem for question 27, we go to the stimulus with eyes peeled for Koch's counterargument. Koch, we learn, is unconvinced by von Pettenkoffer's dramatic demonstration. When, after drinking a bottle of bacteria, von Pettenkoffer doesn't develop cholera, he claims to have proved that the bacterium doesn't cause cholera. Koch disagrees, saying that von Pettenkoffer's stomach acid killed the bacteria before it could affect him. Be careful; we don't want to strengthen Koch's original argument—that the bacterium causes cholera—but rather his second argument— that von Pettenkoffer's stomach acid killed the bacteria. Koch says that stomach acid kills *most* bacteria. But does it kill the specific bacteria that are alleged to cause cholera? We need some evidence that stomach acid does, in fact, kill that bacteria too.

(E) does this—if neutralizing stomach acid increases the risk of cholera infection, then acid clearly harms the bacteria.

(A) does the opposite—it seems to show that stomach acid does not harm cholera. (C) has the same problem. If cholera is caused by drinking water, then stomach acid doesn't seem to have much effect. (D) is irrelevant, as it doesn't address whether stomach acid kills cholera bacteria. (B) is a very tempting kind of wrong answer choice. It provides a *different* counterargument to von Pettenkoffer. It's a good one, but it doesn't strengthen *Koch's* counterargument, which is based on stomach acid. Thus it is not the correct answer to the question.

28. E

Whenever a sentence has an action that started in the past and continues into the present, often indicated by the word "since" and a time (in this case, 1972), the correct tense is the present perfect—using "has/have" and the past participle tense of the verb. The future tense in *since . . . 1972 . . . will continue* doesn't make sense. So, the only answer choice that limits itself to the present perfect, (E), is correct.

Alternately, we can eliminate (A) and (B) based on the pronoun error of *it* vs. *they*. (D) can be ruled out because it is incredibly wordy. Finally, (C) makes a parallelism error: the *and* creates parallel structure, but that would mean that *has* and *will* are both matched to *perpetuate*, and *has perpetuate* is grammatically incorrect.

29. C

There's a clear difference among the beginnings of the answer choices: "in," "that," or nothing. Notice that immediately before the underlined portion is *and*. The underlined portion must be parallel to whatever comes before. The sentence says "proved *that* minority clients . . .," so the underlined portion must begin with *that*. Eliminate (A) and (B).

There are also differences among the verbs. One difference is singular/plural. *Were* in (A) and E) is plural; *has* in (C) and (D) is singular. *Legislation* is a singular noun, so eliminate (A) and (E). Many of the answer choices have "mitigated/mitigating" and "abolished/abolishing." Since these verbs are joined by *rather than*, they must be in parallel form. That eliminates (B) and (D). Only (C) remains.

By the way, to get a better sense of awkward construction, compare (D) and (E) to (C).

30. A

We are asked to weaken the judge's decision, so make sure that we focus on that aspect of the stimulus. The judge based his decision on precedent set by asbestos exposure cases. For the judge's reasoning to be valid, asbestos exposure cases and repetitive stress injury cases must be similar. We're looking for the right answer to explain why repetitive stress cases are different from asbestos exposure cases.

(A) is exactly what we're looking for—a clear difference between the two.

(B) is sneaky. It distorts the question. We're not asked to weaken the idea that the judge's decision is detrimental to the defense but just to weaken the reasoning behind his decision. Whether it helps or hurts the defense is outside the scope of the question. (D) is also a tricky one, as it also draws a distinction between asbestos and repetitive stress. But that distinction is only in *severity of injury*, whereas the scope of the argument is a parallel between the workplaces.

(C) and (E) may or may not be factual, but they are irrelevant to the issue of whether asbestos exposure and repetitive stress are similar.

31. C

The GMAT often uses expletive phrases (which is to say, words set off by commas, dashes, or parentheses that are not vital to the meaning of the sentence . . . sort of like this one) to hide errors by creating distance between mismatching elements. It's often helpful to ignore these phrases when reading the sentence the first time. Reading it that way helps us see a big error: "*Each* of William Kennedy's *novels* in the Albany Trilogy *are* set . . . ." *Each* is singular. (D) and (E) repeat this error ("every one" in (E) is also singular). (B) makes a similar error within its expletive phrase: "each of them novels" means that each of the three titles is composed of multiple novels. It should read "each of them a novel," so it can be eliminated.

32. B

We're told that from 1977 to 1989, the percentage of their own income that the richest 1 percent of Americans paid in federal taxes decreased. At the same time, the proportion (or percentage) of all federal tax revenues that was paid by these same rich Americans increased. So a lighter tax burden on the wealthy resulted in their carrying more of the overall tax load. We need to find an answer that resolves that apparent discrepancy.

(A) doesn't do the trick—it doesn't explain how increased collection efficiency would lower the percentage of income paid by the wealthiest 1 percent.

But if (B) is true, and the top 1 percent are earning much more money, they could reduce the percentage of their income paid to taxes while still increasing the actual amount they pay. (B) is correct. The fact that a *rate* (like a percent) is different from an *actual amount* is frequently tested in Critical Reasoning—and in Data Sufficiency too!

(C) could explain why the rich are paying a lower tax rate, as they are moving their money to untaxable assets. But it does not explain how they would then be paying a higher share of the overall tax burden. (D) has a similar problem. It explains how the rich's share of the tax burden may have gone up (the middle class are paying less, so the amount of overall tax goes down). But it doesn't explain how this is possible when the rich also see their tax burden reduced. If anything, the "several tax loopholes were eliminated" idea suggests the opposite—that the tax burden went *up*. (E) shows how the richest 1 percent account for a higher percentage of overall tax revenues. They've paid an additional $45 billion while everyone else has only had to come up with an additional $5 billion— the $5 billion left from the $50 billion after subtracting the $45 billion that the very rich paid. However, this leaves out the other part of the dilemma—it doesn't show how they can be paying less of their income.

Passage 4—Food Contamination

PASSAGE	ANALYSIS
Contamination is the unintended presence of harmful substances or organisms in food. **While . . . it is still necessary to guard against** the practices that can increase the likelihood of food contamination. **Because** food-borne illness poses a potentially **serious threat** to public health, **preventing** contamination of safe food needs to be a **prime objective . . . Furthermore . . .**	Food contamination seems to be the topic. It's a serious threat, so we need to guard against it.
The **most serious** risk associated with food is the biological hazard. Biological hazards are . . . one of the **most frequently** reported diseases of this type is salmonellosis . . .	Biological hazards and the most common disease
The **other major** form of biologically induced food-borne illness is intoxication . . . *Staphylococcus* food intoxication is one of the **most common** types . . .	Another kind—food-borne intoxication

¶1 Food contamination a potentially serious threat

¶2 Biological hazards

¶3 Food-borne intoxication

Topic: Food contamination

Source: Sources of

Purpose: Describe

33. C

We need the answer that reflects the passage's Topic, Scope, Purpose, and overall structure. (A) and (E) are tempting but only tell parts of the story. (A) is the point of ¶1, and (E) is the point of ¶2 and ¶3. (C) correctly expresses all three paragraphs working together. The last two paragraphs summarize the knowledge of contamination sources, and the first paragraph discusses why this knowledge is essential.

(B) and (D) both distort ¶2 and ¶3, as well as leaving out ¶1.

34. A

The author discusses food service managers in ¶1. The author uses a lot of strong, prescriptive language: "preventing contamination of safe food needs to be a prime objective of every food service manager" and "a food service manager must possess accurate information on the different hazards associated with the contamination of food." The author clearly thinks that a food service manager's comprehension of food hazards is very important. This fits perfectly with (A).

(B) is a distortion. Although the sources of contamination seem varied and complex, there is nothing here to suggest that a diligent food service manager will be restricted in the amount she can know about contamination.

(C) misses the scope of the passage by focusing on the decision to *hire* a manager. Even if we infer that a manager's understanding of these issues must be a consideration in hiring, since it's so important, we still can't say it's the *primary* consideration. (D) uses the extreme word *exclusively* and consequently is too extreme. In fact, the author states that prevention is only part of the battle—knowledge is also necessary so that

a manager knows what to do "in the event that a … crisis does arise."

(E)'s pessimism is reminiscent of (B). A clear understanding of the author's purpose and tone allows us to eliminate choices like these that don't match either. The first few words of (E) are on the right track; in fact, "vitally important" is synonymous with (A)'s "crucial." But the whole choice needs to fit, and the rest of (E) misses the point.

35. D

The striking term *pathogenic organisms* that appears in the question stem is relatively easy to locate in paragraph 2. Correct choice (D) comes right out of lines 24–28, with the keywords *such as* acting as the link between pathogenic microorganisms and bacteria and parasites. Even in a passage with lots of unfamiliar terms, it all boils down to good critical reading. Let's look at the wrong choices. In (A), the passage doesn't tell us what the most common form is. Nothing in paragraph 2 suggests (B), but paragraph 3 actually suggests the opposite—some microorganisms can cause disease even after being killed. A careful reading of the sentence in which "pathogenic organisms" appears shows that choice (C) distorts the meaning of the sentence. Toxins are not the same as pathogenic microorganisms. (E)—how hard it is to detect pathogenic organisms—is outside the scope, as it is never mentioned or implied.

36. B

The beginning of the answer choices are different: "new technology," "modern-day biological taxonomists," "using new technology," or "when modern day biological taxonomists." Immediately before the underlined portion is a descriptive phrase, and we must eliminate any answer choices that do not present a logical description. That phrase says "employing the system of binomial nomenclature." You don't need to know what "binomial nomenclature" means to know that only people can use a system. So we'll eliminate every answer choice that doesn't begin with a person or a group of people. Clearly (A), (C), and (D) are out. (E) is close, but *when* is appropriate only for actual times. Only (B) is correct.

Note also that (A), (D), and (E) do not correctly follow *not only* with *but also*. Also note the awkward "are enabled to" in (D) and the passive "are enabled by" in (E).

37. B

GMAT English is precise. In everyday speech, you can get away with "I have a lot of pressure at work," when you mean "I am under pressure." On the GMAT, you can't. You have to use the correct idiomatic phrase, which is "under pressure to show high profits." Choices (C) and (D) both use "showing"; always be wary of "–ing" verbs. (E) adds needless verbiage.

38. B

When a question is as long as this one, it's very reassuring to know the right strategy—we can confidently and critically attack the question without panicking over its length. Because the question stem says we are looking for an *explanation*, this is an Explain question. Kaplan's strategy for Explain questions is to find the two seemingly discrepant facts, then to look for the answer choice that explains how both could be true.

The two facts presented in the stimulus are (1) demand for the crops produced by Region A and for those produced by Region B dropped only slightly and (2) Region B was better able to

survive the crisis, while Region A's economy was devastated. Interestingly, the stimulus already seems to give part of the answer, signified by the keyword *because*—"[Region B] could adjust the supply of its crops." We might well predict that this ability will play an important part of the correct explanation.

(A) might seem to explain Region A's difficulty in an economic crisis. But the stimulus says that demand fell only slightly for Region A's foodstuffs and that the demand for Region B's dropped by the same amount. So (A) is irrelevant.

(B) shows us how Region B can adjust the supply of its crops and why Region A cannot. Even if you don't know what *perennial* means, the answer choice explicitly says that such crops cannot be easily adjusted. It completes the explanation begun in the stimulus and is, therefore, the correct answer.

(C) explains why one might expect Region A to do well in an economic downturn, so it hardly constitutes an explanation for why it didn't. (D) is also a 180—if anything, it would explain why Region B did poorly, not well. (E) is consistent with only part of the facts. It shows why Region B's demand didn't fall much, but we know that Region A's demand was affected similarly. So this answer doesn't explain the differing fortunes of the two regions' economies.

39. A

There's a 3-2 split at the beginning of the answer choices; some say "when" and others say "while." *When* is the appropriate word for describing a time, which is what the preceding phrase ("the late 19th century") is. So eliminate (C) and (D). There's a similar split at the end. We can eliminate (D) and (E) on those grounds.

You may have noticed that (B) repeats the phrase "in a given year" unnecessarily and can be eliminated on those grounds. There's also a difference in phrasing midway through. If you hadn't already eliminated (B), the unnecessary *just* would be grounds for doing so. Only (A) remains and is correct.

Notice how much text is underlined in this sentence. There will only be a few such questions in each section, and they're good ones to take a quick guess on if you're pressed for time.

40. E

There's a difference among the choices at the beginning. All say "as much as," but what follows is slightly different. The gist of the sentence is that Chesnutt's work reflected one thing to the same degree that it reflected another. That repeating verb is the key to the proper construction. (A) does not have a verb after "as much as" and so should be eliminated. The other verbs differ in tense. (B) and (D) are in the past tense, (C) is in the past perfect, and (E) is in the present. We're not sure when Chesnutt wrote, but this sentence is about his *work*—in other words, his stories. His stories are still around, doing whatever they do, so the present is correct. (E) is the right answer.

Also, note the unnecessarily complicated wording at the end of the choices. They all have the same meaning, but (E) conveys that meaning most simply.

41. A

Be familiar with idioms likely to appear on the GMAT. The correct idiomatic construction is "just as . . ., so . . ." Knowing this, you can narrow down the choices to (A) and (E) here. What follows "just as" must parallel what follows "so." That's why (E) can't be right: "Just as the various languages" isn't parallel to "so it is in U.S. culture." In (A), "the various languages" correctly parallels "the many musical traditions."

This question presents another opportunity for you to train your ear to spot awkward construction. The end of all the wrong answers are awkward compared to (A).

## Part Six

RESOURCES

APPENDIX: MATH SKILLS REFRESHER

- Arithmetic

- Algebra

- Geometry

There are many different math concepts throughout the GMAT. The good news is that you likely covered the relevant math content in high school. In fact, the math that appears on the GMAT is almost identical to the math tested on the SAT or ACT. You don't need to know trigonometry. You don't need to know calculus. No surprises—it's all material you've seen before. The bad news is that you may not have seen it since high school.

This chapter is an overview of essential GMAT math topics. It is a refresher for doing math without a calculator, and it also shows you the math techniques that the GMAT will call on you to use over and over. Some of these techniques—like *canceling*, *factoring*, and *prime factorization*—will give you those "shortcut" solutions that will save you valuable time.

As you study for the GMAT, if you are comfortable with all of the math concepts, great! Use this section to brush up on any concepts that seem slightly unfamiliar or that you'd like a little more practice with. Additionally, review any topic that seems to take too long or is difficult for you without a calculator.

On the other hand, if math is an extreme concern of yours—maybe you never understood these concepts in the first place or they used to make sense but now seem like a brand new topic—use this section to your advantage and study it fully.

The GMAT tests a limited number of core math concepts in predictable ways. Certain topics come up in every test. Even some of the words and phrases appearing in the questions are predictable. Since the test is so formulaic, we can show you the math you're bound to encounter.

After working through this chapter, you may find that you require a more intensive review of math skills and concepts or you want more practice with a particular topic. If that's the case, check out Kaplan's *GMAT Math Foundations* workbook. It provides a comprehensive, back-to-basics, tutor-led approach to math skills review, along with hundreds of skill-building exercises to improve your speed, confidence, and accuracy on test day.

EXPERT EXCLUSIVE

Some of the GMAT's hardest problems are arithmetic questions.

EXPERT EXCLUSIVE

It's highly unlikely that you'll get a question that uses the terms *rational* or *irrational*, but you WILL see many questions that use the term *integer*.

EXPERT EXCLUSIVE

If a question doesn't say "a number is an integer," then the number could be a fraction. Some Data Sufficiency right answers depend upon this possibility.

ARITHMETIC

Most of the math problems you will see on the GMAT involve arithmetic to some extent. Among the most important topics are number properties, ratios, and percents. You should know the basic definitions, such as what an integer is and what even numbers are.

NUMBER OPERATIONS

Number Types

Real Numbers: All numbers on the number line. All of the numbers on the GMAT are real.

Integers: All of the numbers with no fractional or decimal parts: multiples of 1. Negative numbers and 0 are integers too.

Rational Numbers: All of the numbers that can be expressed as the ratio of two integers (all integers and fractions).

Irrational Numbers: All real numbers that are not rational, both positive and negative (e.g., π, $-\sqrt{3}$).

Order of Operations

P = Parentheses
E = Exponents
M = Multiplication
D = Division } in order from left to right
A = Addition
S = Subtraction } in order from left to right

If an expression has parentheses within parentheses, work from the innermost out. This mnemonic will help you remember the order of operations: Please Excuse My Dear Aunt Sally (PEMDAS).

Example: $30 - 5 \times 4 + (7 - 3)^2 \div 8$

First, perform any operations within **Parentheses**. $30 - 5 \times 4 + 4^2 \div 8$

Next, raise to any powers indicated by **Exponents**. $30 - 5 \times 4 + 16 \div 8$

Then do all **Multiplication** and **Division**
in order from left to right.

$$30 - 20 + 2$$

Last, do all **Addition** and **Subtraction** in order
from left to right.

$$10 + 2$$

Answer:

$$12$$

Laws of Operations

Commutative Law: It doesn't matter in what order the operation is performed. Addition and multiplication are both commutative, while division and subtraction are not commutative.

Example:
$$5 + 8 = 8 + 5$$
$$2 \times 6 = 6 \times 2$$
$$3 - 2 \neq 2 - 3$$
$$6 \div 2 \neq 2 \div 6$$

Associative Law: The terms can be regrouped without changing the result. Addition and multiplication are also associative, while division and subtraction are not.

Example:

$$(a + b) + c = a + (b + c)$$
$$(3 + 5) + 8 = 3 + (5 + 8)$$
$$8 + 8 = 3 + 13$$
$$16 = 16$$

$$(a \times b) \times c = a \times (b \times c)$$
$$(4 \times 5) \times 6 = 4 \times (5 \times 6)$$
$$20 \times 6 = 4 \times 30$$
$$120 = 120$$

> **EXPERT EXCLUSIVE**
>
> While you won't be asked for the definitions of *commutative*, *associative*, or *distributive*, you will be expected to *use* these laws. And some arithmetic calculations are easier if you take advantage of these laws:
> $64 \times 102 = 64 \times (100 + 2) =$
> $(64 \times 100) + (64 \times 2) =$
> $6,400 + 128 = 6,528$

Distributive Law: The distributive law allows us to "distribute" a factor among the terms being added or subtracted. In general, $a(b + c) = ab + ac$.

Example:
$$4(3 + 7) = 4 \times 3 + 4 \times 7$$
$$4 \times 10 = 12 + 28$$
$$40 = 40$$

Division can be distributed in a similar way.

Example:
$$\frac{4+6}{2} = \frac{4}{2} + \frac{6}{2}$$

$$\frac{10}{2} = 2 + 3$$

$$5 = 5$$

However, when the sum or difference is in the **denominator**, no distribution is possible.

Example: $\frac{9}{4+5}$ is *not* equal to $\frac{9}{4} + \frac{9}{5}$.

Factoring: The technique called *factoring* uses the distributive law in its reverse form. You can *factor* to simplify some calculations.

EXPERT EXCLUSIVE

Factoring is one the highest-yield concepts you can learn for the GMAT. It is the vital step in many very difficult Algebra and Exponent problems.

Example:

$$11 + 22 + 33 + 44$$
$$(11 \times 1) + (11 \times 2) + (11 \times 3) + (11 \times 4)$$
$$11 \times (1 + 2 + 3 + 4)$$
$$11 \times 10$$
$$110$$

Fractions

4 ← numerator (also known as the *dividend*)

— ← fraction bar (means "*divided by*")

5 ← denominator (also known as the *divisor*)

Equivalent Fractions: When you multiply the numerator and denominator by the same number (any number other than zero), the fraction is unchanged. You simply get an equivalent fraction.

Example: $\dfrac{1}{2} = \dfrac{1 \times 2}{2 \times 2} = \dfrac{2}{4}$

Similarly, dividing the top and bottom by the same nonzero number leaves the fraction unchanged.

Example: $\dfrac{5}{10} = \dfrac{5 \div 5}{10 \div 5} = \dfrac{1}{2}$

The GMAT uses this technique to change the form of fractions that have radicals in the denominator.

Example: $\dfrac{9}{\sqrt{2}} = \dfrac{9 \times \sqrt{2}}{\sqrt{2} \times \sqrt{2}} = \dfrac{9\sqrt{2}}{2}$

Canceling and Reducing Fractions: Generally speaking, when you work with fractions on the GMAT, you'll need to put them in the **lowest terms**. That means that the numerator and the denominator are not divisible by any common integer greater than 1.

EXPERT EXCLUSIVE

Canceling is another high-yield arithmetic technique. You'll see why on the next page.

Example: The fraction $\dfrac{1}{2}$ is in lowest terms, but the fraction $\dfrac{3}{6}$ is not, since 3 and 6 are both divisible by 3.

The method we use to take a fraction and put it in lowest terms is called **reducing**. That simply means to factor and divide out any **common multiples** from both the numerator and denominator. This process is also commonly called **canceling**.

Example: Reduce $\dfrac{15}{35}$ to lowest terms.

First, determine the largest common factor of the numerator and denominator. Then, divide the top and bottom by that number to reduce.

$$\frac{15}{35} = \frac{3 \times 5}{7 \times 5} = \frac{3 \times 5 \div 5}{7 \times 5 \div 5} = \frac{3}{7}$$

Adding and Subtracting Fractions: We can't add or subtract two fractions directly unless they have the same, or "common," denominator.

A common denominator is just a **common multiple** of the denominators of the fractions. The **least common denominator** (LCD) is the **least common multiple** (LCM), the smallest positive number that is a multiple of all the terms.

Example: $\dfrac{3}{5}+\dfrac{2}{3}-\dfrac{1}{2}$

Denominators are 5, 3, 2.
Least Common Denominator (LCD) = 30.

For each fraction, divide the LCD by the denominator.

$$5 \times 6 = 30 \div 5 = 6$$
$$3 \times 10 = 30 \div 3 = 10$$
$$2 \times 15 = 30 \div 2 = 15$$

Then, multiply the numerator and denominator by that result.

$$\left(\frac{3}{5}\times\frac{6}{6}\right)+\left(\frac{2}{3}\times\frac{10}{10}\right)-\left(\frac{1}{2}\times\frac{15}{15}\right)$$

$$=\frac{18}{30}+\frac{20}{30}-\frac{15}{30}$$

Combine the numerators by adding or subtracting and keep the LCD as the denominator.

$$=\frac{18+20-15}{30}=\frac{23}{30}$$

Multiplying Fractions:

Example: $\dfrac{10}{9}\times\dfrac{3}{4}\times\dfrac{8}{15}$

First, reduce (cancel) diagonally and vertically. $\dfrac{\overset{2}{\cancel{10}}}{\underset{3}{\cancel{9}}}\times\dfrac{\overset{1}{\cancel{3}}}{\underset{1}{\cancel{4}}}\times\dfrac{\overset{2}{\cancel{8}}}{\underset{3}{\cancel{15}}}$

Then multiply the numerators together and the denominators together.

$$\frac{2\times1\times2}{3\times1\times3}=\frac{4}{9}$$

EXPERT EXCLUSIVE

See how powerful canceling is? It's much nicer than this:

$$\frac{10}{9}\times\frac{3}{4}\times\frac{8}{15}=\frac{10\times3\times8}{9\times4\times15}=\frac{240}{540}$$

Yuck!

Dividing Fractions: To divide one fraction by another, you actually multiply the first fraction by the **reciprocal** of the divisor (the second fraction). To get the reciprocal of a fraction, invert it! Simply switch around the numerator and the denominator.

For example, the reciprocal of the fraction $\dfrac{3}{7}$ is $\dfrac{7}{3}$.

Example: $\dfrac{4}{3} \div \dfrac{4}{9}$

Invert the divisor, then multiply as usual. $\dfrac{4}{3} \div \dfrac{4}{9}$

$$= \dfrac{4}{3} \times \dfrac{9}{4}$$

$$= \dfrac{{}^{1}\cancel{4}}{{}_{1}\cancel{3}} \times \dfrac{\cancel{9}^{3}}{\cancel{4}_{1}}$$

$$= \dfrac{1 \times 3}{1 \times 1} = \dfrac{3}{1}$$

$$= 3$$

Complex Fractions: A complex fraction is a fraction that contains one or more fractions in its numerator or denominator. There are two methods for simplifying complex fractions.

> **EXPERT EXCLUSIVE**
>
> Complex fractions are one of the GMAT's most common arithmetic setups. You're very likely to see one on test day.

Method I: Use the distributive law. Find the least common multiple of all the denominators and multiply all the terms in the top and bottom of the complex fraction by the LCM. This will eliminate all the denominators, greatly simplifying the calculation.

Example: $\dfrac{\dfrac{7}{9} - \dfrac{1}{6}}{\dfrac{1}{3} + \dfrac{1}{2}}$ LCM of all the denominators is 18.

$$= \dfrac{18 \times \left(\dfrac{7}{9} - \dfrac{1}{6} \right)}{18 \times \left(\dfrac{1}{3} + \dfrac{1}{2} \right)}$$

$$= \dfrac{\dfrac{{}^{2}\cancel{18}}{1} \times \dfrac{7}{\cancel{9}_{1}} - \dfrac{{}^{3}\cancel{18}}{1} \times \dfrac{1}{\cancel{6}_{1}}}{\dfrac{{}^{6}\cancel{18}}{1} \times \dfrac{1}{\cancel{3}_{1}} + \dfrac{{}^{9}\cancel{18}}{1} \times \dfrac{1}{\cancel{2}_{1}}}$$

$$= \dfrac{2 \times 7 - 3 \times 1}{6 \times 1 + 9 \times 1}$$

$$= \dfrac{14 - 3}{6 + 9}$$

$$= \dfrac{11}{15}$$

Method II: Treat the numerator and denominator separately. Combine the terms in each to get a single fraction on top and a single fraction on bottom. We are left with the division of two fractions, which we perform by multiplying the top fraction by the reciprocal of the bottom one. This method is preferable when it is difficult to get an LCM for all of the denominators.

Example:

$$\frac{\dfrac{5}{11}-\dfrac{5}{22}}{\dfrac{7}{16}+\dfrac{3}{8}}$$

LCM of the numerator is 22.

LCM of the denominator is 16.

$$=\frac{\dfrac{10}{22}-\dfrac{5}{22}}{\dfrac{7}{16}+\dfrac{6}{16}}=\frac{\dfrac{5}{22}}{\dfrac{13}{16}}=\frac{5}{\cancel{22}_{11}}\times\frac{\cancel{16}^{8}}{13}=\frac{40}{143}$$

Comparing Positive Fractions: If the numerators are the same, the fraction with the smaller denominator will have the larger value, since the numerator is divided into a smaller number of parts.

Example: $\dfrac{4}{5}>\dfrac{4}{7}$

If the denominators are the same, the fraction with the larger numerator will have the larger value.

Example: $\dfrac{5}{8}>\dfrac{3}{8}$

If neither the numerators nor the denominators are the same, express all of the fractions in terms of some common denominator. The fraction with the largest numerator will be the largest.

> **EXPERT EXCLUSIVE**
>
> If you forget these rules, you can quickly recall them by testing some "obvious" fractions:
>
> $\dfrac{1}{2}>\dfrac{1}{3}$
>
> $\dfrac{3}{2}>\dfrac{1}{2}$

One version of this method is to multiply the numerator of the left fraction by the denominator of the right fraction and vice versa (similar to cross multiplying). Then compare the products obtained this way. If the left product is greater, then the left fraction was greater to start with.

Example: Compare $\dfrac{5}{7}$ and $\dfrac{9}{11}$.

Compare 5×11 and 9×7.

Because $55 < 63$, $\dfrac{5}{7} < \dfrac{9}{11}$.

Example: Compare $\dfrac{22}{19}$ and $\dfrac{11}{9}$.

As before, the comparison can be made by cross mutiplying.

Compare 22×9 and 11×19.

> **EXPERT EXCLUSIVE**
>
> Don't pick just one way to deal with fractions and stick to it relentlessly. The test makers deliberately use a variety of setups, some of which are most easily solved one way. They do this to reward people who consider different approaches. Choose your approach based on what would be the easiest way to deal with the numbers in front of you!

Because $198 < 209$, $\dfrac{22}{19} < \dfrac{11}{9}$.

You could also convert the fractions to percents or decimals for easy comparison.

Example: Compare $\dfrac{5}{8}$ and $\dfrac{7}{11}$.

$\dfrac{5}{8} = 0.625$ and $\dfrac{7}{11} = 0.636363\ldots$

Because $0.625 < 0.6363\ldots$, $\dfrac{5}{8} < \dfrac{7}{11}$.

Converting fractions to decimals or percents frequently comes up on the GMAT. Often the problem gives you fractions in the question but percents in the answer choices. Later in this chapter, you'll see some common equivalencies.

Another way to compare fractions is to find a "benchmark value" against which the fractions can be compared.

Example: Compare $\dfrac{13}{24}$ and $\dfrac{33}{68}$.

Both are very close to $\dfrac{1}{2}$.

$\dfrac{1}{2} = \dfrac{12}{24}$ and $\dfrac{1}{2} = \dfrac{34}{68}$.

Because $\dfrac{13}{24} > \dfrac{1}{2}$ and $\dfrac{33}{68} < \dfrac{1}{2}$, $\dfrac{13}{24} > \dfrac{33}{68}$.

> **EXPERT EXCLUSIVE**
>
> If the numbers seem too scary to do calculations with, that's a good sign that there is another way to do the problem—such as comparing to a benchmark.

Mixed Numbers: Fractions whose numerators are greater than their denominators may be converted into mixed numbers and vice versa. Mixed numbers consist of an integer and a fraction. For example, $3\dfrac{1}{4}, 12\dfrac{2}{5}$, and $5\dfrac{7}{8}$ are all mixed numbers.

Example: Convert $\dfrac{23}{4}$ to a mixed number.

$\dfrac{23}{4} = \dfrac{20}{4} + \dfrac{3}{4}$

$\quad\ = 5\dfrac{3}{4}$

Example: Convert $2\dfrac{3}{7}$ to a fraction.

$2\dfrac{3}{7} = 2 + \dfrac{3}{7}$

$\quad\ = \dfrac{14}{7} + \dfrac{3}{7}$

$\quad\ = \dfrac{17}{7}$

Decimals

Decimals can be converted to common fractions with a power of 10 in the denominator.

Example: $0.053 = \dfrac{53}{10^3} = \dfrac{53}{1,000}$

Numbers are made up of **digits** in specific **places**. The GMAT occasionally asks questions using the terms *digit* and *place*, so you should be familiar with the naming convention:

hundreds	tens	units	tenths	hundredths	thousandths
3	1	5	.2	4	6

> **EXPERT EXCLUSIVE**
>
> When a GMAT question specifies that a variable is a *digit*, remember that the only possible values are the integers 0, 1, 2, 3, 4, 5, 6, 7, 8, and 9. This is a very limited range, and that limitation is usually the key to the solution.

Comparing Decimals: To compare decimals, add zeros after the last digit to the right of the decimal point until all the decimals have the same number of digits. Doing this will make all the denominators of the fractions the same. Therefore, comparing the numerators will determine the order of values.

Example: Arrange in order from smallest to largest: 0.7, 0.77, 0.07, 0.707, and 0.077.

$$0.7 = 0.700 = \frac{700}{1,000}$$

$$0.77 = 0.770 = \frac{770}{1,000}$$

$$0.07 = 0.070 = \frac{70}{1,000}$$

$$0.707 = 0.707 = \frac{707}{1,000}$$

$$0.077 = 0.077 = \frac{77}{1,000}$$

Because $70 < 77 < 700 < 707 < 770$, $0.07 < 0.077 < 0.7 < 0.707 < 0.77$.

Adding and Subtracting Decimals: When adding or subtracting decimals, make sure that the decimal points are lined up, one under the other. This will ensure that the same places are added; that is, tenths are added to tenths, hundredths to hundredths, etc.

Example: $0.5 + 0.05 + 0.005 =$

$$
\begin{array}{r}
0.5 \\
0.05 \\
+\ \underline{0.005} \\
0.555
\end{array}
$$

Multiplying and Dividing Decimals: To multiply two decimals, initially multiply them as you would integers and ignore the decimal places. The number of decimal places in the product will be the sum of the number of decimal places in the factors that are multiplied together.

Example: $0.675 \times 0.42 =$

$$
\begin{array}{rl}
0.675 & \text{(3 decimal places)} \\
\underline{\times\ 0.42} & \underline{+\ \text{(2 decimal places)}} \\
1350 & \\
\underline{27000} & \\
0.28350 & \text{(5 decimal places)}
\end{array}
$$

> ## EXPERT EXCLUSIVE
>
> For each power of 10 you *multiply* a number by, the decimal point moves one place to the *right*. For each power of 10, you *divide* a number by, move the decimal point moves one place to the *left* (e.g., $2.75 \times 100 = 275$; $2.75 \div 100 = 0.0275$).

Division—Method I: When dividing a decimal by another decimal, multiply each by a power of 10 such that the divisor becomes an integer; that is, move the decimal point of each the same number of places. (This doesn't change the value of the quotient.) Then carry out the division as you would with integers, placing the decimal point in the quotient directly above the decimal point in the dividend.

Example: $0.675 \div 0.25 =$

$67.5 \div 25 =$ Move the decimal point over two places to the right to make 0.25 an integer.

$$
\begin{array}{r}
2.7 \\
25\overline{)67.5} \\
\underline{50} \\
175 \\
\underline{175} \\
0
\end{array}
$$

Division—Method II: Turn the division problem into a fraction. It is best when the numbers have common factors. Move the decimal point in the numerator and the denominator an equivalent number of places. Then, cancel common factors.

Example: $0.675 \div 0.25$

$$\frac{0.675}{0.25}$$

$$\frac{675}{250}$$

$$\frac{\cancel{675}^{135}}{\cancel{250}_{50}} = \frac{\cancel{135}^{27}}{\cancel{50}_{10}} = \frac{27}{10} = 2.7$$

NUMBER OPERATIONS PRACTICE SET.

Answers are on page 626.

1. Which of the following is less than $\frac{1}{6}$?

    ○   0.1667

    ○ $\frac{3}{18}$

    ○   0.167

    ○   0.1666

    ○ $\frac{8}{47}$

2. Which of the following is equal to $25(27 + 29 + 31)$?

    ○ $25(27 + 29) + 31$

    ○ $25(27) + 29 + 31$

    ○ $25(27) + 25(29 + 31)$

    ○ $25 + (27)(29)(31)$

    ○ $25(27 + 29) + 25(29 + 31)$

3. $\frac{7}{5} \times \left(\frac{3}{7} - \frac{2}{5} \right) =$

    ○ $\frac{1}{165}$

    ○ $\frac{1}{35}$

    ○ $\frac{1}{25}$

    ○ $\frac{9}{15}$

    ○   1

4.

$$\frac{5}{9}, \frac{5}{12}, \frac{23}{48}, \frac{11}{24}, \frac{3}{7}$$

What is the positive difference between the largest and smallest of the fractions above?

Advanced

5. For which of the following expressions would the value be greater if 160 were replaced by 120?

I. $1,000 - 160$

II. $\dfrac{160}{1+160}$

III. $\dfrac{1}{1-\dfrac{1}{160}}$

○ None

○ I only

○ III only

○ I and II

○ I and III

NUMBER PROPERTIES

Absolute Value

The **absolute value** of a number is the number's distance from zero on the number line. It is denoted by two vertical lines. Since absolute value is a distance, it is always positive. For instance, both +3 and −3 are 3 units from zero, so their absolute values are both 3.

Example: $|-3| = 3$
$|+3| = 3$

The GMAT will increase the degree of an absolute value question's difficulty (and, therefore, the benefit of getting it right) by using variables.

Example: $|z| = 3$

We don't know what z equals. Since z is 3 units from 0, we can deduce that it either equals +3 or −3.

So we can rewrite this one equation as two:
$z = 3$ OR $z = -3$

Another way to conceptualize this is as follows:

$|z| = 3$
$\pm z = 3$
$+z = 3$ OR $-z = 3$
$z = 3$ OR $z = -3$

These problems are fairly straightforward when only one number is involved. But what about expressions? Treat the absolute value bars as parentheses and figure out the value of what's inside *before* you perform the operation. Needless to say, the GMAT will base wrong answers on performing these operations in the wrong order.

INCORRECT: $|-3| + |5| = |-3 + 5| = |2| = 2$

CORRECT: $|-3| + |5|$
$= 3 + 5$
$= 8$

Now, let's look at what happens when we are given expressions with variables.

Example: $|x - 3| = 3$

Believe it or not, this isn't any different from our earlier example:

$|z| = 3$
$z = 3$ OR $z = -3$

Think of it this way:

$|<< chunk >>| = 3$

$<< chunk >> = 3$ OR $<< chunk >> = -3$

Since our $<< chunk >>$ is $x - 3$, that gives us the following:

$|x - 3| = 3$

$x - 3 = 3$ OR $x - 3 = -3$

$x = 6$ OR $x = 0$

The GMAT sometimes adds one more layer of complexity to absolute value: inequalities. The key is to remember that *when considering the possible negative value, the inequality sign changes direction*:

$|x - z| > 3$

$x - z > 3$ OR $x - z < -3$

Don't worry if that seems a little weird to you right now. We'll explore this idea further when we discuss inequalities in the Algebra portion of this chapter.

Properties of −1, 0, 1, and Numbers in Between

Properties of Zero: Adding or subtracting zero from a number does not change the number.

EXPERT EXCLUSIVE

The special properties of −1, 0, and 1 make them important numbers for consideration in Data Sufficiency questions, as well as the "could be/must be" kinds of Problem Solving questions.

Example: $2 + 0 = 2$
$4 - 0 = 4$

Any number multiplied by zero equals zero.

Example: $12 \times 0 = 0$

Division by zero is **undefined**. When given an algebraic expression, be sure that the denominator is not zero. The fraction $\dfrac{0}{0}$ is likewise undefined.

Properties of 1 and −1: Multiplying or dividing a number by 1 does not change the number.

Examples: $4 \times 1 = 4$
$-3 \div 1 = -3$

Multiplying or dividing a number by −1 changes the sign, but not the absolute value.

Examples: $6 \times (-1) = -6$
$-2 \div (-1) = -(-2) = 2$

Note: The sum of a number and −1 times that number is equal to zero.

The **reciprocal** of a number is 1 divided by the number. The product of a number and its reciprocal is 1. Zero has no reciprocal, since $\dfrac{1}{0}$ is undefined.

Properties of Numbers between −1 and 1: The reciprocal of a number between 0 and 1 is greater than the number itself.

EXPERT EXCLUSIVE

Because numbers between −1 and 1 can make things larger or smaller in different ways than do other numbers, they are good numbers to pick when testing whether one expression always has to be bigger or smaller than another.

Example: The reciprocal of $\dfrac{2}{3}$ is $\dfrac{1}{\frac{2}{3}}$.

$$\frac{1}{\frac{2}{3}} = 1 \div \frac{2}{3} = 1 \times \frac{3}{2} = \frac{3}{2}$$

$$\frac{3}{2} > \frac{2}{3}$$

The reciprocal of a number between −1 and 0 is less than the number itself.

Example: The reciprocal of $-\dfrac{2}{3}$ is $-\dfrac{1}{\frac{2}{3}}$.

$$-\frac{1}{\frac{2}{3}} = 1 \div -\frac{2}{3} = 1 \times -\frac{3}{2} = -\frac{3}{2}$$

$$-\frac{3}{2} < -\frac{2}{3}$$

The square of a number between 0 and 1 is less than the number itself.

Example: $\left(\dfrac{1}{2}\right)^2 = \dfrac{1}{2} \times \dfrac{1}{2} = \dfrac{1}{4}$, which is less than $\dfrac{1}{2}$.

Multiplying any positive number by a fraction between 0 and 1 gives a product smaller than the original number.

Example: $6 \times \dfrac{1}{4} = \dfrac{6}{4} = \dfrac{3}{2}$, which is less than 6.

Multiplying any negative number by a fraction between 0 and 1 gives a product greater than the original number.

Example: $-3 \times \dfrac{1}{6} = -\dfrac{3}{6} = -\dfrac{1}{2}$, which is greater than -3.

All these properties can best be seen by observation rather than by memorization.

Operations with Signed Numbers

Addition:

With like signs: Add the absolute values and keep the same sign.

Example: $(-6) + (-3) = -9$

With unlike signs: Take the difference of the absolute values and keep the sign of the number with the larger absolute value.

Example: $(-7) + (+3) = -4$

Subtraction: Subtraction is the inverse operation of addition, so subtracting a number is the same as adding its negation.

Example:
$(-5) - (-10)$
$= (-5) + (+10)$
$= 5$

Multiplication and Division: The product or the quotient of two numbers with the same sign is positive.

Examples: $(-2) \times (-5) = +10$ and $\dfrac{-50}{-5} = +10$

The product or the quotient of two numbers with opposite signs is negative.

Examples: $(-2) \times (+3) = -6$ and $\dfrac{-6}{2} = -3$

> **EXPERT EXCLUSIVE**
>
> Adding a negative number is the same as subtracting a positive number. Subtracting a negative number is the same as adding a positive number.

> **EXPERT EXCLUSIVE**
>
> It doesn't matter whether the negative sign is in the numerator or in the denominator. The fraction $\dfrac{-6}{2}$ is the same as $\dfrac{6}{-2}$ and $-\dfrac{6}{2}$.

Odd and Even

The terms *odd* and *even* apply only to integers. Even numbers are integers that are divisible by 2, and odd numbers are integers that are not. Odd and even numbers may be negative; 0 is even.

A number needs just a single factor of 2 to be even, so the product of an even number and *any* integer will always be even.

EXPERT EXCLUSIVE

Even × Any Integer = Even

The GMAT often sets up questions that can be quickly solved with this combined version of the multiplication rules.

Rules for Odds and Evens

Odd + Odd = Even	Odd × Odd = Odd
Even + Even = Even	Even × Even = Even
Odd + Even = Odd	Odd × Even = Even

Using rules, we have important results involving exponents:

Exponent Rules for Odds and Evens

$$\text{Odd}^{\text{any positive integer}} = \text{Odd}$$
$$\text{Even}^{\text{any positive integer}} = \text{Even}$$

Factors, Primes, and Divisibility

Multiples: An integer that is divisible by another integer without a remainder is a **multiple** of that integer.

Example: 12 is a multiple of 3, since 12 is divisible by 3.

EXPERT EXCLUSIVE

Some useful things to keep in mind when Picking Numbers:

• Every number is both a factor and a multiple of itself.

• 1 is a factor of every number.

• 0 is a multiple of every number.

Remainders: The **remainder** is what is left over in a division problem. A remainder is always smaller than the number we are dividing by.

Example: 17 divided by 3 is 5 with a remainder of 2.

Factors: The **factors**, or **divisors**, of a number are the positive integers that divide into that number without a remainder (or a remainder of 0).

Example: The number 36 has nine factors: 1, 2, 3, 4, 6, 9, 12, 18, and 36.

We can group these factors in pairs: $1 \times 36 = 2 \times 18 = 3 \times 12 = 4 \times 9 = 6 \times 6$

The **greatest common factor**, or **greatest common divisor**, of a pair of numbers is the largest factor shared by the two numbers.

EXPERT EXCLUSIVE

Most GMAT remainder problems are best solved by the strategy of Picking Numbers, which is discussed in greater detail in the Problem Solving chapter of this book.

Prime number: A **prime** number is an integer greater than 1 that has only two factors, 1 and itself. The number 1 is not considered a prime. The number 2 is the first prime number and the only even prime. (Do you see why? Any other even number has 2 as a factor and, therefore, is not prime.) The GMAT expects test-takers to recognize the prime numbers up to 50. They are: 2, 3, 5, 7, 11, 13, 17, 19, 23, 29, 31, 37, 41, 43, 47

EXPERT EXCLUSIVE

These rules can be synthesized into one:

$$\frac{Multiple}{Factor} = Integer$$

Prime factorization: The **prime factorization** of a number is the expression of the number as the product of its prime factors. No matter how you factor a number, its prime factors will always be the same.

Example: $36 = 6 \times 6 = 2 \times 3 \times 2 \times 3$ or $2 \times 2 \times 3 \times 3$ or $2^2 \times 3^2$.

Example: $480 = 48 \times 10 = 8 \times 6 \times 2 \times 5$
$$= 4 \times 2 \times 2 \times 3 \times 2 \times 5$$
$$= 2 \times 2 \times 2 \times 2 \times 3 \times 2 \times 5$$
$$= 2^5 \times 3 \times 5$$

The easiest way to determine a number's prime factorization is to figure out a pair of factors of the number and then determine their factors, continuing the process until you're left with only prime numbers. Those primes will be the prime factorization.

Example: Find the prime factorization of 1,050.

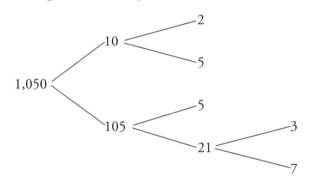

> **EXPERT EXCLUSIVE**
>
> Prime factorization is one of the most valuable tools for the entire Quant section. Any question about multiples or factors is really, at its heart, a question about prime factors. Quickly jotting down the prime factorizations of the numbers in such questions can provide the key to the solution.

So the prime factorization of 1,050 is $2 \times 3 \times 5^2 \times 7$.

Distinct Prime Factors: The GMAT has in the past asked not only about prime factors, but also about distinct prime factors. *Distinct* simply means "different." Thus, $1050 = 2 \times 3 \times 5 \times 5 \times 7$, five numbers with 5 repeating once; it has five prime factors, but only four distinct ones.

Divisibility Tests: Several tests can quickly determine whether a given number is a multiple of 2, 3, 4, 5, 9, and 11.

A number is divisible by 2 if its last digit is even.

> 138 is divisible by 2 because 8 is even.
> 177 is not divisible by 2 because 7 is not even.

A number is divisible by 3 if the sum of its digits is divisible by 3.

> 4,317 is divisible by 3 because $4 + 3 + 1 + 7 = 15$ and 15 is divisible by 3.
> 32,872 is not divisible by 3 because $3 + 2 + 8 + 7 + 2 = 22$ and 22 is not divisible by 3.

A number is divisible by 4 if its last two digits compose a two-digit number that is itself divisible by 4.

> **EXPERT EXCLUSIVE**
>
> Prime factorization is often the key to dealing with scary exponents as well. If a GMAT problem gives you 35^8, rewriting it as $(5 \times 7)^8 = 5^8 \times 7^8$ is almost certainly the way to go.

1,732 is divisible by 4 because 32 is divisible by 4.
1,746 is not divisible by 4 because 46 is not divisible by 4.

A number is divisible by 5 if its last digit is either a 5 or a 0.

26,985 is divisible by 5.
55,783 is not divisible by 5.

A number is divisible by 9 if the sum of its digits is divisible by 9.

16,956 is divisible by 9 because $1 + 6 + 9 + 5 + 6 = 27$, and 27 is divisible by 9.
4,317 is not divisible by 9 because $4 + 3 + 1 + 7 = 15$, and 15 is not divisible by 9.

A number is divisible by 11 if the difference between the sum of its odd-placed digits and the sum of its even-placed digits is divisible by 11.

5,181 is divisible by 11 because $(5 + 8) - (1 + 1) = 11$, which is divisible by 11.
827 is not divisible by 11 because $(8 + 7) - 2 = 13$, which is not divisible by 11.

> **EXPERT EXCLUSIVE**
>
> Divisibility by 11 shows up with surprising regularity in the GMAT's tougher Quant problems.

Bonus rule for 11: If the digit in the tens place of a three-digit number is equal to the sum of the digits in that number's hundreds and units places, then that number is divisible by 11. Furthermore, the quotient of the number divided by 11 will be a two-digit number composed of the digits in the original number's hundreds and units places.

341 is divisible by 11 because $3 + 1 = 4$. Furthermore, $341 = 31 \times 11$.
792 is divisible by 11 because $7 + 2 = 9$. Furthermore, $792 = 72 \times 11$.

This rule *cannot* be used to rule out divisibility, only to rule it in:
715 is divisible by 11, even though $7 + 5 \neq 1$ ($715 = 65 \times 11$).

You can combine these rules above with factorization to figure out whether a number is divisible by other numbers.

To be divisible by 6, a number must pass the divisibility tests for both 2 and 3, since $6 = 2 \times 3$.
534 is divisible by 6 because 4 is divisible by 2 *and* $5 + 3 + 4 = 12$, which is divisible by 3.

To be divisible by 44, a number must pass the divisibility tests for both 4 and 11, since $44 = 4 \times 11$.
8,184 is divisible by 44 because 84 is divisible by 4 *and* $(8 + 8) - (1 + 4) = 11$, which is divisible by 11.

Consecutive Numbers

A list of numbers is **consecutive** if the numbers either occur at a fixed interval or exhibit a fixed pattern. All the consecutive numbers you will encounter on the exam are integers. Consecutive numbers could be in ascending or descending order.

A series of consecutive positive integers: 1, 2, 3, 4, 5, 6
A series of consecutive even numbers: −6, −4, −2, 0, 2, 4
A series of consecutive prime numbers: 5, 7, 11, 13, 17, 19

A series of consecutive integers has a pretty fantastic property: its **median** is the same as its **average**. In just a few pages, we'll go into this in further detail and show you how to quickly solve one of the GMAT's most puzzling arithmetic questions. But for now, let's try some practice problems.

NUMBER PROPERTIES PRACTICE SET

Answers are on page 629.

1. If the product of three integers is odd, which of the following must be true?

   ○   The sum of any two of the integers is even.

   ○   The product of any two of the integers is even.

   ○   The sum of the three integers is even.

   ○   The average (arithmetic mean) of the three integers is even.

   ○   The median of the three integers is even.

2. If the integer P leaves a remainder of 4 when divided by 9, all of the following must be true EXCEPT

   ○   the number that is 4 less than P is a multiple of 9.

   ○   the number that is 5 more than P is a multiple of 9.

   ○   the number that is 2 more than P is a multiple of 3.

   ○   when divided by 3, P will leave a remainder of 1.

   ○   when divided by 2, P will leave a remainder of 1.

3. If *a* and *b* are integers and the sum of *ab* and *b* is odd, which of the following could be true?

  I.   *a* and *b* are both odd.

  II. *a* is even and *b* is odd.

  III. *a* is odd and *b* is even.

  ○ I only

  ○ II only

  ○ III only

  ○ I and II

  ○ I and III

4. If $x = 8y$, where *y* is a prime number greater than 2, how many different positive odd factors does *x* have?

Advanced

5. What is the positive difference between the number of distinct prime factors of 15^2 and the number of distinct prime factors of 64^3?

6. A wire is cut into 3 equal parts. The resulting segments are then cut into 4, 6, and 8 equal parts, respectively. If each of the resulting segments has an integer length, what is the minimum length of the wire?

EXPERT EXCLUSIVE

The average formula is fairly well known. So to make an average-based problem hard, the test makers create problems for which a formula-based approach is difficult. Look to Pick Numbers on many GMAT average questions to make them easier.

CLASSIC FORMULAS

The GMAT assumes that you have a working knowledge of several classic formulas. You should be comfortable using these so that you don't have to waste time trying to remember them.

Averages

The average (arithmetic mean) of a group of numbers is defined as the sum of the values divided by the number of values.

$$\text{Average value} = \frac{\text{Sum of values}}{\text{Number of values}}$$

Example: Henry buys three items costing $2.00, $0.75, and $0.25. What is the average price?

$$\text{Average price} = \frac{\text{Sum of prices}}{\text{Number of prices}}$$

$$= \frac{\text{Total price}}{\text{Number of prices}}$$

$$= \frac{\$2.00 + \$0.75 + \$0.25}{3}$$

$$= \frac{\$3.00}{3}$$

$$= \$1.00$$

Median: If a group of numbers is arranged in numerical order, the median is the middle value.

Example: What is the median of 4, 5, 100, 1, and 6?

Arrange the numbers in numerical order: 1, 4, 5, 6, and 100.
The middle number (the median) is 5.

If a set has an even number of terms, then the median is the average of the two middle terms after the terms are arranged in numerical order.

Example: What is the median value of 2, 9, 8, 17, 11, and 37?

Arrange the values in numerical order: 2, 8, 9, 11, 17, 37.
The two middle numbers are 9 and 11.
The median is the average of 9 and 11; that is, 10.

The median can be quite different from the average. For instance, in the previous example for averages, the average is $1.00, while the median is the middle of the three prices given, or $0.75.

Mode: The mode is the number that appears most frequently in a set. For example, in the set {1, 2, 2, 2, 3, 4, 4, 5, 6} the mode is 2.

Standard Deviation: If you've worked with the standard deviation formula in high school or college, it's probably looked something like this:

$$\sqrt{\frac{1}{N}[(x_1 - \mu)^2 + (x_2 - \mu)^2 + \cdots + (x_N - \mu)^2]}$$

It's not much easier to parse in plain English. Calculating the standard deviation involves (1) subtracting the average of a set from each term in that set, (2) squaring each result, (3) taking the average of those squares, and (4) calculating the square root of that average.

Fortunately, the GMAT will *never* require you to apply this formula! When the standard deviation is tested, all you will need to understand is the basic concept: standard deviation represents how close or far the terms in a list are from the average.

Thus, {1, 2, 3} and {101, 102, 103} have the same standard deviation, since they both have one term on the average and two terms exactly one unit away from the average. A quickly sketched number line can confirm this:

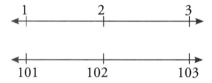

So, {1, 3, 5} will have a smaller standard deviation than {0, 3, 6}. Both sets have an average of 3, but the first has terms 2, 0, and 2 units from the average while the second has terms 3, 0, and 3 units from the average. Again, we can confirm this with a quick sketch:

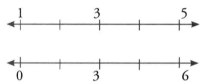

In other words, the GMAT is trying to trick you into using complex mathematical solutions for simple concepts! Trust that the test makers won't require you to know the standard deviation formula, and use your common sense to judge the approximate spread of any sets you see.

Average and Median of Consecutive Integers: As mentioned, the average of a set of consecutive integers will equal its median.

Example: What is the average of 1, 2, 3, 4, and 5?

$$\frac{1+2+3+4+5}{5} = \frac{15}{5} = 3$$

There is another way to calculate this. The average of a series of consecutive integers is also the same as the average of its first and last terms. For the last example, that works out to $\frac{(1+5)}{2} = \frac{6}{2} = 3$.

Sum of Numbers: If we know the average of a group of numbers and the number of numbers in the group, we can find the sum of the numbers. It's as if all the numbers in the group are the average value.

$$\boxed{\text{Sum of values} = \text{Average value} \times \text{Number of values}}$$

Example: What is the sum of all the integers between 1 and 66 inclusive?

Since this is a series of consecutive integers, we can find its average by averaging the first and last terms: $\dfrac{1+66}{2}=\dfrac{67}{2}$.

Sum = Average × Number of Values

Sum $= \dfrac{67}{2} \times 66 = \dfrac{67}{\cancel{2}} \times \cancel{66}^{\,33} = 2,211$

Granted, one still has to calculate 67 × 33, but that is much nicer than adding all 66 numbers!

You may also have to find a sum in what might seem a normal average problem.

Example: The average daily temperature for the first week in January was 31 degrees. If the average temperature for the first six days was 30 degrees, what was the temperature on the seventh day?

The sum for all 7 days = 31 × 7 = 217 degrees.
The sum of the first 6 days = 30 × 6 = 180 degrees.
The temperature on the seventh day = 217 − 180 = 37 degrees.

You can save yourself a lot of arithmetic if you think of the average as a "balancing point" between the numbers in the series. That is, the difference between the average and every number below it will equal the difference between the average and every number above it.

> **EXPERT EXCLUSIVE**
> The "balance" approach dramatically reduces the difficulty of the arithmetic.

We've already seen that the average of $2.00, $0.75, and $0.25 is $1.00. Here's how that balances:

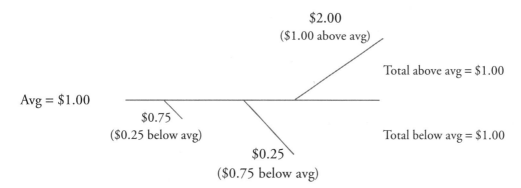

Now let's use this to solve a problem.

Example: The average of 43, 44, 45, and x is 45. What is the value of x?

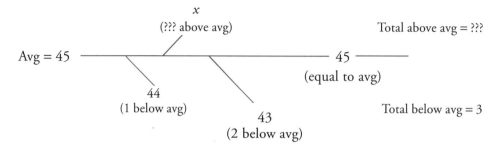

Since the amount above the average must equal the amount below the average, the amount above must be 3. Therefore x is 3 above the average: $3 + 45 = 48$; $x = 48$.

Rates (*A* per *B*)

The most common rate is a speed—miles per hour—but anything with the word *per* is a rate: kilometers per second, miles per gallon, ounces of cheese per party guest, and so forth.

$$\boxed{\text{Rate } A \text{ per } B = \frac{\text{Quantity of } A}{\text{Quantity of } B}}$$

Most basic rate problems involve conversions from one rate to another. These are best handled by multiplying the various rates so that measurements cancel.

Example: If a car averages 25 miles per gallon and each gallon of gas costs $2.40, what's the value of the gas consumed in a trip of 175 miles?

> **EXPERT EXCLUSIVE**
> You may have to invert some of the rates to make the measurements cancel.

$$\frac{\$2.40}{\text{gallon}} \times \frac{\text{gallon}}{25 \text{ miles}} \times 175 \text{ miles}$$

$$\frac{\$2.40}{\text{gallon}} \times \frac{\text{gallon}}{25^1 \text{ miles}} \times 175^7 \text{ miles}$$

$$\$2.40 \times 7$$

$$\$16.80$$

> **EXPERT EXCLUSIVE**
> It's very tempting in "average rate" problems simply to average the different individual rates. Don't! The GMAT writes its problems so that this is *never* the correct solution.

Average Rate (Average *A* per *B*):

$$\boxed{\text{Average } A \text{ per } B = \frac{\text{Total } A}{\text{Total } B}}$$

Example: John travels 30 miles in 2 hours and then 60 miles in 3 hours. What is his average speed in miles per hour?

$$\text{Average miles per hour} = \frac{\text{Total miles}}{\text{Total hours}}$$

$$= \frac{(30+60) \text{ miles}}{(2+3) \text{ hours}} = \frac{90 \text{ miles}}{5 \text{ hours}} = 18 \text{ miles/hour}$$

The GMAT likes to write very complex "average rate" problems. Any time the GMAT asks a question in which somebody moves at different rates at different times, it can be tricky to keep track of all the data. We recommend doing so by jotting down this chart on your scratch booklet:

	Rate	Time	Distance
part 1 of trip			
part 2 of trip			
entire trip			

This chart folds many equations into one:

- Rate × Time = Distance; boxes multiply across.
- Time (part 1) + Time (part 2) = Time (entire trip); time boxes add down.
- Distance (part 1) + Distance (part 2) = Distance (entire trip); distance boxes add down.
- Rates *do not* add, they are calculated by dividing distance by time. Rate boxes *do not* add down.

Example: A motorcyclist drives from Town A to Town B at 40 miles per hour and proceeds immediately to Town C without stopping. The distance from Town A to Town B is 120 miles. If the total speed for the entire journey is 45 miles per hour, and the distance from Town B to Town C is half of the distance from Town A to Town B, then what was the motorcyclist's speed from Town B to Town C?

It's enough to make your head spin! But see how straightforward the problem becomes when you plug the data into the chart:

	Rate	Time	Distance
A to B	40		120
B to C			60
entire trip	45		

Now we can calculate the entire distance (120 + 60) and the time from A to B (120 ÷ 40):

	Rate	Time	Distance
A to B	40	3	120
B to C			60
entire trip	45		180

Now we can calculate the entire time (180 ÷ 45):

	Rate	Time	Distance
A to B	40	3	120
B to C			60
entire trip	45	4	180

Now we can calculate the time from B to C (4 − 3):

	Rate	Time	Distance
A to B	40	3	120
B to C		1	60
entire trip	45	4	180

And finally, what we're solving for, the rate of speed from B to C (60 ÷ 1):

	Rate	Time	Distance
A to B	40	3	120
B to C	60	1	60
entire trip	45	4	180

The answer is 60 miles per hour.

Combined Work

EXPERT EXCLUSIVE

The GMAT usually has a wrong answer based on the reciprocal of the total time. It's safer to use the formula that's specifically for two people/machines if you can.

EXPERT EXCLUSIVE

Avoid one of the most common errors—there are 60 minutes in an hour, not 100. So $\frac{1}{5}$ of an hour is 12 minutes, not 20 minutes.

These questions give you different people or machines that can perform the same job in different times. This question type might seem like a rate problem at first, but in practice it's slightly different. There are two formulas you can use:

$$\text{Total Time} = \frac{AB}{A+B}$$

Use this one if there are two people/machines.

$$\frac{1}{\text{Total Time}} = \frac{1}{A} + \frac{1}{B} + \frac{1}{C} + \cdots + \frac{1}{N}$$

This is the general version that you can use with any number of people/machines.

A, B, C, etc. represent the time it takes the individual people or machines to do the job by themselves.

Example: Bob can clean a room in 3 hours, and George can clean the same room in 2 hours. How many hours does it take Bob and George to clean the room if they work together but independently?

$$\text{Total time} = \frac{3 \times 2}{3 + 2}$$

$$\text{Total time} = \frac{6}{5} \text{ hours, or 1 hour 12 minutes.}$$

Overlapping Sets

Another classic GMAT setup involves a large group that is subdivided into two potentially overlapping subgroups. For example, let's say that in a room of 20 people, there are 12 dog owners and 14 cat owners. Since 12 plus 14 is more than 20, the only way this situation makes any sense is if some people own both a dog and a cat. And it's possible that some own neither. Essentially there are four different subgroups to consider: (1) those who own a dog but not a cat, (2) those who own a cat but not a dog, (3) those who own both a cat and a dog, and (4) those who own neither a cat nor a dog. We could also combine some of these groups to consider both the total number of dog owners and the total number of cat owners.

> **EXPERT EXCLUSIVE**
>
> Sound confusing? That's the point—the GMAT is trying to bury you with the complexity. It's vital to use your scratch material to reorganize the data in a way that makes things more clear.

There are three ways to work these problems. Let's look at each.

Approach 1: A formula:

$$\boxed{\text{Group 1} + \text{Group 2} - \text{Both} + \text{Neither} = \text{Total}}$$

Example: A frat house orders 27 pizzas for a party. Of these, 15 have pepperoni, and 10 have mushrooms. If 4 pizzas have no toppings at all, and no other toppings are ordered, then how many pizzas were ordered with both pepperoni and mushrooms?

Group 1 + Group 2 − Both + Neither = Total
Pepperoni + Mushrooms − Both + None = Total
15 + 10 − Both + 4 = 27
29 − Both = 27
Both = 2

Approach 2: A Venn diagram. This is more visual. This is often best if there is no one in the "neither" group or if you are visually oriented.

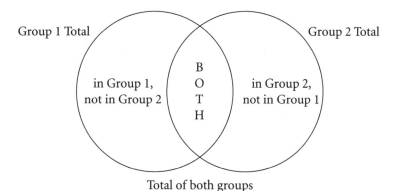

Total of both groups

Example: All the students in a class study either French or Spanish. There are 16 French students, 3 of whom also study Spanish. How many Spanish students are in the class if the class has 25 students altogether?

EXPERT EXCLUSIVE

Each approach has its plusses and minuses. Your own personal thinking style will respond best to one of these over the others. Practice all of them so you get a sense of which approach you like with different problems.

Because 3 of the French students also study Spanish, there must be 13 who study only French. If the "French only" and "Both" groups total 16 and there are 25 students in the class, then 9, or $25 - 16$, students study only Spanish. Thus, $9 + 3 = 12$, the total number of Spanish students. Putting all these numbers into the Venn diagram as we go helps us to see these relationships clearly:

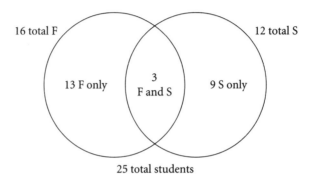

Approach 3: Draw a chart. This way works best with complicated overlapping set problems because it has a separate place for each of the nine data points we might be given:

	in Group 1	not in Group 1	Total
in Group 2			
not in Group 2			
Total			

Example: A company has 200 employees, 90 of whom belong to a union. If there are 95 part-time nonunion employees and 80 full-time union employees, then how many full-time employees are in the company?

Start by putting the data into the chart:

	in union	not in union	Total
full-time	80		
part-time		95	
Total	90		200

Now you can calculate the total number of nonunion employees ($200 - 90$) and the number of part-time union employees ($90 - 80$):

	in union	not in union	Total
full-time	80		
part-time	10	95	
Total	90	110	200

And now either calculate full-time nonunion employees (110 − 95) or the total number of part-time employees (10 + 95):

EXPERT EXCLUSIVE
Take your time organizing the chart, and the problem will almost solve itself!

	in union	not in union	Total
full-time	80	**15**	
part-time	10	95	**105**
Total	90	110	200

Either way, you can then calculate the total number of full-time employees (80 + 15 or 200 − 105):

	in union	not in union	Total
full-time	80	15	**95**
part-time	10	95	105
Total	90	110	200

There are 95 full-time employees.

Combinations and Permutations

Some GMAT questions ask you to count the number of possible ways to select a small subgroup from a larger group. If the selection is **unordered**, then it's a combinations problem. But if the selection is **ordered**, it is a permutations question. For example, if a question asks you to count the possible number of slates of officers to elect to class office, then order matters—President Bob and Vice President Thelma is a different slate than President Thelma and Vice President Bob. You use permutations. But if you had to count the number of pairs of flavors of jelly beans, you are solving a combinations question; cherry and lemon is the same pair as lemon and cherry, so order does not matter (i.e., you wouldn't count those as two different pairs).

EXPERT EXCLUSIVE
The very first thing you need to do is figure out whether you need an ordered or an unordered selection—otherwise, you won't know which formula to use.

Combinations: The combinations formula is used when solving for the number of *k* unordered selections one can make from a group of *n* items. This will often be referred to as *n*C*k*, which is often said as "*n* choose *k*." Not that the GMAT is an oral exam, of course, but it's helpful to say it that way to yourself because that's what making combinations is—an act of choosing. Here's the formula:

EXPERT EXCLUSIVE
n!, or *n*-factorial, is the product of *n* and every positive integer smaller than *n*. For example, $5! = 5 \times 4 \times 3 \times 2 \times 1$.

$$n\mathrm{C}k = \frac{n!}{k!(n-k)!}$$

Example: A company is selecting 4 members of its board of directors to sit on an ethics subcommittee. If the board has 9 members, any of whom may serve, how many different selections of members could be made?

Since the order in which we select the members doesn't change the committee in any way, this is a combinations question. The size of the group from which we choose is n, and the size of the selected group is k. So $n = 9$ and $k = 4$.

$$9C4 = \frac{9!}{4!(9-4)!}$$

EXPERT EXCLUSIVE

Save yourself some work. There's rarely a need to multiply out factorials, since many of the factors will quickly be canceled.

$$\frac{9!}{4!5!}$$

$$\frac{9 \times 8 \times 7 \times 6 \times 5 \times 4 \times 3 \times 2 \times 1}{4 \times 3 \times 2 \times 1 \times 5 \times 4 \times 3 \times 2 \times 1}$$

$$\frac{9 \times 8^2 \times 7 \times \cancel{6} \times \cancel{5 \times 4 \times 3 \times 2 \times 1}}{\cancel{4} \times \cancel{3 \times 2} \times 1 \times \cancel{5 \times 4 \times 3 \times 2 \times 1}}$$

$$9 \times 2 \times 7 = 126$$

Sometimes the problems will be more complicated and will require multiple iterations of the formula.

Example: County X holds an annual math competition, where each county high school sends a team of 4 students. If School A has 6 boys and 7 girls whose math grades qualify them to be on their school's team, and competition rules stipulate that the team must consist of 2 boys and 2 girls, how many different teams might school A send to the competition?

EXPERT EXCLUSIVE

In combinations, permutations, and probability, *and* translates to *multiply*; *or* translates to *add*.

The order of selection doesn't matter here, so we'll use the combinations formula. But hang on a sec . . . if we lump all the students together in a group of 13 and calculate 13C4, we'd wind up including some all-boy teams and all-girl teams. The question explicitly says we can only select 2 boys and 2 girls. So we aren't really choosing 4 students from 13 but rather choosing 2 boys from 6 and 2 girls from 7.

6C2 and 7C2

$$\frac{6!}{2!4!} \times \frac{7!}{2!5!}$$

$$\frac{6 \times 5 \times 4 \times 3 \times 2 \times 1}{2 \times 1 \times 4 \times 3 \times 2 \times 1} \times \frac{7 \times 6 \times 5 \times 4 \times 3 \times 2 \times 1}{2 \times 1 \times 5 \times 4 \times 3 \times 2 \times 1}$$

$$\frac{6^3 \times 5 \times \cancel{4 \times 3 \times 2 \times 1}}{\cancel{2} \times 1 \times \cancel{4 \times 3 \times 2 \times 1}} \times \frac{7 \times 6^3 \times \cancel{5 \times 4 \times 3 \times 2 \times 1}}{\cancel{2} \times 1 \times \cancel{5 \times 4 \times 3 \times 2 \times 1}}$$

$$3 \times 5 \times 7 \times 3 = 315$$

Permutations: If the order of selection matters, you can use the permutation formulas:

number of permutations of n items	number of permutations of k items selected from n
$n!$	$\dfrac{n!}{(n-k)!}$

Example: How many ways are there to rearrange the letters in the word ASCENT?

Clearly order matters here, since ASCENT is different from TNECSA. There are 6 letters in the word, so we must calculate the permutations of 6 items: $6! = 6 \times 5 \times 4 \times 3 \times 2 \times 1 = 720$.

Another way to solve is to draw a quick sketch of the problem, with blanks for the arranged items. Then write in the number of possibilities for each blank in order. Finally, multiply the numbers together. Here's how the ASCENT problem would solve with this technique:

Okay, ASCENT has 6 letters, so we need 6 blanks:

$$\underline{\quad} \times \underline{\quad} \times \underline{\quad} \times \underline{\quad} \times \underline{\quad} \times \underline{\quad}$$

> **EXPERT EXCLUSIVE**
>
> Most upper-level GMAT permutation questions resist formulaic treatment but are easier to complete with the "draw blanks" approach.

There are 6 letters we might place in the first blank (A, S, C, E, N, or T):

$$\underline{\ 6\ } \times \underline{\quad} \times \underline{\quad} \times \underline{\quad} \times \underline{\quad} \times \underline{\quad}$$

No matter which letter we placed there, th re will be 5 possibilities for the next blank:

$$\underline{\ 6\ } \times \underline{\ 5\ } \times \underline{\quad} \times \underline{\quad} \times \underline{\quad} \times \underline{\quad}$$

There will be 4 for the next, 3 thereafter, 2 after that, and just 1 left for the last:

$$\underline{\ 6\ } \times \underline{\ 5\ } \times \underline{\ 4\ } \times \underline{\ 3\ } \times \underline{\ 2\ } \times \underline{\ 1\ } = 720$$

Notice that we wind up reproducing the appropriate formula? It's quite possible to solve most permutation problems without figuring out the right formula ahead of time!

Example: There are 6 children at a family reunion, 3 boys and 3 girls. They will be lined up single-file for a photo, alternating genders. How many arrangements of the children are possible for this photo?

Hmm . . . not sure how to approach this with a formula. So let's draw a picture. We know we'll have 6 "blanks," but we don't know whether to begin with a boy or with a girl. It could be either one. So we'll do both:

bgbgbg OR gbgbgb

Any of the three boys could go in the first spot, and any of the three girls in the second:

__3__×__3__×____×____×____×____+____×____×____×____×____×____

The next spot can be filled with any of the remaining two boys; the one after by any of the two remaining girls. Then the last boy and the last girl take their places:

__3__×__3__×__2__×__2__×__1__×__1__+____×____×____×____×____

That's the boy-first possibility. The same numbers of boys and girls apply to the girl-first possibility, and so we get:

__3__×__3__×__2__×__2__×__1__×__1__+__3__×__3__×__2__×__2__×__1__×__1__

$$9 \times 4 \times 1 + 9 \times 4 \times 1$$
$$36 + 36$$
$$72$$

Hybrids of Combinations and Permutations: Some questions involve elements of both ordered and unordered selection.

Example: How many ways are there to rearrange the letters in the word ASSETS?

Earlier we saw that the rearrangement of ASCENT was a permutation. But what about ASSETS? The order of the E, the A, the T, and the S's matter . . . but the order of the S's themselves does not.

Think about it this way: Put a "tag" on the S's . . . $AS_1S_2ETS_3$. If we just calculated 6! again, we'd be counting $AS_1S_2ETS_3$ and $AS_3S_1ETS_2$ as different words, even though with the tags gone, we can clearly see that they aren't (ASSETS is the same as ASSETS and shouldn't be counted as different). We'll need to eliminate all the redundant arrangements from the 6! total.

So how many ways are there to rearrange those 3 S's within one arrangement of ASSETS? Wait a minute . . . "rearrange"? You guessed it; it's another permutation. Since there are 3 S's in ASSETS, there are 3! ways to rearrange those S's without changing the word. We need to count every group of 3! within the 6! total as only 1.

So instead of 6! arrangements, as there were for ASCENT, the word ASSETS has $\frac{6!}{3!}$.

$$\frac{6!}{3!} = \frac{6 \times 5 \times 4 \times 3 \times 2 \times 1}{3 \times 2 \times 1} = 6 \times 5 \times 4 = 120$$

The same logic would apply to the arrangements of ASSESS . . . $\frac{6!}{4!}$.

And if two letters repeat, you need two corrections: the arrangements of REASSESS is $\frac{8!}{4!2!}$.

Some tricky GMAT problems boil down to this "rearranging letters" problem.

Example: A restaurant is hanging 7 large tiles on its wall in single file. How many arrangements of tiles are possible if there are 3 white tiles and 4 blue tiles?

This problem essentially asks for the arrangements of WWWBBBB. That's $\frac{7!}{3!4!}$.

$$\frac{7\times6\times5\times4\times3\times2\times1}{3\times2\times1\times4\times3\times2\times1} = 7 \times 5 = 35$$

Probability

Probability is the likelihood of a desired outcome to occur.

$$\text{Probability} = \frac{\text{Number of desired outcomes}}{\text{Number of total possible outcomes}}$$

Example: If you have 12 shirts in a drawer and 9 of them are white, the probability of picking a white shirt at random is $\frac{9}{12} = \frac{3}{4}$. The probability can also be expressed as 0.75 or 75%.

Many hard probability questions involve finding the probability of a certain outcome after multiple repetitions of the same experiment or different experiments (a coin being tossed several times, etc.).

Broadly speaking, there are five approaches you can take to probability questions.

Approach 1: Multiply the probabilities of individual events.

This works best when you know the probability for each event and you need to find the probability of all the events occurring (e.g., the probability that on the first flip of a coin a head lands up and on the second flip a tail lands up). Make sure to pay attention to what effect the outcome of the first event has on the second, the second on the third, and so on.

Example: If 2 students are chosen at random from a class with 5 girls and 5 boys, what is the probability that both students chosen will be girls?

The probability that the first student chosen will be a girl is $\frac{5}{10}$, or $\frac{1}{2}$.

> **EXPERT EXCLUSIVE**
>
> Did you notice that $\frac{7!}{3!4!}$ is the same as 7C3? Which is also the same as 7C4, $\frac{7!}{4!3!}$? Well, you're right. They are exactly the same. Whether you think "rearrange WWWBBBB," "choose 4 of the 7 tiles to be blue (the rest will be white)," or "choose 3 of the 7 tiles to be white (the rest will be blue)," the result is the same.
>
> As we'll soon see, many probability questions involve just this kind of calculation.

> **EXPERT EXCLUSIVE**
>
> Take your time thinking probability questions through—often the hardest part is figuring out which approach you want to take.

After that girl is chosen, there are 9 students remaining, 4 of whom are girls. So the probability of choosing a girl for the second student is $\frac{4}{9}$.

The probability that both students chosen will be girls is $\frac{1}{2} \times \frac{4}{9} = \frac{4}{18} = \frac{2}{9}$.

Approach 2: Subtract the probability of the *undesired* outcomes from the total.

This works best when you cannot readily calculate the probability of the desired outcomes but you can readily do so for the undesired ones. In probability, the total is always 1.

Example: If a fair coin is flipped three times, what is the probability of getting at least one tail?

What's desired is one tail, two tails, or three tails in three flips. That's a lot to keep track of. But what's undesired is very clear—three heads in a row.

Total − Undesired

$1 - HHH$

$1 - \frac{1}{2} \times \frac{1}{2} \times \frac{1}{2}$

$1 - \frac{1}{8}$

$\frac{7}{8}$

EXPERT EXCLUSIVE

The "Total − Undesired" approach works well for many kinds of GMAT questions, not just for probability. For example, it's how you'd calculate the shaded area of ▢.

Approach 3: Solve for the probability of one possible desired outcome, then multiply by all the permutations of that outcome.

This works best when what you want is very specific but the order in which it happens is not.

Example: If a fair coin is flipped 5 times, what is the probability of getting exactly 3 heads?

EXPERT EXCLUSIVE

"Fair" just means that every outcome is equally possible. A fair coin will land heads-up 50 percent of the time.

It's clear what we desire—3 heads and 2 tails—but we don't have to get it in any particular order. HTHTH would be fine, as would HHHTT, TTHHH, and so forth. So Approach #1 wouldn't work well for this problem. But we can use Approach #1 to figure out the probability of *one* of these outcomes:

$HHHTT = \frac{1}{2} \times \frac{1}{2} \times \frac{1}{2} \times \frac{1}{2} \times \frac{1}{2} = \frac{1}{32}$.

Now we can multiply this by the number of ways we could get this outcome—in other words, by the number of ways we could rearrange the letters in HHHTT. We saw how to do this earlier, in our discussion of "hybrid" problems a few pages ago.

# of arrangements of $\text{HHHTT} = \dfrac{5!}{3!2!} = \dfrac{5\times4\times3\times2\times1}{3\times2\times1\times2\times1} = 5\times2 = 10$

There are 10 different ways to get 3 heads and 2 tails.

Each one has a probability of $\dfrac{1}{32}$.

The chances of getting exactly 3 heads in 5 coin flips is $\dfrac{1}{32}\times 10 = \dfrac{5}{16}$.

EXPERT EXCLUSIVE

Approaches #3 and #4 are more or less the same, just set up in a different order. Different people prefer different approaches. Practice both and discover which you like best.

Approach 4: We could work with the numerator and denominator of the probability formula separately, then lump the results together in one calculation. We calculate the total number of possible outcomes and the total number of desired outcomes, then put them together in one big fraction (instead of multiplying lots of little fractions together).

Like Approach 3, this one also works best when what you want is very specific but the order in which it happens is not.

Example: A bag holds 4 red marbles, 5 blue marbles, and 2 green marbles. If 5 marbles are selected one after another without replacement, what is the probability of drawing 2 red marbles, 2 blue marbles, and 1 green marble?

$$\text{Probability} = \dfrac{\text{Number of desired outcomes}}{\text{Number of total possible outcomes}}$$

Let's start by thinking about the possible outcomes. We are reaching into a bag of 11 marbles and pulling out 5. (The fact that they are pulled out one by one doesn't change anything; in the end, we still have 5 marbles.) Quite literally, this is "11 choose 5," 11C5.

$$\#\text{possible} = 11\text{C}5 = \dfrac{11!}{5!6!} = \dfrac{11\times10\times9\times8\times7\times6\times5\times4\times3\times2\times1}{5\times4\times3\times2\times1\times6\times5\times4\times3\times2\times1} = 11\times3\times2\times7$$

Now, what is desired? We want 2 of the 4 red marbles, literally "4 choose 2," or 4C2. We also want 2 of the 5 blue marbles (5C2) and 1 of the 2 green marbles (2C1).

EXPERT EXCLUSIVE

Save yourself some work: don't multiply out factors that may later cancel. 11×7 is a much easier calculation than $11\times3\times2\times7$.

#desired = 4C2 and 5C2 and 2C1

$$\dfrac{4!}{2!2!}\times\dfrac{5!}{2!3!}\times\dfrac{2!}{1!1!}$$

$$\dfrac{4\times3\times2\times1}{2\times1\times2\times1}\times\dfrac{5\times4\times3\times2\times1}{2\times1\times3\times2\times1}\times\dfrac{2\times1}{1\times1}$$

$$6\times10\times2$$

Now we'll put the fraction together:

$$\dfrac{\text{Number of desired outcomes}}{\text{Number of total possible outcomes}} = \dfrac{6\times10\times2}{11\times3\times2\times7} = \dfrac{10\times2}{11\times7} = \dfrac{20}{77}$$

Approach 5: Don't do any math at all! Just count the various outcomes.

This works best when the numbers involved are small. In this circumstance, there's really no need to waste time thinking of the right arithmetic calculation.

Example: If a fair coin is flipped two times, what is the probability of getting exactly one head?

> Two coin flips isn't very much. List out the possible results:
> HH, HT, TH, or TT.
> Of these 4 possibilities, 2 have exactly one head—HT and TH.
> So the probability of getting exactly 1 head in 2 flips is $\frac{2}{4}$, or $\frac{1}{2}$.

That's it for the classic formulas. Practice them enough so that you can solve intermediate-level questions quickly and correctly. That way you can reach the high-value, high-difficulty questions with enough time and confidence to think them through.

CLASSIC FORMULAS PRACTICE SET

Answers are on page 632.

1. If the average (arithmetic mean) of b and 2 is equal to the average of b, 3, and 4, what is the value of b?

  ○ 2

  ○ 4

  ○ 8

  ○ 10

  ○ 16

2. A violinist practices 1 hour a day from Monday through Friday. How many hours must she practice on Saturday in order to average 2 hours a day for the 6-day period?

3. If a rocket travels at 1,800 miles per hour, how many miles would it travel in 24 seconds?

  ○ 12

  ○ 35

  ○ 75

  ○ 208

  ○ 720

4. If Ron's closet has 4 pairs of pants, 6 shirts, and 3 jackets, how many outfits of 1 pair of pants, 1 shirt, and 1 jacket could he assemble?

   ○ 6

   ○ 13

   ○ 24

   ○ 72

   ○ 103,680

5. The average (arithmetic mean) of six numbers is 6. If 3 is subtracted from each of four of the numbers, what is the new average?

   ○ $1\frac{1}{2}$

   ○ 2

   ○ 3

   ○ 4

   ○ $4\frac{1}{2}$

6. The average (arithmetic mean) of a set of four numbers is 8.75. When a fifth number is introduced to the set, the average of the set becomes 8. What is the fifth number?

   ○ −3

   ○ 5

   ○ 8.375

   ○ 8.6

   ○ 10.3

7. Jerry's average (arithmetic mean) score on the first three of four tests is 85. If Jerry wants to raise his average by 2 points, what score must he earn on the fourth test?

8. Lucy and Eli take 4 hours working together to stuff envelopes for a fundraiser. If Eli would have taken 12 hours to stuff all the envelopes by himself, how many hours would it have taken Lucy to stuff half the envelopes by herself?

   ○ 2

   ○ 3

   ○ 4

   ○ 5

   ○ 6

9. A work crew orders 50 sandwiches for lunch. Of these, 30 have lettuce, 35 have tomatoes, and 5 have neither lettuce nor tomatoes. How many of the sandwiches have both lettuce and tomatoes?

   ○ 5

   ○ 10

   ○ 15

   ○ 20

   ○ 65

Advanced

10. If the average of $27 - x$, $x - 8$, and $3x + 11$ is y, what is the average of $2y$ and $\frac{2y}{3}$?

    ○ $4x + 40$
    ○ $x + 10$
    ○ $\dfrac{8x + 80}{3}$
    ○ $\dfrac{4x + 40}{3}$
    ○ $\dfrac{2x + 20}{3}$

11. George drives the first 30 miles of a trip at a constant rate of 40 miles per hour. If he drives the remaining 75 miles of the trip at a constant rate of 50 miles per hour, what is his average speed for the entire trip?

12. A company has 13 employees, 8 of whom belong to the union. If 5 people work any one shift, and the union contract specifies that at least 4 union members work each shift, then how many different combinations of employees might work any given shift?

   ○ 10

   ○ 231

   ○ 336

   ○ 350

   ○ 406

13. At Valley High School, 115 graduating seniors failed to make the honor roll. In all, 150 seniors graduated. Ten more seniors made the honor roll than the number who played varsity sports. If 10 graduating seniors both made the honor roll and played varsity sports, what is the probability that any given graduating senior neither made the honor roll nor played varsity sports?

   ○ $\dfrac{1}{15}$

   ○ $\dfrac{1}{3}$

   ○ $\dfrac{2}{5}$

   ○ $\dfrac{2}{3}$

   ○ $\dfrac{27}{30}$

RATIOS

A ratio is a comparison of two quantities by division. Ratios may be written either with a fraction bar $\left(\dfrac{x}{y}\right)$ with a colon (x:y) or in English (ratio of x to y). Ratios can (and in most cases, should) be reduced to lowest terms, just as fractions are reduced.

Example: Joe is 16 years old and Mary is 12. The ratio of Joe's age to Mary's age is 16 to 12.

$$\frac{16}{12} = \frac{4}{3} \text{ or } 4{:}3$$

> **EXPERT EXCLUSIVE**
>
> Some GMAT questions deal with three-part ratios. Always represent them with colons (x:y:z).

In a ratio of two numbers, the numerator is often associated with the word *of* and the denominator with the word *to*.

$$\text{Ratio} = \frac{\text{of...}}{\text{to...}}$$

Example: In a box of doughnuts, 12 are sugar and 18 are chocolate. What is the ratio of sugar doughnuts to chocolate doughnuts?

$$\text{Ratio} = \frac{\text{of sugar}}{\text{to chocolate}} = \frac{12}{18} = \frac{2}{3}$$

Proportions

We frequently deal with ratios by working with a proportion. A proportion is simply a comparison of two ratios. Usually, it's an equation in which two ratios are set equal to one another.

EXPERT EXCLUSIVE

When dealing with proportions, pay close attention to what something is a proportion *of*. A common "twist" is to use different denominators in the same problem.

In the proportion $\frac{a}{b} = \frac{c}{d}$, *a* and *d* are identified as the **extremes**, and *c* and *b* are identified as the **means**. These terms stem from the alternate notation for these ratios, *a* : *b* = *c* : *d*, in which the extremes occupy the end position of the equation. But despite that terminology, it's usually easier to express proportions as fractions when solving GMAT problems.

To solve a proportion, multiply the numerator from the first ratio by the denominator from the second ratio, then the denominator from the first ratio by the numerator of the second ratio, and set the values equal to each other. In other words, multiply the means and set the product equal to the product of the extremes. After this step, divide each side of this new equation by the number with the variable to get your solution.

Example: Solve for *x*: $\frac{6}{11} = \frac{x}{33}$.

Using cross multiplication, the equation becomes $6 \times 33 = x \times 11$. This simplifies to $198 = 11x$. Then divide each side of this new equation by 11. Thus, $x = 18$.

In word problems, proportions are set up so that corresponding units are either one above the other or directly across from one another.

Example: The ratio of T-shirts to sweaters in a closet is 4:5. If there are 12 T-shirts in the closet, how many sweaters are there?

Set up a proportion to solve this question, being careful to line up the units. There are different ways you can approach this problem to get the correct answer. One possible proportion would be $\frac{4 \text{ T-shirts}}{5 \text{ sweaters}} = \frac{12 \text{ T-shirts}}{x \text{ sweaters}}$.

Note that the label of T-shirts appears in both numerators and the label of sweaters appears in both denominators. Another possible proportion would be $\dfrac{4 \text{ T-shirts}}{12 \text{ T-shirts}} = \dfrac{5 \text{ sweaters}}{x \text{ sweaters}}$, where the numbers corresponding with T-shirts appear on the left side and the values corresponding with sweaters appear on the right side. Either way, cross multiplying the means and the extremes results in the equation $4x = 60$. Therefore, $x = 15$. There are 15 sweaters in the closet.

Part:Part Ratios and Part:Whole Ratios

A ratio can compare either a part to another part or a part to a whole. One type of ratio can readily be converted to the other *if* all the parts together equal the whole and there is no overlap among the parts (that is, if the whole is equal to the sum of its parts).

Example: The ratio of domestic sales to foreign sales of a certain product is 3:5. What fraction of the total sales is domestic sales? (Note: This is the same as asking for the ratio of the amount of domestic sales to the amount of total sales.)

In this case, the whole (total sales) is equal to the sum of the parts (domestic and foreign sales). We can convert from a part:part ratio to a part:whole ratio. Of every 8 sales of the product, 3 are domestic and 5 are foreign. The ratio of domestic sales to total sales is $\dfrac{3}{8}$ or 3:8.

Example: The ratio of domestic to European sales of a certain product is 3:5. What is the ratio of domestic sales to total sales?

Here we cannot convert from a part:part ratio (domestic sales:European sales) to a part:whole ratio (domestic sales:total sales) because we don't know if there are any other sales besides domestic and European sales. The question doesn't say that the product is sold only domestically and in Europe, so we cannot assume there are no other sales. The ratio asked for here cannot be determined.

Ratios with More Than Two Terms

Ratios involving more than two terms are governed by the same principles. These ratios contain more relationships, so they convey more information than two-term ratios. Ratios involving more than two terms are usually ratios of various parts, and it is usually the case that the sum of these parts does equal the whole, which makes it possible to find part:whole ratios as well.

Example: Given that the ratio of men to women to children in a room is 4:3:2, what other ratios can be determined?

The whole here is the number of people in the room, and since every person is either a man, a woman, or a child, we can determine part:whole ratios for each of these parts. Of every nine (4 + 3 + 2) people in the room, 4 are men, 3 are women, and 2 are children. This gives us three part:whole ratios:

Ratio of men:total people = 4:9 or $\dfrac{4}{9}$.

Ratio of women:total people = 3:9 = 1:3 or $\dfrac{1}{3}$.

Ratio of children:total people = 2:9 or $\dfrac{2}{9}$.

In addition, from any ratio of more than two terms, we can determine various two-term ratios among the parts.

Ratio of women:men = 3:4 or $\dfrac{3}{4}$.

Ratio of men:children = 4:2 = 2:1 or $\dfrac{2}{1}$.

Ratio of children:women = 2:3 or $\dfrac{2}{3}$.

And finally, if we were asked to establish a relationship between the number of adults and the number of children in the room, we would find that this would be possible as well. For every 2 children, there are 4 men and 3 women, which is 4 + 3 or 7 adults. Thus,

Ratio of children:adults = 2:7 or $\dfrac{2}{7}$.

Ratio of adults:children = 7:2 or $\dfrac{7}{2}$.

> **EXPERT EXCLUSIVE**
> Read carefully! Some questions will give you *A:B:C* and ask you for *A:B+C* rather than *A*:Whole. In those cases, solving for the whole is unnecessary work.

Naturally, a test question will require you to determine only one or at most two of these ratios, but knowing how much information is contained in a given ratio will help you to quickly determine which questions are solvable and which, if any, are not.

Ratios versus Actual Numbers

Ratios are always reduced to simplest form. If a team's ratio of wins to losses is 5:3, this does not necessarily mean that the team has won 5 games and lost 3. For instance, if a team has won 30 games and lost 18, the ratio is still 5:3. Unless we know the actual number of games played (or the actual number won or lost), we don't know the actual values of the parts in the ratio.

Example: In a classroom of 30 students, the ratio of the boys in the class to students in the class is 2:5. How many students are boys?

We are given a part-to-whole ratio (boys:students). This ratio is a fraction. Multiplying this fraction by the whole gives the value of the corresponding part. There are 30 students; $\frac{2}{5}$ of them are boys, so the number of boys must be $\frac{2}{5} \times 30$.

EXPERT EXCLUSIVE

It's usually most helpful to set up ratio scratchwork in columns so you see the relationships clearly.

$$\frac{2 \text{ boys}}{{}_1\cancel{5} \text{ students}} \times \cancel{30}^{6} \text{ students} = 2 \times 6 \text{ boys} = 12 \text{ boys}$$

You can make some deductions about the actual values, though, even when you aren't given a total directly. Often, this is the key to solving a very puzzling proportions question.

Let's say that a car dealership has used and new cars in stock in a ratio of 2:5. We don't know the actual number. We know that if there are 2 used cars, there will be 5 new cars. And if there are 4 (or 2 × 2) used cars, there will be 10 (5 × 2) new cars. If there are 6 used cars (2 × 3), then there are 15 new cars (5 × 3). In other words, the actual numbers will always equal the figures in the ratio multiplied by the same (unknown) factor.

We can translate from ratios into algebra:

used:new = 2:5
used = $2x$; new = $5x$

Example: A homecoming party at College Y is initially attended by students and alumni in a ratio of 1 to 5. But after two hours, 36 more students arrive, changing the ratio of students to alumni to 1 to 2. If the number of alumni did not change over those two hours, how many people were at the party when it began?

Besides the 36 additional students who arrive, nowhere are actual numbers referred to directly. But we can jot down the two ratios we're given in a slightly more useable form:

$S{:}A$	$S{+}36{:}A$
1:5	1:2

We can translate into algebra. Let x be the number of students initially at the party.

$S{:}A$	$S{+}36{:}A$
1:5	1:2
$x{:}5x$	$x + 36 : 2(x + 36)$

Now we've got some equations to work with:

$A = 5x$
$A = 2x + 72$

Aha! We've got two different expressions for *A* that are equal. Thus,

$$5x = 2x + 72$$
$$3x = 72$$
$$x = 24$$

Now we know that there were 24 students initially.

Substitute 24 for *x* to solve for alumni:

$$A = 5 \times 24$$
$$A = 120$$

The party started with 24 students and 120 alumni, for a total of 144 people.

Guessing with Ratios

You may have noticed that many GMAT ratio problems involve things like students, women, children, cars, and so forth—things that cannot really exist as a fraction. (You can't have $43\frac{1}{5}$ people at a party!)

There's a valuable deduction to be made here—if the entities in a problem cannot logically be fractions, then the factor by which the ratio is multiplied must be an integer. Therefore, *the actual number of something must be a multiple of its value in the ratio.*

Example: A movie buff owns movies on DVD and on Blu-ray in a ratio of 7:2. If she buys 6 more Blu-ray movies, that ratio would change to 11:4. If she owns movies on no other medium, what was the original number of movies in her library before the extra purchase?

- ○ 22
- ○ 28
- ○ 77
- ○ 99
- ○ 105

The question asks for the whole of the ratio for which we are initially given only two parts. The question specifies that there are no other parts to the whole, so we can add the two parts together:

DVD:Blu-ray:Total
7:2:9

There's no such thing as "a fraction of a disc" (okay, there is, but half a DVD isn't part of a library—it's in the trash can). Therefore, the common factor by which you'd multiply 7, 2, and 9 to find the actual numbers must be an integer. That means the number of DVDs is a multiple of 7, the number of Blu-rays is a multiple of 2, and the total—what we're looking for—must be a multiple of 9.

Take a look at the answers—only (D) is a multiple of 9, so there's no need to do any more math; (D) must be the answer!

RATIOS PRACTICE SET

Answers are on page 638.

1. A subway car passes 3 stations every 10 minutes. At this rate, how many stations will it pass in 1 hour?

   ○ 2

   ○ 12

   ○ 15

   ○ 18

   ○ 30

2. The ratio of $3\frac{1}{2}$ to $5\frac{1}{4}$ is equivalent to the ratio of

   ○ 3 to 5

   ○ 2 to 3

   ○ 5 to 7

   ○ 7 to 5

   ○ 5 to 3

3. If the ratio of boys to girls in a class is 5 to 3, which of the following could not be the number of students in the class?

   ○ 32

   ○ 36

   ○ 40

   ○ 48

   ○ 56

4. In a certain class, 3 out of 24 students are in student organizations. What is the ratio of students in student organizations to students not in student organizations?

- ○ $\dfrac{1}{8}$

- ○ $\dfrac{1}{7}$

- ○ $\dfrac{1}{6}$

- ○ $\dfrac{1}{5}$

- ○ $\dfrac{1}{4}$

5. In a local election, votes were cast for Mr. Dyer, Ms. Frau, and Mr. Borak in the ratio of 4:3:2. If there were no other candidates and none of the 1,800 voters cast more than one vote, how many votes did Ms. Frau receive?

Advanced

6. If $\dfrac{1}{2}$ of the number of white mice in a certain laboratory is $\dfrac{1}{8}$ of the total number of mice, and $\dfrac{1}{3}$ of the number of gray mice is $\dfrac{1}{9}$ of the total number of mice, then what is the ratio of the number of white mice to the number of gray mice?

- ○ 2:3

- ○ 3:4

- ○ 4:5

- ○ 8:9

- ○ 16:27

PERCENTS

Percent is just another word for "per one hundred."

Therefore, 19% (19 percent) means 19 hundredths

or $\dfrac{19}{100}$

or 0.19

or 19 out of every 100 things

or 19 parts out of a whole of 100 parts

Making and Dropping Percents

To make a percent from decimals or fractions, multiply by 100%. Since 100% means 100 hundredths or 1, multiplying by 100% will not change the number.

Example: $0.17 = 0.17 \times 100\% = 17\%$

Example: $\dfrac{1}{4} = \dfrac{1}{4} \times 100\% = 25\%$

To drop a percent, divide by 100%. Once again, dividing by 100% will not change the number.

Example: $32\% = \dfrac{32\%}{100\%} = \dfrac{32}{100} = \dfrac{8}{25}$

Example: $\dfrac{1}{2}\% = \dfrac{\frac{1}{2}\%}{100\%} = \dfrac{1}{200}$

To change a percent to a decimal, just drop the percent and move the decimal point two places to the left. (This is the same as dividing by 100%.)

Example: $0.8\% = 0.008$

> **EXPERT EXCLUSIVE**
>
> The ability to change a percent into a fraction or a decimal means that you have some choices when you have to do arithmetic with percents. "60% of 30" could be 30×0.6 or $30 \times \dfrac{60}{100}$, whichever you find easier.

Common Percent and Fraction Equivalents

$\dfrac{1}{20} = 5\%$	$\dfrac{1}{11} = 9\dfrac{1}{11}\%$	$\dfrac{1}{10} = 10\%$	$\dfrac{1}{9} = 11\dfrac{1}{9}\%$	$\dfrac{1}{8} = 12\dfrac{1}{2}\%$
$\dfrac{1}{6} = 16\dfrac{2}{3}\%$	$\dfrac{1}{5} = 20\%$	$\dfrac{1}{4} = 25\%$	$\dfrac{1}{3} = 33\dfrac{1}{3}\%$	$\dfrac{1}{2} = 50\%$

$$10\% = \frac{1}{10}$$

$$12\frac{1}{2}\% = \frac{1}{8}$$

$$20\% = \frac{2}{10} = \frac{1}{5}$$

$$25\% = \frac{2}{8} = \frac{1}{4}$$

$$16\frac{2}{3}\% = \frac{1}{6}$$

$$30\% = \frac{3}{10}$$

$$40\% = \frac{4}{10} = \frac{2}{5}$$

$$37\frac{1}{2}\% = \frac{3}{8}$$

$$33\frac{1}{3}\% = \frac{2}{6} = \frac{1}{3}$$

$$50\% = \frac{5}{10} = \frac{1}{2}$$

$$50\% = \frac{4}{8} = \frac{2}{4} = \frac{1}{2}$$

$$50\% = \frac{3}{6} = \frac{1}{2}$$

$$60\% = \frac{6}{10} = \frac{3}{5}$$

$$62\frac{1}{2}\% = \frac{5}{8}$$

$$66\frac{2}{3}\% = \frac{4}{6} = \frac{2}{3}$$

$$70\% = \frac{7}{10}$$

$$80\% = \frac{8}{10} = \frac{4}{5}$$

$$75\% = \frac{6}{8} = \frac{3}{4}$$

$$83\frac{1}{3}\% = \frac{5}{6}$$

$$90\% = \frac{9}{10}$$

$$87\frac{1}{2}\% = \frac{7}{8}$$

$$100\% = \frac{10}{10} = 1$$

Being familiar with these equivalents can save you a lot of time!

Percent Problems

Percent problems will usually give you two of the variables from the formula below and ask for the third. It is usually easiest to change the percent to a common fraction and do the calculation. Most percent problems can be solved by plugging into one formula:

$$\boxed{\text{Percent} \times \text{Whole} = \text{Part}}$$

In percent problems, generally, the whole will be associated with the word *of*; the part will be associated with the word *is*. The percent can be represented as the ratio of the part to the whole, or the *is* to the *of*.

Example: What is 25% of 36?

Here we are given the percent and the whole. To find the part, change the percent to a fraction, then multiply. Use the formula above.

Since $25\% = \dfrac{1}{4}$, we are really being asked what one-fourth of 36 is.

$$\frac{1}{4} \times 36 = 9$$

Example: 13 is $33\dfrac{1}{3}\%$ of what number?

Recall that $33\dfrac{1}{3}\% = \dfrac{1}{3}$.

$$13 = \frac{1}{3}n$$

$$39 = n$$

Example: 18 is what percent of 3?

$$m \times 3 = 18$$

$$m = 6$$

$$6 \times 100\% = 600\%$$

Other problems will ask you to calculate "percent greater than" or "percent less than." In these cases, it is the number that follows the word *than* to which the percentage is applied.

> **EXPERT EXCLUSIVE**
> You may find it faster to convert *percent greater/less than* to *percent of.* "*x*% greater than" becomes "$(100 + x)\%$ of." "*x*% less than" becomes "$(100 - x)\%$ of."

Example: What number is 15% less than 60?

$$n = 60 - 15\% \times 60$$
$$n = 60 - \frac{15}{100} \times 60$$
$$n = 60 - 9$$
$$n = 51$$

Example: What is the price of a television that costs 28% more than a $50 radio?

$$t = r + (28\% \times r)$$
$$t = 50 + \left(\frac{28}{100} \times 50 \right)$$
$$t = 50 + \frac{28}{2}$$
$$t = 50 + 14$$
$$t = \$64$$

Percent Increase and Decrease

$$\text{Percent increase} = \frac{\text{Amount of increase}}{\text{Original whole}}(100\%)$$

$$\text{Percent decrease} = \frac{\text{Amount of decrease}}{\text{Original whole}}(100\%)$$

$$\text{New whole} = \text{Original whole} \pm \text{Amount of change}$$

When dealing with percent increase and percent decrease, always be careful to put the amount of increase or decrease over the *original* whole, not the new whole.

Example: If a dress is offered for a discounted price of $120, what is the percent discount if the regular price is $150?

$$\text{Percent decrease} = \frac{\text{Amount of decrease}}{\text{Original whole}} \times 100\%$$

Since we're asked to calculate the discount, the original price is the regular selling price of $150. The difference in prices is $150 − $120, or $30.

$$\text{Percent discount} = \frac{\$30}{\$150} \times 100\%$$

$$\text{Percent discount} = \frac{1}{5} \times 100\% = 20\%$$

> **EXPERT EXCLUSIVE**
>
> On the GMAT, you'll almost never be asked to simply add percentages.

> **EXPERT EXCLUSIVE**
>
> In this example, a 20% reduction followed by a 10% reduction totals not to a 30% reduction but to one of 28%. This will always happen—two decreases cause a total percent decrease of *less* than the sum of the two individual percents. Likewise, two increases cause a total increase of *more* than the sum of the two individually. You can use this fact to estimate an answer quickly.

Combining Percents: On some problems, you'll need to find more than one percent, or a percent of a percent. Be careful. You can't just add percents, unless you're taking the percents of the same whole. Let's look at an example.

Example: The price of an antique is reduced by 20 percent, and then this discount price is further reduced by 10 percent. If the antique originally cost $200, what is its final price?

First, we know that the price is reduced by 20%. That's the same thing as saying that the price becomes (100% − 20%), or 80% of what it originally was. Eighty percent of $200 is equal to $\frac{8}{10} \times \$200$, or $160. Then, *this price* is reduced by 10%. So 10% × $160 = $16, and the final price of the antique is $160 − $16 = $144.

A common error in this kind of problem is to assume that the final price is simply a 30 percent reduction of the original price. That would mean that the final price is 70 percent of the original, or 70% × $200 = $140. But, as we've just seen, this is *not* correct. Adding or subtracting percents directly only works if those percents are being taken of the same whole. In this example, since we took 20% of the original price, and then 10% of that reduced price, we can't just add the percents together.

PERCENT PRACTICE SET

Answers are on page 640.

1. In a certain class, if Edie's average rose from 72 to 84, by what percent did her average increase?

   ○ 12%

   ○ $14\frac{2}{7}$%

   ○ $16\frac{2}{3}$%

   ○ $66\frac{2}{3}$%

   ○ $85\frac{5}{7}$%

2. A closet contains 24 pairs of shoes. If 25 percent of those pairs of shoes are black, how many pairs are not black?

   ○ 4

   ○ 6

   ○ 12

   ○ 18

   ○ 20

3. If 65 percent of x is 195, what is 75 percent of x?

   ○ 215

   ○ 225

   ○ 250

   ○ 260

   ○ 300

4. A store sells a watch for a profit of 25 percent of the wholesale cost. What percent of the selling price of the watch is the store's profit?

    ○ 12.5%

    ○ 20%

    ○ 25%

    ○ 50%

    ○ 75%

5. In 2002, 30 percent of the 200 apartment units on a certain street were condominiums. By 2003, the total number of units on the street had increased by 25 percent, and 40 percent of the units were condominiums. What was the percent increase of condominiums during this period?

    ○ $10\frac{1}{5}\%$

    ○ 30%

    ○ $33\frac{1}{3}\%$

    ○ 40%

    ○ $66\frac{2}{3}\%$

Advanced

6. In a certain school, 50 percent of all male students and 60 percent of all female students play a varsity sport. If 40 percent of the students at the school are male, what percent of the students do not play a varsity sport?

    ○ 44%

    ○ 50%

    ○ 55%

    ○ 56%

    ○ 60%

7. If increasing 20 by P percent gives the same result as decreasing 60 by P percent, what is P percent of 70?

POWERS AND ROOTS

Rules of Operation with Powers

In the term $3x^2$, 3 is the **coefficient,** x is the **base,** and 2 is the **exponent.**
The exponent refers to the number of times the base is multiplied by itself.
For instance, in 4^3, you multiply 4 by itself 3 times: $4^3 = 4 \times 4 \times 4 = 64$.

Note: In the expression $3x^2$, only the x is being squared, not the 3. In other
words, $3x^2 = 3(x^2)$. If we wanted to square the 3 as well, we would write
$(3x)^2$. (Remember that in the order of operations, we raise to a power *before*
we multiply, so in $3x^2$, we square x and *then* multiply by 3.)

A number multiplied by itself twice is called the **square** of that number (e.g., 5^2 is 5
squared).

A number multiplied by itself three times is called the **cube** of that number (e.g., 4^3 is
4 cubed).

To multiply two terms with the same base, keep the base and add the
exponents.

Example: $2^2 \times 2^3 = 2^{2+3}$
$= 2^5$

To divide two terms with the same base, keep the base and subtract the
exponent of the denominator from the exponent of the numerator.

Example: $4^4 \div 4^2 = 4^{4-2}$
$= 4^2$

To raise a power to another power, multiply the exponents.

Example: $(3^2)^4 = 3^{2 \times 4}$
$= 3^8$

Any number raised to the first power equals itself: $a^1 = a$.

Any number except zero that is raised to the zero power is equal to 1. So $a^0 = 1$, if $a \neq 0$. (0^0 is undefined.)

A negative exponent indicates a reciprocal. To arrive at an equivalent
expression, take the reciprocal of the base and change the sign of the exponent.

$$a^{-n} = \frac{1}{a^n} \text{ or } \left(\frac{1}{a}\right)^n$$

EXPERT EXCLUSIVE

The GMAT asks you to
calculate squares and cubes
so often that they are worth
memorizing. Learn the squares
through $15^2 = 225$ and the
cubes through $5^3 = 125$.

EXPERT EXCLUSIVE

If you're unsure about these
rules, you can easily discover
the logic beneath them by
expanding the numbers: $2^2 \times 2^3 = (2 \times 2) \times (2 \times 2 \times 2) = 2 \times 2 \times 2 \times 2 \times 2$. That's five 2s, so
$2^2 \times 2^3 = 2^5 = 2^{2+3}$.

EXPERT EXCLUSIVE

The special properties of 0
and 1 as exponents make them
important numbers to pick if
you have a variable exponent.

Example: $2^{-3} = \dfrac{1}{2^3} = \left(\dfrac{1}{2}\right)^3 = \dfrac{1}{8}$

Roots

A fractional exponent indicates a root. So $(a)^{\frac{1}{n}} = \sqrt[n]{a}$ (Read "the nth root of a.") If no "n" is present, the radical sign means a square root.

Example: $8^{\frac{1}{3}} = \sqrt[3]{8} = 2$

Rules of Operations with Roots

By convention, the symbol $\sqrt{}$ (called "radical") means the *positive* square root only. Even though there are two different numbers whose square is 9 (both 3 and −3), we say that $\sqrt{9}$ is the positive number 3 only.

Example: $\sqrt{9} = +3; \quad -\sqrt{9} = -3$

When it comes to the four basic arithmetic operations, we treat radicals in much the same way we would treat variables.

Addition and Subtraction: Only like radicals can be added to or subtracted from one another.

Example: $2\sqrt{3} + 4\sqrt{2} - \sqrt{2} - 3\sqrt{3} = \left(4\sqrt{2} - \sqrt{2}\right) + \left(2\sqrt{3} - 3\sqrt{3}\right)$ $\left[\text{Note: } \sqrt{2} = 1\sqrt{2}\right]$

$$= 3\sqrt{2} + \left(-\sqrt{3}\right)$$
$$= 3\sqrt{2} - \sqrt{3}$$

Multiplication and Division: To multiply or divide one radical by another, multiply or divide the numbers outside the radical signs, then the numbers inside the radical signs.

Example: $\left(6\sqrt{3}\right) \times \left(2\sqrt{5}\right) = (6 \times 2) \times \left(\sqrt{3} \times \sqrt{5}\right) = 12\sqrt{3 \times 5} = 12\sqrt{15}$

Example: $12\sqrt{15} \div 2\sqrt{5} = (12 \div 2) \times \left(\sqrt{15} \div \sqrt{5}\right) = 6\sqrt{\dfrac{15}{5}} = 6\sqrt{3}$

Example: $\dfrac{4\sqrt{18}}{2\sqrt{6}} = \left(\dfrac{4}{2}\right)\left(\dfrac{\sqrt{18}}{\sqrt{6}}\right) = 2\left(\sqrt{\dfrac{18}{6}}\right) = 2\sqrt{3}$

EXPERT EXCLUSIVE

If you multiply $\sqrt{x}$ by $\sqrt{x}$, you wind up with x. Another way to think of that is $(\sqrt{x})^2 = x$. Squaring both sides of an equation, therefore, is a nice way to make radicals "disappear."

If the number inside the radical is a multiple of a perfect square, the expression can be simplified by factoring out the perfect square.

Example: $\sqrt{72}=\sqrt{36\times 2}=\sqrt{36}\times\sqrt{2}=6\sqrt{2}$

Warning: You *cannot* "split up" addition underneath a radical sign, although the GMAT will try to talk you into thinking you can.

Example: $\sqrt{100}=10$

$\sqrt{100}=\sqrt{36+64}$

$\sqrt{100}\neq\sqrt{36}+\sqrt{64}$

$\sqrt{100}\neq 6+8$

$\sqrt{100}\neq 14$

Powers of 10

The exponent of a power of 10 tells us how many zeros the number would contain if written out.

Example: $10^6 = 1,000,000$ (6 zeros) since 10 multiplied by itself six times is equal to 1,000,000.

When multiplying a number by a power of 10, move the decimal point to the right the same number of places as in the exponent; that is, the number of zeros in that power of 10.

When dividing by a power of 10, move the decimal point the corresponding number of places to the left. (Note that dividing by 10^4 is the same as multiplying by 10^{-4}.)

Exponents and Powers of 10 with Radicals

If an exponent is under the square root sign, just divide the exponent by two. If an exponent is under a cube root sign, divide it by three.

Examples: $\sqrt{13^4}=13^2$

$\sqrt[3]{7^6}=7^2$

If decimals are under a square root sign, take the square root of the number and divide the number of decimal places by two. Likewise, if a decimal is under a cube root sign, take the cube root of the number and divide the number of decimal places by three.

Examples: $\sqrt{0.0009}=0.03$

$\sqrt[3]{0.000125}=0.05$

POWERS AND ROOTS PRACTICE SET

Answers are on page 644.

1. Which of the following is not equal to 0.0675?

   ○ 67.5×10^{-3}

   ○ 6.75×10^{-2}

   ○ 0.675×10^{-1}

   ○ 0.00675×10^{2}

   ○ 0.0000675×10^{3}

2. If $x > 0$, then $(4^x)(8^x) =$

   ○ 2^{9x}

   ○ 2^{8x}

   ○ 2^{6x}

   ○ 2^{5x}

   ○ 2^{4x}

3. Which of the following is equal to 8^5?

   I. $2^5 \times 4^5$
   II. 2^{15}
   III. $2^5 \times 2^{10}$

   ○ II only

   ○ I and II only

   ○ I and III only

   ○ II and III only

   ○ I, II, and III

4. If $s^2 t^{-2} = 1$ and $st = -4$, what is the value of $s + t$?

Advanced

5. If $x^a x^b = 1$ and $x \neq \pm 1$, then $a + b =$

   ○ x

   ○ -1

   ○ 0

   ○ 1

   ○ It cannot be determined from the information given.

6. If $5^n > 10,000$ and n is an integer, what is the smallest possible value of n?

ALGEBRA

There won't be that many problems that involve only algebra—maybe 20 percent of the Quantitative section. But a lot of the questions on the test will involve algebra to some degree or another. This makes algebra a necessary skill—you have to understand basic equations and how to solve them.

TERMINOLOGY

Terms: A **term** is a numerical constant or the product of a numerical constant and one or more variables. Examples of terms are $3x$, $4x^2yz$, and $2ac$.

Expressions: An **algebraic expression** is a combination of one or more terms. Terms in an expression are separated by either $+$ or $-$ signs. Examples of expressions are $3xy$, $4ab + 5cd$, and $x^2 - 1$.

In the term $3xy$, the numerical constant 3 is called a **coefficient.** In a simple term such as z, 1 is the coefficient. A number without any variables is called a **constant term.** An expression with one term, such as $3xy$, is called a **monomial;** one with two terms, such as $4a + 2d$, is a **binomial**; one with three terms, such as $xy + z - a$, is a **trinomial**. The general name for expressions with more than one term is **polynomial.**

SUBSTITUTION

Substitution is a method that we employ to evaluate an algebraic expression or to express an algebraic expression in terms of other variables.

Example: Evaluate $3x^2 - 4x$ when $x = 2$.

Replace every x in the expression with 2 and then carry out the designated operations.

Remember to follow the order of operations (PEMDAS).

$3x^2 - 4x = 3(2)^2 - 4(2) = 3 \times 4 - 4 \times 2 = 12 - 8 = 4$

Example: Express $\dfrac{a}{b-a}$ in terms of x and y if $a = 2x$ and $b = 3y$.

Here, we replace every a with $2x$ and every b with $3y$: $\dfrac{a}{b-a} = \dfrac{2x}{3y-2x}$.

OPERATIONS WITH POLYNOMIALS

All of the laws of arithmetic operations, such as the commutative, associative, and distributive laws, are also applicable to polynomials.

Commutative Law: $\quad 2x + 5y = 5y + 2x$

$$5a \times 3b = 3b \times 5a = 15ab$$

Associative Law: $\quad 2x - 3x + 5y + 2y = (2x - 3x) + (5y + 2y) = -x + 7y$

$$(-2x)\left(\frac{1}{2}x\right)(3y)(-2y) = (-x^2)(-6y^2) = 6x^2y^2$$

Note: The process of simplifying an expression by subtracting or adding together those terms with the same variable component is called **combining like terms.**

Distributive Law: $\quad 3a(2b - 5c) = (3a \times 2b) - (3a \times 5c) = 6ab - 15ac$

Note: The product of two binomials can be calculated by applying the distributive law twice.

Example: $\quad (x+5)(x-2)$

$$= x \bullet (x-2) + 5 \bullet (x-2)$$
$$= x \bullet x - x \bullet 2 + 5 \bullet x - 5 \bullet 2$$
$$= x^2 - 2x + 5x - 10$$
$$= x^2 + 3x - 10$$

You multiply the First terms first, then the Outer terms, then the Inner terms, and finally the Last terms. A simple mnemonic for this is the word **FOIL**.

EXPERT EXCLUSIVE

Making problems look more complicated than they are by distributing a common factor is a classic GMAT trick. Whenever algebra looks scary, check whether common factors could be factored out.

FACTORING ALGEBRAIC EXPRESSIONS

Factoring a polynomial means expressing it as a product of two or more simpler expressions.

Common Monomial Factor: When there is a monomial factor common to every term in the polynomial, it can be factored out by using the distributive law.

Example: $\quad 2a + 6ac = 2a(1 + 3c)$

Here, $2a$ is the greatest common factor of $2a$ and $6ac$.

Difference of Two Perfect Squares: The difference of two squares can be factored into a product: $a^2 - b^2 = (a - b)(a + b)$.

Example: $d^2 - 16 = (d - 4)(d + 4)$

Polynomials of the Form $a^2 + 2ab + b^2$: Any polynomial of this form is equivalent to the square of a binomial. Notice that $(a + b)^2 = a^2 + 2ab + b^2$ (try FOIL).

Factoring such a polynomial is just reversing this procedure.

Example: $x^2 + 6x + 9 = (x)^2 + 2(x)(3) + (3)^2 = (x + 3)^2$.

Polynomials of the Form $a^2 - 2ab + b^2$: Any polynomial of this form is equivalent to the square of a binomial as in the previous example. Here though, the binomial is the difference of two terms: $(a - b)^2 = a^2 - 2ab + b^2$.

Example: $x^2 - 10x + 25 = (x)^2 - 2(x)(5) + (5)^2 = (x - 5)^2$

> **CAUTION**
>
> $(a - b)^2 \neq a^2 - b^2$
> $(a + b)^2 \neq a^2 + b^2$
> The GMAT will try to trick you into believing otherwise.

The GMAT uses these forms over and over. Review them thoroughly and look out for them as you practice. Notice that all the forms begin and end in a perfect square:

$$a^2 - b^2$$
$$a^2 + 2ab + b^2$$
$$a^2 - 2ab + b^2$$

That's your signal that the test is using one of these "classic polynomials." Picking up on that will save you lots of work, especially in the difficult questions. Imagine seeing this show up:

$$4x^4 + 52x^2 + 169$$

But if you say, "Hang on . . . 169 is 13^2, and $4x^4$ is $(2x^2)^2$ . . . I'll bet this is just $(2x^2 + 13)^2$ . . . " then you only have to confirm that $52x^2 = 2 \times 2x^2 \times 13$ (which it is) to start making the problem easier. (Especially if it asks for the value of $2x^2 + 13$, which a question like this probably would!)

Polynomials of the Form $x^2 + bx + c$: Many polynomials of this form can be factored into a product of two binomials. The product of the first term in each binomial must equal the first term of the polynomial. The product of the last term of each binomial must equal the last term of the polynomial. The sum of the remaining products must equal the second term of the polynomial. Factoring can be thought of as the FOIL method backwards, or "reverse FOIL."

Example: $x^2 - 3x + 2$

We can factor this into two binomials, each containing an x term. Start by writing down what we know.

$$x^2 - 3x + 2 = (x \quad)(x \quad)$$

In each binomial on the right, we need to fill in the missing term. The product of the two missing terms will be the last term in the polynomial: 2. The sum of the two missing terms will be the coefficient of the second term of the polynomial: −3. Try the possible factors of 2 until we get a pair that adds up to −3. There are two possibilities: 1 and 2 or −1 and −2. Since (−1) + (−2) = −3, we can fill −1 and −2 into the empty spaces.

Thus, $x^2 - 3x + 2 = (x - 1)(x - 2)$.

If the coefficient of the constant (the last term) is negative, then your binomials will have different signs (one + and one −). If the coefficient of the constant is positive, then your binomials will both have the same sign (two +'s or two −'s); they will have the same sign as the coefficient in the middle term. Check out the example above: Both binomials have a minus sign because of the −3 coefficient in −3x.

Note: Whenever you factor a polynomial, you can check your answer by using FOIL to obtain the original polynomial.

Linear Equations

An **equation** is an algebraic sentence that says that two expressions are equal to each other. The two expressions consist of numbers, variables, and arithmetic operations to be performed on these numbers and variables.

Solving Equations

To **solve** for some variable, we can manipulate the equation until we have isolated that variable on one side of the equals sign, leaving any numbers or other variables on the other side. Of course, we must be careful to manipulate the equation only in accordance with the equality postulate: *Whenever we perform an operation on one side of the equation, we must perform the same operation on the other side.* Otherwise, the two sides of the equation will no longer be equal.

Linear, or First-Degree, Equations: This is an equation in which all the variables are raised to the first power (there are no squares or cubes). To solve such an equation, we'll perform operations on both sides of the equation in order to get the variable we're solving for all alone on one side. The operations we can perform without upsetting the balance of the equation are addition and subtraction, as well as multiplication or division by a number other than 0. At each step in the process, we'll need to use the reverse of the operation that's being applied to the variable in order to isolate the variable.

Example: If $4x - 7 = 2x + 5$, what is x?

1. Get all the terms with the variable on one side of the equation. Combine the terms.

$$4x - 7 = 2x + 5$$
$$4x - 2x - 7 = 2x - 2x + 5$$
$$2x - 7 = 5$$

2. Get all constant terms on the other side of the equation.

$$2x - 7 + 7 = 5 + 7$$
$$2x = 12$$

3. Isolate the variable by dividing both sides by its coefficient.

$$\frac{2x}{2} = \frac{12}{2}$$
$$x = 6$$

We can easily check our work when solving this kind of equation. The answer we arrive at represents the value of the variable that makes the equation hold true. Therefore, to check that it's correct, we can just substitute this value for the variable in the original equation. If the equation holds true, we've found the correct answer. In the previous example, we got a value of 6 for x. Replacing x with 6 in our original equation gives us $4(6) - 7 = 2(6) + 5$, or $17 = 17$. That's clearly true, so our answer is indeed correct.

Equations with Fractions: These can be solved using the same approach, although this often leads to rather involved calculations. Instead, they can be transformed into an equivalent equation that does not involve fractions. Let's see how to solve such a problem.

Example: Solve $\dfrac{x-2}{3} + \dfrac{x-4}{10} = \dfrac{x}{2}$

1. Multiply both sides of the equation by the least common denominator (LCD). Here the LCD is 30.

$$30\left(\frac{x-2}{3}\right) + 30\left(\frac{x-4}{10}\right) = 30\left(\frac{x}{2}\right)$$
$$10(x-2) + 3(x-4) = 15(x)$$

2. Clear parentheses using the distributive property and combine like terms.

$$10x - 20 + 3x - 12 = 15x$$
$$13x - 32 = 15x$$

3. Isolate the variable. Again, combine like terms.

$$-32 = 15x - 13x$$
$$-32 = 2x$$

4. Divide both sides by the coefficient of the variable.

$$x = \frac{-32}{2} = -16$$

> **EXPERT EXCLUSIVE**
> The GMAT loves to make algebra problems look harder than they need to be by using fractions. Whenever you see a fraction in an algebra question, *always* get rid of the fraction as your very first step.

INEQUALITIES

Inequality Symbols:

> greater than

Example: $x > 4$ means x is greater than 4.

< less than

Example: $x < 0$ means x is less than zero (a negative number).

≥ greater than or equal to

Example: $x \geq -2$ means x can be -2 or any number greater than -2.

≤ less than or equal to

Example: $x \leq \dfrac{1}{2}$ means x can be $\dfrac{1}{2}$ or any number less than $\dfrac{1}{2}$.

> **EXPERT EXCLUSIVE**
> Another good way to get rid of a fraction is to cancel common factors:
> $$\frac{x^2 - y^2}{x+y} = \frac{(x+y)(x-y)}{(x+y)}$$
> $$= \frac{(x+y)(x-y)}{(x+y)} = x - y$$

EXPERT EXCLUSIVE

Sketching a number line is a great way to help yourself to visualize inequalities.

A range of values is often expressed on a number line. Two ranges are shown below.

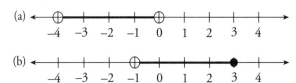

(a) represents the set of all numbers between −4 and 0 *excluding* the endpoints −4 and 0, or −4 < *x* < 0.

(b) represents the set of all numbers greater than −1, up to and *including* 3, or −1 < *x* ≤ 3.

Three-Part Inequalities: If you are given a three-part inequality, you can still do calculations with it. But instead of saying, "What I do to one side, I must also do to the other," you say, "What I do to one part, I must do to *all* parts."

Example: Simplify −11 < 2*x* − 5 < 1.

$$-11 < 2x - 5 < 1$$

add 5 to all sides: $\qquad -11 + 5 < 2x - 5 + 5 < 1 + 5$

combine like terms: $\qquad\qquad -6 < 2x < 6$

divide all sides by 2: $\qquad\qquad -3 < x < 3$

EXPERT EXCLUSIVE

The GMAT tests this concept frequently, especially in Data Sufficiency questions.

Solving Inequalities: We use the same methods as used in solving equations with one exception: *If the inequality is multiplied or divided by a negative number, the direction of the inequality is reversed.*

If the inequality −3*x* < 2 is multiplied by −1, the resulting inequality is 3*x* > −2.

Example: Solve for *x* and represent the solution set on a number line: $3 - \dfrac{x}{4} \geq 2$.

1. Multiply both sides by 4. $\qquad\qquad\qquad\qquad\qquad\qquad\qquad 12 - x \geq 8$

2. Subtract 12 from both sides. $\qquad\qquad\qquad\qquad\qquad\qquad -x \geq -4$

3. Divide both sides by −1 and change the direction of the sign. $\quad x \leq 4$

Note: The solution set to an inequality is not a single value but a range of possible values. Here, the values include 4 and all numbers below 4.

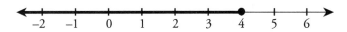

Example: Describe the possible values for *x* if |2*x* − 5| < 3.

With an absolute value, we split the inequality into two, one with a positive number and one with a negative number. But we *must reverse the sign of the inequality in the negative case*:

$$|2x - 5| < 3$$

$2x - 5 < 3$	$2x - 5 > -3$
$2x < 8$	$2x > 2$
$x < 4$	$x > 1$

$$1 < x < 4$$

We also need to watch out for this possibility when multiplying or dividing variables.

Example: Simplify $3b < 2b^2$.

$$3b < 2b^2$$

Divide both sides by b:

Write down both possibilities:

Wait! Is b negative? We don't know!

if b is neg	if b is pos
$3 > 2b$	$3 < 2b$

Divide by 2:

$\dfrac{3}{2} > b$	$\dfrac{3}{2} < b$

All negative numbers are less than $\dfrac{3}{2}$, so b could equal any negative number at all or any positive number greater than $\dfrac{3}{2}$.

$$b < 0 \qquad \text{OR} \qquad \frac{3}{2} < b$$

LITERAL EQUATIONS

If a problem involves more than one variable, we cannot find a specific value for a variable; we can only solve for one variable in terms of the others. To do this, try to get the desired variable alone on one side and all the other variables on the other side.

Example: In the formula $V = \dfrac{PN}{R + NT}$, solve for N in terms of P, R, T, and V.

1.   Clear denominators by cross multiplying.

$$\frac{V}{1} = \frac{PN}{R + NT}$$

$$V(R + NT) = PN$$

2.   Remove parentheses by distributing.

$$VR + VNT = PN$$

3.   Put all terms containing N on one side and all other terms on the other side.

$$VNT - PN = -VR$$

4.   Factor out the common factor N.

$$N(VT - P) = -VR$$

5.   Divide by $(VT - P)$ to get N alone.

$$N = \frac{-VR}{VT - P}$$

Note: We can reduce the number of negative terms in the answer by multiplying both the numerator and the denominator of the fraction on the right-hand side by -1.

$$N = \frac{VR}{P - VT}$$

EXPERT EXCLUSIVE

The GMAT tends to write its answer choices with as few negative terms as possible. It also uses this technique to remove radicals from the denominator:

$$\frac{2}{\sqrt{3}} = \frac{2 \times \sqrt{3}}{\sqrt{3} \times \sqrt{3}} = \frac{2\sqrt{3}}{3}.$$

SIMULTANEOUS EQUATIONS

In general, if you want to find numerical values for all your variables, you will need as many distinct equations as you have variables. If we are given two *distinct* equations with two variables, we can combine the equations to obtain a unique solution set.

Approach 1: Isolate one variable in one equation. Then plug the expression that it equals into its place in the other equation.

Example: Find the values of m and n if $m = 4n + 2$ and $3m + 2n = 16$.

<table>
<tr><td>

EXPERT EXCLUSIVE

Keep your eyes open for opportunities to combine equations. The GMAT rewards those who find clever combinations with quick solutions.

</td><td>

1. We know that $m = 4n + 2$. Substitute $4n + 2$ for m in the second equation.

2. Solve for n.

</td><td>

$3(4n + 2) + 2n = 16$

$12n + 6 + 2n = 16$
$14n + 6 = 16$
$14n = 10$
$n = \dfrac{10}{14} = \dfrac{5}{7}$

</td></tr>
</table>

3. To find the value of m, substitute $\dfrac{5}{7}$ for n in the first equation and solve.

$$m = 4n + 2$$
$$m = 4\left(\frac{5}{7}\right) + 2$$
$$m = \frac{20}{7} + \frac{14}{7} = \frac{34}{7}$$

Approach 2: Add or subtract whole equations from each other to eliminate a variable.

Example: Find the values of x and y if $4x + 3y = 27$ and $3x - 6y = -21$.

There's no obvious isolation/substitution to be done. But if we multiplied the first equation by 2, we'd be able to get rid of the y's.

$$2(4x + 3y) = 2(27)$$

Distribute: $8x + 6y = 54$

Now add the new equation to the second, carefully lining them up so we combine like terms:

$$
\begin{array}{r}
8x + 6y = 54 \\
+[3x - 6y = -21] \\
\hline
11x = 33
\end{array}
$$

Divide by 11: $x = 3$

This can now be substituted back into either equation to yield the other value.

$$4x + 3y = 27$$
$$4(3) + 3y = 27$$
$$12 + 3y = 27$$
$$3y = 15$$
$$y = 5$$

QUADRATIC EQUATIONS

If we set the polynomial $ax^2 + bx + c$ equal to 0, we have a special name for it: we call it a quadratic equation. Since it is an equation, we can find the value(s) for x that make the equation work.

Example: $x^2 - 3x + 2 = 0$

To find the solutions, or **roots**, let's start by doing what we did earlier in this chapter and factoring. Let's factor $x^2 - 3x + 2$ into $(x - 2)(x - 1)$, making our quadratic equation

$$(x - 2)(x - 1) = 0$$

Now, we have a product of two binomials that is equal to 0. When does a product of two terms equal to 0? The only time that happens is when at least one of the terms is 0. If the product of $(x - 2)$ and $(x - 1)$ is equal to 0, that means either the first term equals 0 or the second term equals 0. So to find the roots, we just need to set the two binomials equal to 0. That gives us

$$x - 2 = 0 \text{ or } x - 1 = 0$$

Solving for x, we get $x = 2$ or $x = 1$. As a check, we can plug in 1 and 2 into the equation $x^2 - 3x + 2 = 0$, and we'll see that either value makes the equation work.

> **EXPERT EXCLUSIVE**
>
> Make sure that the quadratic equation is equal to zero before you reverse-FOIL. Otherwise, you won't be able to figure out the possible values of the variable.

FUNCTIONS AND SYMBOLISM

The test uses classic function notation that you may recall from your later high school algebra classes. It also uses some untraditional notation, like ◊, ♠, or ⊗. Both types boil down to substitution.

The basic idea is that you're substituting things in a unique way described by the problem. Here's a classic function problem.

Example: What is the minimum value of the function $f(x) = x^2 - 1$?

What this problem is telling us is that whatever number is between those parentheses gets substituted in place of x in $x^2 - 1$. For instance, $f(2) = 2^2 - 1 = 3$.

A very easy way to solve would be to substitute whatever answer choices the GMAT gives us as the answer to the function. Some may not be possible; some will be. For example, $x^2 = -4$ isn't possible, since the GMAT uses only "real" numbers. The smallest of the possible answers is the correct response.

We could solve it logically, too. The function will be smallest when x^2 is smallest. Squaring a negative number produces a positive number, so x^2 can never be negative. The smallest we could get is $x^2 = 0$. So the smallest $x^2 - 1$ can be is $0 - 1$, or -1.

Some questions offer odd symbols but work basically the same way—as rules for what to substitute.

EXPERT EXCLUSIVE

No need ever to be frightened by weird symbols. Symbols = Substitution. If you can plug numbers in place of letters, you can solve symbol-based questions.

Example: If $x \clubsuit y = 3x - y^2$, then what is the value of $8 \clubsuit 2$?

The scary-looking equation is really just a rule for substitution. Whatever is to the left of the $\clubsuit$ symbol is x and should be substituted in place of x in $3x - y^2$. Similarly, anything to the right of $\clubsuit$ is y and should be substituted for y.

$$x \clubsuit y = 3x - y^2$$
$$8 \clubsuit 2 = 3(8) - (2)^2$$
$$8 \clubsuit 2 = 24 - 4$$
$$8 \clubsuit 2 = 20$$

ALGEBRA PRACTICE SET

Answers are on page 646.

1. If $6x + 7y = 53$ and $8x - 2y = 14$, what is the value of x?

   ○ 2

   ○ 3

   ○ 4

   ○ 5

   ○ 6

2. $p + 3s - (2p - 4s) =$

   ○ $-3p - s$

   ○ $-p - s$

   ○ $s - 3p$

   ○ $7s - p$

   ○ $7s + 3p$

3. If $5j + 3k = 84$ and $7k - 11j = -8$, what are the values of j and k?

   ○ $j = 6$ and $k = 18$

   ○ $j = 6$ and $k = 38$

   ○ $j = 9$ and $k = 13$

   ○ $j = 9$ and $k = 20$

   ○ $j = 9$ and $k = 43$

4. If $f(x) = x^2 + 6$, then $f(-4) =$

   ○ -10

   ○ -2

   ○ 4

   ○ 10

   ○ 22

5. If $c = 4$ and $d = 2$, then $\dfrac{8c^8 d^6}{2c^7 d^8} = ?$

6. Which of the following is a factor of $x^2 - 7x + 10$?

   ○ $x - 7$

   ○ $x - 5$

   ○ $x + 1$

   ○ $x + 2$

   ○ $x + 10$

7. If $3y + 10 = 12x + 2$, $x =$

   ○ $\dfrac{y}{4} + \dfrac{2}{3}$

   ○ $\dfrac{y-3}{4}$

   ○ $\dfrac{y}{4} + 1$

   ○ $\dfrac{y+2}{3}$

   ○ $\dfrac{y}{3} + \dfrac{3}{4}$

8. Look at this number line.

   The number line gives the solution to which inequality?

   ○ $4x + 4 < 7x + 9$

   ○ $5x - 1 \leq 10x + 14$

   ○ $5x + 7 \leq 9x - 5$

   ○ $6x - 23 \leq 3x - 5$

   ○ $6x + 11 \leq 3x + 1$

Advanced

9. What is the solution of $4x - 7y + 12 = 20x + y - 4$ for y?

   ○ $y = 1 - 2x$

   ○ $y = 2 - 2x$

   ○ $y = 2x + 1$

   ○ $y = 3x + 2$

   ○ $y = 3x - 2$

10. If $3x^2 + 24x - 144 = 0$, then $x =$

    ○ -36 and -4

    ○ -36 and 4

    ○ -12 and 4

    ○ -12 and 12

    ○ 36 and -4

GEOMETRY

The geometry tested on the GMAT is fairly basic, such as lines, triangles, and circles. There are only a few fundamental definitions and formulas you need to know. The exam emphasizes ways of applying a couple of elementary rules.

EXPERT EXCLUSIVE

Prioritize your study time wisely. Most test takers see only four to six geometry questions.

LINES AND ANGLES

Lines

A line is a one-dimensional abstraction—infinitely long with no width. Two points determine a straight line; given any two points, there is exactly one straight line that passes through them.

A line **segment** is a section of a straight line of finite length with two endpoints. A line segment is named for its endpoints, as in segment *AB* below. The **midpoint** is the point that divides a line segment into two equal parts.

EXPERT EXCLUSIVE

You can (more or less) trust your eyes on the GMAT. Lines that look straight are straight. Lines that seem to intersect do intersect. Any diagrams in Problem Solving questions will be drawn to scale. But Data Sufficiency diagrams will only match the facts in the question stem, and may not be to the scale of the information in the statements.

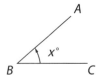

Example: In the figure above, *A* and *B* are the endpoints of the line segment *AB*, and *M* is the midpoint (*AM* = *MB*). What is the length of *AB*?

Since *AM* is 6, *MB* is also 6, so *AB* is 6 + 6, or 12.

Two lines are **parallel** if they lie in the same plane and never intersect each other regardless of how far they are extended. If line ℓ_1 is parallel to line ℓ_2, we write $\ell_1 \parallel \ell_2$.

Two lines are **perpendicular** if they intersect at a 90° angle. The shortest distance from a point to a line is the line segment drawn from the point to the line such that it is perpendicular to the line. If line ℓ_1 is perpendicular to line ℓ_2, we write $\ell_1 \perp \ell_2$. If $\ell_1 \perp \ell_2$ and $\ell_2 \perp \ell_3$, then $\ell_1 \parallel \ell_3$.

Angles

An angle is formed by two lines or line segments intersecting at a point. The point of intersection is called the **vertex** of the angle. Angles are measured in degrees(°).

Angle *x*, ∠*ABC*, and ∠*B* all denote the same angle shown in the diagram above.

Acute, Right, and Obtuse Angles: An **acute angle** is an angle whose degree measure is between 0° and 90°. A **right angle** is an angle whose degree measure is exactly 90°. An

obtuse angle is an angle whose degree measure is between 90° and 180°. A **straight angle** is an angle whose degree measure is exactly 180° (half of a circle, which contains 360°).

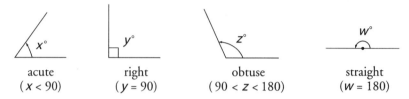

acute	right	obtuse	straight
($x < 90$)	($y = 90$)	($90 < z < 180$)	($w = 180$)

Sums of Angle Measures: The sum of the measures of the angles on one side of a straight line is 180°.

straight
$x + y + z = 180$

EXPERT EXCLUSIVE

The basic fact that all the angles on a straight line add up to 180° is often the key to complex geometry questions.

The sum of the measures of the angles around a point is 360°.

$$a + b + c + d + e = 360$$

Two angles are **supplementary** if together they make up a straight angle (i.e., if the sum of their measures is 180°). Two angles are **complementary** if together they make up a right angle (i.e., if the sum of their measures is 90°).

$c + d = 180$
supplementary

$a + b = 90$
complementary

A line or line segment **bisects** an angle if it splits the angle into two smaller, equal angles. Line segment *BD* below bisects ∠*ABC*, and ∠*ABD* has the same measure as ∠*DBC*. The two smaller angles are each half the size of ∠*ABC*.

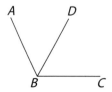

Vertical Angles: Vertical angles are a pair of opposite angles formed by two intersecting line segments. At the point of intersection, two pairs of vertical angles are formed. Angles *a* and *c* below are vertical angles, as are *b* and *d*.

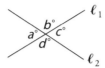

The two angles in a pair of vertical angles have the same degree measure. In the previous diagram, $a = c$ and $b = d$. In addition, since ℓ_1 and line ℓ_2 are straight lines,

$$a + b = c + d = a + d = b + c = 180$$

In other words, each angle is supplementary to each of its two adjacent angles.

If two parallel lines intersect with a third line (called a *transversal*), each of the parallel lines will intersect the third line at the same angle. In the figure below, $a = e$ because they intersect the line at the same angle. Since a and e are equal, and $c = a$ and $e = g$ (vertical angles), we know that $a = c = e = g$. Similarly, $b = d = f = h$.

EXPERT EXCLUSIVE

Whenever the GMAT sets two lines parallel, look for a transversal. Once you find it, look for the equal angles—especially the "opposite interior angles" (inside the parallel lines) like $d = f$ and $c = e$. The key to the problem will almost certainly involve those angles.

In other words, when two parallel lines intersect with a third line, all acute angles formed are equal, all obtuse angles formed are equal, and any acute angle is supplementary to any obtuse angle.

SLOPE

The slope of a line on a coordinate plane tells you how steeply that line goes up or down. If a line gets higher as you move to the right, it has a positive slope. If it goes down as you move to the right, it has a negative slope. To find the slope of a line, use the following formula:

$$\text{Slope} = \frac{\text{Rise}}{\text{Run}} = \frac{\text{Change in } y}{\text{Change in } x}$$

Rise means the difference between the y-coordinate values of the two points on the line, and *run* means the difference between the x-coordinate values.

Example: What is the slope of the line that contains the points $(1,2)$ and $(4,-5)$?

$$\text{Slope} = \frac{-5 - 2}{4 - 1} = \frac{-7}{3} = -\frac{7}{3}$$

EXPERT EXCLUSIVE

Difficult geometry questions often present lines in the form $x = cy + d$. c is NOT the slope! You need to put the line in $y = mx + b$ form first.

To determine the slope of a line from an equation, put the equation into slope-intercept form: $y = mx + b$, where the slope is m.

Example: What is the slope of the equation $3x + 2y = 4$?

$$3x + 2y = 4$$
$$2y = -3x + 4$$
$$y = -\frac{3}{2}x + 2, \text{ so } m \text{ is} -\frac{3}{2}$$

> **EXPERT EXCLUSIVE**
>
> Any point (x, y) on a line will solve the equation for that line if its x- and y-values are plugged in. No point off the line will fit.

The word *intercept* in "slope-intercept form" is there because b is the value of the y-intercept—the point at which the line crosses the y-axis. Another way to think of that is that $(0, b)$ will be a point on the line.

LINES AND ANGLES PRACTICE SET

Answers are on page 651.

1. What is the value of x in the figure below?

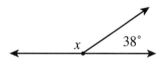

- ○ 38°

- ○ 52°

- ○ 90°

- ○ 142°

- ○ 152°

2. What is the y-intercept of the line in the figure below?

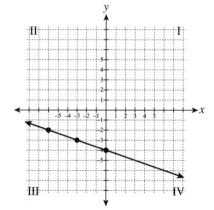

○ $\dfrac{1}{3}$

○ $-\dfrac{1}{3}$

○ $\dfrac{1}{4}$

○ -4

○ 4

3. The measure of one angle is 30 degrees more than twice its supplement. What is the measure of the smaller angle?

    ○   30°

    ○   50°

    ○   75°

    ○   100°

    ○   130°

4. Lines r and s intersect in the figure below. What is the measure of $\angle ABD$?

    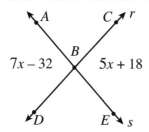

    Note: Figure not drawn to scale.

    ○   16.16°

    ○   25°

    ○   37°

    ○   118°

    ○   143°

5. What is the slope of the line containing the two points (8,−4) and (−13,10)?

    ○   −3

    ○ $-\dfrac{3}{2}$

    ○ $-\dfrac{2}{3}$

    ○ $\dfrac{2}{3}$

    ○ $\dfrac{3}{2}$

Advanced

6. Which of the following is the graph of the equation $2y - 2 = 6x$?

    ○

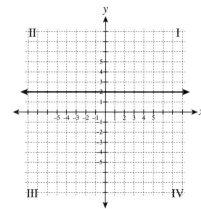

    ○

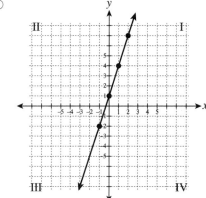

○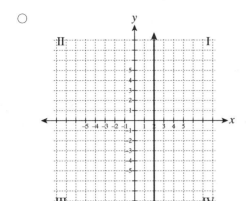

○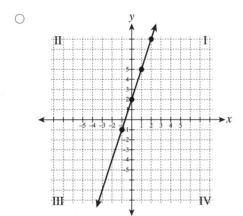

○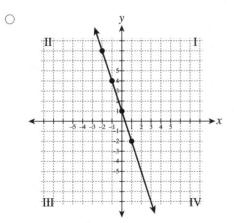

TRIANGLES

A triangle is a closed figure with three angles and three straight sides.

The sum of the **interior angles** of any triangle is 180 degrees.

EXPERT EXCLUSIVE

The triangle is the GMAT's favorite shape. Learn these rules well, as you are likely to need them.

Each interior angle is supplementary to an adjacent **exterior angle.** The degree measure of an exterior angle is equal to the sum of the measures of the two nonadjacent (remote) interior angles.

In the figure below, a, b, and c are interior angles. Therefore $a + b + c = 180$. In addition, d is supplementary to c; therefore $d + c = 180$. So $d + c = a + b + c$, and $d = a + b$. Thus, the exterior angle d is equal to the sum of the two remote interior angles a and b.

The **altitude** (or height) of a triangle is the perpendicular distance from a vertex to the side opposite the vertex. The altitude can fall inside the triangle, outside the triangle, or on one of the sides.

Altitude = *AD*

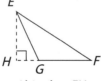
Altitude = *EH*

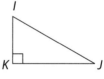
Altitude = *IK*

Sides and Angles: The length of any side of a triangle is less than the sum of the lengths of the other two sides, and it is greater than the positive difference of the lengths of the other two sides.

$b + c > a > |b - c|$

$a + b > c > |a - b|$

$a + c > b > |a - c|$

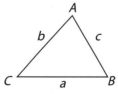

If the lengths of two sides of a triangle are unequal, the greater angle lies opposite the longer side and vice versa. In the figure above, if $\angle A > \angle B > \angle C$, then $a > b > c$.

Area of a Triangle: $\frac{1}{2} \times \text{base} \times \text{height}$.

Example: In the diagram below, the base has length 4 and the altitude length 3, so we write

$$A = \frac{1}{2}bh$$

$$= \frac{1}{2} \times 4 \times 3 = 6$$

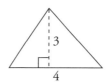

Remember that the height (or altitude) is perpendicular to the base. Therefore, when two sides of a triangle are perpendicular to each other, the area is easy to find. In a right triangle, we call the two sides that form the 90° angle the **legs.** Then the area is one-half the product of the legs, or

$$A = \frac{1}{2}bh$$

$$= \frac{1}{2}\ell_1 \times \ell_2$$

> **EXPERT EXCLUSIVE**
> Don't automatically use the side on the bottom as the base. Any side can be the base, so pick the one that makes for the easiest calculation.

Example: In the triangle below, we could treat the hypotenuse as the base, since that is the way the figure is drawn. If we did this, we would need to know the distance from the hypotenuse to the opposite vertex to determine the area of the triangle. A more straightforward method is to notice that this is a right triangle with legs of lengths 6 and 8, which allows us to use the alternative formula for area:

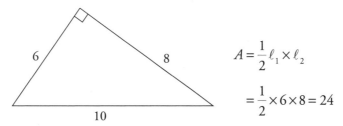

$$A = \frac{1}{2}\ell_1 \times \ell_2$$

$$= \frac{1}{2} \times 6 \times 8 = 24$$

Perimeter of a Triangle: The perimeter of a triangle is the distance around the triangle. In other words, the perimeter is equal to the sum of the lengths of the sides.

Example: In the triangle below, the sides are of length 5, 6, and 8. Therefore, the perimeter is 5 + 6 + 8, or 19.

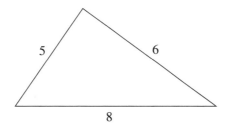

Isosceles Triangles: An isosceles triangle is a triangle that has two sides of equal length. The two equal sides are called **legs,** and the third side is called the **base.**

EXPERT EXCLUSIVE

In an isosceles triangle, the altitude dropped to the base bisects the base (divides it into two equal parts).

Since the two legs have the same length, the two angles opposite the legs must have the same measure. In the figure below, $PQ = PR$, and $\angle Q = \angle R$.

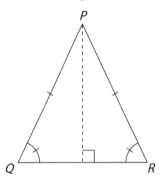

Equilateral Triangles: An equilateral triangle has three sides of equal length and three 60° angles.

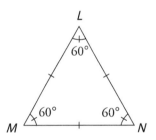

Similar Triangles: Triangles are **similar** if they have the same shape—if corresponding angles have the same measure. For instance, any two triangles whose angles measure 30°, 60°, and 90° are similar. In similar triangles, corresponding sides are proportional to one another. Triangles are **congruent** if corresponding angles have the same measure and corresponding sides have the same length.

Example: What is the perimeter of $\triangle DEF$ below?

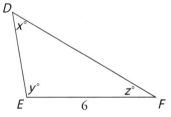

Each triangle has an $x°$ angle, a $y°$ angle, and a $z°$ angle; therefore, they are similar, and corresponding sides are proportional to one another. BC and EF are corresponding sides; each is opposite the $x°$ angle. Since EF is twice the length of BC, each side of △*DEF* will be twice the length of the corresponding side of △*ABC*. Therefore, *DE* = 2(*AB*) or 4, and *DF* = 2(*AC*) or 8. The perimeter of △*DEF* is 4 + 6 + 8 = 18.

The ratio of the areas of two similar triangles is the square of the ratio of corresponding lengths. For instance, in the example above, since each side of △*DEF* is 2 times the length of the corresponding side of △*ABC*, △*DEF* must have 2^2 or 4 times the area of △*ABC*.

$$\frac{\text{Area } \triangle DEF}{\text{Area } \triangle ABC} = \left(\frac{DE}{AB}\right)^2 = \left(\frac{2}{1}\right)^2 = 4$$

EXPERT EXCLUSIVE

This ratio is tested in some of the GMAT's toughest triangle-based geometry questions. Learning it now may save you a lot of calculation on test day.

Right Triangles

A right triangle has one interior angle of 90°, which is also the largest angle of the triangle. The longest side, which lies opposite the right angle, is called the **hypotenuse.** The other two sides are called the **legs.**

Pythagorean Theorem

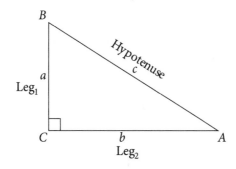

$$(\text{Leg}_1)^2 + (\text{Leg}_2)^2 = (\text{Hypotenuse})^2$$
$$\text{or}$$
$$a^2 + b^2 = c^2$$

Pythagorean Theorem: The **Pythagorean theorem** holds for all right triangles and states that the square of the hypotenuse is equal to the sum of the squares of the legs.

Some sets of integers happen to satisfy the Pythagorean theorem. These sets of integers are commonly referred to as "Pythagorean triples." One very common set that you might remember is 3, 4, and 5. Since $3^2 + 4^2 = 5^2$, you can have a right triangle with legs of lengths 3 and 4 and hypotenuse of length 5. This is the most common kind of right triangle on the GMAT. You should be familiar with the numbers so that whenever you see a right triangle

EXPERT EXCLUSIVE

Some common Pythagorean triples:

    3:4:5
    5:12:13

Some others that may show up in very high-level questions:

    7:24:25
    8:15:17
    9:40:41

with legs of 3 and 4, you will immediately know the hypotenuse must have length 5. In addition, any multiple of these lengths makes a Pythagorean triple; for instance, $6^2 + 8^2 = 10^2$, so 6, 8, and 10 also make a right triangle. One other triple that appears regularly is 5, 12, and 13.

Don't overuse the Pythagorean Theorem. Easily recognizable right triangle patterns such as the triples allow you to avoid spending time on the formula when solving the majority of GMAT geometry problems. But from time to time the GMAT may challenge you with a triangle that doesn't offer any convenient shortcuts, so make sure you can apply the theorem when necessary.

Example: What is the length of the hypotenuse of a right triangle with legs of length 9 and 10?

Use the theorem: The square of the length of the hypotenuse equals the sum of the squares of the lengths of the legs. Here the legs are 9 and 10, so we have

$$\text{Hypotenuse}^2 = 9^2 + 10^2$$
$$= 81 + 100 = 181$$
$$\text{Hypotenuse} = \sqrt{181}$$

The Pythagorean theorem is also how one calculates lengths of lines on a coordinate plane.

Example: What is the length of *AB*?

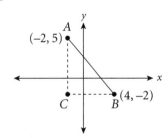

Sketch lines from points *A* and *B* parallel to the axes. They will form a right triangle, and the intersection will have the same *x*-coordinate as one point and the same *y*-coordinate as the other. Because the new lines aren't diagonal, their length is easy to figure out. In this example, the length of *AC* is 7 because the line drops down 5 from *A* to the *x*-axis and then another 2 to *C*. Similarly, the length of *BC* is 6.

EXPERT EXCLUSIVE

The solutions to many coordinate plane problems depend on creating triangles.

Now you can use the Pythagorean theorem to calculate *AB*:

$$AB^2 = BC^2 + AC^2$$
$$AB^2 = 6^2 + 7^2$$
$$AB^2 = 36 + 49$$
$$AB^2 = 85$$
$$AB = \sqrt{85}$$

Special Right Triangles: You can always use the Pythagorean theorem to find the lengths of the sides in a right triangle. There are two special kinds of right triangles, though, that always have the same ratios:

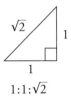

$1:1:\sqrt{2}$

(for isosceles right triangles)

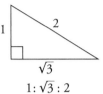

$1:\sqrt{3}:2$

(for 30-60-90 triangles)

EXPERT EXCLUSIVE

The GMAT will try to subvert your expectations about where the radical would be. For example, the legs of an isosceles right triangle might be $\dfrac{9}{\sqrt{2}}$ and the hypotenuse 9.

These two special right triangles appear frequently, and you are very likely to see them. However, the GMAT can hide them in unexpected ways. For example, the diagonal of a square creates two isosceles right triangles. And bisecting an equilateral triangle creates two 30-60-90 triangles:

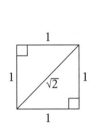

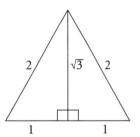

TRIANGLES PRACTICE SET

Answers are on page 653.

1. Which answer choice could not represent the length of three sides of a triangle?

    ○ 2, 2, 3

    ○ 2, 2, 5

    ○ 6, 8, 10

    ○ 4, 4, 4

    ○ 7, 10, 12.5

2. Which segment(s) is the longest side of the triangle below?

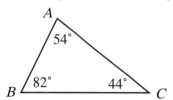

Note: Figure not drawn to scale.

○ Side *AB*

○ Side *BC*

○ Side *AC*

○ Sides *AB* and *AC*

○ All sides are congruent.

3. If the measure of the unique angle of an isosceles triangle is twice the measure of one of the two equal angles, what is the angle measure of the unique angle of this triangle?

○ 35°

○ 45°

○ 70°

○ 90°

○ 135°

4. An equilateral triangle has sides that are 18 cm in length. What is the length of the altitude of this triangle?

○ $9\sqrt{3}$ cm

○ 18 cm

○ $18\sqrt{3}$ cm

○ 36 cm

○ $36\sqrt{3}$ cm

Advanced

5. What is the length of a leg of an isosceles right triangle with a hypotenuse of 8 inches?

   ○ $2\sqrt{2}$

   ○ 4

   ○ $4\sqrt{2}$

   ○ 8

   ○ $8\sqrt{2}$

6. What is the length in feet of a ladder that rests on the ground 24 feet from the foot of a building and reaches 18 feet up the wall of the building?

   ○ 26

   ○ 28

   ○ 29

   ○ 30

   ○ 32

POLYGONS

A polygon is a closed figure whose sides are straight line segments.

The **perimeter** of a polygon is the distance around the polygon, or the sum of the lengths of the sides.

A **vertex** of a polygon is the point where two adjacent sides meet.

A **diagonal** of a polygon is a line segment connecting two nonadjacent vertices.

A **regular** polygon has sides of equal length and interior angles of equal measure.

The number of sides determines the specific name of the polygon. A **triangle** has three sides, a **quadrilateral** has four sides, a **pentagon** has five sides, and a **hexagon** has six sides. Triangles and quadrilaterals are by far the most important polygons on the GMAT.

Interior and Exterior Angles: A polygon can be divided into triangles by drawing diagonals from a given vertex to all other nonadjacent vertices. For instance, the pentagon below can be divided into three triangles. Since the sum of the interior angles of each triangle is 180°, the sum of the interior angles of a pentagon is $3 \times 180° = 540°$.

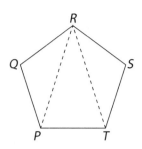

> **EXPERT EXCLUSIVE**
> Breaking down complicated or unusual shapes into several simpler shapes is almost always a good idea on the GMAT.

Example: What is the measure of one interior angle of the regular hexagon below?

> **EXPERT EXCLUSIVE**
> An easy way to determine the sum of the interior angles of a polygon is to use the formula:
> Sum = (# of sides − 2) * 180

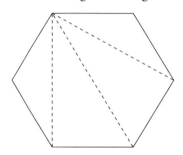

We need to find the sum of the interior angles and divide by the number of interior angles, or 6. Since the hexagon is regular, all angles are equal, so each of them is equal to one-sixth of the sum. Since we can draw four triangles in a six-sided figure, the sum of the interior angles will be 4 × 180°, or 720°. Therefore, each of the six interior angles measures $\frac{720}{6}$, or 120 degrees.

Quadrilaterals

The most important quadrilaterals to know for the GMAT are the rectangle and square. Anything could show up on the test, but concentrate on the most important figures and principles. The lesser-known properties can readily be deduced from the way the figure looks and from your knowledge of geometry.

Quadrilateral: A four-sided polygon. The sum of its four interior angles is 360°.

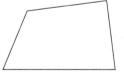

> **EXPERT EXCLUSIVE**
> The diagonal of a rectangle divides it into two congruent right triangles. A square's diagonal creates two congruent isosceles right triangles.

Rectangle: A quadrilateral with four equal angles, each a right angle.

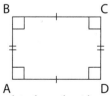

The opposite sides of a rectangle are equal in length. Also, the diagonals of a rectangle have equal length.

Square: A rectangle with four equal sides.

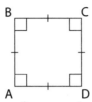

Areas of Quadrilaterals: For the case of a rectangle, we multiply the lengths of any two adjacent sides, called the length and width. Area of a rectangle = length × width = *lw*.

For the case of a square, since length and width are equal, we say:
Area of a square = (side)^2 = s^2.

In the rare event that you have to find the area of a parallelogram (a quadrilateral with equal and parallel opposite sides), multiply the base and the height. Area of a parallelogram = *bh*.

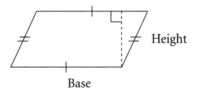

POLYGONS PRACTICE SET

Answers are on page 656.

1. How many sides does a pentagon have?

   ○ 3

   ○ 4

   ○ 5

   ○ 6

   ○ 8

2. What is the length of side *ST* in the rectangle below?

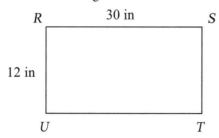

R   30 in   S

12 in

U   T

○ 12 in

○ 18 in

○ 24 in

○ 30 in

○ 42 in

3. If the perimeter of the following hexagon is 98 inches, what is the value of *x*?

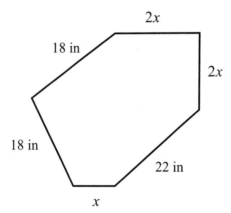

2*x*

18 in

2*x*

18 in

22 in

x

○ 8 in

○ 16 in

○ 19.6 in

○ 31.2 in

○ 40 in

4. If the sum of the measures of the interior angles of a regular polygon is 540°, what is the name of the polygon?

   ○ Triangle

   ○ Quadrilateral

   ○ Pentagon

   ○ Hexagon

   ○ Octagon

5. In square *ABCD* below, diagonal *AC* = 28 cm. What is the length of segment *DE*?

   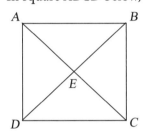

   ○ 7 cm

   ○ 10 cm

   ○ 14 cm

   ○ 28 cm

   ○ 56 cm

6. The sides of a rectangle are in the ratio of 3:7. If the longer side is 630 m, what is the length of the shorter side?

   ○ 63 m

   ○ 90 m

   ○ 210 m

   ○ 270 m

   ○ 1,470 m

7. Given that the length and width of a rectangle are in the ratio of 7:4, what is the width of the rectangle if the area is 448 cm²?

   ○ 4 cm

   ○ 16 cm

   ○ 28 cm

   ○ 32 cm

   ○ 56 cm

8. What is the perimeter of the figure below?

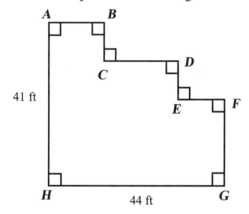

   ○ 42.5 ft

   ○ 85 ft

   ○ 126 ft

   ○ 170 ft

   ○ 1,804 ft

Advanced

9. The length of each side of square *A* is increased by 100 percent to make square *B*. If the length of the side of square *B* is increased by 50 percent to make square *C*, by what percent is the area of square *C* greater than the sum of the areas of squares *A* and *B*?

CIRCLES

Terminology

A circle is the set of all points in a plane at the same distance from a certain point. This point is called the **center** of the circle.

A circle is labeled by its center point: circle O means the circle with center point O. Two circles of different size with the same center are called **concentric**.

Diameter: A line segment that connects two points on the circle and passes through the center of the circle. In circle O, AB is a diameter.

EXPERT EXCLUSIVE

Almost all circle calculations depend on the length of the radius. Begin work on circle problems by identifying a radius and solving for its length, if you can. (All radii from the same circle will have the same length.)

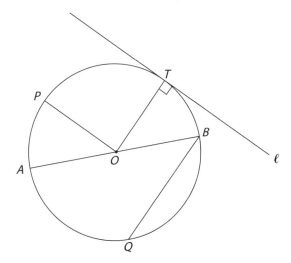

Radius: A line segment from the center of the circle to any point on the circle. The radius of a circle is one-half the length of the diameter. In circle O, OA, OB, OP, and OT are radii.

Chord: A line segment joining two points on the circle. In circle O, QB and AB are chords. The diameter of the circle is the longest chord of the circle.

Central Angle: An angle formed by two radii. In circle O, $\angle AOP$, $\angle POB$, $\angle AOB$, along with others, are central angles.

Tangent: A line that touches only one point on the circumference of the circle. A line drawn tangent to a circle is perpendicular to the radius at the point of tangency. Line ℓ is tangent to circle O at point T.

Circumference and Arc Length

The distance around a circle is called the **circumference**. The number π ("pi") is the ratio of a circle's circumference to its diameter. The value of π is 3.1415926 . . ., usually approximated as 3.14. For the GMAT, it is usually sufficient to remember that π is a little more than 3.

Since π equals the ratio of the circumference to the diameter, a formula for the circumference is

$$C = \pi d$$
or
$$C = 2\pi r$$

EXPERT EXCLUSIVE

Sometimes arcs are designated by three letters. Here, "major arc *AB*" is the same as "arc *AXB*."

An **arc** is a portion of the circumference of a circle. In the figure below, *AB* is an arc of the circle that spans central angle *AOB*. The shorter distance between *A* and *B* along the circle is called the **minor arc**; the longer distance *AXB* is the **major arc**. An arc that is exactly half the circumference of the circle is called a **semicircle** (in other words, half a circle).

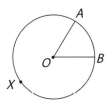

The length of an arc is the same fraction of a circle's circumference as its degree measure is of the degree measure of the circle (360°). For an arc with a central angle measuring *n* degrees,

$$\text{Arc length} = \left(\frac{n}{360}\right)(\text{circumference})$$

$$= \frac{n}{360} \times 2\pi r$$

Example:

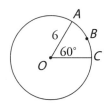

What is the length of arc *ABC* of the circle with center *O* above?

Since circumference = $2\pi r$ and the radius is 6, the circumference is $2 \times \pi \times 6 = 12\pi$.

Since $\angle AOC$ measures 60°, the arc is $\frac{60}{360}$, or one-sixth, of the circumference.

Therefore, the length of the arc is one-sixth of 12π, or 2π.

Inscribed Angle and Arc Length

An **inscribed angle** is one that opens up from the edge of a circle instead of its center. Here, angle *ABC* is inscribed.

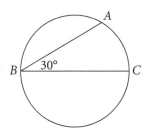

An inscribed angle also has a relationship with minor arc length. For an inscribed angle measuring n degrees,

$$\text{Arc length} = \left(\frac{n}{180}\right) \times \text{circumference}$$

EXPERT EXCLUSIVE

If a right triangle is inscribed in a circle, its hypotenuse will be the circle's diameter.

In other words, an angle that's inscribed defines an arc twice as long as one defined by a central angle of equal angle measure.

Area of a Circle

The area of a circle is given by this formula:

$$\boxed{\text{Area} = \pi r^2}$$

A **sector** is a portion of the circle bounded by two radii and an arc. In the circle below with center O, OAB is a sector. To determine the area of a sector of a circle, use the same method we used to find the length of an arc: Determine what fraction of 360° is in the degree measure of the central angle of the sector, then multiply that fraction by the area of the circle.

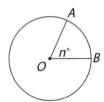

$$\text{Area of sector} = \left(\frac{n}{360}\right) \times (\text{Area of circle})$$

$$= \frac{n}{360} \times \pi r^2$$

Example:

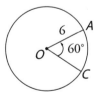

What is the area of sector AOC in the circle with center O above?

Since $\angle AOC$ measures 60°, a 60° "slice" is $\dfrac{60}{360}$, or one-sixth, of the circle. So the sector has area $\dfrac{1}{6} \times \pi r^2 = \dfrac{1}{6} \times \pi(6)^2 = \dfrac{1}{6} \times 36\pi = 6\pi$.

CIRCLES PRACTICE SET

Answers are on page 659.

1. If the area of a circle is 64π, then the circumference of the circle is

   ○ 8π

   ○ 16π

   ○ 32π

   ○ 64π

   ○ 128π

2. If the circumference of a circle is 1, what is the radius of the circle?

   ○ $\dfrac{1}{2\pi}$

   ○ $\dfrac{1}{\pi}$

   ○ $\dfrac{1}{2}$

   ○ $\dfrac{\pi}{2}$

   ○ π

3.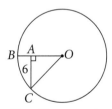

   Note: Figure not drawn to scale.

   In the figure above, if the area of the circle with center O is 100π and CA has a length of 6, what is the length of AB?

   ○ 2

   ○ 3

   ○ 4

   ○ 5

   ○ 6

4.

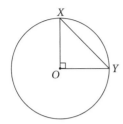

Note: Figure not drawn to scale.

In the figure above, O is the center of the circle. If the area of triangle XOY is 25, what is the area of the circle?

○ 25π

○ $25\pi\sqrt{2}$

○ 50π

○ $50\pi\sqrt{3}$

○ 625π

5.

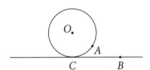

Note: Figure not drawn to scale.

In the figure above, O is the center of the circle with radius x (not shown), and $\overline{OB}$ passes through A. If $\overline{CB}$ is tangent to the circle at C and $\overline{CB} = 2x$, what is the measure of $\overline{AB}$ (not shown)?

○ $x\sqrt{5} - x$

○ $x\sqrt{5}$

○ 5

○ $5x - x$

○ $5x$

Advanced

6. If an arc with a length of 12π is $\dfrac{3}{4}$ of the circumference of a circle, what is the shortest distance between the endpoints of the arc?

○ 4

○ $4\sqrt{2}$

○ 8

○ $8\sqrt{2}$

○ 16

7.

The total area of the four equal circles in the figure above is 36π, and the circles are all tangent to one another. What is the diameter of the small circle?

○ $6\sqrt{2}$

○ $6 + \sqrt{2}$

○ $3\sqrt{2} - 3$

○ $6\sqrt{2} - 6$

○ $6\sqrt{2} + 6$

EXPERT EXCLUSIVE

Be goal oriented in multiple-figure problems. It can be very easy to start calculating measurements of things that have nothing to do with the answer. Doing so will only cost you time.

MULTIPLE FIGURES

You can expect to see some problems on the exam that deal with multiple figures. They test your understanding of various geometrical concepts and relationships, not just your ability to memorize a few formulas. The hypotenuse of a right triangle may be the side of a neighboring rectangle or the diameter of a circumscribed circle. Keep looking for the relationships between the different figures until you find one that leads you to the answer.

One common kind of multiple-figures question involves irregularly shaped regions formed by two or more overlapping figures, often with one region shaded. When you are asked to find the area of such a region, either or both of the following methods may work:

(1) Break up that shaded area into smaller pieces you know the formula for; find the area of each using the proper formula; add those areas together.

(2) Find the area of the whole figure and the area of the unshaded region and subtract the latter from the former.

Example:

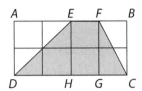

Rectangle *ABCD* above has an area of 72 and is composed of 8 equal squares. Find the area of the shaded region.

For this problem, you can use either of the two approaches. First, divide 8 into 72 to get the area of each square, which is 9. Since the area of a square equals the length of its side squared, each side of the small squares must have length 3. Now you have a choice of methods.

(1) You can break up the trapezoid into right triangle *DEH*, rectangle *EFGH*, and right triangle *FGC*. The area of triangle *DEH* is $\frac{1}{2} \times 6 \times 6$, or 18. The area of rectangle *EFGH* is 3×6, or 18. The area of triangle *FGC* is $\frac{1}{2} \times 6 \times 3$, or 9. The total area is $18 + 18 + 9$, or 45.

(2) The area of the whole rectangle *ABCD* is 72. The area of unshaded triangle *AED* is $\frac{1}{2} \times 6 \times 6$, or 18. The area of unshaded triangle *FBC* is $\frac{1}{2} \times 6 \times 3$, or 9.

Therefore, the total unshaded area is $18 + 9 = 27$. The area of the shaded region is the area of the rectangle minus the unshaded area, or $72 - 27 = 45$.

Inscribed and Circumscribed Figures

A polygon is **inscribed** in a circle if all the vertices of the polygon lie on the circle. A polygon is **circumscribed** about a circle if all the sides of the polygon are tangent to the circle.

Square *ABCD* is inscribed in circle *O*.
(We can also say that circle *O* is circumscribed about square *ABCD*.)

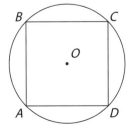

Square *PQRS* is circumscribed about circle *O*.
(We can also say that circle *O* is inscribed in square *PQRS*.)

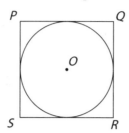

A triangle inscribed in a semicircle such that one side of the triangle coincides with the diameter of the semicircle is a right triangle.

MULTIPLE FIGURES PRACTICE SET

Answers are on page 662.

1. A triangle of height 5 and base 4 has an area exactly $\frac{1}{3}$ that of a rectangle with height 5. What is the width of the rectangle?

   ○ 4

   ○ 5

   ○ 6

   ○ 8

   ○ 10

2.

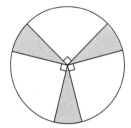

In the circle above, three right angles have vertices at the center of the circle. If the radius of the circle is 8, what is the combined area of the shaded regions?

○ 8π

○ 9π

○ 12π

○ 13π

○ 16π

3.

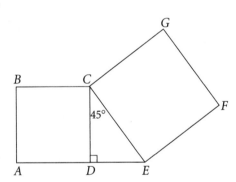

Note: Figure not drawn to scale.

In the figure above, *ABCD* and *CEFG* are squares. If the area of *CEFG* is 36, what is the area of *ABCD*?

○ 6

○ 6√2

○ 9

○ 18

○ 24

4. A triangle and a circle have equal areas. If the base of the triangle and the diameter of the circle each have length 5, what is the height of the triangle?

   ○ $\dfrac{5}{2}$

   ○ $\dfrac{5}{2}\pi$

   ○ 5π

   ○ 10π

   ○ It cannot be determined from the information given.

Advanced

5.

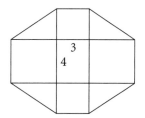

The figure above is composed of 9 regions: 4 squares, 4 triangles, and 1 rectangle. If the rectangle has length 4 and width 3, what is the perimeter of the entire figure?

6.

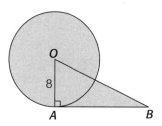

Note: Figure not drawn to scale.

In the figure above, if radius OA is 8 and the area of right triangle OAB is 32, what is the area of the shaded region?

   ○ $64\pi + 32$

   ○ $60\pi + 32$

   ○ $56\pi + 32$

   ○ $32\pi + 32$

   ○ $16\pi + 32$

SOLIDS

A **solid** is a three-dimensional figure (a figure having length, width, and height) and is, therefore, rather difficult to represent accurately on a two-dimensional page. Figures are drawn "in perspective," giving them the appearance of depth. If a diagram represents a three-dimensional figure, that fact will be specified in the accompanying text.

Fortunately, only a few types of solids appear with any frequency on the GMAT: rectangular solids (including cubes) and cylinders.

Other types, such as spheres, may appear, but these questions typically will involve only understanding the solid's properties and not any special formula. Here are the terms used to describe the common solids:

Vertex: The vertices of a solid are the points at its corners. For example, a cube has 8 vertices.

Edge: The edges of a solid are the line segments that connect the vertices and form the sides of each face of the solid. A cube has 12 edges.

Face: The faces of a solid are the polygons that are the boundaries of the solid. A cube has 6 faces, all squares.

Volume: The volume of a solid is the amount of space enclosed by that solid. The volume of any uniform solid is equal to the area of its base times its height.

Surface Area: In general, the surface area of a solid is equal to the sum of the areas of the solid's faces.

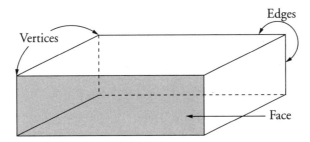

Rectangular Solid

This is a solid with six rectangular faces (all edges meet at right angles). Examples are cereal boxes, bricks, etc.

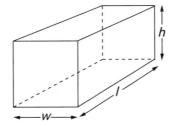

Volume = area of base × height = length × width × height.

$$V = \ell \times w \times h$$

Surface Area = sum of areas of faces.

$$SA = 2\ell w + 2\ell h + 2wh$$

***Diagonals in Rectangular Solids*:** It's common for upper-level geometry questions to ask you to calculate the length of a rectangular solid's diagonal (one that runs from lower-front-left to upper-back-right, for example).

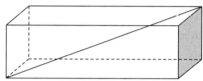

There's a simple formula to calculate the diagonal. It looks a lot like the Pythagorean theorem (in fact, it's derived using that theorem).

$$\text{diagonal}^2 = \text{length}^2 + \text{width}^2 + \text{height}^2$$

***Cube*:** A special rectangular solid with all edges equal ($\ell = w = h$), such as a die or a sugar cube. All faces of a cube are squares.

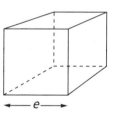

EXPERT EXCLUSIVE

The longest distance between any two points on the surface of a rectangular solid is the diagonal.

Volume = area of base × height.

$$V = l \times w \times h = e^3$$

Surface Area = sum of areas of faces.

$$SA = 2\ell w + 2\ell h + 2wh = 6e^2$$

Cylinder

This is a uniform solid whose horizontal cross section is a circle; for example, a soup can. We need two pieces of information for a cylinder: the radius of the base and the height.

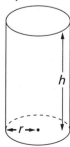

Volume = area of base × height.

$$V = \pi r^2 \times h$$

Lateral Surface Area (LSA) = circumference of base × height.

$$LSA = 2\pi r \times h$$

Total Surface Area = areas of bases + LSA.

$$SA = 2\pi r^2 + 2\pi rh$$

You can think of the surface area of a cylinder as having two parts: One part is the top and bottom (the circles), and the other part is the lateral surface. In a can, for example, the area of either the top or the bottom is just the area of the circle, or lid, which represents the top; hence, πr^2 for the top and πr^2 for the bottom, yielding a total of $2\pi r^2$. For the lateral surface, the area around the can, think of removing the can's label. When unrolled, it's actually in the shape of a rectangle. One side is the height of the can, and the other side is the distance around the circle, or circumference. Hence, its area is $h \times (2\pi r)$, or $2\pi rh$. Thus, the total surface area is $2\pi r^2 + 2\pi rh$.

Sphere

A sphere is made up of all the points in space a certain distance from a center point; it's like a three-dimensional circle. The distance from the center to a point on the sphere is the radius of the sphere. A basketball is a good example of a sphere. A sphere is not a uniform solid; the cross sections are all circles, but they are of different sizes. (In other words, a slice of a basketball from the middle is bigger than a slice from the top.)

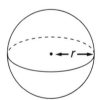

It is not important to know how to find the volume or surface area of a sphere, but occasionally a question might require you to understand what a sphere is.

SOLIDS PRACTICE SET

Answers are on page 664.

1. What is the volume of a cube with sides that are 5 cm in length?

   ○ 15 cm³

   ○ 25 cm³

   ○ 30 cm³

   ○ 125 cm³

   ○ 150 cm³

2. What is the volume of a cylinder with radius of 11 cm and a height of 4 cm?

   ○ 44π cm³

   ○ 88π cm³

   ○ 161.3π cm³

   ○ 484π cm³

   ○ 968π cm³

3. What is the surface area of a rectangular prism with a length of 10 inches, a width of 20 inches, and a height of 14 inches?

   ○ 44 in²

   ○ 620 in²

   ○ 1,240 in²

   ○ 2,480 in²

   ○ 2,800 in²

4. What is the surface area of a cylinder with a base radius of 7 meters and a height of 3 meters?

   ○ 21π m²

   ○ 42π m²

   ○ 49π m²

   ○ 98π m²

   ○ 140π m²

5. If the volume of the rectangular prism below is 1,960 mm³, what is the value of x?

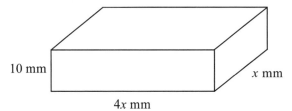

Note: Figure not drawn to scale.

- ○ 7
- ○ 14
- ○ 22.14
- ○ 49
- ○ 390

Advanced

6. What is the length of an edge of a cube whose surface area is 486 m²?

- ○ 9 m
- ○ 54 m
- ○ 81 m
- ○ 121.5 m
- ○ 243 m

7. If the volume of a cylinder is 600π mm³ and the height is 6 mm, what is the diameter of the cylinder?

- ○ 5 mm
- ○ 10 mm
- ○ 20 mm
- ○ 50 mm
- ○ 100 mm

ANSWERS AND EXPLANATIONS FOR MATH SKILLS REFRESHER PRACTICE SETS

NUMBER OPERATIONS PRACTICE SET ANSWERS AND EXPLANATIONS

1. D

You are asked which of the five values is less than $\frac{1}{6}$. Keep in mind that $\frac{1}{6} = 0.166\overline{6}$ (the bar indicates that the 6 repeats forever).

Choice (A): $0.1667 > 0.166\overline{6}$. No good.

Choice (B): $\frac{3}{18} = \frac{\cancel{3}^1}{\cancel{18}_6} = \frac{1}{6}$. No good.

Choice (C): $0.167 > 0.16\overline{6}$. No good.

Choice (D): 0.1666 is less than $0.166\overline{6}$, which has 6s trailing on to the right forever $(0.1666666666\ldots)$. That means (D) is less than $\frac{1}{6}$, so this is the correct answer.

Choice (E): $\frac{1}{6} = \frac{8}{48}$ and $\frac{8}{47} > \frac{8}{48}$; therefore, $\frac{8}{47} > \frac{1}{6}$. No good.

> **EXPERT EXCLUSIVE**
>
> Knowing that $\frac{1}{6} = 0.1\overline{6}$ would really pay off here. Memorize the most common equivalencies by test day.

2. C

Using the distributive law: $25(27 + 29 + 31)$

$$25(27) + 25(29) + 25(31)$$

That eliminates (A), (B), and (E), which all incorrectly distribute the 25. (D) confuses the operations, switching multiplication with addition. The right answer, (C), factors two of the 25s back together again:

$$25(27) + 25(29) + 25(31)$$
$$25(27) + 25(29 + 31)$$

> **EXPERT EXCLUSIVE**
>
> Notice that you didn't have to do $27 + 29 + 31 = 87$ or $25 \times 87 = 2,175$. Long arithmetic calculations are usually not necessary for GMAT problems.

3. C

You've got two choices here: (1) do the subtraction inside the parentheses first, then multiply or (2) distribute first, then multiply, then subtract.

Option 1: $\frac{7}{5} \times \left(\frac{3}{7} - \frac{2}{5} \right)$

Common denominators:

$$\frac{7}{5} \times \left(\frac{3 \times 5}{7 \times 5} - \frac{2 \times 7}{5 \times 7} \right)$$

$$\frac{7}{5} \times \left(\frac{15}{35} - \frac{14}{35} \right)$$

$$\frac{7}{5} \times \frac{1}{35}$$

> **EXPERT EXCLUSIVE**
>
> There's rarely one "right way" to do GMAT arithmetic. As long as you cancel common factors to keep things easy, do whichever arithmetic approach feels more straightforward to you.

Cancel common factors:	$\dfrac{\cancel{7}^{1}}{5} \times \dfrac{1}{\cancel{35}_{5}} = \dfrac{1}{5} \times \dfrac{1}{5}$
	$\dfrac{1}{25}$
Option 2:	$\dfrac{7}{5} \times \left(\dfrac{3}{7} - \dfrac{2}{5} \right)$
Distribute:	$\left(\dfrac{7}{5} \times \dfrac{3}{7} \right) - \left(\dfrac{7}{5} \times \dfrac{2}{5} \right)$
Cancel common factors:	$\left(\dfrac{\cancel{7}^{1}}{5} \times \dfrac{3}{\cancel{7}_{1}} \right) - \left(\dfrac{7}{5} \times \dfrac{2}{5} \right)$
	$\dfrac{3}{5} - \dfrac{14}{25}$
Common denominators:	$\dfrac{3 \times 5}{5 \times 5} - \dfrac{14}{25}$
Subtract:	$\dfrac{15}{25} - \dfrac{14}{25}$
	$\dfrac{1}{25}$

4. $\dfrac{5}{36}$

Like many GMAT problems, you need to think carefully about how you're going to approach this one. The easiest way to compare these fractions is to look for a benchmark. They are all around $\dfrac{1}{2}$. Because $\dfrac{5}{9}$ is the only fraction above $\dfrac{1}{2}$, that's the biggest. Because $\dfrac{5}{12}$ is the fraction furthest from $\dfrac{1}{2}$, it is the smallest.

Alternately, you could quickly compare $\dfrac{5}{12}$, $\dfrac{23}{48}$, and $\dfrac{11}{24}$ by themselves because they could be easily converted to have a common denominator: $\dfrac{5}{12} = \dfrac{20}{48}$; $\dfrac{11}{24} = \dfrac{22}{48}$. Of this group, $\dfrac{5}{12}$ is the smallest, and $\dfrac{23}{48}$ is the largest.

Of the two that remain, $\dfrac{5}{9}$ is the larger and $\dfrac{3}{7}$ is the smaller. (This could be determined by converting to decimal equivalents, comparing with common denominators, using a benchmark, or using the "cross multiply" method—whichever you find easiest.)

So to determine the largest of all five, you need to compare $\frac{5}{9}$ and $\frac{23}{48}$. To determine the smallest, you need to compare $\frac{3}{7}$ and $\frac{5}{12}$. Let's look at the cross multiplication method:

$$\frac{5}{9} \; vs \; \frac{23}{48} \qquad\qquad \frac{3}{7} \; vs \; \frac{5}{12}$$

$$(5 \times 48) \; vs \; (23 \times 9) \qquad\qquad (3 \times 12) \; vs \; (5 \times 7)$$

$$240 \; vs \; 207 \qquad\qquad 36 \; vs \; 35$$

$$\frac{5}{9} \text{ is bigger.} \qquad\qquad \frac{5}{12} \text{ is smaller.}$$

Now, just finish off with the subtraction by finding the LCM:

$$\frac{5}{9} - \frac{5}{12}$$

$$\frac{5 \times 4}{9 \times 4} - \frac{5 \times 3}{12 \times 3}$$

$$\frac{20}{36} - \frac{15}{36}$$

$$\frac{5}{36}$$

Advanced

5. E

In statement I, if we were to subtract a smaller number from 1,000, our result would be larger. Since substituting 120 for 160 in this expression would produce a greater result, we can eliminate choices (A) and (C), which do not include statement I.

Statement II is equivalent to $\frac{160}{161}$. If we replaced 160 with 120, our result would be $\frac{120}{121}$. Which is greater?

That's a difficult comparison to make directly, but it's not too difficult to compare them each to a benchmark value. Both fractions are a tiny bit less than 1.

Imagine a number line: $\frac{160}{161}$ is $\frac{1}{161}$ to the left of (or less than) 1.

$\frac{120}{121}$ is $\frac{1}{121}$ to the left of (or less than) 1.

EXPERT EXCLUSIVE

Dividing by fractions is something the GMAT is very likely to call on you to do.

Because $\dfrac{1}{161}$ is less than $\dfrac{1}{121}$, $\dfrac{160}{161}$ is *closer* to 1. It's a little to the right of, and therefore greater than, $\dfrac{120}{121}$. That eliminates (D).

In statement III, we're dividing 1 by a fraction, which is the same as multiplying 1 by the reciprocal of the fraction. To get a *larger* reciprocal, we need to start with a *smaller* fraction. Which is smaller, $1-\dfrac{1}{160}$ or $1-\dfrac{1}{120}$? We know that $1-\dfrac{1}{120}$ is smaller, since it is farther to the left from 1 on the number line. By replacing 160 with 120, we get a smaller fraction in the denominator of our expression and, therefore, a *larger* reciprocal. That gives the expression a larger value. So III is part of the correct answer. If this is difficult to see, we can actually do the math:

$$\dfrac{1}{1-\dfrac{1}{160}} = \dfrac{1}{\dfrac{159}{160}} = 1 \times \dfrac{160}{159} = 1\dfrac{1}{159}$$

$$\dfrac{1}{1-\dfrac{1}{120}} = \dfrac{1}{\dfrac{119}{120}} = 1 \times \dfrac{120}{119} = 1\dfrac{1}{119}$$

$$1\dfrac{1}{119} > 1\dfrac{1}{159}$$

Statements I and III are larger when 160 is replaced with 120, so the answer is choice (E).

NUMBER PROPERTIES ANSWERS AND EXPLANATIONS

1. A

Since Even × Anything = Even, the only way to have the product of three integers be odd is if all those integers are themselves odd. (Picking Numbers would make this more concrete: $3 \times 3 \times 5 = 45$ or $3 \times 3 \times 3 = 27$, but $2 \times 3 \times 3 = 18$.)

Therefore, the sum of any two of these numbers would be Odd + Odd, which is Even. (A) is correct.

Knowing that (A) must be true means that the others can't be correct. The most efficient approach would be to stop work after (A). For the sake of reinforcing the rules, though, let's look at the others. (B) can be eliminated because Odd × Odd = Odd. (C) is wrong because Odd + Odd = Even, and then Even + Odd = Odd. So (D) is not the correct answer. An odd number divided by 3 cannot be an even number. Otherwise, 2 would be a factor of the odd number, and then it would not be odd. (E) is wrong because *median* means "middle value"; in a set of three odd numbers, the median would have to be odd.

> **EXPERT EXCLUSIVE**
>
> The solutions to many GMAT problems depend upon making deductions from the information given in the question stem before charging ahead to the answer choices.

2. E

Pick a number for P that fits the description ("a remainder of 4 when divided by 9"). You could pick 13, but if you try 13 in each answer choice, you'll find that all five seem to be true. No worries, just pick a different number. We could go up by 9 to 22 or down by 9 to 4. Either one is fine, although 4 is a little more manageable than 22. And either 22 or 4 is consistent with every answer choice but (E). So (E) is the correct answer.

EXPERT EXCLUSIVE

See how much simpler the Picking Numbers approach is? Picking Numbers is almost always the best approach to any question involving remainders.

Here's the "straightforward math" way to do it. We need to find the one choice that isn't *always* true. To find it, let's test each choice. Choice (A) is always true: Since $P \div 9$ has a remainder of 4, P is 4 greater than some multiple of 9, so the number 4 less than P is a multiple of 9.

If $P - 4$ is a multiple of 9, then the next multiple of 9 would be $(P - 4) + 9$, or $P + 5$; thus, choice (B) is also true. With choice (C), we know that since $P - 4$ is a multiple of 9, it is also a multiple of 3. By adding 3s, we know that $(P - 4) + 3$, or $P - 1$, and $(P - 4) + 3 + 3$, or $P + 2$, are also multiples of 3. Choice (C) must be true. And since $P - 1$ is a multiple of 3, when P is divided by 3, it will have a remainder of 1, and choice (D) is always true.

This leaves only choice (E). In simpler terms, choice (E) states that P is always odd. Since multiples of 9 are alternately odd and even (9, 18, 27, 36 . . .), $P - 4$ could be either even or odd, so P also could be either even or odd. Choice (E) is not always true, so it is the correct answer choice.

3. B

Like many GMAT problems, this one gets much easier if you use the information in the question stem to make deductions. We are told that $ab + b$ is odd. Since only Even + Odd equals Odd, we know that either ab is odd and b even, or vice versa. But if b were even, then ab would be even too. So it must be the other way around: b is odd and ab even. And if ab is even and b is odd, a must be even. So we've deduced that b is odd and a is even. Now it's clear that only Statement II is true, so (B) is the answer.

We could also have worked backwards from the statements. Statement I says that both a and b are odd. That would produce the following substitution:

$ab + b$

(Odd × Odd) + Odd

Odd + Odd

Even

But we are told that $ab + b$ is odd, so Statement I is false; (A), (D), and (E) are eliminated.

Statement III explicitly violates the question stem, which only works if *b* is odd. So (C) is eliminated, and (B) is shown to be correct.

Picking Numbers would also work well on this question. Let's say that *b* = 3.

> **EXPERT EXCLUSIVE**
>
> Many Number Properties questions are very abstract but can be quickly solved by Picking Numbers.

Now we have 3*a* + 3 = Odd. Let's say that the odd number is 9.

3*a* + 3 = 9
3*a* = 6
a = 2

b = 3 and *a* = 2 is consistent with Statement II, so only (B) and (D) remain as possible answers. You'd have to test a few other numbers to be sure that no odd value of *a* is possible.

4. 2

If *y* is a prime number greater than 2, it must be odd. Since $8 = 2 \times 2 \times 2$, the only odd factors of *x* will be 1 and *y* itself.

Picking Numbers works great here, getting us around the highly abstract "math solution." Say *y* = 3. Then *x* = 24. The only odd factors of 24 are 1 and 3.

Advanced

5. 1

$15^2 = (15)(15) = (3 \times 5)^2$. So 3 and 5 are the *two* distinct prime factors of 15^2.

$64^3 = (2 \times 2 \times 2 \times 2 \times 2 \times 2)^3$. So 2 is the *one* distinct prime factor of 64^3. Don't forget to do the last part of the problem—find the positive difference between the number of distinct prime factors: $2 - 1 = 1$.

> **EXPERT EXCLUSIVE**
>
> Some GMAT Quant problems are difficult only because they look intimidating. Get past the scariness of 15^2 and 64^3 by factoring, and this problem isn't too bad.

6. 72

Each third of the wire is cut into 4, 6, and 8 parts respectively, and all the resulting segments have integer lengths. This means that each third of the wire has a length that is evenly divisible by 4, 6, and 8. The smallest positive integer divisible by 4, 6, and 8 is 24, so each third of the wire has a minimum length of 24. So the minimum length of the whole wire is three times 24, or 72.

CLASSIC FORMULAS PRACTICE SET ANSWERS AND EXPLANATIONS

1. C

If we translate the English into math, "the average of b and 2 equals the average of b, 3, and 4," becomes

$$\frac{b+2}{2} = \frac{b+3+4}{3}$$

EXPERT EXCLUSIVE

When the numbers are pretty small, so the "balance" approach doesn't save you much work. But try using it on this problem so that you get comfortable with it.

Cross multiply: $\qquad 3(b + 2) = 2(b + 7)$

Distribute: $\qquad\qquad 3b + 6 = 2b + 14$

Subtract $2b$ from each side: $b + 6 = 14$

Subtract 6 from each side: $\qquad b = 8$

We also could have tested numbers from the answer choices by substituting them for b to find the one that makes the averages equal. This technique is called Backsolving, and it's discussed in depth in the Problem Solving chapter of this book.

2. 7

To average 2 hours a day over 6 days, the violinist must practice 2×6, or 12 hours. From Monday through Friday, the violinist practices 1 hour per day. That's a total of 5 hours. To total 12 hours, she must practice $12 - 5$, or 7, hours on Saturday.

EXPERT EXCLUSIVE

Don't shy away from an answer just because it's smaller or larger than the others. Sometimes those answers are correct!

We also could have solved this using the "balance" approach:

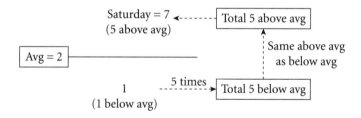

3. A

Here's how this rate conversion should be set up:

$$\frac{1{,}800 \text{ miles}}{\text{hour}} \times \frac{\text{hour}}{60 \text{ minutes}} \times \frac{\text{minute}}{60 \text{ seconds}} \times 24 \text{ seconds}$$

$$\frac{1{,}800 \text{ miles}}{\cancel{\text{hour}}} \times \frac{\cancel{\text{hour}}}{60 \cancel{\text{ minutes}}} \times \frac{\cancel{\text{minute}}}{60 \cancel{\text{ seconds}}} \times 24 \cancel{\text{ seconds}}$$

$$\frac{1{,}800 \times 24 \text{ miles}}{60 \times 60}$$

$$\frac{\cancel{1{,}800}^{\,30} \times \cancel{24}^{\,2} \text{ miles}}{\cancel{60}^{\,1} \times \cancel{60}^{\,5}} = \frac{60}{5} \text{ miles} = 12 \text{ miles}$$

4. D

Since the order in which he selects the pieces of an outfit doesn't really matter (it's safe to assume that he won't try to wear his jacket on his legs), we are dealing with a Combinations question. He's choosing 1 of his 4 pairs of pants, so that's literally "4 choose 1," or 4C1. Similarly, he can choose 6C1 shirts and 3C1 jackets.

4C1 and 6C1 and 3C1

$$= \frac{4!}{1!3!} \times \frac{6!}{1!5!} \times \frac{3!}{1!2!}$$

$$= \frac{4 \times 3 \times 2 \times 1}{1 \times 3 \times 2 \times 1} \times \frac{6 \times 5 \times 4 \times 3 \times 2 \times 1}{1 \times 5 \times 4 \times 3 \times 2 \times 1} \times \frac{3 \times 2 \times 1}{1 \times 2 \times 1}$$

$$= 4 \times 6 \times 3$$

$$= 72$$

If instead of doing this calculation, you just said, "There's 4 pants, and Ron takes 1 of them, so there's 4 possible choices for pants," you wouldn't have been wrong to do so. *n*C1 always equals *n*. Incidentally, *n*C*n* always equals 1.

5. D

If 6 numbers have an average of 6, their sum is 6 × 6, or 36. To subtract 3 from 4 of the numbers, we subtract 4 × 3, or 12, from the sum. The new sum is 36 − 12, or 24; the new average is $\frac{24}{6}$ or 4.

You also could have picked six numbers that average to be 6. Six 6s would be a great choice. Then subtract 3 from four of those, and you've got 3, 3, 3, 3, 6, and 6. Average them, and you'll get 4.

6. B

This question involves two separate but related applications of the average formula. First we can figure out the sum of the first four numbers:

$$8.75 = \frac{\text{sum}}{4}$$

$$\text{sum} = 8.75 \times 4$$

$$\text{sum} = 35$$

Now we're adding another number. The sum will be 35 + *n*, and there will be 5 numbers that together average 8. So our second use of the average formula is as follows:

$$8 = \frac{35 + n}{5}$$

$$40 = 35 + n$$

$$n = 5$$

> **EXPERT EXCLUSIVE**
>
> Read the question carefully! Many intermediate and difficult GMAT questions have some kind of "twist."

EXPERT EXCLUSIVE

The larger the values, the more helpful the "balance" approach will be.

We also could have solved this using the "balance" approach, setting the value of all four of the first numbers to equal the first average, 8.75:

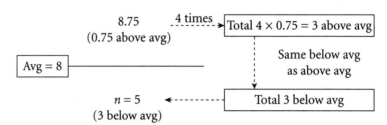

7. 93

This is really just the same problem as the one before. His first tests total

$$85 = \frac{\text{sum}}{3}$$

$$\text{sum} = 85 \times 3$$

$$\text{sum} = 255$$

Now we add in the fourth test (t for test), and his average rises to 85 + 2, or 87:

$$87 = \frac{255 + t}{4}$$

$$348 = 255 + t$$

$$t = 93$$

Now the numbers are getting bigger, and the "balance" approach can save us lots of annoying arithmetic:

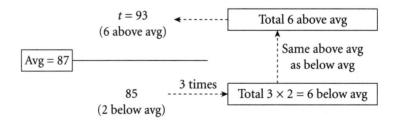

8. B

Since the question addresses two people working together, we'll use the combined work formula to figure out Lucy's time by herself:

$$4 = \frac{L \times 12}{L + 12}$$

Cross multiply: $\qquad\qquad 4L + 48 = 12L$

Subtract $4L$ from each side: $\qquad 48 = 8L$

Divide by 8: $\qquad\qquad\qquad 6 = L$

But the question asks for the time it would take Lucy to do *half* the job, not the whole thing. If Lucy takes 6 hours to do the whole job, she can get half the job done in half the time, 3 hours.

9. D

Whether it's the "neither lettuce nor tomatoes" phrase that tipped you off or the fact that 30 + 35 + 5 doesn't equal 50, the key to solving this one quickly is recognizing it as an Overlapping Sets question. This one fits the formula very well:

Total = Group 1 + Group 2 − Both + Neither
Total = Lettuce + Tomatoes − Both + Neither
50 = 30 + 35 − Both + 5
50 = 70 − Both
Both = 20

You could also use the chart. Here's how you would enter the data:

	with lettuce	no lettuce	Total
with tomatoes	?		35
no tomatoes		5	
Total	30		50

And here's how you might complete it to solve for the sandwiches with both lettuce and tomatoes:

	with lettuce	no lettuce	Total
with tomatoes	20		35
no tomatoes	10	5	15
Total	30		50

Advanced

10. D

In terms of y, the average of $2y$ and $\frac{2y}{3}$ is

$$\frac{2y+\frac{2y}{3}}{2} = \frac{\frac{6y}{3}+\frac{2y}{3}}{2}$$

$$= \frac{8y}{3} \times \frac{1}{2}$$

$$= \frac{8y}{6}$$

$$= \frac{4y}{3}$$

Next, solve for y as the average of $27 - x$, $x - 8$, and $3x + 11$:

$$y = \frac{27 - x + x - 8 + 3x + 11}{3}$$

$$y = \frac{30 + 3x}{3}$$

$$y = \frac{3(x + 10)}{3}$$

$$y = x + 10$$

EXPERT EXCLUSIVE

Most complex average questions are solved much more efficiently by Picking Numbers than by algebra.

Plug this into $\frac{4y}{3}$:

$$= \frac{4(x + 10)}{3}$$

$$= \frac{4x + 40}{3}$$

We also could have Picked Numbers and avoided much of the algebra. Let's say that $x = 2$. Now instead of averaging $27 - x$, $x - 8$, and $3x + 11$, we're averaging 25, −6, and 17. That's much nicer.

$$\frac{25 - 6 + 17}{3} = \frac{36}{3} = 12$$

So $y = 12$. Now we solve for the average of $2(12)$ and $\frac{2(12)}{3}$, or 24 and 8:

$$\frac{24 + 8}{2} = \frac{32}{2} = 16$$

Plug $x = 2$ into all the answer choices, and only (D) yields 16.

11. $46\frac{2}{3}$ or $\frac{140}{3}$

Whenever a GMAT question gives you a problem about someone (or something) moving at two different speeds at two different times, the Rate-Time-Distance chart can carry you through:

	Rate	Time	Distance
part 1 of trip	40		30
part 2 of trip	50		75
entire trip			

Now fill in the remaining boxes, remembering that the chart multiplies from left to right and adds from top to bottom for Time and Distance (not for Rate):

	Rate	Time	Distance
part 1 of trip	40	$\frac{30}{40} = \frac{3}{4}$	30
part 2 of trip	50	$\frac{75}{50} = \frac{3}{2}$	75
entire trip		$\frac{3}{4} + \frac{3}{2} = \frac{9}{4}$	105

	Rate	Time	Distance
part 1 of trip	40	$\dfrac{3}{4}$	30
part 2 of trip	50	$\dfrac{3}{2}$	75
entire trip	$105 \div \dfrac{9}{4}$	$\dfrac{9}{4}$	105

$$105 \div \frac{9}{4} = \frac{\overset{35}{\cancel{105}} \times 4}{\underset{3}{\cancel{9}}} = \frac{35 \times 4}{3} = \frac{140}{3}$$

12. E

This Combinations question is a little tricky since it asks for *at least* 4 union members to work each shift. So we need to count not only the number of ways to select 4 union and 1 nonunion workers but also the number of ways to select 5 union workers.

There are 8 union workers and 13 total employees. So there must be 13 – 8, or 5, nonunion workers.

We are, therefore, trying to count up the number of ways to choose *either* 4 of 8 union and 1 of 5 nonunion *or* 5 of 8 union.

(8C4 and 5C1) or 8C5

$$\left(\frac{8!}{4!4!} \times \frac{5!}{1!4!} \right) + \frac{8!}{5!3!}$$

$$\left(\frac{\overset{2}{\cancel{8}} \times 7 \times \cancel{6} \times 5 \times \cancel{4 \times 3 \times 2 \times 1}}{\cancel{4} \times \cancel{3 \times 2} \times 1 \times \cancel{4 \times 3 \times 2 \times 1}} \times \frac{5 \times \cancel{4 \times 3 \times 2 \times 1}}{1 \times \cancel{4 \times 3 \times 2 \times 1}} \right) + \frac{8 \times 7 \times \cancel{6} \times \cancel{5 \times 4 \times 3 \times 2 \times 1}}{\cancel{5 \times 4 \times 3 \times 2 \times 1} \times \cancel{3 \times 2} \times 1}$$

$$(2 \times 7 \times 5 \times 5) + 8 \times 7$$

$$350 + 56$$

$$406$$

> **EXPERT EXCLUSIVE**
>
> Use your answer choices to help reduce your work. As soon as you know that "8C4 and 5C1" is 350 and that you still have to add to that number, you know that (E) is the only possible answer.

13. D

This combines Overlapping Sets with Probability. Spotting "both made the honor roll and played varsity sports," should tip us off to Overlapping Sets and inspire us to set up a chart. (The more complex the problem, the more helpful the chart will be.)

	varsity	not varsity	Total
honor roll			
not honor roll			
Total			

Now that our scratch paper is a little more organized, we can enter the data from the question stem:

EXPERT EXCLUSIVE

Many difficult GMAT questions test different content areas simultaneously. Just work one aspect of the problem at a time, instead of trying to do it all at once, and it won't seem so hard.

	varsity	not varsity	Total
honor roll	10		$10 + x$
not honor roll			115
Total	x		150

Looks like we can solve for x pretty straightforwardly:

$$(10 + x) + 115 = 150$$
$$x + 125 = 150$$
$$x = 25$$

And now back to the chart:

	varsity	not varsity	Total
honor roll	10		35
not honor roll			115
Total	25		150

And fill in the rest:

	varsity	not varsity	Total
honor roll	10	25	35
not honor roll	15	100	115
Total	25	125	150

The question asks for the probability that any given student would neither be on the honor roll nor play varsity sports. There are 150 students total and 100 who meet the desired criteria. So the answer is $\frac{100}{150}$, which reduces to $\frac{2}{3}$.

RATIOS PRACTICE SET ANSWERS AND EXPLANATIONS

EXPERT EXCLUSIVE

Did you solve this one as a rate conversion? You weren't wrong to do so.

1. D

Since there are 60 minutes in an hour, the subway will pass $\frac{60}{10}$ or 6 times as many stations in 1 hour as it passes in 10 minutes. In 10 minutes it passes 3 stations; in 60 minutes it must pass 6×3 or 18 stations.

2. B

We are asked which ratio is equivalent to $3\frac{1}{2}$ to $5\frac{1}{4}$. Let's start by converting these out

of mixed numbers, which are hard to use in calculations: $\frac{7}{2}$ to $\frac{21}{4}$.

Use either the fraction form or the colon form to calculate the ratio:

$$\frac{\frac{7}{2}}{\frac{21}{4}} \qquad \frac{7}{2}:\frac{21}{4}$$

$$\frac{7}{2}\times\frac{4}{21} \qquad \frac{14}{4}:\frac{21}{4}$$

$$\frac{\cancel{7}^{1}}{\cancel{2}_{1}}\times\frac{\cancel{4}^{2}}{\cancel{21}_{3}} \qquad 14:21$$

$$\frac{2}{3} \qquad 2:3$$

> **EXPERT EXCLUSIVE**
>
> Think logically about the answers. Just by recognizing that $3\frac{1}{2}$ is smaller than $5\frac{1}{4}$, we can eliminate (D) and (E).

3. B

The ratio of 5 boys to 3 girls tells you that for every 5 boys in the class, there must be 3 girls in the class. So the total number of students in the class must be a multiple of 8, since the smallest possible total is 5 + 3, or 8. Since 36 is not divisible by 8, 36 cannot be the total number of students.

4. B

Since 3 out of 24 students are in student organizations, the remaining 24 − 3, or 21, students are not in student organizations. Therefore, the ratio of students in organizations to students not in organizations is

$$\frac{\#\text{in organizations}}{\#\text{not in organizations}}=\frac{3}{21}=\frac{1}{7}.$$

> **EXPERT EXCLUSIVE**
>
> This is a classic GMAT pattern— to give you information about one part of a situation and then to require you to think about the *other* part in order to solve.

5. 600

The ratio of parts is 4:3:2, making a total of 9 parts. Since 9 parts are equal

to 1,800 votes, each part represents $\frac{1,800}{9}$, or 200 votes. Since Ms. Frau

represents 3 parts, she received a total of 3 × 200, or 600 votes. (Another

way to think about it: Out of every 9 votes, Ms. Frau gets 3, which is

$\frac{3}{9}$ or $\frac{1}{3}$ the total number of votes, and $\frac{1}{3}$ of 1,800 is 600.)

> **EXPERT EXCLUSIVE**
>
> Very rarely is there only one "right way" to solve. Choose the approach that seems easiest to you for the particular question that you're working on.

We could also have solved this algebraically by setting up a proportion with F as Ms. Frau's votes:

$$\frac{3}{9} = \frac{F}{1,800}$$

$$\frac{3}{\cancel{9}^{1}} \times \cancel{1,800}^{200} = F$$

$$600 = F$$

Advanced

6. B

This question mixes two kinds of proportions—ratios and fractions. There's absolutely no information given about actual numbers whatsoever. That's a golden opportunity to Pick Numbers.

In this case, we can pick a number for the total number of mice. Pick one that will facilitate calculations. Let's try 72, since it's a multiple of all the denominators of the fractions in the ratios (2, 3, 8, and 9). Now we can get values for the number of white mice and gray mice by using the given information. For the white mice, we have this:

$\frac{1}{2}$ the # of white mice $= \frac{1}{8}$ the total # of mice $= \frac{1}{8} \times 72 = 9$.

If 9 is $\frac{1}{2}$ of the number of white mice, there must be 2×9, or 18, white mice altogether.

As for the gray mice, the following applies:

$\frac{1}{3}$ the # of gray mice $= \frac{1}{9}$ the total # of mice $= \frac{1}{9} \times 72 = 8$.

If 8 is $\frac{1}{3}$ of the number of gray mice, there must be 3×8, or 24, gray mice altogether. The ratio of white mice to gray mice, then, is 18:24, or 3:4.

PERCENT PRACTICE SET ANSWERS AND EXPLANATIONS

1. C

Percent increase $= \dfrac{\text{amount of increase}}{\text{original whole}} \times 100\%$. So if Edie's average rose from 72 to 84, the amount of the increase is $84 - 72 = 12$. The percent increase is $\dfrac{12}{72} \times 100\%$, or $16\frac{2}{3}\%$, and choice (C) is correct.

2. D

If 25% of the shoes are black, then $100\% - 25\%$, or 75% of the shoes are not black. We have 75% of $24 = \dfrac{3}{4} \times 24 = 18$.

Of course, you also could have solved by calculating the number of black shoes . . .

$$25\% \times 24 = \frac{1}{4} \times 24 = 6$$

. . . and then subtracting from the total:

$$24 - 6 = 18$$

3. B

You first need to find what x is. If 65% of $x = 195$, then $(0.65)(x) = 195$.

$$x = \frac{195}{0.65} = 300$$

Then 75% of 300 = 0.75 × 300 = 225.

4. B

The easiest approach is to pick a sample value for the wholesale cost of the watch and, from that, work out the profit and selling price. As usual with percent problems, it's simplest to pick 100. If the watch cost the store $100, then the profit will be 25% of $100, or $25. The selling price equals the cost to the store plus the profit: $100 + $25, or $125.

The profit represents $\frac{25}{125}$ or $\frac{1}{5}$ of the selling price.
The percent equivalent of $\frac{1}{5}$ is 20%.

> **EXPERT EXCLUSIVE**
> Whenever you can get away with picking 100 as the base value in a question, you should.

5. E

There's a surprisingly large amount of data to keep track of in this question, so setting up your scratchwork carefully and clearly is a good idea. Something like this would work well:

> **EXPERT EXCLUSIVE**
> The harder version of this problem would ask you for the percent change in *noncondominium* units. The answer is a $7\frac{1}{7}$% increase. Try figuring out why.

	2002	2003
# condos	30% of 200	
# units	200	+25% of 200

30% of 200 = (0.3)(200) = 60
200 increased by 25% = 200 + (0.25)(200) = 200 + 50 = 250

	2002	2003
# condos	60	40% of 250
# units	200	250

40% of 250 = (0.4)(250) = 100

	2002	2003
# condos	60	100
# units	200	250

$$\text{Percent increase} = \frac{\text{Amount of increase}}{\text{Original whole}} \times 100\%$$

$$= \frac{40}{60} \times 100\%$$

$$= \frac{2}{3} \times 100\%$$

$$= 66\frac{2}{3}\%$$

Advanced

6. A

Varsity or nonvarsity . . . male or female . . . if you pegged this as an Overlapping Sets question, then you are well on your way to mastering the GMAT.

EXPERT EXCLUSIVE

Overlapping Sets and Percentage calculations are both frequently tested concepts. Getting comfortable with both will really help your score.

	male	female	Total
varsity	50% of male	60% of female	
nonvarsity			
Total	40% of total		

Sure, we could try to impress ourselves with our mathematical abilities by sticking with the percents, but why bother? It is much more efficient to impress ourselves with our *GMAT abilities* by picking 100 as the base value—the total students at the school:

	male	female	Total
varsity	20	60% of female	
nonvarsity			
Total	40		100

Now it's a straightforward matter to find the rest of the data:

	male	female	Total
varsity	20	60% of female	
nonvarsity	20		
Total	40	60	100

	male	female	Total
varsity	20	36	56
nonvarsity	20	24	44
Total	40	60	100

Of the 100 students, 44 don't play a varsity sport—that's 44%.

It is possible to solve this one without Picking Numbers or using the chart. Here's one way to do that.

First, what percent of all students are males who play a varsity sport? We know that 50 percent of the males play a varsity sport; that is, 50 percent (or half) of 40 percent = $0.5 \times 0.4 = 0.20 = 20\%$ of all the students.

Now for the women. We know that 60 percent of the females play a varsity sport; that is, 60 percent of 60 percent = $0.6 \times 0.6 = 0.36 = 36\%$ of all the students.

Sum the percents of the males and females who play a varsity sport: 20% + 36% = 56% of the total student population.

The percent of all students who do *not* play a varsity sport is 100% − 56% = 44%.

7. 35

Increasing 20 by P percent means adding P percent of 20 to 20, so we can write, "Increasing 20 by P percent gives the same result as decreasing 60 by P percent," as

$$20\left(1+\frac{P}{100}\right)=60\left(1-\frac{P}{100}\right) \text{ or } 20+\frac{20P}{100}=60-\frac{60P}{100}$$

This equation simplifies to $\frac{80P}{100}=40$. Therefore, $P=50$. Now we need to find P percent of 70, which is $0.5(70) = 35$.

> **EXPERT EXCLUSIVE**
>
> Don't freak out if you have to read something two or three times. Many GMAT questions are intentionally written to confuse test takers. You have enough time for two or three readings.

POWERS AND ROOTS PRACTICE SET ANSWERS AND EXPLANATIONS

1. D

To multiply or divide a number by a power of 10, we move the decimal point to the right or left, respectively, the same number of places as the number in the exponent.

Multiplying by a negative power of 10 is the same as dividing by a positive power. For instance, $3 \times 10^{-2} = \dfrac{3}{10^2}$. Keeping this in mind, let's go over the choices one by one. Remember: We are looking for the choice that is *not* equal to 0.0675.

Choice (A): $67.5 \times 10^{-3} = 0.0675$. No good.

Choice (B): $6.75 \times 10^{-2} = 0.0675$. No good.

Choice (C): $0.675 \times 10^{-1} = 0.0675$. No good.

Choice (D): $0.00675 \times 10^2 = 0.675$. Because $0.675 \neq 0.0675$, this is the correct answer.

Let's go over choice (E) for practice.

Choice (E): $0.0000675 \times 10^3 = 0.0675$. No good.

2. D

EXPERT EXCLUSIVE

Some GMAT questions require you to use the classic exponent rules, such as $(a^b)^c = a^{bc}$, "in reverse."

Remember the rules for operations with exponents. First you have to get both powers in terms of the same base so you can combine the exponents. Note that the answer choices all have base 2. Start by expressing 4 and 8 as powers of 2:

$(4^x)(8^x) = (2^2)^x \times (2^3)^x$

To raise a power to an exponent, multiply the exponents:

$(2^2)^x = 2^{2x}$
$(2^3)^x = 2^{3x}$

EXPERT EXCLUSIVE

Whenever you see exponents with different bases, break the bases down into prime factors. The problem will probably become much easier.

To multiply powers with the same base, add the exponents:

$2^{2x} \times 2^{3x} = 2^{(2x + 3x)}$
$\qquad = 2^{5x}$

The purpose of this chapter is to brush up your math skills, so it's good to do this problem using prime factors and the exponent rules. But think of how easy this problem would be if you picked $x = 1$ . . . it would just be $4 \times 8 = 32$ and running through the powers of 2 until you came to $2^5 = 32$.

3. E

Look at this question as a good review of the rules for the product of exponential expressions. To make the comparisons easier, transform 8^5 and each of the three options so that they have a common base. Since 2 is the smallest base among the expressions to be compared, choose it as your common base. Since $8^5 = (2^3)^5 = 2^{3 \times 5} = 2^{15}$, look for options equivalent to 2^{15}.

I: $2^5 \times 4^5 = 2^5 \times (2^2)^5 = 2^5 \times 2^{2 \times 5} = 2^5 \times 2^{10} = 2^{5 + 10} = 2^{15}$. Okay.

II: 2^{15}. Okay.

III: $2^5 \times 2^{10} = 2^{5 + 10} = 2^{15}$. Okay.

All three are equivalent to 2^{15} or 8^5.

4. 0

First, solve one equation for s in terms of t:

$st = -4$, so $s = \dfrac{-4}{t}$.

Then plug this into the first equation:

$$s^2 t^{-2} = \frac{s^2}{t^2} = \frac{\left(\dfrac{-4}{t}\right)^2}{t^2} = \frac{\dfrac{16}{t^2}}{t^2} = \frac{16}{t^4} = 1$$

$$16 = t^4$$

$$t = 2 \text{ or } t = -2$$

> **EXPERT EXCLUSIVE**
>
> It's very common to be able to solve for a "chunk," such as $s + t$, without knowing the value of the individual variables themselves. This is especially true for Data Sufficiency questions.

Then plug the value of t back into the second equation to find the value of s:

$s = \dfrac{-4}{2} = -2$ or $s = \dfrac{-4}{-2} = 2$.

So either $s = 2$ and $t = -2$, or $s = -2$ and $t = 2$. In either case, $s + t = 2 + -2 = 0$.

Advanced

5. C

We are told that $x^a x^b = 1$. Since $x^a x^b = x^{a+b}$, we know that $x^{a+b} = 1$. If a power is equal to 1, either the base is 1 or -1, or the exponent is 0. Since we are told $x \neq 1$ or -1, the exponent must be 0; therefore, $a + b = 0$.

This could also be solved with a more traditional algebra approach:

$$x^a x^b = 1$$

$$x^a = \frac{1}{x^b}$$

$$x^a = x^{-b}$$

> **EXPERT EXCLUSIVE**
>
> If two exponential expressions with identical bases are equal, then the exponents themselves are equal. For example, if $2^x = 2^3$, then $x = 3$.

Eliminate bases: $\qquad\qquad a = -b$

Substitute into $a + b$: $\qquad -b + b = 0$

6. 6

This problem really shows the value of thinking about prime factors when faced with exponents and large numbers.

$$5^n > 10,000$$
$$5^n > 10^4$$
$$5^n > (2 \times 5)^4$$
$$5^n > 2^4 \times 5^4$$

Clearly $n > 4$. But how much greater? We can't calculate *exactly* how many powers of 5 are in 2^4, but we don't have to . . . all we have to do to answer the question is figure out the smallest power of 5 that would be bigger than 2^4.

We know that $2^4 = 16$. Then $5^1 = 5$, so $5^5 < 2^4 \times 5^4$. We know that $5^2 = 25$, so $5^6 > 2^4 \times 5^4$.

Therefore, the smallest possible value of n is 6.

It would also have been possible to approximate the values of 5^n.

$5^2 = 25$; $5^3 = 125$, so $5^3 > 100$.

Then $5^4 > 100 \times 5$, or $5^4 > 500$.

$5^5 > 500 \times 5$, or $5^5 > 2,500$.

$5^6 > 2,500 \times 5$, or $5^6 > 12,500$.

Thus, 5^6 must be greater than 10,000, but 5^5 clearly is much less than 10,000. So for 5^n to be greater than 10,000, n must be at least 6.

Algebra Practice Set Answers and Explanations

1. B

This question involves a system of equations. One way to solve a system of two equations is first to solve one of the equations for one of the variables.

Take the equation $8x - 2y = 14$ and solve it for y.

$$8x - 2y = 14$$
$$-2y = 14 - 8x$$
$$-y = 7 - 4x$$
$$y = 4x - 7$$

Now that we have solved one equation for y, we can substitute its value into the other equation. So we take $6x + 7y = 53$ and substitute $4x - 7$ for y:

$$6x + 7(4x - 7) = 53$$

Now we can simplify the equation and solve it for x:

$$6x + 28x - 49 = 53$$
$$34x = 102$$
$$x = 3$$

So (B) is the correct answer. You might have selected (D) if you had reported the value of y.

EXPERT EXCLUSIVE

The right answer to the wrong question is the Quant section's most common wrong answer trap.

2. D

$$p + 3s - (2p - 4s)$$

Distribute the minus sign: $p + 3s - 2p + 4s$

Rearrange (the commutative property): $p - 2p + 3s + 4s$

Combine like terms: $-p + 7s$

That isn't an answer choice, so rearrange: $7s - p$

Choice (B) is the result of not correctly distributing the minus sign in $(2p - 4s)$. If $4s$ is subtracted rather than added, then you would get $-s$ instead of $7s$. Choice (E) is the result of not distributing the minus sign in $(2p - 4s)$, such that $2p$ is added rather than subtracted.

EXPERT EXCLUSIVE

Most commonly made errors will lead to wrong answers. This is why it's critical not to rush through GMAT problems—a careless error will lead you to mistake a wrong answer for a right one.

3. C

This question lends itself to substitution. Solving both equations for one variable would involve too much work. Instead, let's solve one equation, $5j + 3k = 84$, for k:

$$5j + 3k = 84$$
$$3k = 84 - 5j$$
$$k = 28 - \frac{5j}{3}$$

Now let's substitute this value of k into the other equation:

$$7\left(28 - \frac{5j}{3}\right) - 11j = -8$$
$$196 - \frac{35j}{3} - 11j = -8$$
$$\frac{35j}{3} + 11j = 204$$
$$\frac{68j}{3} = 204$$
$$68j = 612$$
$$j = 9$$

EXPERT EXCLUSIVE

It would also have been fairly straightforward to plug the values from the answer choices into the equations, looking for one that works for both.

To find the value of k, replace j with 9 in one of the equations and solve:

$$5(9) + 3k = 84$$
$$45 + 3k = 84$$
$$3k = 39$$
$$k = 13$$

(A) and (B) result from getting 6 instead of 9 as the value of j in $68j = 612$. Plugging that value into $5j + 3k = 84$ would get you $k = 18$, (A). You would get 38, (B), if you added 30 to 84 instead of subtracting when solving $30 + 3k = 84$. (E) has the correct value of 9 for j, but the value of 43 for k is incorrect, perhaps as a result of adding 45 to 84 instead of subtracting when solving $45 + 3k = 84$.

4. E

Functions are all about substitution. To solve for $f(-4)$, substitute -4 for x:

$$f(x) = x^2 + 6$$
Substitute:
$$f(-4) = (-4)^2 + 6$$
$$f(-4) = 16 + 6$$
$$f(-4) = 22$$

Choice (C) could be the result of squaring the sum of -4 and 6. You might have gotten (A) if you got -16 instead of 16 when squaring -4.

5. 4

> **EXPERT EXCLUSIVE**
>
> Simplify expressions whenever you can. And *always* begin by trying to clear up fractions.

About the least efficient thing you could do here is substitute first. It's much easier here to use the rules of exponents to simplify the expression:

Since $8 \div 2 = 4$, $c^8 \div c^7 = c^{8-7} = c^1 = c$, and $d^6 \div d^8 = d^{6-8} = d^{-2}$,

$\dfrac{8c^8 d^6}{2c^7 d^8} = \dfrac{4c}{d^2}$. If $c = 4$ and $d = 2$, then $\dfrac{4c}{d^2} = \dfrac{4(4)}{2^2} = \dfrac{16}{4} = 4$.

6. B

Factoring polynomials (reverse-FOILing) is a vital concept for the GMAT. The goal is to turn $x^2 - 7x + 10$ into $(x + \text{something})$ $(x + \text{something else})$. Those two things will multiply to equal $+10$ and add to be -7.

Two things that multiply together to be 10 are, by definition, factor pairs. It's easiest to list them out:

1 and 10
2 and 5

Since they multiply to be *positive* 10, the pair in question will either both be positive or both be negative. The only way for them to sum to *negative* 7, then, is if they are both negative.

Because $-2 + (-5) = -7$, the two factors are $(x - 2)(x - 5)$. (B) is the latter.

7. A

This question involves an equation with two variables. You're asked to solve it for one variable, x. That is the same as solving it "in terms of y."

$$3y + 10 = 12x + 2$$

$$\frac{-2 \qquad -2}{3y + 8 = 12x}$$

Since our goal is to get x alone, we need to cancel out the number in the operation involving x. So we must divide both sides by 12.

$$\frac{3y + 8}{12} = \frac{12x}{12}$$

$$\frac{3y + 8}{12} = x$$

$$\frac{3y + 8}{12} = \frac{3y}{12} + \frac{8}{12}$$

Since $\frac{3y}{12}$ can be simplified to $\frac{y}{4}$ and $\frac{8}{12}$ can be simplified to $\frac{2}{3}$, $\frac{y}{4} + \frac{2}{3}$ is the solution of the equation for x.

This problem could also be solved by picking a number for y (12 would be a good candidate because y is divided both by 3 and by 4 in the answer choices) and solving for x. Then just check to see which answer choice matches that value.

8. C

The number line shows the graph of $x \geq 3$. That inequality must be the solution to one of the answer choices. So you can find the correct answer by solving each inequality. Only $5x + 7 \leq 9x - 5$ has a solution of $x \geq 3$.

Several answer choices can be quickly eliminated—even before they are fully solved. (A) has "<" instead of "≤". (B) and (E) relate x to a negative number instead of a positive one.

> **EXPERT EXCLUSIVE**
> Keep your eyes open. You can often eliminate answer choices halfway through the problem.

Advanced

9. B

$$4x - 7y + 12 = 20x + y - 4$$

Since we're solving for y, start by collecting the y's together. We could do this on the left side of the equation, but that would give us a negative coefficient for y. So let's collect the y's on the right.

Add $7y$ to each side:	$4x + 12 = 20x + 8y - 4$
Subtract $20x$ from each side:	$-16x + 12 = 8y - 4$
Add 4 to each side:	$-16x + 16 = 8y$
Divide by 8:	$-2x + 2 = y$
Re-express as:	$y = 2 - 2x$

10. C

EXPERT EXCLUSIVE

The test makers know that in the real world, you have calculators and computers. When scary-looking arithmetic shows up, there's usually a way around it. More often than not, that "side door" approach involves common factors.

Keep your eyes open for efficient solutions. Reverse-FOILing this quadratic would probably not be too fun, but the possible solutions are just sitting there in the answer choices, waiting to be tested!

Starting with the easiest makes sense, so let's begin by testing whether x could be 4.

$3x^2 + 24x - 144 = 0$

$3(4)^2 + 24(4) - 144 = 0$

$3(16) + 96 - 144 = 0$

$48 + 96 - 144 = 0$

$144 - 144 = 0$

Looks like $x = 4$ works just fine. That eliminates all but (B) and (C). Squaring -36 doesn't sound like any fun, so let's test $x = -12$.

$3(-12)^2 + 24(-12) - 144 = 0$

$3(144) + 2(12)(-12) - 144 = 0$

$3(144) + 2(-144) - 144 = 0$

$3(144) - 144 \, (2 + 1) = 0$

$3(144) - 144(3) = 0$

Looks like $x = -12$ works too. That makes (C) the answer.

Of course, you could have done the math also. Here you can factor out a 3.

$3(x^2 + 8x - 48) = 0$

$x^2 + 8x - 48 = 0$

$(x - 4)(x + 12) = 0$

$x = 4$ or $x = -12$

Lines and Angles Practice Set Answers and Explanations

1. D

The angles in the diagram are supplementary. The sum of their measures, therefore, is 180 degrees. To find the value of x, subtract the given angle of 38 degrees from the sum total of 180 degrees: $180 - 38 = 142$. The value of x is 142 degrees.

Choice (A) is the measure of the given angle. Choice (B) is the complement of the given angle; this measure added to 38 degrees is equal to 90 degrees. Choice (E) could be the result of a mathematical error in subtraction.

2. D

The y-intercept of the graph of a line is the location where the line crosses the y-axis. In this figure the line crosses the y-axis at the point $(0, -4)$. Thus, the y-intercept is -4. Choice (A) is the opposite of the slope of the line. Choice (B) is the slope of the line. Choice (E) is the opposite of the y-intercept, and choice (C) is the reciprocal of this value.

3. B

The first step in solving this question is to realize that the two angles are supplementary. Therefore, the sum of their angle measures is 180 degrees. The question states that one angle is 30 degrees more than twice its supplement. Using this information, let x represent the measure of the smaller angle and $2x + 30$ equal the measure of the larger angle.

Write an equation that sets the sum of these measures equal to 180 degrees:	$x + 2x + 30 = 180$
Combine like terms:	$3x + 30 = 180$
Subtract 30 from each side of the equation:	$3x + 30 - 30 = 180 - 30$
The equation becomes:	$3x = 150$
Divide each side of the equation by 3 to get x alone:	$\dfrac{3x}{3} = \dfrac{150}{3}$
	$x = 50$

Since the value of x is 50, the measure of the smaller angle is 50 degrees. Choice (E) is the measure of the larger angle.

4. E

When two lines intersect, the vertical (nonadjacent) angles formed are congruent. Expressions for $\angle ABD$ and $\angle CBE$ are given. These two angles are vertical angles, so their measures are equal. Write an equation that sets the expressions for each angle equal to each other. Then, solve the equation to find the value of x in order to find the correct answer choice.

When the two expressions are set equal to each other,

the equation can be written as: $7x - 32 = 5x + 18$

Subtract $5x$ from each side of the equation: $7x - 5x - 32 = 5x - 5x + 18$

The equation simplifies to: $2x - 32 = 18$

Add 32 to each side of the equation: $2x - 32 + 32 = 18 + 32$

The equation becomes: $2x = 50$

Divide each side of the equal sign by 2 to get x alone: $\dfrac{2x}{2} = \dfrac{50}{2}$

$x = 25$

This question asks for the measure of $\angle ABD$. This angle is represented by the expression $7x - 32$.

Substitute $x = 25$ into this expression

to find the number of degrees in the angle: $7(25) - 32$

Multiply first, then subtract: $175 - 32 = 143$

The number of degrees in $\angle ABD$ is 143 degrees.

Choice (A) is the result of finding the sum of the expressions and setting it equal to 180 degrees. Choice (B) is the correct value of x, but the question asks for the number of degrees in $\angle ABD$. Choice (C) is the supplement of a 143-degree angle and would represent the two other angles in the diagram. Choice (D) could be the result of a mathematical error when multiplying 7 and 25.

5. C

To find the slope between any two points, substitute the values for each coordinate into the slope formula and simplify. Use the point $(8, -4)$ as (x_1, y_1) and $(-13, 10)$ as (x_2, y_2).

$$m = \frac{y_1 - y_2}{x_1 - x_2}$$

EXPERT EXCLUSIVE

You could also use $\dfrac{y_2 - y_1}{x_2 - x_1}$ and get the right slope. You just can't use $\dfrac{y_2 - y_1}{x_1 - x_2}$.

Substitute into the formula: $m = \dfrac{-4 - 10}{8 - (-13)}$

Simplify the numerator and denominator: $m = \dfrac{-14}{21}$

Simplify the fraction: $m = -\dfrac{2}{3}$

The slope of the line between the two points is $-\dfrac{2}{3}$.

Choice (B) is the reciprocal of the correct choice. If you selected choice (D), you found a positive value, but the slope of this line is negative. Choice (E) is the opposite of the reciprocal of the correct choice. Either (B) or (E) may have been chosen if the *x*-values were placed in the numerator, instead of the denominator, and the *y*-values were reversed as well.

Advanced

6. B

First, change the given equation to slope-intercept form, or $y = mx + b$ form. To change the equation $2y - 2 = 6x$, do the following:

First, add 2 to each side of the equation:	$2y - 2 + 2 = 6x + 2$
The equation simplifies to:	$2y = 6x + 2$
Divide each side of the equation by 2:	$\dfrac{2y}{2} = \dfrac{6x}{2} + \dfrac{2}{2}$
Simplify the equation:	$y = 3x + 1$

In this equation, the value of $m = 3$, so the slope of the line is 3. The value of $b = 1$, so the *y*-intercept is 1. The correct answer choice is the graph of a line with a slope of 3 and a *y*-intercept of 1. Therefore, the correct answer is choice (B).

Choice (A) is the graph of the equation $y = 2$. Choice (C) is the graph of the equation $x = 2$. Choice (D) is the graph of the equation $y = 3x + 2$. Choice (E) is the graph of the equation $y = -3x + 1$.

TRIANGLES PRACTICE SET ANSWERS AND EXPLANATIONS

1. B

In any triangle, the sum of the lengths of the two smaller sides must be greater than the length of the third side. This relationship is true for each answer choice, except for choice (B). In this choice, the values for the sides of the triangle are 2, 2, and 5. If the two smaller sides are added together, the sum is $2 + 2 = 4$. This sum is less than the measure of the third side, since $4 < 5$. Thus, the measures in choice (B) could not represent the sides of a triangle.

2. C

An important relationship involving triangles is that the longest side of a triangle is across from the largest angle in the triangle. In the figure, the largest angle is $\angle B$. This angle measures 82 degrees. Since this is the largest angle, the longest side is across from this angle. This is side *AC*.

Choice (A) is the smallest side of the triangle because it is across from the smallest angle. Choice (B) is longer than side *AB* but shorter than side *AC*, since the angle across from it has a measure that is between the other two angles. Choice (D) is not correct, because two of the angles are not congruent and the triangle is not an isosceles triangle. All sides are not congruent because all angles are not the same measure, so choice (E) is incorrect.

3. D

In any isosceles triangle, there are two identical angles and a third angle with a different angle measure. We know from the prompt that if the two paired angles each have a measure of x, then the unique angle has a measure of $2x$. We also know that any triangle has angles totaling 180 degrees. Use this fact to write an equation for the angle measures of the triangle:

Add each expression for the three angles of the triangle:	$x + x + 2x = 180$
Combine like terms:	$4x = 180$
Divide each side of the equation by 4:	$\dfrac{4x}{4} = \dfrac{180}{4}$
The value of x is:	$x = 45$

x equals 45, but that is the measure of one of the paired base angles; the third angle will have a measure of $2x$, or 90 degrees—choice (D).

Choice (B) is one of the paired angles, and choice (E) is 180 minus the paired angle measure.

4. A

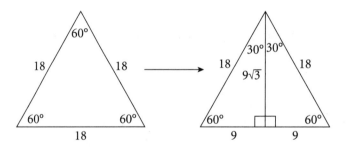

> **EXPERT EXCLUSIVE**
>
> Even if a geometry problem is all text, draw a picture to help yourself visualize it.

The altitude of an equilateral triangle forms two smaller 30-60-90 degree right triangles, where the hypotenuse is the side of the equilateral triangle that is 18 cm. The shorter leg of the right triangle is one-half of this hypotenuse, or 9 cm. The altitude, the longer leg of the right triangle, is thus $9\sqrt{3}$ cm in length.

If you chose (B), you gave the length of the hypotenuse. Choice (C) would be incorrectly arrived at by multiplying the hypotenuse by $\sqrt{3}$ instead of multiplying the shorter leg by $\sqrt{3}$. Choice (D) is twice the length of the hypotenuse.

Advanced

5. C

In an isosceles right triangle, the ratio of leg:leg:hypotenuse is $1:1:\sqrt{2}$, or $x:x:x\sqrt{2}$.
Since the hypotenuse is 8, we could solve for the leg by setting up this equation:

$$x\sqrt{2} = 8$$

Divide both sides by $\sqrt{2}$: $\quad x = \dfrac{8}{\sqrt{2}}$

Multiply by $\dfrac{\sqrt{2}}{\sqrt{2}}$: $\quad x = \dfrac{8}{\sqrt{2}} \times \dfrac{\sqrt{2}}{\sqrt{2}}$

$$x = \dfrac{8\sqrt{2}}{2}$$

$$x = 4\sqrt{2}$$

> **EXPERT EXCLUSIVE**
> Upper-level questions are more likely to have the radical in the leg of an isosceles right triangle than in the hypotenuse.

Each leg measures $4\sqrt{2}$.

6. D

Drawing a diagram makes visualizing the situation much easier. Picture a ladder leaning against a building:

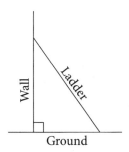

This forms a right triangle, since the side of the building is perpendicular to the ground. The length of the ladder, then, is the hypotenuse of the triangle; the distance from the foot of the building to the base of the ladder is one leg; the distance from the foot of the building to where the top of the ladder touches the wall is the other leg. We can write these dimensions into our diagram:

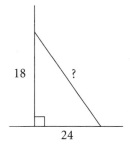

EXPERT EXCLUSIVE

Always be on the lookout for the special right triangles and the Pythagorean triples. Spotting them will save you enormous amounts of calculation.

The one dimension we're missing (what we're asked to find) is the length of the ladder, or the hypotenuse. Well, we could use the Pythagorean theorem to find that, but these numbers are fairly large, and calculating the squares would be troublesome. When you see numbers this large in a right triangle, you should be a little suspicious; perhaps the sides are a multiple of a more familiar Pythagorean triple. One leg is 18, and another leg is 24; 18 is just 6×3, and 24 is just 6×4. So we have a multiple of the familiar 3-4-5 right triangle. That means that our hypotenuse, the length of the ladder, is 6×5, or 30.

Polygons Practice Set Answers and Explanations

1. C

Polygons are classified according to the number of sides they have. A pentagon has five sides. A three-sided polygon is a triangle. A four-sided polygon is a quadrilateral. A six-sided polygon is called a hexagon. An eight-sided polygon is called an octagon.

2. A

In a rectangle, as is true for any parallelogram, opposite sides are congruent. The side opposite ST is RU with a length of 12 inches, choice (A). Choice (B) is the difference between length RS and RU. Choice (D) is the length of side UT. Choice (E) is the sum of the two given lengths.

3. A

The perimeter is the distance around a polygon. You are given the perimeter and asked to find the value of the variable x.

Set up an equation:	$2x + 2x + x + 18 + 18 + 22 = 98$
Combine like terms on the left-hand side:	$5x + 58 = 98$
Subtract 58 from both sides:	$5x + 58 - 58 = 98 - 58$
Simplify and divide both sides by 5:	$\dfrac{5x}{5} = \dfrac{40}{5}$
	$x = 8$

If your answer was choice (B), you found the value of the expression $2x$, or $2(8) = 16$. If you ignored the numerical sides and set up the incorrect equation as $5x = 98$, your answer would have been choice (C). If you had added 58 to both sides of the equation in the second step, instead of subtracting 58, your answer choice would have been (D). Choice (E) is the value of $5x$, not the value of x.

4. C

For this problem, you can use the formula $S = 180 (n - 2)$, where S represents the sum of the interior angles in a regular polygon and n represents the number of sides in the regular polygon. Substituting into the formula, you get this:

The equation is:	$540 = 180(n - 2)$
Divide both sides of this equation by 180:	$\dfrac{540}{180} = \dfrac{180(n - 2)}{180}$
Simplify:	$3 = n - 2$
Add 2 to both sides to isolate n:	$3 + 2 = n - 2 + 2$
	$n = 5$

A five-sided polygon is a pentagon.

You also can work backwards from the answer choices. (A) and (B) are quickly eliminated because triangles and quadrilaterals have interior angle measurements of 180° and 360°, respectively. Draw a quick pentagon, break it into triangles, and you can see that it has an interior angle measurement of 180° × 3, or 540°.

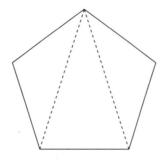

5. C

In any parallelogram, the diagonals bisect each other. And in any rectangle, the diagonals are congruent. Therefore, *BD* is 28 cm, the same as *AC*. Because the diagonals bisect one another, *DE* is one half of 28, or 14 cm, choice (C). You may have chosen (A) if you thought that the length was one-fourth of the length of the diagonal. If your choice was (E), you may have mistakenly multiplied by 2 instead of dividing.

EXPERT EXCLUSIVE

A rectangle is a special kind of parallelogram; a square is a special kind of rectangle. So a square isn't just a square; it's also both a rectangle and a parallelogram.

6. D

If the sides are in the ratio of 3:7, you can multiply each part of the ratio by x to get an equivalent ratio of $3x:7x$. You are told that the longer side, $7x$, is 630 m in length.

So set up the equation: $7x = 630$

Divide each side of this equation by 7: $\dfrac{7x}{7} = \dfrac{630}{7}$

$x = 90$

If $x = 90$, then $3x = 270$.

7. B

The length and width are given as the ratio of 7:4. You can multiply each part of the ratio by the variable x to get an equivalent ratio of $7x:4x$. This means that the length is represented as $7x$ and the width as $4x$. Use the formula for the area of a rectangle, *Area = (Base)(Height)*, where the base is the length and the height is the width. Substitute the value of the area and the expressions for the length and width.

The equation is: $(7x)(4x) = 448$

Multiply on the left-hand side: $28x^2 = 448$

Divide both sides by 28: $\dfrac{28x^2}{28} = \dfrac{448}{28}$

Simplify: $x^2 = 16$

Take the square root of both sides: $\sqrt{x^2} = \sqrt{16}$

$x = 4$

The value of x is 4, so the width, $4x$, is $4(4) = 16$ cm.

Don't fall into the common trap of choice (A), which is the value of the variable, not the measure of the width. A second common mistake is choice (C), which is the measure of the length, not the width. If you chose (D) or (E), you divided 16 by 2 instead of taking the square root of 16, resulting in the incorrect value of $x = 8$. Choice (D) would be the incorrect value of the width with this error, and choice (E) the incorrect value of the length.

8. D

> **EXPERT EXCLUSIVE**
>
> You don't always have to solve for all the individual values to be able to solve for a sum (or any other kind of expression).

At first glance, it appears that not enough information is given. But because this irregular figure is made up of rectangles, look closely and notice that the length of *AH*, 41, is equal to $BC + DE + FG$. Likewise, *HG*, 44, is equal to $AB + CD + EF$. So the perimeter is simply $41 + 44 + 41 + 44 = 85 + 85 = 170$ ft.

If your choice was (A), you divided the sum of 41 and 44 by 2 instead of multiplying by 2. If you chose answer choice (B), you just added the two numbers given in the figure. If your answer was (C), you added $41 + 41 + 44$ and forgot to add in the other value of 44. Choice (E) would be the area of a rectangle with base of 44 and height of 41.

Advanced

9. 80%

The best way to solve this problem is to pick a value for the length of a side of square A. We want our numbers to be easy to work with, so let's pick 10 for the length of each side of square A. The length of each side of square B is 100 percent greater, or twice as great as a side of square A. So the length of a side of square B is 2×10, or 20. The length of each side of square C is 50 percent greater, or $1\frac{1}{2}$ times as great, as a side of square B. So the length of a side of square C is $1\frac{1}{2} \times 20$, or 30. The area of square A is 10^2, or 100. The area of square B is 20^2, or 400. The sum of the areas of squares A and B is $100 + 400$, or 500. The area of square C is 30^2, or 900. The area of square C is greater than the sum of the areas of squares A and B by $900 - 500$, or 400. The percent that the area of square C is greater than the sum of the areas of squares A and B is $\frac{400}{500} \times 100\%$, or 80%.

CIRCLES PRACTICE SET ANSWERS AND EXPLANATIONS

1. B

We need to find the radius to get the circumference. The area is 64π, so use the area formula to get the radius:

$$\text{Area} = \pi r^2 = 64\pi$$
$$r^2 = 64$$
$$r = 8$$

The circumference, which is $2\pi r$, is $2\pi(8)$, or 16π.

EXPERT EXCLUSIVE

No need to be intimidated by calculations with π. It's just a letter—a Greek letter, sure, but a letter all the same. Anything you'd do with an x, you can do with π.

2. A

$C = \pi d = 2\pi r = 1$. If $2\pi r = 1$, then $r = \dfrac{1}{2\pi}$.

3. A

Since we know the area of circle O, we can find the radius of the circle. And if we find the length of OA, then AB is just the difference between OB and OA.

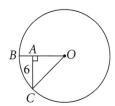

Since the area of the circle is 100π, the radius must be $\sqrt{100}$ or 10. Radius OC, line segment CA, and line segment OA together form a right triangle, so we could use the

Pythagorean theorem to find the length of *OA*. But notice that 10 is twice 5 and 6 is twice 3, so right triangle *ACO* has sides whose lengths are in a 3:4:5 ratio.

OA must have a length of twice 4, or 8. *AB* is the segment of radius *OB* that's not a part of *OA*; its length equals the length of *OB* minus the length of *OA*, or $10 - 8 = 2$.

4. C

Each leg of right triangle *XOY* is also a radius of circle *O*. If we call the radius *r*, then the area of $\triangle XOY$ is $\frac{1}{2}(r)(r)$, or $\frac{r^2}{2}$. At the same time, the area of circle *O* is πr^2. So we can use the area of $\triangle XOY$ to find r^2, then multiply r^2 by π to get the area of the circle.

EXPERT EXCLUSIVE

Keep your eyes open. The GMAT rewards those who think critically about problems and take opportunities to skip unnecessary work.

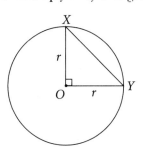

$$\text{Area of } \triangle XOY = \frac{r^2}{2} = 25$$

$$r^2 = 50$$

$$\text{Area of circle } O = \pi r^2 = \pi(50) = 50\pi.$$

Note: It is unnecessary (and extra work) to find the actual value of *r*, since the value of r^2 is sufficient to find the area.

5. A

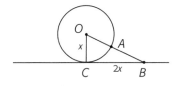

$OC = x$, and you're given that $CB = 2x$, so use the Pythagorean theorem to solve for *OB*:

$$x^2 + (2x)^2 = (OB)^2$$
$$x^2 + 4x^2 = (OB)^2$$
$$5x^2 = (OB)^2$$
$$x\sqrt{5} = OB$$

OA is a radius of the circle and is, therefore, equal to *x*, so $AB = OB - OA = x\sqrt{5} - x$.

Advanced

6. D

Call the endpoints of the arc A and B and the center of the circle C. Major arc AB represents $\frac{3}{4}$ of 360 degrees, or 270 degrees. Therefore, minor arc AB is $360° - 270°$, or $90°$. Since AC and CB are both radii of the circle, $\triangle ABC$ must be an isosceles right triangle:

EXPERT EXCLUSIVE

Creating isosceles triangles inside circles is a favorite GMAT trick. Keep your eyes open for it!

You can find the distance between A and B if you know the radius of the circle. Major arc AB, which takes up $\frac{3}{4}$ of the circumference, has a length of 12π, so the entire circumference is 16π. The circumference of any circle is 2π times the radius, so a circle with circumference 16π must have radius 8. The ratio of a leg to the hypotenuse in an isosceles right triangle is $1:\sqrt{2}$. The length of AB is $\sqrt{2}$ times the length of a leg, or $8\sqrt{2}$.

7. D

Connect the centers of the circles O, P, and Q as shown. Each leg in this right triangle consists of 2 radii. The hypotenuse consists of 2 radii plus the diameter of the small circle.

You can find the radii of the large circles from the given information. Since the total area of the 4 large circles is 36π, each large circle has area 9π. Since the area of a circle is πr^2, we know that the radii of the large circles all have length 3.

EXPERT EXCLUSIVE

Circle problems are almost *always* about the radii, even when no radii are drawn in the diagram!

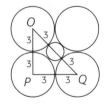

Therefore, each leg in the isosceles right triangle OPQ is 6. The hypotenuse then has length $6\sqrt{2}$ (The hypotenuse of an isosceles right triangle is always $\sqrt{2}$ times a leg.) The hypotenuse is equal to 2 radii plus the diameter of the small circle, so $6\sqrt{2} = (2 \times 3) + (\text{diameter})$, or diameter $= 6\sqrt{2} - 6$.

MULTIPLE FIGURES PRACTICE SET ANSWERS AND EXPLANATIONS

1. C

Let's call the width of the rectangle w. The area of the rectangle, then, is w times 5, its height. The area of the triangle is $\frac{1}{2}$ times the base times the height, or $\frac{1}{2} \times 4 \times 5 = 10$. The area of the triangle is $\frac{1}{3}$ the area of the rectangle, so we know that $\frac{1}{3} \times w \times 5 = 10$. Multiply both sides of this equation by 3 to get $5w = 30$, so $w = 6$.

2. E

The three right angles define three sectors of the circle, each with a central angle of 90°.

> **EXPERT EXCLUSIVE**
>
> Remember, you can solve for sums without knowing individual values.

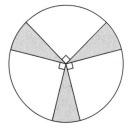

Together, the three sectors account for $\frac{270°}{360°}$, or $\frac{3}{4}$ of the area of the circle, leaving $\frac{1}{4}$ of the circle for the shaded regions. So the total area of the shaded regions $= \frac{1}{4} \times \pi(8)^2$, or 16π.

3. D

Notice that both squares share a side with right triangle CDE. Since square $CEFG$ has an area of 36, CE has a length of $\sqrt{36}$, or 6. Since right triangle CDE has a 45-degree angle, CDE must be an isosceles right triangle. Therefore, CD and DE are the same length. Let's call that length x.

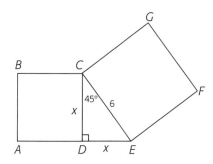

Remember, we're looking for the area of square *ABCD*, which will be x^2. Using the Pythagorean theorem on ΔCDE, we get this:

$$(\text{leg})^2 + (\text{leg})^2 = (\text{hypotenuse})$$
$$x^2 + x^2 = 6^2$$
$$2x^2 = 36$$
$$x^2 = 18$$

So the area is 18. (There's no need to find *x*.)

4. B

The diameter of the circle is 5, so the radius is $\dfrac{5}{2}$ and the area is $\pi\left(\dfrac{5}{2}\right)^2$ or $\dfrac{25}{4}\pi$. This is equal to the area of the triangle. Since the base of the triangle is 5, we can solve for the height:

$$\left(\frac{1}{2}\right)(5)(h) = \frac{25}{4}\pi$$
$$5h = \frac{50}{4}\pi$$
$$h = \frac{50}{20}\pi$$
$$h = \frac{5}{2}\pi$$

Advanced

5. 34

The central rectangle shares a side with each of the 4 squares, and the 4 squares form the legs of the 4 right triangles. Two of the rectangle's sides have a length of 4, so the 2 squares that share these sides must also have sides of length 4. The other 2 sides of the rectangle have a length of 3, so the other 2 squares, which share these sides, must also have sides of length 3. Each triangle shares a side with a small square and a side with a large square, so the legs of each triangle have lengths of 3 and 4, respectively.

> **EXPERT EXCLUSIVE**
>
> On the GMAT, complicated shapes are merely collections of basic ones.

Since the legs are of length 3 and 4, the hypotenuse of each triangle must have a length of 5. (This is the familiar 3-4-5 right triangle.) The perimeter is the sum of the hypotenuses of the triangles and a side from each square:

$$Perimeter = 4(5) + 2(4) + 2(3)$$
$$= 20 + 8 + 6$$
$$= 34$$

6. C

If you picked answer choice (A), you probably added the area of the circle to the area of the triangle. However, this double-counts the area of the figure that is part of both shapes; we need to handle these overlapping figures in a manner similar to how we'd solve overlapping sets. For that reason, the total area of the shaded region equals (the area of the circle) + (the area of the right triangle) − (the area of overlap). The area of circle O is $\pi(8)^2$, or 64π. The area of right triangle OAB is 32. So we just need to find the area of overlap, the area of right triangle OAB inside circle O, which forms a sector of the circle. Let's see what we can find out about $\angle AOB$, the central angle of the sector.

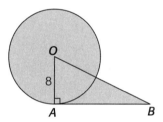

The area of right triangle OAB is 32, and its height is the radius of circle O. So $\frac{1}{2}$ $(8)(AB) = 32$, or $AB = 8$. Since $AB = OA$, $\triangle OAB$ is an isosceles right triangle. Therefore, $\angle AOB$ has a measure of 45°. The area of the sector is $\frac{45}{360}(64\pi)$, or 8π. Now we can get the total area of the shaded region: $64\pi + 32 - 8\pi = 56\pi + 32$.

SOLIDS PRACTICE SET ANSWERS AND EXPLANATIONS

1. D

The formula for the volume of a cube is $V = e^3$, where e is the length of a side, which in this problem is 5 cm. Substitute in this value to get $V = 5^3$, or $V = 5 \times 5 \times 5 = 125$ cm^3.

If you chose answer (A), you multiplied 5×3 instead of $5 \times 5 \times 5$. Answer choice (B) is the area of the base of the prism. If you chose (C), you multiplied the number of faces of the prism, 6, by the side length. Choice (E) is the surface area of the prism, not the volume.

2. D

Use the formula for the volume of a cylinder, $V = \pi r^2 h$. Substitute in the values of radius r, 11 cm, and height h, 4 cm. The volume is $V = \pi \times 11^2 \times 4$. Use the correct order of operations and evaluate the exponent first: $V = \pi \times 121 \times 4$. Multiply to get $V = 484\pi$ cm^3.

If your answer was choice (A), you did not square the radius. Answer choice (B) would be arrived at if you multiplied 11×2 instead of 11×11. Choice (C) is the volume of a cone with these dimensions. Choice (E) is two times the volume of the cylinder.

3. C

To find the surface area, first find the correct formula. The formula for the surface area of a rectangular prism is $SA = 2lw + 2lh + 2wh$, where l is the length, w is the width, and h is the height of the prism.

> **EXPERT EXCLUSIVE**
>
> Be thorough—a common mistake in surface area questions is to forget about half the sides.

Next, locate all of the known values for the formula and substitute these values for the variables in the formula. In this problem, the length is 10 inches, so $l = 10$. The width is 20 inches, so $w = 20$. The height is 14 inches, so $h = 14$. After substituting, use the correct order of operations to evaluate the formula.

Write the formula:	$SA = 2lw + 2lh + 2wh$
Substitute the given values:	$SA = 2(10)(20) + 2(10)(14) + 2(20)(14)$
Multiply each term first:	$SA = 2(200) + 2(140) + 2(280)$
	$SA = 400 + 280 + 560$
Then add to find the surface area:	$SA = 1{,}240$ square inches

If you selected choice (A), you may have just added the three dimensions together. If you chose (B), you may have forgotten to multiply by 2 in each term because this value is equal to one-half of the surface area. Choice (D) is the surface area doubled and could be the result of multiplying by 2 an extra time. Choice (E) is the volume of the figure, or the result of simply multiplying the three dimensions together.

4. E

The formula for the surface area of a cylinder is $SA = 2\pi r^2 + 2\pi rh$, where r is the radius of the base and h is the height of the cylinder. Find all of the known values for the formula and substitute these values for the variables in the formula. In this problem, the radius of the base is 7 meters, so $r = 7$. The height of the cylinder is 3 meters, so $h = 3$. After substituting, use the correct order of operations to evaluate the formula.

Write the formula:	$SA = 2\pi r^2 + 2\pi rh$
Substitute the given values:	$SA = 2\pi(7)^2 + 2\pi(7)(3)$
Apply the exponent first:	$SA = 2\pi(49) + 2\pi(7)(3)$
Then multiply:	$SA = 98\pi + 42\pi$
Last, add to find the surface area:	$SA = 140\pi$ square meters

Choice (A) is the result of multiplying the radius of the base by the height of the cylinder and π. Choice (B) is the surface area of the rectangular region that forms the height of the cylinder. Choice (C) is the area of one of the circular bases. Choice (D) is the area of both circular bases.

EXPERT EXCLUSIVE

There's no need to be intimidated by solids–if you learn the appropriate formulas, applying them is very straightforward.

5. A

To answer this problem, first determine the correct formula. The formula for the volume of a rectangular prism is $V = lwh$. The volume, V, is given as 1,960 mm³; the length, l, is represented as $4x$; the width, w, is represented as x; and the height, h, is given as 10 mm. Substitute into the formula and then solve for the variable.

Write the formula:	$V = lwh$
Substitute the values:	$1,960 = 4x \times x \times 10$
Multiply the terms on the right-hand side:	$1,960 = 40x^2$
Divide both sides by 40:	$\dfrac{1,960}{40} = \dfrac{40x^2}{40}$
Simplify:	$49 = x^2$
Take the square root of both sides:	$\sqrt{49} = \sqrt{x^2}$
Simplify:	$7 = x$

If your answer was choice (B), you omitted the coefficient of 4 and had the incorrect equation of $1,960 = 10x^2$. Choice (C) would be incorrectly arrived at if you forgot to factor in the height in the formula and had the equation $1,960 = 4x^2$. Choice (D) is the value of x^2, not the value of x. If your answer was choice (E), you may have added the dimensions, instead of multiplying, to get the incorrect equation $1,960 = 5x + 10$.

Advanced

6. A

The first step in solving for the length of an edge is to find the appropriate formula to use. The formula for the surface area of a cube is $SA = 6e^2$, where e represents the length of an edge of the cube. The surface area is 486 m^2, so $SA = 486$.

First, write the formula:	$SA = 6e^2$
Substitute the given value:	$486 = 6e^2$
Divide by 6 on each side of the equation to get e^2 alone:	$\dfrac{486}{6} = \dfrac{6e^2}{6}$

The equation simplifies to: $81 = e^2$

To solve for e, take the square root of each side of the equation: $9 = e$

The length of an edge of the cube is 9 m.

Choice (B) is the result of multiplying 9 by 6. Choice (C) is the correct value of e^2, but you need to find the value of e by taking the square root in the final step. Choices (D) and (E) are the result of dividing values into 486 to find factors and not using the formula for surface area.

7. C

Use the formula for the volume of a cylinder; that is, $V = \pi r^2 h$. It is given that the volume, V, is 600π mm^3 and the height, h, is 6 mm. Use the formula to solve for the radius, r, and then determine the diameter as twice the radius.

Write the formula: $V = \pi r^2 h$

Substitute in the values: $600\pi = \pi \times r^2 \times 6$

Divide both sides by 6π: $\dfrac{600\pi}{6\pi} = \dfrac{6\pi r^2}{6\pi}$

Simplify: $100 = r^2$

Take the square root of both sides: $\sqrt{100} = \sqrt{r^2}$

Simplify: $10 = r$

The radius is 10 mm, so the diameter is 20 mm.

Choice (A) is one half the value of the radius. Choice (B) is the length of the radius. Choice (D) would be your answer if you had divided 100 by 2 when solving the equation, instead of taking the square root. Choice (E) is the incorrect value of the diameter if you had divided 100 by 2 when solving the equation for the radius, instead of taking the square root.

For more on the key math concepts you'll need for the GMAT, as well as hundreds of practice drills and even more test-like practice questions, pick up a copy of Kaplan's *GMAT Math Workbook!*